Introduction to Learning and Behavior

Introduction to Learning and Behavior

Fifth Edition

RUSSELL A. POWELL
MacEwan University

P. LYNNE HONEY
MacEwan University

DIANE G. SYMBALUK
MacEwan University

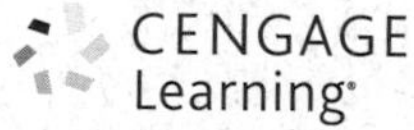

Australia • Brazil • Mexico • Singapore • United Kingdom • United States

***Introduction to Learning and Behavior*, Fifth Edition**
Russell A. Powell,
P. Lynne Honey and
Diane G. Symbaluk

Product Director: Jon-David Hague

Content Developer: Michelle Clark

Product Assistant: Kimiya Hojjat

Marketing Manager: Melissa Larmon

Art and Cover Direction, Production Management, and Composition: Lumina Datamatics, Inc.

Manufacturing Planner: Karen Hunt

Cover Image: Peter Cade/The Image Bank/Getty Images

Library of Congress Control Number: 2015951184

ISBN: 978-1-305-65294-1

Cengage Learning
20 Channel Center Street
Boston, MA 02210
USA

Cengage Learning is a leading provider of customized learning solutions with employees residing in nearly 40 different countries and sales in more than 125 countries around the world. Find your local representative at **www.cengage.com**.

Cengage Learning products are represented in Canada by Nelson Education, Ltd.

To learn more about Cengage Learning Solutions, visit **www.cengage.com**.

Purchase any of our products at your local college store or at our preferred online store **www.cengagebrain.com**.

Printed in the United States of America
Print Number: 01 Print Year: 2015

To parents, mentors, and students who shaped our behavior so well as to make this book a reality.

Brief Contents

Contents

CHAPTER 4 Classical Conditioning: Basic Phenomena and Various Complexities 132

CHAPTER 5 Classical Conditioning: Underlying Processes and Practical Applications 167

CHAPTER 6 Operant Conditioning: Introduction 209

CHAPTER 7 Schedules and Theories of Reinforcement 254

CHAPTER 10 Choice, Matching, and Self-Control 373

CHAPTER 11 Observational Learning and Rule-Governed Behavior 416

Preface

"I wouldn't do this to my budgie," a student once muttered following a lecture in which I (the senior author of this text) had discussed the process of reinforcement. She apparently saw the use of reinforcement as manipulative and reprehensible. I can't remember how I responded (probably with something a bit more diplomatic than what follows), but I could have said that she actually does "this" to her budgie all the time and is simply not aware of it. Moreover, because she's not aware of it, she may be reinforcing her budgie's behavior quite erratically, with the result that the two of them are having a much less satisfying relationship than they could be having. Unfortunately, this student's negative reaction to behavioral principles of conditioning is not uncommon, and most instructors who teach such courses can probably recount similar instances. Thus, one goal of this text is to help convince students that conditioning is not a dangerous form of manipulation but rather a natural process that we do far better to understand and apply wisely than to ignore and apply carelessly.

Another opinion sometimes voiced is that the principles of conditioning, many of which have been derived from research with animals, are largely irrelevant to important aspects of human behavior. After all, how can studies of lever-pressing rats or key-pecking pigeons say anything meaningful about what truly matters to us? This was the very conclusion that I (the senior author again) came to when, as an undergraduate, I first encountered a demonstration of operant conditioning in my introductory psychology class. We were shown a film in which pigeons were taught to peck a little plastic disk (which I later learned is called a "response key") to earn food. The whole endeavor struck me as so completely artificial—not to mention mind-numbingly boring—that I couldn't understand why anyone would waste his or her time on it. Little did I know that some years later I would find myself sitting in a pigeon lab, thrilled that I had been given an opportunity to study something so interesting and important! What I had learned in the interim was that: (1) you have to be careful what you criticize (fate has a way of making us pay for our arrogance) and (2) many of the principles derived from conditioning experiments with animals are among the most useful principles ever discovered by psychologists. Thus, a second goal of this text is to help convince students that the principles derived from behavioral research are far from irrelevant, and that they often have useful and provocative things to say about human behavior.

An even more basic goal of this text is to provide students with a clear introduction to the basic principles of learning and behavior that is both accessible and engaging, especially for those who may have had only limited prior exposure to these principles (such as in an introductory psychology course). Those students who later proceed to a higher-level course in the subject matter will then have a solid foundation on which to build. Students who do not proceed to a higher-level course will nevertheless have gained an appreciation for the behavioral perspective and learned much that may be of relevance to their everyday lives and future careers.

Key Characteristics

The following summarizes some key characteristics of this text:

- **It emphasizes basic principles of learning and behavior rather than theory.** To the extent that theory is discussed, it is either because the theory itself has something meaningful and provocative to say about human behavior (e.g., melioration theory as discussed in Chapter 10) or because a general overview of certain theories (e.g., the Rescorla-Wagner theory, as presented in Chapter 5) can help prepare students for a more in-depth discussion of those theories in a higher-level course.
- **It attempts to strike an appropriate balance between basic research findings, many of which are derived from animal research, and the application of those findings to important and interesting aspects of human behavior.** Although many texts make this claim, we feel that this text represents a truly concerted effort in that regard. Wherever possible, examples from research paradigms with rats or pigeons are juxtaposed with everyday examples with humans. And although some of the applications to humans are highly speculative, they nevertheless represent the type of speculation that behaviorists themselves often engage in and that many students find interesting and memorable.
- **Following from the above, this text is especially innovative in the many examples given of the application of behavioral principles to understanding certain aspects of romantic relationships.** In particular, scattered throughout the text are *Advice for the Lovelorn* columns in which hypothetical students are given behavioral-type advice concerning their relationship difficulties. Personal relationships are, of course, a key concern for many students, and they are often fascinated by the notion that

behavioral principles may be helpful in understanding and resolving problematic relationships. These columns have thus proven to be an effective way to maintain students' interest in the material, enhance their grasp of certain concepts, and provide them with a sense of what it means to think like a behaviorist. (Students are of course given due warning that the advice in these columns is quite speculative and not to be taken too seriously.)

- **The text contains many interesting and thought-provoking topics not normally found in textbooks on learning and behavior.** This includes such topics as what it means to have "willpower," the controversy over the inadvertent creation of multiple personalities during psychotherapy, and how difficulties in life often contribute to a sense of "meaning" in life, all discussed from a behavioral perspective. Many of these topics are presented in special boxed inserts titled *And Furthermore*, which are intended to expand on material presented in the preceding section.
- **This text contains numerous pedagogical features that are designed to facilitate students' ability to study and understand the material.** These features are described later in the section on learning aids. See also the discussion below on the "Study Tips" and self-management features that are new to this edition.

Changes to the Fifth Edition

In the preface to the last edition, we commented on how difficult it is to revise a textbook that seems to be working well for so many students and instructors. Unfortunately (or fortunately), we found ourselves in very much the same boat with respect to this revision. Although some reviewers did have major suggestions for improving certain aspects of the text, these were often contradicted by feedback from other reviewers and instructors who indicated that they very much liked those aspects. Even some of our own suggestions for improvement resulted in such strong reactions from reviewers that we quickly dropped them. It also made us realize the extent to which a successful textbook is no longer the sole property of the publisher and authors but is a shared endeavor with those who have come to rely on it, and we therefore became duly cautious in considering which changes to make. As a result, the most significant changes in this edition consist of value-added material in the form of study tips and advice on behavior self-management, as well as paring down one chapter that, in our experience, was a bit too complicated for many students to handle. We also strove to simplify or shorten sections wherever possible to try and counter the dreaded disease of the ever-expanding textbook.

Thus, one of the most significant changes to this edition is the inclusion of an appendix, titled "A Brief Guide to Behavior Self-Management." This appendix provides practical advice on the use of behavioral principles to enhance self-control and complements the more theoretical presentation of self-control in Chapter 10. It should prove especially useful for students who are asked to do a behavior self-management project as a course assignment, as well as for students who personally struggle with such issues as procrastination. Related to this, a boxed "Study Tips" insert has also been added to each chapter (except the last), which offers specific advice to students on how to improve and manage their study behavior. The Study Tips insert in Chapter 1, for example, describes the 3R (read-recite-review) method for reading a textbook, something that many students have never been taught. Study tips in other chapters generally build upon behavioral concepts covered in those chapters. For example, the study tips insert for Chapter 7 (which covers schedules of reinforcement) discusses the "just-get-started" tactic for overcoming procrastination and relates it to the "break-and-run" pattern of behavior that is typically found in fixed ratio schedules of reinforcement. Our hope is that this material will provide students with the skills needed to become "independent learners," which is a commonly cited goal in higher education but one that educators often make little effort in trying to achieve. The study tips and self-management advice offered in this text therefore represent a concerted attempt to correct that situation.

The other major change in this edition involves Chapter 4, which in our experience many students found rather confusing. We have therefore simplified this chapter by (1) moving the discussion of pseudoconditioning and temporal conditioning to Chapter 3, (2) eliminating the discussion of external inhibition, and (3) consolidating the remaining conditioning procedures under the two categories of extensions to conditioning and specificity in conditioning. This chapter will hopefully now be considerably less difficult for students to work through.

Other changes (many of which were suggested by reviewers) include the following: In the Chapter 1 section on radical behaviorism, the separate discussion of molar versus molecular approaches to the study of behavior has been dropped. Chapter 1 also includes a brief description of the Board Certification program in applied behavior analysis to alert students to the growing number of career opportunities in applied behavior analysis. In Chapter 2, the term "establishing operation" has been updated to the more global term "motivating operation," which encompasses both establishing operations and abolishing operations. In Chapter 3, the brief discussion of preparedness in backward conditioning has been moved to the Chapter 12 discussion of biological preparedness in conditioning. In Chapter 5, the discussion of S-S versus S-R models of conditioning has been dropped; it overlaps too much with other theories of conditioning, which students found confusing. As well, the And Furthermore box on the search for Little Albert has been updated to include the recent discovery of a person who is very likely to have been the real Little Albert.

Chapter 9 eliminates the And Furthermore discussion of "Repression as Avoidance" and replaces it with a description of approach-avoidance conflict.

Students seem to find the concept of approach-avoidance quite interesting, given its relevance for understanding certain relationship issues. In Chapter 10, the And Furthermore box, "Self-Control: How Sweet It Is! Or Is It?", has been updated to include recent findings that seem to contradict Baumeister's strength model of self-control. And Chapter 11 now includes a brief description of Skinner's general approach to verbal behavior, thereby providing a context to the following discussion of rule-governed behavior.

Finally, the number of study questions at the end of each chapter has been somewhat reduced, often by combining two or more related concepts into the same question. The hope is that this will prompt students to more often ponder the similarities and differences between concepts, and thereby enhance their understanding of those concepts.

Learning Aids

This text contains many pedagogical features designed to facilitate students' reading and comprehension of the material. These include the following:

- **Quick Quizzes.** Scattered throughout each chapter are several fill-in-the-blank quizzes. The purpose of these quizzes is to help students actively work with the material as they read it. Although an early reviewer of the first edition commented that such frequent quizzing might frustrate students by interrupting their reading, actual use of the material in class revealed quite the opposite. Students commented that the quizzes were extremely beneficial in helping them engage with the material. They especially appreciated quizzes that were embedded within sections that they perceived as quite technical, simply because the quizzes broke the material up into short chunks that they were better able to assimilate. Students therefore demanded more quizzes, not fewer, and the authors duly complied.
- **Study Questions.** A focused set of around 10–15 study questions is included at the end of each chapter. These study questions cover the most basic concepts discussed in that chapter. Students can be motivated to answer these questions if instructors inform them that some of these questions may appear as short-answer items on quizzes or exams. In fact, the senior author's own strategy is to give students a random sample of four or five of these questions as a weekly chapter test, with students in each class being unaware of which questions they will be asked.
- **Concept Reviews.** Each chapter is followed by a concept review, which lists all key terms and definitions in the chapter. These key terms and definitions are then reiterated in the glossary at the end of the text.
- **Chapter Tests.** Each chapter ends with a chapter test, consisting mostly of fill-in-the-blank items. This test provides comprehensive coverage of the material presented in the chapter. It differs from the *Quick Quizzes* in that more items are of a conceptual, rather than factual or definitional,

nature, thereby encouraging students to think more deeply about the material. These test items are numbered in random order, so that students can immediately look up the answer to any particular item without having to worry about inadvertently seeing the answer to the next item.

- **Opening Vignettes.** Each chapter begins with a chapter outline, followed by either a quotation or a vignette related to the material presented in that chapter. The vignettes usually consist of a short, fictional scenario illustrating a particular concept. The exact concept involved is not immediately revealed, however, thus encouraging students to actively ponder how the material they are reading may be related to the scenario. (An explanation of the concept each scenario is intended to illustrate can be found in the instructor's manual.)

Instructor's Manual

The instructor's manual includes a revised test bank that contains a large number of multiple-choice items per chapter. Many of these items are conceptual in nature, and they are organized by textbook headings and subheadings. The instructor's manual also contains answers to all of the *Quick Quiz* and study question items for each chapter, as well as a set of annotated Web links where students will find information of interest. The manual also contains a description of how the *Advice for the Lovelorn* column can be adapted as a student assignment (along with additional examples of such columns that can be provided to students to facilitate their own efforts).

Sniffy™ the Virtual Rat Lite, Version 2.0: An Available Option

Sniffy the Virtual Rat Lite provides every student with hands-on experience in applying, either at home or in school, the principles of operant and classical conditioning. Sniffy is a computer-generated rat that can be taught to press a lever to earn food, a protocol that is then used to demonstrate many aspects of both operant and classical conditioning. Students purchasing Sniffy receive a laboratory manual with instructions, and a hybrid CD-ROM that operates on Mac OS Version 8.6 or later and Windows 95 SE, ME, 2000, or XP.

The Lite version of Sniffy includes 16 exercises that cover the essential phenomena of learning psychology. The stimulant operant phenomena covered include magazine training; shaping; primary and secondary reinforcement; variable-interval, variable-ratio, fixed-interval, and fixed-ratio schedule effects; and the partial-reinforcement effect. The classical conditioning phenomena covered include acquisition, extinction, and spontaneous recovery.

Students enjoy working with Sniffy and report that these exercises greatly enhance their understanding of the basic principles. We do not, of course, propose that Sniffy can fully substitute for the actual experience of working with live animals. Unfortunately, for various reasons, most institutions are no longer able to offer this valuable opportunity to their undergraduates. Sniffy was created precisely to fill this void. Additionally, some schools use Sniffy as a warm-up before allowing students to work with real animals. For more information about Sniffy the Virtual Rat Lite, Version 2.0, visit cengagebrain.com. Sniffy's creators discuss how they use Sniffy in their classes, and students describe their experiences working with Sniffy.

Acknowledgments

We wish to thank "Dr. Dee," Ally McBeal (who was all the rage on television when this text was first conceived), and all the other people (real and fictional) who inspired the Advice to the Lovelorn features and other aspects of this text. We also thank the following reviewers for their comments and suggestions, which contributed greatly to the improvements made in this edition: Joseph J. Benz, University of Nebraska, Kearney; James MacDonall, Fordham University; Christy Porter, College of William and Mary; and Elizabeth Cooper, University of Tennessee, Knoxville.

In addition, we thank the people at Cengage Learning, including Jon-David Hague, Michelle Clark, Kimiya Hojjat, Kailash Rawat, Kristina Mose-Lebon, Nicole Sala, Brittani Morgan, Veerabhagu Nagarajan, and Pinky Subi for all their support in helping to create this edition. This was an especially great team to work with, and they made the process of revising much easier than it might otherwise have been.

Finally, a special thanks to Dr. Suzanne E. MacDonald, who served as coauthor on early editions of the text and whose influence can still be seen within certain chapters.

Russ Powell
Lynne Honey
Diane Symbaluk

About the Authors

Russell A. Powell

Russ Powell earned his Ph.D. in psychology under the engaging mentorship of Frank Epling and David Pierce at the University of Alberta. As a veteran faculty member at MacEwan University, Russ has taught classes in learning and behavior for over 30 years using a variety of behaviorally inspired formats. He has also conducted and published research on a wide range of topics, including operant conditioning (choice behavior), dissociative identity disorder, sleep paralysis nightmares, self-regulation, and the history of psychology. Most recently, he helped identify the individual now believed to have been Little Albert, the infant in whom Watson & Rayner (1920) famously (or infamously) attempted to condition a phobia of furry animals (e.g., Powell, Digdon, Harris, & Smithson, 2014).

P. Lynne Honey

Lynne Honey—a self-described "evolutionary behaviorist"—completed a Ph.D. in experimental psychology in Jeff Galef's lab at McMaster University, studying the role of social learning on alcohol consumption in rats. She has published a number of papers on this topic and considers social learning to be one of the most powerful adaptations available to our species and others. Dr. Honey joined the Department of Psychology at MacEwan University in 2003 because of its focus on teaching and student engagement. She currently conducts research on human social behavior in an evolutionary context, including studies of social dominance and the influence of personality traits on social behaviors. She also studies the effectiveness of various teaching methods, including peer review and various uses of technology for learning, and has won an award for innovation in teaching.

Diane G. Symbaluk

Diane Symbaluk received her Ph.D. in sociology from the University of Alberta in 1997, with a specialization in criminology and social psychology. She joined MacEwan University in 1996 in order to pursue her joint passion for teaching and research. She has taught courses in a variety of areas including social psychology, criminology, statistics, and research methods. She is presently the faculty advisor for MacEwan University's Community-Based Sociology Project, a student-led research program. Her extensive list of publications includes textbooks, journal articles, and more than 40 pedagogical resources (e.g., study guides, test banks, instructor manuals, and online resources). A Distinguished Teaching Award winner, Diane is currently conducting research on published student ratings of instruction and character strengths of award-winning instructors.

Introduction to Learning and Behavior

CHAPTER 1

INTRODUCTION

CHAPTER OUTLINE

> A review of Gerald Zuriff's *Behaviorism: A Conceptual Reconstruction* (1985)...begins with a story about two behaviorists. They make love and then one of them says, "That was fine for you. How was it for me?" The reviewer, P. N. Johnson-Laird, insists that [this story has a ring of truth about it]. Behaviorists are not supposed to have feelings, or at least to admit that they have them. Of the many ways in which behaviorism has been misunderstood for so many years, that is perhaps the commonest. ...[In fact,] how people feel is often as important as what they do.
>
> **B. F. SKINNER, 1989, p. 3**

> Of all contemporary psychologists, B. F. Skinner is perhaps the most honored and the most maligned, the most widely recognized and the most misrepresented, the most cited and the most misunderstood.
>
> **A. CHARLES CATANIA, 1988, p. 3**

Imagine that while flipping through a new textbook you see that it spends a lot of time discussing experiments with rats and pigeons. Pretty boring, huh? But what if the principles discovered in those experiments could help you improve your study habits, understand your eating disorder, and overcome your fear of spiders? In fact, what if those same principles could even help you improve your romantic relationships? Hmm, perhaps not so boring after all. Well, you might be holding just such a book in your hands. Let's consider a few of these claims in more detail.

Improving self-control. Do you too often find yourself watching television rather than studying? Or hanging out with friends rather than heading to the gym? In other words, do you often find yourself being sidetracked from your long-term goals by activities that are more immediately pleasurable? This book outlines the principles by which the environment around us affects our behavior, including behaviors involved in issues of self-control. Chapter 10, in particular, provides a theoretical account of why self-control is so often difficult for us to achieve, while the appendix, *A Brief Guide to Behavior Self-Management*, offers practical advice on how to improve self-control. In addition, as noted in the preface, scattered throughout the text are boxed inserts on Study Tips that offer specific advice on how to improve both the quality and quantity of studying that you do. The first one, in particular, which directly follows this section, offers research-based advice on how to effectively study a textbook, something that many students have never been taught. Additional information on improving study behavior, as well as other behaviors we may wish we had more control over, can be found scattered throughout the textbook.

Understanding eating disorders. Contrary to popular belief, eating disorders are not necessarily indicative of a psychological problem. For example, through a simple manipulation of a rat's feeding schedule, the rat can be induced to stop eating and engage in extreme levels of exercise. In this book, you will learn how similar processes might account for the development of a clinical disorder in humans known as anorexia nervosa.

Overcoming fears and phobias. Whether you fear spiders, snakes, or exams, this textbook will provide you with insight into how these fears develop. You will learn how the principles of classical conditioning and negative reinforcement underlie many of our fears and anxieties, and how these same principles suggest effective means for treating such symptoms.

Improving relationships with others. In this text, we often use relationship issues to illustrate basic principles of learning and behavior. As well, each chapter contains an *Advice for the Lovelorn* column, in which relationship problems are discussed from a behavioral perspective. Although the advice given is necessarily speculative—and as such should not be taken too seriously—these columns highlight the manner in which behavioral principles have the potential to enrich our understanding of human relationships.

Raising children. Our students sometimes comment that "no one should be allowed to have children until they have taken a course like this." Although this is admittedly an exaggeration, it is nevertheless the case that many of the principles discussed in this text are directly applicable to many common parenting problems.

In general, a proper grounding in the basic principles of learning and behavior will help you understand why you behave the way you do and how your behavior can often be changed for the better. This knowledge can make you a better student, a better parent, a better worker, and a better friend or partner. In a very real sense, the principles described in this text have the potential to enrich both your life and the lives of others—even though many of these principles have been derived from research with rats and pigeons!

Study Tip: Many students are unaware of how best to study a textbook. Too often, for example, they simply read and reread the material in the hope that something will sink in. But research has shown that, for most students, this method is largely ineffective. Better approaches involve the "testing effect," in which testing your ability to recall the information you just read can greatly enhance your memory for it (e.g., Dunlosky, Rawson, Marsh, Nathan, & Willingham, 2013). A recent version of this approach is the 3R method of studying (McDaniel, Howard, & Einstein, 2009). The 3R strategy, which stands for *read-recite-review*, involves the following steps:

1. You first *read* a short section of material, such as the material under a particular subheading—though it could be shorter or longer than this depending on the difficulty or complexity of the material.
2. Once you finish reading, you then *recite* to yourself, without looking at the material, the main points in what you just read. Don't worry about how well you do at this point—you may in fact find it quite difficult—just do the best you can.
3. After attempting to recite the material, then *review* the material by going back over it, paying particular attention to anything you missed in step 2.

Research has shown that, for many students, this approach can significantly enhance learning. Unfortunately, students tend not to study this way because it is difficult and effortful, unaware of the fact that *it is the effort that makes it effective.*

Many students also like to underline (or highlight) as they read, but they unfortunately do so in ways that contribute little to learning (Dunlosky et al., 2013). A frequent problem is that students underline too much information, both important and unimportant. An alternate approach, which we'll call "selective underlining," is to first read the paragraph *without underlining*; you instead simply search for the important points you will want to underline later. After finishing the paragraph, you then go back and underline just the important points. This means that you will often be underlining only parts of sentences rather than whole sentences. This process is slower and more effortful than the typical way students underline, but your recall for the information is likely to be much greater. The underlined passages also provide an excellent summary of the chapter for you to review or use as a basis for making study notes.

As you no doubt noticed, the paragraph you just read provides an example of selective underlining (though you yourself may have chosen a somewhat different set of phrases). Another possibility that you may wish to experiment with would be to combine selective underlining with the 3R approach; for example, selectively underline each paragraph within a section, then when you finish the section try to recite the information you underlined.

You can find plenty of how-to-study advice on the Internet—but be careful with it; the Internet contains a lot of advice, both good and bad—or at your campus counseling center. The important thing is to find the combination of study tactics that works best for you, which may be rather different from what works best for someone else. Of course, this advice is of little use if you tend to procrastinate and rarely study in the first place. In that case, you may wish to consult the appendix at the end of this text for advice on behavior self-management. Even if your instructor has not assigned the appendix as part of your course, you may find useful advice in it that could help decrease your tendency to procrastinate.

Let's begin with a brief outline of what this textbook is about. Simply put, ***behavior*** is any activity of an organism that can be observed or somehow measured. As we discuss in Chapter 2, the activity may be internal or external and may or may not be visible to others. ***Learning*** is a relatively permanent change in behavior that results from some type of experience. For example, reading this text is an example of a behavior, and any lasting change in your behavior as a result of reading this text (e.g., a change in your ability to speak knowledgeably about the subject matter) is an example of learning.

Note that the change in behavior does not have to be immediate, and in some circumstances the change might not become evident until long after the experience has occurred.

This text emphasizes two fundamental forms of learning: classical and operant conditioning. Although these will be discussed in more detail later, a brief description of each is useful at this point. At its most basic level, *classical conditioning* (also known as Pavlovian or respondent conditioning) is the process by which certain inborn behaviors come to be elicited in new circumstances. The behaviors involved are often what the average person regards as reflexive or "involuntary," such as sneezing in response to dust or salivating in response to food. A familiar example of classical conditioning, which is often presented in introductory psychology textbooks, is that of a dog learning to salivate in response to a bell that was previously followed by food. This process can be diagrammed as follows:

Bell: Food → *Salivation*
Bell → *Salivation*

(See "Notation for Conditioning Diagrams" in the And Furthermore box.)

And Furthermore

Notation for Conditioning Diagrams

In this text, you will encounter many diagrams of conditioning procedures. In these diagrams, a colon separating two events indicates that the events occur in sequence. For example, the term "Bell: Food" means that the sound of a bell is followed by the presentation of food. An arrow between two events also indicates that they occur in sequence, but with an emphasis on the fact that the first event *produces* or *causes* the second. For example, "Food → *Salivation*" means that the presentation of food causes the dog to salivate. Thus, with respect to a standard classical conditioning procedure, the term:

Bell: Food → *Salivation*

means that the bell is presented just before the food, and the food in turn causes salivation. This is followed by:

Bell → *Salivation*

which indicates that the presentation of the bell itself now causes the dog to salivate (because of the bell's previous pairing with food). For clarity, we will usually italicize the behavior that is being conditioned (which is often called the "target behavior"). In writing out your notes, however, you may find it easier to indicate the target behavior by underlining it. For example:

Bell: Food → <u>Salivation</u>
Bell → <u>Salivation</u>

As you will learn in this text, classical conditioning underlies many of our emotional responses and contributes to the development of our likes and dislikes. It can also lead to the development of debilitating fears and powerful feelings of sexual attraction.

In contrast to classical conditioning, *operant conditioning* involves the strengthening or weakening of a behavior as a result of its consequences. The behaviors involved are often those that the average person regards as goal-directed or "voluntary." A common experimental example is that of a rat that has learned to press a lever (the behavior) to obtain food (the consequence), the future effect of which is an increase in the rat's tendency to press the lever. This can be diagrammed as follows:

Lever press **→ Food pellet**
Future effect: Likelihood of lever pressing increases

Because the lever press produced a food pellet, the rat is subsequently more likely to press the lever again. In other words, the consequence of the behavior (the food pellet) has served to strengthen future occurrences of that behavior. Many of the behaviors that concern us each day are motivated by such consequences; we hit the remote button to turn on a favorite television show, compliment a loved one because it produces a smile, and study diligently to obtain a passing grade. The consequences can be either immediate, as in the first two examples, or delayed, as in the last example—though, as we will later discuss, the effect of delayed consequences on behavior can involve certain complexities. Because of its importance for humans, operant conditioning is the type of learning most strongly emphasized in this text.

Although the text concentrates on classical and operant conditioning, other types of behavioral processes are also discussed. For example, in *observational learning* the act of observing someone else's behavior facilitates the occurrence of similar behavior in oneself. Certain types of largely inherited (non-learned) behavior patterns, such as *fixed action patterns*, are also discussed, as is the effect of inherited dispositions in either facilitating or inhibiting certain types of learning. Let's begin, however, with a brief overview of the historical background to the study of learning and behavior.

QUICK QUIZ A

While reading the text, you will frequently encounter fill-in-the-blank quizzes. Students report that these quizzes greatly facilitate the task of reading by dividing the material into small chunks and by encouraging them to be actively involved with the material. Also, if you are using the 3R or underlining approach mentioned in the earlier section on study tips, the quizzes provide a way for you to assess how well these techniques are working for you. Note that many of the items contain helpful hints, usually in the form of the initial letter or two of the word that should be inserted into the blank. We have not, however, provided the answer key. This is partly because most of the answers can easily be found in the text; more importantly, though, a certain amount of uncertainty can actually facilitate learning (Dunlosky et al., 2013; Karpicke & Blunt, 2011; Schmidt & Bjork, 1992). In other words, even if you are uncertain about the answer to a particular item, your struggle to figure out the answer will very likely lead you to a better understanding of the relevant concept.

1. The term *behavior* refers to any activity of an organism that can be o__________ or somehow m__________, whereas the term *learning* refers to a relatively p__________ change in behavior as a result of some type of ex__________.
2. In __________ conditioning, behaviors that the average person typically regards as (voluntary/involuntary) *[for these types of items, simply underline the correct answer]* come to be elicited in new situations.
3. In __________ conditioning, a behavior produces some type of consequence that strengthens or weakens its occurrence. Such behaviors are typically those that are generally regarded as "g__________-directed" and which the average person often perceives as being "v__________" in nature.
4. Feeling anxious as you enter a dentist's office is an example of a behavior that has most likely been learned through __________ conditioning. *[Think: Is anxiety the type of behavior you perceive as reflexive and involuntary or as goal-directed and voluntary?]*
5. Speaking with a loud voice in a noisy environment so that others will be able to hear you is an example of a behavior that has most likely been learned through __________ conditioning.
6. According to the notational system to be used in this text, the term "A: B" means that event A (produces/is followed by) event B, and the term "X → Y" means that event X (produces/is followed by) event Y.

Historical Background

Just as it is impossible to outline all of the experiences that have made you who you are, it is impossible to outline all of the historical events that have contributed to the modern-day study of learning and behavior. Some particularly important contributions, however, are discussed in this section.

Aristotle: Empiricism and the Laws of Association

Aristotle was a Greek philosopher who lived between 384 and 322 B.C. Aristotle's teacher, Plato, believed that everything we know is inborn (which he conceived of as "residing in our soul"); thus, learning is simply a process of inner reflection to uncover the knowledge that already exists within. Aristotle, however, disagreed with Plato and argued that knowledge is not inborn but instead is acquired through experience.

Aristotle's disagreement with Plato is an early example of the classic debate between nativism and empiricism, or nature and nurture. The ***nativist*** (***nature***) perspective assumes that a person's abilities and tendencies are largely inborn, whereas the ***empiricist*** (***nurture***) perspective assumes that a person's abilities and tendencies are mostly learned. Plato is thus an early example of a nativist and Aristotle is an early example of an empiricist.[1]

Aristotle also suggested that ideas come to be connected or associated with each other via four laws of association (well, actually three, but he also hinted at a fourth that later philosophers expanded upon).

1. **The Law of Similarity.** According to this law, events that are similar to each other are readily associated with each other. For example, cars and trucks are readily associated because they are similar in appearance (wheels, doors, headlights, etc.) and function (both are used to carry passengers and materials along roadways). These similarities enable us to learn to view cars and trucks as instances of a larger category of objects known as automobiles.
2. **The Law of Contrast.** According to this law, events that are opposite from each other are readily associated. For example, on a word association test the word *black* often brings to mind the word *white*, and the word *tall* often brings to mind the word *short*. Likewise, the sight of your unwashed car reminds you of how nice it would look if you washed it, and an evening of studying reminds you of how enjoyable it would be to spend the evening not studying.
3. **The Law of Contiguity.** This law states that events that occur in close proximity to each other are readily associated (*contiguity* means "closeness"). For example, a child quickly learns to associate thunder and lightning because the sound of thunder soon follows the flash of lightning. Thunder and lightning are also perceived as coming from the same direction. Imagine how difficult it would be to associate thunder and lightning if the thunder occurred several minutes after the lightning flash and came from a different direction.
4. **The Law of Frequency.** In addition to the three preceding laws, Aristotle mentioned a supplement to the law of contiguity, which is that the more frequently two items occur together, the more strongly they are associated. You will more strongly associate a friend with a certain perfume the more frequently you smell that perfume upon meeting her. Likewise, you will more strongly associate a term (such as the law of frequency) with its definition the more frequently you practice saying that definition whenever you see the term (as when using flash cards to help memorize basic terminology).

[1]In philosophy, the term *empiricism* usually refers to the notion that *knowledge* can be gained only through sensory experience rather than through heredity or by pure reasoning. In psychology, the term has a slightly altered meaning, which is that a certain *behavior* or *ability* is the result of experience rather than heredity. Thus, the notion that great musicians have inherited a "gift" for music is a nativist viewpoint, whereas the notion that almost anyone can become a great musician given the right kind of experiences is an empiricist viewpoint. But the word *empiricism* can also be used in a methodological sense to refer to the gathering of information through systematic observation and experimentation, as in "behavioral psychology is an empirical approach to the study of behavior."

Aristotle's laws of association are not merely of historical interest. As you will read later, *the laws of contiguity and frequency are still considered important aspects of learning*. After all, how well could a dog learn to salivate to the sound of a bell if the bell preceded the presentation of food by several minutes, or if there was only one pairing of bell and food?

QUICK QUIZ B

1. The nativist position, as exemplified by the Greek philosopher ________, emphasizes the role of (learning/heredity); the empiricist position, as exemplified by the Greek philosopher ________, emphasizes the role of (learning/heredity).
2. Nativist is to (nature/nurture) as empiricist is to (nature/nurture). (*If you find analogy questions like this confusing, a search of the Internet will yield helpful information on how to handle such questions.*)
3. The law of ________ states that we associate events that are opposite to each other, whereas the law of ________ states that we associate events that occur in close proximity to each other.
4. According to the law of ________, we easily associate events that resemble each other. According to the law of ________, the more often two events occur together, the stronger the association.
5. Animals that have fur, four legs, a tail, and can bark are quickly perceived as belonging to the same species. This is an example of the law of ________.
6. The fact that the words *full* and *empty* are easily associated with each other is an example of the law of ________.
7. The *more often* one practices a particular move in wrestling, the more likely one is to perform that move in a real match. This is an example of the law of ________.
8. After once encountering a snake in her garage, Lisa is now quite nervous each time she enters the garage. This is an example of the law of ________. This is also an example of (classical/operant) conditioning.

Bettmann/CORBIS

René Descartes
(1596–1650)

Descartes: Mind-Body Dualism and the Reflex

René Descartes (1596–1650) is the French philosopher who wrote the famous line "I think, therefore I am." Fortunately for psychology, this was not his only contribution. In Descartes' time, many people assumed that human behavior was governed entirely by free will or "reason." Descartes disputed this notion and proposed a dualistic model of human nature. On the one hand, he claimed, we have a body that functions like a machine and produces involuntary, reflexive behaviors in response to external stimulation (such as sneezing in response to dust). On the other hand, we have a mind that has free will and produces behaviors that we regard as voluntary (such as choosing what to eat for dinner). Thus, Descartes' notion of ***mind–body dualism*** proposes that some human behaviors are reflexes that are automatically elicited by external stimulation, while other behaviors are freely chosen and controlled by the mind. Descartes also believed that only humans possess free will, while the behavior of nonhuman animals is entirely reflexive.

Descartes' dualistic view of human nature was a major step in the scientific study of learning and behavior because it suggested that at least some behaviors—namely, reflexive behaviors—are mechanistic and could therefore be scientifically investigated. It also suggested that the study of animal behavior might yield useful information about the reflexive aspects of human behavior.

The British Empiricists

Although Descartes believed that the human mind has free will, he also assumed, like Plato, that some of the ideas contained within it (e.g., the concepts of time and space) are inborn. By contrast, a group of British philosophers, known as the ***British empiricists***, maintained that almost all knowledge is a function of experience. For example, one of the major proponents of British empiricism, John Locke (1632–1704), proposed that a newborn's mind is a *blank slate* (in Latin, *tabula rasa*) upon which environmental experiences are written. The British empiricists also believed that the conscious mind is composed of a finite set of basic elements (specific colors, sounds, smells, etc.) that are combined through the principles of association into complex sensations and thought patterns—a sort of psychological version of the notion that all physical matter consists of various combinations of the basic elements.

QUICK QUIZ C

1. Descartes' dualistic model proposed that human behavior has two aspects: an inv__________ or ref__________ aspect that functions like a machine, and a v__________ aspect that is f__________ chosen. By contrast, the behavior of animals was believed to be entirely __________.
2. The British __________, such as John __________, maintained that knowledge was largely a function of ex__________ and that the mind of a newborn infant is a (in Latin) t__________ r__________ (which means __________ __________).
3. They also believed that the mind is composed of a finite set of basic __________ that are combined through the principles of __________ to form our conscious experiences.

Structuralism: The Experimental Study of Human Consciousness

The British empiricists did not conduct any experiments to test their notion that the mind is composed of basic elements; their conclusions were instead based upon logical reasoning and the subjective examination of their own

Edward B. Titchener
(1867–1927)

conscious experience. Realizing the deficiencies in this approach, the German philosopher Wilhelm Wundt (1832–1920) proposed using the scientific method to investigate the issue. This approach was strongly promoted by an American student of his, Edward Titchener (1867–1927), and became known as structuralism. ***Structuralism*** assumes that it is possible to determine the structure of the mind by identifying the basic elements that compose it.

Structuralists made great use of the method of ***introspection***, in which the subject in an experiment attempts to accurately describe his or her conscious thoughts, emotions, and sensations. To get a feel for how difficult this is, try to describe your conscious experience as you listen to the ticking of a clock (and just saying, "I'm bored" doesn't cut it). One thing you might report is that the ticks seem to have a certain rhythm, with a series of two or three clicks being clustered together. You might also report a slight feeling of tension (is it pleasant or unpleasant?) that builds or decreases during each series of ticks. As you can see, an accurate report of what we introspectively observe can be quite difficult.

Although this approach to psychology died out by the early 1900s (for reasons described shortly), its emphasis on systematic observation helped establish psychology as a scientific discipline. More importantly, its extreme emphasis on conscious experience as the proper subject matter for psychology resulted in a great deal of frustration and dissatisfaction—which eventually led to the later establishment of a more objective approach to psychology, known as behaviorism.

William James
(1842–1910)

Functionalism: The Study of the Adaptive Mind

William James (1842–1910), often regarded as the founder of American psychology, helped establish the approach to psychology known as functionalism. ***Functionalism*** assumes that the mind evolved to help us adapt to the world around us and that the focus of psychology should be the study of those adaptive processes. This proposition was partially derived from Darwin's theory of evolution, which proposes that adaptive characteristics that enable a species to survive and reproduce tend to increase in frequency across generations while nonadaptive characteristics tend to die out. Thus, according to a functionalist perspective, characteristics that are highly typical of a species, such as the characteristic of consciousness in humans, must have some type of adaptive value.

Based on such reasoning, functionalists believed that psychologists should not study the structure of the mind, but instead study the adaptive significance of the mind. Learning, as an adaptive process, was therefore a topic of great interest to the functionalists. Moreover, although functionalists still made use of introspection and still emphasized the analysis of conscious experience (in this manner, being similar to the structuralists), they were not opposed to the study of animal behavior. Like Darwin, they believed that humans evolved in the same manner as other animals and that much of what we learn from studying animals might therefore be of direct relevance to humans. Not surprisingly, two of the most important figures in the early history of behaviorism, E. L. Thorndike (discussed in Chapter 6) and John B. Watson (discussed later in this chapter), were students of functionalist psychologists.

QUICK QUIZ D

1. The st__________ approach proposed that the goal of psychology should be to identify the basic elements of the mind. The primary research method used for accomplishing this was the method of i__________.
2. Those who adopted the f__________ approach to psychology emphasized the adaptive processes of the mind and were thus very interested in the study of learning.
3. The __________ approach viewed animal research as (relevant/irrelevant) to the study of human behavior in that humans were assumed to have evolved in a (similar/dissimilar) way to other animals.
4. The functionalists were similar to the structuralists in that they emphasized the study of c__________ experience and often used the method of i__________.
5. William James was a (functionalist/structuralist), and Edward Titchener was a __________.

Philip Gendreau/Bettmann/CORBIS

Charles Darwin
(1809–1882)

The Theory of Evolution: Humans as Animals

As we have seen, the theory of evolution had a significant influence on the development of behaviorism, which continues today. We should therefore take some time to discuss this theory more fully. Charles Darwin published the theory of evolution in 1859 in his book, *On the Origin of Species by Means of Natural Selection* (often simply called *The Origin of Species*). It describes how species, including humans, change across generations in response to environmental pressures. The basis of this theory is the principle of ***natural***

selection, which is the concept that individuals or species that are capable of adapting to environmental pressures are more likely to reproduce and pass along their adaptive characteristics than those that cannot adapt.

There are three main components to the principle of natural selection. The first is that *traits vary, both within a species* (e.g., some dogs are larger than other dogs) *and between species* (e.g., humans have a slower metabolism than hummingbirds). The second is that *many traits are heritable*, meaning that they have a genetic basis and can be inherited by offspring. The third component of natural selection is that *organisms must compete for limited resources* (bearing in mind, however, that being an effective competitor might sometimes involve cooperation as much as conflict).

Now let us put all three ideas together. Some individuals will acquire more resources than others based on certain inherited traits that give them an advantage. These individuals are therefore better able to survive—which is commonly referred to as "survival of the fittest." However, the real driving force behind evolution is not survival of the fittest but the *reproductive advantage held by those individuals possessing traits that are best suited to the environment*. In other words, successful individuals are more likely to have offspring who, when they inherit the successful traits from their parents, are also more likely to survive and have offspring. As this process continues through succeeding generations, the proportion of individuals possessing the successful traits increases while the proportion of individuals possessing the unsuccessful traits decreases. Eventually, the changed population might differ so much from the original population that it becomes a new species.

Thus, an ***evolutionary adaptation*** is an adaptive trait that evolves as a result of natural selection. We usually think of such adaptations as physical characteristics (e.g., the trunk of an elephant), but adaptations can also be behaviors. For example, as you will learn in Chapter 3, if you inadvertently place your hand over a flame, a *flexion response* will cause you automatically to pull your hand away from the damaging fire even before you consciously feel pain. You can imagine how an inborn reflex like this would help an individual live long enough to reproduce, compared to an individual who lacked such reflexes.

A particularly important evolutionary adaptation, which is the focus of this text, is the ability to learn. From an evolutionary perspective, the ability to learn evolved because it conferred significant survival advantages on those who had this ability. Thus, the distinction between nature and nurture can be seen as highly simplistic, since the ability to learn (nurture) is itself inherited (nature).

In this text, you will learn about features of learning that are common across a variety of species, which suggests that the ancestors of these species faced similar environmental pressures that resulted in the evolution of similar features. Nevertheless, you will also learn about certain between-species differences in learning ability.

As noted, Darwin's theory of evolution had a strong effect on the early development of behaviorism, especially through its influence on the functionalist school of psychology out of which behaviorism developed.

It continues to have an effect through the increased attention given these days to the role of genetic factors in learning, and through the recent establishment of "evolutionary psychology" as a major area of study within psychology.

QUICK QUIZ E

1. The three main components to the theory of natural selection are:
   a. traits vary, within and between species
   b. many traits are variable
   c. organisms must compete for limited resources

2. To say that a trait is heritable means that it has a genetic basis and can be inherited by offspring.

3. The real driving force behind evolution is not survival of the fittest, but rather the reproductive advantage held by individuals who possess adaptive traits.

4. It is simplistic to assume that one can draw a clear distinction between nature and nurture, because the way we learn is itself an inherited trait.

Psychology Archives/The University of Akron

John B. Watson
(1878–1958)

Behaviorism: The Study of Observable Behavior

In 1913, a flamboyant young psychologist by the name of John B. Watson published a paper titled "Psychology as the Behaviorist Views It." In it, he lamented the lack of progress achieved by experimental psychologists up to that time, particularly the lack of findings that had any practical significance. A major difficulty, Watson believed, was the then-current emphasis on the study of conscious experience, especially as promoted by the structuralists. In particular, the method of introspection was proving to be highly unreliable. Researchers frequently failed to replicate each other's findings, which often led to bitter squabbles. Watson mockingly described the types of arguments that often ensued:

> If you fail to reproduce my findings, it is not due to some fault in your apparatus or in the control of your stimulus, but it is due to the fact that your introspection is untrained.... If you can't observe 3–9 states of clearness in attention, your introspection is poor. If, on the other hand, a feeling seems reasonably clear to you, your introspection is again faulty. You are seeing too much. Feelings are never clear. (Watson, 1913, p. 163)

The difficulty, of course, is that we are unable to directly observe another person's thoughts and feelings. We therefore have to make an *inference* that the person's verbal reports about those thoughts and feelings are accurate.[2] It is also the case that many of the questions being tackled by the structuralists were essentially unanswerable, such as whether sound has the quality of "extension in space" and whether there is a difference in "texture" between an imagined perception of an object and the actual perception of the object (Watson, 1913, p. 164). In a very real sense, experimental psychology seemed to be drowning in a sea of vaguely perceived images and difficult-to-describe mental events. Moreover, the notion that the proper subject matter of psychology was the study of consciousness was so strongly entrenched that it affected even those who studied animal behavior. As Watson exclaimed,

> On this view, after having determined our animal's ability to learn, the simplicity or complexity of its methods of learning, the effect of past habit upon present response...we should still feel that the task is unfinished and that the results are worthless, until we can interpret them by analogy in the light of consciousness. [In other words,] we feel forced to say something about the possible mental processes of the animal. (Watson, 1913, p. 160)

Watson reasoned that the only solution to this dilemma was to make psychology a purely "objective science" based solely on the study of directly observable behavior and the environmental events that surround it. All reference to internal processes, such as thoughts and feelings, were to be stricken from analysis. By objectifying psychology in this manner, Watson hoped that psychology could then join the ranks of the *natural sciences*—biology, chemistry, and physics—which had traditionally emphasized the study of observable phenomena. In Watson's now-classic words,

> Psychology as the behaviorist views it is a purely objective experimental branch of natural science. Its theoretical goal is the prediction and control of behavior. Introspection forms no essential part of its methods, nor is the scientific value of its data dependent upon the readiness with which they lend themselves to interpretation in terms of consciousness. (Watson, 1913, p. 154)

Thus, as originally defined by Watson, ***behaviorism*** is a natural science approach to psychology that focuses on the study of environmental influences on observable behavior.

---

[2]An *inference* is a supposition or guess based on logical deduction rather than on observation. For example, if you describe to me a dream that you had last night, your report is based on your direct observation of a subjective experience. But if I accept that description (because there seems to be no reason for you to lie about it), I am making an inference that your report is accurate. Now suppose I interpret the dream as indicating that you have some unresolved, unconscious conflict, and you accept that interpretation as true. We are now both making an inference that this unconscious conflict exists, because neither you nor I have directly observed it. Needless to say, inferences about unconscious processes are even more problematic than inferences about conscious processes, because not even the person in whom the unconscious process exists is able to directly observe it.

Watson also believed strongly in the value of animal research. In keeping with his functionalist background—in turn following from Darwin's theory of evolution—he believed that the principles governing the behavior of nonhuman species might also be relevant to the behavior of humans. Thus, traditional behavioral research is often conducted using nonhuman animals, primarily rats and pigeons. As many of the examples in this text illustrate, the results obtained from such research are often highly applicable to human behavior.

It is worth noting that Watson was not the first psychologist to recommend a more objective, natural science approach to psychology. He simply reflected a growing sentiment among many researchers at that time that such a move was necessary. Watson's arguments, however, were the most clearly stated and therefore had a strong effect. Thus, while his 1913 paper (which later became known as the "Behaviorist Manifesto") did not have an immediate impact, its influence slowly grew until, by the 1920s, the behaviorist revolution was well under way. (For a brief discussion of Watson's personal life, see "John B. Watson: Behaviorism's Controversial Founder" in the And Furthermore box.)

And Furthermore

John B. Watson: Behaviorism's Controversial Founder

John B. Watson was a charismatic and aggressive individual and as such was perhaps ideally suited for lifting psychology out of the mentalistic quagmire in which it had become immersed. Unfortunately, those same traits led to a life of conflict. The most infamous story concerns the manner in which Watson was forced to resign from his university position. One version has it that he and a female student were caught conducting intimate experiments on human sexual responding, and he was forced to resign over the resultant scandal. There is, however, little evidence for this story (see Benjamin, Whitaker, Ramsey, & Zeve, 2007, for a description of how this rumor became established), and the real events appear to be as follows.

In 1920, at the height of his academic career, Watson began an affair with Rosalie Rayner, a graduate student whose family was well connected and powerful. Catching wind of the affair, Watson's wife entered Rosalie's room during a social visit to the Rayners and stole the letters Watson had written to his young lover. She then filed for divorce and used the letters to help win a lucrative settlement. Meanwhile, the university ordered Watson to end his affair with Rosalie. Watson refused and immediately tendered his resignation. Soon after, news of Watson's divorce and of the affair found its way into the media, with one of Watson's love letters even appearing in several newspapers. Watson's academic career was ruined.

Cast adrift, Watson married Rayner and obtained a job with a New York advertising firm. In his new position, he attempted to promote a more scientific approach to the discipline of advertising—though the extent to which he had any significant influence on the industry is questionable (Coon, 1994). He also continued to publish books and magazine articles promoting his behavioristic views. In fact, Watson was very much the pop psychologist of his era, much like the present-day Dr. Phil. Unfortunately, as with pop psychology today, some of his advice was based more on personal opinion than on well-established principles. For example, Watson believed that children should be trained to act like adults and even recommended giving them a handshake, rather than a hug or a kiss, when sending them to bed! In fact, the only time he ever showed affection to his own children was when his wife died in 1935. Teary eyed, Watson lightly put his arms around his children as he told them that their mother had passed away, then never again mentioned her name. Not surprisingly, his children retained bitter memories of their upbringing, and one son later committed suicide.

It has been suggested that Watson had an underlying fear of emotions. In his love relationships (and he had numerous affairs throughout his life), he was extremely impulsive and amorous; yet in a group setting he would reportedly flee the room when the discussion turned to emotional issues. Thus, although Watson's proposal to banish thoughts and feelings from psychology helped establish it as a more objective science, it may also have reflected some personal difficulties.

In his later years, Watson became something of a recluse, living in the country and raising animals. He had always been fond of animals—sometimes claiming he preferred their company to that of humans—which may account for his early interest in animal research. He died in 1958 at the age of 80. (See Buckley, 1989, for a comprehensive biography of Watson.)

QUICK QUIZ F

1. Watson noted that a major problem with the method of ________ was that the results obtained were often unreliable.
2. A basic problem with relying on someone's report about his or her thoughts and feelings is that we are making an i________ that the report is accurate. This term is defined in the footnote as a supposition or guess based on logical d________ rather than direct o________.
3. The notion that the proper subject matter of psychology should be the study of consciousness was so strong that even those who studied ________ behavior felt compelled to make inferences about mental processes in their subjects.
4. Watson argued that psychology needed to become a n________ science (like biology, chemistry, and physics) based solely on the study of directly ob________ events.

Five Schools of Behaviorism

Many people mistakenly believe that behaviorism is a monolithic entity, with Watson's views being the same views held by other behaviorists. In fact, there are several schools of behaviorism, each based on a somewhat different set of assumptions about how best to study environmental influences on behavior. In this section, we describe five of these schools, beginning with Watson's original brand of behaviorism, which is sometimes referred to as methodological behaviorism (e.g., O'Donohue & Ferguson, 2001).[3]

Watson's Methodological Behaviorism

One of the most extreme versions of behaviorism is the one originally proposed by Watson (1913). ***Methodological behaviorism*** asserts that, for methodological reasons, psychologists should study only those behaviors that can be directly observed (see Figure 1.1). Subjectively perceived activities, such as thinking, are methodologically too difficult to assess to be of much use in a scientific analysis of behavior. Such activities can be included for analysis only if they can, in some way, be directly measured. Watson, for example, hypothesized that thinking involves minute movements of the vocal cords in the larynx—and he enjoyed goading his critics by referring to his own thoughts as "laryngeal activity" (Buckley, 1989). If this were true, and if such movements could be precisely measured, then the act of thinking could be subjected to scientific analysis. (As it turns out, laryngeal activity is not a reliable measure of thinking.)

It is important to emphasize that Watson's behavioristic proposal to ignore thoughts and feelings in scientific analysis was not simply an attempt to dehumanize people or to pretend that thoughts and feelings do not exist (whatever his own personal biases may have been); rather, it was in part a logical response to a crisis. If the discipline of psychology was to survive, it would need to break free from the extreme mentalism of the time and adopt

FIGURE 1.1 In methodological behaviorism, internal events, such as consciously perceived thoughts and feelings as well as unconscious drives and motives, are excluded from the analysis of behavior. Instead, one studies the direct relationship between changes in the environment and changes in observable behavior.

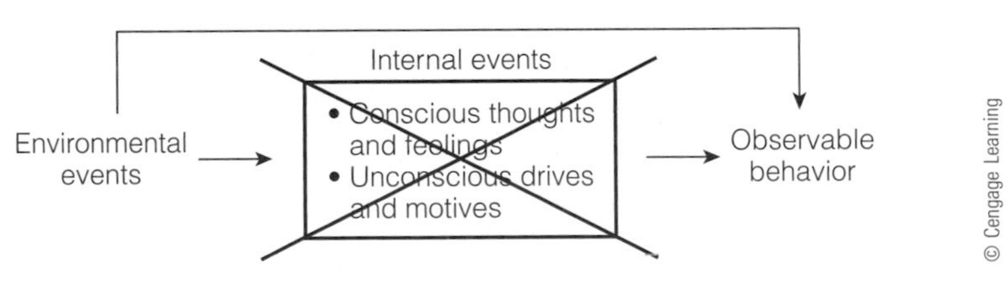

[3]Be aware that the names of the different schools presented here are not at all standardized. For example, a quick search of scholarly postings on the Internet will soon reveal alternative names for Watson's approach, such as *classical behaviorism* and even *radical behaviorism* (which is usually reserved for Skinner's version of behaviorism). And the term *methodological behaviorism* is sometimes applied to any approach that rejects the value of data gathered through introspection, including many cognitive approaches to psychology.

a much different perspective. Watson's behavioristic call to arms, though extreme, accomplished just that.

From a theoretical perspective, Watson's specific view of learning was rather mechanistic. Drawing from Pavlov's work on classical conditioning, he came to believe that all learning involves the development of a simple connection between an environmental event (the "stimulus") and a specific behavior (the "response"). Watson's theory of learning is therefore regarded as a type of ***stimulus-response (S-R) theory***, in which a connection is formed between a specific stimulus and a specific response. Complex behavior is presumed to involve extremely long chains of these S-R connections.

Over time, Watson also became something of an extremist regarding the nature–nurture issue. In his original 1913 article, he had emphasized the influence of both heredity and environment on behavior. In fact, he was one of the first individuals to systematically study innate behavior patterns in animals (he spent several strenuous summers engaged in field research with a type of seabird). Later, however, following extensive observations of human infants, he came to the conclusion that humans inherit only a few fundamental reflexes along with three basic emotions: love, rage, and fear. Everything else, he believed, is learned. This led Watson, in 1930, to make one of his most famous claims:

> Give me a dozen healthy infants, well-formed, and my own specified world to bring them up in and I'll guarantee to take any one at random and train him to become any type of specialist I might select—doctor, lawyer, artist, merchant-chief, and, yes, even beggar-man and thief, regardless of his talents, penchants, tendencies, abilities, vocations, and race of his ancestors. (p. 104)

Unfortunately, many textbooks quote only this passage and omit the very next sentence, which reads, "I am going beyond my facts, but so have the advocates of the contrary and they have been doing it for many thousands of years" (p. 104). And this was precisely Watson's point: The supposition that a person's abilities are largely inherited has been strongly promoted throughout history (and has often been used to justify acts of discrimination and racism). Watson was one of the first to issue a strong challenge to this assumption, arguing instead that there is at least as much evidence suggesting that human abilities are mostly learned. For this reason, Watson's behavioral model became quite popular among the reformists of his day who were attempting to combat racism. (For recent evidence on the importance of learning as opposed to innate ability, see "Deliberate Practice and Expert Performance" in the And Furthermore box.)

As we previously noted, many people mistakenly equate behaviorism with Watson's rather extreme version. In fact, few behaviorists were this extreme; instead, they developed approaches that were considerably more moderate. One of the most influential of these was Hull's neobehaviorism, which we discuss next.

QUICK QUIZ G

1. Watson's brand of behaviorism is often referred to as ______ behaviorism.
2. According to this type of behaviorism, psychologists should study only those behaviors that can be ______.
3. Watson believed that all reference to ______ events should be eliminated from the study of behavior.
4. Watson proposed a(n) ______-______ theory of learning, which hypothesizes that learning involves the formation of a direct connection between a st______ and a r______.
5. In his 1913 article on behaviorism, Watson emphasized the influence of (heredity/environment/both) in the development of behavior. In his later theorizing, he downplayed the role of ______ in the development of human behavior.
6. In his later theorizing, Watson proposed that humans inherit (many/a few) basic reflexes, along with three basic emotions: ______, ______, and ______.

And Furthermore

Deliberate Practice and Expert Performance

Watson's emphasis on the importance of nurture over nature in determining human behavior is often viewed with skepticism. This is especially the case when it comes to behaviors that are indicative of exceptional ability. Most people, including many psychologists (e.g., Gardner, 1993), assume that, unless a person is born with a certain amount of talent, there are limits in how far he or she will be able to progress in a particular endeavor. Indeed, the notion that a Babe Ruth, Albert Einstein, or Wolfgang Amadeus Mozart is to a large extent born, and not made, is part of the mystique surrounding these individuals. But consider the following:

- Expert performers in almost all fields of endeavor, ranging from music to athletics to chess, require a minimum of 10 years of intensive training before achieving a high level of performance. Even Mozart, who started composing at age 4, did not compose world-class music until his late teens. Mozart's father was also a professional musician who published the first book on violin instruction and provided his children with intensive musical training from an early age. (Mozart's reputation has also benefitted from certain dubious claims: For example, the notion that he could compose entire works in memory and then write them down with little or no editing is based on a single passage in a supposed letter of his that is now believed to be a forgery [Colvin, 2008]).
- As an experiment, a Hungarian educator, Polgar, set out to systematically train his daughters to become expert chess players. All three daughters have achieved high rankings in international chess, and one daughter, Judit, at one point held the record for becoming the youngest grand master ever, at 15 years of age.
- The superlative abilities shown by experts are almost always specific to their field of endeavor. For example, chess experts have the ability to memorize the exact positions of all the chess pieces in a game after only a few seconds' glance at the chessboard.

But they perform no better than non-chess players at memorizing chess pieces randomly distributed around the board in a non-game pattern.

- Almost all of the remarkable feats displayed by *savants*—individuals of low intellectual ability who nevertheless possess some remarkable skill—have been taught to normal individuals. For example, the ability of some savants to name the day of the week for any arbitrary date (e.g., "What day of the week was June 30, 1854?") has been duplicated by ordinary college students after only a few weeks of training.

Based on findings such as these, Ericsson, Krampe, and Tesch-Römer (1993; see also Ericsson & Charness, 1994) argued that the most critical factor in determining expert performance is not innate ability but deliberate practice. Deliberate practice is practice that is not inherently enjoyable; it instead involves intense concentration and considerable effort with a view toward improving one's performance. More than any other variable, the accumulated amount of deliberate practice in an activity is strongly predictive of an individual's level of performance.

Because deliberate practice is so effortful, the amount that can be tolerated each day is necessarily limited. For this reason, elite performers often practice about 4 hours per day. Ericsson et al. (1993), for example, found that the best violin students engaged in solitary practice (which was judged to be the most important type of practice) for approximately 3.5 hours per day, spread out across two to three sessions, each session lasting an average of 80 minutes. Note that this did not include time spent receiving instruction, giving performances, or playing for enjoyment. The students also devoted about 3.5 hours a day to rest and recreation and obtained more than average amounts of sleep.

Top-level performers in intellectual pursuits display similar characteristics. Novelists typically write for about 3 to 4 hours each day, usually in the morning. Eminent scientists likewise write for a few hours each morning—the writing of articles arguably being the most important activity determining their success—and then devote the rest of the day to other duties. B. F. Skinner is especially instructive in this regard. In his later life, he would rise at midnight and write for 1 hour, then rise again at 5:00 A.M. and write for another 2 hours. The remainder of the morning was devoted to correspondence and other professional tasks, while much of the afternoon was devoted to leisure activities such as tinkering in his workshop and listening to music. He deliberately resisted any urge to engage in serious writing at other times of the day, feeling that this often resulted in poor-quality writing the next morning. However, the limited amount of writing he did each day was more than compensated for by the consistency with which he wrote, resulting in a steady stream of influential articles and books throughout his career (Bjork, 1993).

Of course, Ericsson et al. (1993) do not completely discount the role of heredity in expert performance. Heredity might well affect the extent to which one becomes interested in an endeavor, as well as one's ability to endure the hard work needed to become a top performer. Nevertheless, the obvious importance of deliberate practice suggests that we should not be too quick to discount our ability to acquire a certain skill. Although many of us might not have the desire, time, or resources to become elite athletes, excellent musicians, or famous scientists, this does not rule out the possibility of becoming better tennis players, learning how to play the guitar, or significantly improving our math skills. After all, the best evidence available suggests that it is largely a matter of practice. (See Ericsson, 2009, for further information on this topic.)

Deane Keller, "Dr. Clark Leonard Hull (1884–1952), M. A. (Hon.) 1929" Yale University Art Gallery, Gift of Colleagues, friends and students of the sitter

Clark L. Hull
(1884–1952)

Hull's Neobehaviorism

A major challenge to methodological behaviorism came from Clark Hull (1884–1952), who claimed that Watson's rejection of unobservable events was scientifically unsound. Hull noted that both physicists and chemists make inferences about events they have never directly observed but that can nevertheless be *operationalized* (i.e., defined in such a way that they can be measured). For example, gravity cannot be directly observed, but its effect on falling objects can be precisely measured. Hull believed that it might likewise be useful for psychologists to infer the existence of internal events that might *mediate* (form a connection) between the environment and behavior.

The mediating events that Hull incorporated into his theory consisted largely of physiological-type reactions, for example, a "hunger drive" that can be operationalized as number of hours of food deprivation. Such mediating events are formally called *intervening variables*, meaning that they intervene between a cause (such as food deprivation) and an effect (such as speed of running toward food). Thus, Hull's ***neobehaviorism*** utilizes intervening variables, in the form of hypothesized physiological processes, to help explain behavior (see Figure 1.2).

It is important to note that Hull's use of intervening variables did not mean that he advocated a return to mentalism. Like Watson, he strongly opposed the use of introspection as a scientific tool, believing that subjective experiences are too vague and unreliable to be of much use. Thus, whether the organism actually experienced a feeling of hunger was of no concern to him. What did concern him was whether the *concept of hunger*, as defined in some measurable way (such as number of hours of food deprivation), was scientifically useful and led to testable hypotheses.

Hull's theory was also an S-R theory because it assumed that learning consists of the establishment of connections between specific stimuli and specific

FIGURE 1.2 In Hull's neobehaviorism, theorists make use of intervening variables in the form of hypothesized physiological processes to help explain the relationship between the environment and behavior.

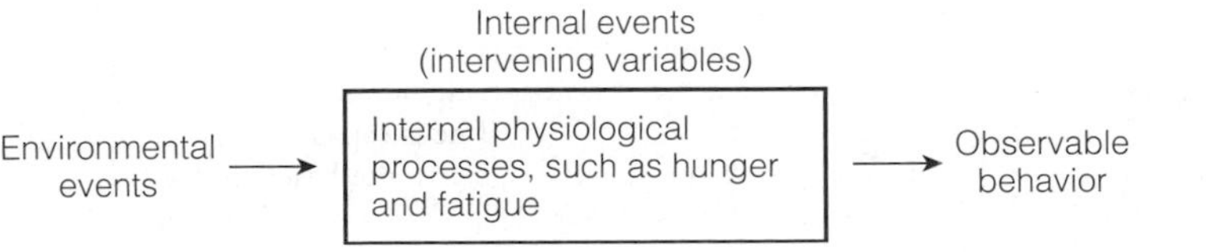

responses. Thus, like Watson, he viewed behavior in a very mechanistic, stimulus-response fashion. Lest this seem dehumanizing, recognize that it is not far removed from some modern-day cognitive approaches, which view humans as analogous to computers that process bits of information from the environment (input) to produce responses (output). This is actually quite similar to Hull's model of behavior. In fact, some versions of modern-day cognitive psychology can even be considered outgrowths of Hull's neobehaviorism.[4]

Hull was the most influential experimental psychologist of the 1940s and 1950s. Unfortunately, many aspects of his theory (which are beyond the scope of this text) were very difficult to test. The theory was also highly mathematical and grew increasingly complex as equations were expanded and modified. Some of these modifications were forced on Hull by his critics, the most famous of whom was Edward C. Tolman. (For an overview of Hull's theory, as well as to gain a sense of its complexity, see Hull, 1943.)

QUICK QUIZ H

1. Hull believed that it might be useful to incorporate internal events into one's theorizing so long as they can be op__________ by defining them in such a way that they can be measured.
2. In Hull's approach, the internal events he included were hypothetical ph__________ processes.
3. Such internal events are called i__________ variables in that they are presumed to m__________ between the environment and behavior.
4. Hull's theory was a(n) __________ theory in that it assumed that the process of learning involves the creation of connections between specific s__________ and specific r__________.

Tolman's Cognitive Behaviorism

Hull's S-R theory of learning is often categorized as a "molecular" theory insofar as it assumed that specific S-R connections are the building blocks of behavior in the same way that molecules are the building blocks of matter. Edward Tolman (1886–1959) disagreed with this approach and believed that it would be more useful to analyze behavior on a "molar" (i.e., broader) level.

---

[4]Interestingly, people seem less critical of the cognitive information-processing approach to psychology, which draws an analogy between humans and computers, than they are of the traditional behavioral approach, which draws an analogy between humans and animals such as rats. Perhaps this is because we are impressed by the ability of computers to perform certain human-like tasks (e.g., play chess), and we are insulted by the notion that humans and rats have anything in common. Yet, outside their specialized abilities, computers are quite inferior to rats. Imagine, for example, that a man, a rat, and a computer are washed up on a deserted island. To the extent that the man emulates the rat (if he is capable of it), he will likely survive; to the extent that he emulates the computer, he will sit on the beach and rot. Rats have a marvelous ability to learn and adapt; present-day computers do not. Fortunately for us, humans are far more rat-like than computer-like.

Edward C. Tolman
(1886–1959)

For example, he felt that we can understand a rat's behavior in a maze more accurately as a goal-directed attempt to obtain food than as a long chain of discrete stimulus-response connections that, in machine-like fashion, lead to food (e.g., Tolman, 1932). This molar approach to learning is similar to the gestalt approach to perception (Kohler, 1947), from which Tolman drew much of his inspiration. To the gestalt psychologists, perception is not simply the summation of different bits of conscious experience but is instead a "holistic" process resulting in an organized, coherent, perceptual experience. We perceive a house as more than just a combination of bricks and boards; it is bricks and boards plus something more. As the classic gestalt saying goes, "the whole is more than the sum of the parts." Similarly, for Tolman, behavior is more than just a chain of discrete responses attached to discrete stimuli. It is instead an overall pattern of behavior directed toward particular outcomes, and it can be properly analyzed only on that level.

Although Tolman disagreed with much of Hull's theorizing, he did agree that intervening variables may be useful in a theory of learning (in fact, it was Tolman who first suggested this). However, while Hull's intervening variables were physiological-type processes like hunger and fatigue, Tolman's were more mentalistic. The Tolmanian rat, as well as the Tolmanian person, was not simply motivated by drives and habits but also had "expectations" and "hypotheses." Thus, Tolman's ***cognitive behaviorism*** (sometimes called "purposive behaviorism") utilizes intervening variables, usually in the form of hypothesized cognitive processes, to help explain behavior (see Figure 1.3).

Tolman's (1948) most famous intervening variable is the ***cognitive map***, which is a mental representation of one's spatial surroundings. Evidence for this concept was provided by a study on "latent learning" by Tolman and Honzik (1930). This experiment was conducted in an attempt to disprove Hull's notion that behavior must be rewarded for learning to take place;

FIGURE 1.3 In Tolman's cognitive behaviorism, theorists make use of intervening variables in the form of hypothesized cognitive processes to help explain the relationship between environment and behavior.

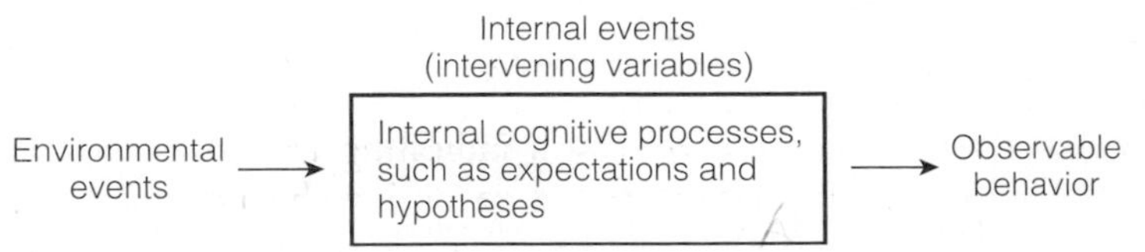

FIGURE 1.4 Maze used by Tolman and Honzik (1930) in their study of latent learning. (Adapted from M. H. Elliott, *The Effect of Change of Reward on the Maze Performance of Rats.* University of California, Publications in Psychology, Volume 4, 1928.).

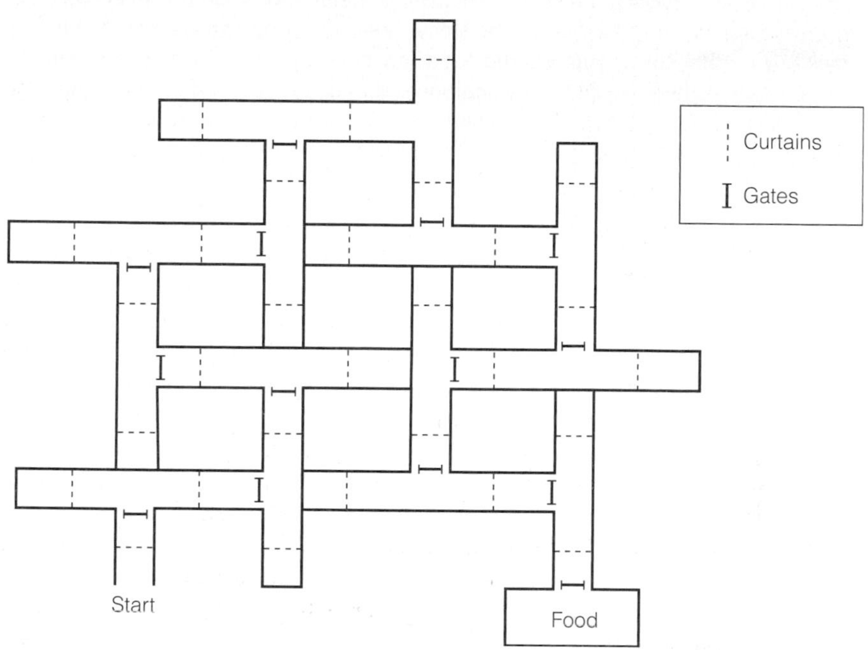

that is, in the absence of some type of reward, nothing can be learned. To test this notion, Tolman and Honzik trained three groups of rats on a complex maze task (see Figure 1.4). The rats in a continuous-reward group always found food when they reached the goal box, but the rats in the two other groups found no food when they reached the goal box (they were simply removed from the maze and then fed several hours later). Training proceeded at the rate of one trial per day for 10 consecutive days. As expected, the rewarded group learned to run quickly to the goal box, whereas the two nonrewarded groups took much longer to do so.

Following this initial phase of training, on day 11 the rats in one of the nonrewarded groups also began receiving food when they reached the goal box. According to Hull, the rats in that group should only then have started to learn their way through the maze, which would have been demonstrated by a gradual improvement in their performance. What Tolman and Honzik found instead was a dramatic improvement in the rats' performance on the very next trial (see Figure 1.5; see also "How to Read a Graph" in the And Furthermore box).

Tolman interpreted these results as indicating that the initially nonrewarded rats had in fact learned the maze during the first 10 trials of the experiment, and that they had learned it at least as well as the group that

FIGURE 1.5 Errors made by the different groups of rats in Tolman and Honzik's (1930) latent learning experiment. The vertical axis represents the average number of wrong turns the rats in each group made before reaching the goal box. Group NR are those rats that never received a reward for reaching the goal box. Group R are those rats that always received a reward for reaching the goal box. Group NR-R received no reward for the first 10 days of the study, then began receiving a reward on day 11. Note that this group was run for a few days longer than the other two groups to see if there would be any additional change in their performance. (Adapted from Tolman, E. C., & Honzik, C. H. (1930). Degrees of hunger, reward and nonreward, and maze learning in rats. *University of California Publications in Psychology, 4,* 241–275.)

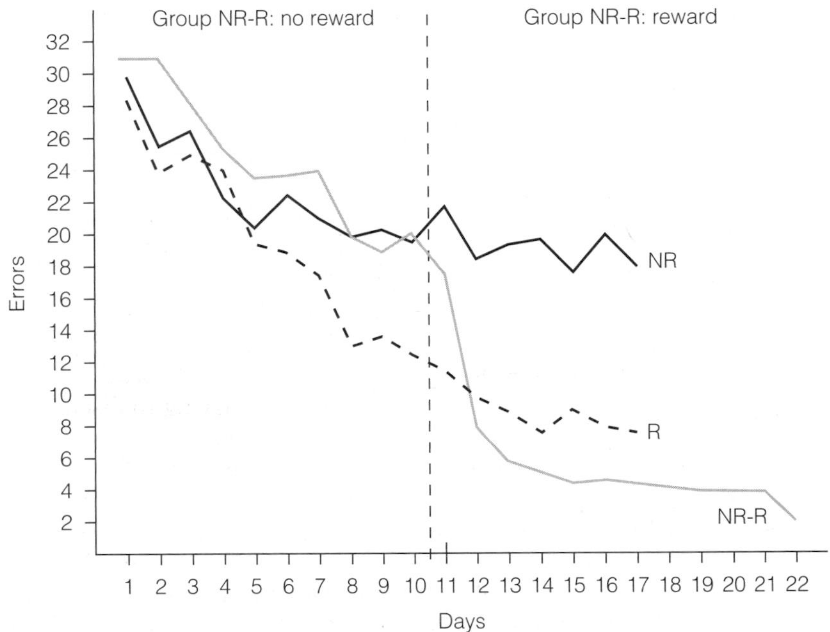

had been receiving food. He would later interpret these findings as indicating that the rats had developed a "cognitive map" of the maze during the early trials (Tolman, 1948), which became apparent only when they began to receive food in the goal box. Thus, this experiment is regarded as a classic demonstration of ***latent learning***, in which learning occurs despite the absence of any observable indication of learning and only becomes apparent at a later time. The experiment is also regarded as demonstrating the distinction between *learning* and *performance*, because learning was apparently taking place even when the subjects showed no evidence of learning in their performance at that time. (See also Jensen, 2006, for a critique of this study and how it has been interpreted.)

And Furthermore

How to Read Graphs

A graph is a concise way of conveying information. It has two axes: the horizontal or x-axis, which is formally called the abscissa, and the vertical or y-axis, which is formally called the ordinate. The vertical axis is usually a measure of the target behavior in which we are interested; in Figure 1.5 this is the number of errors the rats made while running through a maze. The horizontal axis usually indicates some aspect of the experimental manipulation, in this case the days on which the rats were run through the maze. The broken line between days 10 and 11 indicates that there was a change in conditions at this time, which is described by the labels on each side of the broken line (namely, that group NR-R switched from receiving no reward to receiving a reward). The three lines within the graph therefore indicate the average number of errors made by each group of rats on each day of the experiment.

Although Tolman believed that it was useful to incorporate cognitive variables into his theory, he remained in many ways a standard behaviorist. Like Hull and Watson, he believed that introspective reports of thoughts and feelings are so unreliable as to be of little scientific value. He maintained that his own theoretical inferences about cognitive processes were based entirely on direct observations of behavior and were thus objectively based. Tolman once even apologized for the "shameful necessity" of having to discuss conscious experience in a textbook he was writing (Tolman, 1932)—a reflection perhaps of how frustrated psychologists had been by the old introspectionist approach. Like other behaviorists, Tolman also believed strongly in the usefulness of animal research for discovering basic processes of learning, and almost all of his research was conducted with rats.

Much of Tolman's research was directly aimed at challenging Hull's theory of learning. Hull responded by modifying his theory, in increasingly complex ways, to account for many of Tolman's findings.[5] As a result, Tolman's cognitive behaviorism never achieved the same popularity

[5]Roughly speaking, Hull (1943) tried to account for the results of Tolman and Honzik's latent learning experiment by hypothesizing that the rats in the nonrewarded conditions found the mere act of being removed from the maze when they reached the empty goal box to be slightly rewarding. This slight reward was sufficient to ensure that the rats learned the pathway to the goal box, but not sufficient to motivate them to greatly reduce the number of errors they were making. Only when the incentive to get to the goal box was increased by the availability of food did the number of errors drop significantly and the degree of learning become evident. Alternatively, Jensen (2006) has recently pointed to evidence indicating that the rats in the nonrewarded group may have found the act of entering a blind alley punishing, thereby reducing their tendency to make incorrect responses. This would again argue against interpreting these particular results as strong evidence of latent learning.

"Bathroom? Sure, it's just down the hall to the left, jog right, left, another left, straight past two more lefts, then right, and it's at the end of the third corridor on your right."

during his lifetime as Hull's neobehavioral approach. With the growth of cognitive psychology, however, many of Tolman's research methods and concepts have been adopted by modern researchers. Cognitive behaviorism is now a flourishing field of study, and the study of cognitive processes in nonhuman animals is now known as "animal cognition" or "comparative cognition" (which is the focus of Chapter 13).

QUICK QUIZ I

1. Tolman's approach is known as ____________ behaviorism because it utilizes mentalistic concepts, such as "expectations," to explain behavior. This approach is also sometimes called p____________ behaviorism.
2. A ____________ ____________ is an internal representation of one's surroundings.
3. The experiment by Tolman and Honzik (1930) has traditionally been regarded as a demonstration of ____________ learning, in which learning appears to take place in the absence of any reward. The experiment has also been regarded as a demonstration of the distinction between learning and ____________.
4. Tolman believed that introspectively observed thoughts and feelings are (useless/useful) in the analysis of behavior. As well, almost all of Tolman's research was conducted using ____________ as subjects.
5. The modern-day study of cognitive processes in nonhuman animals is known as a____________ c____________ or com____________ c____________.

Albert Bandura
(b. 1925)

Bandura's Social Learning Theory

If Tolman's use of cognitive concepts seems to represent a partial return to mentalism, Albert Bandura's social learning theory is an even stronger step in that direction. The roots of social learning theory can be partly traced to Hull's neobehaviorism in that Bandura had considerable exposure to Hullian theorists during his graduate training. In fact, the term *social learning theory* was first used by followers of Hull who were attempting to apply Hullian concepts to human social behavior, particularly the process of imitation (Miller & Dollard, 1941). Bandura was very much interested in imitation, which he referred to as *observational learning*, and he eventually became the dominant researcher in the field. His most famous investigations concern the effect of observational learning on aggressive behavior (Bandura, 1973).

Although Bandura's interests were partially influenced by Hullian psychologists, his interpretation of the learning process is more closely aligned with Tolman. Like Tolman, Bandura focuses on broad behavior patterns (i.e., he uses a molar approach) and strongly emphasizes the distinction between learning and performance. Unlike Tolman, however, he views internal events as more than just theoretically useful; they are seen as actual events occurring within us that strongly influence our behavior. This means that, unlike the other behaviorists we have discussed, Bandura does not dismiss the value of introspectively observed thoughts and feelings in explaining behavior. Thus, ***social learning theory*** (also called *cognitive social learning theory* or *social-cognitive theory*) strongly emphasizes the importance of observational learning and cognitive variables in explaining human behavior (Bandura, 1977, 1997).

Bandura also has a distinct view of determinism (the notion that each behavior has a cause). ***Reciprocal determinism*** is the assumption that environmental events, observable behavior, and "person variables" (including thoughts and feelings) reciprocally influence each other (see Figure 1.6). Thus, according to Bandura, how we think and behave can influence our environment—through the environments we choose to be in as well as how we perceive those environments—as much as the environment influences how we think and behave. And behavior can influence our thoughts and feelings ("I'm stammering, therefore I must be anxious") as much as our thoughts and feelings can influence our behavior. This can be contrasted with the other models we've discussed in which environment causes behavior, and internal events, if included, serve only a mediational role (Environment → Internal events → Behavior).

FIGURE 1.6 Bandura's model of reciprocal determinism, in which observable behavior, environmental events, and internal events are all viewed as interacting with each other.

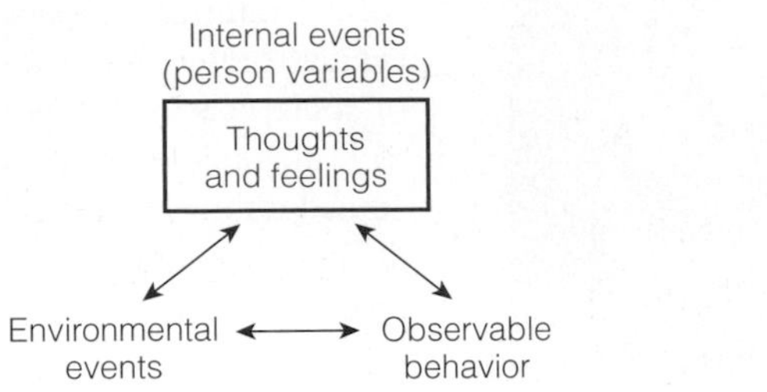

Social learning theory has stimulated a considerable amount of research, particularly in the area of observational learning. It has also stimulated the development of *cognitive-behavior therapy*, in which psychological disorders are treated by altering both environmental variables and cognitive processes. For example, a cognitive-behavioral treatment for an irrational fear of spiders might involve some type of safe exposure to spiders (an environmental manipulation) along with instructions to replace fearful thoughts with certain types of calming thoughts (a cognitive manipulation). Cognitive-behavioral treatments have become quite popular in recent years. Social learning theory (along with its cousin, animal cognition) has become a dominant force in behavioral psychology and is rivaled by only one other school of thought—B. F. Skinner's radical behaviorism.

QUICK QUIZ J

1. Bandura's ______ ______ theory emphasizes the importance of o______ learning and c______ variables.
2. The concept of ______ ______ proposes that three variables: e______, b______, and p______ variables, all interact with each other.
3. Bandura's work has influenced the development of a type of therapy known as ______-______ therapy, in which an attempt is made to change behavior by altering both environmental and c______ factors.

Skinner's Radical Behaviorism

From Watson to Bandura, we see a steady increase in the use of internal events to help explain behavior. Not everyone has agreed with this trend. Burrhus Frederic Skinner argued for a return to a stricter form of behaviorism. Skinner's version of behaviorism, known as ***radical behaviorism***, emphasizes the influence of the environment on observable (overt) behavior, rejects the use of internal events to explain behavior, and views thoughts and feelings as behaviors that themselves need to be explained. Thus, unlike

Burrhus Frederic Skinner
(1904–1990)

Watson's methodological behaviorism, radical behaviorism does not completely reject the inclusion of internal events in a science of behavior; it merely rejects the use of these events as explanations for behavior (Skinner, 1953, 1974). We explain this notion more fully in the following section.

Skinner's View of Internal Events Skinner viewed internal events, such as sensing, thinking, and feeling, as "covert" or private behaviors that are subject to the same laws of learning as "overt" or publicly observable behaviors. Thus, internal events can be included in an analysis of behavior, but only as more behavior that needs to be explained. For example, whereas a social learning theorist might say that a student studies because she expects that studying will result in a high mark, Skinner would say that both the act of studying and the thoughts about achieving a high mark by studying are the result of some experience, such as a history of doing well on exams when the student did study.

For several reasons, Skinner was loath to consider internal events as explanations for behavior. First, he agreed with Watson's concern that, since we do not have direct access to the internal events of others, we must rely on their verbal reports of such events, which are often unreliable. Skinner further noted that such unreliability is to be expected, given the manner in which people learn to label their internal events. Specifically, young children need to be taught by their caretakers to describe their internal experiences. Because these caretakers (usually parents) cannot directly observe internal events in their children, they must infer their occurrence from the children's observable behaviors.

Consider, for example, the task of teaching a young boy to correctly label the feeling of pain. The parent must wait until the child is displaying some observable behavior that typically accompanies pain, such as crying in response to a stubbed toe. Based on this behavior, the parent then infers that the child is experiencing pain and says something like, "My, your toe must really hurt!" After a few experiences like this, the child will himself begin using the word *hurt* to describe what he is feeling in such circumstances.

Pain is probably one of the easier feelings to teach, given that the observable behaviors accompanying it are usually quite distinct (although even here, there may be considerable variability across individuals in the intensity of sensation required before something is called painful). Consider how much more difficult it is to teach a child to accurately describe more subtle emotions such as contentment or discomfort, for which the observable behaviors are often much less distinct. Because the parents have less reliable information on which to base their inferences about such states, the labels they provide to the child may only approximate the child's actual feelings. As a result of these experiences, the labels people use to describe their feelings may often be only crude approximations of what they actually feel. For this reason, Skinner was uninterested in using a person's description of an internal emotional state as an explanation for behavior; he was, however, quite interested in how people come to label their internal states (Skinner, 1957).

A second problem with using internal events to explain behavior is that it is often difficult to determine the actual relationship of thoughts and feelings to behavior. Take, for example, the act of providing help in an emergency. Do you provide help because you feel concern for the person involved? Or do you provide help and feel concerned at the same time, with no necessary link between the two? After all, people often take action in an emergency quite quickly, without reflecting upon how they feel. Or do your feelings of concern for someone sometimes arise *after* you have tried to help them? Lest this notion seem strange to you, consider that people's "feelings" can often be altered by manipulating their overt behavior. For example, people can often be induced to change their opinion about a certain issue—such as whether capital punishment should be abolished—by asking them to write an essay promoting a different point of view. If they do not already hold a strong opinion about that issue and do not feel that they are being forced to write the essay, many people will alter their opinion to be consistent with what they have written (Cialdini, 1993). In similar fashion, the concern you feel for others might sometimes result from, or at least be strengthened by, the act of helping them.

A third difficulty with using internal events to explain behavior is that we do not have any means of directly changing these internal events. Our only means of changing both covert behavior and overt behavior is to change some aspect of the environment. For example, if I instruct a client to think calm, relaxing thoughts whenever he or she is in an anxiety-arousing situation, and this effectively reduces the anxiety, a radical behaviorist would say that the effective treatment is not the calm, relaxing thoughts but the instructions I have given the person about thinking calm, relaxing thoughts. And since exposing the client to these instructions is really a manipulation of the client's environment, then it is really a change in the environment that is ultimately responsible for reducing the level of anxiety. Therefore, if changing the environment is the only manner in which behavior can be influenced, then why not emphasize the environment as the ultimate cause of behavior?

A fourth problem with using internal events to explain behavior is that (as with explanations based on instinct) such explanations are sometimes only pseudo-explanations. For example, if I say that I "feel like going to the movies," am I really referring to a bodily condition of some sort? Or am I simply making a prediction about my future behavior? In other words, I am simply saying that I am quite likely to go to the movies under these particular circumstances, given that nothing prevents me from doing so. Thus, my "feeling" statement is really a statement about potential behavior more than about a bodily feeling. For this reason, saying that I am going to the movies because I "feel like going to the movies," or studying because I "feel like studying," is really no explanation at all.

For reasons such as these, Skinner (1953) rejected internal events as explanations for behavior; instead, he focused on the environment as the ultimate cause of both observable behavior (overt behavior) and internal events (covert behavior). But neither did he believe that we are helpless pawns of our environment. He assumed that once we understand the manner in which the environment affects us, we can then change the environment so it will exert a more beneficial influence on our behavior. We can refer to this process as ***countercontrol***, which is the deliberate manipulation of environmental events to alter their impact on our behavior. Nevertheless, in Skinner's view, even such acts of countercontrol can ultimately be traced to environmental influence. Consider, for example, Jamie, who decides to improve her study habits by rearranging her study environment. At first glance, Jamie's decision (the thoughts she has had about this issue) seems to be the cause of the improvement in her study habits. On the other hand, Jamie would not have made this decision unless she had first been exposed to information about its usefulness. The source of this information (such as reading about such tactics in the appendix on self-management in this textbook) is an environmental influence and is, in Skinner's view, the ultimate cause of the improvement in Jamie's study habits.

As for the notion of free will, radical behaviorists are, by definition, interested in the principles by which the environment determines behavior; hence, the notion that a behavior has been freely chosen is not an assumption they would make. They are, however, quite interested in why people might perceive that a behavior has been freely chosen. One possibility is that our behavior seems to be freely chosen when the controlling variables are subtle and not easily identified. As previously noted, there is a good deal of evidence suggesting that behavior can be subtly influenced in ways we are not aware of (e.g., Cialdini, 1993). Skinner (1971) also pointed out that we are especially likely to perceive a *lack of freedom* when behavior is being controlled through the use of aversive consequences. It is for reasons such as this that Skinner strongly argued that society should "engineer" the environment to maximize the use of positive reinforcement (which is perceived as less constraining) and minimize the use of punishment.[6]

In general, Skinner seems to agree with some aspects of Bandura's notion of reciprocal determinism, in the sense that environmental events, internal events, and observable behavior can be viewed as interacting with each other. Like Bandura (and Tolman), he also analyzed behavior from a molar,

---

[6]While reading about such issues, bear in mind that behavioristic assumptions are just that—assumptions. They do not necessarily reflect some type of absolute truth, nor do they necessarily reflect the private beliefs of the scientist. Thus, one can adopt these assumptions as a useful way of looking at behavior without abandoning other assumptions, such as a religious belief about the existence of free will. After all, even if free will does exist, the environment still has a major impact on our behavior, and it would be foolish not to learn the principles by which the environment influences behavior. In this regard, the first author recalls a seminary student he once taught who could always be seen carrying around his two favorite textbooks—his behavior analysis text and the Bible.

FIGURE 1.7 A diagrammatic representation of Skinner's view of the relationship between environmental events, internal events, and observable behavior. Although all three components are capable of influencing each other, the emphasis is on environmental events as the ultimate cause of both observable behavior and internal events (as indicated by the solid arrows).

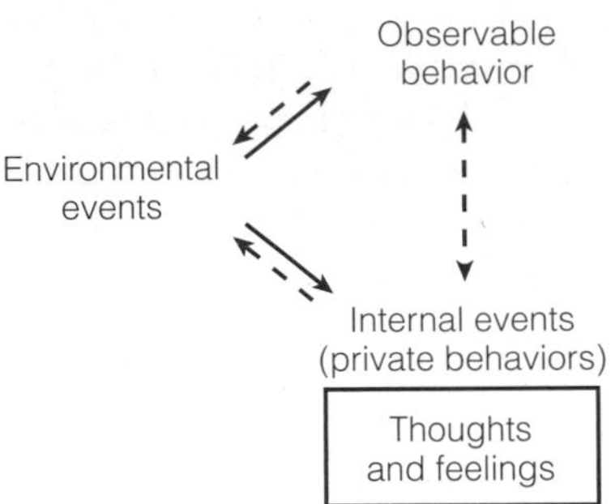

rather than a molecular (S-R), perspective. Where Skinner differs, however, is in his assumption that the environment (in combination with genes; see below) ultimately determines both observable behavior and internal events. A diagrammatic depiction of Skinner's approach might therefore look something like Figure 1.7. (See Skinner [1953, 1987, 1989] for a discussion of his perspective on private events; also see Anderson, Hawkins, Freeman, and Scotti [2000] for the many issues involved in incorporating private events into a science of behavior.)

QUICK QUIZ K

1. Skinner's ______________ behaviorism emphasizes both internal and external behaviors as resulting from e______________ influences.
2. Skinner views thoughts and feelings as pr______________ behaviors that themselves need to be explained.
3. In teaching children to label their feelings, parents first have to make an inf______________ about what the child is feeling based on the child's (external/internal) behavior.
4. In determining the relationship of thoughts and feelings to overt behavior, it is sometimes difficult to know if the thoughts and feelings pr______________ or f______________ the behavior.
5. Yet another issue with respect to using internal events to explain behavior is that we (can/cannot) directly change such events.
6. Saying that you went skiing because you "felt like it" is, from Skinner's perspective, an example of using feelings as a ps______________ explanation for your behavior.
7. Altering the environment in order to control our own behavior is referred to as c______________ control. However, in Skinner's view, even this type of behavior is ultimately the result of some type of e______________ influence.

ADVICE FOR THE LOVELORN

While reading this text you will occasionally encounter advice columns, like this one, in which behavioral concepts are applied to relationship problems. Bear in mind that the advice given is often quite speculative and that real relationship difficulties are too complex to be properly assessed and dealt with through simplistic advice columns. Nevertheless, these columns will, in a fun manner, give you a sense for how behavioral concepts can offer a unique perspective on important aspects of human behavior.

Dear Dr. Dee,

I have very strong feelings for my new girlfriend, but I can't tell if these are feelings of infatuation or love. My friends tell me I'm in love, but my parents tell me I'm infatuated. How can I tell the difference?

So Confused

Dear So,

The distinction between love and infatuation is a tough one, and many people find it difficult to differentiate between the two. Interestingly, Skinner (1989) suggested that the more subtle an emotional state, the more value there is in analyzing that emotion in terms of the circumstances that surround it. In what circumstance, for example, are we most likely to use the term *infatuation*? For starters, are we not more likely to use that term when the level of attachment seems to greatly exceed the rewards available in the relationship? In particular, isn't it the case that we often apply the word *infatuation* to a relationship that is driven by short-term sexual rewards with few long-term prospects? By contrast, the word *love* is typically applied to a relationship in which a strong level of attachment seems to properly match the available rewards. The relationship seems to have good long-term prospects and is not driven merely by short-term sexual rewards. Thus, for many people, the word *infatuation* implies an "unhealthy" relationship that is doomed to failure, whereas the word *love* implies a "healthy" relationship that has the potential to prosper.

A little thought will likely reveal other differences between infatuation and love. Nevertheless, our brief analysis suggests that if you wish to determine whether you are "in love" or "merely infatuated," you might do well to ponder the rewards offered by that relationship and forget about trying to detect minute differences in feelings.

Behaviorally yours,

Dr. Dee

Skinner's View of Genetic Factors What about the role of genetic influences on behavior? In discussing these various schools of behaviorism, we have focused on the role of the environment; but we have done so simply because that is what behaviorists generally do—they study the effects of environmental experiences on behavior. Traditionally, they leave it to other disciplines, such as ethology or evolutionary psychology, to study the role of genetic influences. But this does not mean that behaviorists discount the role of heredity. As noted earlier, Darwin's theory of evolution played a strong role in the establishment of behaviorism, and many behaviorists recognize that heredity can profoundly influence animal and human behavior. Skinner (e.g., 1953, 1987, 1989), in fact, repeatedly acknowledged that behavior was fundamentally the result of the interaction between genes and the environment. And far from being dismayed by research indicating genetic limitations on operant conditioning (some of which is discussed in Chapter 12), he was fascinated by it and even initiated some early research along these lines (Skinner, 1987).

Skinner also noted that operant conditioning bears a striking resemblance to the evolutionary principle of natural selection. As earlier discussed, according to the principle of natural selection, members of a species that inherit certain adaptive characteristics are more likely to survive and propagate, thereby passing those characteristics on to their offspring. Thus, over many generations, the frequency of those adaptive characteristics within the population increases and becomes well established. In similar fashion, in operant conditioning, behaviors that lead to reinforcing consequences are more likely to be repeated, whereas those that do not lead to reinforcing consequences are less likely to be repeated. In other words, operant conditioning is sort of a mini-evolution in which an organism's behaviors that are adaptive (that lead to reinforcers) increase in frequency while behaviors that are nonadaptive (that do not lead to reinforcers) decrease in frequency. The processes of natural selection and operant conditioning are therefore quite similar. The basic difference is that natural selection is concerned with the evolution of inherited characteristics within a species, whereas operant conditioning is concerned with the evolution of learned behavior patterns within an individual.

Although Skinner (1953) was more accepting of the potential effects of heredity on behavior than was Watson, he nevertheless remained wary about placing too much emphasis on such factors. Genetic factors are largely unmodifiable, and to assume that a behavior pattern has a strong genetic basis is to assume also that little can be done to alter it (except perhaps through some type of physiological intervention). When dealing with maladaptive characteristics such as learning difficulties or aggressive tendencies in children, this assumption can have serious implications. Think about it: If you had a son who was having difficulty in math, would you want his teacher to be a strong empiricist (who emphasizes the role of experience in determining behavior) or a strong nativist (who emphasizes the role of genetics and heredity)? Almost certainly, you would want a teacher who is a strong empiricist and who believes the child's math problems are the result of poor learning experiences, which can therefore potentially be corrected by providing better experiences. Thus, a strong empiricist approach, such as that exemplified by Skinner and other behaviorists, tends to be more optimistic about the possibility of changing behavior for the better. Behaviorists nevertheless have a growing appreciation for the influence of genetic factors on learning and behavior, and recent years have seen a significant increase in research in this area.

QUICK QUIZ L

1. Although he emphasized the role of the environment, Skinner also believed that behavior was fundamentally the result of the interaction of g________ and the environment. He was in fact quite interested in evidence indicating g________ limitations on ________ conditioning.
2. Skinner believed that the processes of ev________ and op________ conditioning were quite similar in that both involved the selection of what was adaptive from what was not adaptive.
3. On a practical level, Skinner was (enthused/cautious) about genetic explanations for behavior because he believed that such explanations tend to be (optimistic/pessimistic) about the possibility of change.

Behavior Analysis and Applied Behavior Analysis More so than other behaviorists, Skinner was careful to distinguish between the philosophical, scientific, and applied aspects of his approach. *Radical behaviorism* refers to the philosophical aspect of Skinner's approach that we have just been discussing, that is, the set of assumptions upon which Skinner's behavioral science is based. The term ***behavior analysis*** (sometimes called the ***experimental analysis of behavior***) is the basic science that grew out of radical behaviorism. Behavior analysts have especially concentrated on researching the various principles of operant conditioning.

Like Watson, Skinner was concerned that the principles discovered through basic research should have practical application. In this regard, he did not disappoint. His work directly led to the establishment of ***applied behavior analysis***, a technology of behavior in which basic principles of behavior are applied to analyzing and solving real-world problems. These applications range from treating or managing clients with clinical disorders (such as depression and schizophrenia), to improving educational practices and athletic performance, to promoting health-related behaviors and reducing pollution. Applied behavior analysis (often abbreviated as ABA) is particularly well established as the treatment of choice for children with developmental and intellectual disabilities, especially autism, and many applied behavior analysts work in this field. Applied behavior analysis is also sometimes referred to as *behavior modification* or *behavior therapy*, although the latter term tends to include cognitive-behavioral approaches to treatment more so than would be found in applied behavior analysis.

After taking a course on learning and behavior, some students become intensely interested in pursuing a career in applied behavior analysis. Fortunately, there is a growing demand for individuals with training in applied behavior analysis, as well as a growing number of programs available to provide such training. Internationally recognized certification exams have also been established to ensure that applied behavior analysts are highly trained and meet a common set of standards. Individuals with graduate degrees and intensive training in applied behavior analysis are eligible to become Board Certified Behavior Analysts (BCBAs). BCBAs conduct behavioral assessments and design, deliver, and supervise behavioral interventions. Individuals with bachelor's degrees and training in applied behavior analysis (either during or following their degree) are eligible to become Board Certified Assistant Behavior Analysts (BCaBAs). BCaBAs can carry out many of the same functions as BCBAs, but do so under the supervision of a BCBA. For detailed information on these accreditations and a list of approved programs for training, go to the Web site of the Behavior Analyst Certification Board at http://www.bacb.com/. For those interested in becoming BCBAs or BCaBAs, this textbook and the course you are presently enrolled in may well be your first step along that path. (See also "The Life of B. F. Skinner" in the And Furthermore box.)

QUICK QUIZ M

1. Skinner's philosophy of behaviorism (meaning the set of basic assumptions for how best to conduct a science of behavior) is called ______ behaviorism.
2. The science that grew out of that philosophy is called b______ a______ (or the e______ a______ of b______).
3. The behavioral technology that has grown out of the basic science is known as ______ ______ ______ (which is often abbreviated as ______).
4. Individuals with graduate degrees who are highly trained in applied behavior analysis are eligible to become ______, while those with bachelor's degrees are eligible to become ______.

And Furthermore

The Life of B. F. Skinner

Though quieter and less colorful than Watson, Skinner was nevertheless also the focus of much controversy. As such, it may be worthwhile to briefly describe his life, especially since he is viewed by many as the prototypical behaviorist. Indeed, in a survey of psychology department chairpersons, Skinner was voted the most influential psychologist of the twentieth century (Haggbloom et al., 2002).

Burrhus Frederic Skinner was born in Susquehanna, Pennsylvania, in 1904. Raised in a traditional Presbyterian household, Skinner had a relatively normal childhood, though it was not without difficulties. For example, although he was never physically punished as a child (apart from once having his mouth washed out with soap for saying a bad word), he was taught through reprimands and warnings "to fear God, the police, and what people will think" (Skinner, 1967, p. 407). Interestingly, as a behaviorist, he would later conclude that punishment is an ineffective means for managing behavior, often creating more problems than it solves.

One of Skinner's strongest traits, even in childhood, was his love of building and inventing:

> I made slingshots, bows and arrows, blow guns and water pistols from lengths of bamboo, and from a discarded water boiler a steam cannon with which I could shoot plugs of potato and carrot over the houses of our neighbors. ... I tried again and again to make a glider in which I might fly. (Skinner, 1967, p. 388)

This inventiveness served Skinner well in later years when he was able to build unique devices for studying the behavior of animals, most notably the operant conditioning chamber (or "Skinner box"; see Chapter 6). Without these inventions, it is conceivable that many of the principles discussed in this text would have remained undiscovered.

Skinner's personality was also characterized by a strange mixture of objectivity and sentimentality (Bjork, 1993). For example, when his younger brother Ebbie suddenly died of a cerebral hemorrhage, Skinner observed the death in a surprisingly detached fashion. Nevertheless, he was greatly distressed by the incident and felt pangs of guilt when he later recalled how he had once injured his brother in play. Skinner's objectivity was also apparent in everyday settings. For example, in describing a family friend, Skinner once wrote:

> The doctor and his dog are becoming more than idle amusement. ... He becomes a fool in the eyes of everyone but me when he attempts to justify the dog's actions. ... [Pep] comes up to us wagging his tail—"He says 'throw me a stick,'" says the doctor. ... Lately I've got the habit too. It's quite fun to make up mental processes to fit a dog's every move. (as quoted in Bjork, 1993, p. 63)

As a radical behaviorist, Skinner would later argue that mentalistic terms are often mere inferences derived from observable behavior.

Skinner graduated from a small liberal arts college and, with some encouragement from the famous poet Robert Frost, spent a year trying to establish himself as a writer. Although quite disciplined about it, he completed only a few stories and poems and eventually gave up in despair. He sometimes claimed that he had failed as a writer because he had nothing important to say; but he also speculated that his writing was simply too "objective" to interest the average reader, with too few references to thoughts and feelings (Bjork, 1993, p. 56). Years later Skinner would publish a novel called *Walden Two*, but it was an "objective" novel about a utopian community founded on behavioral principles.

Following his failure at becoming a writer, Skinner came to the conclusion that his real interests lay in the study of behavior. Impressed by the writings of John B. Watson, he entered graduate studies at Harvard in 1928. He thrived in that environment. Much of his graduate and postdoctoral training was surprisingly unstructured, and he was often left to his own devices to study whatever he wished. In later years, he would write that he had no sense of ever devising a theory or testing a hypothesis; he simply followed his interests. He discounted the notion of science as a formal system of theory building and hypothesis testing, asserting that real science is much less structured than most scientists describe it to be (Skinner, 1956).

Like Watson before him, Skinner was sometimes the target of false rumors. For example, when Skinner's wife, Eve, did not adjust well to the "joys" of motherhood, Skinner built an "air crib" (or "baby tender") to ease the burden of raising their youngest daughter, Deborah. The crib was a large, enclosed space with an unbreakable glass window. The baby, wearing only a diaper, lay on a woven plastic sheet (the surface of which felt like linen), while the surrounding air was carefully filtered and maintained at a precise temperature (see Figure 1.8). Skinner believed the air crib to be far superior to the jail-like bars, uncertain temperature fluctuations, and loose bedding of the standard crib. It was also much easier to keep clean. Enthused by his invention and by the way Deborah seemed to thrive, Skinner wrote an article on the device for *Ladies' Home Journal* and set out to market it. Unfortunately, a story arose that Skinner was isolating his daughter in an "operant conditioning chamber" and experimenting on her. According to one version of the story, the daughter eventually went insane and killed herself. The reality is that she had a happy childhood, spent no more time in the air crib than other

FIGURE 1.8 Skinner's daughter, Deborah, seemed to thrive in the "air crib" or "baby tender" her father had built for her, so Skinner set out to market it as an improvement over the standard crib with its jail-like bars and poor hygiene. Unfortunately, it led to the completely false rumor that he was conducting conditioning experiments on his daughters and that they developed severe psychological problems as a result.

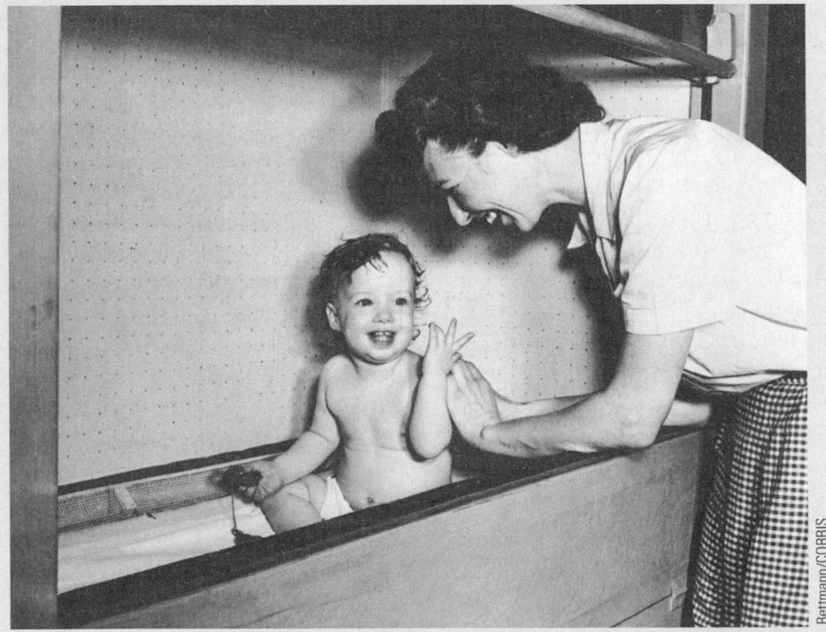

Bettmann/CORBIS

children do in a regular crib, and grew up to be quite normal. Nevertheless, the damage was done, and few air cribs were ever sold.[7]

In the early 1970s, Skinner was severely criticized by numerous intellectuals and politicians for his book *Beyond Freedom and Dignity*. In the book, Skinner (1971) rejected the concept of free will and argued that we must instead "engineer" society to more effectively control human behavior. He had hoped the book would encourage people to devise better programs for eliminating pollution, preventing crime, and so on, and he became quite depressed over the criticism he received. Skinner received a more favorable reaction for his invention of the "teaching machine" and programmed instruction—although in later years, he lamented that this notion too had been largely ignored and never utilized to its full potential. But the widespread use of personal computers, which are ideally suited for programmed instruction, may be starting to change that.

Throughout his later years, Skinner remained intellectually active, carefully engineering his environment to compensate for the effects of aging. He even wrote a book, *Enjoy Old Age*, offering advice on behavior self-management for the elderly (Skinner & Vaughan, 1983). His final public appearance was on August 10, 1990, when he was presented with a Lifetime Contribution Award by the American Psychological Association. Terminally ill, but with little fear of death and as independent as ever, Skinner used his acceptance speech to lambaste the psychological community for its return to mentalistic explanations of behavior. Eight days later he passed away from leukemia at the age of 86. (See Vargas, 1990, for a touching description of Skinner's final days.)

SUMMARY

This text introduces the basic principles of learning and behavior. It particularly emphasizes the principles of classical conditioning, in which reflexive behaviors come to be elicited in new situations, and operant conditioning, in which the strength of a behavior is influenced by its consequences.

Individuals of historical significance in the study of learning include Aristotle, who assumed that knowledge is gained largely from experience (as opposed to being inborn) and believed that learning is based on four laws of association: similarity, contrast, contiguity, and frequency. Descartes proposed that involuntary behaviors, which occur in both humans and animals, are automatically elicited by external stimulation, whereas voluntary behaviors, which occur only in humans, are controlled by free will. The

[7]Unfortunately, the myth that Skinner experimented on his daughter still makes the rounds today. A notable example is a book by Laura Slater (2004) entitled *Opening Skinner's Box: Great Psychological Experiments of the Twentieth Century* in which she repeats the rumors of Deborah's insanity. This prompted an angry response from Deborah, entitled "I Was Not a Lab Rat," in which she demands that people stop spreading these vicious rumors (Skinner-Buzan, 2004).

British empiricists argued that all knowledge is a function of experience, and they strongly emphasized the laws of association in their study of learning. Structuralists, such as Titchener, assumed that the mind is composed of a finite number of basic elements that can be discovered using the method of introspection. Darwin's theory of evolution proposed the notion that adaptive characteristics, including the ability to learn, evolve through the process of natural selection. This influenced the functionalists, such as William James, who believed that psychologists should study the adaptive processes of the mind. Functionalism led to the establishment of behaviorism, with its emphasis on the study of publicly observable behavior and the environmental events that influence it.

There are several schools of behaviorism. Watson's methodological behaviorism rejects all references to internal events that cannot be directly observed. Hull's neobehaviorism includes references to hypothetical internal events, usually of a physiological nature (such as fatigue or hunger), that mediate between the environment and behavior. Tolman's cognitive behaviorism utilizes hypothesized intervening variables that are mentalistic in nature, such as expectations and cognitive maps. This approach led to Bandura's social learning theory, which emphasizes the importance of observational learning and cognitive variables in learning, as well as the notion that internal events, environment, and observable behavior reciprocally interact with each other. By contrast, Skinner's radical behaviorism views internal events as private behaviors subject to the same laws of learning as publicly observable behaviors. Skinner's perspective emphasizes the influence of the environment on behavior but does not discount the influence of genetic factors. The science that has grown out of radical behaviorism is called behavior analysis, which in turn has led to applied behavior analysis, in which basic principles of behavior are applied to solving real-world problems.

SUGGESTED READINGS

Watson, J. B. (1913). Psychology as the behaviorist views it. *Psychological Review*, 20, 154–177. The article that started it all.

Skinner, B. F. (1953). *Science and human behavior*. New York: Macmillan. A book that many regard as the bible of radical behaviorism.

Skinner, B. F. (1974). *About behaviorism*. New York: Knopf. For the average undergraduate, this introduction to radical behaviorism is probably more accessible than *Science and Human Behavior*.

Barash, D. P. (1982). How it works: Evolution as a process. In *Sociobiology and behavior* (2nd ed.). New York: Elsevier Science. A good introduction to evolution and behavior.

Hergenhahn, B. R. (2009). *An introduction to theories of learning* (8th ed.). Englewood Cliffs, NJ: Prentice-Hall. Contains extensive descriptions of the different approaches to learning and behavior, such as those by Hull and Tolman.

Buckley, K. W. (1989). *Mechanical man: John Broadus Watson and the beginnings of behaviorism*. New York: Guilford Press. A well-written biography of John B. Watson and the controversies that swirled around him.

Bjork, D. W. (1993). *B. F. Skinner: A life*. New York: Basic Books. A very readable biography of Skinner's life.

STUDY QUESTIONS

Many of the following study questions ask you to compare and contrast different concepts, and as such, the answers may not always be immediately obvious. As noted earlier, however, having to struggle with the material is often an excellent way to learn it.

1. Name and briefly describe the two fundamental forms of learning emphasized in this textbook. How do these two forms of learning differ from each other?
2. Describe the nativist versus empiricist approaches to knowledge. How would a nativist versus an empiricist explain how Picasso became such a great artist?
3. Name and provide examples of the four laws of association. Which two laws are most important in modern approaches to learning?
4. Outline Descartes' dualistic model of human behavior. In his view, what is a basic distinction between the behavior of humans and the behavior of other animals?
5. How did the British empiricists view the acquisition of knowledge?
6. Describe the structuralist approach to psychology and the basic method by which they gathered data. How did the functionalist approach differ from this? Which of these approaches was in favor of animal experimentation, and why?
7. Describe Darwin's principle of natural selection. What are the three main components of the principle of natural selection?
8. What is the basic difference between Watson's methodological behaviorism and Hull's neobehaviorism? How did Watson's position on the nature–nurture debate change over time?
9. How is Bandura's social learning approach similar to Tolman's cognitive behaviorism, and how does it differ?
10. How is Skinner's radical behaviorism similar to Watson's methodological behaviorism, and how does it differ?
11. What is reciprocal determinism? In what ways would Skinner and Bandura have agreed versus disagreed in their views of how behavior is determined?
12. Outline the distinction between radical behaviorism, behavior analysis, and applied behavior analysis.

CONCEPT REVIEW

applied behavior analysis. A technology of behavior in which basic principles of behavior are applied to solving real-world issues.

behavior. Any activity of an organism that can be observed or somehow measured.

behavior analysis. The behavioral science that grew out of Skinner's philosophy of radical behaviorism. Also known as the "experimental analysis of behavior."

behaviorism. A natural science approach to psychology that traditionally focuses on the study of environmental influences on observable behavior.

British empiricism. A philosophical school of thought that maintains that almost all knowledge is a function of experience.

cognitive behaviorism. A brand of behaviorism that utilizes intervening variables, usually in the form of hypothesized cognitive processes, to help explain behavior. Sometimes called "purposive behaviorism."

cognitive map. The mental representation of one's spatial surroundings.

countercontrol. The deliberate manipulation of environmental events to alter their impact on our behavior.

empiricism. In psychology, the assumption that behavior patterns are mostly learned rather than inherited. Also known as the *nurture* perspective (or, rarely, as *nurturism*).

evolutionary adaptation. An inherited trait (physical or behavioral) that has been shaped through natural selection.

functionalism. An approach to psychology that proposes that the mind evolved to help us adapt to the world around us and that the focus of psychology should be the study of those adaptive processes.

introspection. The attempt to accurately describe one's conscious thoughts, emotions, and sensory experiences.

latent learning. Learning that occurs in the absence of any observable indication of learning and only becomes apparent at a later time.

law of contiguity. A law of association in which events that occur in close proximity to each other in time or space are readily associated with each other.

law of contrast. A law of association in which events that are opposite from each other are readily associated with each other.

law of frequency. A law of association in which the more frequently two items occur together, the more strongly they are associated with each other.

law of similarity. A law of association in which events that are similar to each other are readily associated with each other.

learning. A relatively permanent change in behavior that results from some type of experience.

methodological behaviorism. A brand of behaviorism that asserts that, for methodological reasons, psychologists should study only those behaviors that can be directly observed.

mind–body dualism. Descartes' philosophical assumption that some human behaviors are bodily reflexes that are automatically elicited by external stimulation, while other behaviors are freely chosen.

nativism. The assumption that a person's characteristics are largely inborn. Also known as the *nature* perspective.

natural selection. The evolutionary principle according to which organisms that are better able to adapt to environmental pressures are more likely to reproduce and pass along those adaptive characteristics than those that cannot adapt.

neobehaviorism. A brand of behaviorism that utilizes intervening variables, in the form of hypothesized physiological processes, to help explain behavior.

radical behaviorism. A brand of behaviorism that emphasizes the influence of the environment on overt behavior, rejects the use of internal events to explain behavior, and views thoughts and feelings as behaviors that themselves need to be explained.

reciprocal determinism. The assumption that environmental events, observable behavior, and "person variables" (including internal events) reciprocally influence each other.

social learning theory. A brand of behaviorism that strongly emphasizes the importance of observational learning and cognitive variables in explaining human behavior. Also known as "cognitive social learning theory" or "social-cognitive theory."

S-R theory (or stimulus-response theory). The theory that learning involves the establishment of a connection between a specific stimulus (S) and a specific response (R).

structuralism. An approach to psychology that assumes that it is possible to determine the structure of the mind by identifying the basic elements that compose it.

CHAPTER TEST

Chapter tests typically contain fewer hints than quick quizzes do—for example, there is usually only a single blank for an answer, even though the answer may require more than a single word. Unlike the quick quizzes, however, an answer key has been provided at the end. Note too that the question numbers have been scrambled (e.g., the first question on this list is number 9). This allows you to look up the answer to a question immediately without having to worry about inadvertently seeing the answer to the next question. Finally, do not worry if you are initially unable to answer some of the items without having to look back through the chapter. Fill-in-the-blank items can be difficult, and this test is designed to be a learning experience more than a form of self-assessment. You may find it difficult to recall some of the information because it is still relatively unfamiliar to you.

9. When Tara saw the lush green lawn, it reminded her of just how dry the lawn had been the previous year. Among the four laws of association, this is best described as an example of the law of contrast.
29. Deanna often gets lost when she drives around the city that she lives in. Tolman would say that she has a faulty cognitive map
17. When Danielle first saw Gina, she immediately thought of Reese Witherspoon. Among the four laws of association, this is most likely an example of the law of similarity
1. Jordan once became terribly ill while visiting Chicago. As a result, whenever he visits Chicago, he thinks of the illness he suffered at that time. Among the four laws of association, this is best described as an example of the law of contiguity.
10. After struggling unsuccessfully to completely eliminate his test anxiety, Andres finally accepts that there are some aspects of himself that he can control and some that he cannot. This conclusion is similar to that of the French philosopher Decartes and his theory of mind-body dualism.
12. In trying to understand her feelings for Juan, Alisha pays close attention to the sensations she feels each time she sees him. This is an example of the method of introspection. This was a favorite method of research by psychologists who followed the approach known as structuralism.
27. Hull's theory is a (molar/molecular) type of theory, whereas Tolman's theory is a molar type.
7. When Anastasia once visited Vancouver, it rained *every day for a month.* As a result, whenever she is trapped in a rainstorm, it reminds her of her trip to Vancouver. Among the four laws of association, this is best described as an example of the law of frequency.
20. Reggie claims that she freely chose to become a musician, despite her parents putting tremendous pressure upon her to choose a different career. A behaviorist like Skinner would say that her decision to become a musician may instead have been the result of environmental influences that are very (subtle/salient).
15. "My cat never gets lost. It's like she has a blueprint in her mind of the exact layout of the entire town." This statement fits best with (name the behaviorist) Tolman's brand of behaviorism, known as cognitive behaviourism.
11. "Babies know nothing," Kristie pronounced when her sister commented on how intelligent her new baby seemed to be. Kristie obviously believes that the mind of a newborn is a blank slate (or, in Latin, tabula rasa), a notion that was promoted by a group of philosophers known as the British Empiricists
31. Although Roberta just sits there throughout the lecture, she can afterward repeat everything the professor said. This is an example of latent learning, which illustrates the distinction between learning and performance.

16. Skinner noted that people are least likely to perceive their behavior to be freely chosen when their behavior is controlled by __________ consequences.
25. Recall the opening vignette to the chapter where, after making love, one behaviorist comments, "That was fine for you, how was it for me?" This joke is most descriptive of which school of behaviorism? __________
23. Shira emphasizes environmental explanations for behavior and believes that thoughts and feelings should be regarded as private behaviors that also need to be explained. As such, she is most likely a(n) __________ behaviorist. To the extent that Shira also conducts research into basic principles of behavior, she can be called a(n) __________. And to the extent that she applies such principles to developing better methods for coaching basketball, she can be called a(n) __________.
2. Aristotle was a(n) (nativist/empiricist), whereas Plato was a(n) (nativist/empiricist).
32. Learning is a relatively __________ change in behavior that results from some type of __________.
22. When I haven't eaten for several hours, I feel a strong sense of hunger and therefore walk quickly as I head to the cafeteria. This statement fits best with (name the behaviorist) __________'s brand of behaviorism, known as __________.
5. Neal was recently stung by a wasp and is now quite fearful of wasps. This is best seen as an example of __________ conditioning.
30. John's therapist tells him that, although she cares about what he feels, she is more interested in what he did and in the environmental circumstances that affected both his behavior and his feelings. This therapist's approach fits best with __________'s brand of behaviorism, known as __________.
19. Descartes believed that the behavior of __________ is entirely reflexive.
14. Mandy found a five-dollar bill when she took out the trash one day. As a result, she now volunteers quite often to take out the trash. This is an example of __________ conditioning.
26. A middleman in a business transaction is analogous to what Tolman and Hull referred to as a(n) __________ variable.
33. As originally defined by Watson, behaviorism is a(n) __________ science approach to psychology that emphasizes the study of __________ influences on __________ behavior.
3. After Jasmine saw her sister talk back to the sassy kid next door, she herself did likewise. The behaviorist who would find this incident most interesting is probably __________.
36. Learning how to swing a bat by watching others is an example of (observable/observational) learning. Actually swinging the bat is an example of __________ behavior.

18. Angie's therapist tells her that he doesn't care what she thinks and feels; he is concerned only about what she did and about the circumstances that affected her behavior. This therapist's approach fits best with (name the behaviorist) ________'s brand of behaviorism, known as ________

8. In considering the process of dreaming, a researcher who followed the approach to psychology known as ________ would have been most concerned with understanding how dreaming facilitates our ability to adapt to the world around us.

35. Lynne persists in teaching her daughter music despite the insistence of her husband that the child "was born tone deaf." Which of these two has an attitude most similar to that of a behaviorist? ________

24. Sal claims that the neglect he suffered as a child resulted in low self-esteem, which in turn resulted in his long history of criminal activity. His parole officer tells him that such an explanation is too simplistic, that it ignores the complex manner in which the various facets of life interact with each other, and that Sal needs to acknowledge that his own attitude played a role in creating his difficulties. Among the theorists in this chapter, the one who would most appreciate this statement is ________, because it agrees with his concept of ________ determinism.

4. "Great musicians are born, not made" is an example of the (nativist/empiricist) perspective on behavior, and "practice makes perfect" is an example of the (nativist/empiricist) perspective.

28. (Hull/Watson/Both) ________ assumed that behavior consists of a long chain of specific stimulus-response connections. This approach is known as a(n) ________ theory of behavior.

13. William James was a (structuralist/functionalist), and Titchener was a (structuralist/functionalist).

6. The defining characteristic of behaviorism, as originally proposed by Watson, is the emphasis on ________ influences on ________ behavior.

21. Removing the television set from your room so you won't be distracted while studying is an example of what Skinner called ________

34. The Rs in the 3R approach to studying stand for ________ ________.

ANSWERS TO CHAPTER TEST

1. contiguity
2. empiricist; nativist
3. Bandura
4. nativist; empiricist
5. classical
6. environmental; observable (or overt)
7. frequency
8. functionalism
9. contrast
10. Descartes; mind–body

11. blank; *tabula rasa*; British empiricists
12. introspection; structuralism
13. functionalist; structuralist
14. operant
15. Tolman's; cognitive (or purposive) behaviorism
16. aversive (or punishing)
17. similarity
18. Watson's; methodological behaviorism
19. animals
20. subtle
21. countercontrol
22. Hull's; neobehaviorism
23. radical; behavior analyst; applied behavior analyst
24. Bandura; reciprocal
25. methodological behaviorism
26. intervening
27. molecular; molar
28. both; S-R (stimulus-response)
29. cognitive map
30. Skinner's; radical behaviorism
31. latent; performance
32. permanent; experience
33. natural; environmental; observable
34. read, recite, review
35. Lynne
36. observational; observable

Chapter 2

RESEARCH METHODS

CHAPTER OUTLINE

Based on an actual conversation that took place between a "relationship expert" and a caller on a radio call-in show:

"Hi, Dr. Kramer. I need some advice. I'm wondering if I should get married or break off my engagement and finish university first."

"How old are you?"

"Twenty-one."

"Break off your engagement. Statistically, your marriage has a much better chance of surviving if you don't get married until your late twenties."

"Oh, okay."

This chapter introduces you to the basic methods of behavioral research. Once a researcher has developed a hypothesis or has decided on a specific topic of interest, such as the effect of reward size on speed of learning, he or she will employ a research method to obtain some behavioral data. Some of the methods for obtaining data include naturalistic observation, control group designs, and single-subject designs.

The methods used in behavioral research are in many ways similar to those used in other fields of psychology. For example, behavioral research often involves comparisons between "experimental" groups that receive some kind of manipulation (or treatment) and "control" groups that do not receive that manipulation. In some cases, however, the methods are quite distinctive. For example, behavior analysts (as discussed in Chapter 1, these are behaviorists who follow Skinner's philosophy of radical behaviorism) have a strong preference for conducting experiments that require only one or, at most, a few subjects. These types of experimental designs, known as *single-subject designs*, have several advantages (as well as disadvantages), which we discuss later in the chapter. Let's begin, however, with an overview of some basic terms and definitions.

Basic Terms and Definitions

Independent and Dependent Variables

All scientific research involves the manipulation and/or measurement of certain variables. A ***variable*** is a characteristic of a person, place, or thing that can change (vary) over time or from one situation to another. Temperature is an example of a variable; temperature varies from day to day, season to season, and place to place. Height and weight are also examples of variables—people come in many different sizes and shapes. Until a person reaches maturity, his or her height will change over a period of time. Weight is even less consistent and can fluctuate endlessly, often in directions we do not particularly like.

Almost anything can be considered a variable. Consider an old-style singles ad:

Brown-haired, S, M, 25, seeks S, F, aged 20–26, for fun and friendship.

The *S* in this ad stands for "single," which is one category of the variable *marital status*, which can range from single, to common-law married, to married, to divorced, and even to widowed. The *M* stands for "male," which is part of the dichotomous (meaning "two categories") variable *gender* (i.e., male and female). *Age*, *hair color*, and preference for *fun and friendship* are examples of other variables in this ad.

Two types of variables are particularly important in an experiment. The ***independent variable*** is the aspect of an experiment that is made to systematically vary across the different conditions in the experiment. In other words, the independent variable is what is *manipulated* in an experiment. For example, we may be interested in whether the size of a reward (or "reinforcer") can affect the efficiency of learning. To test this notion, we might conduct a maze learning experiment with rats. Each rat is given 10 trials in which it is placed in a maze and allowed to find its way to the goal box. Depending on the "experimental condition" to which the rat has been randomly assigned, it receives one, two, or three pellets of food each time it reaches the goal box. Thus, the independent variable in this experiment is the number of food pellets the rats in each group receive when they reach the goal box.

The ***dependent variable*** is the aspect of an experiment that is allowed to vary freely to see if it is affected by changes in the independent variable. In other words, the dependent variable is what we measure in an experiment. In a psychology experiment, this is almost always some type of behavior. Changes in the dependent variable are *dependent upon* changes in the independent variable (which is a useful phrase to remember to help you distinguish between dependent and independent variables). In our rat experiment, the dependent variable could be the total number of errors (i.e., number of wrong turns) the rat makes while trying to find its way to the goal box. Alternatively, we might simply look at the speed with which the rat reaches the goal box. Either way, a significant difference between groups on this measure will indicate whether the number of food pellets found in the goal box affects the rat's efficiency in learning the maze. In turn, this will provide supportive evidence for our more general notion—which is what we are really interested in—that the size of a reinforcer affects the efficiency of learning.

Functional Relationships

In behavioral research, the dependent variable is almost always some behavior, and the independent variable is some environmental event or experience that is presumed to influence the behavior. The relationship between changes in an independent variable and changes in a dependent variable is known as a ***functional relationship***. Thus, behaviorists are typically interested in discovering functional relationships between changes in environmental events and changes in behavior. A functional relationship can also be thought of as a cause-and-effect relationship, with changes in the independent variable being the cause and changes in the dependent variable being the effect.

QUICK QUIZ A

1. A researcher is interested in studying the effects of viewing television violence on aggression in children. She shows one group of participants an extremely violent movie, another group a moderately violent movie, and a third group a nonviolent movie. In this case, the level of movie violence shown to the children would be considered the ____________ variable, and the children's subsequent level of aggressive behavior would be the ____________ variable.
2. A change in the dependent variable is considered to be the (cause/effect) in an experiment, whereas a change in the independent variable is considered to be the ____________.
3. A ____________ relationship is the relationship between a change in an independent variable and an associated change in a dependent variable. Behaviorists are typically concerned with discovering the relationship between changes in e____________ events and changes in b____________.

Stimulus and Response

Two terms commonly encountered in behavioral textbooks are *stimulus* and *response*. A ***stimulus*** is any event that can potentially influence behavior, and a ***response*** is a particular instance of a behavior. For example, food is a stimulus that elicits the response of salivation when presented to a hungry dog. Similarly, loud music (a stimulus) might cause your neighbor to bang on the wall (a response), and a high mark on a test (a stimulus) might cause you to grin with delight (a response). Note that the terms *response* and *behavior* can often be used interchangeably; however, the term *behavior* tends to be used when referring to a category of responses (as in the *behavior* of lever pressing for food throughout an experimental session, with each specific lever press being a *response*).

The plural for the word *stimulus* is *stimuli*. Thus, a red light is a stimulus, and a red light and a green light are stimuli. A stimulus is sometimes also referred to as a *cue* in that it signals (cues) the occurrence of a certain behavior, such as when a red traffic light serves as a cue for stopping and a green traffic light serves as a cue for proceeding.

Note that the response of one organism can act as a stimulus that influences the response of another organism. For example, when one rat bites another, the bite is a stimulus that might elicit a retaliatory response from the other rat. In turn, this retaliatory response might then act as a stimulus that induces the first rat to retreat. Likewise, a smile from Shane is a stimulus that encourages Tami to say hello; Tami's hello is in turn a stimulus that encourages Shane to introduce himself. Thus, social interactions generally consist of a chain of alternating responses, with each person's response acting as a stimulus for the next response from the other person.

Overt and Covert Behavior

It is also important to distinguish between overt and covert behavior. ***Overt behavior*** is behavior that can potentially be observed by an individual other than the one performing the behavior. In other words, it is behavior that could be publicly observed if others were present. A person's response of saying hello and a rat's response of pressing a lever are both instances of overt behavior. As noted in Chapter 1, behaviorists traditionally have emphasized the study of overt (observable) behavior.

Skinner, however, maintained that internal events such as thoughts, feelings, and even sensory experiences (e.g., seeing and hearing) should also be classified as behaviors. Skinner referred to such behaviors as "private behaviors" or "private events," although they are more commonly referred to as covert behaviors. Thus, ***covert behavior*** is behavior that can be perceived only by the person performing the behavior. In other words, it is behavior that is *subjectively perceived* and is not publicly observable. Dreaming, thinking about your next chess move, visualizing how your date will go on the weekend, and feeling anxious are all examples of covert behavior. Of course, some covert behaviors have components that could be made publicly observable. A feeling of anxiety, for example, is likely to involve increases in heart rate and muscle tension, both of which could be electronically measured. If such measurements are made, then those particular components of anxiety can be considered overt—which from a behavioral perspective is much preferred over a purely subjective report of anxiety.

Just as the behavior of one person can serve as a stimulus for the behavior of another, covert and overt behaviors within the same person can act as stimuli for each other. For example, thinking about one's next move in chess (a covert behavior) is a stimulus that influences which chess piece you actually move (an overt behavior), while accidentally moving the wrong chess piece (an overt behavior) is a stimulus that induces you to think unpleasant thoughts about yourself (a covert behavior). As behavior analysts put it, the environment does not stop with the skin: events both outside the skin and inside the skin can influence our behavior—though behavior analysts maintain that the ultimate cause of the behavior is often to be found outside the skin. (For example, what might a behavior analyst consider to be the ultimate cause of a person thinking about a certain chess move and then making that move?)

Appetitive and Aversive Stimuli

Many stimuli, both internal and external, can be classified as appetitive or aversive. An ***appetitive stimulus*** is an event that an organism will seek out. Food is an appetitive stimulus when we are hungry; water is an appetitive stimulus when we are thirsty. An ***aversive stimulus*** is an event that an organism will avoid. Electric shock and extreme heat are examples of aversive stimuli. (Note that the word is *aversive* and not *adversive*.)

Appetitive and aversive stimuli could also be defined as those events that people usually describe as pleasant or unpleasant. Such descriptions are often

Calvin and Hobbes **by Bill Watterson**

accurate, but one has to be careful not to rely on them too much. As the *Calvin and Hobbes* cartoon illustrates, people can vary widely in the types of events they regard as appetitive versus aversive—a point that many parents overlook when they attempt to reinforce or punish a child's behavior. As well, a person may claim that a certain experience is unpleasant, yet work actively to obtain it. For example, someone might describe her pack-a-day smoking habit as "disgusting," yet move heaven and earth to make it to the store in time to buy another pack. Despite what she says, tobacco is clearly an appetitive stimulus for her. The moral of the story is that talk is cheap—or, as behavior analysts sometimes put it, "just verbal behavior." It may or may not accurately reflect the nonverbal behavior it presumably describes.

QUICK QUIZ B

1. A(n) _stimulus_ is any event that can potentially influence behavior; a(n) _response_ is a specific instance of behavior.
2. A tone is a s_timulus_ and a tone and a bell are s_timuli_.
3. In a social interaction, one person's response can be another person's _stimulus_.
4. Julie dislikes Jake, one of the sales personnel who works in her department. Because Julie avoids Jake like the plague, Jake can be considered an (appetitive/adversive/aversive) stimulus.
5. Julie closes her office door when Jake is nearby, which is an example of a(n) (overt/covert) behavior. Julie also thinks unkind thoughts about Jake and feels nervous when he is around, both of which are examples of _covert_ behavior.
6. Jake is strongly attracted to Julie and often hangs around her office just to get a glimpse of her. Julie is thus a(n) _appetitive_ stimulus for Jake.
7. If we think before we act, then our (covert/overt) behavior serves as a stimulus that influences our _overt_ behavior. If we act first and feel regret later, then our _overt_ behavior serves as a stimulus that influences our _covert_ behavior.
8. Covert behaviors can also be called p_erceived_ behaviors or events.

Motivating Operations

You may have noticed in some of the preceding examples that how we react to an event depends on a particular state or condition. Any procedure that affects the appetitiveness or aversiveness of an event is called a ***motivating operation***. There are two types of motivating operations: establishing operations and abolishing operations. An ***establishing operation*** is a procedure that *increases* the appetitiveness or aversiveness of an event, and an ***abolishing operation*** is a procedure that *decreases* the appetitiveness or aversiveness of an event. For example, depriving an animal of food is an establishing operation that increases the appetitive value of food, while "satiating" an animal on food—that is, feeding it until it is no longer hungry—is an abolishing operation that decreases the appetitive value of food. Thus, *deprivation* (the prolonged absence of an event) and *satiation* (the prolonged exposure to or consumption of an event) are common types of motivating operations. If the event is being used as a reinforcer for some behavior—such as food being used as a reinforcer for lever pressing—then we could also regard deprivation and satiation as procedures that respectively increase or decrease the effectiveness of a reinforcer.

The manner in which deprivation and satiation affect the appetitiveness of food is obvious. Less obviously, deprivation and satiation can also affect our reactions to many other events. If you have ever gone without television for an extended period of time (deprivation), you may have found it surprisingly interesting when you finally saw it again. Likewise, if you hear a favorite song too often (satiation), you may lose interest in it.

Although the general rule is that deprivation increases the appetitiveness of an event and satiation decreases its appetitiveness, exceptions can occur. For example, people (and even rats, as you will see in a later chapter) who undertake severe diets sometimes acquire a disorder known as anorexia nervosa. In these cases, severe food deprivation seems to decrease the appetitive value of food rather than increase it, and these individuals begin to eat even less food than the diet allows. Many people who have anorexia also engage in extremely high levels of activity yet seem to find the activity more, not less, reinforcing—that is, they do not seem to "satiate" on the activity. These processes are discussed more fully in Chapter 12.[1]

Contiguity and Contingency

Two terms that are often confused are *contiguity* and *contingency*. Although they sound similar, they have very different meanings. *Contiguity*, as mentioned in the opening chapter, means "closeness or nearness." Thus, ***temporal contiguity*** is the extent to which events occur close together in time.

---

[1]If you are uncertain how to pronounce *satiation*, or any other word in this text, audio examples of pronunciation can be found on the Internet, such as at the Merriam-Webster site: http://www.merriam-webster.com/help/audiofaq.htm.

Thunder and lightning are temporally contiguous—we see the lightning and shortly afterward hear the thunder. Temporal contiguity is an important aspect of learning. A rat will more readily learn to press a lever for food if the food immediately follows the lever press than if it appears several seconds later. Likewise, a child will more quickly learn to throw a tantrum for candy if he is immediately given candy each time he does so.

Spatial contiguity is the extent to which events are situated close to each other in space. This type of contiguity also affects learning. It is easier for a rat to learn to press a lever for food if the food dispenser is close to the lever as opposed to being several feet away. Likewise, it may take a young child (or a young puppy) somewhat longer to learn that a doorbell, as opposed to a knock, indicates that someone is at the front door. The sound of the knock is spatially contiguous with the door (the sound comes from the door), whereas the sound of the doorbell is not (the sound usually comes from a box located elsewhere in the house).

The term *contingency* has a quite different meaning from contiguity. A ***contingency*** is a predictive (or functional) relationship between two events, such that the occurrence of one event predicts the probable occurrence of another. If a rat receives a food pellet whenever it presses a lever, then a contingency exists between lever pressing and food. We then say that the presentation of food is contingent on lever pressing. Likewise, if a child receives a big balloon each time she goes to the dentist, then a contingency exists between visiting the dentist and receiving the balloon. In other words, receiving the balloon is contingent upon visiting the dentist. As you will see later, contingency is an extremely important aspect of learning.

QUICK QUIZ C

1. A m__________ o__________ is a procedure that affects the appetitiveness or aversiveness of a stimulus.
2. An a__________ o__________ is a procedure that makes an event less attractive or less aversive, while an e__________ o__________ makes an event more attractive or more aversive.
3. Farah has been working out of town and has not seen a movie for over a year. It is likely that, for her, the reward value of going to a movie has (increased/decreased) as a function of (satiation/deprivation), which is an example of a (n) __________ operation.
4. The term __________ means "closeness or nearness."
5. Erin claims that she once experienced a sharp pain in her leg at the precise moment that her son, who was on a mountain-climbing expedition, broke his leg. Because of the t__________ c__________ between her feeling of pain and her son's injury, Erin now believes that she has some type of psychic ability.
6. People who live close to each other are more likely to date and fall in love. In other words, s__________ c__________ seems to have a strong effect on the development of romantic relationships.

7. Sasha obtains a high mark on her exams only when she studies diligently. For Sasha, there is a (contingency/contiguity) between studying diligently and doing well on her exams.
8. The fact that a dog receives a treat only when it begs means that the treat is (contiguous with/contingent upon) the behavior of begging. The fact that the treat closely follows begging also means that the two events are (contiguous with/contingent upon) each other.

Measurement of Behavior

Behavioral Definitions

When we study the effects of particular variables on a certain behavior (which is often referred to as the "target behavior"), it is important that we properly define the behavior. Such behavioral definitions should be *objective* in the sense that they refer to some observable aspect of the individual's behavior. For example, yelling and striking are observable aspects of aggressive behavior, but feelings of anger are not. Therefore, defining aggression in terms of the physical characteristics of yelling and striking is more precise than defining it as feelings of anger.

Behavioral definitions should also be clearly defined, that is, *unambiguous*. For example, we might define yelling as a loud vocalization that continues for more than 5 seconds and can be heard outside a closed door. Striking might be defined as a rapid arm or leg movement that results in physical contact. From a scientific perspective, an unambiguous definition will ensure that our measurements of the behavior are relatively consistent over time and across settings. What counts as an aggressive incident today will also count as an aggressive incident tomorrow. Further, if we are investigating various treatments to reduce the number of aggressive incidents (e.g., by rewarding the child for acting nonaggressively), we can be more certain that any observed change in the aggressive behavior is the result of our treatment as opposed to an unconscious shift in our definition of aggression. Finally, an unambiguous definition will make it easier for other researchers to replicate our results.

Clear definitions of behavior are also beneficial outside the clinical or research setting, particularly in such tasks as child rearing (the ultimate challenge in behavior management). A major problem faced by many children is that parents often shift their standards as to what constitutes appropriate behavior. For example, a parent might constantly tell a child that eating in the living room is wrong, but then allow eating in the living room when visitors arrive or when the family is watching a movie. A clearer definition of what behaviors are appropriate versus inappropriate would be less confusing to the child and would reduce the probability of the child violating the rules. One parent we know of uses a "three-warning" rule for situations that require compliance. For example, if one of the children is asked to get ready to go swimming with her aunt, she must comply by the third warning or else suffer a negative consequence (e.g., she will not be allowed to go swimming that day). Because the rule is so well defined and allows the child a certain amount of time "to get mobilized," negative consequences rarely have to be imposed. And even when the child does not comply and does suffer the consequences, she rarely makes a fuss about it because she was well aware of the contingencies from the outset. (This does not mean that the children in this family are rigidly controlled. In fact, one's first impression upon entering the household is that it is quite chaotic, with children running everywhere, laughing and playing. Within clearly defined limits, the children are allowed a great deal of freedom, which they very much appreciate.)

Recording Methods

Depending on how we define a target behavior, there are several ways in which we can go about measuring it. Let's look at a few of these methods.

Rate of Response One of the most popular measures in behavioral research is ***rate of response***, which is the frequency with which a response occurs in a certain period of time. Rate measurements are most appropriate when the response is of brief duration, with a well-defined start and finish (i.e., onset and offset). The number of cigarettes smoked per day, the number of words written in a 1-hour writing session, and the number of body stomps in a half-hour broadcast of professional wrestling are all rate measures of behavior. (When defining or giving examples of rate, be sure to include the time aspect. For example, *number of lever presses per hour* is a rate measure of behavior, but *number of lever presses* by itself, with no mention of time, is not.)

Certain experimental procedures have been explicitly designed to facilitate measuring behavior in terms of rate. For example, operant conditioning experiments often involve rats pressing levers to earn food. The lever press is a very definable response, because once the lever is pressed sufficiently for the microswitch to be activated, a response is electronically recorded. Number of lever presses per session thus provides a precise measure of the rat's food-directed behavior. Rate is a particularly favored measure among some behaviorists (especially radical behaviorists), because it tends to be highly sensitive to the influence of other variables. For example, the rate at which a rat presses a lever for food will vary closely with the number of hours of food deprivation, the type of food being delivered (preferred or non-preferred), and the amount of effort required to press the lever. Likewise, the rate at which you can say aloud the definitions of the concepts in this text (e.g., the number of terms you are able to define per minute while sorting through your flash cards) may be a good indicator of the extent to which you are now fluent enough with the concept to begin applying it to different situations. In fact, such fluency measures of learning are a basic aspect of a behavioral approach to instruction known as *precision learning* (e.g., Lindsley, 1991; Binder, 1996).

A ***cumulative recorder*** is a classic device that measures the total number of responses over time and provides a graphic depiction of the rate of behavior.

This instrument consists of a roll of paper that unravels at a slow, constant pace and a movable pen that makes tracks across it (see Figure 2.1). If there are no responses for a period of time, the pen remains stationary while the paper unrolls beneath it. This results in a flat, horizontal line along the paper, with longer lines indicating longer periods of no responding. When a response occurs (e.g., the rat presses the lever), electronic equipment registers the response and produces a slight upward movement of the pen. Thus, a low rate of response produces a line that slopes upward at a shallow angle (because the pen is slowly moving upward while the paper passes beneath it), whereas a high rate of response produces a line that slopes upward at a steep angle. *The important thing to remember is that the steeper the line, the higher the rate of response.* A cumulative record thereby provides an easily read, graphic depiction of changes in the subject's rate of response over time. (Needless to say, these days, response rates are more often recorded by computer software programs. This allows for the generation of various types of descriptive records, including cumulative records.)

Intensity The ***intensity*** of a behavior is the force or magnitude of the behavior. For example, in Pavlov's classical conditioning procedure with dogs, in which a tone was followed by food:

Tone: Food → *Salivation*
Tone → *Salivation*

the strength of conditioning was typically measured as the amount (magnitude) of saliva produced whenever the tone was presented by itself. More saliva indicated stronger conditioning. Another example of intensity is the force with which a rat presses a lever to obtain food. Likewise, it is intensity that we are concerned with when we teach a child to speak softly and print firmly.

FIGURE 2.1 Illustration of a cumulative recorder. This device consists of a roll of paper that unravels at a slow, constant pace. If no response is made, the pen remains stationary, resulting in a horizontal line. A high rate of response produces a steep line, and a low rate of response produces a shallow line. The short slashes indicate the points at which reinforcers were delivered, for example, food pellets delivered to a rat for making a certain number of lever presses. (*Source*: Malone, 1990.)

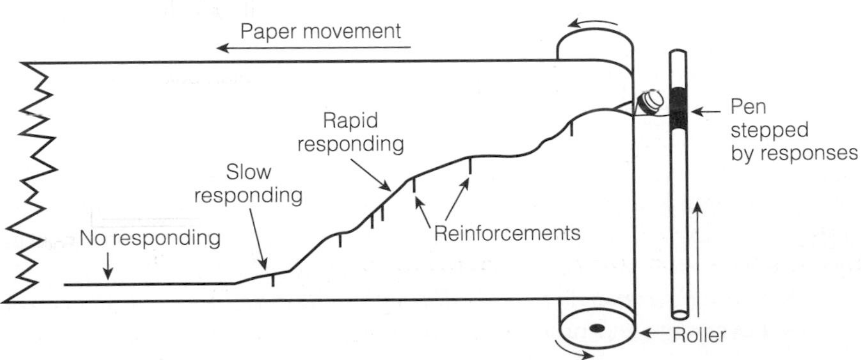

Duration ***Duration*** is the length of time that an individual repeatedly or continuously performs a behavior. This measure is appropriate when we are concerned with either increasing or decreasing the length of time the behavior occurs. For example, a student may attempt to increase the amount of time he spends studying each week, as well as decrease the amount of time spent watching television.

Speed Although duration measures are sometimes useful, they are in some ways imprecise. You may run for an hour, but the speed at which you run (as indicated by the amount of distance covered during that hour) will be a more accurate indicator of your fitness level. Thus, ***speed*** is the length of time it takes for an episode of behavior to occur from start to finish. The length of time it takes for a rat to run through a maze from the start box to the goal box is a measure of speed. (See Figure 2.2 for examples of mazes that have been used in behavioral research.) We are also concerned with speed when we teach a child to eat a meal more quickly (if he tends to dawdle at the dinner table) or more slowly (if he tends to fling food everywhere in a rush to get finished). Studies on activity levels in rats often

FIGURE 2.2 Three classic mazes used in behavioral research. Although the Hampton Court maze was often used by researchers in the early 1900s, it was later largely supplanted by the T-maze and the straight-alley "maze," which, because of their simplicity, proved more useful for investigating basic principles of behavior. (*Source*: Lieberman, 2000.)

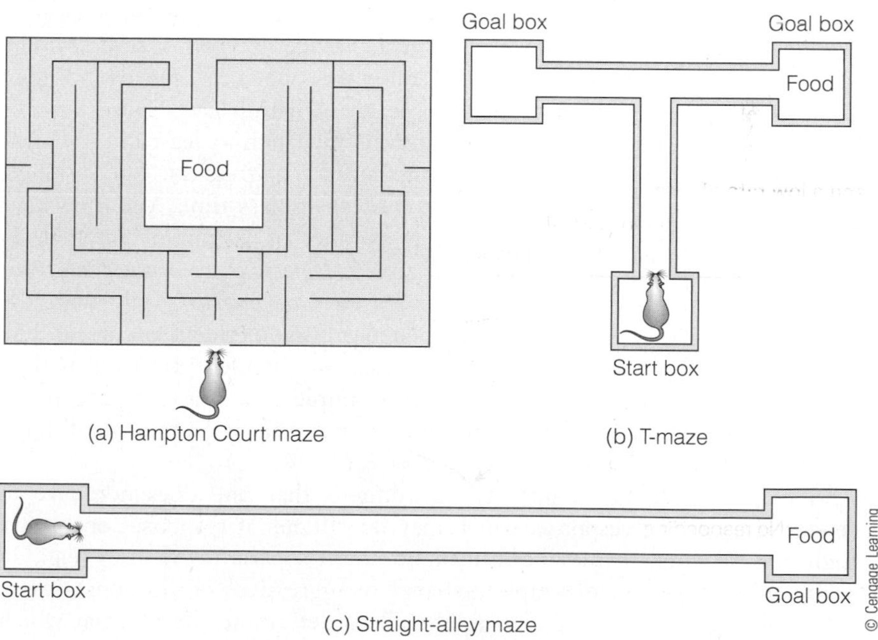

measure both the duration of running (the amount of time the rats spend running in the wheel) as well as the speed of running (the distance covered per hour or per day). But note that we could also use a rate measure of wheel running, that is, the number of wheel turns per hour.

Latency The ***latency*** of a behavior is the length of time required for a behavior to begin. With respect to conditioning of salivation, the strength of conditioning can be measured not only in terms of the amount of saliva, but also in terms of how soon the dog begins salivating after it hears the tone. Likewise, the number of days it takes for a student to begin working on a term paper after it has been assigned might be a useful measure of the extent to which she procrastinates on such tasks. TV game shows that require contestants to press buzzers when they believe they have the right answer are using a latency measure of the contestants' performance.

Latency, speed, and duration are often confused because they all involve some type of time measurement. To help distinguish between them, consider the behavior of an athlete who specializes in the 100-meter sprint. The amount of time it takes for her to commence running when she hears the starting pistol—which is only a fraction of a second—is a measure of latency, whereas the amount of time it takes for her to complete the race (start to finish) is a measure of speed. Conversely, the total amount of time she trains each day is a measure of duration.

Interval Recording A particularly efficient way of measuring behavior, often utilized in applied settings, is ***interval recording***: the measurement of whether or not a behavior occurs during each interval within a series of continuous intervals. For example, if we wish to measure the amount of aggressive behavior in a classroom, we might make a video record of several hours of class time. We would then have observers view the video and note whether or not an aggressive incident occurred within each successive 10-minute interval. The proportion of intervals in which at least one incident occurred would then be our overall measure of aggression. For instance, imagine that we record 3 hours (180 minutes) of class time. We then have observers view the video and count the number of 10-minute intervals in which least one aggressive incident occurred. *Note that we are not concerned with how many aggressive incidents occurred in each interval*, only with the number of intervals in which at least one aggressive incident occurred. The percentage of intervals during which at least one incident occurred is then our overall measure of the behavior. For example, if at least one aggressive incident occurred in 12 of the 18 ten-minute intervals, then the overall measure of aggression would be $12/18 \times 100 = 66.7\%$.

A major advantage of interval recording is that one does not have to record every single response, which may be difficult if responses occur at a high rate or where it may be difficult to count separate responses (e.g., an argument that consists of a rapid exchange of aggressive vocalizations). Interval recording is also useful if it is difficult to determine the point at which the target behavior starts and stops. Arguments would be a good example of this in that they sometimes build slowly, and trying to determine the exact moment when the argument begins may be difficult.

Time-Sample Recording A variant of interval recording is time-sample recording. In ***time-sample recording***, one measures whether or not a behavior occurs during each interval within a series of discontinuous intervals (intervals that are spaced apart). For example, to assess the level of aggression in a classroom, we might have an observer unobtrusively enter the classroom for a 10-minute interval at the start of each half hour and record whether at least one aggressive incident occurred during that interval. The behavior of the students is thus intermittently sampled, and the percentage of these sampled intervals in which an aggressive incident occurred is our overall measure of aggression. Imagine, for example, that over a period of 6 hours we are able to sample 12 ten-minute intervals. If one or more aggressive incidents occurred in nine of those intervals, then the overall level of aggression is calculated as $9/12 \times 100 = 75\%$. Although we will not have observed every act of aggression using such a method, we will nevertheless have obtained a fairly good approximation of the level of aggression in that setting. As well, this method of recording is very time efficient for our observer, who can spend most of the day working on other tasks or making observations in other classrooms.

Topography Sometimes we are concerned with the ***topography*** of a behavior, which is the physical form of the behavior. For example, rather than record the rate at which a rat presses a lever, we might observe *how* it presses the lever, such as whether it uses its left paw or right paw. Similarly, it is the topography of the behavior that we are concerned with when we teach a child how to dress appropriately, write neatly, and brush his teeth properly. Training a dolphin (or your pet goldfish) to swim through a hoop to obtain a food reward is yet another example in which the topography of the behavior is the focus of concern.

Number of Errors Any behavior in which responses can be categorized as right or wrong can be assessed in terms of the number of errors. For example, the number of wrong turns a rat takes before it finds its way through a maze to the goal box is one measure of how well the rat has learned the maze. Likewise, the number of errors a student makes on an exam is the traditional method for determining how well the student knows the material.

Assessing Reliability

One thing you may have wondered about in reading some of the preceding examples is the reliability or trustworthiness of the data that we are gathering using these methods. This is an important issue when the data is being gathered by observers who might vary widely in their judgments as to whether or

TABLE 2.1 **Recordings of aggressive behavior by two independent observers in each of 12 intervals. A ✓ indicates that at least one aggressive incident was judged to have occurred in that interval. The observers were in disagreement only in intervals 4 and 5, yielding an interobserver reliability measure of 10/12 = 83.3%.**

INTERNAL	1	2	3	4*	5*	6	7	8	9	10	11	12
Observer A	✓		✓		✓	✓		✓	✓		✓	
Observer B	✓		✓	✓		✓		✓	✓		✓	

not a particular behavior has occurred. For this reason, whenever possible, researchers attempt to utilize two or more independent observers for at least part of the assessment period and then calculate the extent to which the observers agree on their observations. For example, in an interval recording procedure in which two observers independently record the occurrence of aggression in each of 12 consecutive intervals, they may agree on whether or not an incident occurred in 10 of the intervals and disagree in 2 of the intervals (see Table 2.1). Our measure of *interobserver reliability* in this case can be calculated as the number of intervals during which the observers agree divided by the total number of intervals: 10/12 = 83.3%. There are no hard and fast rules for what constitutes adequate reliability, but 80% is often regarded as the minimum acceptable level and 90% as the preferred level. If reliability is considered to be inadequate, then our behavioral definition may need to be revised or our observers may need further training in identifying aggressive incidents. (For additional information on assessing reliability, see Kazdin, 2011.)

QUICK QUIZ D

1. Behavioral definitions should be (subjective/objective) as well as (ambiguous/unambiguous).
2. The force with which a person can squeeze a device that measures grip strength is a measure of i__________.
3. How long it takes a musician to play a musical piece from beginning to end is a measure of __________, whereas the number of hours the musician practices each week is a measure of __________. The amount of time it takes the musician to commence playing following the conductor's cue to begin is a measure of __________.
4. The exact manner in which Jana lifts a dumbbell and presses it overhead is called the t__________ of the behavior.
5. The number of fish a person catches in a 1-hour period is the measure of the r__________ at which fish are being caught.
6. Recording whether or not Ashley hiccups during a continuous series of 5-minute time periods is an example of __________ recording, whereas recording whether or not hiccupping occurs during 5-minute periods at the

start of each hour throughout the day is an example of ____________ ____________ recording.

7. A device commonly used to measure the ongoing rate of a behavior is a c____________ r____________. On this device, a flat line indicates (no/slow/fast) responding, while a steep line indicates ____________ responding and a shallow line indicates ____________ responding.

8. Which of the following is an example of a rate measure of writing? (a) number of words written, (b) number of words written per hour.

9. In an interval recording procedure, our two classroom observers agreed on whether Mika was being disruptive or not during 15 of 20 observed intervals. The level of interobserver reliability in this example is ____________%, which is generally considered (adequate/inadequate).

Research Designs

Deciding how to measure a behavior is only part of the problem. We must also determine which method to use to assess the impact of certain variables on that behavior. Several methods are available, and they can be divided into two general types: descriptive methods and experimental methods.

Descriptive Research

Descriptive research involves gathering information about a behavior and the circumstances within which it occurs. It does not involve the manipulation of any variables. Descriptive methods include the survey approach, in which individuals answer a series of questions, and the case study approach, which involves the intensive study of a single individual, such as someone who has a rare type of disorder. The descriptive method most relevant to behavioral research, however, is ***naturalistic observation***, in which one systematically observes and records the occurrence of a behavior in its natural environment. Note the word *systematically*. We are not talking here about casual observations, which may be strongly biased by the researcher's preconceptions. Behavioral scientists have as many preconceptions about behavior as the average person does—perhaps more, because it is their job to study behavior—and are therefore susceptible to viewing behavior from a biased perspective. To avoid, or at least minimize, such biases, researchers attempt to define their variables precisely and make their observations in a consistent and uniform manner.

Jane Goodall's systematic study of chimpanzee behavior in the wild is a classic example of naturalistic observation. Through her detailed observations, we now know that chimpanzees eat meat (they sometimes kill and devour monkeys), use primitive tools (they sometimes dip a twig into a termite hill to capture termites for food), and engage in warfare (chimpanzees from one group have been observed stalking, attacking, and killing members of a neighboring group; see Goodall, 1990).

Naturalistic observation is a commonly used approach in *ethology* (or *behavioral ecology*), a branch of zoology that focuses on the study of inherited behavior patterns in animals. Such patterns have presumably evolved to help the animal cope with certain aspects of its natural environment. For this reason, inherited behavior patterns are usually best studied within the natural environment (or a close approximation to it), because the behavior may not occur when the animal is removed from that environment. Displays of dominance and submission, for instance, may not be evident unless an animal is allowed to freely interact with members of its own species. For example, a dog's behavior of rolling over on its back and displaying its underside can be more clearly seen as a submissive gesture when dogs interact with each other than when they interact with us. One of the authors first realized this when he witnessed the family dog being attacked by a much larger dog. Following a brief skirmish, Trixie rolled over on her back and displayed her underside, the same behavior she often displayed toward us. What had always seemed like a simple request for a tummy scratch also functioned as an inborn gesture of submission.

Although naturalistic observation is ideal for studying inherited behavior patterns, it also contributes to our understanding of learning. A famous example of this is the "cultural adoption" of food-washing behavior among a troop of macaque monkeys off the coast of Japan. When one monkey acquired the habit of washing sand off a sweet potato by dipping it in lake water (the researchers had left the potatoes on a sandy beach to attract the monkeys to that area), other monkeys in the troop soon imitated this behavior. Interestingly, the oldest monkeys in the troop never adopted this "newfangled way" of cleaning food (Kawamura, 1963).

The naturalistic observation approach is excellent for gaining rich, detailed information about a behavior and the circumstances in which it typically occurs. The main problem with this approach is that it often leaves us uncertain as to which variables affect the occurrence of the behavior; in other words, it is difficult to determine cause-and-effect (or functional) relationships. For example, if you study childhood aggression by observing children interacting on a playground, you may see many displays of aggressive behavior (e.g., grabbing a toy away from another child, pushing, yelling, etc.). However, it will be difficult to determine *why* these aggressive behaviors are occurring. You might not know, for example, whether an aggressive child has had a long history of aggression, is experiencing considerable frustration that day, or has had frequent exposure to violence in the home. In a sense, the natural environment is a vast sea of variables, and sorting out which variables are responsible for which behavior can be a daunting task. Thus, the naturalistic observation approach is often insufficient for gaining a full understanding of a behavior and the variables that influence it.

QUICK QUIZ E

1. Shannon and her students spend each spring and summer in the local river valley studying the vocalizations of squirrels. If they only observe and record occurrences of the behavior and the circumstances in which it occurs, they are engaging in the naturalistic observation method of research, which is a type of descriptive research.

2. Shannon clearly defines the behavior they are studying and carefully assesses the level of interobserver reliability among her students. By doing so, she is attempting to minimize the possibility of researcher bias, in which the beliefs and expectations of the researchers can unduly influence their observations.

3. The major limitation of the naturalistic observation approach to research is that it is often difficult to determine functional (or cause-and-effect) relationships.

Experimental Research

Although naturalistic observations can provide detailed information about behavior, they usually do not allow us to draw firm conclusions about the causes of a behavior. To draw such conclusions, it is usually necessary to conduct an experiment. Thus, in their quest to discover functional relationships between environmental events and behavior, behavioral researchers have a strong preference for the experimental approach to research.

In ***experimental research***, one or more independent variables are systematically varied to determine their effect on a dependent variable (i.e., the behavior you suspect will change as a result of changes in the independent variable). Any differences in behavior across the different conditions of the experiment are presumed to be caused by the differences in the independent variable.

Behavioral researchers use two main types of experimental designs: group designs and single-subject designs. As will be seen, each type of design has its advantages and disadvantages, and the decision to employ one method or the other largely has to do with the nature of the issue being investigated.

Group Designs The most common type of experimental design is the ***group design***, in which one manipulates one or more independent variables across groups of subjects. For example, in a simple ***control group design***, individuals are randomly assigned to either an experimental (or treatment) group or a control group; the experimental group is then exposed to a certain manipulation or treatment, while the control group is not. Imagine, for example, that 20 rats are randomly assigned to either an experimental group or a control group. Rats in the experimental group are individually placed in an experimental chamber for 30 minutes, during which time they receive a free food pellet every minute. The rats in the control group are treated exactly the same except they receive no food during the 30-minute session. They are simply allowed to snoop around the chamber. The rats in each group receive one session per day for 10 consecutive days. On day 11, a mechanical lever is placed in each chamber, and the rats must learn to press the lever to obtain food. The question of interest is whether the rats that previously received free food will learn to press the lever more readily or less readily than the rats that did not receive free food. Thus, the *independent variable* in this experiment is the presence versus absence of free food during the initial phase of the experiment, and the *dependent variable* is the average amount of time it takes for the rats in each group to learn to press the lever for food. (By the way, research has shown that animals that receive free food subsequently have more difficulty learning how to respond for food [Welker, 1976; Wheatley, Welker, & Miles, 1977]. This suggests that exposure to free reinforcers can sometimes impair an animal's ability to learn how to respond for reinforcers.)

Group designs are usually more complicated than the simple control group design we just described. In a ***factorial design***, one examines the effects of two or more independent variables (or factors) across groups of subjects. For example, we might wonder if the damaging effects of free food on ability to learn are dependent on age. Thus, we might rerun this experiment with groups of old rats, middle-aged rats, and young rats. This approach would yield what is known as a 2 × 3 *factorial design*, in which there are two independent variables (food and age), the first of which has two levels (free food versus no food) and the second of which has three levels (old age versus middle age versus young age). This experiment would therefore involve a total of six groups (old with free food, old with no food, middle-aged with free food, middle-aged with no food, young with free food, and young with no food; see Table 2.2). If the results indicate that free food affects learning ability only in rats of a certain age, then we say that there is an *interaction* between the effects of free food and age. Such interaction effects give us a finer understanding of the variables in which we are interested, and research is often designed to search for such effects.

A variant on a group design that is used in certain types of animal research is a comparative design. A ***comparative design*** is a type of group design in which different species constitute one of the independent variables. It is often used to test evolutionary hypotheses regarding the differences in selective pressures for a particular trait between species. For example, if you hypothesize that rats have evolved to deal with small, enclosed environments better than dogs have (or that dogs have evolved to deal with large, open environments better than rats have), you could examine how quickly dogs

TABLE 2.2 Six experimental conditions (groups of participants) in a 2 × 3 factorial experiment involving two levels of a "food" variable and three levels of an "age" variable.

	YOUNG (Y)	MIDDLE-AGED (M)	OLD (O)
No food (NF)	NFY	NFM	NFO
Free food (FF)	FFY	FFM	FFO

and rats learn to find a target in an enclosed maze versus a large open area. This is a 2 × 2 factorial design in which there are two independent variables (species and environment), each of which has two levels (rat versus dog; maze versus open area). Of course, you would not use exactly the same apparatus for a rat that you would for a dog; rather, you would attempt to equate the equipment to the relative size and other important traits of each species. This includes recognizing that different species may exhibit certain abilities in very different ways. For example, in a comparison of dogs versus hedgehogs in their ability to learn to avoid danger, one must consider the fact that dogs and hedgehogs cope with danger in very different ways, with dogs tending to run away whereas hedgehogs tend to roll up into a ball and freeze.

Group designs are excellent for assessing the average effects of certain variables. Cause-and-effect conclusions are possible due to the strict control over the environment that allows the experimenter to rule out alternative explanations. Because all subjects receive identical experiences except for the independent variable that is being manipulated, we can be fairly confident that differences between groups in performance are the result of differences in the independent variable. *Random assignment* of subjects to each condition, where suitable, also ensures that various characteristics of the subjects in each group are likely to be evenly distributed across the different conditions. Thus, the groups in each condition will be pretty much alike at the onset of the experiment, and any differences found at the end of the experiment will most likely be due to our manipulation of the independent variable.

Group designs, however, are not without their drawbacks. To begin with, this type of design usually requires a large number of subjects (often 10 or more per group). In fact, for statistical reasons, the larger the number of subjects in a group, the more trustworthy the results. But what if you wished to conduct research on the effectiveness of a behavioral treatment for one individual? It would be impractical to conduct an experiment with a large number of subjects just to determine if a certain treatment might be effective for one person. Group designs are therefore not well suited for investigating the effect of a certain treatment on a particular individual.

A second difficulty with group designs is that they typically focus on the *average* performance of all subjects in each group. Little attention is given to the performance of individual subjects, even if some subjects differ markedly from the average. For example, going back to our rat study, suppose that 2 out of the 10 rats previously given free food learned to press the lever almost immediately, while the others took much longer. Even if, on average, the rats in this free-food group learned more slowly than the rats in the no-food group, what about the two quick learners? Should we regard them as mere aberrations ("I guess some rats are just brighter than others"), or is it the case that exposure to free food actually facilitates learning in some individuals? Using similar reasoning, one behavior analyst (himself a victim of brain cancer) has questioned the heavy reliance on large-scale clinical trials to determine the efficacy of new drugs in treating cancer, his argument being that a drug that appears ineffective for the average patient might nevertheless be effective for a subset of patients (Williams, 2010). By ignoring individual data, we might never consider such a possibility. In other words, group data is combined to produce a statistical average, but the scores of some individuals within the group may deviate markedly from this average; therefore, average results may have little relevance to particular individuals. (Question: What implication does this have for the value of the advice given during the radio call-in show in the vignette presented at the start of this chapter?)

A third limitation of group designs is that the results are often analyzed and interpreted only at the end of the experiment, rather than during the experiment. In some situations, this may be undesirable. If, for example, we are treating a child for self-injurious behavior, we need to be aware throughout whether our treatment is having a positive effect. If the effect is positive, we can maintain the treatment; if the effect is negative, we should immediately halt our treatment and try something different. By contrast, group designs that measure effects only at the end of the study usually do not provide us with this type of flexibility.

In conclusion, although group designs are excellent for assessing the average effects of independent variables among large numbers of subjects, there are limitations. Alternative designs that do not suffer from these limitations—but have their own limitations—are single-subject designs, which we discuss in the next section.

QUICK QUIZ F

1. In an experiment, a(n) independent variable is systematically manipulated to determine its effects on a(n) dependent variable.
2. In a behavioral experiment, the independent variable is usually a change in some type of environmental experience and the dependent variable is a change in behavior.
3. In the simplest form of a control group design, individuals are randomly assigned to either an experimental (or treatment) group or a control group.
4. Group designs that are used to assess behavioral differences between species are called comparative designs, in which different species constitute one of the independent variables.
5. Briefly stated, three problems with control group designs are:
   a. need a large number of participants
   b. typically focuses on the average of the group
   c. analyzed and interpreted at the end of the experiment rather than during

Single-Subject Designs Unlike group designs, ***single-subject designs*** require only one or a few subjects to conduct an entire experiment. Also known as *single-case* or *small-n* designs, there are several types of such designs, four of which are described here.

Simple-Comparison (AB) Design In a ***simple-comparison design***, behavior in a baseline condition is compared to behavior in a treatment condition.

Suppose, for example, that Cory wishes to cut down on smoking (as a first step toward quitting) and wonders if he might be able to do so by punishing himself. In a *self-punishment* procedure, people apply an aversive consequence to themselves each time they engage in an unwanted target behavior. Self-punishment of smoking might consist of Cory giving his buddy a dollar for each cigarette he smokes. (Another way of looking at this is that Cory has implemented a fine or tax on himself to try to reduce the amount he smokes.)

The first step in the program would be for Cory to take a baseline measure of the number of cigarettes he typically smokes each day. The ***baseline*** of a behavior is the normal frequency of the behavior that occurs before some type of intervention. Cory could, for example, keep an index card tucked inside the flap of his cigarette pack and make a check mark on it for each cigarette he smokes prior to implementing his self-punishment program.

The baseline period should last several days (two weeks is often recommended) to provide an assessment of the typical frequency of Cory's smoking. If it appears that there is a gradual upward or downward trend in the amount smoked during baseline—sometimes the mere act of closely monitoring a behavior can result in some improvement, a process known as *reactivity* (see Study Tip)—Cory should continue the baseline phase until the behavior stabilizes. Following the baseline, he should then institute the self-punishment procedure for several days. If the treatment is effective, the frequency of smoking during the treatment period should be consistently lower than it was during the baseline period (see Figure 2.3).

In this type of study, the baseline period is called the A phase, and the treatment period is called the B phase. Thus, this design is sometimes referred to as an AB design. (Students sometimes think the baseline phase

FIGURE 2.3 Simple-comparison (AB) design. Hypothetical results using a simple-comparison design to assess the effectiveness of a treatment (self-punishment) on number of cigarettes smoked. The dashed vertical line divides the baseline condition from the treatment condition. Results are consistent with, but do not provide strong evidence for, the notion that the treatment was effective.

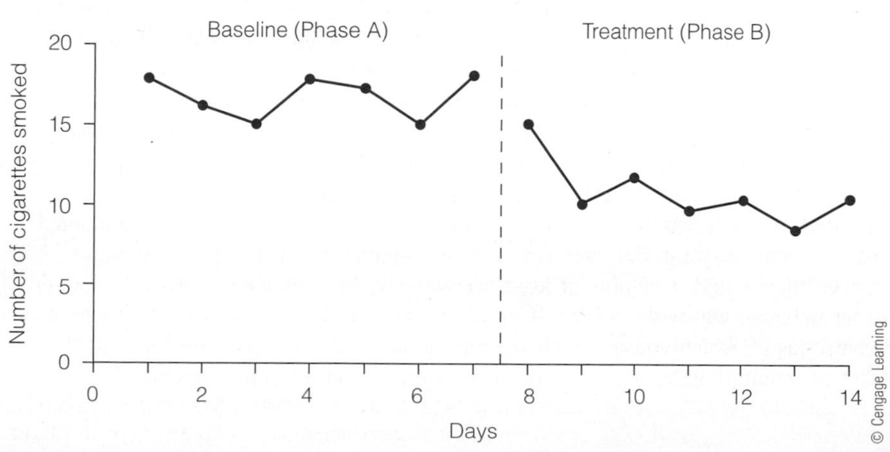

is the B phase because the word *baseline* starts with a B. Don't think that way. The *baseline phase is the A phase* because that is the phase we start with, and the treatment phase is the B phase because it follows the A phase.)

The major problem with the simple-comparison design is that it does not control for the possibility that some other event occurred at the same time that the treatment was implemented, and it was this other event that caused the change in the behavior. For example, perhaps Cory caught a cold at the same time that he began self-punishment, and it is actually the cold that accounts for the reduction in smoking. The simple-comparison design does not allow us to assess this possibility and thus constitutes a poor experimental design. In other words, it does not clearly demonstrate a functional relationship between the independent variable (self-punishment) and the dependent variable (smoking). At best, it provides only suggestive evidence that the treatment was effective. If, however, you are simply interested in obtaining some type of improvement in the behavior, then a simple-comparison design may be sufficient.

Study Tip: *Reactivity* is a change in behavior that often occurs when a behavior is being observed or somehow monitored, even by oneself. The change that occurs is often in a positive direction, which means that self-monitoring can sometimes, by itself, produce an improvement in behavior. Unfortunately, the reactivity effect is often temporary, with much of the improvement eventually disappearing. Nevertheless, one can also find examples of a more enduring effect, resulting in a long-lasting improvement in behavior.

For example, I (one of the coauthors of this textbook) once counseled a college freshman who was feeling overwhelmed by all the work she had been assigned in her classes that fall. Among other things, I suggested that she track her study behavior each day (start times, stop times, and total time studied) using a simple recording sheet. We met only a few times after that as she quickly got on track with her courses. Interestingly, though, I came across that same student a few years later when she was studying in the library. Much to my surprise, she had beside her a photocopy of the recording sheet I had given her years earlier when she had come to see me. She told me that she had used it to track each and every study session throughout her undergraduate program, claiming that it played a major role in keeping her motivated. Although this is only anecdotal evidence and she was no doubt doing many other things right—she graduated with excellent marks and eventually went on to graduate studies—it is not unusual to find examples of highly successful people who claim to have found the act of tracking their behavior to be extremely useful. Skinner (1987) is a prime example in this regard, for years having carefully recorded the amount of writing that he did each day (see also Epstein, 1997). Many famous novelists, such as Earnest Hemingway, have done likewise, carefully tracking their daily output to ensure that they maintain a consistent pace (Watson & Tharp, 2014).

As noted in the appendix, self-monitoring is a basic aspect of a properly conducted self-management program. But even if you're not conducting such a program, you might nevertheless find it helpful, at least occasionally, to track your study behavior—or any other behavior you wish to alter. If nothing else, it will make you aware of where the behavior is at, which you can then work to improve. But it's also possible that the mere act of monitoring, by itself, will result in some degree of improvement.

Reversal Design A much better design is the reversal design, which is sometimes also called an ABA or ABAB design (depending on the number of reversals carried out). A ***reversal design*** consists of repeated alternations between a baseline phase and a treatment phase. If the behavior systematically changes each time the treatment is instituted and later withdrawn, then a functional relationship has been demonstrated between the treatment and the behavior. In Cory's case, he would begin with the baseline phase, then institute a self-punishment phase, then revert to baseline, and then revert to self-punishment. If the results are something like those depicted in Figure 2.4, with smoking decreasing each time the treatment is implemented and increasing each time the treatment is withdrawn, then we have obtained fairly strong evidence that the treatment is the cause of the improvement. It is unlikely that some other event, such as illness, coincided precisely with each application of the treatment to produce such systematic changes in behavior.

The reversal design has many strengths. First, unlike the control group design, it allows an entire experiment to be conducted with a single subject. As such, the reversal design is often ideal for determining the effectiveness of a behavioral intervention for a particular person. Second, some behaviorists argue that statistical tests are not needed to determine if the changes in behavior are meaningful (Sidman, 1960). One can often just "eyeball" the graph to see if the treatment is working. The underlying logic is that if the results are not clear enough to be judged meaningful by visual inspection alone, then the treatment should be altered to produce a stronger effect. This forces the investigator to attain precise control over the variables influencing the target behavior and to strive for powerful treatments that produce large effects.

FIGURE 2.4 Reversal (ABAB) design. Hypothetical results using a reversal design to assess the effectiveness of a treatment (self-punishment) on number of cigarettes smoked. The systematic change in smoking across the alternating conditions provides strong evidence that the treatment was the cause of the improvement.

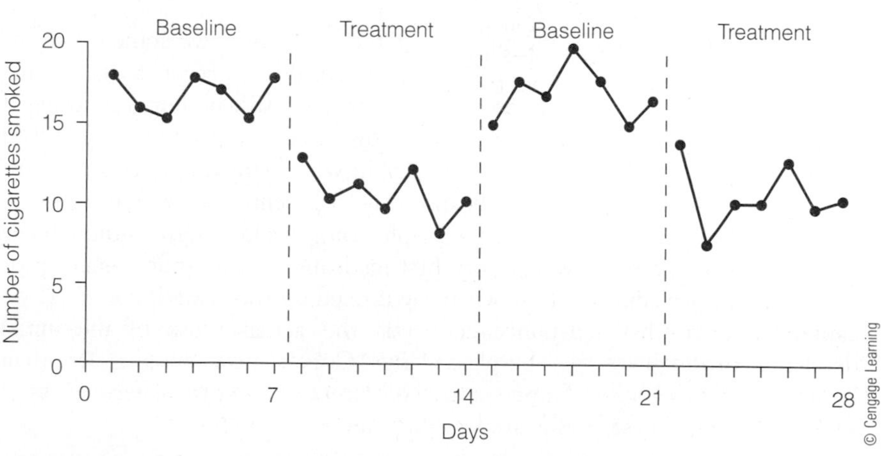

You might be wondering whether results from a reversal design can be generalized to other subjects, since we have demonstrated the effect with only one subject. This is an important question, because in science we are concerned with finding effects that have generality. With single-subject designs, this issue is dealt with by conducting the study with more than one subject. Since each subject in the study constitutes an entire experiment, *each additional subject constitutes a replication of that experiment*. And insofar as replication (or reproducibility) is considered a key factor in establishing the validity of a scientific finding, then finding the same pattern of results for all of the subjects exposed to these procedures would indicate that the results of the experiment are probably valid and have good generality. For example, if we tried the self-punishment treatment with four individuals and they all showed consistent decreases in smoking during the treatment phase, then it is quite likely that this treatment will be effective for many other individuals (although the nature of the punishing consequence might have to be tailored to each individual; what is punishing for one person might not be punishing for another). Thus, studies that utilize single-subject designs are often conducted with four or more individuals to assess the extent to which the findings can be replicated across individuals. For radical behaviorists in particular, this type of replication is considered a strong indicator of the generality and validity of one's findings.

It is also possible to use a reversal design to assess the effectiveness of more than one treatment. For example, imagine that Cory's initial treatment turns out to be relatively ineffective and results in little if any improvement. Rather than withdrawing the treatment and returning to baseline, a better strategy would be to implement a new treatment and see if it produces a stronger effect. In Cory's case, he might decide that the $1 fine for each cigarette smoked is insufficiently punishing and that he should instead fine himself $2. The implementation of this larger punisher constitutes a new phase of treatment, phase C. If after a week that treatment appears to be successful, Cory can revert to the baseline for a week and then return again to the treatment to confirm its effectiveness. This would then be called an ABCAC design (see Figure 2.5).

Reversal designs have some advantages, but they also have some disadvantages. The first disadvantage is that if the behavior doesn't revert to its original baseline level when the treatment is withdrawn, we will be left wondering if the treatment was effective. If, for example, the results for Cory's study looked something like those depicted in Figure 2.6, in which smoking does not return to its pretreatment level during the reversal to baseline, we would be in no better situation than if we had run a simple-comparison design. Although the rate of smoking dropped when Cory first instituted the self-punishment procedure, it did not climb back up when the procedure was halted; therefore, we cannot be sure that self-punishment was the actual cause of the initial decrease. Although we may be pleased that Cory is now smoking less than he used to, from a scientific perspective of demonstrating the effectiveness of self-punishment, these results are less than ideal.

FIGURE 2.5 Two-treatment reversal design. Hypothetical results in which a reversal design was used to assess the effectiveness of two treatment procedures on the number of cigarettes smoked. When the first treatment (B) produced little improvement, a second treatment (C) was implemented. This treatment was then alternated with a baseline period to confirm its effectiveness. This would therefore be called an ABCAC design.

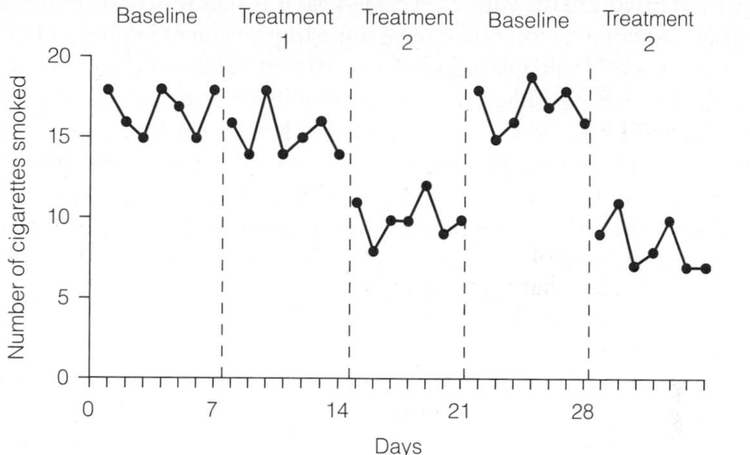

FIGURE 2.6 Reversal (ABAB) design. Hypothetical results in which a reversal design was used to assess the effectiveness of a self-punishment treatment on smoking. In this case, the behavior did not revert to its baseline level when the treatment was withdrawn. Thus, although it is possible that the treatment was the cause of the improvement, these results do not provide strong evidence in that regard.

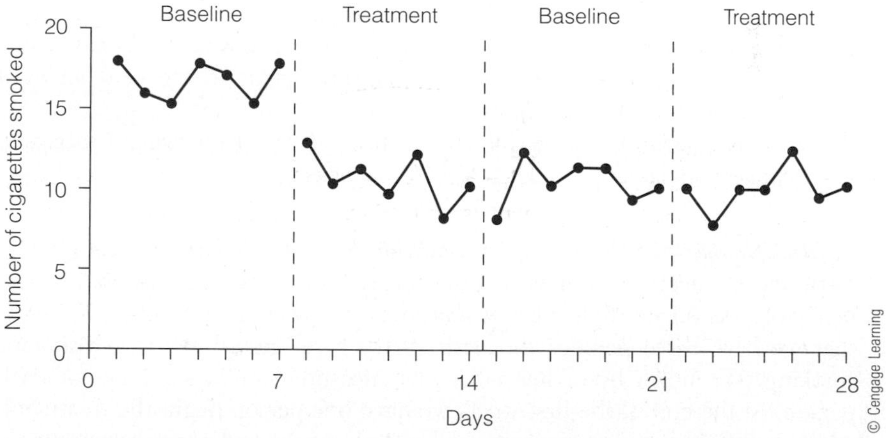

A second, related disadvantage is that the design is inappropriate for situations in which the treatment is intended to produce a long-lasting effect. For example, a student who is exposed to a new method of teaching math will hopefully experience a permanent increase in his or her math ability. A reversal design would not be appropriate for assessing the effect of such an intervention, because the improvement should remain evident long after the intervention has ended.

A third disadvantage with a reversal design is that it may be ethically inappropriate to remove a treatment once some improvement has been obtained. If, for example, the implementation of a treatment results in the elimination of a person's severe drug addiction, is it reasonable for us to temporarily withdraw the treatment in the hope that the addictive behavior will reappear? Although from a scientific perspective removing the treatment would help confirm its effectiveness, such removal would not be ethical. In such cases, we must instead look for another method of demonstrating a functional relationship between the implementation of the treatment and the improvement in behavior. One alternative is to use a multiple-baseline design.

QUICK QUIZ G

1. In a simple-comparison design, behavior in a b__________ condition is compared to behavior in a t__________ condition.
2. A simple-comparison design (does/does not) allow us to determine if there is a f__________ relationship between the independent and dependent variables.
3. A reversal design, also called a(n) __________ design, involves repeated alternations between a(n) __________ period and a(n) __________ period.
4. What type of result do we need to see during the second baseline phase to determine whether our treatment is the cause of the change in the behavior? ______________________________
5. A reversal design is inappropriate for an experiment in which the treatment is expected to produce a (temporary/permanent) change in the behavior even after the treatment is withdrawn.
6. A reversal design is also inappropriate when the act of removing a successful treatment would lead to e__________ problems.

Multiple-Baseline Design In a ***multiple-baseline design***, a treatment is instituted at successive points in time for two or more persons, settings, or behaviors. As an example of a *multiple-baseline-across-persons* design, imagine that we have three people who wish to try a self-punishment program for smoking. We begin by taking a baseline measurement of smoking for each person. At the end of the first week, we have one person begin the treatment, while the other two carry on with the baseline. At the end of the second week, we have a second person begin the treatment while the third person carries on with the baseline. Finally, at the end of the third week, the third person also begins the treatment. Thus, across the three individuals, the treatment is implemented at different points in time. If the improvement in behavior coincides with the implementation of the treatment for each individual, then a functional relationship between the treatment and the improvement in behavior has been demonstrated (see Figure 2.7).

As an example of a *multiple-baseline-across-settings* design, imagine that the three graphs in Figure 2.7 represent Cory's rate of smoking in three different settings: at work, at home, and at the coffee shop. After a week of baseline, Cory begins self-punishing his smoking, but only at work. After the second week, he begins self-punishing smoking at home while continuing to punish it at work. Finally, after the third week, he also starts punishing his smoking behavior at the coffee shop. If his rate of smoking in each setting drops only when the self-punishment procedure is implemented there, then the procedure is highly likely to be the cause of the improvement.

As an example of a *multiple-baseline-across-behaviors* design, imagine that the three graphs in Figure 2.7 represent three of Cory's problem behaviors—for example, smoking, swearing, and nail-biting. In this case, we implement the treatment at different times for each behavior. If each behavior shows improvement only when the treatment is implemented, then we have again demonstrated a functional relationship between the treatment and behavior.

The multiple-baseline design is a good alternative to the reversal design in that we do not have to worry about withdrawing the treatment to determine that it is effective. This design is therefore appropriate for situations in which the treatment is likely to produce a permanent change in behavior, or in which it may be unethical to withdraw the treatment once some improvement has been achieved. Nevertheless, this design is limited because we need to have more than one person, setting, or behavior to which the treatment can be applied. Another limitation is that the treatment effect might generalize across the different settings or behaviors before the treatment is instituted within those settings or behaviors. For example, as Cory begins to exert more control over his smoking at work, this effect might generalize to his smoking patterns at home and at the coffee shop even before the treatment is applied in those settings. Under such circumstances, it would be difficult to determine whether the treatment was in fact the cause of the improvement.

QUICK QUIZ H

1. With a multiple-baseline design, the treatment is instituted at different points in t________ for one or more p____________, s____________, or b________.
2. A key advantage of the multiple-baseline design is that we do not have to w__________ the treatment to determine if it is effective.
3. It is therefore a preferable design for situations in which the treatment might result in a (temporary/permanent) change in behavior, or where it might be une________ to withdraw the treatment.

FIGURE 2.7 Multiple-baseline design. Hypothetical results using a multiple-baseline-across-persons design to assess the effectiveness of a treatment (self-punishment) on number of cigarettes smoked. The three graphs represent the data for three different persons. For each person, the improvement in behavior coincides with the point at which the treatment was implemented. This result shows a functional relationship between the treatment and the improvement in behavior.

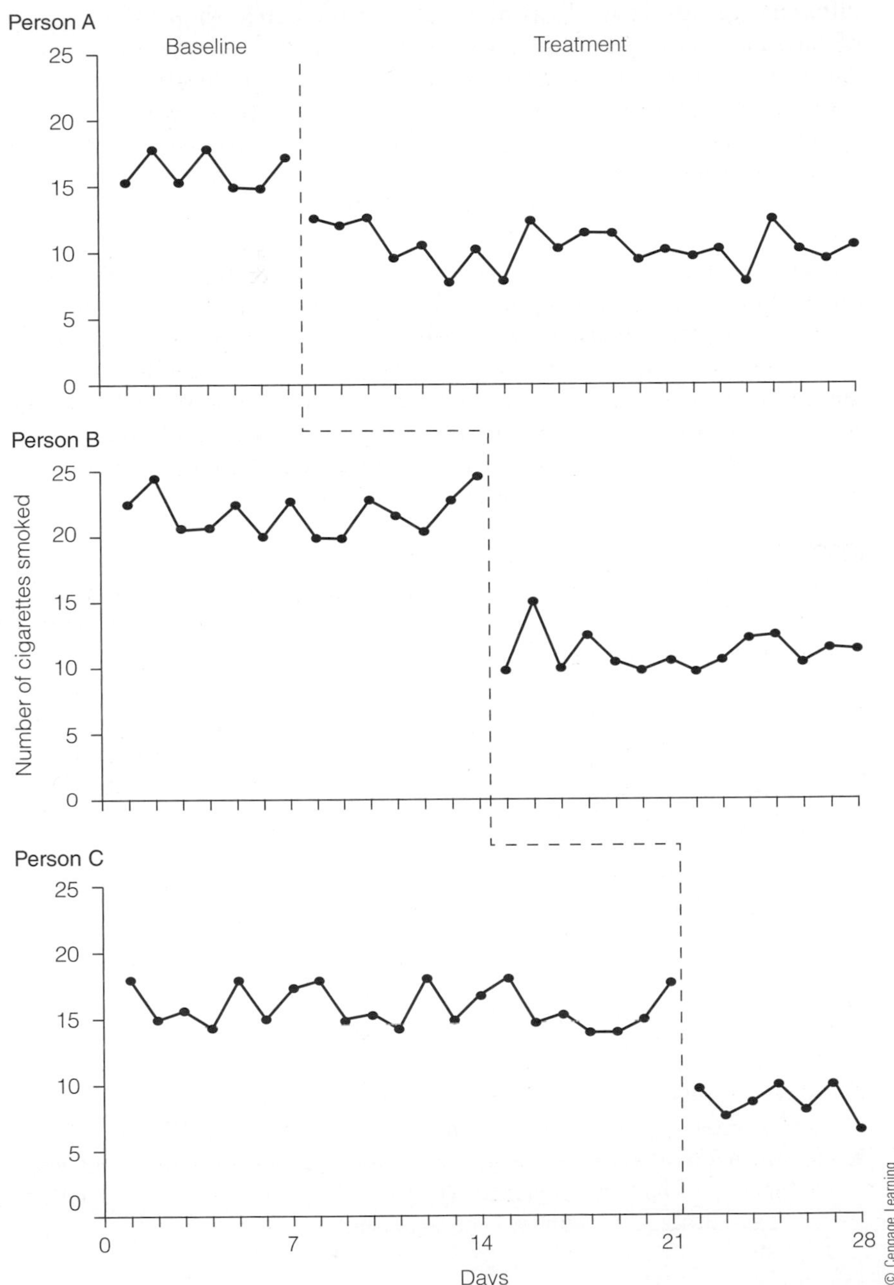

Changing-Criterion Design In some circumstances, the treatment is not intended to produce a large, immediate change in behavior but rather a gradual change over time. A useful design for measuring such changes is a ***changing-criterion design***, in which the effect of the treatment is demonstrated by how closely the behavior matches a criterion that is being systematically altered.

Imagine, for example, that Cory decides to use self-punishment to gradually reduce his smoking behavior. Following a baseline period, he sets a certain criterion for an allowable number of cigarettes that is slightly less than the average number of cigarettes he smoked during the baseline. If he successfully meets this criterion for 3 consecutive days, he reduces the allowable limit by two cigarettes. If he meets that criterion for 3 consecutive days, he reduces the limit by two more cigarettes. He repeats this process until the eventual goal of no smoking has been achieved. The self-punishment procedure consists of tearing up a dollar bill for every cigarette that is smoked over the allowable limit (see Axelrod, Hall, Weiss, & Rohrer, 1974, for a case report of such a procedure).

Hypothetical results for this program are displayed in Figure 2.8. Cory was usually successful in meeting each criterion, with the number of cigarettes smoked per day either matching or falling below the criterion for that day. The three exceptions occurred on days 29, 33, and 34. Because Cory exceeded the criterion on these days, he would have implemented the self-punishment contingency of tearing up a dollar bill.

FIGURE 2.8 Changing-criterion design. Hypothetical data using a changing-criterion design to assess the effectiveness of self-punishment to gradually reduce smoking. The dashed horizontal lines indicate the changing criterion for the allowable number of cigarettes smoked per day.

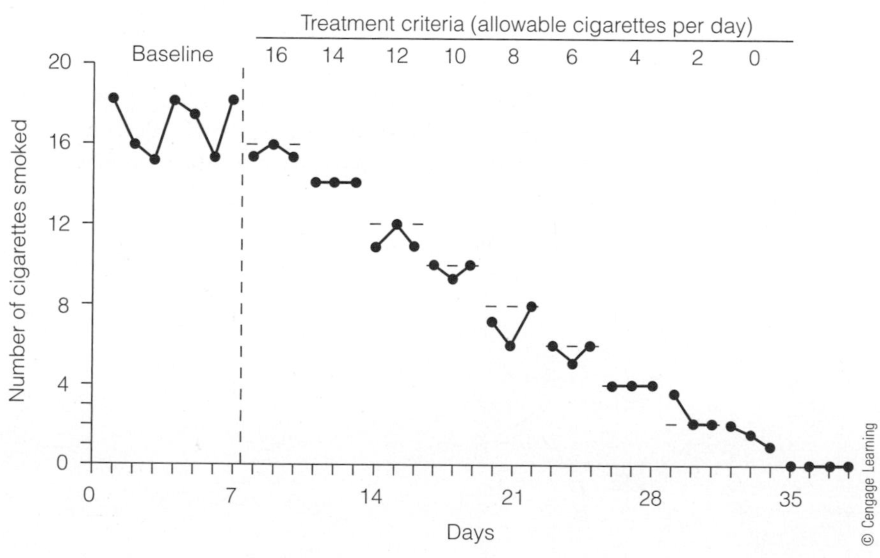

ADVICE FOR THE LOVELORN

Dear Dr. Dee,

I am suspicious that my boyfriend is having an affair with his former girlfriend. Whenever she's in town, he phones me significantly less often. For example, between May and August, when I know for a fact that she was in town, he phoned me an average of 5.8 times per week, while between September and December, when she was out of town, he phoned an average of 6.4 times per week. I worked it out, and sure enough, this is a statistically significant difference! But when I confronted him with this hard evidence of his unfaithfulness, he denied it and said that I'm being paranoid.

Am I Being Paranoid?

Dear Am I,

Given the evidence that you have presented, I would have to say yes, you are being paranoid. Worse than that, you are being a poor scientist. For example, you have neglected to consider other factors that might account for the observed difference. Quite apart from his former girlfriend being in town, your boyfriend may be calling less often between May and August for other reasons, such as spending more time in outdoor activities. Such possibilities need to be considered before you can draw any conclusions about your boyfriend's unfaithfulness.

You also need to recognize that statistically significant differences do not provide hard evidence of anything. What they provide is *supportive* evidence for a certain possibility. Even with a highly significant difference between two sets of scores, there is still a slight possibility that the difference is actually due to chance variation. As well, you need to consider that a difference that is *statistically* significant may not be *meaningfully* significant. In fact, the difference you have described seems quite small. I bet that if you chart the number of phone calls week by week, as in a simple-comparison design, you won't see much of a difference between the May–August period and the September–December period. And if you don't see much of a difference by eyeballing the data, then maybe there isn't much of a difference.

Behaviorally yours,

Dr. Dee

As noted previously, the changing-criterion design is appropriate for situations in which the behavior is intended to change gradually by some specified amount. Thus, it would be an appropriate design for gradually increasing the amount of time one studies each day or decreasing the amount of time spent playing computer games. It is important, however, that the behavior closely match the changing criteria; otherwise, it will be difficult to determine if the change in behavior is the result of the treatment or of some other factor. The design can, however, be greatly strengthened by including periods in which the criteria suddenly change in the opposite direction (for example, in the case of Cory, the number of cigarettes allowed would sometimes be raised for a few days). If the behavior continues to track the criteria closely even when they change direction, then we will have obtained strong evidence for the effectiveness of the treatment. In a sense, we have created a changing-criterion design that incorporates aspects of a reversal design.

The reversal design and multiple-baseline design are the most basic single-subject designs—with the reversal design often regarded as the strongest design—while the changing-criterion design is less often utilized. Other types of single-subject designs have also been devised, each having its advantages and disadvantages (see Kazdin, 2011). Most of these designs have been developed for use in applied settings. In experimental research, the control group design is often employed in studies of classical conditioning, while the reversal design (or some variant of it) is often employed in studies of operant conditioning, especially by behavior analysts.

QUICK QUIZ I

1. A changing-criterion design is most appropriate for assessing the effect of programs designed to produce a (sudden/gradual) change in behavior.
2. In a changing-criterion design, it is important that the level of behavior (exceed/closely match/lag behind) the changes in the criterion for that behavior.
3. The changing-criterion design can be strengthened by including periods in which the criterion suddenly ______________.

Use of Animals in Behavioral Research

Animal research has greatly contributed to our understanding and treatment of serious diseases and illnesses, as well as to our understanding of basic physiological processes. Similarly, many of the basic principles of behavior have been discovered through research with animals, especially rats and pigeons. But if the ultimate goal of such research is to discover principles of behavior that are applicable to humans, why use animals at all? In this section we outline some of the advantages and disadvantages of animal research that may help inform your opinion in this highly controversial debate.

Two advantages of using animals in research are the ability to control their genetic makeup and their learning history. Knowledge of an animal's genetic makeup can help us eliminate, or assess, the effects of inherited differences on learning and behavior. Rats, for example, can be bred so that entire batches are genetically identical or highly similar. We can try to control for genetic differences in humans by studying identical twins, but the number of people we can obtain for such research is necessarily quite limited. Similarly, animals bred for research have had somewhat identical experiences during their upbringing, along with a fairly limited learning history. By comparison, it is impossible to control for the learning histories of humans who volunteer for psychological research. If we are conducting experiments designed to assess basic principles of learning, then the learning histories of one's subjects could critically influence the outcome of the experiment.

A third advantage to using animals as subjects is that researchers are often able to more strictly control the experimental environment for animals than for humans. This advantage is especially important in behavioral research, in which we are attempting to isolate and manipulate certain aspects of the environment to determine their effect on behavior. For example, if we are interested in the effect of food deprivation on activity level in rats (as discussed in Chapter 12), then it is highly advantageous to strictly control the rat's feeding schedule—to a degree that would be difficult to attain in humans. Human subjects participating in ongoing research also have an unfortunate tendency to discuss the research task with their friends when they leave the lab each day, even when they are asked not to do so. These conversations can easily lead to a significant change in the person's behavior during the next experimental session. By contrast, rats tend not to give each other suggestions while lounging about in their home cages following a hard day of lever pressing. Their behavior therefore tends to be more consistent from day to day. In general, because animals are more easily isolated from extraneous influences during the course of the experiment, their behavior is more likely to reflect the true influence of the independent variable.

A fourth reason for using animals in behavioral research is that some research cannot ethically be conducted with humans. This is particularly the case with experimental manipulations that are potentially aversive or harmful. For example, rats have been used to investigate the manner in which classical conditioning might account for unusual instances of drug overdose (this finding is discussed in Chapter 5). Investigations using such an *animal model* of drug addiction have the potential to save lives but would be impossible to conduct with human subjects. (An *animal model* is a procedure that uses animals to mimic a particular human characteristic or symptom, such as drug addiction or anorexia nervosa.)

In reaction to these claimed benefits of animal research, critics have offered several counterarguments. One criticism is that because animals are not humans, the findings from animal research necessarily have limited applicability to humans. The physiological processes, genetic tendencies, and learning histories of animals are simply too different for research with animals to be of much relevance to humans. In this text we hope to convince you of the opposite, but the argument should not be dismissed out of hand. Despite the demonstrated benefits of animal research, some research with animals almost certainly does have little applicability to humans. Unfortunately, determining ahead of time which research findings are likely to be applicable to humans is a difficult task. Some of the most applicable findings from animal research, such as basic research on schedules of reinforcement (discussed in Chapter 7), initially would have struck some people as trivial and unimportant. (In fact, some people opposed to behaviorism still regard these findings as trivial and unimportant.)

Perhaps the most fundamental criticism of animal research is that it is morally wrong and that animals have rights similar to humans. Animal rights activists oppose "inhumane" research practices, such as confining animals to cages, subjecting them to electric shock, depriving them of food, and so on. From this perspective, even the reported benefits of animal research for saving lives and improving the human condition are insufficient to justify submitting animals to such morally reprehensible practices. (See the And Furthermore box: Cruel Starvation or a Healthy Diet.)

Beginning in the 1800s, researchers have reacted to such criticism by developing guidelines that weigh the benefits of research against the injurious or aversive nature of the procedures. The first guidelines were formulated in 1876, with the introduction of the British Cruelty to Animals Act. It was in the 1960s, however, that animal care committees and review boards became strongly established. Today, researchers in most professional organizations, including the American Psychological Association, are regulated by ethical standards that provide strict guidelines for the care and use of animals.

It is also worth noting that animal researchers are themselves concerned about the welfare of their animals. Skinner, for example, disliked shocking rats and therefore conducted few studies of punishment (Bjork, 1993). And researchers generally acknowledge that the animal rights movement has served a valuable purpose by ensuring the development of strict standards of ethical conduct. They likewise recognize that the extent to which animal research is justified is a difficult question that individuals must answer for themselves. The important thing, however, is to make it an informed decision. (For a discussion of these issues, see Smoo & Resnick, 2009.)

QUICK QUIZ J

1. Two advantages to using animals for behavioral research is that one can more strictly control an animal's g__________ makeup and l__________ history.
2. A third advantage to using animals is that the ex__________ environment can more easily be controlled for animals than for humans.
3. A fourth advantage to using animals for research is that it would be u__________ to conduct certain types of studies with humans, such as examining the effects of brain lesions on learning ability.

And Furthermore

Cruel Starvation or a Healthy Diet: The Ethics of Food Restriction

In many of the animal studies described in this text, food is used as a reward (reinforcer) for performing certain behaviors. As such, the animals are typically food deprived to ensure that they are well motivated to work for food. Pigeons, for example, are typically placed on a diet until their weight is about 80 to 85% of their *free-feeding weight*, which is the amount they weigh when food is constantly available. Some people regard such food restriction procedures as inhumane. But is this really the case?

First, we have to remember that the 80 to 85% level is calculated relative to the pigeon's weight when food is freely available. Free food is an unnatural state of affairs for a pigeon, which in its natural environment must constantly forage for food. The result is that the weight of a pigeon on free food is well beyond its natural weight. Poling, Nickel, and Alling (1990), for example, found that wild pigeons placed on free food for 42 days experienced an average weight increase of 17%, with some pigeons gaining as much as 30%. (This latter figure is equivalent to a 160-pound individual who, with little to do but eat, balloons up to 208 pounds!) Thus, the weight of a pigeon at 80% of its free-feeding weight may be quite close to what it would be if it were foraging for food in its natural environment.

A second point to bear in mind is that a certain amount of food restriction can be healthy. In fact, calorie restriction is the most reliable means known for slowing the aging process. Many species show significant increases in both health status and life span when raised on diets that provide 30 to 50% fewer calories than normal (e.g., Weindruch, 1996; Koubova, 2003). And humans too seem to benefit from a certain degree of calorie restriction or intermittent fasting (e.g., Longo & Mattson, 2014). (But see also the discussion on activity anorexia in Chapter 12 for a warning of what can happen when calorie restriction is taken too far.)

4. Two arguments against the use of animals in research are:

a. limited applicability to humans

b. morally wrong

SUMMARY

Behavioral research involves the manipulation and measurement of variables. The independent variable is that aspect of an experiment that is systematically varied across conditions or over time and is believed to affect the dependent variable, which is the behavior being measured. Appetitive stimuli are events that are sought out by an organism, whereas aversive stimuli are events that are avoided. Motivating operations are procedures that affect the appetitiveness or aversiveness of an event. Procedures that increase the appetitiveness or aversiveness of an event (such as deprivation) are called establishing operations; procedures that decrease the appetitiveness or aversiveness of an event (such as satiation) are called abolishing operations. A contingency exists if the occurrence of one event predicts the likely occurrence of another. This is often the case in experimental research where changes in an independent variable produce changes in a dependent variable.

Behavioral researchers strive to employ objective, unambiguous definitions of behavior. Depending on the research question, there are several ways to measure behavior. Rate of response indicates the frequency with which a response occurs within a certain period of time, and intensity is the force or magnitude of a behavior. Duration is the total amount of time a behavior is performed, speed is the length of time required to perform a complete episode of behavior from start to finish, and latency is the amount of time it takes for a behavior to begin. In interval recording, one records whether or not a behavior occurs within a series of continuous intervals; in time-sample recording, one records whether or not a behavior occurs within a series of discontinuous intervals. Other behavioral measures include topography (the physical form of a behavior) and number of errors. Interobserver reliability is assessed by calculating the extent to which two or more independent observers agree in their observations.

In addition to selecting a measure of behavior, researchers need to determine the most appropriate method for conducting research. Descriptive methods of research, such as naturalistic observation, can provide rich, detailed information but do not demonstrate causal relationships. Experimental methods can demonstrate causal relationships and generally take the form of group designs or single-subject designs. Group designs involve comparing groups of subjects that have been exposed to different levels of an independent variable. Group designs have certain drawbacks, such as requiring large numbers of participants. In contrast, single-subject designs can be used to demonstrate cause-and-effect relationships using only one or a few individuals. Single-subject designs include the simple-comparison design, reversal design, multiple-baseline design, and changing-criterion design, each of which has its strengths and weaknesses.

Advantages of using animals as subjects in behavioral research include enhanced control over learning history, genetic background, and experimental environment relative to research conducted with human participants. Also, animals can be used in studies that cannot ethically be conducted on humans. Disadvantages of using animals are the possibility that findings may have limited application to humans and the notion that animals have the same rights as humans. Ethics committees have been established to weigh the costs and benefits of proposed research involving animals.

SUGGESTED READINGS

Skinner, B. F. (1956). A case history in scientific method. *American Psychologist, 11*, 221–233. Skinner's interesting and sometimes irreverent view of what the "scientific method" *really* involves, at least from the perspective of his own experience.

Sidman, M. (1960). *Tactics of scientific research: Evaluating experimental data in psychology*. New York: Basic Books. The classic text on single-subject research designs. Although this book is a bit beyond most undergraduates, a quick perusal will give you a sense of the radical behaviorist approach to research.

Kazdin, A. E. (2011). *Single-case research designs* (2nd ed.). New York: Oxford University Press. Contains an extensive discussion of research methods in applied behavior analysis.

STUDY QUESTIONS

1. Distinguish between independent and dependent variables. What is a functional relationship? In experimenting on the effectiveness of a certain study technique on test performance, what would be the independent and dependent variable? What would indicate a functional relationship?
2. Define stimulus and response. Differentiate between the terms *stimulus* and *stimuli*.
3. Distinguish between overt and covert behavior, and between appetitive and aversive stimuli.
4. What is a motivating operation? Name and describe two types of motivating operations. Provide an example of each that makes use of the procedure of deprivation or satiation.
5. Distinguish between contiguity and contingency. How might contiguity affect the perception of a contingency in determining whether a certain food is causing you to break out in a rash?
6. Define rate of response. How does one distinguish between a high rate of response versus a low rate of response versus a period of no response on a cumulative record?
7. What is the distinction between speed, duration, and latency measures of behavior? Describe how each could be used in assessing the behavior of studying.
8. Define the intensity and topography of a behavior. Describe how each could be used in assessing the behavior of throwing a ball.
9. Describe interval recording and time-sample recording. Describe how each could be used in assessing the extent to which a child is playing computer games during the evenings. What constitutes the overall measure of behavior in these recording procedures?
10. How does one calculate the reliability of the behavioral observations when using an interval recording procedure? What is the generally acceptable level of reliability?

11. What are descriptive research methods? Describe the use of naturalistic observation to assess the foraging behavior of a squirrel. What is the major benefit and the major limitation of such research methods?
12. What is experimental research? Describe the simplest type of group design that could be used to assess the effectiveness of the 3R approach to studying. What are three limitations of group designs?
13. What are single-subject designs? Describe a simple-comparison design and draw a graph of some hypothetical results using such a design. (For both this and the following three items, make sure that the graph is properly drawn and labeled.) In what sense is the simple-comparison design a "flawed" design?
14. Describe a reversal design and draw a graph of some hypothetical results using such a design. How is it superior to a simple-comparison design? What are three disadvantages of reversal designs?
15. Describe a multiple-baseline design and draw a graph of some hypothetical results using one version of this design. What is the advantage of this design over a reversal design? What are two limitations of this design?
16. Describe a changing-criterion design and draw a graph of some hypothetical results using such a design. For what types of treatments is this design most appropriate?
17. List four advantages and two disadvantages of using animals as subjects in behavioral research.

CONCEPT REVIEW

abolishing operation. A procedure that decreases the appetitiveness or aversiveness of a stimulus.

appetitive stimulus. An event that an organism will seek out.

aversive stimulus. An event that an organism will avoid.

baseline. The normal frequency of a behavior prior to an intervention.

changing-criterion design. A type of single-subject design in which the effect of the treatment is demonstrated by how closely the behavior matches a criterion that is systematically altered.

comparative design. A type of group design in which different species constitute one of the independent variables.

contingency. A predictive relationship between two events such that the occurrence of one event predicts the probable occurrence of the other.

control group design. A type of group design in which, at its simplest, subjects are randomly assigned to either an experimental (or treatment) group or a control group.

covert behavior. Behavior that can be subjectively perceived only by the person performing the behavior. Thoughts and feelings are covert behaviors. Also known as *private events* or *private behavior*.

cumulative recorder. A device that records total number of responses over time and provides a graphic depiction of the rate of response.

dependent variable. That aspect of an experiment that is allowed to freely vary to determine if it is affected by changes in the independent variable.

descriptive research. Research that focuses on describing behavior and the circumstances within which it occurs.

duration. The total amount of time that an individual repeatedly or continuously performs a certain behavior.

establishing operation. A procedure that increases the appetitiveness or aversiveness of a stimulus.

experimental research. A research method in which one or more independent variables are systematically varied to determine their effect on a dependent variable.

functional relationship. The relationship between changes in an independent variable and changes in a dependent variable; a cause-and-effect relationship.

factorial design. A type of group design in which one examines the effects of two or more independent variables (or factors) across groups of subjects.

group design. A type of experimental research in which one manipulates one or more independent variables across groups of subjects.

independent variable. That aspect of an experiment that is made to systematically vary across the different conditions in an experiment.

intensity. The force or magnitude of a behavior.

interval recording. The measurement of whether or not a behavior occurs within a series of continuous intervals. (The number of times the behavior occurs within each interval is irrelevant.)

latency. The length of time required for a behavior to begin.

motivating operation. A procedure that affects the appetitiveness or aversiveness of a stimulus. (There are two types: establishing operations and abolishing operations.)

multiple-baseline design. A type of single-subject design in which a treatment is instituted at successive points in time for two or more persons, settings, or behaviors.

naturalistic observation. A descriptive research approach that involves the systematic observation and recording of behavior in its natural environment.

overt behavior. Behavior that can potentially be observed by an individual other than the one performing the behavior.

rate of response. The frequency with which a response occurs in a certain period of time.

response. A particular instance of a behavior.

reversal design. A type of single-subject design that involves repeated alternations between a baseline period and a treatment period.

simple-comparison design. A type of single-subject design in which behavior in a baseline condition is compared to behavior in a subsequent treatment condition.

single-subject design. A research design that requires only one or a few subjects in order to conduct an entire experiment. (Also known as *single-case* or *small-n* designs.)

spatial contiguity. The extent to which events are situated close to each other in space.

speed. The length of time required to perform a complete episode of a behavior from start to finish.

stimulus. Any event that can potentially influence behavior. (The plural for stimulus is *stimuli*.)

temporal contiguity. The extent to which events occur close together in time.

time-sample recording. The measurement of whether or not a behavior occurs within a series of discontinuous intervals. (The number of times that it occurs within each interval is irrelevant.)

topography. The physical form of a behavior.

variable. A characteristic of a person, place, or thing that can change (vary) over time or from one situation to another.

CHAPTER TEST

12. Using a(n) ____________ recording procedure that lasted 10 minutes, Erik's classmate observed that he blew his nose at least once during the first and second minute, as well as the fourth, seventh, ninth, and tenth minutes. His overall level of nose blowing is calculated as ____________%.

27. James decides to implement a program to gradually reduce the amount of time he plays computer games. A useful design for determining the effectiveness of this program would be a ____________ design.

3. Each time it rains, there is an increase in the number of umbrellas being carried on the street. There appears to be a ____________ relationship between rain and the appearance of umbrellas.

23. The length of time it takes Robert to read a chapter from start to end is a(n) ____________ measure of behavior, while the amount of time it took before he started reading is a(n) ____________ measure of behavior. The total amount of time he spends reading each day is a(n) ____________ measure of behavior.

28. The reversal design is also known as a(n) ____________ design.

15. In a simple ____________ group design, subjects are randomly assigned to a treatment or nontreatment condition.

11. Number of cigarettes smoked per day is a(n) ____________ measure of smoking.

19. Animals are often used in behavioral research because this practice allows for greater ____________ over learning history, genetic influences, and experimental environment than is possible with humans. As

well, animals are often used when the use of humans would be _______________.

10. In measuring the force with which a boxer delivers a blow, we are measuring the _______________ of the behavior.

26. I wish to test a new drug that I believe will permanently remove the symptoms of a rare neurological disorder. Three patients who suffer from the disorder have volunteered to take the drug. What would be a useful type of design to demonstrate the effectiveness of this drug? _______________

16. The strongest type of single-subject design for determining the effectiveness of a behavioral intervention (given that it can suitably be used) is a(n) _______________ design. On the other hand, if I'm only interested in obtaining an improvement in the behavior, then a _______________ design may suffice.

4. A flash of light is called a _______________, while a beep and a flash of light are called _______________. Lever pressing would typically be called a (response/behavior), while a specific lever press would be called a _______________.

20. After Trish told Jen that Ryan was the most popular guy in school, Jen became extremely interested in him. Trish's statement about Ryan apparently functioned as a(n) _______________ operation that increased Ryan's value as a(n) _______________ stimulus.

25. You have just eaten a large pizza. It is likely that the reward value of eating a pizza has now (increased/decreased) as a function of s_______________. This is an example of a type of _______________ operation known as a(n) _______________ operation.

1. Any characteristic of a person, place, or thing that can change is called a _______________.

9. Robbie is afraid of spiders, but Tami finds them interesting. A spider is a(n) _______________ stimulus to Robbie, and a(n) _______________ stimulus to Tami.

24. When people feel confident, they tend to stand straight. In this case, we are using the _______________ of a behavior as a measure of confidence.

6. A knife and spoon are placed side by side in a dinner setting, creating spatial (contiguity/contingency) between the two utensils.

18. Dr. Jansen wonders whether the crows that he is studying can solve certain types of problems better than dogs can. In testing this notion, he would use a type of experimental design known as a(n) _______________ design.

7. Krista has not seen her boyfriend in four months. It is likely that the appetitive value of seeing her boyfriend has (increased/decreased) as a function of d_______________. This is an example of a type of _______________ operation known as a(n) _______________ operation.

13. Using a(n) __________ recording procedure, a school psychologist unobtrusively observes a class for a 20-minute period four times each day and notes whether some type of disruption occurs during those times.
17. A useful type of group design to determine whether both selective underlining *and* the 3R approach would result in more effective studying would be a(n) __________ design.
2. In a classical conditioning experiment, one group of dogs first hears a tone and then receives food, while another group of dogs receives food and then hears a tone. Following this, the researcher measures how much the dogs in each group salivate when they simply hear the tone. In this experiment, the order in which tone and food are presented is the __________ variable, and the amount of salivation to the tone is the __________ variable.
22. On a cumulative recorder, (25/75) lever presses per minute would produce a steeper line in comparison to 50 lever presses per minute. A __________ line would indicate a period of time with no lever presses.
14. The two main approaches to behavioral research are the __________ approach and the __________ approach.
29. Two independent observers agree on whether or not the target behavior occurred during 14 of the observed intervals and disagree on whether or not it occurred during 6 of the observed intervals. Interobserver reliability is therefore calculated as __________%, which is (below/at/above) the minimum acceptable level of reliability.
5. Blinking is a(n) __________ behavior, while thinking about blinking is a(n) __________ behavior.
8. Dr. Ross studies schizoid personality disorder by sitting in the park each day and observing the behavior of street people who are known to be suffering from the disorder. Dr. Ross is using a descriptive research method known as __________.
21. To determine whether drinking coffee in the evening keeps me awake at night, I observe my sleep patterns for a 2-week period during which I drink coffee each evening, followed by a 2-week period during which I do not drink coffee in the evening. I am using a __________ design to conduct this study, which will likely give me (strong/questionable) evidence concerning how coffee affects my sleep patterns.

ANSWERS TO CHAPTER TEST

1. variable
2. independent; dependent
3. functional (or contingent)
4. stimulus; stimuli; behavior; response
5. overt; covert (or private)
6. contiguity
7. increased; deprivation; motivating; establishing

8. naturalistic observation
9. aversive; appetitive
10. magnitude (or intensity)
11. rate
12. interval; 60%
13. time-sample
14. descriptive; experimental
15. control
16. reversal (or ABAB); simple-comparison
17. factorial
18. comparative
19. control; unethical
20. establishing; appetitive
21. simple comparison (or AB); questionable
22. 75%; flat
23. speed; latency; duration
24. topography
25. decreased; satiation; motivating; abolishing
26. multiple-baseline-across-persons
27. changing-criterion
28. ABAB (or ABA)
29. 70%; below

CHAPTER 3

ELICITED BEHAVIORS AND CLASSICAL CONDITIONING

CHAPTER OUTLINE

At a friend's party, Uma witnessed her boyfriend flagrantly flirting with another woman. She was initially angry, but when he later apologized for his actions and was very attentive to her, she experienced unusually strong feelings of attraction toward him. Still, she somehow felt manipulated by the whole affair. After all, her friends had warned her that he had a terrible reputation for playing "mind games."

Elicited Behaviors

The word *elicit* means "to draw out or bring forth." Thus, an ***elicited behavior*** (also known as a *respondent behavior*) is a behavior that is drawn out by a preceding stimulus. (Note that the word is *elicit* and not *illicit*, which refers to something illegal, such as an illicit drug.) A sneeze produced by a particle of dust or a startle reaction to the sound of a gunshot are examples of elicited behaviors. They are elicited in the sense that they are automatically drawn out by the stimuli that precede them. In this sense, many elicited behaviors are those that we consider to be involuntary. For example, you do not choose to be startled by a gunshot; your startle reaction is an involuntary response to the gunshot. Similarly, you do not choose to salivate when you bite into a lemon; salivating is an involuntary response to the taste of the lemon.

In this chapter, we begin by describing different types of elicited behaviors as well as some simple mechanisms by which they can be modified. This will include a discussion of the opponent-process theory of emotion, an intriguing theory that explains a wide variety of emotional phenomena ranging from drug cravings to the sense of loss you feel following a breakup. The remainder of the chapter will then be devoted to introducing the concept of classical conditioning, the first major type of learning to be discussed in this text.

Reflexes

Reflexes are the most basic form of elicited behavior. A ***reflex*** is a relatively simple, automatic response to a stimulus. (It can also be defined as the relationship between such a response and the stimulus that elicits it.) Some reflexes involve only a single gland or set of muscles, such as when you salivate in response to a drop of lemon juice or blink in response to a puff of air. Other reflexes involve the coordinated action of several body parts. For example, the ***startle response***—a defensive reaction to a sudden, unexpected stimulus—involves the automatic tightening of skeletal muscles as well as various hormonal and visceral (internal organ) changes. Similarly, the ***orienting response***—in which we automatically position ourselves to facilitate attending to a stimulus—can involve a relatively major body movement, such as when we automatically turn in response to an unfamiliar noise behind us.

Many reflexes are closely tied to survival. For example, food consumption involves a chain of reflexes that include salivation, peristalsis (wave-like actions that push food down the esophagus and through the digestive system), and secretion of digestive juices in the stomach. Conversely, the vomiting reflex serves a protective function by expelling potentially poisonous substances from the digestive system. Other protective reflexes include the ***flexion response***, in which we automatically jerk our hand or foot away from a hot or sharp object that we have inadvertently contacted, and the aforementioned startle reaction, designed to ready us for fight or flight if an unexpected stimulus should prove dangerous.

Newborns come "prepackaged" with a host of reflexes that facilitate their survival. For example, if you touch a baby's cheek with your finger, the baby will automatically turn his or her head in that direction. This reflex is designed to facilitate taking a nipple into the mouth. Once the nipple is in the mouth, the baby's sucking reflex is activated (which in turn elicits a "milk letdown" reflex in the mother). Some of these reflexes disappear within a few years (e.g., the sucking reflex), but others, such as salivating and vomiting, remain with us throughout life.

Many of the simpler reflexes are activated through a ***reflex arc***: a neural structure underlying some reflexes that consists of a sensory neuron, an interneuron, and a motor neuron. For example, when you quickly jerk your hand away from an open flame, your flexion response is being activated through a reflex arc. Upon touching the flame, receptors in the hand stimulate sensory neurons that carry a danger message (in the form of a burst of nerve impulses) toward the spinal cord. Within the spinal cord, interneurons receive this message and immediately pass it on to the motor neurons. These motor neurons then activate the muscles in the arm that pull the hand away from the flame. Simultaneously, pain messages are also sent up the spinal cord to the brain; but by the time they are received and you consciously feel the pain, your hand is already being withdrawn from the flame. Thus, we do not withdraw our hand from the flame because of the pain; we actually begin withdrawing our hand before feeling any pain. Because the flexion response utilizes a simple reflex arc through the spinal cord, we are able to withdraw our hand from the flame much quicker than if the message had to be routed all the way through the brain and then back down to the arm muscles (see Figure 3.1).

QUICK QUIZ A

1. A simple, involuntary response to a stimulus is called a __________.
2. Reflexes are e__________ in the sense that they are drawn out by stimuli that precede their occurrence.
3. A s__________ response is an automatic defensive response to a sudden, unexpected stimulus; the o__________ response is an elicited set of movements designed to facilitate attending to a stimulus.
4. Many simple reflexes are activated through a r__________ a__________ that consists of a(n) __________ neuron, a(n) __________neuron, and a(n) __________ neuron (in that order).
5. Quickly jerking your hand or foot away from contact with an open flame or sharp object is a reflexive action known as a fl__________ response. In such cases, the perception of pain generally (precedes/follows) the occurrence of the response.

FIGURE 3.1 Schematic diagram of a reflex arc underlying a flexion response. Upon touching a hot or sharp object, sensory neurons carry the message via nerve impulses toward the spinal cord. Interneurons within the spinal cord then receive the message and pass it directly to motor neurons. The motor neurons in turn activate muscles in the arm or leg that carry out the reflex action. At the same time that this reflex arc is being activated, a pain message is sent to the brain. Thus, the reflex arc enables a person to withdraw his or her arm or leg from the damaging stimulus prior to actually feeling any pain.

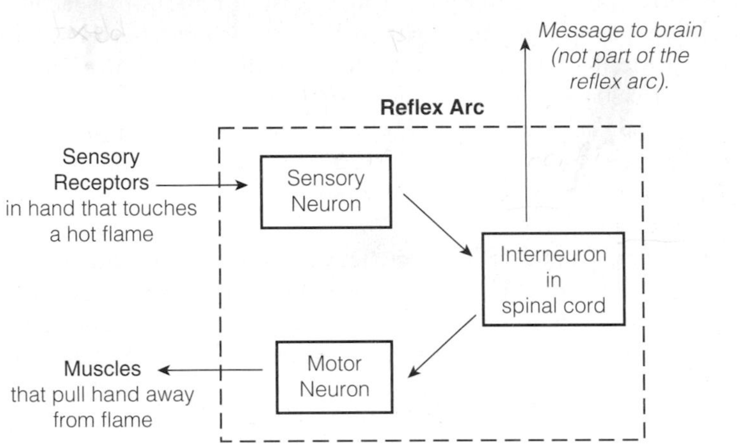

Fixed Action Patterns

Some types of elicited behaviors are more complex than simple reflexes. A ***fixed action pattern*** is a fixed sequence of responses elicited by a specific stimulus. Examples include web building by spiders, V-shaped formation flying by ducks, and nut burying by some species of squirrels. Dogs and cats display numerous fixed action patterns. Cats compulsively scratch the ground to cover up urine and feces (effective in a litter box but completely ineffective on your carpet) and rub up against the legs of visitors to "mark" them as belonging to their territory. Dogs indicate their desire to play by wagging their tails, stretching out their front legs, and lowering their heads to the ground (see Figure 3.2). In fact, by adopting this posture (and looking completely foolish in front of any visitors), you can effectively ask your dog if it wishes to play (which of course it will not, given that it now has you looking like an idiot).

For many fixed action patterns, we are able to identify a specific stimulus that sets it in motion. The specific stimulus that elicits a fixed action pattern is called a ***sign stimulus*** or ***releaser***. For example, a male *Betta splendens*, better known as a Siamese fighting fish, immediately takes an aggressive posture at the sight of another male (the releaser), spreading out its fins and flaring its gills. Similarly, during mating season, a male stickleback fish

FIGURE 3.2 Example of a fixed action pattern. A dog will indicate its desire for play by stretching out its front legs and lowering its head to the ground.

WilleeCole Photography/Shutterstock.com

displays a fixed sequence of aggressive actions when another male enters its territory (Tinbergen, 1951). Interestingly, the sign stimulus for the stickleback's aggressive actions is not the presence of the other male but the sight of its red underbelly. If the red belly is covered up or painted a different color, the intruder will not be attacked. Conversely, a pie-shaped or cigar-shaped piece of wood with a red patch on the bottom will be attacked.

Fixed action patterns tend to be unique to certain species and are therefore sometimes called *species-specific behaviors*. They can also be called instincts, but some researchers dislike this term because it implies that the behavior is more rigid and inflexible than is actually the case. For example, if two rats are subjected to a painful stimulus, such as an electric shock, they will automatically attack each other (Ulrich & Azrin, 1962). In fact, many species will become aggressive in reaction to pain, but in rats it often takes the form of a fixed action pattern in which the two combatants rear up on their hind legs and essentially box by striking out at each other with their front paws. Interestingly, this aggression is more likely to occur in rats that have been trained to be aggressive than in those that have not been trained to be aggressive (Baeninger & Ulm, 1969). Thus, the rats' fixed action pattern of aggression is actually somewhat variable and can be significantly modified by experience.

Fixed action patterns are adaptive responses that have evolved to help animals cope with consistent aspects of their environment. The difficulty with such inherited patterns is that a sudden, large-scale change in the environment may render the pattern useless—or even harmful. For example, deer have an inborn tendency to run a zigzag pattern when being pursued by a predator. This action, which confuses the predator, greatly increases the deer's chances of survival in the wild; unfortunately, it also greatly reduces the deer's chances of survival when it is being pursued by a modern automobile. By comparison, an animal that can modify its behavior patterns through learning can better adapt to a changing environment, which is why the ability to learn was such an important evolutionary advancement.

QUICK QUIZ B

1. A(n) __________ __________ __________ is a fixed sequence of responses that occurs in reaction to a specific stimulus. The specific stimulus that elicits this behavior is called a s__________ stimulus or re__________.
2. Different species of spiders spin different kinds of webs. Web spinning of this sort can thus be considered a sp__________ -sp__________ behavior. Such behaviors used to be called i__________, but some researchers dislike this term because it implies that the behavior is more (flexible/inflexible) than is actually the case.

Simple Mechanisms of Learning

Habituation and Sensitization

The repeated presentation of an eliciting stimulus can alter the strength of the elicited behavior. ***Habituation*** is a decrease in the strength of an elicited behavior following repeated presentations of the eliciting stimulus. For example, we quickly stop attending to low-intensity background noises such as the ticking of a clock or the distant noise of traffic. Similarly, a sudden, unexpected tap on the shoulder may elicit a startle response, whereas any additional taps might have no such effect.

By contrast, ***sensitization*** is an increase in the strength of an elicited behavior following repeated presentations of the eliciting stimulus. For example, soldiers under attack generally do not habituate to the sound of artillery shells exploding nearby. Instead, their startle reaction grows stronger. Needless to say, this greatly contributes to the stress they experience and the inevitable breakdown virtually all soldiers will suffer after too much exposure to battle conditions (though Hollywood would often have you think otherwise).

The effects of habituation and sensitization usually disappear when the stimulus is not presented for a period of time, meaning that the strength of the behavior returns to its original level. For example, you might habituate to the sound of a neighbor's stereo one evening, only to be once more bothered by it when she first turns it on the next morning. In the few hours since you last heard the music, your habituation to it disappeared and you again responded to the noise like you normally would. But note that habituation can occur over varying time spans. The examples so far given represent *short-term habituation*, in which the response *quickly* decreases as a result of repeated stimulation and the ability to respond then *quickly* recovers in the absence of stimulation. Conversely, in *long-term habituation*, the response *slowly* decreases as a result of repeated stimulation, and the ability to respond then *slowly* recovers in the absence of stimulation. For example, if you move into an apartment from which you hear the sound of a train each morning, your reaction to the noise will probably be most intense on the first day and then slowly decrease thereafter. Moreover, once you become fully habituated to the noise, you would have to be away from your apartment for several weeks or even months before your reaction to the noise would return to its original level. Additionally, long-term habituation tends to occur when presentations of the stimulus are widely spaced (e.g., a train going by your apartment each morning), whereas short-term habituation tends to occur when presentations of the stimulus are narrowly spaced or continuous (e.g., a child next door repeatedly banging on a drum). And finally, repeated sessions of short-term habituation, spread out over time, can eventually lead to long-term habituation. The outside traffic noise that you to habituate to each time you come home in the evening eventually becomes unnoticeable even when you first walk in the door.

Note that sensitization often generalizes to other stimuli. A shell-shocked soldier is likely to jump not only in response to artillery explosions but also to any sudden stimulus. By contrast, habituation tends to be more stimulus specific, such that even small changes in the stimulus may result in the reappearance of the response. Thus, many people suddenly become aware of the sound of their car when the motor sounds a bit different or when the car has a slightly different feel to it as they are driving along. Only a minor change is needed to alert the driver that something is potentially wrong (and hopefully, inexpensive to fix). One version of this process is known as the *Coolidge effect*, based on an old joke about former U.S. president Calvin Coolidge. The story has it that he and his wife were once being separately escorted around a chicken farm. When Mrs. Coolidge was informed that the resident rooster was capable of mating several times a day, she remarked, "You should tell that to the president." Informed about this, the president asked whether the repeated matings occurred with the same chicken or different chickens. When told that it was different chickens, he said, "You should tell that to my wife." The Coolidge effect therefore is the enhanced sexual arousal displayed by the males of some species when presented with different sexual partners as opposed to the same sexual partner to whom it has habituated.

In what is known as ***dishabituation***, habituated responses can also reappear following the presentation of a seemingly irrelevant novel stimulus. For example, Sherri might quickly habituate to the sound of gunshots at a shooting range. If, however, a handsome stranger approaches and stands nearby, she might again be startled when the next shot is fired. Likewise, couples can sometimes rekindle their romance by traveling to a new and different environment—or even by treating themselves to a night in a hotel room rather than staying at home.

QUICK QUIZ C

1. An increase in the strength of a behavior following repeated presentations of the eliciting stimulus is called __________.
2. A decrease in the strength of a behavior following repeated presentations of the eliciting stimulus is called __________.
3. Learning to ignore the sound of dripping water is an example of __________; becoming increasingly aware of the sound of a jackhammer on the street below your apartment is an example of __________.
4. The fact that it has been several months since you noticed the sound of the morning and evening whistles at a nearby factory is an example of __________-t__________ habituation. Such habituation tends to build up (quickly/slowly), following which, when the stimulus is no longer presented, the ability to respond recovers (quickly/slowly).
5. In general, sensitization is (less/more) stimulus specific than habituation.
6. In what is known as dis__________ the presentation of a (familiar/novel) stimulus during a period of habituation can sometimes result in the (reappearance/disappearance) of the habituated response.

Why does repeated exposure to certain stimuli sometimes result in habituation and sometimes in sensitization? One factor is the intensity of the eliciting stimulus. A *low-intensity stimulus*, such as the ticking of a clock, typically results in habituation, while a *high-intensity stimulus*, such as exploding artillery shells, typically results in sensitization. A *stimulus of intermediate intensity* often results in an initial period of sensitization, followed by habituation. For example, at a shooting range, the first few shots you hear might produce an increasingly strong startle reaction. But you then begin to habituate to the shots, and after a while you hardly notice them.

Another factor that influences habituation versus sensitization, which can often override the intensity factor, is the evolutionary (adaptive) significance of the stimulus. Habituation and sensitization are processes that we see across species, even in simple organisms like worms and snails (e.g., Wicks & Rankin, 1997). From an evolutionary perspective, this suggests that these processes have tremendous survival advantages. They enable us to categorize stimuli into those that are currently irrelevant, which we tend to habituate to, and those that are currently relevant, which we tend not to habituate to and may even become sensitized to (Eisenstein, Eisenstein, & Smith, 2001). Thus, we find it easier to habituate to the harmless sound of a locomotive shuttling railcars back and forth in a nearby rail yard than the buzzing sound of a wasp in our room that could sting us. Likewise, most people quickly habituate to the smell of onions and spices, even if strong, but become increasingly bothered by the smell of something rotten, which could poison us. This perspective also explains why stimulus intensity can make a difference: low-intensity stimuli are often insignificant while high-intensity stimuli are often highly significant and sometimes dangerous.

Of course, we don't always get it right and sometimes become sensitized to things that are not dangerous. Wouldn't you love to be able to habituate quickly to the sound of the barking dog next door? Unfortunately (or fortunately), organisms behave in ways that increase their likelihood of survival and reproduction, which often means erring on the side of caution. Add to this individual differences in the tendency to habituate and sensitize (LaRowe, Patrick, Curtin, & Kline, 2006), and sleepless nights due to barking dogs are an unfortunate reality for many of us.

Finally, it is worth noting that habituation and sensitization, although relatively simple processes, have proven to be highly useful in illuminating some of the basic neurological processes involved in learning. For example, Kandel and colleagues (e.g., Hawkins, Bailey, & Kandel, 2010) have carried out extensive investigations into the neural mechanisms that underlie habituation in *Aplysia*, a large marine snail. When lightly touched, *Aplysia* withdraws its gill beneath a protective mantle (a "gill-withdrawal reflex"), which habituates with repeated stimulation. Insofar as *Aplysia* has an extremely simple nervous system—consisting of only a few thousand neurons compared to the many millions of neurons found in even a mouse—it has proven to be an ideal organism for mapping the sequence of neural and biochemical events that lead to habituation. This work in turn has led to key insights into the biological processes that govern learning and memory in general, for which Kandel was awarded a Nobel Prize in 2000. Considerable work has also gone into the neurological processes involved in classical and operant conditioning, which are likewise fundamental forms of learning (e.g., Guerra & Silva, 2010). Thus, although the present text focuses on behavior rather than the biological processes that underlie it, the basic principles and concepts presented herein constitute essential knowledge for anyone interested in the neuroscience of learning and memory.

QUICK QUIZ D

1. In general, repeated presentations of a low-intensity stimulus result in ____________ and repeated presentations of a high-intensity stimulus result in ____________.
2. A stimulus of intermediate intensity will initially result in a period of ____________ which is then followed by ____________.
3. From an evolutionary standpoint, if a stimulus is irrelevant or "safe," we tend to ____________ to it, whereas if a stimulus is potentially dangerous we become ____________ to it.

Opponent-Process Theory of Emotion

Habituation and sensitization represent two opposing tendencies: weaker reactivity to a stimulus versus stronger reactivity. Solomon (1980; see also Solomon & Corbit, 1974) has proposed an intriguing theory of emotion that involves a similar dual mechanism. Known as the opponent-process theory, it is particularly good at explaining the aftereffects of strong emotional responses. Consider, for example, the following anecdote:

> My neighbor's son was struck by lightning as he was returning from a golf course. He was thrown to the ground. His shorts were torn to shreds and he was burned across his thighs. When his companion sat him up, he screamed "I'm dead, I'm dead." His legs were numb and blue and he could not move. By the time he reached the nearest hospital he was *euphoric* [italics added]. (Taussig, as quoted in Solomon, 1980, p. 691)

In one sense, the boy's euphoria is logical in that he was lucky to be alive. But in another sense, it is illogical because he was injured and decidedly worse off than before the incident. Should he not have remained at least somewhat distressed about the incident?

Consider, too, the following scenario. Suppose you purchase a lottery ticket during a visit home. Next weekend, your mom phones to tell you the winning numbers—and lo and behold, you discover that you have won $50,000! Wow! You are absolutely elated. Unfortunately, an hour later you receive another call from your mom informing you that she made a mistake on the numbers. It turns out that you won $50. You are now extremely disappointed even though you are still $50 better off than when you climbed out of bed that morning. Within a day, however, your disappointment wears off and you carry on with your impoverished lifestyle as usual.

Now consider an experiment in which a dog is exposed to electric shock (e.g., Katcher et al., 1969). During the shock, the dog's heart rate quickly rises to a peak, decreases slightly, and then stabilizes at a relatively high level. Now guess what happens when the shock is turned off. Does the dog's heart rate return to normal? No, it does not. When the shock is removed, the dog's heart rate plunges to *below* normal and then after a few minutes moves back up to normal (see Figure 3.3). In fact, the pattern of changes in heart rate during and after the shock—an index of the dog's emotional response to shock—is very similar to the emotional pattern displayed in the preceding lottery scenario. In both cases, an event elicits a strong emotional response; but when the event is withdrawn, an opposite response is elicited and then gradually disappears.

An explanation for such emotional changes is provided by the opponent-process theory of emotion. The ***opponent-process theory*** proposes that an emotional event elicits two competing processes: (1) an a-process (or primary process) that is directly elicited by the event, and (2) a b-process (or opponent process) that is elicited by the a-process and serves to counteract the a-process. For example, the presentation of shock directly elicits a tendency for the dog's heart rate to increase, which is the a-process. This increase in heart rate in turn elicits a compensatory reaction that tries to decrease heart rate, which is the b-process. The purpose of this compensatory b-process is to counter the sudden increase in heart rate, thereby maintaining a state of internal balance (known as *homeostasis*). In other words, the b-process tries to prevent the increase in heart rate from becoming too extreme, which could be damaging or even fatal. The actual heart rate during the shock is

FIGURE 3.3 Heart rate changes accompanying the application and withdrawal of shock. Our emotional responses often follow a similar pattern, with the onset of the emotional event followed by one type of response and the offset of the event followed by an opposite response.

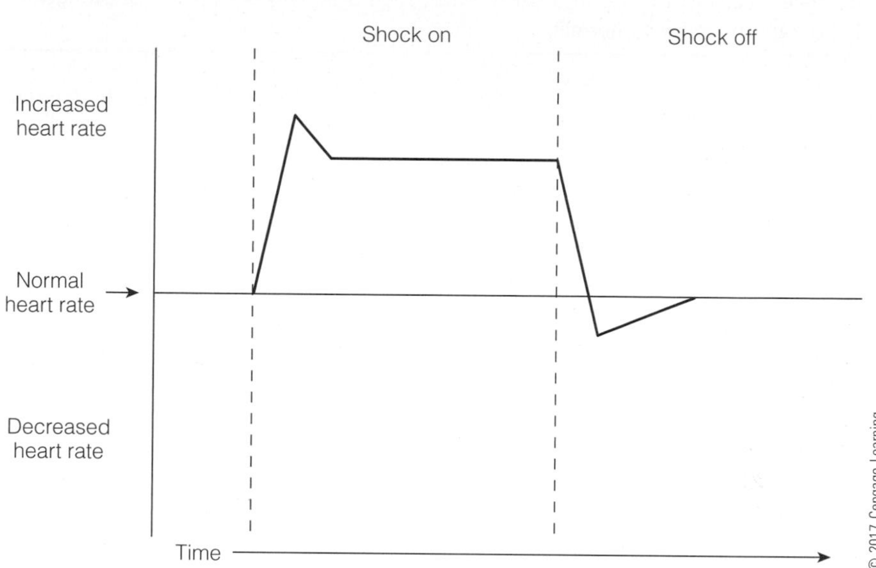

therefore the net result of the tendency for heart rate to increase in the presence of shock (the a-process), minus the compensatory tendency for heart rate to decrease (the b-process; see Figure 3.4). Similarly, in the lottery example, the feeling of elation you experience when you think you have won the lottery is the emotional response directly elicited by the thought of winning (the a-process) minus the compensatory reaction to this elation (the b-process), which is trying to keep your elation from becoming too extreme.

QUICK QUIZ E

1. The opponent-process theory of emotion accounts for why a strong emotional response is often followed by a(n) (similar/opposite) emotional response.
2. The ____________-____________ is directly elicited by the emotional event; this in turn elicits the ____________-____________, the purpose of which is to maintain a relatively balanced internal state known as h____________.
3. The a-process is also known as the pr____________ process, and the b-process is also known as the o____________ process.

The a- and b-processes have some important characteristics:

1. **The a-process correlates closely with the presence of the emotional event.** As shown in Figure 3.4, the tendency for the heart rate to increase in response to shock is directly tied to the presence of the

FIGURE 3.4 Opponent-process mechanisms that underlie changes in heart rate due to the onset and offset of shock. During the shock, as the b-process acquires strength, it pulls heart rate down from its initial peak and stabilizes it at a moderately high level. Following shock, when the a-process is no longer active, the b-process pulls heart rate to below normal, then gradually disappears, allowing the heart rate to return to normal.

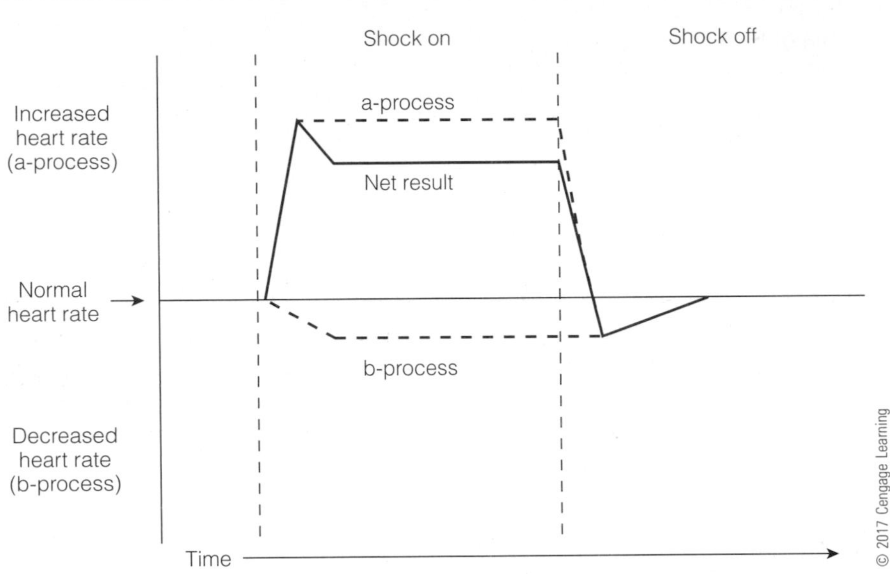

shock. When the shock is presented, heart rate immediately increases; when the shock is removed, heart rate immediately decreases. Similarly, you immediately become elated when you think you have won the lottery, and your elation immediately disappears when you discover that you have not.

2. **The b-process is slow to increase and slow to decrease.** The slow buildup in the b-process accounts for why our emotional response to an event is often strongest at the outset. If you look again at Figure 3.4, you can see that when the shock is first turned on, the dog's heart rate quickly peaks and then declines slightly before stabilizing. The immediate peak happens during the early moments of shock when the b-process is not yet strong enough to counteract the a-process, thereby allowing the a-process free rein to increase heart rate. After a few moments, though, the b-process becomes strong enough to moderate the a-process, causing a slight decrease in heart rate before stabilizing. When the shock is removed, the a-process immediately disappears; but the b-process only slowly declines. For this reason, when the shock is turned off, the dog's heart rate plunges to well below normal, because all that remains is the b-process that has been trying to pull heart rate down. (It is as though,

in a tug-of-war, the other team suddenly let go of the rope, sending your team flying backward in the direction you were pulling.) Similarly, when you discover that you have not won the lottery, you immediately feel depressed because the counterreaction to the elation you have been feeling is all that remains. As this b-process gradually weakens, however, your emotional response slowly returns to normal, just as the dog's heart rate slowly returns to normal.

3. **With repeated presentations of the emotional event, the b-process increases in both strength and duration.** This is the most interesting part of the theory. For example, what happens to the dog's heart rate if it is repeatedly shocked? As it turns out, the increase in heart rate during each shock becomes less and less extreme. Additionally, each time the shock is turned off, the dog's heart rate plunges more and more deeply and takes increasingly longer to return to normal (see Figure 3.5). The dog's overt emotional response matches these changes in heart rate. Whereas in the early sessions the dog shows considerable distress in response to the shock, in later sessions it appears more annoyed than distressed. More surprising, though, is the change in the dog's emotional response following the shock. Whereas in the early sessions the dog appears somewhat relieved when the shock is turned off,

FIGURE 3.5 Effects of repeated stimulus presentations on primary and opponent processes. With repeated stimulation, the b-process (opponent process) becomes stronger and takes longer to disappear. The result is that heart rate rises only slightly above normal during the shock, then drops considerably below normal following the shock and takes a relatively long time to return to normal.

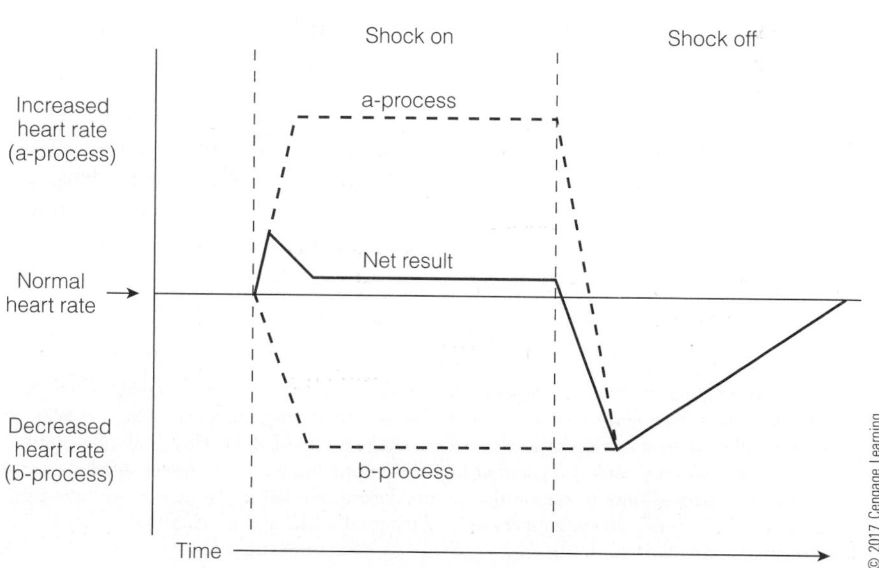

in the later sessions it shows signs of extreme pleasure, jumping about and greeting the experimenter with enthusiasm.

4. **The a-process and the b-process tend to be hedonically opposite from each other.** The word *hedonic* refers to the extent to which something is experienced as pleasurable versus unpleasurable. In general, if the a-process is experienced as unpleasurable (as shown by the dog's distress while being shocked), the b-process will be experienced as pleasurable (as shown by the dog's euphoria when the shock was withdrawn). Conversely, if the a-process is experienced as pleasurable (as in the elation one feels from having won the lottery), the b-process will be experienced as unpleasurable (as in the disappointment one feels in discovering that one did not win the lottery after all).

Similar emotional patterns have been found in humans. For example, Epstein (1967) found that military parachutists became less and less terrified with repeated jumps and became more and more elated following each jump. This sense of elation can last several hours among veteran jumpers and probably accounts, at least partially, for the strong attraction some people feel toward parachuting and other high-risk activities.[1]

The opponent-process theory of emotion also has implications for a phenomenon known as revictimization (van der Kolk, 1989). Some people repeatedly become involved in abusive relationships or have great difficulty leaving such relationships. A contributing factor may be that the person has become hooked on the powerful feelings of pleasure that occur during the "honeymoon period" of forgiveness that often follows an abusive episode. This intense pleasure is the compensatory after-reaction (the b-process), which has become greatly strengthened during repeated episodes of abuse. As suggested in the opening vignette to this chapter, a weaker version of this honeymoon effect might even occur in relationships in which one is exposed to intermittent periods of emotional distress rather than actual abuse.

Not all research has supported opponent-process theory (e.g., Newton, Kalechstein, Tervo, & Ling, 2003). Furthermore, as you will see in Chapter 5, it appears that classical conditioning often plays a role in the elicitation of opponent processes, especially those associated with drug use. Nevertheless, opponent-process theory has stimulated a considerable amount of research and has proven extremely useful for enhancing our understanding of emotional behavior.

---

[1]Note, however, that emotional changes during skydiving can be a bit more complex than this. Veteran skydivers experience a peak of anxiety just before leaving the plane (a high-risk moment), followed by a strong sense of elation during the free fall, another peak of anxiety when the chute is being deployed (another high-risk moment), and then a sense of elation after they land. The strong sense of elation that occurs during free fall might be a contributing factor to accidents because veteran jumpers may be tempted to delay deploying the chute until the last possible moment (Delk, 1980).

QUICK QUIZ F

1. With repeated presentations of the emotional event, the b-process (increases/ decreases) in both s__________ and d__________.
2. The __________ process is directly tied to the presence of the emotional event, whereas the __________ process is (slow/quick) to increase and __________ to decrease.
3. Feeling elated while talking on the phone to someone with whom you are in love is an example of the __________-__________ process; feeling lovesick after you hang up is an example of the __________-__________ process.
4. The above example is also an illustration of how the a- and b-processes are h__________ (opposite/similar) to each other; for example, if the a-process is pleasurable, then the b-process is __________.

Classical Conditioning

We have so far discussed those situations in which a certain stimulus (e.g., lemon juice) elicits a particular response (e.g., salivation). We have also noted that repeated presentations of a stimulus can sometimes change the nature of the response, either strengthening it (sensitization), weakening it (habituation), or by eliciting a compensatory reaction (an opponent process). But these are relatively simple means of adaptation. Insofar as the world is a complex place filled with a vast array of stimuli, we often need to anticipate whether an event is about to occur and to recognize whether certain events are meaningfully related to other events. For example, when we are first stung by a wasp, it is adaptive for us to associate the pain with the sight and sound of the wasp. It is also adaptive for us to be wary of insects that resemble wasps, because many of them (e.g., honeybees and hornets) also sting. Thus, the ability to relate one event to another allows us to better anticipate the future, thereby greatly facilitating our chances of survival.

In ***classical conditioning***, a stimulus comes to elicit a response because it has been paired (or associated) with another stimulus. Classical conditioning is also known as *Pavlovian conditioning*, after Pavlov, who discovered many of the basic principles of classical conditioning. Behavior analysts, who follow Skinner's approach to behaviorism, typically refer to this type of conditioning as *respondent conditioning*, with the elicited behaviors, as previously noted, being called *respondent behaviors* or simply *respondents*.

Pavlov's Discovery of Classical Conditioning

Ivan P. Pavlov (1849–1936), a Russian physiologist, is generally credited with the first systematic investigations into classical conditioning.[2] Beginning in

[2]At about the same time, an American graduate student by the name of E. B. Twitmyer also conducted experiments on this type of conditioning, and even reported his results at the 1904 conference of the American Psychological Association (Hothersall, 1984). However, his report generated little interest, and he abandoned the topic—which is fortunate, because the term "Twitmyerian conditioning" is a mouthful.

ADVICE FOR THE LOVELORN

Dear Dr. Dee,

Several months ago I broke up with my boyfriend when he took a job in another city. We were together 5 years, and it had turned into a pretty monotonous relationship by the time it ended. But it sure is taking me a long time to get over it. My friend tells me that I must have some kind of "unresolved dependency issue" for me to be this depressed. She recently broke up with her boyfriend—she went out with him for only a month but claims that she was madly in love—and got over it in a week. Is there something wrong with me, or is my friend just superficial?

Still Depressed

Dear Still,

There may be several reasons why some people take longer than others to recover from a breakup. The opponent-process theory, however, might be particularly applicable in your case. Remember that our primary emotional response to an event (the a-process) typically weakens with repeated exposure, while the emotional after-reaction (the b-process) typically strengthens. Solomon (1980) suggested that these processes are also applicable to love relationships. Couples that have been together a long time often have weaker feelings of affection for each other than do couples that have been together a short time. When relationships end, however, couples that have been together a long time experience a much deeper and longer-lasting sense of loss than do couples that have been together a short time. According to opponent-process theory, this sense of loss is the compensatory reaction to the relationship, which will be much stronger in those couples that have been together longer. For this reason, it will naturally take more time for you to get over your long-term "monotonous" relationship than for your friend to get over her brief "madly-in-love" relationship.

Behaviorally yours,

Dr. Dee

the late 1800s, Pavlov conducted important research on digestive secretions as well as the neural mechanisms that control them. He is, in fact, responsible for much of what we now know about digestion and won the Nobel Prize for his discoveries.

As part of this research enterprise, Pavlov also investigated salivation, the initial step in the digestive process. By this time, Pavlov was well aware that salivation could be initiated by psychic factors such as the sight of food (visual perception being regarded as a psychic, meaning a psychological, process). He

Ivan P. Pavlov
(1849–1936)

was nevertheless surprised at the amount of control exerted by these factors. He noted, for instance, that different substances affected both the quantity and quality of saliva produced. For example, a moist, edible substance such as meat elicited a small amount of slimy saliva whereas a dry, inedible substance such as sand elicited a large amount of watery saliva (to facilitate spitting it out). These differences existed both when the substances were actually placed in the dogs' mouths and, later, when the dogs were merely shown these substances. Subsequent research confirmed that these psychic secretions exhibited a great deal of regularity and lawfulness, and Pavlov began to devote more and more resources to their investigation. By 1907, classical conditioning, as it would come to be known, had become the sole focus of his research efforts.

In the decades that followed, Pavlov discovered most of the basic principles of classical conditioning and explored their application in such diverse areas as personality, hypnosis, sleep, and psychopathology. The epitome of the devoted scientist, Pavlov could be a tough taskmaster with students and assistants (once refusing to accept an assistant's excuse that he was late because he had to avoid the revolutionary battles going on in the streets). Yet in other ways he seems to have been a devoted humanitarian. When the Soviet regime took control—fortunately, they continued to support his research endeavors—he was reported to have been openly critical of its denial of basic rights and religious freedoms. Pavlov also showed great concern for the welfare of his dogs. He invested considerable effort in devising surgical procedures that allowed for the accurate observation of internal mechanisms of digestion while minimizing the animals' discomfort and ensuring a full postoperative recovery.

Basic Procedure and Definitions

We will illustrate the process of classical conditioning using one of Pavlov's basic procedures in which a dog was trained to salivate to the sound of a metronome. During these experiments, the dog was restrained in a harness, and a tube was inserted into an incision that had been made in its cheek. Whenever the dog salivated, the saliva would run down the tube into a container where it could be precisely measured (see Figure 3.6). Although the apparatus appears uncomfortable, the dogs in fact quickly got used to it.

Pavlov's basic procedure worked as follows. Before conditioning, the dogs automatically salivated in response to the taste of food. Because salivation to food occurs naturally and does not require prior training (conditioning), it is called an *unconditioned response* (UR), and the food is called an *unconditioned stimulus* (US). The sound of a metronome, however, does not elicit salivation

FIGURE 3.6 Pavlov's conditioning apparatus. In some of Pavlov's early experiments, a dog was trained to salivate to the sound of a metronome. The dog was restrained in a harness, and a tube was inserted into an incision in its cheek. Whenever the dog salivated, the tube carried the saliva to a container that activated a recording device. (*Source*: Coon, 1998.)

and is therefore said to be a *neutral stimulus* (NS) with respect to salivation. During conditioning, the sound of the metronome is presented just before the food, which of course continues to elicit salivation. After conditioning, as a result of having been paired with the food, the metronome itself now elicits salivation. Because salivating to the metronome requires prior training (conditioning), it is called a *conditioned response* (CR), and the sound of the metronome is called a *conditioned stimulus* (CS)[3] (see Figure 3.7).

This procedure can be schematically diagrammed as follows.

Before conditioning:

Food → *Salivation*
US UR
Metronome → No salivation
NS —

[3]Note that the Russian terms used by Pavlov were originally translated as conditioned and unconditioned. They are, however, more precisely translated as "conditional" and "unconditional." In this text, however, we will continue to use the former terms because they remain more commonly used.

FIGURE 3.7 Classical conditioning of salivation. Before conditioning, the dog automatically salivates to the taste of food. During conditioning, the sound of a metronome is presented just before the presentation of food. After conditioning, the metronome itself elicits salivation. (*Source*: Nairne, 2000.)

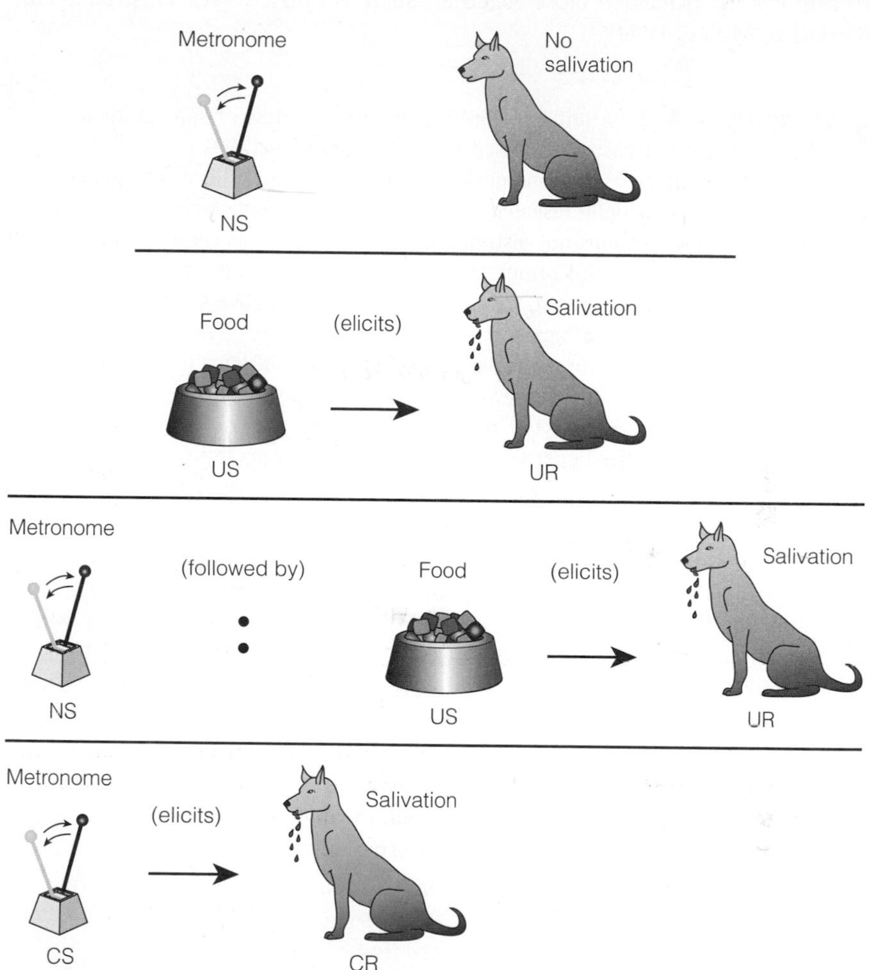

During conditioning:

Metronome: Food → *Salivation*
NS (or CS) US UR

(During conditioning, the metronome can be labeled as either an NS or a CS, because during this phase it begins as an NS and then becomes a CS.)

After conditioning:

Metronome → *Salivation*
CS CR

Each pairing of the NS and US during conditioning is called a *conditioning trial.*[4] Several conditioning trials are often needed before the NS becomes established as a CS. In general, conditioning is more effective (requires fewer conditioning trials) when the trials are spaced far apart, such as every 10 minutes, than massed close together, such as every 30 seconds (e.g., Yin, Barnet, & Miller, 1994).

Study Tip: It is important to note that the effectiveness of spaced (or distributed) learning trials over massed learning trials—which has come to be known as the *spacing effect*—applies to most learning situations, not just classical conditioning. For example, research has shown that studying is significantly more effective when study sessions are distributed over time (such as regular study sessions spread throughout a semester) rather than massed close together (such as cramming the night before an exam). In fact, in a recent review of effective study techniques, the only techniques found to have high levels of empirical support were *self-testing* (as in the 3R method of studying discussed earlier) and *distributed practice* (Dunlosky et al., 2013). This also means that regularly reviewing older material as you proceed through this course—such as regularly testing your recall for earlier material or redoing earlier practice tests—could significantly boost your overall performance in the course.

Measuring the level of conditioning can be done in various ways. One method is to intersperse the conditioning trials with an occasional *test trial* in which the NS is presented by itself. For example, every once in a while, the metronome can be presented alone to see if it elicits salivation. Alternatively, one can continue to pair the metronome with the food and simply observe whether salivation occurs during the short interval between the start of the metronome and the presentation of food.

As an everyday example of classical conditioning, let us suppose that a child is bitten by a dog and subsequently develops a fear of dogs. This process can be diagrammed as follows (omitting the "before conditioning" phase):

Dog: Bite → *Fear*
NS US UR
Dog → *Fear*
CS CR

The bite can be considered an unconditioned stimulus that elicits an unconditioned response of fear (actually more pain than fear, but we will simplify matters a bit). As a result of the bite, the sight of the dog becomes a conditioned stimulus that elicits in the child a conditioned response of fear.

Let us now look more closely at each component of the classical conditioning procedure. The ***unconditioned stimulus (US)*** is a stimulus that naturally elicits a

[4]It is also sometimes referred to as a *reinforcement trial*, but in this text we will reserve the term *reinforcement* for operant conditioning procedures that involve the use of a "reward" (or more precisely, a "reinforcer").

Fortunately, Pavlov realized that the value of such experiments lay in their ability to reveal basic principles of behavior, not simply in their ability to make a dog salivate.

response, and the ***unconditioned response (UR)*** is the response that is naturally elicited by the US. When we say here that the response is *naturally* elicited by the US, we mean that it is an *unlearned* or *innate* reaction to that stimulus. For example, food naturally elicits the response of salivation, and a bite naturally elicits the response of fear (and pain). (Note that the US and UR are sometimes given the abbreviations of UCS and UCR.)

The ***conditioned stimulus (CS)*** is any stimulus that, although initially neutral, comes to elicit a response because it has been associated (or paired) with an unconditioned stimulus. The metronome is initially neutral with respect to salivation in that it does not naturally elicit salivation.[5] After the metronome has been associated with food, however, it does elicit salivation. The ***conditioned response (CR)*** is the response, *often similar* to the UR, that is elicited by the CS. Note that the conditioned response is at most only similar to the unconditioned response. It is never identical (a fact that is overlooked in many introductory psychology textbooks). Even when the UR and CR appear identical, as in the case of salivation elicited by the food (US) and by the metronome (CS), there are always some differences. For example, the CR is usually weaker or less intense than the UR. Thus, the dog will typically salivate less to the metronome

[5]Although the sound of the metronome is neutral with respect to salivation, it might not be neutral with respect to other types of responses. For example, the sound will very likely function as a US for an orienting response (turn on the metronome and the dog will naturally prick up its ears and turn toward it).

than it will to the food. The CR is also sometimes quite different from the UR. For example, as noted earlier, the unconditioned response elicited by a dog bite is actually different from the conditioned response elicited by the sight of the dog that bit us. For simplicity, we labeled both responses as fear responses; however, the response to the bite is mostly what we would describe as a pain reaction ("Yeow!"), whereas the subsequent response to the dog would be one that is more clearly identified as fear (e.g., freezing). The extent to which the CR can differ from the UR is discussed more fully in Chapter 5.

QUICK QUIZ G

1. Classical conditioning is also known as P____________ conditioning or r____________ conditioning. In the latter case, the behaviors themselves are called r____________ behaviors or simply ____________.
2. In the metronome example, the metronome is initially a(n) ____________ stimulus because it (does/does not) elicit salivation. The food, however, is a(n) ____________ stimulus that elicits a(n) ____________ response of salivation.
3. During conditioning, the metronome can be labeled as either a(n) ____________ stimulus or a(n) ____________ stimulus.
4. Following conditioning, the metronome is a(n) ____________ stimulus, and the salivation elicited by the metronome is a(n) ____________ response.
5. Each pairing of the metronome and the food is called a c____________ tr____________; learning is most effective when these are spaced (far apart/close together).
6. In the basic classical conditioning procedure, the (US/NS) is followed by the (CS/US/NS), which in turn elicits the (CR/UR). As a result, the first stimulus becomes a (CS/US/NS), which elicits a (CR/UR).
7. Using the appropriate abbreviations, label each component in the following diagram of a conditioning procedure:

   Wasp: Painful sting → *Fear*

   Wasp → *Fear*

8. Using the format in question 7, diagram a classical conditioning procedure involving the stimuli of "nurse" and "painful injection," and the response of "anxiety." Label each component using the appropriate abbreviations.
9. The UR is the (learned/innate) response to the (NS/CS/US). The CR is the ____________ response to the ____________.
10. The CS was originally a(n) (NS/US/UR). The CR is (often/always) (similar/identical) to the UR.

Appetitive and Aversive Conditioning

Most classical conditioning procedures can be divided into two categories based on whether the US is pleasant or unpleasant. In ***appetitive conditioning***, the US is an appetitive event (one that an organism approaches or seeks out); in mentalistic terms, it is something usually regarded as pleasant. Examples include food (if the organism is hungry), water (if the organism is thirsty), or addictive drugs. Sexual stimuli too are regarded as appetitive stimuli, and there is good evidence that sexual responses can be classically conditioned. For example, Rachman and Hodgson (1968) took seven male volunteers and presented them with conditioning trials in which a picture of black, knee-length boots was followed by a picture of a nude woman. After about 30 trials, five of the males became sexually aroused by the sight of the boots. (Don't worry. The researchers later eliminated the conditioning by repeatedly presenting the picture of the boots without the picture of the nude—this process, known as *extinction*, is discussed later.)

In ***aversive conditioning***, the US is an aversive event (one that an organism avoids); that is, in mentalistic terms, it is something usually regarded as unpleasant. Examples of aversive USs include an electric shock, a painful bite, and an unpleasant odor. Aversive conditioning often occurs rapidly, perhaps with only one or two conditioning trials, especially when the aversive stimulus is quite strong. This reflects the close relationship between aversive conditioning and survival; to survive, we have evolved in such a way as to quickly learn to dislike those events that cause pain or illness.

Given how easily aversive conditioning can occur, it is not surprising that this type of conditioning helps account for many of our fears and anxieties. When the fear is appropriate—as in learning to fear a vicious dog that has bitten us—such conditioning is beneficial. When the fear is inappropriate—as when we begin to fear all dogs—such conditioning can be problematic. Therefore, a great deal of effort has gone into the study of fear conditioning, as well as into how such fears can be eliminated. This research has yielded important information on how real-world fears and anxieties can be treated (which is discussed more fully in Chapter 5).

When conducting research on fear conditioning in animals, measuring the level of fear can be problematic. Changes in certain physiological responses, such as heart rate, that might indicate fear are difficult to record, especially in small experimental animals such as rats. An ingenious solution to this problem was developed by Estes and Skinner (1941); it is known as the *conditioned suppression* or *conditioned emotional response (CER) paradigm*. In the basic paradigm, the rat is first trained to engage in an ongoing behavior in the form of lever pressing to obtain food (with many lever presses being required to obtain a single pellet). When a steady rate of lever pressing has been established, a fear-conditioning procedure is introduced in which, say, a 30-second tone is presented followed by a 1-second shock. Thus:

30″ Tone: 1″ Shock → ***Fear***
NS US UR

In the initial phase, the rat will become emotionally upset (fearful) whenever it receives a shock and will stop pressing the lever for food. As conditioning proceeds, however, the tone also will come to elicit fear:

30″ Tone → ***Fear***
CS CR

and the rat will stop pressing the lever when it hears the tone. Thus, the degree to which lever pressing for food is suppressed in the presence of the 30-second tone can be used as an indirect measure of the extent to which the tone elicits fear. Think of the procedure as similar to a gunfighter walking in and out of a saloon. The extent to which the saloon patrons fear the gunfighter can be accurately measured by the extent to which they stop talking to each other when he is in the saloon (you can hear a pin drop!) and resume talking when he leaves. Similarly, the rat's level of fear can be assessed by the extent to which it stops lever pressing for food when the tone is sounding and resumes lever pressing for food when the tone is not sounding.

On a more formal level, conditioned suppression is measured in the form of a suppression ratio. A *suppression ratio* is the number of responses emitted during the CS period divided by the total number emitted during the CS period and the same length period immediately preceding the CS. Thus,

$$\textbf{Suppression Ratio} = \frac{\textbf{\# of CS responses}}{\textbf{\# of CS responses} + \textbf{\# of pre-CS responses}}$$

For example, imagine that a rat emits 20 responses during a 30-second pre-CS period followed by 0 responses during the 30-second CS period. In other words, there is total suppression of responding during the CS period. The suppression ratio would be:

$$\frac{\mathbf{0}}{\mathbf{0+20}} = \mathbf{0}$$

Thus, a suppression ratio of 0 indicates total suppression of responding. But what if instead there was only a partial suppression of responding during the CS? For example, what if the rat emitted 10 responses during the CS period? In this case, the suppression ratio would be:

$$\frac{\mathbf{10}}{\mathbf{10+20}} = \frac{\mathbf{10}}{\mathbf{30}} = \mathbf{.33}$$

And if there was no suppression of responding—that is, the rat emitted the same number of responses during the CS period as during the pre-CS period—the suppression ratio would be:

$$\frac{\mathbf{20}}{\mathbf{20+20}} = \frac{\mathbf{20}}{\mathbf{40}} = \mathbf{.5}$$

Note how the suppression ratio will generally vary between 0 and .5, with a lower ratio indicating greater suppression and more effective conditioning. A ratio of 0 indicates greater suppression and stronger fear conditioning than a ratio of .33, which in turn indicates greater suppression and stronger fear conditioning than a ratio of .5. Students often find this confusing since the stronger conditioning is indicated by the lower number, which is opposite to the way most ratios work. To keep it straight, simply remember that *a lower number indicates less responding (greater suppression) of behavior*.

The CER paradigm has proven to be a useful method for investigating fear conditioning in animals and is, in fact, commonly used to study classical conditioning processes. But be careful to remember that the CR in this type of procedure is the covert response of fear; it is *not* the reduction in lever pressing, which simply serves as the indirect measure of fear.

Note that classical conditioning can also transform a normally aversive stimulus into an appetitive stimulus. Pavlov found that if a dog received a shock to one of its paws and then received food, the dog would eventually begin to salivate in response to the shock. The dog's overt reactions to the shock, such as tail wagging, further indicated that the shock had lost its aversiveness. Interestingly, if the shock was then applied to a different paw, the dog would not salivate but would instead react with discomfort. The perception of shock as pleasurable appeared to be quite specific to the body part involved in the conditioning.

As you may already have guessed, this same process might partially account for the development of masochistic tendencies (the tendency to perceive painful stimulation as pleasurable) in humans. The painful stimulation from being whipped, for example, has for some people become associated with feelings of sexual arousal, as a result of which the painful stimulation itself can now elicit arousal. Interestingly, as with Pavlov's dogs, people who are masochistic do not perceive all pain as pleasurable; rather, it is only the type of pain that is connected with their erotic experiences (e.g., being whipped) that is perceived as pleasurable. The pain they feel from accidentally stubbing a toe or banging a shin is typically as aversive for them as it is for anyone else (Rathus, Nevid, & Fichner-Rathus, 2000).

QUICK QUIZ H

1. In ____________ conditioning, the US is an event that the organism typically avoids; in ____________ conditioning, the US is an event that the organism typically seeks out.
2. Learning to associate the corner bar with the happy times you experience in that bar is an example of (aversive/appetitive) conditioning; learning to associate your refrigerator with the nauseating smell of spoiled food is an example of (aversive/appetitive) conditioning.
3. In a c__________ e__________ response (CER) paradigm, the level of fear elicited by a CS is indicated by the degree to which the rat's rate of lever pressing for food (decreases/increases) in the presence of that stimulus.
4. The CER paradigm is also known as a c__________ s__________ procedure.
5. The suppression ratio is the number of (pre-CS/CS/post-CS) responses divided by the number of ____________ responses plus ____________ responses.
6. Intense fear in a CER procedure is indicated by a suppression ratio of (.5/0); no fear is indicated by a suppression ratio of around (.5/0).

And Furthermore

Classical Conditioning and Interpersonal Attraction

Classical conditioning may play an important role in interpersonal attraction. According to the reinforcement-affect model of attraction (Byrne & Clore, 1970), the extent to which we are attracted to someone can be significantly affected by the degree to which the person is associated with events that elicit positive emotions. For this reason, we are generally attracted to people who say and do the kinds of things that make us feel good.

Even events as innocuous as pleasant background music or a positive news story on the radio can heighten our perception of someone as attractive. This means that associating ourselves with pleasant stimuli—pleasant music, attractive clothing, and even a clean car—during an initial date can greatly facilitate the possibility of a second date.

The reinforcement-affect model also suggests that we are less attracted to someone who is associated with aversive events. Obviously, dressing like a slob or drinking to the point of vomiting during a first date is probably not a good idea. But hearing bad news on the radio or really annoying music could also undermine your prospects for a second date. On the other hand, there may be times when you *want* to be perceived as less attractive. A letter once appeared in a newspaper advice column in which a woman described how she finally managed to dissuade a persistent acquaintance from continually asking her out. She agreed to a date and then ate plenty of garlic beforehand! Her suitor was apparently not a big garlic fan, and she had no further problems with him.

Excitatory and Inhibitory Conditioning

In all of the examples so far, and as it is traditionally defined, the NS is associated with the presentation of a US. The metronome is associated with the presentation of food, the dog is associated with a painful bite, and the tone is associated with shock. Conditioning in which the NS is associated with the presentation of a US is known as ***excitatory conditioning***. The result of excitatory conditioning is that the CS comes to elicit a certain response, such as salivation or fear.

But what if a stimulus is associated with the absence of the US rather than its presentation? What if, for example, a vicious dog always bites you except when its owner is present? The owner then is a sort of safety signal that indicates the absence of a painful bite. Conditioning in which the NS is associated with the absence or removal of a US is known as ***inhibitory conditioning***. The result of inhibitory conditioning is that the CS comes to inhibit the occurrence of a certain response—that is, the response is less likely to occur when that stimulus is present. Thus, although the dog is an excitatory CS for fear, the owner is an inhibitory CS for fear, and your fear of the dog will be suppressed when the owner is present. Similarly, if a rat is consistently shocked after a tone is presented, the tone will become an excitatory stimulus for fear. But if the rat is never shocked after a tone and a light are presented together, the light will become an inhibitory CS for fear because it signals the absence of shock. In such procedures, the excitatory CS is usually labeled a CS+, and the inhibitory CS is labeled a CS–.

Traditionally, researchers have focused on the study of excitatory conditioning, and most of the basic principles of classical conditioning have been established using excitatory procedures. For this reason, most of the examples in this text are examples of excitatory conditioning. In recent years, however, the study of inhibitory conditioning has begun to attract a good deal of attention (Domjan, 2015).

QUICK QUIZ I

1. Conditioning trials in which the NS is followed by the presentation of a US will produce _____________ conditioning; conditioning trials in which the NS is followed by the absence or removal of a US will produce _____________ conditioning.
2. Your grandmother always cooks great meals except when your vegetarian sister is present. As a result, you usually salivate a great deal when sitting at your grandmother's table for a meal, but not when your sister is present. Your grandmother's table is a(n) _____________ CS for salivation, while your vegetarian sister is a(n) _____________ CS for salivation.
3. Most of the basic principles of classical conditioning have been established using procedures that involve _____________ conditioning.
4. An excitatory CS is one that is associated with the (presentation/removal) of a US; an inhibitory CS is one that is associated with the (presentation/removal) of a US.
5. An excitatory CS for fear is one that will (elicit/suppress) a fear response; an inhibitory CS for fear is one that will (elicit/suppress) a fear response.
6. For the residents of Berlin and London during World War II, an air-raid siren would have been a (CS+/CS–) for anxiety, while the all-clear siren would have been a (CS+/CS–) for anxiety.
7. A click is followed by food, while a click and a buzzing noise is never followed by food. In this case, the click will become a (CS+/CS–) for salivation and the buzzing noise will become a (CS+/CS–).

Temporal Factors in Conditioning

In the classical conditioning examples discussed to this point, the NS was always presented before the US. This arrangement, however, is only one of several ways to present the NS and US. In this section, we outline four NS-US arrangements and note their effectiveness in producing conditioning. We then consider a form of conditioning, temporal conditioning, in which the NS (CS) is not an external stimulus but is itself the passage of time.

Four Temporal NS-US Arrangements There are essentially four ways in which presentations of the NS and US can be temporally arranged. We outline these arrangements below and note the effectiveness of each for producing a conditioned response.

1. **Delayed Conditioning.** In ***delayed conditioning***, the onset of the NS precedes the onset of the US, and the two stimuli overlap. For example, if we want a rat to associate a tone with a brief shock, we first present the tone and then, while the tone is still on, present a shock. As shown in Figure 3.8a, the onset of the tone precedes the onset of the shock and the tone is still on when the shock is presented. (Note that it is the point at which the two stimuli are turned on, rather than turned off, that is critical.) A delayed conditioning procedure is often the best arrangement for conditioning, especially if the time between the onset of the NS and the onset of the US (known as the *interstimulus interval* or ISI) is relatively brief. When conditioning certain autonomic responses (responses controlled by the autonomic nervous system), such as salivation, the optimal ISI is generally in the range of a few seconds. When conditioning skeletal responses (responses controlled by skeletal muscles), such as the eyeblink reflex, the optimal ISI is about a half second. Thus, conditioning generally works best when the onset of the NS is soon followed by the onset of the US; this fact is consistent with the idea that the NS serves as a predictor of the US, a notion that is discussed in Chapter 5. (Nevertheless, some forms of classical conditioning do not require a close temporal pairing between the NS and US. One such form, known as taste aversion conditioning, is described in Chapter 12.)
2. **Trace Conditioning.** In ***trace conditioning***, the onset and offset of the NS precede the onset of the US. In other words, the NS occurs before the US, and the two stimuli do not overlap. For example, a tone is turned on and then off, and this is then followed by the presentation of a shock (see Figure 3.8b). The time between the offset of the NS and the onset of the US (e.g., between the point when the tone was turned off and the shock was turned on) is called the *trace interval*. Because the tone is no longer present when the shock occurs, you might say that the organism has to "remember" the occurrence of the tone (or, in cognitive terms, have a "memory trace" of it) to be able to associate the two. Trace conditioning can be almost as effective as delayed conditioning if the trace interval is relatively short (no more than a few seconds). If the trace interval is longer than that, conditioning is, in most cases, much less likely to occur.
3. **Simultaneous Conditioning.** In ***simultaneous conditioning***, the onset of the NS and the onset of the US occur simultaneously. For example, a tone and a shock are turned on at the same time (see Figure 3.8c).

FIGURE 3.8 Four ways in which presentation of the NS and US can be temporally arranged.

(a) Delayed conditioning procedure

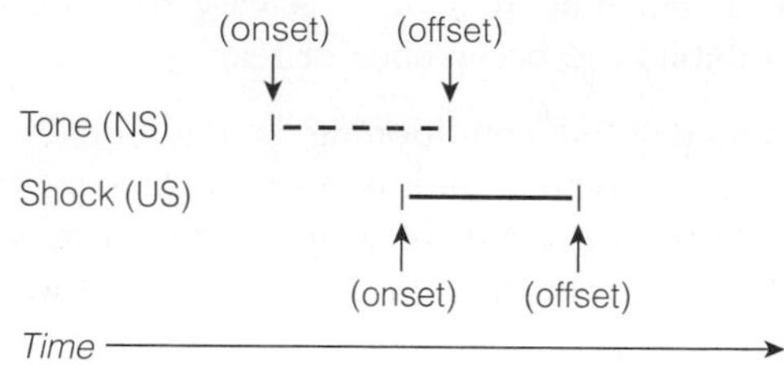

(b) Trace conditioning procedure

Tone (NS)

Shock (US)

Time

(c) Simultaneous conditioning procedure

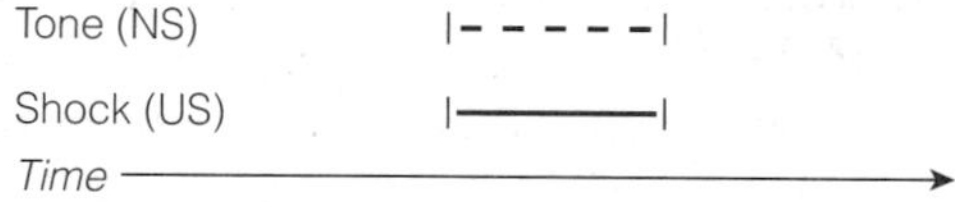

(d) Backward conditioning procedure

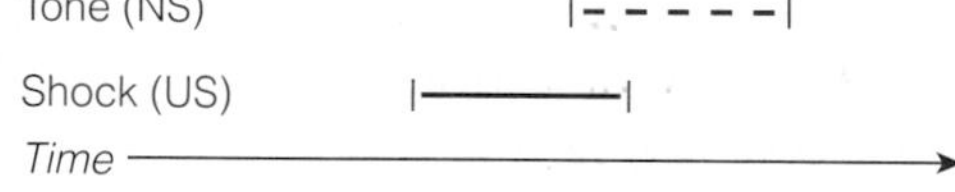

Although simultaneous conditioning involves the closest possible contiguity between the NS and the US, this procedure usually results in poor conditioning. One reason for this is that if the NS occurs at the same time as the US, the NS is no longer a good predictor of the US (in the same way that an air-raid siren is essentially useless if it starts wailing at precisely the same time as the first explosions occur).

4. **Backward Conditioning.** In ***backward conditioning***, the onset of the NS follows the onset of the US. In other words, the US is presented first and the NS is presented later. For example, the rat receives a shock and then hears a tone (see Figure 3.8d). Backward conditioning has traditionally been regarded as the least effective procedure for conditioning, especially with respect to conditioning of an excitatory response (although, as you will see in Chapter 12, exceptions

can occur, such as with stimuli that we may have an innate tendency to fear). Backward conditioning can, however, sometimes result in conditioning of an inhibitory response. For example, if a tone sounds just before a shock is *terminated*, then the tone reliably predicts the removal of shock. The tone in this case can become a safety signal (CS–) that inhibits the occurrence of fear.

Thus, although delayed conditioning is traditionally thought of as the most effective arrangement, conditioning can occur with other arrangements. In fact, although beyond the scope of this text, recent evidence suggests that all of these arrangements can, in complex ways, impact behavior (see Domjan, 2015).

Temporal Conditioning In all of the examples presented to this point, the CS has been a distinctive, external stimulus of some sort, such as a light, a metronome, or a dog. But this need not be the case. ***Temporal conditioning*** is a form of classical conditioning in which the CS is the passage of time. For example, if a dog is given a bite of food every 10 minutes, it will eventually salivate more strongly toward the end of each 10-minute interval than at the start of the interval. The end of the 10-minute interval is the effective CS for salivation. Similarly, residents of a city who experience a bombing attack each night at 2:00 A.M. for several nights in a row will likely start feeling anxious as 2:00 A.M. approaches, even in the absence of any clock indicating the time. The various cues that we use to estimate time, some of which are internal, are sufficient to elicit the feelings of anxiety.

QUICK QUIZ J

1. The most effective temporal arrangement for conditioning is __________ conditioning, in which the onset of the NS (precedes/follows) the onset of the US, and the two stimuli (overlap/do not overlap).
2. In delayed conditioning, the time between the onset of the NS and the onset of the US is called the __________ interval (abbreviated __________).
3. In trace conditioning, the (onset/offset/onset & offset) of the NS precedes the __________ of the US.
4. In trace conditioning, the time between the __________ of the NS and the __________ of the US is called the __________ interval. Trace conditioning can be effective if this interval is relatively (long/short).
5. In simultaneous conditioning, the __________ of the NS occurs at the same time as the __________ of the US.
6. In backward conditioning, the (NS/US) is presented first and the (NS/US) is presented later. Backward conditioning can result in inhibitory conditioning when the NS signals the (presentation/removal) of the US.
7. Simultaneous and backward conditioning procedures have traditionally been considered as (less/more) effective than delayed and trace conditioning procedures.

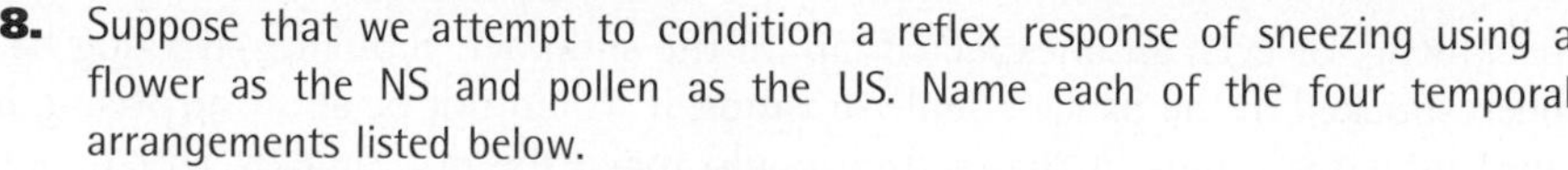

8. Suppose that we attempt to condition a reflex response of sneezing using a flower as the NS and pollen as the US. Name each of the four temporal arrangements listed below.

a. ________ conditioning: **Flower** |----|
Pollen |——|

b. ________ conditioning: **Flower** |--------|
Pollen |——|

c. ________ conditioning: **Flower** |----|
Pollen |———|

d. ________ conditioning: **Flower** |----|
Pollen |——|

9. In ________ conditioning, the (NS/US) is presented at regular intervals, with the result that the passage of time becomes a (CS/US).

Pseudoconditioning

We hope you are now pretty familiar with the basic classical conditioning procedure and some of the phenomena associated with it. Be aware, however, that determining whether classical conditioning has occurred is not always as straightforward as it might seem. A phenomenon known as *pseudoconditioning* poses a particular problem. In ***pseudoconditioning***, an elicited response that appears to be a CR is actually the result of sensitization rather than conditioning. Suppose, for example, that we try to condition a leg withdrawal reflex (leg flexion) in a dog by presenting a light flash followed by a slight shock to its paw.

Light flash: Shock → *Leg flexion*

After a few pairings of the light with the shock, we now find that a fairly strong flexion response occurs immediately when the light is flashed.

Light flash → *Leg flexion*

On the surface, it seems that the light flash has become a CS and that we have successfully conditioned a flexion response. But have we? What if instead of flashing a light, we sound a beep and find that, lo and behold, it too elicits a response?

Beep → *Leg flexion*

What is going on here?

Remember the process of sensitization, in which the repeated presentation of an eliciting stimulus can sometimes increase the strength of the elicited response? Well, sensitization can result in the response also being elicited by other stimuli. For example, soldiers with war trauma exhibit an enhanced startle response, not just to the sound of exploding mortar shells but to certain other stimuli as well, including doors slamming, cars backfiring, or even an unexpected tap on the shoulder. Similarly, if a dog has been shocked in the paw a couple of times, it would not be at all surprising if any sudden stimulus in that setting could make the dog quickly jerk its leg up. Therefore, although we thought we had established a CR—which is the result of a CS having been paired with a US—in reality we have simply produced a hypersensitive dog that automatically reacts to almost any sudden stimulus.

Pseudoconditioning is a potential problem whenever the US is some type of emotionally arousing stimulus. Fortunately, there are ways of assessing the extent to which a response is the result of pseudoconditioning rather than real conditioning. One alternative is to employ a control condition in which the NS and US are presented separately. For example, while subjects in the experimental group receive several pairings of the light flash and the shock, subjects in the control group receive light flashes and shocks that are well separated in time.

Experimental group	***Control group***
Light flash: Shock → *Leg flexion*	**Light flash / / Shock → *Leg flexion***

(The symbol / / for the control group means that the light flash and the shock are *not* paired together and are instead presented apart from each other.) When the animals in each group are then exposed to the light flash presented on its own, we find the following:

Experimental group	***Control group***
Light flash → *Leg flexion*	**Light flash → *Weak leg flexion***

The level of responding shown by the control group is presumed to reflect the amount of sensitization (pseudoconditioning) due to the use of an upsetting stimulus such as a shock. However, because the response shown by the experimental group is stronger than that shown by the control group, conditioning is assumed to have occurred, with the difference between the two groups indicating the strength of conditioning. Classical conditioning experiments typically utilize one or more control groups like this to assess how much actual conditioning has taken place versus how much the subject's responses are the result of nonconditioning factors such as sensitization.

QUICK QUIZ K

1. When an elicited response that appears to be a CR is actually the result of sensitization, we say that ____________ has taken place.
2. The above phenomenon is a potential problem whenever the US produces a strong em____________ response.
3. An appropriate control procedure to test for this phenomenon involves a control group of subjects being presented the NS and US (together/apart). Responding that is later elicited by the NS in this group is assumed to be the result of s____________ rather than real conditioning.

SUMMARY

In general, elicited behaviors are involuntary reactions to specific stimuli. Examples of elicited behaviors include reflexes and fixed action patterns. Repeated presentations of the same stimulus may decrease the strength of a behavior (known as habituation) or increase the strength of a behavior (known as sensitization). A similar dual mechanism is evident in the opponent-process theory of emotion, in which an event elicits an emotional response (the a-process) that in turn elicits a compensatory response (the b-process).

In classical conditioning, a neutral stimulus is paired with some other stimulus that naturally elicits a response; as a result, the neutral stimulus also comes to elicit a response. In Pavlov's basic procedure, the unconditioned stimulus (US) is the stimulus that naturally elicits a response, and the unconditioned response (UR) is the response that is naturally elicited by the US. The conditioned stimulus (CS) is the stimulus that, although initially a neutral stimulus (NS), comes to elicit a response because it has been associated with the US. The conditioned response (CR) is the response that, following conditioning, is elicited by the CS.

In appetitive conditioning, the US is an appetitive stimulus such a food; in aversive conditioning, the US is an aversive stimulus such as a shock. Studies of aversive conditioning are often carried out using a conditioned suppression procedure in which a rat stops lever pressing for food in the presence of a tone that has been paired with a shock. In excitatory conditioning, the CS predicts the presentation of the US; in inhibitory conditioning, the CS predicts the removal of the US.

There can be various temporal arrangements of the NS and US in classical conditioning. In delayed conditioning, the onset of the NS precedes the onset of the US and overlaps with it. In trace conditioning, the onset and offset of the NS precede the onset of the US. In simultaneous conditioning, the NS and US are presented at the same time. In backward conditioning, the onset of the NS follows the onset of the US. Delayed conditioning and trace conditioning are traditionally considered the most effective conditioning procedures. In temporal conditioning, the NS (CS) is the passage of time between USs that are presented at regular intervals. Pseudoconditioning is a false form of conditioning in which the response is actually the result of sensitization rather than classical conditioning.

SUGGESTED READINGS

Babkin, B. P. (1949). *Pavlov: A biography.* Chicago, IL: University of Chicago Press. An excellent biography of Pavlov by a former student of his.

Pavlov, I. P. (1927). *Conditioned reflexes* (G. V. Anrep, Trans.). London: Oxford University Press. The best of Pavlov's own books on classical conditioning.

Windholz, G. (1997). Ivan P. Pavlov: An overview of his life and psychological work. *American Psychologist, 52*, 941–946. The commemorative issue of *American Psychologist* in which this article appears also contains several other articles on Pavlov's work and on the modern-day status of classical conditioning.

STUDY QUESTIONS

1. What is a reflex? Diagram the sequence of events in a reflex arc that underlies a flexion response when one's hand touches a sharp object.
2. Define fixed action pattern. What is a sign stimulus or releaser? Give an example of a fixed action pattern and its releaser.
3. Define habituation and sensitization. What is the effect of stimulus intensity on habituation and sensitization?
4. Distinguish between long-term and short-term habituation. Describe the phenomenon of dishabituation.
5. Define the opponent-process theory of emotion. What are four characteristics of opponent processes?
6. Define classical conditioning. Diagram an example of a classical conditioning procedure. Be sure to label each component using the appropriate abbreviations.
7. Define the terms unconditioned stimulus, unconditioned response, conditioned stimulus, and conditioned response.
8. Distinguish between appetitive and aversive conditioning. Describe the conditioned suppression (or CER) procedure.
9. How do excitatory conditioning and inhibitory conditioning differ from each other? Give an example of each.
10. Name and diagram (or describe) four temporal arrangements of the NS and US. Which two arrangements are traditionally considered to be most effective? What is temporal conditioning?
11. What is pseudoconditioning and how is it assessed?

CONCEPT REVIEW

appetitive conditioning. Conditioning procedure in which the US is an appetitive event (one that an organism approaches or seeks out).

aversive conditioning. Conditioning procedure in which the US is an aversive event (one that an organism avoids).

backward conditioning. Conditioning procedure in which the onset of the NS follows the onset of the US.

classical conditioning. A process whereby a stimulus comes to elicit a response because it has been paired with (or associated with) another stimulus. Also known as Pavlovian conditioning or respondent conditioning.

conditioned response (CR). The response, often similar to the unconditioned response, that is elicited by the conditioned stimulus.

conditioned stimulus (CS). Any stimulus that, although initially neutral, comes to elicit a response because it has been associated with (paired with) an unconditioned stimulus.

delayed conditioning. Conditioning procedure in which the onset of the NS precedes the onset of the US, and the two stimuli overlap.

dishabituation. The reappearance of a habituated response to a stimulus following the presentation of another, seemingly irrelevant novel stimulus.

elicited behavior. Behavior that is drawn out (elicited) by a preceding stimulus. Also known as *respondent behavior*.

excitatory conditioning. Conditioning procedure in which the NS is associated with the *presentation* of a US.

fixed action pattern. A fixed sequence of responses elicited by a specific stimulus.

flexion response. The automatic response of jerking one's hand or foot away from a hot or sharp object.

habituation. A decrease in the strength of an elicited behavior following repeated presentations of the eliciting stimulus.

inhibitory conditioning. Conditioning procedure in which the NS is associated with the *absence* or *removal* of a US.

opponent-process theory. A theory proposing that an emotional event elicits two competing processes: (1) an a-process (or primary process) that is directly elicited by the event, and (2) a b-process (or opponent process) that is elicited by the a-process and serves to counteract the a-process.

orienting response. The automatic positioning of oneself to facilitate attending to a stimulus.

pseudoconditioning. A situation in which an elicited response that appears to be a CR is actually the result of sensitization rather than conditioning.

reflex. A relatively simple, involuntary response to a stimulus.

reflex arc. A neural structure that underlies many simple reflexes and consists of a sensory neuron, an interneuron, and a motor neuron.

sensitization. An increase in the strength of an elicited response following repeated presentations of the eliciting stimulus.

sign stimulus (or releaser). A specific stimulus that elicits a fixed action pattern.

simultaneous conditioning. Conditioning procedure in which the onset of the NS and the onset of the US are simultaneous.

startle response. A defensive reaction to a sudden, unexpected stimulus, which involves the automatic tightening of skeletal muscles and various hormonal and visceral changes.

temporal conditioning. A form of classical conditioning in which the CS is the passage of time.

trace conditioning. Conditioning procedure in which the onset and offset of the NS precede the onset of the US.

unconditioned response (UR). The response that is naturally (without prior learning) elicited by the unconditioned stimulus.

unconditioned stimulus (US). A stimulus that naturally (without prior learning) elicits a response.

CHAPTER TEST

4. A sudden loud noise is likely to elicit a(n) ____________ response, which is a reflexive defensive response to a sudden, unexpected stimulus.
13. With repeated presentations of the emotional event, the b-process (increases/decreases) in both ____________ and ____________.
23. Seeing a wasp land on your arm and then watching it as it stings you is an example of a(n) ____________ conditioning procedure; noticing the wasp at the same moment that you feel the sting is an example of a(n) ____________ conditioning procedure.
6. When a subordinate dog submits to a threatening display from a dominant dog, it will often roll over on its back and display its belly. This type of action sequence is called a(n) ____________, and the threatening display from the dominant dog is called the ____________ stimulus or ____________ for these actions.
14. Classical conditioning is also known as P____________ conditioning or ____________ conditioning. In the latter case, the elicited behaviors are referred to as ____________.
9. The faint sound of a jackhammer several blocks away will likely result in ____________, but the extremely loud sound of a jackhammer right outside your window may result in ____________. The moderately loud sound of a jackhammer half a block away may result in a period of ____________ followed by ____________.
26. In general, aversive conditioning occurs (more/less) readily than appetitive conditioning.
12. According to the opponent-process theory of emotion, b-processes are (slow/quick) to increase and (slow/quick) to decrease.
18. Imagine an eyeblink conditioning procedure in which the sound of a click is paired with a puff of air to the eye. Each pairing of the click and air puff during conditioning is referred to as a(n) ____________.
2. During an eyeblink conditioning procedure, you blinked not only in response to the sound of the click but also when someone tapped you on the shoulder. Your response to the tap on the shoulder may be indicative of ____________ conditioning, which means that the elicited eyeblink may be the result of ____________ rather than classical conditioning.

11. In the opening scenario to this chapter, Uma witnessed her boyfriend flirting with another woman. First, she experienced intense anger. Later, however, when he apologized for his actions and was very attentive to her, she experienced unusually strong feelings of attraction toward him. An explanation for this pattern of emotional changes is provided by the __________ theory of emotion. In this case, Uma's feelings of anger are an example of the __________ process, and her feelings of affection following his apology are an example of the __________ process.

1. Behaviors that are automatically drawn out by the stimuli that precede them are referred to as __________ behaviors (or __________ behaviors).

20. When you opened the broken refrigerator yesterday, the putrid smell of rotten eggs made you nauseous. Today, when you are about to open the refrigerator, you again find yourself becoming nauseous, even though the refrigerator has been thoroughly cleaned. In classical conditioning terms, the refrigerator has become a(n) __________ stimulus that now elicits a(n) __________ response of nausea. In this case, the nausea produced by the sight of the refrigerator is likely to be (less/more) severe than the nausea produced by the smell of rotten eggs.

5. The reflexive action of pulling your hand away from a hot plate is activated through a(n) __________: a neural structure underlying simple reflexes that consists of a(n) (in correct order) __________________________.

25. A conditioning procedure is likely to be more effective if the conditioning trials are spaced (one minute/one hour) apart. This is in keeping with what is known as the __________ effect, in which learning occurs more readily when practice sessions are spaced (close together/far apart).

10. You finally habituate to the faint sound of a jackhammer half a block away, such that you cease to notice it. The lights in your house then go out, at which point you again notice the sound of the jackhammer. This is an example of the process of __________.

15. Imagine an eyeblink conditioning procedure in which the sound of a click is paired with a puff of air to the eye. The puff of air is called the __________ stimulus (abbreviated __________), and the eyeblink that it elicits is called the __________ response (abbreviated __________).

30. In general, long-term habituation is most likely to occur when the stimulus is presented at (narrowly/widely) spaced intervals; in this case, the ability to respond tends to recover (slowly/quickly) when the stimulus is no longer presented.

19. When you opened the broken refrigerator one evening, the putrid smell of rotten eggs made you nauseous. In classical conditioning terms, the

putrid smell is a(n) __________ stimulus that elicits a(n) __________ response of nausea.

28. Inadvertently touching a hot object is likely to elicit a(n) __________ response, which is controlled through a simple sequence of neurons known as a __________.

7. Fixed action patterns are sometimes called __________ behaviors because they are often unique to a certain species.

3. The reflexive action of a dog pricking up its ears in response to a sound is an example of a(n) __________ response, which consists of movements designed to facilitate __________ __________.

31. How does one calculate a suppression ratio? __________

17. Imagine an eyeblink conditioning procedure in which the sound of a click is paired with a puff of air to the eye. After conditioning, the click becomes a(n) __________ stimulus (abbreviated __________) because it now elicits an eyeblink. The eyeblink elicited by the click is called the __________ response (abbreviated __________).

27. Dana always feels relaxed when she takes her large dog for a walk, even though the neighborhood is relatively dangerous. This appears to be an example of __________, with the dog functioning as a(n) __________ CS (which can be abbreviated __________).

21. When you opened the broken refrigerator one evening, the putrid smell of rotten eggs made you nauseous. Your later response of nausea to the sight of the refrigerator is an example of (aversive/appetitive) conditioning as well as (excitatory/inhibitory) conditioning.

32. Jared's parents always start arguing at around midnight each night. As a result, he wakes up feeling anxious each night just before midnight. This seems to be an example of __________ conditioning.

16. Imagine an eyeblink conditioning procedure in which the sound of a click is paired with a puff of air to the eye. Before conditioning, the sound of the click does not elicit an eyeblink; it is therefore considered a(n) __________ stimulus.

29. In a conditioned suppression ratio, a score of __________ indicates total suppression of the behavior, while a score of around __________ indicates no suppression.

8. In a restaurant, the parents of a noisy child hardly notice the commotion. This is an example of __________. However, the customers at neighboring tables are becoming increasingly annoyed by the child. This is an example of __________.

22. Brett is allergic to bee stings. He eats and drinks heartily when he is inside the restaurant, but not when he is seated on the outdoor patio surrounded by flowers. This circumstance is similar to the __________ paradigm, which is also known as the __________ (CER) procedure.

24. In an experiment involving the conditioning of an eyeblink response to the sound of a click, hearing the click and then two seconds later feeling the puff of air in your eye is an example of a(n) trace conditioning procedure. Conversely, feeling the puff of air and then hearing the click is an example of a(n) backward conditioning procedure. In general, the (former/latter) procedure is likely to be more effective.

ANSWERS TO CHAPTER TEST

1. elicited; respondent
2. pseudo; sensitization
3. orienting; attending to a stimulus
4. startle
5. reflex arc; sensory neuron; interneuron; motor neuron
6. fixed action pattern; sign; releaser
7. species-specific
8. habituation (or long-term habituation); sensitization
9. habituation; sensitization; sensitization; habituation
10. dishabituation
11. opponent-process; primary (or a-); opponent (or b-)
12. slow; slow
13. increases; strength; duration
14. Pavlovian; respondent; respondents
15. unconditioned; US; unconditioned; UR
16. neutral
17. conditioned; CS; conditioned; CR
18. conditioning trial
19. unconditioned; unconditioned
20. conditioned; conditioned; less
21. aversive; excitatory
22. conditioned suppression; conditioned emotional response
23. delayed; simultaneous
24. trace; backward; former
25. one hour; spacing; far apart
26. more
27. inhibitory conditioning; inhibitory; CS–
28. flexion; reflex arc
29. 0; .5
30. widely; slowly
31. Assuming CS and pre-CS periods of equal length (e.g., 30 seconds each), divide the number of CS responses by the number of CS responses plus pre-CS responses
32. temporal

Chapter 4

CLASSICAL CONDITIONING: BASIC PHENOMENA AND VARIOUS COMPLEXITIES

CHAPTER OUTLINE

Jana enjoys being wildly unpredictable in her relationships, believing that most men find unpredictable women exciting. She cancels dates at the last minute, shows up on the guy's doorstep at odd hours of the day or night, and tries as much as possible to be completely spontaneous. Unfortunately, many of the guys she goes out with seem to be rather stressed out and neurotic, though it usually takes a while before this becomes apparent. She is starting to wonder if there are any good men around these days.

Some Basic Conditioning Phenomena

Acquisition

In classical conditioning, ***acquisition*** refers to the process of developing and strengthening a conditioned response through repeated pairings of a neutral stimulus (NS) with an unconditioned stimulus (US). In general, acquisition proceeds rapidly during early conditioning trials and then gradually levels off. The maximum amount of conditioning that can take place in a particular situation is known as the *asymptote* of conditioning (see Figure 4.1).

The asymptote of conditioning, as well as the speed of conditioning, is dependent on several factors. In general, *more intense USs produce stronger and more rapid conditioning than do less intense USs*. For example, we can obtain stronger conditioning of a salivary response when the US consists of a large

FIGURE 4.1 A typical acquisition curve in which strength of conditioning increases rapidly during the first few trials and then gradually levels off over subsequent trials.

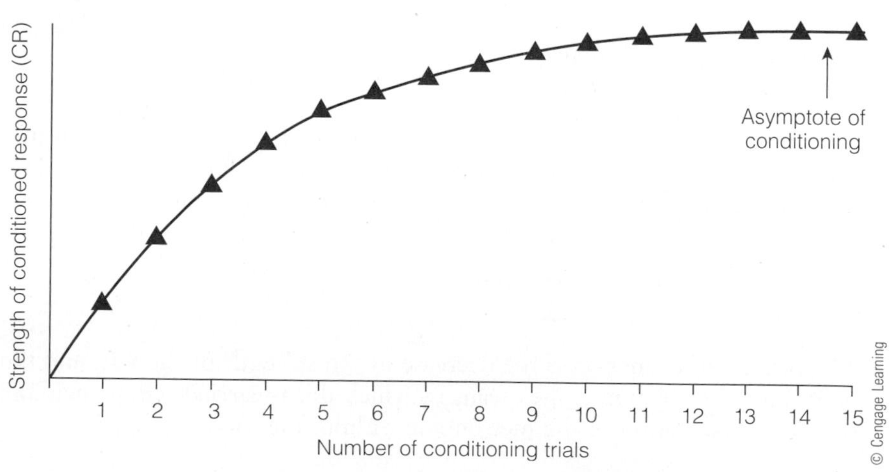

amount of food or a highly preferred food than if it consists of a small amount or less preferred food. Likewise, a severe bite from a dog will result in a stronger fear than a minor bite will. Similarly, *more intense* NSs *result in stronger and more rapid conditioning than do less intense* NSs. For example, a loud metronome that has been paired with food produces a stronger response of salivation than a faint metronome that has been paired with food. And, not surprisingly, conditioned fear responses to dogs are more readily acquired if the person is bitten by a large dog rather than by a small dog.

QUICK QUIZ A

1. The process of strengthening a conditioned response through repeated pairings of an NS with a US is known as __________. In general, conditioning proceeds more (rapidly/slowly) during the early trials of a conditioning procedure.
2. The maximum amount of learning (or conditioning) that can take place in a given situation is known as the __________ of learning.
3. In general, a (more/less) intense US produces stronger conditioning, and a (more/less) intense NS produces stronger conditioning.

Extinction and Related Phenomena

Given that a certain stimulus now elicits a conditioned response, is there any way to eliminate the response? In the *process* known as ***extinction***, a conditioned response is weakened or eliminated when the conditioned stimulus (CS) is repeatedly presented in the absence of the US. The term *extinction* also applies to the *procedure* whereby this happens, namely the repeated presentation of the CS in the absence of the US.

Suppose, for example, that a metronome has been paired with food such that it now elicits a conditioned response of salivation:

Metronome: Food → *Salivation*
NS US UR

Metronome → *Salivation*
CS CR

If we now continue to present the metronome by itself and never again pair it with food (each presentation of the metronome being known as an "extinction trial"), the conditioned response of salivation will eventually die out—that is, the CR of salivation will have been *extinguished*.

Metronome → No salivation
"NS" —

The process of extinction is the decrease in the strength of the CR, and the procedure of extinction is the means by which this is carried out, namely the repeated presentation of the metronome without the food.

In a similar manner, if a dog that once bit me never again bites me, my fear response to the dog should eventually extinguish. Unfortunately, some people who were once bitten by a dog continue to fear that dog as well as other dogs, in which case we might say that they have a "phobia" about dogs. But if the person has never again been bitten by the dog, why is his or her fear so persistent? One reason is that people who fear dogs tend to avoid them, and to the extent that they avoid them, their fear response cannot be extinguished. As you will see in later chapters, this tendency to avoid a feared event is a major factor in the development and maintenance of a phobia, and treatment procedures for phobias are often based on preventing this avoidance response from occurring.

Once a CR has been extinguished, one should not assume that the effects of conditioning have been completely eliminated. For this reason, in the preceding diagram the "NS" following extinction has been placed in quotation marks, since it is no longer a pure neutral stimulus. For one thing, *a response that has been extinguished can be reacquired quite rapidly when the CS (or NS) is once again paired with the US*. If we again pair the metronome with food following an extinction procedure, it may take only a few pairings before we achieve a fairly strong level of conditioning. Likewise, if I somehow manage to overcome my phobia of dogs, I might rapidly reacquire that phobia if I again have a frightening experience with dogs.

As further evidence that extinction does not completely eliminate the effects of conditioning, an extinguished response can reappear even in the absence of further pairings between the CS and US. Suppose, for example, that we do extinguish a dog's conditioned salivary response to a metronome by repeatedly presenting the metronome without food. By the end of the extinction session, the metronome no longer elicits salivation. However, if we come back the next morning and sound the metronome, the dog will very likely salivate. In everyday terms, it is almost as if the dog has forgotten that the metronome no longer predicts food. As a result, we are forced to conduct another series of extinction trials, repeatedly sounding the metronome without the food. After several trials, the response is again extinguished. The next day, however, the dog again starts salivating when we first present the metronome. At this point, we might be tempted to conclude that we have an awfully dumb dog on our hands. The dog, however, is simply displaying a phenomenon known as spontaneous recovery.

Spontaneous recovery is the reappearance of a conditioned response to a CS following a rest period after extinction. Fortunately, spontaneous recovery does not last forever. Each time the response recovers it is usually weaker and extinguishes more quickly than before (see Figure 4.2). Therefore, after several extinction sessions, we should be able to sound the metronome at the start of the session and find little or no salivation.

The phenomenon of spontaneous recovery is particularly important to remember when attempting to extinguish a conditioned fear response. For example, we might arrange for a dog-phobic child to spend several hours with a dog. At the end of that time, the child's fear of the dog might seem

FIGURE 4.2 Hypothetical results illustrating a decline in spontaneous recovery across repeated sessions of extinction.

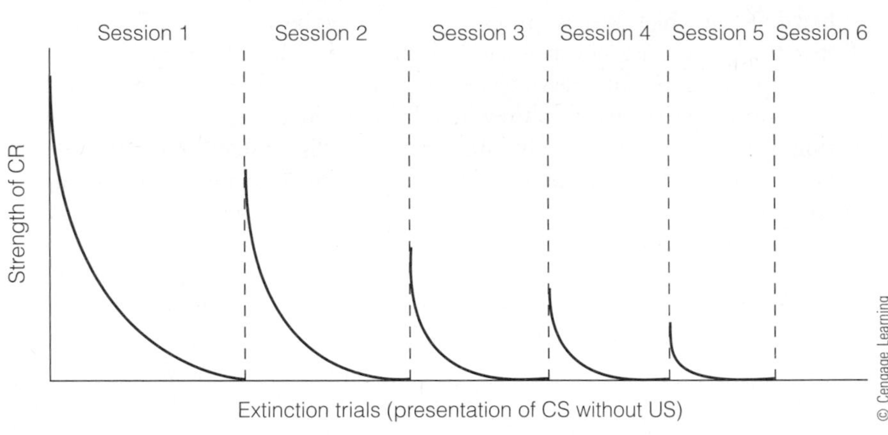

to have been totally eliminated. Nevertheless, it is quite possible that the fear will at least partially recover the next time the child is confronted with a dog, and that several sessions of extinction may be needed before the fear is completely eliminated. Similarly, if you feel terribly anxious with a new date at the start of the evening but more at ease after a couple of hours, do not be disappointed if you again find yourself becoming anxious at the start of your next date. It may take several dates with that person before you feel comfortable right from the outset. Likewise, following a breakup, it may take a while before your feelings of attraction to the other person are finally extinguished, and even then they may intermittently reappear for a considerable period of time.

To Pavlov (1927), the phenomenon of spontaneous recovery indicated that extinction is not simply a process of unlearning the conditioning that has taken place. Rather, extinction involves learning something new, namely, to inhibit the occurrence of the CR in the presence of the CS. For example, rather than unlearning the response of salivation to the metronome during extinction, the dog learns to inhibit the response of salivation to the metronome, with the connection between the metronome and salivation still remaining intact on some underlying level. Spontaneous recovery may therefore represent the partial weakening of this inhibition during the rest period between extinction sessions.

Support for the notion that extinction involves a buildup of inhibition is also provided by a phenomenon known as disinhibition. ***Disinhibition*** is the sudden recovery of a conditioned response during an extinction procedure when a novel (unfamiliar) stimulus is introduced. For example, if we are in the process of extinguishing conditioning to a metronome but then present an unusual humming noise in the background, the sound of the metronome may again elicit a considerable amount of salivation. In diagram form:

(**Step 1:** First condition the metronome as a CS for salivation)

Metronome: Food → *Salivation*
NS US UR

Metronome → *Salivation*
CS CR

(**Step 2:** Begin extinction trials by repeatedly presenting the metronome by itself, as a result of which the CR is greatly weakened)

Metronome → *Weak salivation* (Partial extinction)
CS CR

(**Step 3:** Present a novel humming noise in background during the extinction procedure, as a result of which the CR recovers in strength)

(Unusual humming noise) Metronome → *Salivation*
CS CR

Similarly, if your anxiety while giving a speech in class gradually fades, it may suddenly recover when a noisy ceiling fan starts up or someone walks in late. (Note that the phenomenon of disinhibition is similar to dishabituation, discussed in Chapter 3, in which the presentation of a novel stimulus results in the reappearance of a habituated response. To distinguish these concepts, it may help to remember that *dishabituation* involves the reappearance of a *habituated* response, and *disinhibition* involves the recovery of a response that has become partially *inhibited* due to extinction.)[1]

QUICK QUIZ B

1. In the *process* of extinction, a conditioned response grows weaker because ______________________________.
2. The *procedure* of extinction involves ______________________________ ______________________________.
3. Once a CR has been extinguished, reacquisition of that response tends to occur (more/less) rapidly than the original conditioning.
4. The sudden recovery of an extinguished response following some delay after extinction is known as s__________ r__________.
5. With repeated sessions of extinction, each time a response recovers, it is usually somewhat (weaker/stronger) and extinguishes more (slowly/quickly).
6. Pavlov believed that this phenomenon indicates that extinction involves the (inhibition/unlearning) of a conditioned response.
7. The sudden recovery of a response during an extinction procedure when a novel stimulus is introduced is called __________.

[1] Another reason that extinction of CRs can be difficult or incomplete is that we might not identify all of the stimuli that are helping to elicit the response. For example, in the case of a dog phobia, stimuli other than the dog—such as the sound of growling or worried looks on the faces of others—may also be involved. Those stimuli may also need to be incorporated into the extinction procedure.

Stimulus Generalization and Discrimination

Classical conditioning would not be very useful if it only enabled us to learn about relationships between particular stimuli. For example, if we are bitten by a spider, it would not be very helpful for us to fear only that particular spider (which, in any case, we probably obliterated the moment it bit us). From an evolutionary perspective, it would be far more adaptive to learn to fear other spiders as well, particularly spiders that look similar to the one that bit us. Fortunately, this is precisely what happens, through a process known as stimulus generalization.

In classical conditioning, ***stimulus generalization*** is the tendency for a CR to occur in the presence of a stimulus that is similar to the CS. In general, the more similar the stimulus is to the original CS, the stronger the response. For example, if a dog is conditioned to salivate to a tone that has a pitch of 2000 Hz, it will salivate to similar tones as well. But it will salivate more strongly to a 1900-Hz tone or a 2100-Hz tone than it will to a 1000-Hz tone or a 3000-Hz tone. In other words, tones that are most similar in pitch to the original CS will elicit the strongest response. Similarly, after being bitten by a dog, a child will probably fear not only that particular dog but other dogs as well. And the child is particularly likely to fear dogs that closely resemble the dog that bit him.

The process of generalization is most apparent when the stimuli involved are physically similar and vary along a continuum. Tones of varying pitch or loudness and lights of varying color or brightness are examples of such stimuli. However, generalization can also occur across nonphysical dimensions, particularly in humans who use language. ***Semantic generalization*** is the generalization of a conditioned response to verbal stimuli that are similar in *meaning* to the CS. For example, if humans are exposed to a conditioning procedure in which the sight of the word *car* is paired with shock, that word eventually becomes a CS that elicits a fear response. When participants are shown other words, generalization of the fear response is more likely to occur to those words that are similar in meaning to *car*, such as *automobile* or *truck*, than to words that look or sound similar, such as *bar* or *tar*. Thus, the meaning of the word is the critical factor in semantic generalization. For this reason, words that have similar meaning for an individual—for example, *Jennifer Lopez* and *J-Lo*—are likely to generate the same conditioned emotional response.

The opposite of stimulus generalization is ***stimulus discrimination***, the tendency for a response to be elicited more by one stimulus than another. For example, if the dog salivates in the presence of the 2000-Hz tone but not in the presence of a 1900-Hz tone, then we say that it is able to *discriminate*, or has *formed a discrimination*, between the two stimuli. Such discriminations can be deliberately trained through a procedure known as *discrimination training*. If we repeatedly present the dog with one type of trial in which a 2000-Hz tone is always followed by food and another type of trial in which a 1900-Hz tone is never followed by food, the dog will soon learn to salivate in the presence of the 2000-Hz tone and not in the presence of the 1900-Hz tone.

Step 1: Conditioning phase (with the two types of trials presented several times in random order)

2000-Hz tone: Food → *Salivation*
NS US UR

1900-Hz tone: No food
NS —

Step 2: Test phase

2000-Hz tone → *Salivation*
CS+ CR

1900-Hz tone → No salivation
CS− —

As a result of training, the 2000-Hz tone has become an excitatory CS (or CS+) because it predicts the presentation of food, and the 1900-Hz tone has become an inhibitory CS (or CS−) because it predicts the absence of food. The discrimination training has, in effect, countered the tendency for generalization to occur. (Note that the two types of trials were presented in random order during the conditioning phase. If they were instead presented in alternating order, the dog might associate the presentation of food with every second tone rather than with the tone that has a pitch of 2000 Hz.)

As you may have already guessed, discrimination training is a useful means for determining the sensory capacities of animals. For example, by presenting an animal with a CS+ tone and a CS− tone that are successively more and more similar, we can determine the animal's ability to discriminate between tones of different pitch. If it salivates to a CS+ of 2000 Hz and does not salivate to a CS− of 1950 Hz, then it has shown us that it can distinguish between the two. But if it salivates equally to both the 2000-Hz tone and the 1950-Hz tone, then it cannot distinguish between the two.

Generalization and discrimination play an important role in many aspects of human behavior. Phobias, for example, involve not only the classical conditioning of a fear response but also an overgeneralization of that fear response to inappropriate stimuli. For example, a woman who has been through an abusive relationship may develop feelings of anxiety and apprehensiveness toward all men. Eventually, however, through repeated interactions with men, this tendency will decrease and she will begin to adaptively discriminate between men who are potentially abusive and those who are not. Unfortunately, such discriminations are not always easily made, and further bad experiences could greatly strengthen her fear. Moreover, if the woman begins to avoid all men, then the tendency to overgeneralize may remain, thereby significantly impairing her social life. As noted earlier, if we avoid that which we are afraid of, it is difficult for us to overcome our fears.

QUICK QUIZ C

1. Stimulus generalization is the tendency for a (CR/UR) to occur in the presence of stimuli that are similar to the original (CS/US). In general, the more (similar/different) the stimulus, the stronger the response.
2. The generalization of a conditioned response to stimuli that are similar in meaning to a verbal CS is called s_____________ generalization.
3. The opposite of stimulus generalization is stimulus _____________. This can be defined as ____.
4. Feeling anxious around all objects that look like a rattlesnake is an example of stimulus _____________, whereas feeling anxious only around rattlesnakes is an example of stimulus _____________.
5. Suppose Cary disliked his physics instructor and, as a result, came to dislike all science instructors. This example illustrates the process of over_____________.

Experimental Neurosis

Overgeneralization is not the only way that processes of discrimination versus generalization influence the development of a psychological disorder. For example, Pavlov (1927, 1928) reported an interesting discovery made by a colleague, Shenger-Krestovnikova, that arose during a discrimination training procedure. In this experiment, an image of a circle signaled the presentation of food and an ellipse signaled no food (see Figure 4.3). In keeping with normal processes of discrimination, the dog duly learned to salivate when it saw the circle (a CS+) and not salivate when it saw the ellipse (a CS−). Following this, the ellipse was gradually made more circular, making it more difficult for the dog to determine when food was about to appear. When the ellipse was almost completely circular, the dog was able to make only a weak discrimination, salivating slightly more in the presence of the circle than in the presence of the ellipse. Interestingly, continued training with these stimuli did not result in any improvement. In fact, after several weeks, the discrimination was lost. More interestingly, however, the hitherto well-behaved dog became extremely agitated during each session—squealing, wriggling about, and biting at the equipment. It acted as though it was suffering a nervous breakdown.

Pavlov called this phenomenon ***experimental neurosis***, an experimentally produced disorder in which animals exposed to unpredictable events develop neurotic-like symptoms. Pavlov hypothesized that human neuroses might

FIGURE 4.3 Discrimination training procedure used by Shenger-Krestovnikova in which the picture of a circle functioned as the CS+ and the picture of the ellipse functioned as the CS−.

develop in a similar manner. Situations of extreme uncertainty can be stressful, and prolonged exposure to such uncertainty might result in the development of neurotic symptoms. Thus, in the opening vignette to this chapter, it is not surprising that Jana's boyfriends often display increasing symptoms of neuroticism as the relationship progresses. A little uncertainty in one's romantic relationships can be exciting, but extreme uncertainty might eventually become aversive.

In carrying out their studies of experimental neurosis, Pavlov and his assistants also discovered that different dogs displayed different symptoms. Some dogs became anxious when exposed to the procedure, while others became catatonic (rigid) and acted almost hypnotized. A few dogs, however, displayed few if any symptoms and did not have a nervous breakdown. Pavlov speculated that such differences reflected underlying differences in temperament. This was an extension of one of Pavlov's earlier observations that certain dogs condition more easily than others. Shy, withdrawn dogs seemed to make the best subjects, conditioning easily, whereas active, outgoing dogs were more difficult to condition (which is quite the opposite of what Pavlov had originally expected).

Based on results such as these, Pavlov formulated a theory of personality in which inherited differences in temperament interact with classical conditioning to produce general patterns of behavior. Eysenck (1957) later utilized certain aspects of Pavlov's work in formulating his own theory of personality. A major aspect of Eysenck's theory is the distinction between introversion and extroversion. In very general terms, introverts are individuals who are highly reactive to external stimulation (hence, cannot tolerate large amounts of stimulation and tend to withdraw from such stimulation), condition easily, and develop anxiety-type symptoms in reaction to stress. By contrast, extroverts are less reactive to external stimulation (hence, can tolerate, and will even seek out, large amounts of stimulation), condition less easily, and develop physical-type symptoms in reaction to stress. Eysenck's theory also proposes that psychopaths, individuals who engage in antisocial behavior, are extreme extroverts who condition very poorly. As a result, they experience little or no conditioned anxiety when harming or taking advantage of others, such anxiety being the underlying basis of a conscience.

Both Pavlov's and Eysenck's theories of personality are considerably more complicated than presented here, involving additional dimensions of personality and finer distinctions between different types of conditioning, especially excitatory and inhibitory conditioning. Thus, extroverts do not always condition more poorly than introverts, and additional factors are presumed to influence the development of neurotic symptoms (Clark, Watson, & Mineka, 1994; Eysenck, 1967; Monte, 1999). Nevertheless, processes of classical conditioning interacting with inherited differences in temperament could well be major factors in determining one's personality.

The experimental neurosis paradigm also suggests that prolonged exposure to unpredictable events can sometimes have serious effects on our well-being. We will explore this topic in more detail in Chapter 9.

QUICK QUIZ D

1. In Shenger-Krestovnikova's experiment the animal suffered a nervous breakdown when exposed to a CS+ and a CS− that were made progressively (more/less) similar.
2. Pavlov referred to this nervous breakdown as e__________ n__________, an experimentally produced disorder in which animals exposed to unp__________ events develop n__________-like symptoms.
3. Pavlov and his assistants noted that the dogs displayed two general patterns of symptoms. Some dogs became __________ while other dogs became __________. In addition, (all/not all) dogs developed symptoms.
4. Pavlov believed that these differences between dogs in the types of symptoms they developed reflected (learned/inherited) differences in t__________.
5. In Eysenck's theory, introverts are (more/less) reactive to external stimulation than extroverts are, and they therefore (can/cannot) tolerate large doses of stimulation. Introverts also condition (more/less) easily than extroverts.
6. Introverts seem to develop a__________-type symptoms in reaction to stress, whereas extroverts develop p__________-type symptoms.
7. Psychopaths are extreme (introverts/extroverts) who condition (very easily/very poorly). They therefore feel little or no conditioned __________ when harming or manipulating others.

Study Tip: The extent to which introverts versus extroverts react to external stimulation also has implications for the type of environment one can effectively study in. In general, extroverts, being less reactive to external stimulation, are better able to cope with potential distractors, like background noise or loud music, and may even prefer such environments. Introverts, on the other hand, being more reactive to external stimulation, function better in environments that are relatively quiet or with soft music playing in the background. The most common finding, however, is that both introverts and extroverts perform best in environments that have minimal distractions with no music (e.g., Chamorro-Premuzic, Swami, Terrado, & Furnham, 2009). That said, remember that such studies are reporting average tendencies found among groups of people, and these findings may or may not apply to you as an individual. As with self-management in general, the key is to discover what works best for you. For example, I (Russ Powell) once ran into a top student who didn't seem particularly extroverted but who was nevertheless studying in the food fair area of a busy mall! She said it was her favorite place to study; it seemed as though the constant background noise maintained her arousal at a high enough level that studying there never became monotonous for her. Conversely, my coauthor, Lynne, a rather extreme extrovert, just mentioned to me that she learns well with almost any kind of background music, loud or soft, but heaven forbid that it include singing; words are extremely distracting to her. I too prefer instrumental music while working, but it has to be very soft music and even then I sometimes have to turn it off. So what kind of environment is best for you to study in?

Three Extensions to Classical Conditioning

The normal classical conditioning procedure involves associating a single neutral stimulus with a US. But stimuli rarely exist in isolation. For example, a neighborhood bully does not exist as an isolated element in a child's world. The bully is associated with a variety of other stimuli, such as the house he lives in, the route he takes to school, and the kids he hangs around with. If a child is assaulted by the bully and learns to fear him, will he also fear the various objects, places, and people with which the bully is associated? In more technical terms, can classical conditioning of a CS also result in the development (or strengthening) of a conditioned response in the absence of a direct pairing between the NS (or CS) and the US? The processes outlined below indicate that it can.

Higher-Order Conditioning

Suppose you are stung by a wasp while out for a run one day and, as a result, develop a terrible fear of wasps. Imagine, too, that following the development of this fear, you notice a lot of wasps hanging around the trash bin outside your apartment building. Could the trash bin also come to elicit a certain amount of fear, or at least a feeling of edginess or discomfort? In ***higher-order conditioning***, a stimulus that is associated with a CS can also become a CS. Thus, the trash bin could very well come to elicit a fear response through its association with wasps. This process can be diagrammed as follows:

(**Step 1:** Basic conditioning of a fear response to wasps. As part of a higher-order conditioning procedure, this first step is called "first-order conditioning," and the original NS and CS are respectively labeled NS_1 and CS_1.)

Wasp: Sting → *Fear*
NS_1 US UR

Wasp → *Fear*
CS_1 CR

(**Step 2:** Higher-order conditioning of the trash bin through its association with wasps. This second step is sometimes also called "second-order conditioning," and the new NS and CS are labeled NS_2 and CS_2.)

Trash bin: Wasp → *Fear*
NS_2 CS_1 CR

Trash bin → *Fear*
CS_2 CR

The CS_2 generally elicits a weaker response than the CS_1 (which, as noted in Chapter 3, generally elicits a weaker response than the US). Thus, the fear response produced by the trash bin is likely to be much weaker than the fear response produced by the wasps. This is not surprising given that the trash bin is only indirectly associated with the unconditioned stimulus (i.e., the wasp sting) upon which the fear response is based.

FIGURE 4.4 In this example of higher-order conditioning, a metronome is paired with food and becomes a CS_1 for salivation, following which a light paired with the metronome becomes a CS_2 for salivation. (*Source*: Nairne, 2000.)

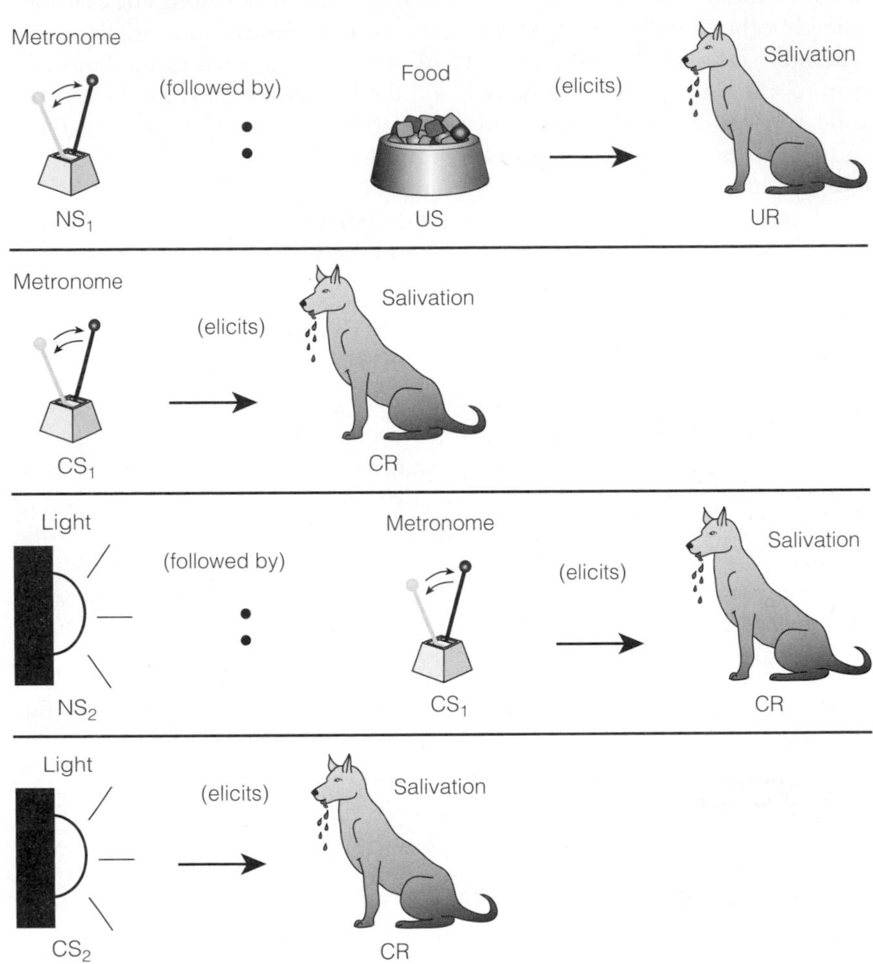

An experimental example of higher-order conditioning might involve pairing a metronome with food so that the metronome becomes a CS_1 for salivation, and then pairing a light with the metronome so that the light becomes a CS_2 for salivation (see Figure 4.4). In diagram form:

(**Step 1:** First-order conditioning)

Metronome: Food → *Salivation*
NS_1 US UR

Metronome → *Salivation*
CS_1 CR

(**Step 2:** Second-order, or higher-order, conditioning)

Light: Metronome → *Salivation*
NS_2 CS_1 CR

Light → *Salivation*
CS_2 CR

The light now elicits salivation although it has never been directly paired with food. (For consistency, we will continue to use Pavlov's salivary conditioning procedure as the basic experimental example throughout much of this chapter. In reality, however, modern researchers use other procedures to study classical conditioning, such as the conditioned suppression procedure discussed in Chapter 3.)

We could also attempt *third-order conditioning* by pairing yet another stimulus, such as the sound of a tone, with the light. However, third-order conditioning can be experimentally difficult to obtain, and when it is obtained, the conditioned response to a third-order conditioned stimulus (the CS_3) is likely to be quite weak.

Higher-order conditioning is commonly used in advertising. For example, advertisements often pair a product with celebrities that, through past conditioning, have come to elicit positive emotional responses in many of us. As discussed in the And Furthermore box, the assumption is that the sight of the celebrity will elicit a positive emotional response in us that will be associated with the product and thereby increase the likelihood that we will purchase the product.

QUICK QUIZ E

1. In higher order conditioning, an already established CS is used to condition a new CS.
2. In general, the CS_2 elicits a (weaker/stronger) response than the CS_1.
3. In higher-order conditioning, conditioning of the CS_1 is often called first-order conditioning, while conditioning of the CS_2 is called second-order conditioning.
4. In a higher-order conditioning procedure in which a car is associated with a famous person, the famous person is the (CS_1/CS_2) and the car is the (CS_1/CS_2).

Sensory Preconditioning

We have seen that an event that is *subsequently* associated with a feared event like wasps, such as trash bins, can become a CS for fear. What about an event that was *previously* associated with wasps, such as a toolshed that once had a wasps' nest hanging in it? Will walking near the shed now also elicit feelings of anxiety?

In ***sensory preconditioning***, when one stimulus is conditioned as a CS, another stimulus with which it was previously paired can also become a CS. If you previously associated the toolshed with wasps and then acquired a fear

And Furthermore

When Celebrities Misbehave

As mentioned, advertisers are aware that we are more likely to buy products that are associated with celebrities ... but will any celebrity do? Some companies will shy away from a celebrity who has been convicted of a crime or implicated in some sort of scandal. For example, when basketball star Kobe Bryant was accused of sexual assault in 2003 (a case that was eventually dismissed), he lost his endorsement deal with McDonald's. When Mary-Kate Olsen checked into a treatment facility in 2004 because of an eating disorder, "Got Milk?" ads featuring the Olsen twins were no longer used by the California Milk Processor Board (CMPB). Companies like McDonald's and CMPB are particularly sensitive to indiscretions by their celebrity endorsers, because their corporate image is aimed at being "wholesome" and "family oriented."

Do all advertisers react this way to celebrity scandal? Not necessarily. When photos were published in 2005 by the *Daily Mirror* (a British tabloid) that showed model Kate Moss allegedly using cocaine, she immediately lost some lucrative endorsements with fashion companies, including H & M and Burberry, as well as several modeling contracts. Interestingly, this short-term loss was not sustained; according to Forbes.com (a leading business and finance news site), not only did Burberry re-sign Moss to an endorsement deal, but other high-end clients were quick to sign her to new contracts. Why would companies want their products associated with a drug-using model?

The fashion industry thrives on what is "edgy," and many designers and retailers want their products to be associated with things that are dark and dangerous, as well as sexy. While some companies (like H & M, which made statements about its antidrug stance in the wake of the Moss cocaine scandal) try to maintain a clean image, others are comfortable being associated with the darker side of life. Thus, if consumers associate a product with the dangerous and less-than-pure image of Kate Moss, then they are making exactly the association the retailer was hoping for. (And they can put on that eyeliner, and feel a little bit dangerous, without having to resort to cocaine use of their own!)

of wasps as a result of being stung, you might also feel anxious when walking near the toolshed. This process can be diagrammed as follows:

(**Step 1:** Preconditioning phase in which the toolshed is associated with wasps)

Toolshed: Wasps
NS_2 NS_1

(**Step 2:** Conditioning of wasps as a CS_1)

Wasp: Sting → *Fear*
NS_1 US UR

Wasp → *Fear*
CS_1 CR

(**Step 3:** Presentation of the toolshed)

Toolshed → *Fear*
CS_2 CR

The toolshed now elicits a fear response, although it was never directly paired with a wasp sting.

An experimental example of sensory preconditioning with dogs involves first presenting several pairings of two neutral stimuli such as a light and a metronome. The metronome is then paired with food to become a CS for salivation. As a result of this conditioning, the light, which has never been directly paired with the food but has been associated with the metronome, also comes to elicit salivation (see Figure 4.5). This process can be diagrammed as follows:

(**Step 1:** Preconditioning phase, in which the light is repeatedly associated with the metronome)

Light: Metronome (10 presentations of light followed by metronome)
NS_2 NS_1

(**Step 2:** Conditioning of the metronome as a CS_1)

Metronome: Food → *Salivation*
NS_1 US UR

Metronome → *Salivation*
CS_1 CR

(**Step 3:** Presentation of the light)

Light → *Salivation*
CS_2 CR

As with higher-order conditioning, the response elicited by the light (CS_2) is generally weaker than the response elicited by the metronome (CS_1). Likewise, the fear response elicited by the toolshed (CS_2) is likely to be weaker than the fear response elicited by the wasps (CS_1).

FIGURE 4.5 In this example of sensory preconditioning, a dog is presented with several pairings of a light and a metronome. The metronome is then paired with food and becomes a conditioned stimulus for salivation. As a result, the light that was previously paired with the metronome also becomes a conditioned stimulus for salivation. (*Source*: Nairne, 2000.)

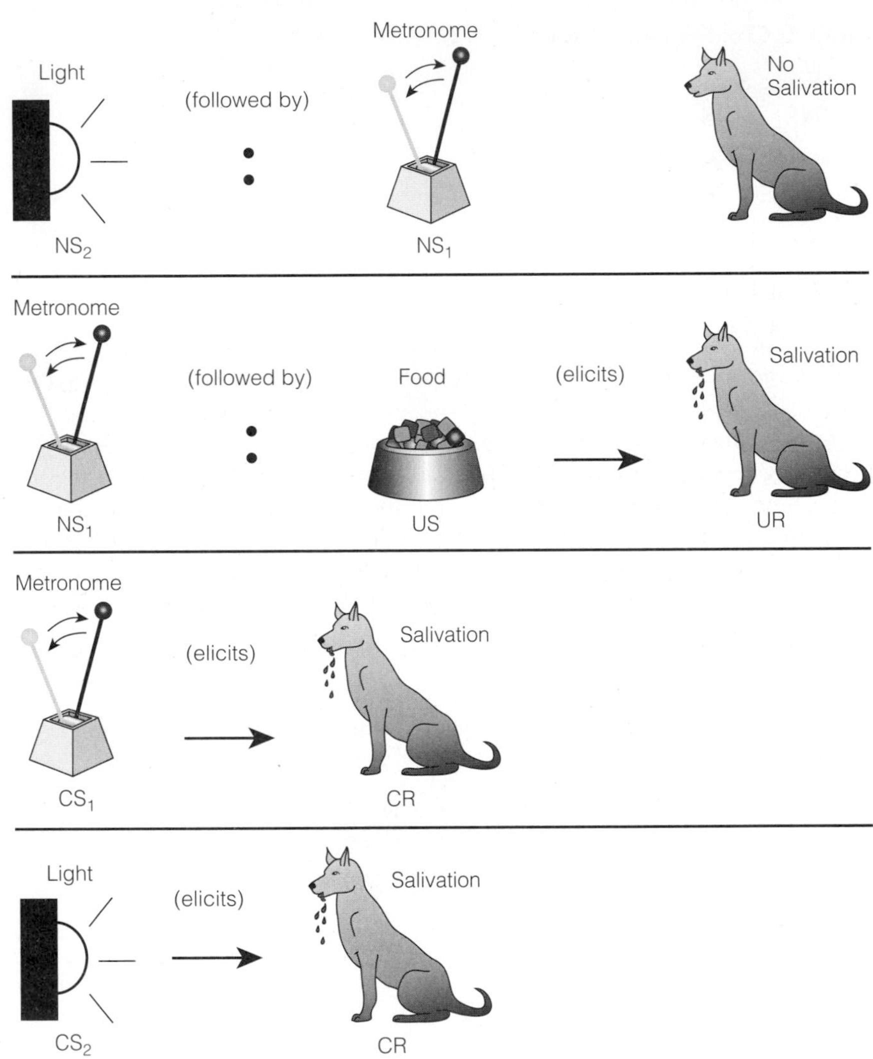

Although it was once believed necessary to pair the neutral stimuli hundreds of times in the preconditioning phase (e.g., Brogden, 1939), it is now known that this type of conditioning works best if the stimuli are paired relatively few times (R. F. Thompson, 1972). This prevents the animal from becoming overly familiar with the stimuli prior to conditioning, which you will later learn can interfere with conditioning. Another unusual finding with sensory preconditioning is that the procedure is sometimes more effective when the two stimuli in the preconditioning phase are presented simultaneously as opposed to sequentially (Rescorla, 1980). This result is unusual because it contradicts what we find with NS-US pairings, in which simultaneous presentation of the two stimuli is relatively ineffective.

Sensory preconditioning is significant because it demonstrates that stimuli can become associated with each other in the absence of any identifiable response (other than an orienting response). In this sense, sensory preconditioning can be viewed as a form of *latent learning*, which was first discussed in Chapter 1. Just as Tolman's rats learned to find their way around a maze even when it seemed as if there were no significant consequences for doing so (i.e., food had not yet been introduced into the goal box), animals will associate stimuli with each other even when those stimuli seem to have little significance for them.

US Revaluation

At the beginning of this chapter, we mentioned how more intense stimuli produce stronger conditioning than do less intense stimuli. For example, a strong shock will produce stronger fear conditioning than a weak shock does. But what would happen if we conducted our conditioning trials with one level of shock and then presented a different level of shock by itself on a subsequent nonconditioning trial? In other words, would changing the intensity or value of the US after the conditioning of a CS also change the strength of response to the CS? Imagine, for example, that the sound of a metronome is followed by a small amount of food, with the result that the metronome comes to elicit a small amount of saliva.

Metronome: Small amount of food → *Weak salivation*
NS US UR

Metronome → *Weak salivation*
CS CR

Once this conditioning has been established, we now present the dog with a large amount of food, which elicits a large amount of saliva.

Large amount of food → *Strong salivation*
US UR

What type of response will now be elicited by the metronome? As it turns out, the dog may react to the metronome as though it predicts a large amount of food rather than a small amount of food.

Metronome → *Strong salivation*
CS CR

Note that the metronome was never directly paired with the large amount of food; the intervening experience with the large amount by itself produced the stronger CR of salivation.

Is this scenario more likely an example of higher-order conditioning or of sensory preconditioning? (You will find the answer when you complete the end-of-chapter test.)

Therefore, ***US revaluation*** is the postconditioning presentation of the US at a different level of intensity, thereby subsequently altering the strength of response to the previously conditioned CS. It is called US *revaluation* because the *value* or magnitude of the US is being changed. Depending on whether the US is increased or decreased in strength, this procedure can also be called *US inflation* or *US deflation*. The preceding scenario is an example of US inflation. As an example of US deflation, imagine that you salivate profusely when you enter Joe's Restaurant because you love their turkey gumbo. You then get a new roommate, who, as it turns out, is a turkey gumbo fanatic and prepares turkey gumbo meals five times a week. Needless to say, so much turkey gumbo can become monotonous (an instance of long-term habituation), and you finally reach a point where you have little interest in turkey gumbo. As a result, when you next enter Joe's Restaurant, you salivate very little. The value of turkey gumbo has been markedly reduced in your eyes, which in turn affects your response to the restaurant that has been associated with it.

In everyday terms, it seems like what is happening in US revaluation is that the animal has learned to *expect* the US whenever it sees the CS; the intensity of its response is thus dependent on the animal's most recent experience with the US. This interpretation fits well with cognitive explanations of conditioning, as will be discussed in the next chapter. (You will also see that US revaluation can play a role in the development or exacerbation of phobias.)

QUICK QUIZ F

1. Suppose you suddenly developed a strong fear of dogs after being severely bitten. As a result, you are also anxious about in-line skating because, on several occasions in the past, you witnessed people walking their dogs on the in-line skating paths. This example illustrates the phenomenon of ________________.
2. In the above example, the in-line skating paths will probably elicit a (stronger/weaker) fear response than will the sight of the dogs.
3. Sensory preconditioning often works best when the two neutral stimuli are paired (relatively few/hundreds of) times in the preconditioning phase.
4. Unlike NS-US pairings in normal conditioning, NS-NS pairings in sensory preconditioning can produce stronger conditioning when the two stimuli are presented (sequentially/simultaneously).
5. The (US/CS) r__________ procedure involves the (preconditioning/postconditioning) presentation of the (CS/US) by itself at a different level of intensity than used in the original conditioning.
6. Nikki feels all excited when she sees her father arrive home each evening because he always brings her some licorice. One day her mother bought her licorice earlier in the day, and Nikki had no desire for licorice when evening came around. As a result, she was not as excited when her father came home that evening. In this example, her father is a (CS/US) through his association with licorice. Being satiated with licorice therefore reduced the value of the (CS/US) that typically followed her father's arrival home. As a result, her (CR/UR) of excitement on seeing her father was greatly reduced.

Four Examples of Specificity in Classical Conditioning

In the preceding section, we examined three ways in which the classical conditioning can be extended or strengthened even in the absence of a direct pairing between an NS (or CS) and a US. In this section, we discuss four procedures—overshadowing, blocking, occasion setting, and latent inhibition—that demonstrate that conditioning doesn't automatically occur simply because an NS and a US have been paired with each other; rather, conditioning often occurs to specific stimuli or in specific circumstances only. Two of these procedures (overshadowing and blocking) involve the presentation of what is known as a compound stimulus. A ***compound stimulus*** consists of the simultaneous presentation of two or more individual stimuli (e.g., the sound of a metronome is presented at the same time as a light).

Overshadowing

If you were stung by a wasp during a walk in the woods, would it make sense to develop a conditioned fear response to every stimulus associated with that event (e.g., the trees surrounding you, the butterfly fluttering by, and the cloud formation in the sky)? No, it would not. Rather, it would make more sense to develop a fear of those stimuli that were most salient (that really stood out) at the time of being stung, such as the sight of the wasp.

In ***overshadowing***, the more salient member of a compound stimulus is more readily conditioned as a CS and thereby interferes with conditioning of the less salient member. In the wasp example, you are likely to develop a conditioned fear response to the most distinctive stimuli associated with that event, such as the sight of the wasp and perhaps the buzzing sound it makes.

An experimental example of overshadowing might involve first pairing a compound stimulus, such as a bright light and a faint-sounding metronome, with food. After several pairings, the compound stimulus becomes a CS that elicits salivation. However, when each member of the compound is tested separately, the bright light elicits salivation while the faint metronome elicits little or no salivation (see Figure 4.6). In diagram form:

(**Step 1:** Conditioning of a compound stimulus as a CS. Note that the compound stimulus consists of the simultaneous presentation of the two bracketed stimuli.)

[Bright light + Faint metronome]: Food → *Salivation*
NS US UR

[Bright light + Faint metronome] → *Salivation*
CS CR

(**Step 2:** Presentation of each member of the compound separately)

Bright light → *Salivation*
CS CR

Faint metronome → No salivation
NS —

Due to the presence of the bright light during the conditioning trials, no conditioning occurred to the faint metronome. This is not because the faint metronome is unnoticeable. If it had been paired with the food by itself, it could easily have become an effective CS. Only in the presence of a more salient stimulus does the less salient stimulus come to elicit little or no response.

Head managers make use of the overshadowing effect when they assign an assistant to announce an unpopular decision. Although the employees might recognize that the head manager is mostly responsible, the assistant is the

FIGURE 4.6 In this example of overshadowing, a bright light and a faint-sounding metronome are simultaneously presented as a compound stimulus and paired with food. After several pairings, the compound stimulus becomes a CS that elicits salivation. However, when each member of the compound is tested separately, the bright light elicits salivation but the faint-sounding metronome does not. (*Source*: Nairne, 2000.)

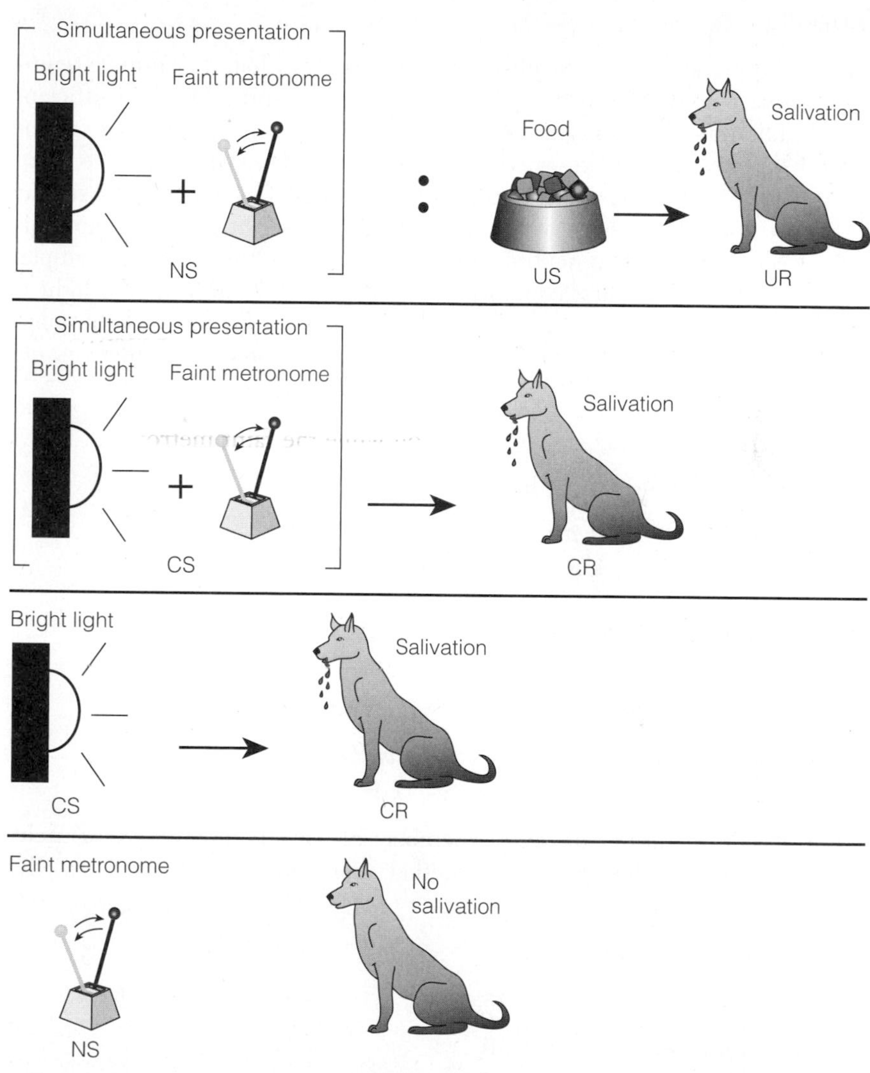

most salient stimulus and will, as a result, bear the brunt of the blame. It is thus the assistant who is likely to become most disliked by the employees. On the other hand, head managers often make a point of personally announcing popular decisions, thereby attracting most of the positive associations to themselves even if they have been only minimally involved in those decisions. Similarly, the positive feelings generated by the music of a rock band will be most strongly associated with the most salient member of that band (usually the lead singer)—a fact that often leads to problems when other band members conclude that they are not receiving their fair share of the accolades.

Blocking

The phenomenon of overshadowing demonstrates that, in some circumstances, mere contiguity between a neutral stimulus and a US is insufficient for conditioning to occur. An even clearer demonstration of this fact is provided by a phenomenon known as blocking. In ***blocking***, the presence of an established CS interferes with conditioning of a new CS. Blocking is similar to overshadowing, except that the compound consists of a neutral stimulus and a CS rather than two neutral stimuli that differ in salience. For example, suppose that a light is first conditioned as a CS for salivation. If the light is then combined with a metronome to form a compound, and this compound is then paired with food, little or no conditioning occurs to the metronome (see Figure 4.7).

In diagram form:

(**Step 1:** Conditioning of the light as a CS)

Light: Food → *Salivation*
NS US UR

Light → *Salivation*
CS CR

(**Step 2:** Several pairings of a compound stimulus with the US)

[Light + Metronome]: Food → *Salivation*
CS NS US UR

(**Step 3:** Presentation of each member of the compound separately. The question at this point is whether conditioning occurred to the metronome.)

Light → *Salivation*
CS CR

Metronome → No salivation
NS —

In step 2, the presence of the light blocked conditioning to the metronome. An everyday (but overly simplistic) way of thinking about what is happening here is that the light already predicts the food, so the dog pays attention only to the light. As a result, the metronome does not become an effective CS despite being paired with the food.

FIGURE 4.7 In this example of blocking, a light is first conditioned as a CS for salivation. When the light is then combined with a metronome to form a compound stimulus, and this compound stimulus is paired with food, the metronome does not become a conditioned stimulus. The presence of the already established CS blocks conditioning to the metronome. (*Source*: Nairne, 2000.)

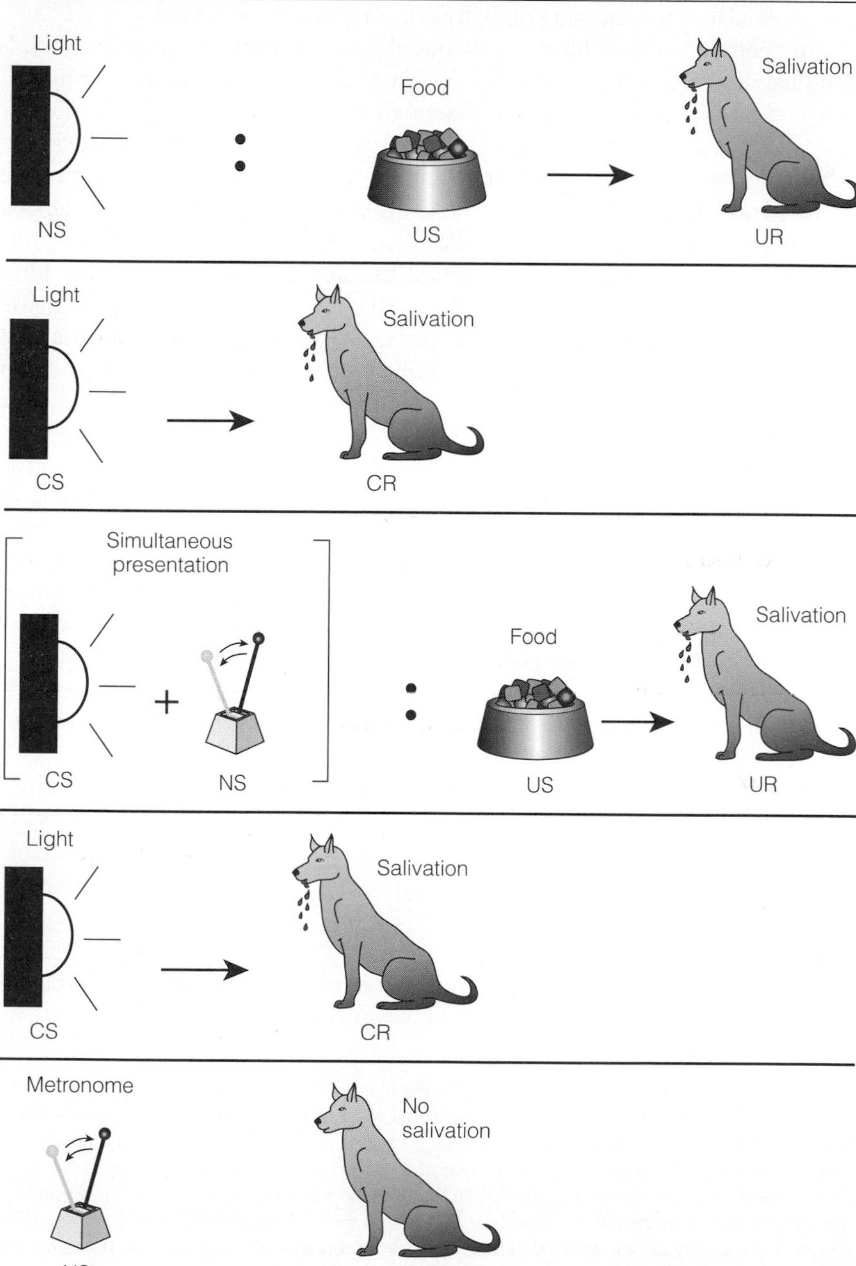

For a real-life example of the blocking effect, imagine that you have to make an unpopular announcement to your employees. The phenomenon of blocking suggests that you would do well to make it a joint announcement with another manager who is already disliked by the employees (one who is already an aversive CS). The employees might then attribute most or all of the bad news to the unpopular manager, and you will be left relatively unscathed.

The phenomenon of blocking garnered a lot of attention when it was first demonstrated (Kamin, 1969). It clearly indicates that mere contiguity between an NS and a US is insufficient to produce conditioning. Rather, it seems that a more crucial factor in conditioning is the extent to which the NS comes to act as a signal or predictor of the US. In more cognitive terms (Tolman would have loved blocking), the act of conditioning can be said to produce an "expectation" that a particular event is about to occur. When the light is conditioned as a CS, the dog comes to expect that food will follow the light. Later, when the metronome is presented at the same time as the light, the metronome provides no additional information about when food will occur; hence, no conditioning occurs to it. We will again encounter this notion of expectations when we discuss the Rescorla-Wagner theory of conditioning in Chapter 5.[2]

QUICK QUIZ G

1. A compound stimulus consists of the (simultaneous/successive) presentation of two or more separate stimuli.
2. In ___________ the most salient member of a compound stimulus is more readily conditioned as a CS and thereby interferes with conditioning of the less salient member. In ___________, the presence of an established CS within a compound interferes with conditioning of another stimulus.
3. In a(n) ___________ procedure, the compound stimulus consists of a neutral stimulus and a CS, whereas in a(n) ___________ procedure, the compound stimulus consists of two neutral stimuli that differ in salience or intensity.
4. Because Jez has a history of getting into trouble, he often catches most of the blame when something goes wrong, even when others are also responsible for what happened. This is most similar to the phenomenon of ___________.

Occasion Setting

As we have learned, classical conditioning involves establishment of an association between two events, such as between the sound of a metronome and

[2] A different way of thinking about this (again, popular with researchers who have a preference for cognitive interpretations of such matters) is that increases in conditioning can occur only to the extent that a US is unexpected or surprising. Once a US is fully expected, such as when a light by itself reliably predicts the occurrence of food, no further conditioning can occur. In more general terms, we learn the most about something when we are placed in a position of uncertainty and must then strive to reduce that uncertainty. Once the uncertainty has been eliminated, learning ceases to occur. Thus, in blocking, no conditioning (no new learning) occurs to the neutral stimulus, because the presence of the CS that it has been combined with ensures that the animal is not surprised when the US soon follows.

the taste of food or between the sight of a wasp and the feel of its sting. To date, however, we have largely ignored the fact that these two events do not exist in isolation but instead occur within a certain context. This context often comes to serve as an overall predictor of the relationship between these two events. Imagine, for example, that presentations of the metronome are followed by food, but only when a background light is on. When the background light is off, presentations of the metronome are not followed by food. The conditioning procedure would look something like this, with the presentation of light-on and light-off phases occurring in random order:

(Light on) Metronome: Food → *Salivation*
NS NS US UR

(Light off) Metronome: No food
— NS —

As a result, we are likely to find that the metronome elicits salivation only when the background light is on and not when it is off:

(Light on) Metronome → *Salivation*
OS CS CR

(Light off) Metronome: No salivation
— "NS" —

(where the abbreviation "OS" stands for occasion setter)

The background light in this instance is an *occasion setter* because it predicts the occasions on which the metronome is followed by food. It does not itself elicit salivation, but its presence controls the extent to which the metronome as a CS elicits salivation. Thus, ***occasion setting*** is a procedure in which a stimulus (an *occasion setter*) signals whether a CS is likely to be followed by a US and thereby controls whether the CS will elicit a CR.

An occasion setter can signal either the presentation of a US or its absence, or even a change in the intensity of the US. Imagine, for example, that an abused child receives his worst beatings from his parents whenever they are drinking alcohol. Thus:

(Alcohol absent) Parents: Mild abuse → *Mild anxiety*
(Alcohol present) Parents: Severe abuse → *Strong anxiety*

Although the child typically feels a mild amount of anxiety around his parents, the sight or smell of alcohol in the presence of his parents greatly increases his anxiety. Thus:

(Alcohol absent) Parents → *Mild anxiety*
(Alcohol present) Parents → *Strong anxiety*

The conditioned response of anxiety to the parents is intensified by the presence of alcohol. The alcohol is therefore an occasion setter that alters the child's level of anxiety in the presence of the parents.

Because the real world consists of a complex mixture of stimuli, occasion setting is an important factor in many instances of classical conditioning. Women are typically more anxious about being harassed while walking by a male worker at a construction site than while walking by a male worker in an office complex. And hikers are more anxious around bears with cubs than they are around bears without cubs. The additional stimuli present in these circumstances (construction site and bear cubs) indicate a higher probability of certain events (harassment and bear attack).

Latent Inhibition

Do we condition more readily to stimuli that are familiar or unfamiliar? You might think that familiar stimuli are more readily conditioned; if we already know something about a topic, it seems easier to learn more about it. In fact, in what is known as ***latent inhibition***, a familiar stimulus is more difficult to condition as a CS than is an unfamiliar (novel) stimulus.[3] Or, stated the other way around, *an unfamiliar stimulus is more readily conditioned as a CS than a familiar stimulus*. For example, if, on many occasions, a dog has heard the sound of a metronome prior to conditioning, then a standard number of conditioning trials might result in little or no conditioning to the metronome (see Figure 4.8). In diagram form:

(**Step 1:** Stimulus pre-exposure phase in which a metronome is repeatedly presented alone)

Metronome (40 presentations)
NS

(**Step 2:** Conditioning trials in which the pre-exposed metronome is now paired with food)

Metronome: Food → *Salivation* (10 trials)
NS US UR

(**Step 3:** Test trial to determine if conditioning has occurred to the metronome)

Metronome → No salivation
NS —

If the dog had not been pre-exposed to the metronome and it had been a novel stimulus when first paired with food, then the 10 conditioning trials would have resulted in significant conditioning to the metronome. Because of the pre-exposure, however, no conditioning occurred. It will take many more pairings of metronome and food before the metronome will reliably elicit salivation.

[3]Latent inhibition is also known as the *CS pre-exposure effect*. A related phenomenon, known as the *US pre-exposure effect*, holds that conditioning is slower with familiar, as opposed to unfamiliar, USs.

FIGURE 4.8 In latent inhibition, familiar stimuli are more difficult to condition as CSs than novel stimuli. If a dog has, on many occasions, heard the sound of a metronome prior to conditioning being implemented, then it will be difficult to obtain conditioning to the metronome using a standard number of conditioning trials. (*Source*: Nairne, 2000.)

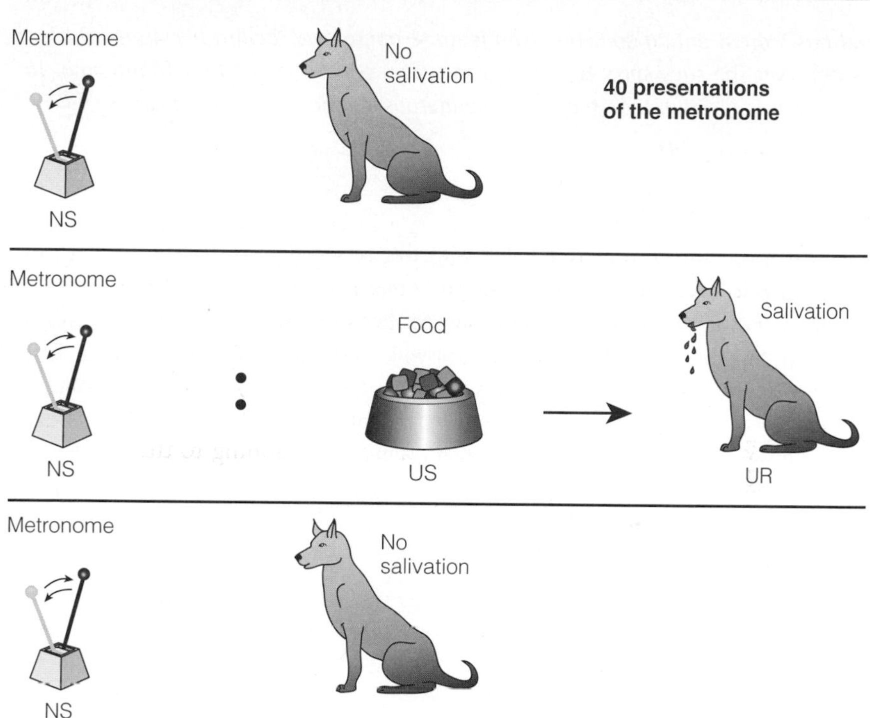

In the same way that habituation prevents the occurrence of unlearned reflexive responses to redundant stimuli (e.g., a startle response to a repeatedly occurring noise), latent inhibition prevents the development of conditioned responses to redundant stimuli that are coincidentally paired with a US. Such stimuli are likely to be inconsequential with respect to the conditioning event. For example, if a rabbit in a grassy field is attacked by a coyote and then escapes, it will be much more adaptive for the rabbit to associate the attack with the novel scent of the coyote than with the familiar scent of grass. The scent of the coyote is a good predictor of a possible attack, and a fear of that scent will help the rabbit avoid such attacks in the future. A fear of the grass, however, will be completely maladaptive because the rabbit is surrounded by grass day in and day out. It is the novel stimuli preceding the presentation of a US that are most likely to be meaningfully related to it.

Difficulties with latent inhibition (as well as habituation) are evident in people who have schizophrenia (Lubow & Gewirtz, 1995). These individuals often have great difficulty attending to relevant stimuli in their environment and are instead distracted by irrelevant stimuli, such as various background noises or

ADVICE FOR THE LOVELORN

Dear Dr. Dee,

My friend has started dating someone who is quite aggressive toward her. I am worried for her safety, yet she says she's known him for years and he is not that frightening. To the rest of us, it is obvious that the guy is dangerous. Is she blinded by love?

Deeply Concerned

Dear Deeply,

On the one hand, your friend is more familiar with this person than you are, so it may be that her judgment is indeed more accurate. On the other hand, her increased familiarity with him might also mean that it will take longer for her to become fearful of him. This is in keeping with the process of latent inhibition, in which we condition less readily to familiar stimuli than to unfamiliar stimuli. This is yet another factor that might contribute to people remaining in an abusive relationship even though the people around them clearly recognize the danger signals. So it may be that she is blinded by latent inhibition, not love.

Behaviorally yours,

people passing nearby. Experiments have revealed that people with schizophrenia display less latent inhibition than is normal—that is, they condition more easily to familiar stimuli—indicating that the disorder partly involves an inability to screen out redundant stimuli. Experiments have also revealed that drugs used to treat schizophrenia tend to increase levels of latent inhibition, thereby normalizing the person's attentional processes.

QUICK QUIZ H

1. In classical conditioning, o_____________ s_____________ is a procedure in which a stimulus signals whether a CS is likely to be followed by the _____________. This stimulus is called a(n) _____________ _____________.
2. In _____________ _____________, a familiar stimulus is more difficult to condition as a CS than is an unfamiliar stimulus.
3. Latent inhibition (prevents/promotes) the development of conditioned associations to redundant stimuli.
4. Being afraid of a stranger in a dark alley, as opposed to on a crowded street, is an example of _____________ _____________; not being afraid of guns (even though you accidentally shot yourself in the foot) because you're a long-time gun owner is an example of _____________ _____________

Warning

In this chapter, you have been exposed to several conditioning procedures, some of which are quite similar (such as overshadowing and blocking). Be sure to *overlearn* these procedures, as students often confuse them, especially under the stress of an examination.

SUMMARY

In general, early conditioning trials produce more rapid acquisition of conditioning than do later trials. Weakening a conditioned response by repeatedly presenting the CS by itself is known as extinction. Spontaneous recovery is the reappearance of a previously extinguished response after a rest period, and disinhibition is the sudden recovery of an extinguished response following introduction of a novel stimulus.

In stimulus generalization, we learn to respond similarly to stimuli that resemble a CS. One version of stimulus generalization, known as semantic generalization, involves generalization of a response to verbal stimuli that are similar in meaning to the CS. In stimulus discrimination, we respond to one stimulus more than another, a process that is established through discrimination training. Pavlov discovered that dogs that were exposed to a difficult discrimination problem often suffered from nervous breakdowns, a phenomenon that he called experimental neurosis.

In higher-order conditioning, a previously conditioned stimulus (CS_1) is used to condition a new stimulus (CS_2). The CS_2 elicits a weaker response than the CS_1 because there is only an indirect association between the CS_2 and the US. In sensory preconditioning, when one stimulus is conditioned as a CS, another stimulus with which it was previously associated also becomes a CS. US revaluation involves exposure to a stronger or weaker US following conditioning, which then alters the strength of response to the CS.

Certain situations can also interfere with the process of conditioning. For example, overshadowing occurs when the most salient member of a compound stimulus is more readily conditioned as a CS and thereby interferes with the conditioning of a less salient member. Blocking occurs when the presence of an established CS during conditioning interferes with conditioning of a new CS. With occasion setting, an additional stimulus (an occasion setter) indicates whether a CS will be followed by a US; the CS therefore elicits a CR only in the presence of the occasion setter. Familiar stimuli are more difficult to condition than unfamiliar stimuli, a phenomenon known as latent inhibition.

SUGGESTED READINGS

Eysenck, H. J. (1967). *The biological basis of personality*. Springfield, IL: Charles C Thomas. Indicates the extent to which Pavlov's work influenced Eysenck's theory of personality and, hence, many other theories of personality.

Lieberman, D. A. (2000). *Learning: Behavior and cognition* (3rd ed.). Belmont, CA: Wadsworth. For students who may find it helpful to read alternative descriptions of these various classical conditioning phenomena.

STUDY QUESTIONS

1. Draw a graph of a typical acquisition curve (remember to properly label each axis), and indicate the asymptote of conditioning.
2. Define the processes of extinction and spontaneous recovery. What typically happens to spontaneous recovery with repeated sessions of extinction?
3. Define disinhibition and give an example. How does disinhibition differ from dishabituation (as covered in Chapter 3)?
4. Describe stimulus generalization and semantic generalization. Give an example of each for a fear conditioning procedure in which the spoken word "rat" was paired with shock, and the stimulus later being presented is the spoken word of either "mouse" or "hat."
5. Describe stimulus discrimination and give an example. Diagram an example of a discrimination training procedure. (When asked to diagram a conditioning procedure like this, be sure to label each component with the appropriate abbreviations, e.g., CS, US, etc.)
6. Define experimental neurosis, and describe Shenger-Krestovnikova's procedure for producing it.
7. Define higher-order conditioning and sensory preconditioning. Note how they are both similar to and different from each other. Diagram an example of each.
8. Define and diagram an example of US revaluation.
9. Define overshadowing and blocking. Note how they are both similar to and different from each other. Diagram an example of each.
10. Define occasion setting and latent inhibition. Diagram an example of each.

CONCEPT REVIEW

acquisition. The process of developing and strengthening a conditioned response through repeated pairings of an NS (or CS) with a US.

blocking. The phenomenon whereby the presence of an established CS interferes with conditioning of a new CS.

compound stimulus. A complex stimulus that consists of the simultaneous presentation of two or more individual stimuli.

disinhibition. The sudden recovery of a conditioned response during an extinction procedure when a novel stimulus is introduced.

experimental neurosis. An experimentally produced disorder in which animals exposed to unpredictable events develop neurotic-like symptoms.

extinction. The process whereby a conditioned response can be weakened or eliminated when the CS is repeatedly presented in the absence of the US; also, the procedure whereby this happens, namely, the repeated presentation of the CS in the absence of the US.

higher-order conditioning. The process whereby a neutral stimulus that is associated with a CS (rather than a US) also becomes a CS.

latent inhibition. The phenomenon whereby a familiar stimulus is more difficult to condition as a CS than is an unfamiliar (novel) stimulus.

occasion setting. A procedure in which a stimulus (known as an occasion setter) signals whether a CS is likely to be followed by a US and thereby controls whether the CS will elicit a CR.

overshadowing. The phenomenon whereby the more salient member of a compound stimulus is more readily conditioned as a CS and thereby interferes with conditioning of the less salient member.

semantic generalization. The generalization of a conditioned response to verbal stimuli that are similar in meaning to the CS.

sensory preconditioning. When one stimulus is conditioned as a CS, another stimulus with which it was previously associated can also become a CS.

spontaneous recovery. The reappearance of a conditioned response to a CS following a rest period after extinction.

stimulus discrimination. The tendency for a response to be elicited more by one stimulus than another.

stimulus generalization. The tendency for a CR to occur in the presence of a stimulus that is similar to the CS.

US revaluation. A process that involves the postconditioning presentation of the US at a different level of intensity, thereby altering the strength of response to the previously conditioned CS.

CHAPTER TEST

12. In higher-order conditioning, the CS_2 generally elicits a (stronger/weaker) response than does the CS_1.
5. The fact that you learned to fear wasps and hornets, as well as bees, after being stung by a bee is an example of stimulus ______. On the other hand, if you fear only poisonous snakes and not nonpoisonous snakes, that would be an example of stimulus ______.
8. Pavlov regarded spontaneous recovery and disinhibition as evidence that extinction involves the (unlearning/inhibition) of the learned response.

18. While playing tennis one day, you suffer a minor ankle sprain. Two weeks later you severely twist your ankle while stepping off a curb. You now find yourself very worried about playing tennis. This is an example of ________.
23. According to Eysenck, psychopaths tend to be extreme (extroverts/introverts) who condition (easily/poorly).
20. Midori feels anxious whenever the manager walks into the store accompanied by the owner because the manager always finds fault with the employees when the owner is there. This is best seen as an example of ________ with the owner functioning as the ________.
14. Two examples of specificity in conditioning, known as ________ and ________, involve pairing a compound stimulus with a US. They both provide evidence that contiguity between the NS and the US (is/is not) a sufficient factor in conditioning.
2. Following an experience in which you were stung by a bee and subsequently developed a fear of bees, you are hired for a 1-day job in which your task is to catch bees for a biologist. During the day, you never once get stung by a bee. As a result, your fear of bees will likely (decrease/increase), a process known as ________.
10. The researcher feels that you have done such a fine job catching bees that she hires you for another day. At the start of the next day, you will likely find that your fear of bees has (completely disappeared/partially returned), a phenomenon known as ________.
22. By the end of the second day, your fear of bees has mostly disappeared. However, you then hear thunder in the distance and become a bit worried about whether you should immediately head back to the lab. You decide first to catch one more bee, but find that your fear of bees is now somewhat stronger. The sudden recovery of your fear response to bees is an example of a process known as ________.
15. Marty once played in an all-star game alongside Bobby Orr (a famous and talented hockey player). Marty scored two goals and an assist, as did Orr. Orr was later voted the game's most valuable player, while Marty's name was barely mentioned. This situation seems analogous to the ________ effect in classical conditioning.
25. Remember the cartoon of Pavlov learning to salivate to the bell after watching the dogs being trained to salivate to the sound of a bell? This situation might have arisen during conditioning if the dogs were being fed bites of juicy steak, the sight of a steak being for many people a (CS_1/CS_2) for salivation. The bell would then become a (CS_1/CS_2) through its association with the sight of the steak. Thus, of the three types of extensions to classical conditioning, this is most similar to the process of ________.
19. If one thinks of a conditioned stimulus as being a particularly salient stimulus, then a blocking procedure is very similar to a(n) ________ procedure.

3. Consider the following example in which the sight of different people comes to elicit feelings of anger:

   (Step 1)
   Seeing John: John's rude behavior → *Anger toward John*
   Seeing John → *Anger toward John*
   (Step 2)
   Seeing Amir: Seeing John → *Anger toward John*
   Seeing Amir → *Anger toward Amir*
   This is an example of ____________ conditioning.

11. In higher-order conditioning, conditioning of the CS_1 is sometimes called ____________ conditioning, and conditioning of the CS_2 is called ____________ conditioning.

6. The *procedure* of extinction involves the ____________; while the *process* of extinction involves the ____________.

24. The gradual strengthening of a classically conditioned fear response by repeated pairings of a tone with a shock is an example of the process of ____________. During this process, the early pairings of tone and shock are likely to produce (larger/smaller) increments in conditioning than the later pairings.

1. The maximum amount of conditioning that can take place in a particular situation is known as the ____________ of conditioning.

9. Consider the following example in which feelings of tension toward your former friend, Yoshi, are also elicited by a restaurant where you often used to meet up with him:

   (Step 1: Repeated experiences in restaurant)
   Restaurant: Yoshi
   (Step 2: Not in restaurant)
   Yoshi: Argument → *Tension*
   Yoshi → *Tension*
   (Step 3)
   Restaurant → *Tension*
   This process is best interpreted as an example of ____________.

4. Based partially on Pavlov's work on experimental neurosis, Eysenck concluded that people who are ____________ tend to be highly reactive to external stimulation, condition easily, and develop anxiety-type symptoms in reaction to stress. By contrast, people who are ____________ tend to be less reactive, condition less easily, and develop physical-type symptoms in reaction to stress.

17. You once played in an all-star game alongside Antonio, an unknown basketball player just like you. Antonio, however, is a very tall and noticeable player on the court. Although you both played equally well,

almost all the credit for the win went to Antonio, which seems analogous to the overshadowing effect in classical conditioning.

13. If the scent of ammonia and the ticking of a clock are combined to form a compound stimulus, then the two stimuli are being presented (simultaneously/successively).
21. Rasheed had never experienced a more difficult multiple-choice test. Virtually every alternative for every question looked equally correct. By the end of the exam, he felt extremely anxious. Rasheed's experience is somewhat analogous to a phenomenon discovered by Pavlov's associates, which they called experimental neurosis
16. A student has great difficulty ignoring irrelevant material sometimes mentioned in class and is easily distracted. This student might also display (stronger/weaker) evidence of latent inhibition compared to the average student.
7. A person who fears dogs also feels anxious when he hears the word canine. This is an example of semantic generalization.

ANSWERS TO CHAPTER TEST

1. asymptote
2. decrease; extinction
3. higher-order
4. introverts; extroverts
5. generalization; discrimination
6. repeated presentations of the CS without the US; resultant decrease in the strength of the conditioned response
7. semantic generalization
8. inhibition
9. sensory preconditioning
10. partially returned; spontaneous recovery
11. first-order; second-order
12. weaker
13. simultaneously
14. blocking; overshadowing; is not
15. blocking (with Orr being analogous to an established CS)
16. weaker; latent
17. Antonio; overshadowing
18. US revaluation (or US inflation)
19. overshadowing
20. occasion setting; occasion setter
21. experimental neurosis
22. disinhibition
23. extroverts; poorly
24. acquisition; larger
25. CS_1; CS_2; higher-order conditioning

CHAPTER 5

CLASSICAL CONDITIONING: UNDERLYING PROCESSES AND PRACTICAL APPLICATIONS

CHAPTER OUTLINE

Estella thought Juan looked a bit tipsy as he left the picnic to drive home. She wondered if she should tell him that the supposedly nonalcoholic punch he had been drinking was actually spiked with vodka. On the other hand, he had only had a single glass. Surely, he couldn't be drunk.

Underlying Processes in Classical Conditioning

By now, you probably realize that classical conditioning is not as simple a process as it first seems. It is a complex phenomenon that is only slowly yielding its secrets to researchers. The following sections discuss major theoretical notions concerning the underlying processes of classical conditioning. You will then learn how some of these theories have resulted in findings of practical importance.

Stimulus-Substitution Theory

We begin with Pavlov (1927) who viewed classical conditioning as largely a matter of replacing one stimulus with another. Thus, according to Pavlov's ***stimulus-substitution theory***, the CS acts as a substitute for the US. For example, pairing a tone with food results in the tone becoming a substitute for the food, the outcome of which is that the tone can now elicit salivation. And pairing the sound of a click with an air puff to the eye results in the click becoming a substitute for the air puff, the outcome of which is that the click can now elicit an eyeblink.

Pavlov was a physiologist who believed that classical conditioning was an indirect way of studying neurological processes in the brain. Thus, he often made inferences about the kinds of neurological processes that are activated during conditioning. He claimed that presentation of a US, such as food, activates an area of the cerebral cortex (the outermost layer of the brain) that is responsible for sensing the occurrence of that event. Activation of this "food center" in the brain in turn activates another part of the cortex (the "salivation center") that produces the unconditioned response of salivation.

Food → *Activates food center in cortex* → *Activates salivation center in cortex* → ***Salivation***

Pavlov also believed that the presentation of a neutral stimulus, such as a light, activates another area of the cortex responsible for detecting that type of stimulus. According to Pavlov, when the light is presented just before the food, a connection is formed between the area of the cortex activated by the light and the area activated by the food. As a result, activation of the light center of the cortex also activates the food center of the cortex, which in turn produces salivation. In other words, Pavlov believed that the presentation of the light set in motion the following sequence of events:

Light → *Activates light center in cortex* → *Activates food center in cortex* → *Activates salivation center in cortex* → ***Salivation***

Pavlov's notions about the kinds of neurological processes underlying classical conditioning are now considered to be incorrect. The actual processes involved are known to be considerably more complex than he presumed. Nevertheless, this does not negate all aspects of Pavlov's theory. For example, consider the notion that the conditioned stimulus (CS) is somehow a direct substitute for the US. In at least some cases, it seems as though animals do react to the CS as if it were the US. The dog salivates to the light just as it does to food. More importantly, the dog may even approach the light and start to lick it, as though pairing the light with the food resulted in the light being perceived as edible (Pavlov, 1941). This sort of phenomenon, now known as sign tracking, is discussed more fully in Chapter 12.

A particular difficulty for stimulus-substitution theory is that if the CS is acting as a substitute for the US, then the CR should always be the same, or at least highly similar, to the UR. Although this is often the case, it sometimes is not the case; in fact, there are sometimes substantial differences between the CR and the UR. For example, a rat that receives a foot shock (the US) will probably jump (the UR). However, if it sees a light (CS) that has been paired with a foot shock, it will often freeze (the CR). Why would the rat jump in one instance and freeze in the other? An examination of the rat's natural response to danger gives us a clue. If a rat is attacked by a snake, jumping straight up (and rats can really jump!) may cause the snake to miss. On the other hand, if a rat detects a snake in the vicinity, tensing its muscles and freezing will minimize the possibility of being detected or, if the rat is attacked, will enable it to jump quickly. This suggests that the purpose of the CR, rather than merely being a version of the UR, is to ready the organism for the occurrence of the US—which brings us to our next theory of conditioning.

Preparatory-Response Theory (and the Compensatory-Response Model)

According to the ***preparatory-response theory*** of conditioning, the purpose of the CR is to prepare the organism for the presentation of the US (Kimble, 1961, 1967). The dog salivates to the tone to get ready for food, and the rat freezes in response to the light to get ready for the shock. Note that in one case, the preparatory response is quite similar to the UR, whereas in the other case it is quite different. Thus, unlike stimulus-substitution theory, preparatory-response theory allows for situations in which the CR and the UR are sometimes different.

An interesting example of conditioned preparatory-responses involves cases in which the CR seems to be the exact opposite of the original UR.

This often occurs with drug reactions, so we will illustrate it using the example of heroin. Imagine that an addict always injects heroin in the presence of certain environmental cues, such as in a particular room. Heroin has several effects on the body, but we will focus on just one of them for now, which is a decrease in blood pressure. Thus, regularly shooting up with heroin in a particular setting involves the following sequence of events:

Heroin-related cues: **Heroin** → ***Decreased blood pressure***
NS **US** **UR**

If this was a normal conditioning procedure, one might expect that the heroin-related cues will eventually become a CS that will itself elicit a decrease in blood pressure. But in reality, the opposite occurs. With repeated drug use, the presence of the heroin-related cues elicits not a decrease in blood pressure, but an increase in blood pressure!

Heroin-related cues → ***Increased blood pressure***
CS **CR**

How can this be? Remember the opponent-process theory of emotion that we learned about in Chapter 3. Recall how certain stimuli can elicit both a primary response (the a-process) and a compensatory response (the b-process). Thus, according to the ***compensatory-response model***, a CS that has been repeatedly associated with the primary response (a-process) to a US will eventually come to elicit a compensatory response (b-process).

To help clarify this, let us examine the heroin example in more detail. Repeatedly injecting heroin does not simply elicit a response, but instead sets in motion a chain of events. The heroin directly elicits an immediate decrease in blood pressure (the a-process) that in turn elicits a compensatory increase in blood pressure (the b-process).

Heroin → *Decreased blood pressure* → *Increased blood pressure*
(a-process) *(b-process)*

In terms of stimuli and responses, the heroin is a US that naturally elicits a decrease in blood pressure, and the decrease in blood pressure is itself a US that naturally elicits an increase in blood pressure. Therefore, the decrease in blood pressure is both an unconditioned response (UR) to heroin and an unconditioned stimulus (US) that elicits a compensatory increase in blood pressure.

Heroin → *Decreased blood pressure* → *Increased blood pressure*
US *UR/US* *UR*

Notice that there are two USs in this sequence that the cues in the environment could potentially become associated with: the heroin and the decrease in blood pressure that results from the heroin.

What happens in compensatory conditioning is that the heroin-related cues, such as being in a certain room, become associated not with the heroin but with the primary response to heroin—that is, with the decrease in blood pressure. As a result, these cues eventually come to elicit the compensatory reaction to that response. So the actual conditioning that takes place with heroin is as follows:

Heroin-related cues: Decreased blood pressure → *Increased blood pressure*
NS US UR

Heroin-related cues → *Increased blood pressure*
CS CR

Why would this type of compensatory conditioning occur? Remember how, in the opponent-process theory, the compensatory reactions to a US serve to maintain a state of homeostasis (internal balance). If these compensatory reactions start occurring before the US is presented, they will be even more effective in minimizing the disturbance produced by the US. For example, if the compensatory reaction to the heroin (an increase in blood pressure) can be elicited just before the injection of heroin, then the immediate physical reaction to the heroin (the decrease in blood pressure) will be effectively moderated. In this sense, a conditioned compensatory response allows the body to prepare itself *ahead of time* for the onslaught of the drug. Conditioned compensatory responses therefore constitute an extreme form of preparatory response to certain environmental events.

QUICK QUIZ A

1. According to ________-________ theory, the CS acts as a substitute for the US. According to this theory, the CR and UR should always be the same or at least highly similar. As it turns out, this is (true/false).
2. According to ________-________ theory, the purpose of the CR is to prepare the organism for the occurrence of the US.
3. According to the ________-________ model of drug conditioning, a CS that has been paired with a drug will eventually come to elicit a c________ reaction to the drug.
4. More precisely, the CS has become associated with the (a-process/b-process) being elicited by the drug and the CS therefore eventually comes to elicit the (a-process/b-process) that was originally elicited by the (a-process/b-process).
5. Diagram the actual events involved in the conditioning of an increase in blood pressure in response to a hypodermic needle that has been consistently associated with heroin administration (hint: the US in this conditioning is not heroin):

   Needle: ________ → ________
   NS US UR

   Needle → ________
   CS CR

6. Shock naturally elicits an increase in heart rate. In this case, shock is the (NS/CS/US) and the increase in heart rate is the (CR/UR).

7. Following from the above, an increase in heart rate naturally elicits a compensatory decrease in heart rate. For this sequence of events, the increase in heart rate is the (NS/CS/US) and the decrease in heart rate is the (CR/UR).
8. Following from the above, a tone that is repeatedly paired with shock will eventually come to elicit a compensatory decrease in heart rate. Diagram the actual events involved in this type of conditioning (pay particular attention to what the US actually consists of).

Tone: shock/increase bp → decrease bp
NS US UR

Tone → decrease bp
CS CR

The compensatory-response model obviously has important implications for *drug addiction*. Drug addictions are partly motivated by a tendency to avoid the symptoms of withdrawal, which are essentially the compensatory responses to the effect of the drug. For example, heroin produces a decrease in blood pressure as well as a combination of other effects, which the drug user experiences as pleasant feelings of relaxation and euphoria. This relaxing effect of heroin in turn elicits compensatory reactions that, on their own, would be experienced as unpleasant feelings of agitation. Repeated heroin use therefore results in the following process of conditioning:

Heroin-related cues: Relaxation effect (from heroin) → ***Compensatory agitation***
NS US UR

Heroin-related cues → ***Compensatory agitation***
CS CR

Thus, an addict will, after repeated heroin use, begin to experience unpleasant feelings of agitation simply by being in the presence of cues associated with heroin use. These symptoms are what the addict perceives as cravings or symptoms of withdrawal.

The presence of drug-related cues is one of the strongest reasons why people continue to battle cravings long after they have stopped using a drug. Think of an individual who always uses heroin in a particular environment, goes into a rehab program, and then returns home to her usual environment. When she returns to the environment in which she had previously used heroin, she will very likely become tense and agitated, which she will interpret as withdrawal symptoms and a craving for heroin. And to escape from these symptoms, she will be sorely tempted to once more take heroin.

To the extent that withdrawal symptoms are elicited by cues associated with drug use, then removing those cues should weaken the withdrawal symptoms and make it easier to remain abstinent. This possibility is supported by anecdotal evidence. Many American soldiers became heroin users during their tour of duty in Vietnam, leading to fears that they would remain addicted when they returned home. These fears, however, did not materialize (Robins, 1974). One explanation for this is that the drastic change in environment when the soldiers returned home removed many of the cues associated with heroin use, thereby alleviating the symptoms of withdrawal and making it easier for them to remain heroin free.

Unfortunately, for many people trying to kick a habit, whether it is alcohol, cigarettes, or heroin, it is often not possible to completely avoid all cues associated with the drug. For this reason, modern treatments for drug addiction often include procedures designed to extinguish the power of drug-related cues. For example, someone attempting to quit smoking may be required to remain in the presence of cigarettes for a long period of time without smoking. Repeated presentations of the CS (the sight of the cigarettes) in the absence of the US (nicotine ingestion) should result in weaker and weaker CRs (cravings for a smoke). Of course, this process can initially be very difficult—and in the case of severe alcoholism, even dangerous due to the severity of withdrawal symptoms. It therefore requires careful management, but once accomplished it can significantly reduce the possibility of a relapse. (See also Sokolowska, Siegel, & Kim, 2002, for a discussion of how some CSs can be internal, such as feelings of stress that lead to smoking, and how the effect of these internal cues may also need to be extinguished.)

The compensatory-response model also has implications for *drug tolerance* (Siegel, 1983, 2005). For example, if you have a habit of always drinking in a particular setting, then the various cues in that setting—people greeting you as you walk in the front door of the bar; the stool you always sit on—become CSs for the effect of alcohol. The presence of these CSs will initiate physiological reactions that compensate for the alcohol you are about to consume. As a result, in the presence of these CSs, you should have greater tolerance for alcohol than you would in their absence.

Research has confirmed this association. In a study by McCusker and Brown (1990), participants consumed alcohol in either an "alcohol expected" environment (i.e., alcohol was consumed in a simulated lounge during the evening with pub noises playing in the background) or an "alcohol unexpected" environment (i.e., alcohol was consumed during the day in an office environment). Those who consumed alcohol in the expected environment performed significantly better on various measures of cognitive and motor functioning compared to those who consumed alcohol in the unexpected environment. They also showed smaller increases in pulse rate. This suggests that the alcohol-related cues in the expected condition (evening, lounge setting) elicited compensatory reactions that partially compensated for the effects of the alcohol (see also Bennett & Samson, 1991).

On the other side of the coin, this also means that if you consume alcohol in an environment where you typically do not drink (e.g., a business luncheon), the alcohol could have a much stronger effect on you than if you consumed it in an environment where you typically do drink (e.g., a bar). This means that your ability to drive safely could be significantly more impaired following a lunchtime martini than after an evening drink at a bar. Worse yet, even if you do consume the drink at a bar, consider what happens when you leave that setting. Your compensatory reactions might be significantly reduced because you have now removed yourself from the alcohol-related cues that elicit those reactions. As a result, you may become more intoxicated during the drive home from the bar than you were in the bar (Linnoila, Stapleton, Lister, Guthrie, & Eckhardt, 1986). This means that the amount of alcohol you consume is not, by itself, a reliable gauge for determining how intoxicated you are. (Thus, going back to the opening vignette for this chapter, why should Estella be concerned about Juan's ability to drive?)[1]

It should be noted that there are exceptions to the typical compensatory reactions to a CS. Stimuli associated with drug use sometimes elicit drug-like reactions rather than drug-compensatory reactions. In other words, the stimuli become associated with the primary response to the drug rather than the compensatory response. For example, in one study, rats became more sensitive to cocaine when it was administered in the usual cocaine administration environment than in a different one (Hinson & Poulos, 1981). The CSs for cocaine administration apparently elicited reactions that mimicked the drug, thereby strengthening its effect. There is also evidence that stimuli associated with drug use sometimes elicit both drug compensatory responses in one system of the body and drug-like responses in another. For example, a cup of decaffeinated coffee (which, appearing as coffee, is normally a cue for caffeine consumption) can produce a caffeine-like increase in alertness and a caffeine-compensatory decrease in salivation (Rozen, Reff, Mark, & Schull, 1984; see also Eikelboom & Stewart, 1982; Lang, Ross, & Glover, 1967). Thus, the circumstances in which conditioning results in drug-like reactions versus drug-compensatory reactions are complex and not entirely understood (Siegel, 1989). (See also "Conditioned Compensatory Responses and Drug Overdose" in the And Furthermore box.)

And Furthermore

Conditioned Compensatory Responses and Drug Overdose

The compensatory-response model has also been used to explain incidents of *drug overdose*. Many "overdose" fatalities do not, in fact, involve an unusually large amount of the drug. For example, heroin addicts often die after injecting a dosage that has been well tolerated on previous occasions. A critical factor appears to be the setting within which the drug is administered. As we have seen, if a heroin addict typically administers the drug in the presence of certain cues, those cues become CSs that elicit compensatory reactions to the drug. An addict's tolerance to heroin therefore is much greater in the

[1]The type of alcohol consumed can also have an effect. People become significantly more intoxicated following consumption of an unusual drink (such as a strange liqueur) rather than a familiar drink (such as beer). The familiar drink can be seen as a CS for alcohol that elicits compensatory reactions to the alcohol (Remington, Roberts, & Glautier, 1997).

presence of those cues than in their absence. Anecdotal evidence supports this possibility. Siegel (1984) interviewed 10 survivors of heroin overdose, 7 of whom reported that the overdose had been preceded by an unusual change in the setting or drug administration procedure. For example, one woman reported that she overdosed after hitting a vein on the first try at injecting the drug, whereas she usually required several tries. Further evidence comes from studies with rats that had become addicted to heroin. When the cues usually associated with heroin were absent, the rats' ability to tolerate a large dose was markedly reduced to the point that many of the rats died. Thus, heroin-tolerant rats who were administered a very strong dose of heroin in a novel setting were more likely to die than those who received the dose in the setting previously associated with the drug (Siegel, Hinson, Krank, & McCully, 1982).

Siegel (1989) describes additional cases that illustrate the dangers of drug overdose resulting from conditioning effects. For example:

> The respondent (E. C.) was a heavy user of heroin for three years. She usually self-administered her first, daily dose of heroin in the bathroom of her apartment, where she lived with her mother. Typically, E. C. would awake earlier than her mother, turn on the water in the bathroom (pretending to take a shower), and self-inject without arousing suspicion. However, on the occasion of the overdose, her mother was already awake when E. C. started her injection ritual, and knocked loudly on the bathroom door telling E. C. to hurry. When E. C. then injected the heroin, she immediately found that she could not breathe. She was unable to call her mother for help (her mother eventually broke down the bathroom door and rushed E. C. to the hospital, where she was successfully treated for heroin overdose). (pp. 155–156)

Siegel goes on to explain that the mother knocking on the bathroom door was an unusual cue that may have disrupted the environmental CSs that would normally have elicited compensatory reactions to the heroin.

QUICK QUIZ B

1. According to the compensatory-response model of drug addiction, symptoms of withdrawal are likely to be (stronger/weaker) in the presence of drug-related cues. This is because the drug-related cues tend to elicit (primary/compensatory) responses to the drug that are experienced as cravings.
2. In keeping with the compensatory-response model, modern treatments for drug addiction often recommend (exposure to/removal of) drug-related cues to allow (conditioning/extinction) of the cravings to take place.
3. We tend to have (higher/lower) tolerance for a drug in the presence of cues associated with taking the drug.
4. Suppose an addict always injects heroin in her bedroom at home, but one time stays overnight at a friend's house and decides to take an injection there. The addict will likely experience a(n) (increased/decreased) reaction to the drug at her friend's house.
5. A person who drinks a glass of wine in a fine restaurant is likely to be (more/less) affected by the alcohol than if she drank the same amount of wine in a courtroom.

Rescorla-Wagner Theory

One of the most influential theories of classical conditioning was proposed by Rescorla and Wagner (1972). Their theory attempted to explain the effect of each conditioning trial on the strength, or what might be called the "associative value," of the CS in its relationship to the US. The ***Rescorla-Wagner theory*** proposes that a given US can support only so much conditioning, and this amount of conditioning must be distributed among the various CSs that are present. Another way of saying this is that there is only so much associative value available to be distributed among the cues associated with the US.

One assumption of this theory is that *stronger stimuli (USs and CSs) support more conditioning than do weaker stimuli.* For example, the use of a highly preferred food as the US produces a stronger conditioned response of salivation than does a less preferred food. Imagine, for example, that a tone paired with a highly preferred food (say, steak) elicits a maximum of 10 drops of saliva, while a tone paired with a much less preferred food (say, dog food) elicits only 5 drops of saliva. If we regard each drop of saliva as a unit of associative value, then we could say that the highly preferred food supports a maximum associative value of 10 units, while the less preferred food supports a maximum associative value of 5 units.

We can use the following format to diagram the changes in associative value (we will assume the highly preferred food is the US):

Tone (V = 0): **Food** (*Max* = 10) → ***Salivation***
Tone (V = 10) → ***Salivation***

The letter V will stand for the associative value of the CS (which at the start of conditioning is 0). The term *Max* will stand for the maximum associative value that can be supported by the US once conditioning is complete. In our example, imagine V as the number of drops of saliva the tone elicits—0 drops of saliva to begin with and 10 drops once the tone is fully associated with the food—and *Max* as the maximum number of drops of saliva that the tone can potentially elicit if it is fully associated with the food. (If this is starting to look a bit mathematical to you, you are correct. In fact, the model can be expressed in the form of an equation. For our purposes, however, the equation is unnecessary.)[2]

Now suppose that a compound stimulus consisting of a tone and a light are repeatedly paired with the food, to the point that the compound stimulus obtains the maximum associative value.

[Tone + Light] (V = 0): **Food** (*Max* = 10) → ***Salivation***
[Tone + Light] (V = 10) → ***Salivation***

---

[2]The equation for the Rescorla-Wagner model is $\Delta V = k(\lambda - V)$, where V is the associative value of the CS, λ ("lambda") represents the maximum associative value that the CS can hold (i.e., the asymptote of learning), and k is a constant that represents the salience of the CS and US (with greater salience supporting more conditioning). For more information on the use of this equation, see Domjan (2015).

This associative value, however, must somehow be distributed between the two component members of the compound. For example, if the tone is a bit more salient than the light, then the tone might have picked up 6 units of associative value while the light picked up only 4 units. In other words, when tested separately, the tone elicits 6 drops of saliva while the light elicits 4.

Tone (V = 6) → ***Salivation***
Light (V = 4) → ***Salivation***

If the tone was even more salient than the light—for example, it was a very loud tone and a very faint light—then *overshadowing* might occur, with the tone picking up 9 units of associative value and the light only 1 unit:

[Loud tone + Faint light] (V = 0): Food (*Max* = 10) → ***Salivation***
Loud tone (V = 9) → ***Salivation***
Faint light (V = 1) → ***Salivation***

The loud tone now elicits 9 drops of saliva (a strong CR) while the faint light elicits only 1 drop of saliva (a weak CR). Thus, the Rescorla-Wagner explanation for the overshadowing effect is that there is only so much associative value available (if you will, only so much spit available) for conditioning, and if the stronger stimulus in the compound picks up most or all of the associative value, then there is little or no associative value left over for the weaker stimulus.

As can be seen, the Rescorla-Wagner theory readily explains conditioning situations involving compound stimuli. Take, for example, a *blocking* procedure. One stimulus is first conditioned to its maximum associative value:

Tone (V = 0): **Food** (*Max* = 10) → ***Salivation***
Tone (V = 10) → ***Salivation***

This stimulus is then combined with another stimulus for further conditioning trials:

[Tone + Light] (V = 10 + 0 = 10): **Food** (*Max* = 10) → ***Salivation***

But note that the food supports a maximum associative value of only 10 units, and the tone has already acquired that much value. The light can therefore acquire no associative value because all of the associative value has already been assigned to the tone. Thus, when the two stimuli are later tested for conditioning, the following occurs:

Tone (V = 10) → ***Salivation***
Light (V = 0) → **No salivation**

So far we have described the Rescorla-Wagner theory in relation to changes in associative value. The theory has also been interpreted in more cognitive terms. To say that a CS has high associative value is similar to saying that it is a strong predictor of the US, or that the subject strongly "expects" the US whenever it encounters the CS. Thus, in the previous example, to say that the tone has high associative value means that it is a good predictor of food and that the dog "expects" food whenever it hears the tone. In the case of blocking, however, the tone is such a good predictor of food that the light with which it is later paired becomes redundant, and the presence of the light does not affect the subject's expectations about food. As a result, no conditioning occurs to the light. In general, then, conditioning can be viewed as a matter of building the subject's expectations that one event will follow another.

The Rescorla-Wagner theory also leads to some counterintuitive predictions. Consider what happens if you first condition two CSs to their maximum associative value and then combine them into a compound stimulus for further conditioning. For example, suppose we condition a tone to its maximum associative value, as follows:

Tone (V = 0): **Food** (*Max* = 10) → ***Salivation***
Tone (V = 10) → ***Salivation***

and then do the same for the light:

Light (V = 0): **Food** (*Max* = 10) → ***Salivation***
Light (V = 10) → ***Salivation***

We now combine the tone and the light into a compound stimulus and conduct further conditioning trials:

[Tone + Light] (V = 10 + 10 = 20): **Food** (*Max* = 10) → ***Salivation***

Note that the tone and the light together have 20 units of associative value (10 for the tone and 10 for the light). However, the maximum associative value that can be supported by the food at any one moment is only 10 units. This means that the associative value of the compound stimulus must decrease to match the maximum value that can be supported by the US. Thus, according to the Rescorla-Wagner theory, after several pairings of the compound stimulus with food, the total associative value of the compound stimulus will be reduced to 10:

[Tone + Light] (V = 10) → ***Salivation***

This in turn means that when each member in the compound is tested separately, its value also will have decreased. For example:

Tone (V = 5) → ***Salivation***
Light (V = 5) → ***Salivation***

Thus, even though the tone and light were subjected to further pairings with the food, the associative value of each decreased (i.e., each stimulus elicited less salivation than it originally did when it had been conditioned individually). This is a counterintuitive result in that one would normally expect further pairings between a CS and US to either maintain or strengthen the conditioning rather than weaken it.

The effect we have just described is known as the ***overexpectation effect***, which is the decrease in the conditioned response that occurs when two separately conditioned CSs are combined into a compound stimulus for further pairings with the US. It is as though presenting the two CSs together leads to an "overexpectation" about what will follow. When this expectation is not fulfilled, the subject's expectations are modified downward. As a result, each CS in the compound loses some of its associative value.

Although the Rescorla-Wagner model has been a source of inspiration for researchers, not all of its predictions have been confirmed. As a result, revisions to the model have been proposed along with alternative models. Some behaviorists have also criticized the common practice of interpreting the Rescorla-Wagner model in cognitive terms by arguing that the concept of associative value, which can be objectively measured by the strength of the CR, makes inferences about mentalistic processes unnecessary (e.g., Pierce & Epling, 1995). Despite these debates, however, few models have been as productive in furthering our understanding of the underlying processes of classical conditioning.

QUICK QUIZ C

1. The Rescorla-Wagner theory proposes that a given ______ can support only so much conditioning, and this amount of conditioning must be distributed among the various ______ available.
2. In general, stronger USs support (more/less) conditioning than weaker USs.
3. According to the Rescorla-Wagner theory, overshadowing occurs because the more salient CS picks up (most/little) of the associative value available in that setting.
4. According to the Rescorla-Wagner theory, blocking occurs because the (CS/NS/US) in the compound has already picked up all of the available associative value.
5. Suppose a compound stimulus has an associative value of 25 following conditioning. According to the Rescorla-Wagner theory, if one CS has acquired 15 units of associative value, the other CS must have acquired ______ units of associative value.
6. Suppose a tone and a light are each conditioned with food to a maximum associative value of 8 units. If the tone and light are combined into a compound stimulus for further conditioning trials, the associative value of each stimulus must necessarily (decrease/increase). This is known as the o______ effect.

Practical Applications of Classical Conditioning

Understanding Phobias

A particularly salient way that classical conditioning affects our lives is through its involvement in the development of fears and anxieties. As already

ADVICE FOR THE LOVELORN

Dear Dr. Dee,

My friend says that if you are deeply and madly in love with someone, then you will necessarily be much less interested in anyone else. I think my friend is wrong. There is no reason why someone can't be deeply in love with more than one person at a time. So who is right?

The Wanderer

Dear Wanderer,

I honestly don't know who is right. But your friend's hypothesis seems somewhat consistent with the Rescorla-Wagner theory. If feelings of love are to some extent classically conditioned responses, then the more love you feel for one person (meaning that he or she is a distinctive CS that has strong associative value), the less love you might feel for alternative partners who are simultaneously available (because there is little associative value left over for those other CSs). In other words, there is only so much love (so much associative value) to go around, and strong romantic feelings for one person will result in weak romantic feelings for others. In keeping with this, you can occasionally encounter people who report being so "in love" with someone—at least in the early stages of a relationship—that they are attracted to no one else. (I remember a movie star once being interviewed who was madly in love. He remarked that he had never thought it possible that he could so completely lose interest in other women.) It is the case, however, that some people are strongly attracted to many different partners, though perhaps what is attracting them is some quality that those partners have in common, such as a high degree of physical attractiveness. But would we then define such attraction as love?

Behaviorally yours,

Dr. Dee

noted, a conditioned fear response can be elicited by a previously neutral stimulus that has been associated with an aversive stimulus. In most cases, this sort of fear conditioning is a highly adaptive process because it motivates the individual to avoid a dangerous situation. A person who is bitten by a dog and learns to fear dogs is less likely to be bitten in the future simply because he or she will tend to avoid dogs.

This process, however, occasionally becomes exaggerated, with the result that we become very fearful of events that are not at all dangerous or only minimally dangerous. Such extreme, irrational fear reactions are known as phobias. In many cases, these phobias seem to represent a process of *overgen-*

eralization, in which a conditioned fear response to one event has become overgeneralized to other harmless events. Thus, although it may be rational to fear a mean-looking dog that once bit you, it is irrational to fear a friendly-looking dog that has never bitten you.

Watson and Rayner's "Little Albert" The importance of classical conditioning and overgeneralization in the development of phobias was first proposed by John B. Watson and Rosalie Rayner. In 1920, Watson and Rayner published a now-famous article in which they described their attempt to condition a fear response in an 11-month-old infant named Albert. Albert was reported to be a healthy, well-developed child, whose mother worked as a wet nurse in the hospital where the tests were conducted. Albert was described as a "stolid and unemotional" child who almost never cried. In fact, he seemed to display an unusual level of emotional stability.

The researchers began the experiment by testing Albert's reactions to a variety of objects. These included a white rat, a rabbit, a dog, some cotton wool, and even a burning newspaper. None of the objects elicited any fear, and in fact Albert often attempted to handle them. He was, however, startled when the experimenters made a loud noise by banging a steel bar with a hammer. The experimenters thus concluded that the loud noise was an unconditioned stimulus that elicited a fear response (or, more specifically, a startle reaction), whereas the other objects, such as the rat, were neutral stimuli with respect to fear:

Loud noise → *Fear* (as indicated by startle reaction)
US UR

Rat → No fear
NS —

In the next part of the experiment, Watson and Rayner (1920) paired the white rat (NS) with the loud noise (US). The rat was presented to Albert, and just as his hand touched it, the steel bar was struck with the hammer. In this first conditioning trial, Albert "jumped violently and fell forward, burying his face in the mattress. He did not cry, however" (p. 4). He reacted similarly when the trial was repeated, except that this time he began to whimper. The conditioning session was ended at that point.

The next session was held a week later. At the start of the session, the rat was handed to Albert to test his reaction to it. He tentatively reached for the rat, but quickly withdrew his hand after touching it. Since, by comparison, he showed no fear of some toy blocks that were handed to him, it seemed that a slight amount of fear conditioning to the rat had occurred during the previous week's session. Albert was then subjected to further pairings of the rat with the noise, during which he became more and more fearful. Finally, at one point, when the rat was presented without the noise, Albert "began to crawl so rapidly that he was caught with difficulty before reaching the edge of the table" (Watson & Rayner, 1920, p. 5). Albert's reaction was interpreted by Watson and Rayner as indicating that the rat had indeed come to

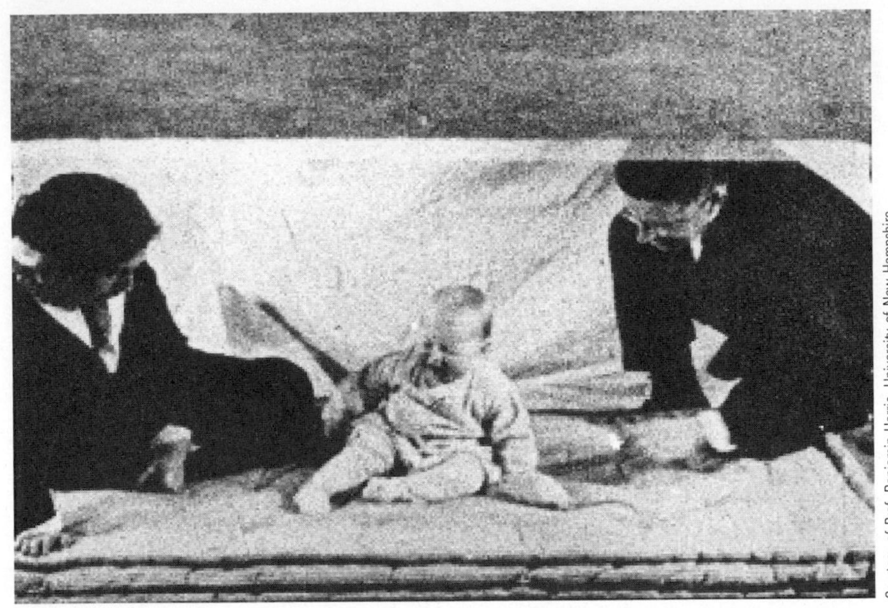

Courtesy of Prof. Benjamin Harris, University of New Hampshire

Watson and Rayner with Little Albert. (The white rat is beside Albert's left arm.)

elicit a conditioned fear response as a result of its association with the noise. This process can be diagrammed as follows:

Rat: Loud noise → ***Fear***
NS US UR

Rat → ***Fear*** (as indicated by crying and crawling away from the rat)
CS CR

In subsequent sessions, during which Albert occasionally received additional conditioning trials, he reportedly showed not only a fear of the rat but also of objects that were in some way similar to the rat, such as a rabbit, a fur coat, a dog, and even a Santa Claus mask. In other words, Albert's fear seemed to have generalized to objects that were similar to the original CS. His apparent fear of the rat, and his generalized fear of similar objects, persisted even following a 30-day break, although the intensity of his reactions was somewhat diminished. At that point, Albert left the hospital, so no further tests could be conducted. Watson and Rayner were also unable to carry out their original plan of using behavioral procedures to eliminate Albert's newly acquired fear response.[3]

[3]If all this seems terribly unethical, well, by today's standards, it is. The lack of established ethical guidelines for psychological research at that time no doubt played a role. But it is also interesting to note that the Little Albert study hardly raised an eyebrow when it was published. In fact, Watson received far more criticism for his research with rats (from animal rights activists of that era) than he did for his research with Albert (Buckley, 1989). Although mistreatment of children was a concern at that time, people then were not as sensitive as we are today about possible long-term problems resulting from adverse childhood experiences.

Although the Little Albert experiment is often depicted as a convincing demonstration of phobic conditioning in a young infant, this is actually highly debatable (Harris, 1979; Powell, Digdon, Harris, & Smithson, 2014). For one thing, there was no control for the possibility of pseudoconditioning; that is, it is possible that Albert was simply sensitized (upset) by the repeated loud noise and it was this that resulted in his subsequent negative reaction to the relatively unfamiliar animals and objects he was being shown (as opposed to the specific pairing of the rat with the noise). It also took several pairings of the rat and the noise before the rat elicited a fear reaction, and the fear reaction would typically weaken considerably by the time the next test session occurred several days later. By contrast, real-life phobias usually require only one pairing of the CS with the US to become established, and they often grow stronger over time. Watson and Rayner (1920) also noted that Albert wasn't afraid of anything so long as he was able to suck his thumb, and they had to repeatedly remove his thumb from his mouth during the sessions to enable a fear reaction to be elicited. This suggests that any fear conditioning that might have occurred was in fact relatively weak since it was easily countered by the pleasure derived from thumb sucking.

Thus, although Watson and Rayner (1920) speculated about the possibility of Albert growing up to be a neurotic individual with a strange fear of furry objects, there are several reasons to believe that this did not occur. More recent evidence suggests that additional factors are often involved in the development of a true phobia, some of which are discussed in the next section.[4] (For further information about this matter, including evidence provided by the recent identification of an individual who probably was the real Little Albert, see "On Searching for Little Albert: A Personal Account" in the And Furthermore box.)

QUICK QUIZ D

1. A phobia is an extreme, irrational fear reaction to an event. From a classical conditioning perspective, it seems to represent a process of over________.
2. In the Little Albert experiment, the rat was originally a(n) ________ stimulus, while the loud noise was a(n) ________ stimulus.
3. Albert's startle response to the noise was a(n) ________ response, while his crying in response to the rat was a(n) ________ response.
4. Differences between Albert's fear conditioning and the conditioning of real-life phobias are that the latter often require (only one/more than one) conditioning trial and often grow (stronger/weaker) over time.
5. Albert's fear response was (present/absent) whenever he was sucking his thumb, which suggests that the fear conditioning was actually relatively (strong/weak).

---

[4]It has been noted that the Little Albert study can also be interpreted as an example of operant conditioning (e.g., Goodwin, 2005). More specifically, because the loud noise occurred when Albert reached for the rat—meaning that the noise followed the reaching response and served to punish that response—the process can be described as an example of "positive punishment" (which is discussed in Chapter 6).

And Furthermore

On Searching for Little Albert: A Personal Account

As noted earlier, Watson and Rayner (1920) reported that Little Albert's mother removed him from the hospital before they could treat him for the phobia they believed they had instilled in him. As a result, people over the years have wondered whatever happened to Little Albert. Did he grow up with a fear of furry objects as Watson and Rayner speculated he might? Unfortunately, various attempts to track him down were unsuccessful—that is, until recently.

In some clever detective work, Beck, Levinson, and Irons (2009) used the 1920 U.S. census records to identify a woman, Arvilla Merritte, who (like Albert's mother) worked in, and resided in, Johns Hopkins Hospital during the time that the Watson and Rayner (1920) experiment was being conducted there. Hospital records indicated that Arvilla had given birth to a son, Douglas, whose age closely matched the reported age of Little Albert at the time the experiment began. Based on such congruencies, the authors concluded that Douglas was almost certainly Little Albert—and that the name given to him by Watson and Rayner, "Albert B," was most likely a pseudonym.

Not surprisingly, the reported discovery of Little Albert's identity resulted in a great deal of fanfare; the *APA Monitor*, for example, proclaimed that "one of psychology's greatest mysteries appears to have been solved" (DeAngelis, 2010, p. 10). But there was also a tinge of sadness and disappointment: Douglas had died from hydrocephalus at age 6, and this in turn nullified any speculation about what had happened to Little Albert when he grew up. Not everyone, however, was convinced that the real Little Albert had been found (e.g., Reese, 2010; Harris, 2011), including the first author of this text (Powell, 2010, 2011). Although it seemed possible that Douglas Merritte was Little Albert, the evidence was perhaps not as strong as many people were assuming.

These concerns grew when a follow-up article, three years later, reported some startling new evidence in the case (Fridlund, Beck, Goldie, & Irons, 2012). The article claimed that Douglas had suffered from hydrocephalus almost from birth and was severely ill during the time of the experiment; moreover, Watson almost certainly knew of the illness when selecting him for the experiment. In other words, Watson, in a severe breach of ethics, had knowingly experimented upon a neurologically impaired child and then deliberately hid this fact by describing the child as healthy! The evidence presented included an analysis of the Little Albert film that purportedly revealed previously unnoticed evidence of neurological impairment in Albert's behavior. Additionally, Douglas Merritte's medical records, once thought to have been lost, confirmed that he had indeed been diagnosed with hydrocephalus soon after birth and had suffered from numerous neurological symptoms throughout his stay in the hospital. Needless to say, this dramatic new version of the Little Albert story garnered considerable attention in the media with Watson being roundly villified (e.g., Coombs, 2013).

I (Russ Powell) discussed my concerns about this case with a colleague, Nancy Digdon, who is a developmental psychologist. After viewing the Little Albert film herself and seeing no evidence of the neurological impairment that Fridlund et al. (2012) claimed to have found, Nancy likewise became concerned that something was amiss. We decided to conduct a thorough analysis of the evidence for Douglas as Albert, as well as search for an alternate candidate for Albert. Ben Harris, a noted Watson historian, and Christopher Smithson, a genealogical researcher, later joined the investigation.

We began our search for Little Albert by focusing on another woman listed in the 1920 census record, Pearl Barger, who likewise resided in the hospital at the time of the Watson and Rayner experiment. Beck et al. (2009) had been unable to find any evidence that Pearl had a baby with her during her stay in the hospital and had therefore dismissed her as a possible candidate for Albert's mother. In our own search, however, we came across a genealogical document that indicated that Pearl Barger had married a Charles Martin in 1921 (less than a year after Pearl's stay in the hospital) and that one of their children was named Albert! Further investigation revealed that their son's full name was William Albert Martin (but almost everyone called him "Albert") and that he had died in 2007. Most important, he was, like Douglas Merritte, around the correct age to have been Little Albert. Based on this information, we were eventually able to track down and interview Albert Martin's niece, Dorothy Parthree, and with her permission view his hospital records, which still existed in the medical archives of Johns Hopkins Hospital.

The results of our investigation strongly suggest that Albert Martin was the real Little Albert (Powell et al., 2014; Digdon, Powell, & Harris, 2014). Key evidence includes the following:

- Albert Martin's name was written in the hospital records as "Albert Barger"—his mother and father were not yet married—which matches the name, "Albert B," reported by Watson and Rayner (1920). It is worth noting that research articles from that era often used participants' actual names or initials, there being no ethical requirement at that time to protect their identities.
- Apart from some common childhood illnesses, Albert Barger was a healthy and robust child throughout much of his stay in the hospital, which matches the description of Little Albert given by Watson and Rayner.
- Albert Barger weighed around 22 pounds at 9 months of age, which approximates the weight of 21 pounds reported by Watson and Rayner for Little Albert. This weight, which is heavy for a 9-month-old, is also consistent with Little Albert's decidedly chubby appearance in the film. (Douglas Merritte, by contrast, was significantly underweight at that age due to his illness.)
- Perhaps most significant, the hospital records indicate that Albert Barger was 12 months 21 days of age when he was discharged from the hospital—which exactly matches the age reported by Watson and Rayner for when Little Albert was discharged. (Conversely, Douglas Merritte was discharged a week earlier.)

Although the preponderance of evidence, at the time of this writing, strongly suggests that Albert Barger was the real Little Albert (Griggs, 2015), there remain some inconsistencies. For example, Watson (1924/1925) reported that Little Albert was "adopted by an out-of-town family" soon after leaving the hospital; Albert Barger, however, like Douglas Merritte, grew up with his mother. On the other hand, Albert was adopted in the sense that his father, Charles Martin, following his marriage to Albert's mother, would have had to adopt him in order for his last name to be changed from Barger to Martin. If Watson heard rumors about this "adoption" and name change, he

William Albert Martin

(1919–2007)

The person now believed to have been "Little Albert."

may have been misled into thinking that Albert, like many children of unwed mothers at that time, had been adopted by another family.

So if Albert Barger (Martin) was the real Little Albert, did he indeed grow up to have a fear of furry animals? In fact, his niece told us that he did have an aversion to dogs and other animals, which at first blush seems to confirm that the experiment had successfully (and unethically) instilled in him a lasting phobia. At second blush, however, the evidence is much less clear. His aversion to animals was more a dislike of animals than a fear of animals and it wasn't particularly strong (his wife used to good-naturedly tease him about it). Moreover, as a child, he once had a dog that he very much loved, and he once told his niece that he acquired his dislike of dogs after the trauma of seeing the dog get run over in the street. Additionally, Albert Martin seems to have been a rather easy-going, if fastidious, individual who led a relatively satisfying life, which seems consistent with Watson and Rayner's belief that the experiment would be unlikely to result in any lasting harm. Thus, it is impossible to say, one way or the other, whether the experiment had a lasting effect on him, but if there was an effect, it seems most likely to have been relatively minor.

So far as we know, Albert Martin had no knowledge of spending the first year of his life in a hospital or of participating in Watson and Rayner's (1920) experiment, his parents apparently having kept it a secret from their children. Interestingly, when his niece was asked in an interview what her uncle (an intellectually curious man who loved to read) would have thought about being Little Albert, she quickly replied, "Oh, he would have been thrilled" (Bartlett, 2014; this news article, along with a clip of the interview, can be found at https://chronicle.com/article/The-Search-for-Psychologys/146747/).

Additional Factors in Phobic Conditioning Not all phobias are acquired through a direct process of classical conditioning. Indeed, many people with phobias are unable to recall any particular conditioning event before the development of their symptoms (Marks, 1969). Additionally, most people are surprisingly resilient when exposed to extremely frightening events and do not develop chronic fears such as occur in phobias and in posttraumatic stress disorder (PTSD). For example, the vast majority of people exposed to air raids during World War II endured them rather well, developing only short-term fears that quickly disappeared (Rachman, 1977). Researchers have therefore suggested several additional variables that, singly or in combination, may be involved in the development of a phobia. These include observational learning, temperament, preparedness, incubation, US revaluation, and selective sensitization.

Observational Learning Many phobias are acquired when observing fearful reactions in others. For example, in World War II a major predictor of whether children developed a fear of air raids was whether their mothers were fearful. As well, airmen who became phobic of combat often developed their symptoms after witnessing fear reactions in a crewmate (Rachman, 1977).

This tendency to acquire conditioned fear reactions through observation may be inherited (Mineka, 1987). If so, a display of fear by another person may be conceptualized as an unconditioned stimulus that elicits an unconditioned fear response in oneself:

Display of fear by others → *Fear in oneself*
US **UR**

A neutral stimulus that is associated with this display might then become a conditioned stimulus for fear:

Snake: Display of fear by others → *Fear in oneself*
NS **US** **UR**

Snake → *Fear in oneself*
CS **CR**

The result is that a person who has had no direct confrontation with snakes may indirectly acquire a conditioned fear of snakes. (The other way in which observational learning of a fear response can occur is through higher-order conditioning, which is discussed in the section on observational learning in Chapter 11.)

Temperament ***Temperament*** is an individual's level of emotional reactivity, which is to a large extent genetically determined. Temperament seems to affect how easily a conditioned response can be acquired, including a fear response. As noted in Chapter 4, Pavlov found that dogs that were shy and withdrawn conditioned more readily than dogs that were active and outgoing. Similarly, individuals with certain temperaments may be more genetically susceptible than others to the development of conditioned fears (Clark, Watson, & Mineka, 1994). Even Watson, who downplayed the role of genetic influences in human behavior, acknowledged the possible influence of temperament. Watson and Rayner (1920) deliberately chose Albert as a subject for their experiment in the belief, accurate or not, that his emotional stability would grant him a good deal of immunity against any harmful effects of their procedures.

Preparedness The concept of ***preparedness*** refers to an innate disposition to learn certain types of behaviors or certain types of associations more easily than others (Seligman, 1971). Thus, with respect to phobias, people in general may have an inherited predisposition to make aversive associations to certain kinds of events, such as snakes as opposed to flowers. This notion was initially proposed by Valentine (1930), who attempted to replicate Watson and Rayner's experiment with his 1-year-old daughter. He did so by blowing a loud whistle when she touched certain objects. When the object she touched was a pair of opera glasses, she displayed no fear, even to the sound of the whistle. When the object was a caterpillar, however, some fear was elicited. Valentine also observed a 2-year-old who became fearful of dogs "at slight provocation." He concluded that humans may have an innate tendency to fear certain kinds of events, such as certain animals, and that Watson had been able to condition Albert to fear rats because of this tendency.

More recent evidence for the role of preparedness in fear conditioning includes a study by Cook and Mineka (1989). They exposed laboratory-raised rhesus monkeys to videotapes edited to show another monkey reacting either fearfully or non-fearfully to either a fear-relevant stimulus (toy snake or toy crocodile) or a fear-irrelevant stimulus (flowers or toy rabbit). Only those monkeys who observed the model reacting fearfully to the fear-relevant stimulus acquired a conditioned fear reaction to that stimulus. Similarly, Soares and Öhman (1993) found that human subjects developed signs of conditioned anxiety when exposed to subliminal stimuli—pictures presented so briefly that subjects were consciously unaware of the content—that were paired with uncomfortable levels of electric shock. This conditioned reaction occurred when the pictures were of fear-relevant stimuli (snakes and spiders) as opposed to fear-irrelevant stimuli (flowers and mushrooms). This result supports the notion that humans, too, may be predisposed to learn to fear certain types of objects and events. (The concept of preparedness is more fully discussed in Chapter 12.)

Students often confuse the concepts of temperament and preparedness. In people, temperament refers to differences between people in how emotionally reactive they are, which in turn affects how easily they can develop a phobia. Preparedness (as it relates to phobias) refers to differences between the types of phobias in how easily they can be acquired. Thus, temperament refers to how easily a certain person can acquire a phobia, while preparedness refers to how easily a certain type of phobia can be acquired. For example, the fact that Jason more easily develops phobias than does Samantha reflects the role of temperament; the fact that, for both of them, a phobia of snakes is more easily acquired than a phobia of toasters reflects the role of preparedness.

QUICK QUIZ E

1. From a conditioning perspective, viewing a display of fear in others can be conceptualized as a(n) ______ stimulus that elicits a(n) ______ response of fear in oneself. The event the other person is reacting to might then become a(n) ______ stimulus that elicits a(n) ______ response of fear in oneself.
2. The term ______ refers to an individual's genetically determined level of emotionality and reactivity to stimulation. It (does/does not) seem to affect the extent to which responses can be classically conditioned.

3. The concept of p________ holds that we are genetically programmed to acquire certain kinds of fears, such as fear of snakes and spiders, more readily than other kinds.
4. Travis rolled his pickup truck, yet he had no qualms about driving home afterward; Cam was in a minor fender bender and was petrified of driving for several days afterward. These different outcomes may reflect (learned/innate) differences in t________ between the two individuals.
5. The fact that people are generally more fearful of encountering snakes than they are of being run over by a car, even though the latter is far more likely in this day and age, may reflect (innate/learned) differences in p________ for acquiring certain kinds of fears.

Incubation When a phobia develops through a direct process of classical conditioning, why does the conditioned fear response not extinguish with subsequent exposures to the CS? To some extent, extinction does not occur because the person tends to avoid the feared stimulus (the CS) so that repeated exposure to the CS in the absence of the US does not take place. Additionally, however, because of this tendency to move away from the feared stimulus, any exposures that do occur are likely to be very brief. According to Eysenck (1968), such brief exposures may result in a phenomenon known as "incubation."

Incubation refers to the strengthening of a conditioned fear response as a result of brief exposures to an aversive CS. For example, a child who is bitten by a dog and then runs away each time he encounters one may find that his fear of dogs grows worse even though he is never again bitten. As a result, what may have started off as a moderate fear of dogs may evolve over time into a severe fear. In fact, this process might even result in a conditioned fear that is stronger than the unconditioned fear that was originally elicited when the child was bitten. It also contradicts the general rule that the presentation of the CS without the US will result in extinction (Sandin & Chorot, 2002). Note, too, that covert exposures to the feared stimulus—as in worrying about it—might also result in incubation (Wells & Papageorgiou, 1995). Incubation is, of course, one reason for the old adage that if you fall off a horse you should immediately get back on; if you wait, you might later become too fearful to get back on.[5]

US Revaluation As noted in Chapter 4, exposure to a US of a different intensity (i.e., a different *value*) than that used during conditioning can alter the strength of the response to a previously conditioned CS. This process could play a major role in human phobias (Davey, 1992). Consider,

[5]The term incubation is also used to refer to a closely related phenomenon, also of relevance to the get-back-on-the-horse adage, in which a conditioned fear response may grow stronger during a rest period after conditioning *without further exposures to either the US or the CS*—a process that is believed to play a role in the delayed onset of PTSD that can occur following a traumatic event (e.g., Pickens, Golden, Adams-Deutch, Nair, & Shaham, 2009).

for example, a skateboarder who experiences a minor injury as a result of a fall:

Skateboarding: Minor injury → *Slight anxiety*
Skateboarding → *Slight anxiety*

Because the injury was relatively minor, skateboarding elicits only a slight amount of conditioned anxiety, most of which will likely extinguish as the skateboarder continues the activity. But imagine that this person later is in a car accident and suffers a severe injury:

Car: Severe injury → *Strong anxiety*

In addition to now experiencing anxiety while being in a car—

Car → *Strong anxiety*

—he might also display a strong degree of anxiety to skateboarding:

Skateboarding → *Strong anxiety*

It is as though the skateboarder finally realizes just how painful an injury can be. And given that skateboarding is associated with being injured, it too now elicits strong feelings of anxiety.

The process of US revaluation can also occur through observational learning. A student of one of the authors reported that she developed a phobia about snowboarding after first spraining her leg in a minor snowboarding accident—which resulted in only minor anxiety about snowboarding—and then witnessing someone else suffer a major accident. In this circumstance, observational learning resulted in US inflation, which then led to the phobia. Note that this differs from pure observational learning to the extent that her earlier minor snowboarding accident set the stage for her later reaction when witnessing someone else suffer a major snowboarding accident.

Finally, US inflation can also occur through verbally transmitted information. Consider the following case described by Davey, de Jong, and Tallis (1993):

> M. F. (male, aged 29 yr) worked as a bank employee. On one occasion the bank was robbed, and during the robbery M. F. was threatened with a gun. He had not been particularly anxious at the time and returned to work the next day without complaining of any residual fear symptoms. However, 10 days after the robbery he was interviewed by the police, and during this interview he was told that he was very lucky to be alive because the bank robber was considered to be a dangerous man who had already killed several people. From this point on M. F. did not return to work and developed severe PTSD symptoms. (p. 496)

This latter example suggests that we have to be particularly careful about the sort of information we convey to people who have suffered potentially traumatic events, because that information itself might induce a traumatic reaction. Indeed, research has shown that individuals who have been exposed to a traumatic event and are then given a *psychological debriefing* (also known as *critical incident stress debriefing*)—which is a structured form of counseling designed to prevent the development of PTSD—are sometimes *more* likely to develop PTSD than those who do not receive such debriefings (e.g., Mayou & Ehlers, 2000; Sijbrandij, Olff, Reitsma, Carlier, & Gersons, 2006). It seems that the debriefing itself sometimes heightens the effect of the trauma, perhaps by giving victims the impression that the trauma was more severe than they would otherwise have thought. Although the use of psychological debriefings is still being promoted by some psychologists, more empirically based procedures have now been developed that are more respectful of a person's individual coping style and are less likely to inadvertently do harm (Gist & Devilly, 2010).

Selective Sensitization Yet another process that could influence the development of a phobia is ***selective sensitization***, which is an increase in one's reactivity to a potentially fearful stimulus following exposure to an unrelated stressful event. For example, people with *agoraphobia* (fear of being alone in a public place) often report that the initial onset of the disorder occurred during a period in which they were emotionally upset or suffered from some type of physical illness (Rachman, 1977). Similarly, an individual going through a stressful divorce might find that her previously minor anxiety about driving in heavy traffic suddenly develops into severe anxiety. The stressful circumstance surrounding the divorce affects her reactions not only to the divorce but to other potentially aversive events as well. Thus, during turbulent times in one's life, minor fears and anxieties may become exacerbated into major fears and anxieties (Barlow, 1988).

QUICK QUIZ F

1. Brief exposures to a feared CS in the absence of the US may result in a phenomenon known as ____________ in which the conditioned fear response grows (stronger/weaker). This runs counter to the general principle that presentation of the CS without the US usually results in e____________.
2. According to the concept of ____________ revaluation, phobic behavior might sometimes develop when the person encounters a (more/less) intense version of the (CS/US) than was used in the original conditioning. This process can also occur through o____________ l____________ or through v____________ transmitted information.
3. The process of s____________ s____________ refers to an increase in one's reactivity to a potentially fearful stimulus following exposure to a stressful event that is (related/unrelated) to the feared stimulus.

Treating Phobias

Perhaps more than any other disorder, phobias are highly susceptible to treatments based on behavioral principles of conditioning. In this section, we discuss the two basic types of treatment: systematic desensitization and flooding.

Systematic Desensitization Recall how Watson and Rayner had intended to treat the phobia they believed they had created in Albert but were unable to do so because his mother suddenly removed him from the hospital. A few years later, Mary Cover Jones (1924) did carry out such a treatment (under Watson's supervision) with Peter, a 2-year-old boy who had an extreme fear of rabbits. Jones's treatment strategy consisted of first feeding Peter cookies while presenting a rabbit at a considerable distance. It was assumed that the positive emotional response elicited by the cookies would overcome the mild anxiety elicited by the distant rabbit. Over successive sessions, the rabbit was gradually brought closer to Peter as he continued to eat cookies. Within a few months, Peter was munching on cookies while holding the rabbit in his lap. As a result of this gradual conditioning procedure, Peter's fear of the rabbit was eliminated.

Although Jones's treatment procedure, carried out in 1924, seemed to have effectively eliminated a phobia, it languished in obscurity until Joseph Wolpe (1958) essentially rediscovered it 30 years later. As a graduate student, Wolpe conducted research on fear conditioning in cats exposed to electric shocks. The cats displayed a strong fear of both the experimental chamber in which they had been shocked and the room containing the chamber. A major indication of this fear was the cats' refusal to eat while in the room (an example of conditioned suppression). Wolpe then devised a treatment plan to eliminate the fear. He began by feeding the cats in a room that was quite dissimilar from the original "shock" room. Then, over a period of days, the cats were fed in rooms that were made progressively similar to the shock room. Eventually they were able to eat in the room in which they had originally been shocked. The procedure effectively eliminated the conditioned fear in all 12 cats that Wolpe studied.

Wolpe (1958) interpreted the cats' improvements to be the result of ***counterconditioning***, in which a CS that elicits one type of response is associated with an event that elicits an incompatible response. In Wolpe's study, the experimental room originally elicited a fear response because of its association with shock. Later, it elicited a positive emotional reaction after it had become associated with food. Wolpe proposed that the underlying process in counterconditioning is ***reciprocal inhibition***, in which the occurrence of one response can be inhibited by the occurrence of an incompatible response. Thus, the positive emotional response elicited by food inhibited the cats' anxiety because the two responses countered each other.

As a result of his success, Wolpe (1958) began to ponder ways of applying this treatment procedure to human phobias. Although both he and Jones had successfully used the response of eating food to counter feelings of anxiety, Wolpe felt that this approach would be impractical for most treatment situations involving humans. He toyed with other types of responses that might counter anxiety, such as anger and assertiveness (i.e., the client was taught to act angry or assertive in situations that were normally associated with fear), but then finally hit upon the use of deep muscle relaxation. Deep muscle relaxation is largely incompatible with the experience of anxiety (Jacobson, 1938), making it ideal from Wolpe's perspective as a tool for counterconditioning.

Wolpe (1958) also realized that real-life exposure to a phobic stimulus was impractical in some treatment scenarios. For example, it would be extremely difficult to expose a person with a fear of thunderstorms to a succession of storms that are made progressively more frightening. To solve this dilemma, Wolpe decided to have the patient simply visualize the feared stimulus. A series of visualized scenarios could then be constructed that would represent varying intensities of the feared event. For example, the person could imagine a storm some distance away that had only a mild amount of thunder and lightning, then a storm that was somewhat closer with a bit more thunder and lightning, and so on. One drawback to this procedure is that the counterconditioning occurs only to the visualized event, and it will then have to generalize to the real event. Nevertheless, if the visualization is fairly vivid, the amount of generalization to the real world should be considerable.

Thus, Wolpe's (1958) procedure, known as ***systematic desensitization***, is a behavioral treatment for phobias that involves pairing relaxation with a succession of stimuli that elicit increasing levels of fear. The three parts of the procedure are as follows:

1. *Training in relaxation.* An abbreviated version of Jacobson's (1938) deep muscle relaxation procedure is commonly employed for inducing relaxation, but other methods such as meditation or hypnosis have also been used.
2. *Creation of a hierarchy of imaginary scenes that elicit progressively intense levels of fear.* Experience has shown that about 10 to 15 scenes are sufficient, starting with a scene that elicits only a minor degree of fear (e.g., for a dog-phobic individual, it might be visualizing a friendly poodle tied to a tree at a distance of several yards) and finishing with a scene that elicits a tremendous amount of anxiety (e.g., visualizing standing beside a large dog that is barking).
3. *Pairing of each item in the hierarchy with relaxation.* Starting with the least fearful scene in the hierarchy, the person is asked to visualize the scene for about 10 to 30 seconds and then engage in a short period of relaxation. This process is repeated until the first scene no longer elicits anxiety, at which point the process is carried out using the next scene. By the time the top item in the hierarchy is reached, most of the person's fear will have been eliminated, leaving only a residual amount of fear to what was once an intensely fearful scene. The fear response to this final scene is also eliminated, at which point it is quite likely that the person will now feel significantly less anxious when confronted with the phobic stimulus in real life.

Although Wolpe (1958) emphasized, mostly for convenience, the use of imaginary stimuli (the procedure then being referred to as *imaginal desensitization*), the treatment can also be carried out with real stimuli. This version of desensitization is sometimes referred to as *in vivo desensitization*. Mary Cover Jones's (1925) treatment of Peter's rabbit phobia is an example of *in vivo* desensitization. As with imaginal desensitization, *in vivo* desensitization usually makes use of relaxation to counter the person's fear response. For example, a dog-phobic client might move gradually closer to a real dog, pausing after each step and relaxing for several seconds. Additionally, the process might first be carried out with a very small dog and then gradually progress to a very large dog. *In vivo* desensitization has an obvious advantage in that one does not have to worry about whether the treatment effect will generalize to a real-life stimulus because one is already working with a real-life stimulus. However, in severely phobic clients, the real stimulus might elicit a tremendous amount of anxiety. In such cases, it might be wiser to first use imaginal desensitization to eliminate much of the fear, and then switch to *in vivo* desensitization to complete the process. More detailed information on systematic desensitization can be found in behavior modification texts such as Spiegler and Guevremont (2010).

Considerable research has been carried out on systematic desensitization. It tends to be very effective with patients who have relatively few phobias that are highly specific in nature (e.g., a fear of spiders). By contrast, people who suffer from social phobias tend to experience a generalized fear of many different social situations and do not respond as well to this form of treatment. Additionally, when using imaginal desensitization, the client must be able to clearly visualize the feared event and experience anxiety while doing so. Unfortunately, some individuals are unable to visualize clearly, or they feel no anxiety even with clear visualization. In these cases, *in vivo* desensitization is the better alternative.

As noted, Wolpe (1958) assumed that systematic desensitization is a counterconditioning procedure that works through the process of reciprocal inhibition. However, some researchers (e.g., Eysenck, 1976) have claimed that systematic desensitization is really just a simple matter of extinction in which a CS is repeatedly presented in the absence of the US. From this perspective, systematic desensitization for a dog-phobic individual works simply because it involves repeated presentations of dogs (or images of dogs) in the absence of anything bad happening, with the relaxation being irrelevant. In fact, relaxation is not always needed for the treatment to be effective; gradual exposure to the feared stimulus is by itself often sufficient. On the other hand, in support of the counterconditioning explanation, severe phobias often respond better to treatment when relaxation is included (Wolpe, 1995). The exact mechanism by which systematic desensitization produces its effects is, however, still unknown, and it may well be that both extinction and counterconditioning are involved.

QUICK QUIZ G

1. Associating a stimulus that already elicits one type of response with an event that elicits an incompatible response is called ______________. Wolpe believed that the underlying process is r______________ i______________, in which certain types of responses are (compatible/incompatible) with each other, and the occurrence of one type of response i______________ the other.
2. Mary Cover Jones used the response of ______ to counter Peter's feelings of anxiety, while Wolpe, in his s________ d________ procedure, used ______________

3. The three basic components of Wolpe's procedure are:

a. ____________________

b. ____________________

c. ____________________

4. A version of Wolpe's procedure that uses real-life rather than imaginary stimuli is called __________ desensitization. A major advantage of this procedure is that there is less worry about whether the treatment effect will g__________ to the real world.

5. Wolpe's procedure is very effective with people who have (few/many) phobias that are (general/specific) in nature. Thus, this procedure (does/does not) work well with people who have a social phobia.

6. One bit of evidence against the counterconditioning explanation for this type of treatment is that relaxation (is/is not) always necessary for the treatment to be effective. On the other hand, in keeping with the counterconditioning explanation, relaxation does seem to facilitate treatment when the phobia is (nonspecific/severe).

Study Tip: Counterconditioning is a process that can be applied to any situation that an individual finds aversive, including studying. Some students, for example, as a result of past frustrations, may find the act of studying distinctly unpleasant and even anxiety arousing. This contributes to their tendency to procrastinate, and when they do study, they find it hard to concentrate. Changing to a new study environment, discussed in Chapter 8, can help alleviate this problem, but another tactic that might help would be to associate studying with pleasant stimuli that will counteract the aversive associations. Good students are often quite fussy about their study environment and arrange for it to be as pleasant as possible, with a comfortable chair, pleasant music, a favorite drink, and maybe even a treat to nibble on. If you presently find studying aversive, you may wish to consider doing likewise (with the treats being gradually faded out if you don't want to get hooked on them). Practicing relaxation or meditation just prior to studying may also be helpful. As always, the trick is to experiment and find what works for you.

Flooding Consider a rat that continues to avoid a goal box in which it was once shocked, even though no further shocks will ever be delivered. One straightforward way to eliminate this phobic behavior is to place the rat in the goal box and insert a barrier that prevents it from leaving. Forced to remain in the box, the rat will initially show considerable distress, but this will disappear as time passes and no shock is delivered. By simply preventing the avoidance response from occurring, we can quickly eliminate the rat's fear.

The treatment procedure that makes use of this response-prevention principle is ***flooding therapy***: a behavioral treatment that involves prolonged exposure to a feared stimulus, thereby providing maximal opportunity for the conditioned fear response to be extinguished (Spiegler & Guevremont, 2010). This method can be contrasted with systematic desensitization, in which exposure to the feared stimulus not only occurs gradually but also involves pairing the feared event with a response that will counteract the fear (such as relaxation). Flooding is more clearly based on the principle of extinction as opposed to counterconditioning.

As with systematic desensitization, there are two basic types of flooding procedures. In *imaginal flooding*, the client is asked to visualize, as clearly as possible, a scenario involving the feared event. For example, an individual who is spider phobic might imagine waking up at night to find a large, hairy spider on the pillow beside her. A person with a fear of heights might imagine having to climb down a fire escape from a 10th-floor apartment. The greater the level of fear induced by the visualized scenario, the better.

The client first visualizes the scenario in the therapist's office and then practices visualizing it at home. Although the level of fear during visualization may initially increase, it should eventually begin to decrease. Once the fear response to one scenario has been extinguished, the fear response to other scenarios (e.g., having to remove a spider from the kitchen sink) can be similarly extinguished. After extinction has occurred within several scenarios, the client will likely experience considerably less fear when encountering the feared event in the real world.

An alternative to imaginal flooding is *in vivo* flooding, which consists of prolonged exposure to the actual feared event. Consider, for example, a woman who is extremely fearful of balloons (perhaps because someone once burst a balloon in her face when she was a child). An *in vivo* flooding procedure might involve filling a room with balloons and then having the woman enter the room, close the door, and remain inside for an hour or more. After a few sessions of this, her fear of balloons might well be eliminated.

Of course, *in vivo* flooding is something that people have been intuitively aware of for centuries. The famous German poet and philosopher Goethe described how, as a young man, he had cured himself of a fear of heights by climbing the tower of the local cathedral and standing on the ledge. He repeated this procedure until his fear was greatly alleviated (Lewes, 1965; see also "Was Sigmund Freud a Behavior Analyst?" in the And Furthermore box.) As with *in vivo* desensitization, *in vivo* flooding is advantageous because it does not require the treatment effect to generalize from an imagined encounter to a real encounter. It is also not dependent on a person's visualization ability. On the other hand, *in vivo* flooding can be highly aversive; neither can it be used with some types of fears, such as house fires, that are impossible to replicate in a therapy setting.

One concern with any type of flooding therapy is that the stress involved may result in medical complications. As well, clients who have a history of other psychiatric disorders may experience an exacerbation of their fears as a

And Furthermore

Was Sigmund Freud a Behavior Analyst?

Students sometimes wonder how, if conditioning principles are so effective in treating certain disorders, other therapeutic systems that use decidedly different methods for treating such disorders could have become so well established. One possibility is that these other systems sometimes make use of behavioral principles but have neglected to advertise the fact. For example, few people are aware that Sigmund Freud, the founder of psychoanalysis, very much appreciated the value of direct exposure to one's fears. This is apparent in the following description of Freud and his followers on a holiday outing in 1921 (Grosskurth, 1991). During an excursion in the mountains, they climbed a tower to a platform that was surrounded by an iron railing at hip level.

> Freud suggested that they all lean forward against the railing with their hands behind their backs, their feet well back, and imagine that there was nothing there to prevent them from falling. This was an exercise Freud had devised for overcoming the fear of heights, from which he had suffered as a young man. Jones [one of Freud's most devoted followers] teased him that it didn't seem very psychoanalytic. (p. 21)

Despite Jones's opinion, Freud (1919/1955) was so impressed with the effectiveness of this technique that he recommended it as an adjunct to psychoanalysis, arguing that a phobia first needs to be weakened through direct exposure before the final resolution of the fear can be achieved through psychoanalysis:

> One starts, therefore, by moderating the phobia [by direct exposure]; and it is only when that has been achieved at the physician's demand that the associations and memories [of unconscious conflicts] come into the patient's mind which enable the phobia to be resolved. (pp. 165–166)

Of course, one might wonder how Freud could have determined that the resolution of the phobia was due to the retrieval of childhood memories rather than the cumulative effects of further exposure. (See also Thyer, 1999, for an example of how Carl Jung, another psychodynamic therapist, used an exposure-based procedure to treat a case of railroad phobia.)

result of this type of treatment. One must be particularly cautious about using flooding to treat clients suffering from PTSD. It is also important that the duration of each exposure, whether *in vivo* or imaginal, be sufficiently long (at least 30 to 45 minutes); otherwise the fear may not be extinguished or, worse yet, it may become stronger. In this sense, flooding is a riskier procedure than systematic desensitization (Spiegler & Guevremont, 2010).

Hybrid Approaches to the Treatment of Phobias Systematic desensitization and flooding are the most basic behavioral approaches to the treatment of phobic behavior. Several variations of these approaches have been devised, which often combine aspects of each along with additional processes such as observational learning. Such approaches are generally known as *exposure-based treatments* or *exposure therapies* and are now considered the treatment of choice for phobic disorders (Spiegler & Guevremont, 2010).

For example, Öst (1989) described a method for rapidly eliminating specific phobias, such as a specific fear of spiders, in a single session. The major component of the treatment package was an *in vivo exposure* procedure in which clients were encouraged to approach the feared object as closely as possible, remain there until the anxiety faded away, and then approach the object even more closely. This process continued until the client had closely approached the object and had experienced at least a 50% reduction in reported level of fear. Note that this exposure procedure is similar to systematic desensitization in that it is somewhat gradual, and similar to flooding in that the client is encouraged to endure a fairly intense level of anxiety each step of the way.

Öst's (1989) treatment package included several additional components. For example, throughout the procedure, most clients were accompanied by the therapist who acted as a model to demonstrate how to interact with the feared object (such as how to use a jar to capture a spider). The therapist also helped the client physically contact the feared object—for example, by first touching the object while the client touched the model's hand, then touching the object while the client also touched the object, and then gradually removing his hand while the patient continued touching the object. This procedure is sometimes called *participant modeling* (or contact desensitization) and has been shown to greatly facilitate treatment (Bandura, 1975; Bandura, Blanchard, & Ritter, 1969).

QUICK QUIZ H

1. In flooding therapy, the avoidance response is (blocked/facilitated), thereby providing maximal opportunity for the conditioned fear to __________.
2. Two types of flooding therapy are __________ flooding in which one visualizes the feared stimulus, and __________ flooding in which one encounters a real example of the feared stimulus.
3. For flooding therapy to be effective, the exposure period must be of relatively (long/short) duration.
4. Modern therapies for phobias are often given the general name of e__________-b__________ treatments.
5. Öst's single-session procedure combines the gradualness of s__________ d__________ with the prolonged exposure time of fl__________. This procedure also makes use of p__________ m__________, in which the therapist demonstrates how to interact with the feared object.

Aversion Therapy for Problem Behaviors

Some behavior problems stem from events being overly enticing rather than overly aversive. For example, nicotine and alcohol can be highly pleasurable, with the result that many people become addicted. Similarly, pedophiles have inappropriate feelings of sexual attraction to young children. Obviously, one way to counter these problem behaviors is to directly reduce the attractiveness of the relevant stimuli.

Aversion therapy is a treatment procedure that reduces the attractiveness of a desired event by associating it with an aversive stimulus (Spiegler & Guevremont, 2010). An ancient version of this treatment was suggested by the Roman writer Pliny the Elder, who recommended treating overindulgence in wine by secretly slipping the putrid body of a large spider into the bottom of the wine drinker's glass. The intention was that the feelings of revulsion elicited by a mouthful of spider would become associated with the wine, thereby significantly reducing the person's desire for wine (Franks, 1963). More recent versions of this therapy are somewhat less primitive. For example, the taste of alcohol has sometimes been paired with painful electric shocks. An alternative version—which is similar to Pliny's treatment in that it makes use of stimuli associated with ingestion—involves pairing the taste of alcohol with nausea. In this case, the client is first given an *emetic*, which is a drug that produces nausea. As the nausea develops, the client takes a mouthful of alcohol. This procedure is repeated several times; as well, the type of alcohol is varied across trials to ensure generalization. Research has shown that such nausea-based treatments are more effective than shock-based treatments, presumably because we have a biological tendency to quickly associate nausea with substances that we ingest (Baker & Cannon, 1979; Masters, Burish, Hollon, & Rimm, 1987). This tendency, known as taste aversion conditioning, is discussed more fully in Chapter 12.

Aversion therapy has also been used with smoking, with similar results. Early attempts to pair smoking and electric shock were relatively ineffective, possibly because physical pain is not a biologically relevant response to smoking. A more effective procedure has been to pair smoking with nicotine-induced nausea. This procedure, known as "rapid smoking," involves having the client smoke continuously, inhaling every 6 to 10 seconds (Danaher, 1977). Within a few minutes, extreme feelings of nausea are elicited and the person will be unable to continue. One session is usually sufficient to produce at least temporary abstinence. This is especially the case with smokers who do not yet have a strong physical addiction to smoking and who smoke more for the pleasure of smoking—which the aversive conditioning counteracts—than for the avoidance of withdrawal symptoms (Zelman, Brandon, Jorenby, & Baker, 1992). Long-term abstinence is much less certain but can be facilitated through the use of additional treatment procedures (such as *relapse prevention training*, in which the person learns to identify and cope with situations in which there is a high risk of resuming the problematic behavior [Marlatt & Gordon, 1985]). Rapid smoking is, however, very stressful, usually resulting in extreme increases in heart rate. Thus, this type of treatment must be employed cautiously, as it could lead to medical difficulties (Lichtenstein & Glasgow, 1977). (In other words, do not try this at home!)

Aversion therapy has also been used to treat sex offenders (Hall, Shondrick, & Hirschman, 1993). In the case of pedophiles, photographic images of unclothed children may be paired with drug-induced nausea or a powerfully unpleasant scent such as ammonia. As part of a comprehensive treatment package, such procedures help reduce the risk that the individual will reoffend following release from prison.[6]

Aversion therapy is sometimes carried out with the use of imaginal stimuli rather than real stimuli. This version of the treatment is usually called *covert sensitization*. For example, a person addicted to smoking might imagine experiencing extreme illness and vomiting each time she tries to smoke. Alternatively, she might visualize being forced to smoke cigarettes that have been smeared with feces. As with imaginal desensitization, the effectiveness of this procedure is dependent on the client's ability to visualize images clearly and to experience strong feelings of revulsion in response to these images. The treatment effect also has to generalize from the visualized event to the real event, which, as in imaginal treatments for phobias, is likely to result in some loss of effectiveness. Thus, covert sensitization will likely be somewhat less effective than aversion therapy, which utilizes exposure to the actual stimulus.

QUICK QUIZ I

1. In ________ therapy, one attempts to reduce the attractiveness of an event by associating that event with an unpleasant stimulus.
2. A standard treatment for alcoholism is to associate the taste of alcohol with feelings of n________ that have been induced by consumption of an e________.
3. A highly effective procedure for reducing cigarette consumption, at least temporarily, is r________ s________.
4. In general, aversion therapy is (more/less) effective when the unpleasant response that is elicited is biologically relevant to the problematic behavior.
5. Aversion therapy is sometimes carried out using ________ stimuli rather than real stimuli. This type of treatment procedure is known as ________ sensitization.

Medical Applications of Classical Conditioning

There is a growing body of evidence indicating that processes of classical conditioning have significant medical implications. For example, Russell et al. (1984) were able to condition guinea pigs to become allergic to certain odors by pairing those odors with an allergy-inducing protein. People who have allergies may experience a similar process, such that their allergic reaction is elicited not only by the substance that originally caused the allergy

[6]Although aversion therapy for pedophiles does reduce the likelihood that they will reoffend, be aware that these treatments have not been demonstrated to be a "cure" for most offenders (Kirsch & Becker, 2006).

but also by stimuli associated with it. Thus, for a person who is allergic to pollen, even the mere sight of flowers might elicit an allergic reaction.

Flowers: Pollen → *Allergic reaction*
NS US UR

Flowers → *Allergic reaction*
CS CR

Other studies have shown that various aspects of the immune system can be classically conditioned. For example, Ader and Cohen (1975) exposed rats to an immunosuppressive drug paired with saccharin-flavored water. These rats were then given an injection of foreign cells, followed by a drink of either saccharin-flavored water or plain water. The rats that drank the saccharin-flavored water produced fewer antibodies in reaction to the foreign cells than did the rats that drank the plain water. The flavored water had apparently become a CS for immunosuppression.

In a real-world extension of this study, Bovbjerg et al. (1990) found that women who received chemotherapy in a hospital setting displayed evidence of immunosuppression when they later returned to the hospital. The hospital environment had become associated with the immunosuppressive effect of the chemotherapy and was now a CS for a conditioned immunosuppressive response. Thus:

Hospital: Chemotherapy → *Immunosuppression*
NS US UR

Hospital → *Immunosuppression*
CS CR

Other studies have shown that classical conditioning can be used to strengthen immune system functioning. For example, one team of researchers gave human subjects a taste of sherbet followed by shots of adrenaline (Buske-Kirschbaum, Kirschbaum, Stierle, Jabaij, & Hellhammer, 1994). Adrenaline tends to increase the activity of natural killer cells, which are an important component of the body's immune system. After pairing the sweet sherbet with the adrenaline, the sweet sherbet itself elicited an increase in natural killer cell activity. Hence:

Sweet sherbet: Adrenaline → *Increased natural killer cell activity*
NS US UR

Sweet sherbet → *Increased natural killer cell activity*
CS CR

(See also Solvason, Ghanta, & Hiramoto, 1988.)

The medical implications of such findings are significant. Many patients would benefit considerably from enhanced immune functioning during the course of their illness. Other patients, however—namely those who suffer from autoimmune diseases, such as arthritis, in which the immune system seems to be overactive—would benefit from a procedure that could weaken their immune system. (See Exton et al., 2000, for a review of research into this issue; also Ader, 2003.)

Classical conditioning also has important implications for our understanding of the *placebo effect* (Siegel, 2002). In drug research, a placebo is an inert substance that appears to be a drug but in reality has no pharmacological value. In double-blind control studies, placebos are given to a control group to assess the effects of "expectancy" upon the patient's symptoms, such effects being known as placebo effects. Only when the drug effect is stronger than the placebo effect is the drug considered effective.

In classical conditioning terms, the placebo effect can be seen as the result of pairing the appearance of the drug (originally an NS) with the active ingredients of the drug (the US). Thus, conditioning a placebo effect for aspirin, in which the active ingredient is acetylsalicylic acid, would involve the following:

White pill: Acetylsalicylic acid → *Headache removal*
NS US UR

White pill → *Headache removal*
CS CR

The possibility that this type of process underlies the placebo effect is supported by the fact that placebo effects are much more likely to occur following a period of treatment with the active drug (e.g., Kantor, Sunshine, Laska, Meisner, & Hopper, 1966). Additionally, repeated administration of a placebo by itself tends to reduce its effectiveness, which suggests that a process of extinction is taking place (Lasagna, Mosteller, von Felsinger, & Beecher, 1954).

If conditioning processes do underlie placebo effects, research into this process might allow us to better control such effects. Placebos could then be used, for example, to reduce the frequency with which a patient has to take the real drug, thereby reducing some of the side effects associated with the drug. Additionally, we may be able to devise ways in which the placebo effect can be combined with the real drug to produce an enhanced form of treatment (see Siegel, 2002).

QUICK QUIZ J

1. Diagram the classical conditioning process in Ader and Cohen's (1975) study of immunosuppression. Label each component using the appropriate abbreviations.

2. Supporting the possibility that placebo effects are classically conditioned responses, such effects are more likely to occur (following/preceding) a period of treatment with the real drug. As well, repeated presentations of the placebo by itself tend to (reduce/increase) its effectiveness, which suggests that e____________ may be taking place.

SUMMARY

Pavlov's stimulus-substitution theory of conditioning assumes that the CS acts as a substitute for the US. The fact that the CR is sometimes different from the UR does not support this theory. According to the preparatory-response theory of conditioning, the CR serves to prepare the organism for the onset of the US. In one version of preparatory-response theory, known as the compensatory-response model, the CS is viewed as eliciting opponent processes that counteract the effect of the US. This approach has significant application to understanding addiction. The Rescorla-Wagner theory accounts for certain conditioning phenomena (e.g., blocking) by proposing that a given US can support only so much conditioning, which must be distributed among the various CSs available.

The principles of classical conditioning are useful in understanding and treating phobias. Watson and Rayner (1920) attempted to condition an 11-month-old infant named Albert to fear a rat by associating presentations of the rat with a loud noise. True phobic conditioning, however, may involve additional factors, including observational learning, temperament, preparedness, incubation, US revaluation, and selective sensitization.

Systematic desensitization is a treatment procedure for phobias that utilizes a counterconditioning procedure in which a CS that elicits one type of response is associated with another stimulus that elicits an incompatible response. The three components of systematic desensitization are training in deep muscle relaxation, creation of a hierarchy of imaginary scenes that elicit progressively intense levels of fear, and pairing each item in the hierarchy with relaxation. In *in vivo* desensitization, the imaginary scenes are replaced by a hierarchy of real-life encounters with the feared stimulus. Flooding is an alternative treatment procedure that involves prolonged exposure to a feared stimulus. Recent exposure-based treatments for phobias often combine characteristics of both systematic desensitization and flooding as well as observational learning.

Aversion therapy attempts to reduce the attractiveness of a desired event by associating it with an aversive stimulus. Examples include associating nausea with alcohol ingestion or cigarette smoking and, in pedophiles, associating the smell of ammonia with the sight of young children. In a technique known as covert sensitization, aversion therapy is carried out with the use of imaginal stimuli rather than real stimuli.

Classical conditioning has medical implications. For example, neutral stimuli that have been associated with an allergy-inducing substance can become CSs that elicit a conditioned allergic response. Related studies provide evidence that classical conditioning may be involved in the creation of the placebo effect, with the placebo being a CS that elicits a drug-like response.

SUGGESTED READINGS

Pavlov, I. P. (1941). *Conditioned reflexes and psychiatry* (W. H. Gantt, Trans.). New York: International Publishers. Pavlov's attempt to apply the principles of conditioning to understanding various forms of human neuroses.

Wolpe, J. (1958). *Psychotherapy by reciprocal inhibition.* Stanford, CA: Stanford University Press. Wolpe's original book describing his development of systematic desensitization.

Spiegler, M. D., & Guevremont, D. C. (2010). *Contemporary behavior therapy* (5th ed.). Pacific Grove, CA: Brooks/Cole. An excellent introductory text on behavior therapy describing many different treatment procedures, including some procedures not mentioned in this chapter.

STUDY QUESTIONS

1. Describe Pavlov's stimulus-substitution theory. What is the preparatory-response theory of conditioning, and what advantage does it have over stimulus-substitution theory?
2. Describe the compensatory-response model of conditioning. How does the compensatory-response model account for drug overdoses that occur when an addict seems to have injected only a normal amount of the drug?
3. Describe the Rescorla-Wagner theory. Describe (or diagram) the Rescorla-Wagner theory account of blocking. Describe (or diagram) how the Rescorla-Wagner theory accounts for the overexpectation effect.
4. Briefly describe the Watson and Rayner experiment with Little Albert and the results obtained. What are some of the weaknesses in this experiment as a demonstration of classical conditioning of a phobia?
5. Assuming that look of fear in others can act as a US, diagram an example of observational learning in a child's acquisition of a phobia to mice. Be sure to include the appropriate abbreviations (NS, US, etc.).
6. Describe how temperament and preparedness can affect the acquisition of a phobia, and give an example of each that helps clearly differentiate between the two.
7. Describe how incubation, selective sensitization, and US revaluation can affect the acquisition of a phobia. Give an example of each that clearly differentiates it from the other two concepts.
8. What is counterconditioning and reciprocal inhibition? Describe how counterconditioning might be used to try to reduce your aversion to your roommate's bad taste in music.
9. Describe the use of imaginal versions of systematic desensitization versus flooding to treat a student's exam anxiety. How do they differ in terms of the underlying process by which each type of treatment is presumed to produce its effect?
10. Define aversion therapy and covert sensitization. Why is shock generally less effective than nausea in producing an aversion to cigarettes or alcohol?
11. Diagram an example of a classical conditioning procedure that alters immune system functioning. In what way might classical conditioning be involved in the creation of a placebo effect?

CONCEPT REVIEW

aversion therapy. A form of behavior therapy that attempts to reduce the attractiveness of a desired event by associating it with an aversive stimulus.

compensatory-response model. A model of conditioning in which a CS that has been repeatedly associated with the primary response (a-process) to a US will eventually come to elicit a compensatory response (b-process).

counterconditioning. The procedure whereby a CS that elicits one type of response is associated with an event that elicits an incompatible response.

flooding therapy. A behavioral treatment for phobias that involves prolonged exposure to a feared stimulus, thereby providing maximal opportunity for the conditioned fear response to be extinguished.

incubation. The strengthening of a conditioned fear response as a result of brief exposures to an aversive CS.

overexpectation effect. The decrease in the conditioned response that occurs when two separately conditioned CSs are combined into a compound stimulus for further pairings with the US.

preparatory-response theory. A theory of classical conditioning that proposes that the purpose of the CR is to prepare the organism for the presentation of the US.

preparedness. An innate predisposition to learn certain kinds of associations more easily than others (e.g., to associate snakes with an aversive event).

reciprocal inhibition. The process whereby the occurrence of a response is inhibited by the occurrence of an incompatible response.

Rescorla-Wagner theory. A theory of classical conditioning that proposes that a given US can support only so much conditioning and that this amount of conditioning must be distributed among the various CSs.

selective sensitization. An increase in one's reactivity to a potentially fearful stimulus following exposure to an unrelated stressful event.

stimulus-substitution theory. A theory of classical conditioning that proposes that the CS acts as a substitute for the US.

systematic desensitization. A behavioral treatment for phobias that involves pairing relaxation with a succession of stimuli that elicit increasing levels of fear.

temperament. An individual's level of emotional reactivity that, to a large extent, is genetically determined.

CHAPTER TEST

8. The three steps in systematic desensitization are training in relaxation, creation of a hierarchy of feared situations, and pairing each item in the hierarchy with relaxation.

21. In the Little Albert study, the loud noise was the (CS/US), while the white rat was the (CS/US). Little Albert's fear of other furry objects illustrates the process of stimulus ________.
3. Lothar's job has recently become quite stressful. Interestingly, he is also developing a fear of driving through rush-hour traffic. This is best described as an example of ________.
12. One weakness in the Little Albert study is that they did not control for the possibility of ________ conditioning. Also, unlike most real-life phobias, Albert's fear conditioning seemed to require (several/one) trial(s) to become established and grew (weaker/stronger) over time.
25. Tara's original slight fear of spiders turns into a major phobia when she witnesses a friend become hospitalized after being bitten by a spider. This is an example of ________.
7. The procedure of pairing a feared dog with an appetitive stimulus such as candy is an example of ________. This type of procedure can be effective due to the underlying process of ________.
20. When Uncle Bob and Aunt Shirley were separated, they each gave Little Lucas great Christmas presents, with the result that he developed positive feelings for both of them. They then resolved their difficulties and moved back together. They now give Little Lucas one great present from the two of them. The Rescorla-Wagner theory predicts that Little Lucas's positive feelings for each will become (stronger/weaker). This is known as the ________ effect.
13. In keeping with ________ theory, Pavlov's dogs would sometimes treat a light that had been paired with food as though it were itself food.
9. Desensitization and flooding procedures that utilize thoughts about the feared stimulus are known as ________ procedures, whereas procedures that involve exposure to the real stimulus are known as ________ procedures.
2. While playing with a spider, Suyen was frightened by the sound of a firecracker. As a result, she acquired a lasting fear of spiders, but not of firecrackers. This is an illustration of the concept of ________.
17. According to the Rescorla-Wagner theory, overshadowing occurs because the ________ stimulus picks up most of the associative value.
26. Fatalities seemingly due to drug overdose may sometimes be the result of taking the drug in a setting that is (associated/not associated) with drug use, thereby resulting in a (weaker/stronger) compensatory response and a (higher/lower) level of drug tolerance.
10. In ________ therapy, one attempts to (decrease/increase) the attractiveness of a desired event by pairing it with an (appetitive/aversive) stimulus. An imagery-based form of this therapy is called ________.
6. Traditional advice has it that if you fall off a horse you should immediately get back on and keep riding until your fear has disappeared. This approach is

similar to the therapeutic technique known as ______________. Furthermore, getting back on immediately allows no opportunity for brief exposures to the feared stimulus, which could result in ______________ of the conditioned fear response.

24. Evidence for the role of conditioning in placebo effects includes the fact that such effects are more likely to occur (following/preceding) a period of treatment with (a fake/the real) drug. Also, repeated administration of a placebo reduces its effectiveness, which suggests that a process of ______________ is taking place.

14. I am likely to become most intoxicated if I drink alcohol in the presence of cues (associated with/not associated with) alcohol.

18. According to the Rescorla-Wagner theory, ______________ occurs because the (CS/NS/US) in the compound stimulus has already picked up most of the associative value.

4. Bo was never afraid of bees until he saw his best friend, Emmet, react with a look of horror to the sight of a bee. Bo now becomes quite anxious each time he sees a bee. This is best described as an example of ______________ learning.

15. A cat salivates to the sound of your alarm clock in anticipation of a breakfast feeding. It also freezes at the sight of another cat in anticipation of an attack. These examples are best accounted for by the ______________ theory of conditioning.

23. Tika's slight fear of snakes turns into a major phobia when she suffers a serious illness. This is an example of the process of ______________.

1. The ease with which an individual can acquire a conditioned fear response may be influenced by that person's emotional reactivity, which is known as ______________. This may, to a large extent, be (genetically/environmentally) determined.

11. Fran experiences an allergic reaction whenever people even talk about dogs. In the terminology of classical conditioning, the talk about dogs appears to be a (use the abbreviation) ______________ while the allergic reaction is a ______________.

19. According to the ______________ effect, if two fully conditioned stimuli are combined into a compound stimulus that is then subjected to further pairings with the US, the associative value of each member of the compound will (increase/decrease).

5. In conditioning of a compensatory response to shock, the actual US for the compensatory response would be the (shock/decrease in heart rate/increase in heart rate).

16. Research on classical conditioning processes in drug addiction suggests that the withdrawal symptoms evoked by the sight of a desired drug are actually ______________ reactions to the drug that have come to be elicited by environmental cues associated with the drug.

22. Tran's slight fear of rats turns into a major phobia when he is told by his parents that rats are much more dangerous than he previously suspected. This is an example of US revaluation

ANSWERS TO CHAPTER TEST

1. temperament; genetically
2. preparedness
3. selective sensitization
4. observational
5. increase in heart rate
6. flooding; incubation
7. counterconditioning; reciprocal inhibition
8. relaxation; hierarchy; each item in the hierarchy with relaxation
9. imaginal; *in vivo*
10. aversion; decrease; aversive; covert sensitization
11. CS; CR
12. pseudo-; several; weaker
13. stimulus-substitution
14. not associated with
15. preparatory-response
16. compensatory (or opponent or b-process)
17. more salient (stronger)
18. blocking; CS
19. overexpectation; decrease
20. weaker; overexpectation
21. US; CS; generalization
22. US revaluation
23. selective sensitization
24. following; the real; extinction
25. US revaluation (in this case combined with observational learning)
26. not associated; weaker; lower

CHAPTER 6

OPERANT CONDITIONING: INTRODUCTION

CHAPTER OUTLINE

"Hurry up," he growled as she carefully searched the selection of videos.

"Oh, don't be so grumpy," she said sweetly, hooking her arm into his.

"Just pick one, damn it!"

She quickly picked out a video, then gave him a hug as they walked to the checkout counter. (Based on a real incident observed in a video store.)

In the last few chapters, we focused on elicited behavior and the type of learning known as classical conditioning. Elicited behavior is controlled by the stimuli that precede it. Recall how in Pavlov's classic experiment food elicited salivation and how, after a tone had been paired with food, it too elicited salivation:

Tone: Food → *Salivation*
Tone → *Salivation*

Note how the target response in this type of learning always occurs at the end of the sequence. The preceding stimulus, by itself, is sufficient to elicit the response. In this sense, the process is very reflexive: Present the stimulus and the response automatically follows.

But is everything we do this reflexive? Does the sight of this text, for example, automatically elicit the response of reading? Obviously it does not (though students who tend to procrastinate might sometimes wish that it did). Rather, if you had to explain why you are reading this text, you are likely to say you are reading it in order to achieve something—such as an understanding of the subject matter or a high grade in a course. Reading the text is oriented toward some goal, a consequence, and this consequence is the reason for the behavior. Indeed, most behaviors that concern us each day are motivated by a consequence. For example, we go to a restaurant for a meal, we turn on a radio to hear music, and we ask someone out on a date hoping he or she will accept. When we fail to achieve the desired outcome, we are unlikely to continue the behavior. How long would you persist in asking someone out on a date if that person never accepted?

Behaviors that are influenced by their consequences are called *operant behaviors* and the effects of those consequences upon behavior are called *operant conditioning*. They are called operant conditioning because the response *operates on the environment* to produce a consequence. This type of learning is also called *instrumental conditioning* because the response is *instrumental* in producing the consequence.

QUICK QUIZ A

1. Operant behaviors are influenced by their ________.
2. Elicited behavior is a function of what (precedes/follows) it; operant behavior is a function of what (precedes/follows) it.
3. Another name for operant conditioning is ________ conditioning.

Historical Background

Although people have used operant conditioning for thousands of years (e.g., in raising children, training animals), this kind of learning was not subjected to scientific analysis until the 1890s when Edwin L. Thorndike investigated the learning ability of animals.

© Psychology Archives/The University of Akron

Edwin L. Thorndike
(1874–1949)

Thorndike's Law of Effect

As a graduate student, Thorndike was interested in animal intelligence. There was considerable speculation at that time that animals were capable of higher forms of reasoning. Particularly impressive were stories about lost dogs and cats finding their way home over long distances. As Thorndike (1898) noted, however, "Dogs get lost hundreds of times and no one ever notices it or sends an account of it to a scientific magazine, but let one find his way from Brooklyn to Yonkers and the fact immediately becomes a circulating anecdote" (p. 4; see also Thorndike, 1911).

Thorndike was not suggesting that animals could not in some ways be intelligent, but rather that we should not accept anecdotes as fact, nor should we assume that animals behaving in a particular way are doing so for intelligent reasons. It was not only the lay public that caused Thorndike to argue for caution in interpreting animal behavior. Some of his contemporary researchers were also guilty of a noncritical analysis of animal intelligence. In particular, George John Romanes (1888/1989) argued that animals engage in thought processes, such as decision making, that are analogous to human thought processes, and he presented various anecdotes to support his case. Thorndike was skeptical, however, and believed that the intellectual ability of animals could be properly assessed only through systematic investigation.

Of the many experiments Thorndike (1898) conducted with animals, the most famous one involved cats. In a typical experiment, a hungry cat was enclosed in a puzzle box, and a dish of food was placed outside. To reach the food, the cat had to learn how to escape from the box, such as by stepping on a treadle that opened a gate. The first time the cat was placed in the puzzle box, several minutes passed before it accidentally stepped on the treadle and opened the gate. Over repeated trials, it learned to escape the box more quickly. There was, however, no sudden improvement in performance as would be expected if the cat had experienced a "flash of insight" about how to solve the problem. Rather, it seemed as though the response that worked (stepping on the treadle) was gradually strengthened, while responses that did not work (e.g., clawing at the gate, chewing on the cage) were gradually weakened (see Figure 6.1). Thorndike suspected that a similar process

A convincing example of animal intelligence.

FIGURE 6.1 Thorndike's puzzle box. In a typical experiment, a hungry cat was enclosed in a puzzle box and a dish of food was placed outside the box. To reach the food, the cat had to learn how to escape from the box by stepping on a treadle that opened the gate. The graph illustrates the general decrease across trials in the amount of time it took the cat to escape. (*Source*: Nairne, 2000.)

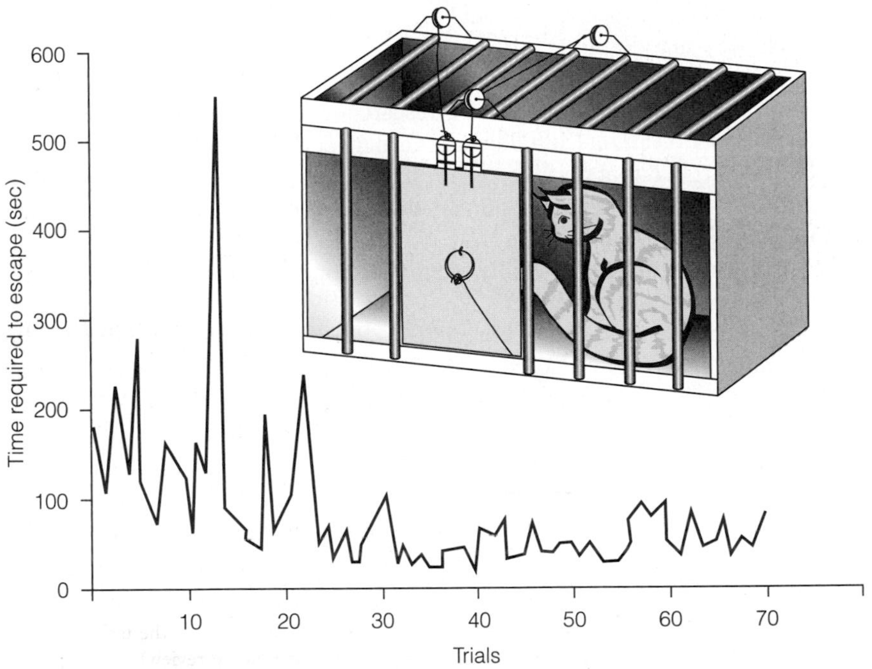

governed all learning, and on this basis he formulated his famous law of effect.[1]

According to the ***law of effect***, behaviors leading to a satisfying state of affairs are strengthened or "stamped in," while behaviors leading to an unsatisfying or annoying state of affairs are weakened or "stamped out." Thus, the extent to which the *consequences* of a behavior are satisfying or annoying determine whether the behavior will be repeated. Thorndike's law of effect is a hallmark in the history of psychology. However, it was another young scientist by the name of Burrhus Frederic Skinner who fully realized the implications of this principle for understanding and changing behavior.

Skinner's Selection by Consequences

Skinner came upon the study of operant conditioning by a somewhat different route. As a graduate student in the late 1920s, he was well aware of Thorndike's law of effect. However, like many psychologists of the time, he believed that behavior could best be analyzed as though it were a reflex. He also realized, like Pavlov, that a scientific analysis of behavior required finding a procedure that yielded regular patterns of behavior. Without such regularity, which could be achieved only in a well-controlled environment, it would be difficult to discover the underlying principles of behavior.

In this context, Skinner set out to devise his own procedure for the study of behavior, eventually producing one of the best-known apparatuses in experimental psychology: the operant conditioning chamber, or "Skinner box." In a standard Skinner box for rats, the rat is able to earn food pellets by pressing a response lever or bar (see Figure 6.2).

Skinner's procedure is known as the "free operant" procedure because the rat freely responds with a particular behavior (like pressing a lever) for food, and it may do so at any rate. The experimenter controls the contingencies within the operant chamber, but the animal is not forced to respond at a particular time. This contrasts with other procedures for studying animal learning, such as maze learning, in which the experimenter initiates each trial by placing the rat in the start box.[2] Skinner demonstrated that the rate of behavior in an operant chamber was controlled by the conditions that he established in his experiments. Later, Skinner invented a variant of the operant chamber for pigeons, in which the pigeon pecks an illuminated plastic disc called a response key (named after the telegraph key) to earn a few seconds of access to food (see Figure 6.3). Many of the principles of operant

---

[1]Although Thorndike's research led to a general tendency to reject anecdotal evidence for "insightful" learning in animals, some researchers believe he may have overstated the case. They claim that there is evidence available for rapid learning, depending on the task and the species examined (see Wasserman & Zentall, 2006, for a comprehensive review).

[2]Although the terms *operant conditioning* and *instrumental conditioning* are often used interchangeably, the latter term is sometimes reserved for procedures that involve distinct learning trials, such as maze learning experiments, as opposed to Skinner's free operant procedure.

FIGURE 6.2 Operant conditioning chamber for rats. When the rat presses the lever (or bar), a food pellet drops into the food tray. Aversive stimuli can be presented by delivering an electric shock through the floor grids. (*Source*: Lieberman, 2000.)

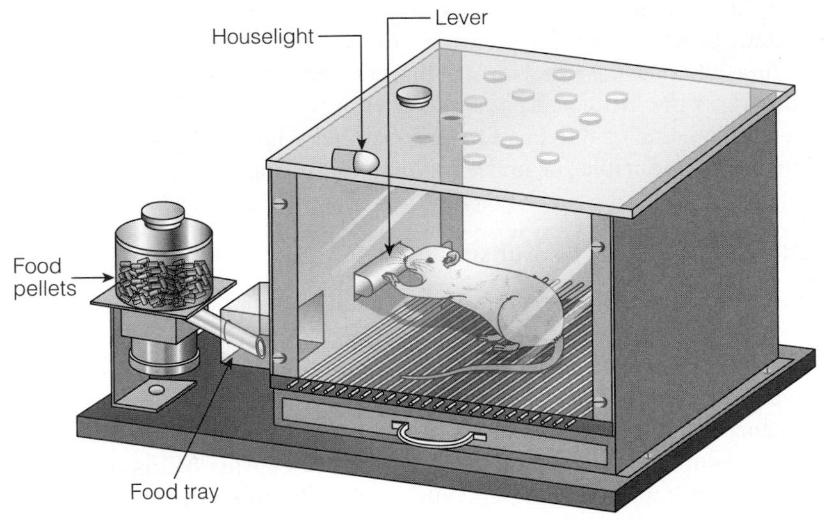

conditioning were discovered with the use of these key-pecking and lever pressing procedures.

With the evolution of the Skinner box, Skinner's beliefs about the nature of behavior also changed. He abandoned the notion that all behavior could be analyzed in terms of reflexes and, along with other learning theorists, came

FIGURE 6.3 Operant conditioning chamber for pigeons. When the pigeon pecks the response key (a translucent plastic disc that can be illuminated with different colored lights), grain is presented in the food cup for a period of a few seconds. (*Source*: Domjan, 2000.)

to believe that behaviors can be conveniently divided into two categories. One category consists of involuntary, reflexive-type behaviors, which as Pavlov had demonstrated can often be classically conditioned to occur in new situations. Skinner referred to such behavior as *respondent behavior*. The other category, which Skinner called *operant behavior*, consists of behaviors that seem more voluntary in nature and are controlled by their consequences rather than by the stimuli that precede them. It was this type of behavior that Thorndike had studied in his puzzle box experiments and upon which he had based his law of effect. It was this type of behavior that most interested Skinner as well. He spent the rest of his life investigating the basic principles of operant conditioning and applying those principles to important aspects of human behavior (Skinner, 1938, 1967; see also Bjork, 1993).

QUICK QUIZ B

1. Thorndike's cats learned to solve the puzzle box problem (gradually/suddenly).
2. Based on his research with cats, Thorndike formulated his famous __________ of __________, which states that behaviors that lead to a(n) __________ state of affairs are strengthened, while behaviors that lead to a(n) __________ state of affairs are weakened.
3. According to Thorndike, behaviors that worked were st__________ i__________, while behaviors that did not work were st__________ o__________.
4. The Skinner box evolved out of Skinner's quest for a procedure that would, among other things, yield (regular/irregular) patterns of behavior.
5. In the original version of the Skinner box, rats earn food by p__________ a l__________; in another version, pigeons earn a few seconds of access to food by p__________ at an illuminated plastic disc known as a __________ __________.
6. Skinner's procedures are also known as fr__________ o__________ procedures in that the animal controls the rate at which it earns food.
7. Skinner originally thought all behavior could be explained in terms of __________, but he eventually decided that this type of behavior could be distinguished from another, seemingly more voluntary type of behavior known as __________ behavior.

Operant Conditioning

Operant conditioning is a type of learning in which the future probability of a behavior is affected by its consequences. Note that this is essentially a restatement of Thorndike's law of effect. Skinner, however, was dissatisfied with Thorndike's mentalistic description of consequences as being either satisfying or annoying. Satisfaction and annoyance are internal states inferred from the animal's behavior. Skinner avoided any speculation about what the animal (or person) might be thinking or feeling and simply emphasized the effect of the consequence on the future *probability* of the behavior.

Note that Skinner's principle of operant conditioning bears a striking resemblance to Darwin's evolutionary principle of natural selection. According to the principle of natural selection, members of a species that inherit certain adaptive characteristics are more likely to survive and propagate, thereby passing that characteristic on to offspring. Thus, over many generations, the frequency of those adaptive characteristics within the population will increase and become well established. Similarly, according to the principle of operant conditioning, behaviors that lead to favorable outcomes are more likely to be repeated than those that do not lead to favorable outcomes. Thus, operant conditioning is sort of a mini-evolution of an organism's behaviors, in which behaviors that are adaptive (lead to favorable outcomes) become more frequent while behaviors that are nonadaptive (do not lead to favorable outcomes) become less frequent.

The operant conditioning process can be conceptualized as involving three components: (1) a response that produces a certain consequence (e.g., lever pressing produces a food pellet), (2) the consequence that serves to either increase or decrease the probability of the response that preceded it (e.g., the consequence of a food pellet increases the rat's tendency to again press the lever), and (3) a discriminative stimulus that precedes the response and signals that a certain consequence is now available (e.g., a tone that signals that a lever press will now produce food). These components are examined in more detail below.

Operant Behavior

An ***operant behavior*** is a class of emitted responses that result in certain consequences; these consequences then affect the future probability or strength of those responses. Operant responses are sometimes simply called *operants*. Suppose, for example, that a rat presses a lever and receives a food pellet, with the result that it is more likely to press the lever in the future.

Lever press→ **Food pellet**

The effect: The future probability of lever pressing increases.

Or Jonathan might tell a joke and receive a frown from the person he tells it to. He is now less likely to tell that person a joke in the future.

Tell a joke → **Person frowns**

The effect: The future probability of telling a joke decreases.

In each case, the behavior in question (the lever pressing or the joke telling) is an operant response (or an "operant") because its occurrence results in a certain consequence *and* that consequence affects the future probability of the response.

In contrast to classically conditioned behaviors, which are said to be *elicited by stimuli* (e.g., food elicits salivation), operant behaviors are technically said to be *emitted by the organism* (e.g., the rat emits lever presses or the person emits the behavior of telling jokes). This wording is used to indicate that operant behavior appears to have a more voluntary, flexible quality to it compared to elicited behavior, which is generally more reflexive and automatic. (Does this mean that operant behavior actually is voluntary? Not necessarily. Insofar as such behavior comes to be controlled by the consequences that follow the behavior, it can be argued that the sense of voluntariness, or "freedom of choice," that accompanies such behavior is merely an illusion [Skinner, 1953].)

Operant behavior is typically defined as a *class of responses*, with all of the responses in that class capable of producing the consequence. For example, there are many ways a rat can press a lever for food: hard or soft, quick or slow, right paw or left paw. All of these responses are effective in depressing the lever and producing food; therefore they all belong to the same class of responses known as "lever presses." Similarly, Jonathan could tell many different jokes, and he could even tell the same joke in many different ways, all of which might produce a laugh. Defining operants in terms of classes has proven fruitful because it is easier to predict the occurrence of a class of responses than it is to predict the *exact* response that will be emitted at a particular point in time. For example, it is easier to predict that a hungry rat will press a lever to obtain food than it is to predict exactly how it will press the lever on any particular occasion.

QUICK QUIZ C

1. Skinner's definition of operant conditioning differs from Thorndike's law of effect in that it is (more/less) mentalistic.
2. Operant conditioning is similar to the principle of natural selection in that behaviors that are (adaptive/nonadaptive) tend to increase in frequency, while behaviors that are __________ tend to decrease in frequency. The difference is that operant conditioning deals with changes within a(n) (species/individual) while the principle of natural selection deals with changes within a(n) __________.
3. The process of operant conditioning involves the following three components: (1) a r__________ that produces a certain __________, (2) a c__________ that serves to either increase or decrease the likelihood of the __________ that preceded it, and (3) a d__________ stimulus that precedes the __________ and signals that a certain __________ is now available.
4. Classically conditioned behaviors are said to be e__________ by the stimulus, while operant behaviors are said to be e__________ by the organism.
5. Operant responses are also simply called __________.
6. Operant behavior is usually defined as a(n) __________ of responses rather than a specific response.

Operant Consequences: Reinforcers and Punishers

The second component of an operant conditioning procedure is the consequence that either increases (strengthens) or decreases (weakens) the frequency of a behavior. Consequences that strengthen a behavior are called reinforcers, and consequences that weaken a behavior are called punishers.

Thus, an event is a ***reinforcer*** if (1) it follows a behavior, and (2) the future probability of that behavior increases. Conversely, an event is a ***punisher*** if (1) it follows a behavior, and (2) the future probability of that behavior decreases.

Diagrams of operant conditioning procedures generally use the following symbols. Reinforcers are usually given the symbol S^R (which stands for *reinforcing stimulus*), and punishers are given the symbol S^P (which stands for *punishing stimulus*). The operant response is given the symbol R. Using these abbreviations, a diagram of a procedure in which a lever press is reinforced by the delivery of a food pellet looks like this:

Lever press → **Food pellet**
R $\mathbf{S^R}$

The food pellet is a reinforcer because it follows the lever press *and* increases the future probability of lever pressing. A diagram of Jonathan's failed attempt at humor, in which a frown punished his behavior of telling jokes, looks like this:

Tell a joke → **Person frowns**
R $\mathbf{S^P}$

The frown is a punisher because it follows the joke *and* the future probability of joke telling decreases.

Note that, from a behavior analysis perspective, it is technically incorrect to say that a person or animal has been reinforced or punished; rather, it is the behavior that has been reinforced or punished. Only the behavior increases or decreases in frequency. (But not everyone is this strict or cautious in their wording, and it is not uncommon to see references to the animal being reinforced. There is value, however, in emphasizing behavior in this way. If you want a child to stop doing something, should you tell her that her behavior displeases you or that she displeases you? Similarly, when your roommate does something that bothers you, will it be more constructive to tell him that his behavior disturbs you or that he disturbs you? Is it easier for people to change their behavior or to change who they are?)

It is also important to differentiate the terms *reinforcer* and *punisher* from *reinforcement* and *punishment*. *Reinforcer* and *punisher* both refer to the specific *consequence* used to strengthen or weaken a behavior. In the previous examples, the food pellet is a reinforcer for lever pressing, and the frown is a punisher for joke telling. In contrast, the terms *reinforcement* and *punishment* usually refer to the *process* or *procedure* by which a certain consequence changes the strength of a behavior. Thus, the use of food to increase the strength of lever pressing is an example of reinforcement, while the food itself is a reinforcer. Similarly, the process of frowning to discourage Jonathan from telling jokes is an example of punishment, while the frown itself is a punisher. In summary, the terms *reinforcer* and *punisher* refer to the actual consequences of the behavior; the terms *reinforcement* and *punishment* refer to the process or procedure of strengthening or weakening a behavior by instituting those consequences.

Note, too, that *reinforcers and punishers are formally defined entirely by their effect on behavior*. For example, a laugh is a reinforcer for the behavior of joke telling only to the extent that joke telling then increases. If, for some reason, joke telling decreases as a result of the laugh (perhaps the person telling the joke delights in disgusting his listeners and does not want them to find his joke funny), the laugh would by definition be a punisher. It is important to remember this, because events that on the surface seem like reinforcers or punishers do not always function in that manner. We encountered this notion in Chapter 2 in our discussion of the distinction between appetitive and aversive events (and particularly in the cartoon depiction of Calvin ravenously eating what he believes to be a bowl of maggot soup). In similar fashion, a teacher might yell at her students for being disruptive, and as a result the students become *more* (not less) disruptive. Although the teacher is clearly trying to punish the disruptive behavior, the yelling is actually having the opposite effect. By definition, therefore, the yelling is a reinforcer because it is causing the disruptive behavior to increase in frequency (perhaps because disruptive students find that other students admire them if they upset the teacher).

Thus, the safest bet is to define consequences as reinforcers and punishers in relation to their effect on behavior and not in relation to how pleasant or unpleasant they seem. It is for this reason that many behaviorists prefer the term *reinforcer* rather than *reward*, the latter term being too strongly associated with events that are seemingly pleasant (e.g., affection, food, money). For example, the teacher's yelling is hardly what anyone would call a reward, but technically speaking it is a reinforcer for the students' disruptive behavior. Not all behaviorists are this strict in their terminology, however, and they sometimes use the terms *reward* and *reinforcer* interchangeably (e.g., Bandura, 1997; Herrnstein, 1997).[3] Moreover, because students often find it helpful to think of consequences in terms of whether they are pleasant or unpleasant, we will sometimes make use of such terms in our discussion of consequences. In other words, to help you gain an initial grasp of this material, we will sometimes be rather informal in the terminology we use. (You should check with your professor, however, to determine if such informality will be acceptable in the course you are taking.)

Finally, you should be aware that punishment is not the only means of weakening a behavior. A response that has been strengthened through reinforcement can also be weakened by the withdrawal of reinforcement. The weakening of a behavior through the nonreinforcement of a previously

[3]Furthermore, some behaviorists use the term *reward* to refer to the effect of the consequence on the animal as opposed to behavior (Rachlin, 1991). For example, a dog biscuit can be both a reinforcer for the dog's *behavior* of begging and a reward to the *dog* for having carried out such a behavior. Or, to put it differently, reinforcers strengthen our behavior, while rewards make us happy.

reinforced behavior is known as ***extinction***. For example, a child who has learned to whine for candy in the supermarket will eventually cease whining when behaving that way no longer results in candy. Likewise, a roommate who tells gross jokes because of the outraged reaction he gets from his religiously inclined roommates will eventually stop telling such jokes if the roommates stop reacting that way. Extinction is usually a much gentler process than punishment; one drawback to it, however, is that it is typically a much slower process. Extinction and the various issues associated with it are more fully discussed in Chapter 8.

QUICK QUIZ D

1. Simply put, reinforcers are those consequences that s____________ a behavior, while punishers are those consequences that w____________ a behavior.
2. A reinforcer is an event that (precedes/follows) a behavior and (increases/decreases) the probability of that behavior. A punisher is an event that (precedes/follows) a behavior and (increases/decreases) the probability of that behavior.
3. The terms *reinforcement* and *punishment* refer to the pr____________ or pr____________ whereby a behavior is strengthened or weakened by its consequences.
4. Strengthening a roommate's tendency toward cleanliness by thanking her when she cleans the bathroom is an example of a (reinforcement/reinforcer), while the thanks itself is a ____________.
5. Eliminating a dog's tendency to jump up on visitors by scolding her when she does so is an example of (punisher/punishment), while the scolding itself is a ____________.
6. Strictly speaking, reinforcers and punishers are defined entirely by their ____________ on behavior. For this reason, the term *reinforcer* is often preferred to the term ____________ because the latter is too closely associated with events that are regarded as pleasant or desirable, and such events may or may not strengthen a behavior.
7. When Moe stuck his finger in a light socket, he received an electric shock. As a result, he now sticks his finger in the light socket as often as possible. By definition, the electric shock was a ____________ because the behavior it followed has increased in frequency.
8. Each time Edna talked in class, her teacher immediately came over and gave her a hug. As a result, Edna no longer talks in class. By definition, the hug is a ____________ because the behavior it follows has decreased in frequency.
9. When labeling an operant conditioning procedure, punishing consequences (punishers) are given the symbol ____________ (which stands for ____________ ____________), while reinforcing consequences (reinforcers) are given the symbol ____________ (which stands for ____________ ____________). The operant response is given the symbol ____________.
10. When we give a dog a treat for fetching a toy, are we attempting to reinforce (a) the behavior of fetching the toy, or (b) the dog that fetched the toy? When

we chastise a child for being rude, are we attempting to punish (a) the child who was rude, or (b) the child's rude behavior?

11. Weakening a behavior through the withdrawal of reinforcement for that behavior is known as extinction. In general, this is a (slower/faster) process than punishment.

12. Clayton stopped using the toaster after he received a shock while doing so. This is an example of (punishment/extinction). Manzar stopped using the toaster after it no longer made good toast. This is an example of extinction.

Operant Antecedents: Discriminative Stimuli

The operant response and its consequence are the most essential components of the operant conditioning procedure. In most circumstances, however, a third component can also be identified. When a behavior is consistently reinforced or punished in the presence of certain stimuli, those stimuli will begin to influence the occurrence of the behavior. For example, if lever pressing produces food only when a tone is sounding, the rat soon learns to press the lever only when it hears the tone. This situation can be diagrammed as follows:

Tone: ***Lever Press*** **→ Food pellet**
S^D R S^R

This sequence can be read as follows: In the presence of the tone, if the rat presses the lever, it will receive food. The tone is called a discriminative stimulus. Discriminative stimuli are traditionally given the symbol S^D (pronounced "es-dee"). A ***discriminative stimulus (S^D)*** is a stimulus in the presence of which responses are reinforced and in the absence of which they are not reinforced. In other words, a discriminative stimulus is a signal that indicates that a response will be followed by a reinforcer.

Another example: If Susan always laughs at Jonathan's jokes, then he is more likely to tell her a joke. The sight of Susan is an S^D for Jonathan's behavior of telling jokes. This can be diagrammed as follows:

Susan: ***Tell her a joke*** **→ She laughs**
S^D R S^R

Discriminative stimuli are said to "set the occasion for" the behavior, meaning that the behavior is more likely to occur in the presence of those stimuli. Discriminative stimuli do not elicit behavior in the manner of a CS or US in classical conditioning. For example, the tone does not automatically elicit a lever press; it merely increases the probability that a lever press will occur. Whether or not lever pressing occurs is still a function of its consequence (food), and the S^D simply indicates that this consequence is now available. Similarly, the presence of Susan does not automatically elicit the behavior of joke telling in Jonathan; rather, he is simply more likely to tell a joke in her presence. Therefore, rather than saying that the S^D elicits the behavior, we say that the person or animal emits the behavior in the presence of the S^D. (Remember, it is only in classical conditioning that we say that the stimulus *elicits* the behavior. In operant conditioning, we say that the organism *emits* the behavior.)

The discriminative stimulus, the operant behavior, and the reinforcer or punisher constitute what is known as the ***three-term contingency***. The three-term contingency can also be viewed as consisting of an *antecedent event* (an antecedent event is a *preceding* event), a *behavior*, and a *consequence* (which can be remembered by the initials ABC).

Antecedent	*Behavior*	*Consequence*
Susan:	***Tell her a joke →***	**She laughs**
S^D	**R**	S^R
Tone:	***Lever press →***	**Food pellet**
S^D	**R**	S^R

Another way of thinking about this sequence is that you notice something (Susan), do something (tell Susan a joke), and get something (Susan laughs at your joke). Similarly, you notice that it is 7:00 P.M., you turn on the TV, and you get to see your favorite sitcom. Or maybe your dog notices that you have popcorn, begs persistently, and gets some of the popcorn. Many students find this sequence easy to remember: Notice something, do something, get something (although, as you will later see, the consequence in some cases involves losing or avoiding something rather than getting something). Analyzing a problem behavior in terms of the three-term contingency—the manner in which the antecedents and consequences affect the strength of the behavior—is considered a fundamental aspect of applied behavior analysis.

So far, we have dealt only with stimuli that are associated with reinforcement. Stimuli can also be associated with punishment. A stimulus that signals that a response will be punished is called a ***discriminative stimulus for punishment*** (which is sometimes given the symbol S^{Dp}). For example, if a water bottle signals that meowing will result in being sprayed with water (rather than being fed), a cat will quickly learn to stop meowing whenever it sees the water bottle.

Water bottle: ***Meow*** **→ Get sprayed**
S^{Dp} **R** S^P

Similarly, a motorist who receives a fine for speeding in the presence of a police car will soon learn to stop speeding in the presence of police cars.

Police car: ***Speed*** **→ Receive fine**
S^{Dp} **R** S^P

For the speeding motorist, the presence of a police car is a discriminative stimulus for punishment.

A discriminative stimulus may also signal the occurrence of *extinction*; that is, the stimulus signals the nonavailability of a previously available reinforcer. If, for example, lever pressing is typically followed by the presentation of food, but only when a tone is sounding and not when a buzzer is sounding, then:

Tone: ***Lever press*** **→ Food pellet**
S^D R S^R

Buzzer: ***Lever press*** **→ No food**
S^Δ R —

The buzzer in this case is a ***discriminative stimulus for extinction***, which is a stimulus that signals the absence of reinforcement. As you can see in the example above, the discriminative stimulus for extinction is typically given the symbol S^Δ (pronounced "es-delta"). As noted earlier, the process of extinction is more fully discussed in Chapter 8.[4]

Finally, you should be aware that processes of operant and classical conditioning overlap such that a particular stimulus can simultaneously act as both a discriminative stimulus and a conditioned stimulus. For example, consider a tone that serves as an S^D for the operant behavior of lever pressing for food:

Tone: ***Lever press*** **→ Food**
S^D R S^R

The tone is closely associated with food, and food, of course, elicits salivation. This means that during the course of our operant conditioning procedure, the tone will also become a conditioned stimulus (CS) that elicits salivation as a conditioned response (CR). Thus, if we ignore the lever pressing and concentrate just on the salivation, then what is happening is this:

Tone: Food → ***Salivation***
NS US UR

Tone → ***Salivation***
CS CR

Whether the tone should be considered an S^D or a CS depends on the response to which one is referring. It is an S^D with respect to the operant response of lever pressing and a CS with respect to the classically conditioned response of salivation. (See Table 6.1 for a summary of the differences between classical and operant conditioning.)

[4]The symbols for discriminative stimuli are not entirely standardized. Some textbooks use S+ (positive discriminative stimulus) to denote the discriminative stimulus for reinforcement, and S– (negative discriminative stimulus) to denote the discriminative stimulus for extinction or punishment.

TABLE 6-1 **Differences between operant and classical conditioning. Note that these are *traditional* differences. As you will see in Chapter 12, the distinction between classical and operant conditioning is sometimes less clear than what is depicted here.**

CLASSICAL CONDITIONING	OPERANT CONDITIONING
Behavior is generally seen as involuntary and inflexible.	Behavior is generally seen as voluntary and flexible.
Behavior is said to be "elicited by the stimulus."	Behavior is said to be "emitted by the organism."
This type of conditioning typically involves innate patterns of behavior (URs).	This type of conditioning often does not involve innate patterns of behavior.
Behavior is a function of what comes before it; that is, the preceding stimulus is critical and the consequences are largely irrelevant.	Behavior is a function of what comes after it; that is, the consequences are critical and the preceding stimulus merely "sets the occasion for the behavior."
Conditioning involves a stimulus-stimulus-response (S-S-R) sequence.	Conditioning involves a stimulus-response-stimulus (S-R-S) sequence.

In general, to determine if operant or classical conditioning is involved, the most important question to ask is whether the behavior is mostly a function of what precedes it (classical conditioning) or what might follow it (operant conditioning).

QUICK QUIZ E

1. The operant conditioning procedure usually consists of three components: (1) a d________ s________, (2) an o________ response, and (3) a c________.
2. A discriminative stimulus is usually indicated by the symbol ________.
3. A discriminative stimulus is said to "________ the ________ for the behavior," meaning that its presence makes the response (more/less) likely to occur.
4. A discriminative stimulus (does/does not) elicit behavior as opposed to a conditioned stimulus that (does/does not) elicit behavior.
5. Using the appropriate symbols, label each component in the following three-term contingency (assume that the behavior will be strengthened):
   Phone rings: *Answer phone* → Conversation with friend
   ________ ________ ________
6. The three-term contingency can also be thought of as an ABC sequence, where A stands for ________ B stands for ________ and C stands for ________.
7. Another way of thinking about the three-term contingency is that you ________ something, ________ something, and ________ something.

8. A stimulus in the presence of which a response is punished is called a ________________ for ________________. It can be given the symbol ________.

9. A bell that signals the start of a round in a boxing match and therefore serves as an S^D for the operant response of beginning to box may also serve as a(n) (S^D/CS) for a fear response. This is an example of how the processes of ________ conditioning and ________ conditioning often overlap.

Four Types of Contingencies

We have seen that there are two main types of consequences in operant conditioning: reinforcers and punishers. If the response is followed by a reinforcer, then we say that a *contingency of reinforcement* exists (meaning that the delivery of the reinforcer is contingent upon the response); if the response is followed by a punisher, we say that a *contingency of punishment* exists. However, contingencies of reinforcement and punishment can be further divided into two subtypes: positive and negative. This results in four basic types of contingencies (response-consequence relationships): positive reinforcement, negative reinforcement, positive punishment, and negative punishment. Because these are sometimes confusing to students, we describe them in some detail below.

As you learned previously, reinforcement is a procedure that strengthens a behavior, and punishment is a procedure that weakens a behavior. That part is pretty straightforward, but this next part can be tricky. When combined with the words *reinforcement* or *punishment*, the word *positive* means only that the behavior is followed by the *presentation* or addition of something (think of a + [positive] sign, which means "add"). Thus, the word *positive*, when combined with the terms *reinforcement* or *punishment*, does *not* mean good or pleasant; it means only that the response has resulted in something being added or presented. The event that is presented could either be pleasant (receiving a compliment) or unpleasant (getting yelled at).

Similarly, the word *negative*, when combined with the words *reinforcement* or *punishment*, means only that the behavior is followed by the *removal* of something; that is, something is subtracted from the situation (think of a – [negative] sign, which means "subtract"). The word *negative*, therefore, in this context, does *not* mean bad or unpleasant; it means only that the response results in the removal of something. The something that is removed could be an event that is pleasant (your dessert is taken away) or unpleasant (the person stops yelling at you).

To summarize, in the case of positive reinforcement and positive punishment, the word *positive* means only that the behavior has resulted in something being presented or added. In negative reinforcement and negative punishment, the word *negative* means only that the behavior has resulted in something being removed or subtracted. The word *reinforcement*, of course, means that the behavior will subsequently increase in strength, and the word *punishment* means that the behavior will subsequently decrease in strength.

Thus, to determine which type of contingency is involved in a particular instance, ask yourself the following two questions: (1) *Does the consequence consist of something being presented or withdrawn?* If the consequence consists of something being presented, then it is a *positive* contingency; if the consequence consists of something being withdrawn, then it is a *negative* contingency; (2) *Does the consequence serve to strengthen or weaken the behavior?* If it strengthens the behavior, then we are dealing with *reinforcement*; if it weakens the behavior, then we are dealing with *punishment*. Apply these two questions to situations that you encounter, and you will almost always (we will deal with some exceptions later) be able to determine which of the four types of contingencies is involved.

Finally, you will see in the examples below that we have used the generic symbols S^R and S^P for both the positive and negative versions of reinforcement and punishment. However, more specific symbols are sometimes used, such as S^{R+} for positive reinforcement, S^{R-} for negative reinforcement, S^{P+} for positive punishment, and S^{P-} for negative punishment. Your professor can let you know if he or she has any preferences in this regard.

QUICK QUIZ F

1. The word *positive*, when combined with the words reinforcement or punishment, means only that the behavior is followed by the ____________ of something. The word *negative*, when combined with the words reinforcement or punishment, means only that the behavior is followed by the ____________ of something.
2. The word *positive*, when combined with the words reinforcement or punishment, (does/does not) mean that the consequence is good or pleasant. Similarly, the term *negative*, when combined with the words reinforcement or punishment, (does/does not) mean that the consequence is bad or unpleasant.
3. Within the context of reinforcement and punishment, positive refers to the (addition/subtraction) of something, and negative refers to the (addition/subtraction) of something.
4. Reinforcement is related to a(n) (increase/decrease) in behavior, whereas punishment is related to a(n) (increase/decrease) in behavior.

Positive Reinforcement

Positive reinforcement consists of the *presentation* of a stimulus (one that is usually considered pleasant or rewarding) following a response, which then leads to an increase in the future strength of that response. Loosely speaking, the behavior results in the delivery of something the recipient likes, so the person or animal is more likely to behave that way in the future. Some of the earlier illustrations have been examples of positive reinforcement. The standard rat procedure in which lever pressing produces food is an example of positive reinforcement because the consequence of food leads to an increase in lever pressing. It is reinforcement because the behavior increases in frequency, and it is positive reinforcement because the consequence involves the presentation of something—namely, food (which we would call a positive reinforcer). Here are other examples of positive reinforcement:

Turn on TV → **See the show**
R S^R

Smile at person → **The person smiles at you**
R S^R

Order coffee → **Receive coffee**
R S^R

Study diligently for quiz → **Obtain an excellent mark**
R S^R

Compliment partner → **Receive a kiss**
R S^R

Negative Reinforcement

Negative reinforcement is the *removal* of a stimulus (one that is usually considered unpleasant or aversive) following a response, which then leads to an increase in the future strength of that response. Loosely speaking, the behavior results in the prevention or removal of something the person or animal hates, so they are more likely to behave that way in the future. For example, if by pressing a lever a rat terminates an electric shock that it is receiving, it will become more likely to press the lever the next time it receives an electric shock. This is an example of reinforcement because the behavior increases in strength; it is negative reinforcement because the consequence consists of taking something away. Here are some additional examples:

Open umbrella → **Escape rain**
R S^R

Claim illness → **Avoid writing an exam**
R S^R

Take aspirin → **Eliminate headache**
R S^R

Turn on the heater → **Escape the cold**
R S^R

The last example is interesting because it illustrates how it is sometimes a matter of interpretation as to whether something is an example of negative reinforcement or positive reinforcement. Does the person turn on the heater to escape the cold (negative reinforcement) or to obtain warmth (positive reinforcement)? Either interpretation would be correct.

Negative reinforcement involves two types of behavior: escape and avoidance. ***Escape behavior*** results in the termination (stopping) of an aversive stimulus. In the example of the person getting rained on, by opening the umbrella the person stops this from happening. Likewise, taking aspirin removes a headache, and turning on the heater allows one to escape the cold. Avoidance is similar to escape except that ***avoidance behavior*** occurs before the aversive stimulus is presented and therefore prevents its delivery. For example, if the umbrella were opened before stepping out into the rain, the person would avoid getting rained on. And by pretending to be ill, a student avoids having to take an exam. Escape and avoidance are discussed in more detail in Chapter 9.

QUICK QUIZ G

1. When you reached toward the dog, he nipped at your hand. You quickly pulled your hand back. As a result, he now nips at your hand whenever you reach toward him. The consequence for the *dog's behavior of nipping* consisted of the (presentation/removal) of a stimulus (namely, your hand), and his behavior of nipping subsequently (increased/decreased) in frequency; therefore, this is an example of positive reinforcement.
2. When the dog sat at your feet and whined during breakfast one morning, you fed him. As a result, he sat at your feet and whined during breakfast the next morning. The consequence for the dog's whining consisted of the (presentation/removal) of a stimulus, and his behavior of whining subsequently (increased/decreased) in frequency; therefore, this is an example of positive reinforcement.
3. Karen cries while saying to her boyfriend, "John, I don't feel as though you love me." John gives Karen a big hug, saying, "That's not true, dear, I love you very much." If John's hug is a reinforcer, Karen is (more/less) likely to cry the next time she feels insecure about her relationship. More specifically, this is an example of negative reinforcement of Karen's crying behavior.
4. With respect to escape and avoidance, an escape response is one that *terminates* an aversive stimulus, while an avoidance response is one that *prevents* an aversive stimulus from occurring. Both types of responses are maintained by (positive/negative) ________ reinforcement.
5. Turning down the heat because you are too hot is an example of an (escape/avoidance) response; turning it down before you become too hot is an example of an (escape/avoidance) response.

Positive Punishment

Positive punishment consists of the *presentation* of a stimulus (one that is usually considered unpleasant or aversive) following a response, which then leads to a *decrease* in the future strength of that response. Loosely speaking, the behavior results in the delivery of something the person or animal hates, so the subject is less likely to behave that way in the future. For example, when a rat received a shock after pressing a lever, it stopped pressing the lever. This is an example of punishment because the behavior decreases in strength, and it is positive punishment because the consequence involves the presentation of something (i.e., shock). Consider some further examples of positive punishment:

Talk back to the boss **→ Get reprimanded**
R $\mathbf{S^P}$

Swat at the wasp **→ Get stung**
R $\mathbf{S^P}$

Meow constantly **→ Get sprayed with water**
R $\mathbf{S^P}$

In each case, the behavior is followed by the presentation of an aversive stimulus, with the result that there is a decrease in the future probability of the behavior.

People frequently confuse positive punishment with negative reinforcement. One reason for this is the fact that many behaviorists use the term *negative reinforcer* to refer to an aversive (unpleasant) stimulus and the term *positive reinforcer* to refer to an appetitive (pleasant) stimulus. Unfortunately, people with less knowledge of the field have then assumed that the presentation of a negative reinforcer is an instance of negative reinforcement, which it is not. Within the framework presented here, it is instead an instance of positive punishment.

Negative Punishment

Negative punishment consists of the *removal* of a stimulus (one that is usually considered pleasant or rewarding) following a response, which then leads to a decrease in the future strength of that response. Loosely speaking, the behavior results in the removal of something the person or animal likes, so the subject is less likely to behave that way in the future. Here are some examples of negative punishment:

Stay out past curfew **→ Lose car privileges**
R $\mathbf{S^P}$

Argue with boss **→ Lose job**
R $\mathbf{S^P}$

Play with food **→ Lose dessert**
R $\mathbf{S^P}$

Tease sister **→ Sent to room (loss of social contact)**
R $\mathbf{S^P}$

In each case, it is punishment because the behavior decreases in strength, and it is negative punishment because the consequence consists of removing something. The last example is known as "time-out" and is employed by many parents as a replacement for spanking. Removal of social contact is usually one consequence of such a procedure; more generally, however, the child loses the opportunity to receive any type of positive reinforcer during the time-out interval. Children usually find such situations unpleasant, with the result that even very brief time-outs can be effective.

Consider another example of negative punishment: Jonathan's girlfriend, who is quite jealous, completely ignored him (withdrew her attention from him) when she observed him having a conversation with another woman at a party. As a result, he stopped talking to the other women at the party.

Jonathan talks to other women **→ His girlfriend ignores him**
R **S^P**

Jonathan's behavior of talking to other women at parties was negatively punished. It is punishment in that the frequency with which he talked to other women at the party declined, and it is negative punishment because the consequence that produced that decline was the withdrawal of his girlfriend's attention.

Question: In this scenario, Jonathan's behavior has been negatively punished. But what contingencies are operating on the girlfriend's behavior? When she ignored him, he stopped talking to other women at the party. Given that this occurred, she might ignore him at future parties if she again sees him talking to other women. If so, her behavior has been negatively reinforced by the fact that it was effective in getting him to stop doing something she disliked. If we diagram this interaction from the perspective of each person, we get the following:

For Jonathan:

I talk to other women **→ My girlfriend ignores me**
R **S^P**

For his girlfriend:

I ignore Jonathan **→ He stops talking to other women**
R **S^R**

As you can see, a reduction in one person's behavior as a result of punishment can negatively reinforce the behavior of the person who implemented the punishment. This is the reason we are so often enticed to use punishment: Punishment is often successful in immediately getting a person to stop behaving in ways that we dislike. That success then reinforces our tendency to use punishment in the future, which of course can create major problems in the long run. We discuss the uses and abuses of punishment more fully in Chapter 9.[5]

Many people mistakenly equate behaviorism with the use of punishment. It is important to recognize that behaviorists actually emphasize the use of positive reinforcement. Indeed, Skinner (1953) believed that many societal problems can be traced to the overuse of punishment as well as negative reinforcement. For example, teachers too often control their students by

[5]Note that the labels for the two types of punishment are not standardized. For example, positive and negative punishment are sometimes called *Type 1* and *Type 2 punishment*.

attempting to punish maladaptive behavior rather than by positively reinforcing adaptive behavior. Moreover, the educational system in general is designed in such a way that students too often study to avoid failure (a negative reinforcer) rather than to obtain knowledge (a positive reinforcer). As a result, schooling is often more onerous and less effective than it could be.

Similarly, in interpersonal relationships, people too often attempt to change each other's behavior through the use of aversive consequences, such as complaining, when positive reinforcement for appropriate behavior might work just as well or better. Marsha, for example, says that Roger forgets to call whenever he is going to be late, even though she often complains about it. Perhaps a more effective approach would be for her to express her appreciation when he does call.

Furthermore, although many people believe that the key to a great relationship is open communication, research has shown that a much more important element is the ratio of positive (pleasant) interactions to negative (aversive) interactions. In fact, one of the best predictors of a successful marriage is when the positives outweigh the negatives by a ratio of about five to one (Gottman, 1994). Even volatile relationships, in which there seems to be an enormous amount of bickering, can thrive if the number of positive exchanges, such as teasing, hugging, and praising, greatly outweigh the number of negative exchanges.

To help strengthen your understanding of the four types of contingencies—positive reinforcement, negative reinforcement, positive punishment, and negative punishment—and deal with examples that are potentially confusing, see also "Four Types of Contingencies: Tricky Examples" in the And Furthermore box.

QUICK QUIZ H

1. When Sasha was teasing the dog, it bit her. As a result, she no longer teases the dog. The consequence for *Sasha's behavior* of teasing the dog was the (presentation/removal) of a stimulus, and the teasing behavior subsequently (increased/decreased) in frequency; therefore, this is an example of ______________.
2. Whenever Sasha pulled the dog's tail, the dog left and went into another room. As a result, Sasha now pulls the dog's tail less often when it is around. The consequence for pulling the dog's tail was the (presentation/removal) of a stimulus, and the behavior of pulling the dog's tail subsequently (increased/decreased) in frequency; therefore, this is an example of ______________.
3. When Alex burped in public, Stephanie got angry with him. Alex now burps quite often when he is around Stephanie. The consequence for burping was the ______________ of a stimulus, and the behavior of belching subsequently ______________ in frequency; therefore, this is an example of ______________.
4. When Alex held the door open for Stephanie, she made a big fuss over what a gentleman he was becoming. Alex no longer holds the door open for her. The consequence for holding open the door was the ______________ of a

stimulus, and the behavior of holding open the door subsequently ________ in frequency; therefore, this is an example of ________ ________.

5. When Tenzing shared his toys with his brother, his mother stopped criticizing him. Tenzing now shares his toys with his brother quite often. The consequence for sharing the toys was the ________ of a stimulus, and the behavior of sharing the toys subsequently ________ in frequency; therefore, this is an example of ________ ________.

And Furthermore

Four Types of Contingencies: Tricky Examples

After learning about the four types of contingencies, students are sometimes dismayed when they encounter examples that suddenly confuse them. When this happens, the contingency has often been worded in an unusual way. For example, suppose a mother tells her son that *if he does not clean his room, then he will not get dessert.* What type of contingency is this? (Think about this for a while before reading further.) To begin with, it sounds like a negative contingency because the consequence seems to involve the threatened loss of something—namely, the dessert. It also sounds like reinforcement because the goal is to increase the probability of a certain behavior—cleaning the room. We might therefore conclude that this is an example of negative reinforcement. But does this make sense? In everyday terms, negative reinforcement involves strengthening a behavior by removing something that the person dislikes, while here we are talking about removing something that the person likes. So what's going on here?

To clarify situations like this, it helps to reword the example in terms of the *occurrence* of a behavior rather than its *nonoccurrence*, because in reality one can only reinforce or punish the occurrence of a behavior. By doing so, and depending on which behavior we focus upon, this example can be interpreted as fitting one of two types of contingencies. On one hand, if the target behavior is cleaning the room, it can be viewed as an example of positive reinforcement: *If the son cleans his room, he can have dessert.* On the other hand, if the target behavior is "doing something other than cleaning the room" (or something other than following his mother's instructions), it can be viewed as an example of negative punishment: *If the son does something other than clean his room, he will not get dessert.* Thus, all behaviors other than room cleaning, such as watching television, will result in the loss of dessert. In fact, to the extent that the mother made her request in a threatening manner, she probably intended something like the latter. But note how she could just as easily have worded her request in the form of positive reinforcement—"If you clean your room, you can have some dessert"—and how much more agreeable that sounds. Unfortunately, parents too often choose the unpleasant version, especially when they are frustrated or angry, which in turn helps to create a decidedly unpleasant atmosphere in the household.

Positive Reinforcement: Further Distinctions

Because behaviorists so strongly emphasize positive reinforcement, let us have a closer look at this type of contingency.

Immediate Versus Delayed Reinforcement

A reinforcer can be presented either immediately after a behavior occurs or following some delay. In general, *the more immediate the reinforcer, the stronger its effect on the behavior*. Suppose, for example, that you wish to reinforce a child's behavior of playing quietly by giving him a treat. The treat should ideally be given while the quiet period is still in progress. If, instead, you deliver the treat several minutes later, while he is engaged in some other behavior (e.g., banging a stick on his toy box), you might inadvertently reinforce that behavior rather than the one you wish to reinforce.

The weak effect of delayed reinforcers on behavior accounts for some major difficulties in life. Do you find it tough to stick to a diet or an exercise regime? This is mainly because the benefits of exercise and proper eating are delayed and therefore weak, whereas the enjoyable effects of alternate activities, such as watching television and drinking a soda, are immediate and therefore powerful. Similarly, have you ever promised yourself that you would study all weekend, only to find that you completely wasted your time watching television and going out with friends? The immediate reinforcement associated with these recreational activities effectively outweighed the delayed reinforcement associated with studying. Of course, what we are talking about here is the issue of self-control, a topic that is more fully discussed in Chapter 10.

The importance of immediate reinforcement is so profound that some behaviorists (e.g., Malott, 1989; Malott & Suarez, 2004) argue that a delayed reinforcer does not, on its own, actually function as a "reinforcer." They point to experimental evidence indicating that delaying a reinforcer by even a few seconds can severely influence its effectiveness (e.g., Grice, 1948; Keesey, 1964; see also J. Williams, 1973). This finding suggests that delayed reinforcers, to the extent that they are effective, may function by a different mechanism from immediate reinforcement, especially in humans. Thus, receiving a good mark on that essay you wrote last week does not reinforce the behavior of essay writing in the same way that immediately receiving a food pellet reinforces a rat's tendency to press a lever (or immediately seeing your mother's smile reinforces your tendency to give her another compliment). Rather, in the case of humans, behaviors that appear to be strengthened by long-delayed reinforcers are often under the control of rules or instructions that we have received from others or generated for ourselves. These rules or instructions describe to us the delayed consequences that can result from a behavior (e.g., "Gee, if I work on that essay tonight, I am likely to get a good mark on it next week"), thereby bridging the gap between the behavior and the consequence.

In this text, for simplicity, we will ignore some of the complexities associated with the issue of rules and delayed reinforcement, though we will briefly discuss rule-governed behavior in Chapter 11. For the present purposes, it is sufficient to note that delayed reinforcement is usually much less potent, and perhaps even qualitatively different, than immediate reinforcement. This also makes clear the crucial importance of immediate reinforcement when dealing with young children (and animals) who have little or no language capacity, since the use of instructions is essentially dependent on language.

QUICK QUIZ I

1. In general, the more ____________ the reinforcer, the stronger its effect on behavior.
2. It is sometimes difficult for students to study in that the reinforcers for studying are ____________ and therefore (weak/strong), whereas the reinforcers for alternative activities are ____________ and therefore ____________.
3. It has been suggested that delayed reinforcers (do/do not) function in the same manner as immediate reinforcers. Rather, the effectiveness of delayed reinforcers in humans is largely dependent on the use of i____________ or r____________ to bridge the gap between the behavior and the delay.

Primary and Secondary Reinforcers

A ***primary reinforcer*** (also called an ***unconditioned reinforcer***) is an event that is innately reinforcing. Loosely speaking, primary reinforcers are things we are born to like rather than learn to like, and that therefore have an innate ability to reinforce our behavior. Examples of primary reinforcers are food, water, proper temperature (neither too hot nor too cold), and sexual contact.

Many primary reinforcers are associated with basic physiological needs, and their effectiveness is closely tied to a state of deprivation. For example, food is a highly effective reinforcer when we are food deprived and hungry but not when we are satiated. Some primary reinforcers, however, do not seem to be associated with a physiological state of deprivation. An animal (or person) cooped up in a boring environment will likely find access to a more stimulating environment highly reinforcing and will perform a response such as lever pressing (or driving to the mall) to gain such access. In cases such as this, the deprivation seems more psychological than physiological.

A ***secondary reinforcer*** (also called a ***conditioned reinforcer***) is an event that is reinforcing because it has been associated with some other reinforcer. Loosely speaking, secondary reinforcers are those events that we have learned to like because they have become associated with other things we like. Much of our behavior is directed toward obtaining secondary reinforcers, such as good marks, fine clothes, and a nice car. Because of our experiences with these events, they can function as effective reinforcers for our current behavior. Thus, if good marks in school are consistently associated with praise, then the good marks themselves can serve as reinforcers for behaviors such as studying. And just seeing a teacher who once provided you with lots of praise may be an effective reinforcer for the behavior of visiting her many years later.

Conditioned stimuli (CSs) that have been classically conditioned using appetitive unconditioned stimuli (USs) can also function as secondary reinforcers. For example, suppose that the sound of a metronome has been paired with food to produce a classically conditioned response of salivation:

Metronome: Food → *Salivation*
NS US UR
Metronome → *Salivation*
CS CR

The metronome, through its association with food, can now be used as a secondary reinforcer for an operant response such as lever pressing:

***Lever press* → Metronome**
R S^R

The animal essentially seeks out the metronome because of its pleasant associations. Similarly, we might frequently seek out certain music that has been closely associated with a romantic episode in our life because of its pleasant associations. (This may partially explain why each generation seems to prefer the music of their youth; it's associated with the good times they once had, or are now having, in their youth.)

Discriminative stimuli associated with reinforcers can likewise function as secondary reinforcers. Consider a tone that has served as an S^D signaling the availability of food for lever pressing:

Tone: *Lever press* → Food
S^D R S^R

This tone can now be used as a secondary reinforcer for some other behavior, such as running in a wheel:

***Run in wheel* → Tone**
R S^R

An important type of secondary reinforcer is known as a generalized reinforcer. A ***generalized reinforcer*** (also known as a ***generalized secondary reinforcer***) is a type of secondary reinforcer that has been associated with several other reinforcers. For example, money is a powerful generalized reinforcer for humans because it is associated with an almost unlimited array of other reinforcers, including food, clothing, furnishings, entertainment, and even dates (insofar as money will likely increase our attractiveness to others). In fact, money can become such a powerful reinforcer that some people would rather just have the money than the things it can buy. Social attention, too, is a highly effective generalized reinforcer, especially for young children (though some aspects of it, such as touching, are probably also primary reinforcers). Attention from caretakers is usually associated with a host of good things such as food and play and comfort, with the result that attention by itself can become a powerful reinforcer. It is so powerful that some children will even misbehave to get someone to pay attention to them, even if the attention consists of the person being angry with them. In fact, this is one of the ways in which punishment can backfire; what is intended to be a punisher actually serves as a positive reinforcer in the form of attention.

Generalized reinforcers are often used in behavior modification programs. In a "token economy," tokens are used in institutional settings—such as mental institutions, prisons, or classrooms for problem children—to increase the frequency of desirable behaviors, such as completing an assigned task, dressing appropriately, or behaving sociably. Attendants deliver the tokens immediately following the occurrence of the behavior. These tokens can later be exchanged for "backup reinforcers" such as treats, fun activities, or television time. In essence, just as the opportunity to earn money motivates many of us to behave appropriately, so too does the opportunity to earn a token motivate the residents of that setting to behave appropriately. (See Miltenberger, 2012, for a more detailed discussion of token economies.)

Note that an event can function as both a primary reinforcer and a secondary reinforcer. A Thanksgiving dinner, for example, can be both a primary reinforcer, in the sense of providing food, and a secondary reinforcer due to its association with a beloved grandmother who prepared many similar dinners in your childhood.

Finally, just as stimuli that are associated with reinforcement can become secondary reinforcers, so can *behaviors* that are associated with reinforcement. For example, children who are consistently praised for helping others might eventually find the behavior of helping others to be reinforcing in and of itself. They will then help others not to receive praise but because they "like to help." We would then describe such children as having an altruistic nature. By a similar mechanism, in what is known as *learned industriousness theory* (Eisenberger, 1992), even hard work can become a secondary reinforcer. Rats, for example, that have received reinforcement for emitting forceful lever presses will later run faster down an alleyway to obtain food (Eisenberger, Carlson, Guile, & Shapiro, 1979). And students who have received reinforcement for solving complex math problems will later write essays of higher quality (Eisenberger, Masterson, & McDermitt, 1982). Experiments have also confirmed the opposite: Rats and humans that have received reinforcers for displaying low effort on a task will often perform poorly on subsequent tasks. (Something to think about if you have a tendency to take the easy way out.)

QUICK QUIZ J

1. Events that are innately reinforcing are called p____________ reinforcers. They are sometimes also called un____________ reinforcers.
2. Events that become reinforcers through their association with other reinforcers are called s____________ reinforcers. They are sometimes also called c____________ reinforcers.
3. Candy would for most people be an example of a ____________ reinforcer, while a coupon that is used to purchase the candy would be an example of a ____________ reinforcer.
4. A (CS/US) that has been associated with an appetitive (CS/US) can serve as a secondary reinforcer for an operant response. As well, a stimulus that serves as a(n) ____________ for an operant response can also serve as a secondary reinforcer for some other response.
5. A generalized reinforcer (or generalized secondary reinforcer) is a secondary reinforcer that has been associated with ________________________.
6. Two generalized reinforcers that have strong effects on human behavior are ____________ and ____________.
7. Behavior modification programs in institutional settings often utilize generalized reinforcers in the form of t____________. This type of arrangement is known as a t____________ ec____________.

Intrinsic and Extrinsic Reinforcement

In the preceding discussion, we noted that operant behavior itself can sometimes be reinforcing. Such a behavior is said to be intrinsically reinforcing or motivating. Thus, ***intrinsic reinforcement*** is reinforcement provided by the mere act of performing the behavior. We go ice skating because it is invigorating, we party with friends because we like their company, and we work hard at something partly because hard work has, through experience, become enjoyable (though you are probably still not convinced about that one). Animals, too, sometimes engage in activities for their own sake. In some of the earliest research on intrinsic motivation, it was found that with no additional incentive, monkeys repeatedly solved mechanical puzzles (Harlow, Harlow, & Meyer, 1950).

Unfortunately, many activities are not intrinsically reinforcing and instead require additional incentives to ensure their performance. ***Extrinsic reinforcement*** is the reinforcement provided by some consequence that is external to the behavior (i.e., an "extrinsic reinforcer"). For example, perhaps you are reading this text solely because of an upcoming exam. Passing the exam is the extrinsic consequence that is motivating your behavior. Other examples of extrinsically motivated behaviors are driving to get somewhere, working for money, and dating an attractive individual merely to enhance your prestige.

Unfortunately, the distinction between intrinsic and extrinsic reinforcers is not always clear. For example, is candy an intrinsic or extrinsic reinforcer?

In one sense, candy seems like an intrinsic reinforcer because eating it is an enjoyable activity; yet the candy exists external to the behavior that is being reinforced. In such cases, it often helps to focus on the behavior that is being strengthened. Imagine, for example, that we offer candy to a child to strengthen the behavior of being quiet in the supermarket. The candy is clearly an extrinsic reinforcer for the behavior of *being quiet* but with respect to the behavior of *eating candy* the candy is the critical component in an intrinsically reinforcing activity. In any case, do not fret too much if you encounter an example that seems confusing. The most important thing is to be able to distinguish situations in which the motivation is clearly intrinsic (taking a bath for the pleasure of it) from those in which the motivation is clearly extrinsic (taking a bath so that your date this evening will be impressed with how nice and clean you are).

Question: What happens if you are given an extrinsic reinforcer for an activity that is already intrinsically reinforcing? What if, for example, you love ice skating and are fortunate enough to be hired one weekend to skate around a public rink while displaying a new line of sportswear? Will the experience of receiving payment for skating increase, decrease, or have no effect on your subsequent enjoyment of the activity?

Although you might think that it would increase your enjoyment of skating (since the activity is not only enjoyable but also associated with money), some researchers claim that experiences like this can *decrease* intrinsic interest. For example, Lepper, Green, and Nisbett (1973) found that children who enjoyed drawing with Magic Markers became less interested following a session in which they had been promised, and then received, a "good player" award for drawing with the markers. In contrast, children who did not receive an award or who received the award unexpectedly after playing with the markers did not show a loss of interest. Similar results have been reported by other investigators (e.g., Deci & Ryan, 1985). However, some researchers have found that extrinsic rewards have no effect on intrinsic interest (e.g., Amabile, Hennessey, & Grossman, 1986) or actually produce an *increase* in intrinsic interest (e.g., Harackiewicz, Manderlink, & Sansone, 1984). Unfortunately, despite these mixed findings, it is the damaging effects of extrinsic rewards on intrinsic motivation that are often presented to the public (e.g., Kohn, 1993). But is this a fair assessment of the evidence? Are the harmful effects of reinforcement the rule or the exception?

Cameron and Pierce (1994) attempted to answer this question by conducting a meta-analysis of 96 well-controlled experiments that examined the effects of extrinsic rewards on intrinsic motivation. (A meta-analysis is a statistical procedure that combines the results of several separate studies, thereby producing a more reliable overall assessment of the variable being studied.) The meta-analysis by Cameron and Pierce indicates that extrinsic rewards usually have little or no effect on intrinsic motivation. External rewards can occasionally undermine intrinsic motivation, but only when *the reward is expected* (i.e., the person has been instructed beforehand that she will receive a reward), *the reward is tangible* (e.g., it consists of money rather than praise), and *the reward is given for simply performing the activity* (and not for how well it is performed). It also turns out that verbal rewards, such as praise, often produce an increase in intrinsic motivation, as do tangible rewards given for high-quality performance (see Deci & Ryan, 1985). Cameron and Pierce (1994) conclude that extrinsic rewards can be safely applied in most circumstances and that the limited circumstances in which they decrease intrinsic motivation are easily avoided. Bandura (1997) likewise has argued that the dangers of extrinsic rewards on intrinsic motivation have been greatly overstated. (See Cameron, 2001; Cameron, Pierce, Banko, & Gear, 2005; Cameron & Pierce, 2002; and Deci, Koestner, & Ryan, 2001a, 2001b, for further contributions to this debate.)[6] (See also "Positive Reinforcement of Artistic Appreciation" in the And Furthermore box.)

And Furthermore

Positive Reinforcement of Artistic Appreciation

B. F. Skinner (1983) once described how two students used positive reinforcement to instill in their new roommate an appreciation of modern art. These students had several items of modern art in their apartment, but the roommate had little interest in them and was instead proceeding to "change the character" of the space. As a counterploy, the students would pay attention to the roommate only when they saw him looking at one of the art works. They also threw a party and arranged for an attractive young woman to engage him in a discussion about modern art. They then arranged for him to receive announcements from local art galleries about upcoming art shows. After about a month, the roommate himself suggested attending a local art museum. Interestingly, while there, he just "happened" to find a five-dollar bill lying at his feet while he was looking at a painting. According to Skinner, "It was not long before [the two students] came again in great excitement—to show me his first painting" (p. 48).

[6] It is also the case that a contingency that seems to involve positive reinforcement might in reality be more aversive in nature. A catcher for a Major League Baseball team once told one of the authors of this text that he hated baseball because there were so many young players trying to replace him. The consequence that now motivated him was apparently the threatened loss of a good salary if he played poorly. According to Skinner (1987), human behavior is too often controlled by such negative consequences—working to avoid the loss of a paycheck and studying to avoid failure (especially prevalent in students who procrastinate until they are in danger of failing). It is therefore not surprising that these activities often seem less than intrinsically interesting.

QUICK QUIZ K

1. A(n) ________ motivated activity is one in which the activity is itself reinforcing; a(n) ________ motivated activity is one in which the reinforcer consists of some type of additional consequence that is external to the activity.
2. Running to lose weight is an example of a(n) ________ motivated activity; running because it "feels good" is an example of a(n) ________ motivated activity.
3. In their meta-analysis of relevant research, Cameron and Pierce (1994) found that extrinsic rewards decrease intrinsic motivation only when they are (expected/unexpected), (tangible/verbal), and given for (performing well/merely engaging in the behavior).
4. They also found that extrinsic rewards generally increased intrinsic motivation when the rewards were (tangible/verbal), and that tangible rewards increased intrinsic motivation when they were delivered contingent upon (high/low)-quality performance.

Study Tip: Students often complain that they find it difficult to study, or even go to lectures, because their courses are so boring. Often, these are students who are doing the minimal amount of work to get by (if that). But the question can be asked: Are they doing minimal work because their courses are boring, or are their courses boring because they're doing minimal work? In support of the latter possibility, students who, for whatever reason, suddenly decide to pull up their marks—perhaps because they've decided they want to do a professional or graduate degree—will sometimes comment that they didn't realize how interesting their courses (or at least some of their courses) can be when they really apply themselves. This change in perception is, of course, in keeping with the notion that being rewarded for high-quality performance can increase one's intrinsic interest in a task. So if you tend to be a "minimalist" student who finds college courses boring, you might consider really applying yourself to your studies as part of the solution.

Natural and Contrived Reinforcers

The distinction between intrinsic and extrinsic reinforcers is closely related to the distinction between natural and contrived reinforcers. ***Natural reinforcers*** are reinforcers that are typically provided for a certain behavior; that is, they are an expected consequence of the behavior within that setting. Money is a natural consequence of selling merchandise; gold medals are a natural consequence of hard training and a great performance. ***Contrived*** (or ***artificial***) ***reinforcers*** are reinforcers that have been deliberately arranged to modify a behavior; they are not a typical consequence of the behavior within that setting. For example, although television is the natural reinforcer for the behavior of turning on the set, it is a contrived reinforcer for the behavior of, say, accomplishing a certain amount of studying. In the latter case, we have created a contrived contingency in an attempt to modify the person's study behavior.

Although contrived reinforcers are often seen as a hallmark of behaviorism, behaviorists strive to utilize natural reinforcers whenever possible (Sulzer-Azaroff & Mayer, 1991). When contrived reinforcers are used, the ultimate intention is to let the "natural contingencies" eventually take over if at all possible. For example, although we might initially use tokens to motivate a patient with schizophrenia to socialize with others, our hope is that the behavior will soon become "trapped" by the natural consequences of socializing (e.g., smiles and pleasant comments from others) such that the tokens can eventually be withdrawn. Similarly, although we might initially use praise to increase the frequency with which a child reads, the natural (and intrinsic) reinforcers associated with reading will hopefully take over so that the child will begin reading even in the absence of praise.

It is important to remember that natural contingencies tend to produce more efficient behavior patterns than do contrived contingencies (Skinner, 1987). Although a coach might use praise to reinforce correct throwing actions by a young quarterback, the most important factor in producing correct throws will be the natural consequence of where the ball goes.

To distinguish between intrinsic versus extrinsic reinforcers and natural versus contrived reinforcers, just remember that the former is concerned with the extent to which the behavior itself is reinforcing while the latter is concerned with the extent to which a reinforcer has been artificially imposed so as to manipulate a behavior. Note, too, that the extent to which a reinforcer has been artificially imposed is not always clear; hence, it is easy to find examples in which it is ambiguous as to whether the reinforcer is contrived or natural. Are grades in school a natural reinforcer or a contrived reinforcer? It depends on whether one's grades are considered as a typical aspect of the learning environment, at least within the school system, or as a contrived aspect. In any event, as with intrinsic versus extrinsic motivation, the important thing is to be able to distinguish those situations in which the reinforcers are clearly contrived—as often occurs in a behavior modification program—from those in which the reinforcers are considerably more natural.

QUICK QUIZ L

1. A(n) ____________ reinforcer is a reinforcer that typically occurs for that behavior in that setting; a(n) ____________ reinforcer is one that typically does not occur for that behavior in that setting.
2. You flip the switch and the light comes on. The light coming on is an example of a(n) (contrived/natural) reinforcer for flipping the switch.
3. You thank your roommate for helping out with the housework in an attempt to motivate her to help more often. To the extent that this works, the thank-you is an example of a (contrived/natural) reinforcer; it is also an example of an (intrinsic/extrinsic) reinforcer.
4. In applied behavior analysis, although one might initially use (contrived/natural) consequences to first develop a behavior, the hope is that the behavior will

become tr_________ by the n_________ c_________ associated with that behavior.

5. In most cases, the most important consequence in developing a highly effective slap shot in hockey will be the (contrived/natural) consequence of where the puck goes and how fast it travels.

Shaping

Positive reinforcement is clearly a great way to strengthen a behavior, but what if the behavior that you wish to reinforce never occurs? For example, what if you want to reinforce a rat's behavior of pressing a lever but are unable to do so because the rat never presses the lever? What can you do? The solution is to use a procedure called shaping.

Shaping is the gradual creation of new behavior through reinforcement of successive approximations to that behavior. With our rat, we could begin by delivering food whenever it stands near the lever. As a result, it begins standing near the lever more often. We then deliver food only when it is facing the lever, at which point it starts engaging in that behavior more often. In a similar manner, step-by-step, we reinforce touching the lever, then placing a paw on the lever, and then pressing down on the lever. When the rat finally presses down on the lever with enough force, it closes the microswitch that activates the food magazine. The rat has now earned a reinforcer on its own. After a few more experiences like this, the rat begins to reliably press the lever to earn food. By reinforcing successive approximations to the target behavior, we have managed to teach the rat an entirely new behavior.

Another example of shaping: How do you teach a dog to catch a Frisbee? Many people simply throw the Frisbee at the dog, at which point the dog probably wonders what on earth has gotten into its owner as the Frisbee sails over its head. Or possibly the dog runs after the Frisbee, picks it up after it falls on the ground, and then makes the owner chase after it to get the Frisbee back. Karen Pryor (1999), a professional animal trainer, recommends the following procedure. First, reinforce the dog's behavior of taking the Frisbee from your hand and immediately returning it. Next, raise the criterion by holding the Frisbee in the air to make the dog jump for it. When this is well established, toss the Frisbee slightly so the dog jumps and catches it in midair. Then toss it a couple of feet so the dog has to run after it to catch it. Now gradually throw it farther and farther so the dog has to run farther and farther to get it. Remember to provide lots of praise each time the dog catches the Frisbee and returns it.

Shaping is obviously a fundamental procedure for teaching animals to perform tricks. During such training, the trainers often use a sound, such as a click from a handheld clicker, to reinforce the behavior. The sound has been repeatedly paired with food so that it has become a secondary reinforcer. The benefit of using a sound as a reinforcer is that it can be presented immediately upon the occurrence of the behavior, even if the animal is some distance away. Also, if food were presented each time the correct behavior occurred, the animal would quickly satiate, at which point the food would

An excellent demonstration of the power of shaping.

ADVICE FOR THE LOVELORN

Dear Dr. Dee,

My boyfriend has a terrible tendency to boss me around. I have tried to counter this tendency by being especially nice to him, but the problem seems to be getting worse. He also refuses to discuss it or see a counselor. He says I am too sensitive and that I am making a mountain out of a molehill. What should I do?

Just About Hadenough

Dear Just,

You should first recognize that some people have a long history of reinforcement for being dominant or aggressive, and that it is sometimes difficult to alter such tendencies. In fact, you might eventually have to bail out of this relationship, particularly because he refuses to discuss what seems to be an obvious problem.

Nevertheless, you might also wish to consider the possibility that you are inadvertently reinforcing his aggressiveness. Remember how, in the opening vignette to this chapter, the young woman reacted to her partner's angry demands by a show of affection. While this might have reduced his anger in the short run, it might also have reinforced his tendency to be aggressive. After all, not only was his anger effective in getting her to hurry up, it also resulted in a hug. The next time he wants her to hurry up or desires affection, what better way than to get angry?

As a first step, you might wish to take note of the situations in which your boyfriend becomes bossy. If it appears that you might be inadvertently reinforcing his bossiness by being nice to him when he acts that way, you could try offering him little or no attention when he behaves that way and lots of attention when he behaves appropriately. Can this work? In her book *Don't Shoot the Dog*, Karen Pryor (1999) relates the following story about a woman who implemented just such a program:

> A young woman married a man who turned out to be very bossy and demanding. Worse yet, his father, who lived with them, was equally given to ordering his daughter-in-law about. It was the girl's mother who told me this story. On her first visit she was horrified at what her daughter was going through. "Don't worry, Mother," the daughter said. "Wait and see." The daughter formed the practice of responding minimally to commands and harsh remarks, while reinforcing with approval and affection any tendency by either man to be pleasant and thoughtful. In a year, she had turned them into decent human beings. Now they greet her with smiles when she comes home and leap up—both of them—to help with the groceries. (p. 30)

By reinforcing successive approximations toward decent behavior and not reinforcing bossy behavior (yet still responding minimally to their requests), this woman was apparently able to shape more appropriate behavior in her husband and father-in-law. Remember, though, that such problems are often difficult to manage and may require professional help. Or you may have to abandon the relationship.

Behaviorally yours,

Dr. Dee

become ineffective as a reinforcer. By using a secondary reinforcer such as a click, with food delivered only intermittently, satiation will take longer to occur, thereby allowing for longer training sessions.

Most of our behaviors have, to some extent, been learned or modified through shaping. For example, when children first learn to eat with a knife and fork, parents might praise even very poor attempts. Over time, though, they expect better and better performance before offering praise. In a similar manner, we gradually shape the child's behavior of dressing appropriately, speaking politely, and writing legibly. And shaping is not confined merely to childhood. All of us are in the position of receiving constant feedback about our performance—be it ironing clothes, cooking a meal, or slam-dunking a basketball—thus allowing us to continually modify our behaviors and improve our skills. In such circumstances, it is usually the natural consequences of the behavior—the extent to which we are successful or unsuccessful—that provide the necessary reinforcement for gradual modifications of the behavior.

And Furthermore

Training Ishmael

Although the principles of reinforcement and shaping are easy enough to understand, applying these principles is another matter. In this case, there is no substitute for the experience of shaping behavior in a live animal. Unfortunately, many students live in apartments or dormitories where trainable pets, such as dogs and cats, are not allowed. Fortunately, apartment dwellers are often allowed to keep fish, and some fish are in fact quite trainable. A quick search of the Internet, for example, will reveal several examples of goldfish that have been trained to swim through hoops, push balls around, and even ring a bell for food.

To illustrate the process of training a fish, let us consider some training that one of the authors conducted with Ishmael, a 2-inch long, dark blue, male *Betta splendens* (Siamese fighting fish). The interesting thing about training a male Betta is that two types of reinforcers are available. One is food; however, Bettas are sometimes fussy eaters (unlike goldfish) and should be given only a few bites of food per day, which can significantly shorten training sessions. The other type of reinforcer is the presentation of a mirror. The mirror image that the fish sees of itself is perceived as another male, which then elicits the fixed action pattern of an aggressive threat display. Bettas being rather feisty in nature, the opportunity to aggress like this can be used as a positive reinforcer to strengthen some other behavior (Melvin, 1985; T. Thompson, 1963).

As a demonstration of the effectiveness of using the mirror to train Ishmael, mirror presentations were made contingent upon the behavior of turning a half circle. During an initial baseline period, Ishmael's clockwise and counterclockwise circling tendencies were recorded throughout a 10-minute session with 10 mirror presentations presented noncontingently (independent of any behavior) at random points in time. (Question: Why include mirror presentations in the baseline period?) During this period, Ishmael showed a slight preference for turning in a counterclockwise direction (see Figure 6.4).

FIGURE 6.4 Number of clockwise and counterclockwise turns made by Ishmael across different phases of the demonstration.

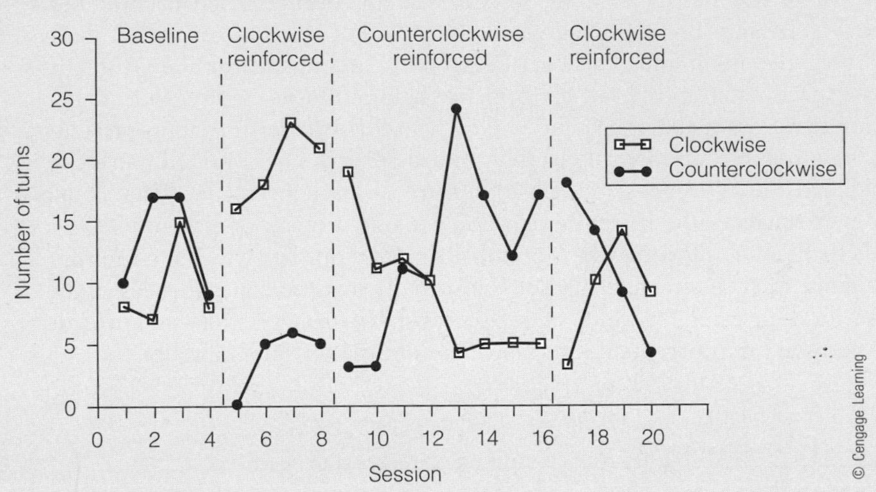

A clockwise turn was therefore selected for initial training. Mirror presentations were initially made contingent upon successive approximations to the required behavior (i.e., slight turns in the correct direction were initially reinforced, with subsequent reinforcement requiring progressively more complete turns). Shaping proceeded rapidly, with Ishmael quickly establishing a pattern of clockwise turns. In session 9, the requirement was reversed, with counterclockwise turns being reinforced and clockwise turns being extinguished. In this phase, even with shaping, counterclockwise turns did not become well established until session 13. A reversal was then attempted in which clockwise turns were again reinforced and counterclockwise turns were extinguished (hence, overall, this was an ABCB design). Unfortunately, although Ishmael's behavior seemed to be changing in the intended direction, in session 20, the number of turns in either direction—as well as, it seemed, his general activity level—dropped sharply. During attempted sessions on subsequent days, he mostly sat at the bottom of the tank and reacted only minimally to the mirror. It appeared as though long-term habituation had set in such that the mirror was no longer sufficiently reinforcing to motivate the target behavior. Training was therefore terminated. Nevertheless, despite this less-than-ideal conclusion, the results obtained do suggest that mirror presentation was, throughout much of the study, functioning as an effective reinforcer for Ishmael's circling behavior.

If you are interested in training your own Betta, there is plenty of information available on the Web, including videos; just search for "Betta training" or "Betta tricks." As for the answer to the question about including mirror presentations in the baseline period, mirror presentation by itself generates a lot of excitement and movement in a Betta. Hence, noncontingent presentation of the mirror during the baseline period controls for the increase in circling that may occur simply due to the increased movement caused by mirror presentation alone.

For further information on shaping, you might wish to visit Karen Pryor's Web site on "clicker training" (shaping through the use of clicks as secondary reinforcers); just search for "Karen Pryor" and "clicker training." Clicker training has become increasingly popular with dog owners and is being used to shape behavior in everything from birds to horses and even llamas and elephants. (See also "Training Ishmael" in the And Furthermore box.)

QUICK QUIZ M

1. Shaping is the creation of new operant behavior through the reinforcement of s____________ a____________ to that behavior.
2. In clicker training with dogs, the click is a s____________ reinforcer that has been established by first pairing it with f____________, which is a p____________ reinforcer.
3. The advantages of using the click as a reinforcer is that it can be delivered i____________. It can also prevent the animal from becoming s____________ on the reinforcer.

SUMMARY

In contrast to elicited behaviors that are automatically elicited by the stimuli that precede them, operant behaviors are controlled by their consequences. Thus, in operant (or instrumental) conditioning, the future probability of a response is affected by its consequence. Reinforcers are consequences that increase the probability of (or strengthen) a response, whereas punishers decrease the probability of (or weaken) a response. In positive reinforcement and positive punishment, the consequence involves the presentation of a stimulus, whereas in negative reinforcement and negative punishment, the consequence involves the removal of a stimulus. A discriminative stimulus is a stimulus in the presence of which a response has been reinforced and in the absence of which it has not been reinforced.

Immediate reinforcers have a much stronger effect than delayed reinforcers. Primary reinforcers are events that are innately reinforcing; secondary reinforcers are events that become reinforcing because they have been associated with other reinforcers. A generalized reinforcer is a secondary reinforcer that has been associated with many other reinforcers. Intrinsic reinforcement occurs when performing a behavior is inherently reinforcing; extrinsic reinforcement occurs when the reinforcer is a consequence that is external to the behavior. Extrinsic reinforcement can undermine intrinsic interest in a task when the reinforcer is expected, tangible, or is made contingent on mere performance of the task. Extrinsic reinforcement can strengthen intrinsic interest when the reinforcer consists of verbal praise or is made contingent on high-quality performance. Natural reinforcers are reinforcing consequences that typically follow a behavior, whereas contrived reinforcers are reinforcing consequences that are artificially arranged in order to deliberately modify a behavior.

Shaping is the creation of novel behavior through the reinforcement of gradual approximations to that behavior. Effective shaping is often carried out with the use of a secondary reinforcer, such as the sound of a whistle or a click that can be delivered immediately following the occurrence of the appropriate behavior.

SUGGESTED READINGS

Thorndike, E. L. (1898). Animal intelligence: An experimental study of the associative processes in animals. *Psychological Review Monograph Supplement, 2*, 1–109. A classic work in the field.

Kohn, A. (1993). *Punished by rewards.* Boston: Houghton Mifflin. One of the harshest criticisms of the use of rewards to motivate people.

Cameron, J., & Pierce, W. D. (2002). *Rewards and intrinsic motivation: Resolving the controversy.* New York: Greenwood Publishing. An ardent defense of the use of rewards to motivate people.

Pryor, K. (1975). *Lads before the wind: Adventures in porpoise training.* New York: Harper & Row. An engaging account of Pryor's experiences in becoming a dolphin trainer.

Pryor, K. (1999). *Don't shoot the dog: The new art of teaching and training* (Rev. ed.). New York: Bantam Books. Pryor's popular book on the art of shaping behavior as applied to everything from dogs to horses to humans.

STUDY QUESTIONS

1. State Thorndike's law of effect. What is operant conditioning (as defined by Skinner), and how does this definition differ from Thorndike's law of effect?
2. Define the terms *reinforcer* and *punisher*. How do those terms differ from the terms *reinforcement* and *punishment*?
3. What is a discriminative stimulus? How does it differ from a conditioned stimulus? Define the three-term contingency and diagram an example. Be sure to include the appropriate symbols for each component.
4. Define positive reinforcement and negative reinforcement and diagram an example of each. Be sure to include the appropriate symbols for each component.
5. Define positive punishment and negative punishment and diagram an example of each. Be sure to include the appropriate symbols for each component.
6. How is negative reinforcement similar to positive punishment? Why are the two terms so often confused with each other?
7. How does immediacy affect the strength of a reinforcer? How does this often lead to difficulties for students in their academic studies?
8. Distinguish between primary reinforcers, secondary reinforcers, and generalized reinforcers, and give an example of each. Why are generalized reinforcers often quite powerful?

9. Define intrinsic and extrinsic reinforcement, and give an example of each. Under what conditions does extrinsic reinforcement undermine versus enhance intrinsic interest?
10. Define natural and contrived reinforcers, and give an example of each. What type of reinforcer is commonly used in the initial stages of behavior modification, and what is the hoped-for result in the long run?
11. Define shaping and give an example. What are two advantages of using a secondary reinforcer, such as a sound, as an aid to shaping?

CONCEPT REVIEW

avoidance behavior. Behavior that occurs before the aversive stimulus is presented and thereby prevents its delivery.

contrived reinforcers. Reinforcers that have been deliberately arranged to modify a behavior; they are not a typical consequence of the behavior in that setting. Also called *artificial reinforcers.*

discriminative stimulus (S^D). A stimulus in the presence of which responses are reinforced and in the absence of which they are not reinforced, that is, a stimulus that signals the availability of reinforcement.

discriminative stimulus for extinction (S^Δ). A stimulus that signals the absence of reinforcement.

discriminative stimulus for punishment (S^{Dp}). A stimulus that signals that a response will be punished.

escape behavior. A behavior that results in the termination of an aversive stimulus.

extinction. The weakening of a behavior through the nonreinforcement of a previously reinforced behavior.

extrinsic reinforcement. The reinforcement provided by a consequence that is external to the behavior, that is, an extrinsic reinforcer.

generalized reinforcer. A type of secondary reinforcer that has been associated with several other reinforcers. Also called a *generalized secondary reinforcer.*

intrinsic reinforcement. Reinforcement provided by the mere act of performing the behavior; the behavior itself is the reinforcer.

law of effect. As stated by Thorndike, the proposition that behaviors that lead to a satisfying state of affairs are strengthened or "stamped in," while behaviors that lead to an unsatisfying or annoying state of affairs are weakened or "stamped out."

natural reinforcers. Reinforcers that are naturally provided for a certain behavior; they are a typical consequence of the behavior within that setting.

negative punishment. The removal of a stimulus (one that is usually considered pleasant or rewarding) following a response, which then leads to a decrease in the future strength of that response.

negative reinforcement. The removal of a stimulus (one that is usually considered unpleasant or aversive) following a response, which then leads to an increase in the future strength of that response.

operant behavior. A class of emitted responses that result in certain consequences; these consequences, in turn, affect the future probability (strength) of those responses.

operant conditioning. A type of learning in which the future probability (strength) of a behavior is affected by its consequences.

positive punishment. The presentation of a stimulus (one that is usually considered unpleasant or aversive) following a response, which then leads to a decrease in the future strength of that response.

positive reinforcement. The presentation of a stimulus (one that is usually considered pleasant or rewarding) following a response, which then leads to an increase in the future strength of that response.

primary reinforcer. An event that is innately reinforcing. Also called an *unconditioned reinforcer*.

punisher. An event that (1) follows a behavior and (2) decreases the future probability of that behavior.

reinforcer. An event that (1) follows a behavior and (2) increases the future probability of that behavior.

secondary reinforcer. An event that is reinforcing because it has been associated with some other reinforcer. Also called a *conditioned reinforcer*.

shaping. The gradual creation of new behavior through reinforcement of successive approximations to that behavior.

three-term contingency. The relationship between a discriminative stimulus, an operant behavior, and a consequence (reinforcer or punisher).

CHAPTER TEST

31. Shaping is: (A) the reinforcement of a new operant behavior, (B) the gradual reinforcement of a new operant behavior, (C) the reinforcement of successive approximations to a new operant behavior, (D) the creation of new operant behavior through successive approximations to reinforcement.

20. A positive reinforcer is a stimulus, (A) the presentation of which increases the strength of a response, (B) the presentation of which follows a response and increases the strength of that response, (C) the presentation of which decreases the strength of a response, (D) the presentation of which follows a response and decreases the strength of that response.

2. Elicited behaviors are controlled by the events that (precede/follow) their occurrence, while operant behaviors are controlled by the events that (precede/follow) their occurrence.

14. An easy way to remember the three-term contingency is that you notice something, do something, and get something.

25. Behaviors that are performed for their own sake are said to be intrinsically motivated; behaviors that are performed to achieve some additional incentive are said to be extrinsically motivated.

11. Reinforcers and punishers are defined entirely by their ____________ on behavior.
8. An event is a punisher if it ____________ a behavior and the future probability of that behavior ____________.
23. Money and praise are common examples of ____________ reinforcers.
12. If the rat does not press the lever, then it does not receive a shock. As a result, the rat no longer presses the lever. This is best considered as an example of (A) negative reinforcement, (B) negative punishment, (C) positive reinforcement, (D) positive punishment. *(Think carefully about this one.)*
28. At the zoo one day, you notice a zookeeper leading a rhinoceros into a pen by repeatedly whistling at it. It is probably the case that the whistle has been paired with ____________ and is now functioning as a ____________.
1. Compared to most elicited behaviors, operant behaviors seem (more/less) automatic and reflexive.
15. The three-term contingency can be thought of as an ABC sequence in which A stands for ____________, B stands for ____________, and C stands for ____________.
27. The gradual development of new operant behavior through reinforcement of successive (instances/approximations) of that behavior is called ____________.
6. Operant behaviors are sometimes simply called ____________. These can be contrasted with elicited behaviors, which Skinner called ____________ behaviors or simply ____________.
21. Each time a student studies at home, she is praised by her parents. As a result, she no longer studies at home. This is an example of (positive/negative) (reinforcement/punishment).
17. When combined with the words *reinforcement* or *punishment*, the word *negative* indicates that the consequence consists of something being (removed/unpleasant), and the word *positive* indicates that the consequence consists of something being (presented/pleasant).
10. The terms *reinforcer* or *punisher* refer to the specific ____________ that follows a behavior, whereas the terms *reinforcement* or *punishment* refer to the ____________ or ____________ whereby the probability of a behavior is altered by its consequences.
24. Harpreet very much enjoys hard work and often volunteers for projects that are quite demanding. It is likely the case that for him the act of expending a lot of effort has often been ____________ and now functions as a ____________ reinforcer.
3. According to Thorndike's ____________, behaviors that lead to a(n) ____________ state of affairs are strengthened, whereas behaviors that lead to a(n) ____________ state of affairs are weakened.
30. A generalized secondary reinforcer is one that has become a reinforcer because it has been associated with: (A) a primary reinforcer,

(B) a secondary reinforcer, (C) several secondary reinforcers, (D) several primary reinforcers, or (E) several reinforcers (either primary or secondary).

19. When Beth tried to pull the tail of her dog, he bared his teeth and growled threateningly. Beth quickly pulled her hand back. The dog growled even more threateningly the next time Beth reached for his tail, and she again pulled her hand away. Eventually Beth gave up, and no longer tries to pull the dog's tail. The dog's behavior of baring his teeth and growling served to (positively/negatively) (punish/reinforce) Beth's behavior of trying to pull his tail. And Beth's behavior of pulling her hand away served to ______ the dog's behavior of growling.

32. Achieving a record number of strikeouts in a game would be a (natural/contrived) reinforcer for pitching well; receiving a bonus for throwing that many strikeouts would be a(n) ______ reinforcer.

5. Operant behaviors are usually defined as a(n) ______ of responses, all of which are capable of producing a certain ______

16. A stimulus that signals that a response will be punished is called a ______ for punishment. It is sometimes given the symbol ______

22. Events that are innately reinforcing are called ______ reinforcers; events that become reinforcers through experience are called ______ reinforcers.

9. A reinforcer is usually given the symbol ______, while a punisher is usually given the symbol ______. The operant response is given the symbol ______. A discriminative stimulus that signals the availability of reinforcement is given the symbol ______.

26. Steven has fond memories of his mother reading fairy tales to him when he was a child. As a result he now enjoys reading fairy tales as an adult. For Steven, the act of reading fairy tales is functioning as what type of reinforcer? (A) primary, (B) secondary, (C) intrinsic, (D) extrinsic, (E) both secondary and intrinsic.

4. Classically conditioned behaviors are said to be e______ by the st______; operant behaviors are said to be e______ by the org______.

18. Referring to this chapter's opening vignette, among the four types of contingencies described in this chapter, the woman's response to her boyfriend most likely resulted in ______ of his behavior, which means that his abusive behavior toward her will likely (increase/decrease) in the future as a result of her actions.

7. An event is a reinforcer if it ______ a behavior and the future probability of that behavior ______.

29. Major advantages of using the sound of a click for shaping are that the click can be delivered ______ and the animal is unlikely to ______ upon it.

13. A discriminative stimulus is a stimulus that signals that a(n) reinforcer is available. It is said to "set the occasion" for the behavior.

ANSWERS TO CHAPTER TEST

1. less
2. precede; follow
3. law of effect; satisfying; unsatisfying (or annoying)
4. elicited; stimulus; emitted; organism
5. class; consequence
6. operants; respondent; respondents
7. follows; increases
8. follows; decreases
9. S^R; S^P; R; S^D
10. consequence (or event or stimulus); process; procedure
11. effect
12. D (because "*lever press*→ shock" is the effective contingency)
13. reinforcer; set the occasion
14. notice; do; get
15. antecedent; behavior; consequence
16. discriminative stimulus; S^{Dp}
17. removed; presented
18. positive reinforcement; increase
19. positively; punish; negatively reinforce
20. B
21. positive punishment
22. primary (or unconditioned); secondary (or conditioned)
23. generalized (or generalized secondary)
24. positively reinforced; secondary (or conditioned)
25. intrinsically; extrinsically
26. E
27. approximations; shaping
28. food; secondary reinforcer
29. immediately; satiate
30. E
31. C
32. natural; contrived

CHAPTER 7

SCHEDULES AND THEORIES OF REINFORCEMENT

CHAPTER OUTLINE

"I don't understand why Alvin is so distant," Mandy commented. "He was great when we started going out. Now it's like pulling teeth to get him to pay attention to me."

"So why do you put up with it?" her sister asked.

"I guess I'm in love with him. Why else would I be so persistent?"

Schedules of Reinforcement

In this section, we discuss schedules of reinforcement. A ***schedule of reinforcement*** is the response requirement that must be met to obtain reinforcement. In other words, a schedule indicates what exactly has to be done for the reinforcer to be delivered. For example, does each lever press by the rat result in a food pellet or are several lever presses required? Did your mom give you a cookie each time you asked for one, or only some of the time? And just how persistent does Mandy have to be before Alvin will pay attention to her? As you will discover in this section, different response requirements can have dramatically different effects on behavior. Many of these effects (known as *schedule effects*) were first observed in experiments with pigeons (Ferster & Skinner, 1957), but they also help explain some puzzling aspects of human behavior that are often attributed to internal traits or desires.

Continuous Versus Intermittent Schedules

A ***continuous reinforcement schedule*** is one in which each specified response is reinforced. For example, each time a rat presses the lever, it obtains a food pellet; each time the dog rolls over on command, it gets a treat; and each time Karen turns the ignition in her car, the motor starts. Continuous reinforcement (abbreviated CRF) is very useful when a behavior is first being shaped or strengthened. For example, when using a shaping procedure to train a rat to press a lever, reinforcement should be delivered for each approximation to the target behavior. Similarly, if we wish to encourage a child to always brush her teeth before bed, we would do well to initially praise her each time she does so.

An ***intermittent (or partial) reinforcement schedule*** is one in which only some responses are reinforced. For example, perhaps only some of the rat's lever presses result in a food pellet, and perhaps only occasionally did your mother give you a cookie when you asked for one. Intermittent reinforcement obviously characterizes much of everyday life. Not all concerts we attend are enjoyable, not every person we invite out on a date accepts, and not every date that we go out on leads to an enjoyable evening. And although we might initially praise a child each time she properly completes her homework, we might soon praise her only occasionally in the belief that such behavior should persist in the absence of praise.

There are four basic (or simple) types of intermittent schedules: fixed ratio, variable ratio, fixed interval, and variable interval. We will describe each one along with the characteristic response pattern produced by each. Note that this characteristic response pattern is the stable pattern that emerges once the organism has had considerable exposure to the schedule. Such stable patterns are known as *steady-state behaviors*, in contrast to the more variable patterns of behavior that are evident when an organism is first learning a schedule.

QUICK QUIZ A

1. A s__________ of reinforcement is the r__________ requirement that must be met in order to obtain reinforcement.
2. On a c__________ reinforcement schedule (abbreviated __________), each response is reinforced, whereas on an i__________ reinforcement schedule, only some responses are reinforced. The latter is also called a p__________ reinforcement schedule.
3. Each time you flick the light switch, the light comes on. The behavior of flicking the light switch is on a(n) __________ schedule of reinforcement.
4. When the weather is very cold, you are sometimes unable to start your car. The behavior of starting your car in very cold weather is on a(n) __________ schedule of reinforcement.
5. S__________ e__________ are the different effects on behavior produced by different response requirements. These are the stable patterns of behavior that emerge once the organism has had sufficient exposure to the schedule. Such stable patterns are known as st__________-st__________ behaviors.

Four Basic Intermittent Schedules

Fixed Ratio Schedules On a ***fixed ratio (FR) schedule***, reinforcement is contingent upon a fixed, predictable number of responses. For example, on a fixed ratio 5 schedule (abbreviated FR 5), a rat has to press the lever 5 times to obtain a food pellet. On an FR 50 schedule, it has to press the lever 50 times to obtain a food pellet. Similarly, earning a dollar for every 10 carburetors assembled on an assembly line is an example of an FR 10 schedule, while earning a dollar for each carburetor assembled is an example of an FR 1 schedule. Note that an FR 1 schedule is the same as a CRF (continuous reinforcement) schedule in which each response is reinforced (thus, such a schedule can be correctly labeled as either an FR 1 or a CRF).

FR schedules generally produce a high rate of response along with a short pause following the attainment of each reinforcer (see Figure 7.1). This short pause is known as a *post-reinforcement pause*. For example, a rat on an FR 25 schedule will rapidly emit 25 lever presses, munch down the food pellet it receives, and then snoop around the chamber for a few seconds before rapidly emitting another 25 lever presses. In other words, it will take a short break following each reinforcer, just as you might take a short break after reading each chapter in a textbook or completing a particular assignment. Note,

FIGURE 7.1 Response patterns for fixed ratio (FR), variable ratio (VR), fixed interval (FI), and variable interval (VI) schedules. This figure shows the characteristic pattern of responding on each of the four basic schedules. Notice the high response rate on the FR and VR schedules, moderate response rate on the VI schedule, and scalloped response pattern on the FI schedule. Also, both the FR and FI schedules are accompanied by post-reinforcement pauses. (*Source*: Adapted from Nairne, J. S., *Psychology: The Adaptive Mind*, 2nd edition. Copyright © 2000 Brooks/Cole. Reprinted by permission of Cengage Learning.)

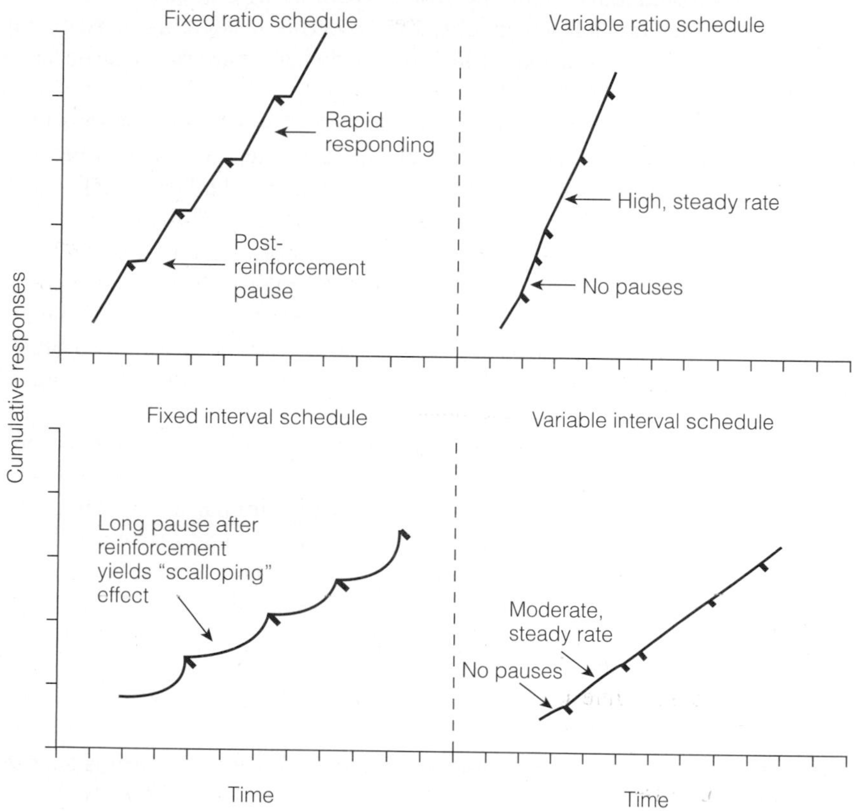

too, that each pause is usually followed by a relatively quick return to a high rate of response. Thus, the typical FR pattern is described as a "break-and-run" pattern—a short break followed by a steady run of responses.

In general, higher ratio requirements produce longer post-reinforcement pauses. This means that you will probably take a longer break after completing a long assignment than after completing a short one. Similarly, a rat will show longer pauses on an FR 100 schedule than on an FR 30 schedule. With very low ratios, such as CRF or FR 2, there may be little or no pausing other than the time it takes for the rat to munch down the food pellet. In such cases, the next reinforcer is so close—only a few lever presses away—that the rat is tempted to immediately go back to work. (If only the reinforcers for studying were so immediate!)

Schedules in which the reinforcer is easily obtained are said to be very *dense* or *rich*, while schedules in which the reinforcer is difficult to obtain are said to be very *lean*. Thus, an FR 5 schedule is considered a very dense schedule of reinforcement compared to an FR 100. During a 1-hour session, a rat can earn many more food pellets on an FR 5 schedule than it can on an FR 100. Likewise, an assembly line worker who earns a dollar for each carburetor assembled (a CRF schedule) is able to earn considerably more during an 8-hour shift than is a worker who earns a dollar for every 10 carburetors assembled (an FR 10 schedule).

In general, "*stretching the ratio*"—moving from a low ratio requirement (a dense schedule) to a high ratio requirement (a lean schedule)—should be done gradually. For example, once lever pressing is well established on a CRF schedule, the requirement can be gradually increased to FR 2, FR 5, FR 10, and so on. If the requirement is increased too quickly—for example, CRF to FR 2 and then a sudden jump to FR 20—the rat's behavior may become erratic and even die out altogether. Likewise, if you try to raise the requirement too high—say, to FR 2000—there may be a similar breakdown in the rat's behavior. Such breakdowns in behavior are technically known as ***ratio strain***, which is a disruption in responding due to an overly demanding response requirement.

Ratio strain is what most people would refer to as burnout, and it can be a big problem for students faced with a heavy workload. Some students, especially those who have a history of getting by with minimal work, may find it increasingly difficult to study under such circumstances and may even choose to drop out of college. If they had instead experienced a gradual increase in workload over a period of several months or years, they might have been able to put forth the needed effort to succeed.

QUICK QUIZ B

1. On a(n) _______________ schedule, reinforcement is contingent upon a fixed number of responses.
2. A schedule in which 15 responses are required for each reinforcer is abbreviated _______________.
3. A mother finds that she always has to make the same request three times before her child complies. The mother's behavior of making requests is on a(n) _______________ schedule of reinforcement.
4. An FR 1 schedule of reinforcement can also be called a _______________ schedule.
5. A fixed ratio schedule tends to produce a (high/low) rate of response, along with a p_______________.
6. An FR 200 schedule of reinforcement will result in a (longer/shorter) pause than an FR 50 schedule.
7. The typical FR pattern is sometimes called a b_______________-and-r_______________ pattern, with a _______________ pause that is followed immediately by a (high/low) rate of response.

8. An FR 12 schedule of reinforcement is (denser/leaner) than an FR 75 schedule.

9. A dense schedule of reinforcement can also be referred to as a r__________ schedule.

10. Over a period of a few months, Aaron changed from complying with each of his mother's requests to complying with every other request, then with every third request, and so on. The mother's behavior of making requests has been subjected to a procedure known as "s__________ the r__________."

11. Graduate students often have to complete an enormous amount of work in the initial year of their program. For some students, the workload involved is far beyond anything they have previously encountered. As a result, their study behavior may become increasingly (erratic/stereotyped) throughout the year, a process known as r__________ s__________.

Study Tip: Post-reinforcement pauses may have important implications for studying. On the one hand, they suggest that there may be a natural tendency for us to take a break after completing a certain amount of work. On the other hand, when students take a break from studying, they often have difficulty starting up again. A possible explanation is that students, unlike pigeons and rats who have little to do during a post-reinforcement pause, tend to engage in highly reinforcing activities during a study break, such as playing computer games or watching television. A possible solution to this problem might be to ensure that study breaks, especially the ones you intend to be brief, do not involve anything particularly interesting; for example, rather than watching television, you might instead do some light housework, a bit of exercise, or perhaps just sit and listen to some quiet music. Like a pigeon with a break-and-run pattern, you may now find it much easier to resume studying. As for more reinforcing activities, such as TV watching, these can be saved for the end of the study session, where you can partake of them as major reinforcers for a job well done (though, as you will learn in Chapter 10, there are questions concerning the extent to which such "self-reinforcement" constitutes real reinforcement).

Another useful trick, which can be used whenever you have difficulty sitting down to study, is the just-get-started (JGS) tactic (e.g., Pychyl, 2010). In this case, you set yourself a very small and easily attained goal, such as to study for at least 5 or 10 minutes with the option to then quit if you still "don't feel like studying." Many students find that once the allotted time has passed, it is surprisingly easy to carry on—in the same way that once a pigeon starts responding on an FR schedule, it has a strong tendency to complete the entire run of responses up to the next reinforcer. Many people report finding the JGS tactic to be very helpful in reducing the tendency to procrastinate (such as when working on term papers), and you may wish to experiment with it yourself.

Variable Ratio Schedules On a ***variable ratio (VR) schedule***, reinforcement is contingent upon a varying, unpredictable number of responses. For example, on a variable ratio 5 (VR 5) schedule, a rat has to emit an *average* of 5 lever presses for each food pellet, with the number of lever responses on any particular trial varying between, say, 1 and 10. Thus, the number of required lever presses might be 3 for the first pellet, 6 for the second pellet, 1 for the third pellet, 7 for the fourth pellet, and so on, with the overall average being 5 lever presses for each reinforcer. Similarly, on a VR 50 schedule, the number of required lever presses may vary between 1 and 100, with the average being 50.

VR schedules generally produce a high and steady rate of response, often with little or no post-reinforcement pause (see Figure 7.1). A post-reinforcement pause is especially unlikely to occur when the minimum response requirement in the schedule is very low, such as a VR 50 schedule in which the requirement varies between 1 and 100 as opposed to a VR 50 in which the requirement varies between, say, 10 and 90 (Schlinger, Derenne, & Baron, 2008). This is understandable if you consider that each response on the former schedule has the potential of resulting in a reinforcer even if a reinforcer has just been obtained.

The real world is filled with examples of VR schedules. Some predatory behaviors, such as that shown by cheetahs, have a strong VR component in that only some attempts at chasing down prey are successful. In humans, only some acts of politeness receive an acknowledgment, only some residents who are called upon by canvassers will make a contribution, and only some TV shows are enjoyable. Many sports activities, such as shooting baskets in basketball and shots on goal in hockey, are also reinforced largely on a VR schedule. As I am writing this passage, a colleague stopped by and joked that his golf drive is probably on a VR 200 schedule. In other words, he figures that an average of about 1 in every 200 drives is a good one. I (Russ Powell) replied that my own drives are on a much leaner schedule with the result that ratio strain has set in, which is fancy behaviorist talk for "I so rarely hit the ball straight that I have just about given up playing."

Variable ratio schedules help to account for the persistence with which some people display certain maladaptive behaviors. Gambling is a prime example in this regard: The unpredictable nature of these activities results in a very high rate of behavior. In fact, the behavior of a gambler playing a slot machine is the classic example of a VR schedule in humans. Certain forms of aberrant social behavior may also be accounted for by VR schedules. For example, why do some men persist in using cute, flippant remarks to introduce themselves to women when the vast majority of women view such remarks negatively? One reason is that a small minority of women actually respond favorably, thereby intermittently reinforcing the use of such remarks. For example, Kleinke, Meeker, and Staneske (1986) found that although 84% of women surveyed rated the opening line "I'm easy. Are you?" as poor to terrible, 14% rated it as either very good or excellent!

Variable ratio schedules of reinforcement may also facilitate the development of an abusive relationship. At the start of a relationship, the individuals involved typically provide each other with an enormous amount of positive reinforcement (a very dense schedule). This strengthens the relationship and increases each partner's attraction to the other. As the relationship progresses, such reinforcement naturally becomes somewhat more intermittent. In some situations, however, this process becomes malignant, with one person (let us call this person the victimizer) providing reinforcement on an extremely intermittent basis, and the other person (the victim) working incredibly hard to obtain that reinforcement. Because the process evolves gradually (a process of slowly "stretching the ratio"), the victim may have little awareness of what is happening until the abusive pattern is well established. What would motivate such an unbalanced process? One source of motivation is that the less often the victimizer reinforces the victim, the more attention (reinforcement) he or she receives from the victim. In other words, the victim works so hard to get the partner's attention that he or she actually reinforces the very process of being largely ignored by that partner. Of course, it does not necessarily have to be a one-way process, and there may be relationships in which the partners alternate the role of victim and victimizer. The result may be a volatile relationship that both partners find exciting but that is constantly on the verge of collapse due to frequent periods in which each partner experiences "ratio strain."

QUICK QUIZ C

1. On a variable ratio schedule, reinforcement is contingent upon a __________ un__________ __________ of responses.
2. A variable ratio schedule typically produces a (high/low) rate of behavior (with/without) a post-reinforcement pause.
3. An average of 1 in 10 people approached by a panhandler actually gives him money. His behavior of panhandling is on a(n) __________ (be precise and use the abbreviation) schedule of reinforcement.
4. As with an FR schedule, an extremely lean VR schedule can result in r__________ s__________.

Fixed Interval Schedules On a ***fixed interval (FI) schedule***, reinforcement is contingent upon the first response after a fixed, predictable period of time. For a rat on a fixed interval 30-second (FI 30-sec) schedule, the first lever press *after* a 30-second interval has elapsed results in a food pellet. Following that, another 30 seconds must elapse before a lever press will again produce a food pellet. Any lever pressing that occurs during the interval, before the 30-second period has elapsed, is ineffective. Similarly, trying to phone a business that opens in exactly 30 minutes will be effective only after the 30 minutes have elapsed, with any phone calls before that being ineffective.

FI schedules often produce a "scalloped" (upwardly curved) pattern of responding, consisting of a post-reinforcement pause followed by a gradually increasing rate of response as the interval draws to a close (see Figure 7.1). For example, a rat on an FI 30-sec schedule will likely emit no lever presses at the start of the 30-second interval. This will be followed by a few tentative lever presses perhaps midway through the interval, with a gradually increasing rate of response thereafter. By the time the interval draws to a close and the reinforcer is imminent, the rat will be emitting a high rate of response, with the result that the reinforcer will be attained as soon as it becomes available.

Would the behavior of trying to phone a business that opens in 30 minutes also follow a scalloped pattern? If we have a watch available, it probably would not. We would simply look at our watch to determine when the 30 minutes have elapsed and then make the phone call. The indicated time would be a discriminative stimulus (S^D) for when the reinforcer is available (i.e., the business is open), and we would wait until the appropriate time before phoning. But what about the behavior of looking at your watch during the 30 minutes (the reinforcer for which would be noticing that the interval has elapsed)? You are unlikely to spend much time looking at your watch at the start of the interval. As time progresses, however, you will begin looking at it more and more frequently. In other words, your behavior will follow the typical scalloped pattern of responding.

The distribution of study sessions throughout the term can also show characteristics of an FI scallop, which can again contribute to students' tendency to procrastinate in their studying. At the start of a course, many students engage in little or no studying, given that the first exam is some distance away. This is followed by a gradual increase in studying as the first exam approaches. The completion of the exam is again followed by little or no studying until the next exam approaches. Unfortunately, these post-reinforcement pauses are often too long, with the result that many students obtain much poorer marks than they would have if they had studied at a steadier pace throughout. (Note, however, that studying for exams is not a pure example of an FI schedule, because a certain amount of work must be accomplished during the interval to obtain the reinforcer of a good mark. On a pure FI schedule, any responding that happens during the interval is essentially irrelevant.)

QUICK QUIZ D

1. On a fixed interval schedule, reinforcement is contingent upon the ________ response following a(n) ________, pr________ period of ________.
2. If I have just missed the bus when I get to the bus stop, I know that I have to wait 15 minutes for the next one to come along. Given that it is absolutely freezing out, I snuggle into my parka as best I can and grimly wait out the interval. Every once in a while, though, I emerge from my cocoon to take a quick glance down the street to see if the bus is coming. My behavior of looking for the bus is on a(n) ________ (use the abbreviation) schedule of reinforcement.
3. In the example in question 2, I will probably engage in (few/frequent) glances at the start of the interval, followed by a gradually (increasing/decreasing) rate of glancing as time passes.
4. Responding on an FI schedule is often characterized by a sc________ pattern of responding consisting of a p________ p________ followed

by a gradually (increasing/decreasing) rate of behavior as the interval draws to a close.

5. On a pure FI schedule, any response that occurs (during/following) the interval is irrelevant.

Variable Interval Schedules On a ***variable interval (VI) schedule***, reinforcement is contingent upon the first response after a varying, unpredictable period of time. For a rat on a variable interval 30-second (VI 30-sec) schedule, the first lever press after an *average* interval of 30 seconds will result in a food pellet, with the actual interval on any particular trial varying between, say, 1 and 60 seconds. Thus, the number of seconds that must pass before a lever press will produce a food pellet could be 8 seconds for the first food pellet, 55 seconds for the second pellet, 24 seconds for the third, and so on, the average of which is 30 seconds. Similarly, if each day you are waiting for a bus and have no idea when it will arrive, then looking down the street for the bus will be reinforced after a varying, unpredictable period of time—for example, 2 minutes the first day, 12 minutes the next day, 9 minutes the third day, and so on, with an average interval of, say, 10 minutes (VI 10-min).

VI schedules usually produce a moderate, steady rate of response, often with little or no post-reinforcement pause (see Figure 7.1). By responding at a relatively steady rate throughout the interval, the rat on a VI 30-sec schedule will attain the reinforcer almost as soon as it becomes available. Similarly, if you need to contact your professor with a last-minute question about an assignment and know that she always arrives in her office sometime between 8:00 A.M. and 8:30 A.M., a good strategy would be to phone every few minutes throughout that time period. By doing so, you will almost certainly contact her within a few minutes of her arrival.

Because VI schedules produce steady, predictable response rates, they are often used to investigate other aspects of operant conditioning, such as those involving choice between alternative sources of reinforcement. You will encounter examples of this when we discuss choice behavior in Chapter 10.

QUICK QUIZ E

1. On a variable interval schedule, reinforcement is contingent upon the __________ response following a __________, un__________ period of __________.
2. You find that by frequently switching stations on your radio, you are able to hear your favorite song an average of once every 20 minutes. Your behavior of switching stations is thus being reinforced on a __________ schedule.
3. In general, variable interval schedules produce a (low/moderate/high) and (steady/fluctuating) rate of response with little or no __________.

Comparing the Four Basic Schedules The four basic schedules produce quite different patterns of behavior, which vary in both the rate of response

TABLE 7.1 Characteristic response rates and post-reinforcement pauses for each of the four basic intermittent schedules. These are only general characteristics; they are not found under all circumstances. For example, an FR schedule with a very low response requirement, such as FR 2, is unlikely to produce a post-reinforcement pause. By contrast, an FR schedule with a very high response requirement, such as FR 2000, may result in ratio strain and a complete cessation of responding.

	FR	VR	FI	VI
Response rate	High	High	Increasing	Moderate
Post-reinforcement pause	Yes	No	Yes	No

and in the presence or absence of a post-reinforcement pause. These characteristics are summarized in Table 7.1. As can be seen, ratio schedules (FR and VR) produce higher rates of response than do interval schedules (FI and VI). This makes sense because the reinforcer in ratio schedules is entirely "response contingent"; that is, it depends entirely on the number of responses emitted. A rat on a VR 100 schedule can double the number of food pellets earned in a 1-hour session by doubling its rate of lever pressing. Similarly, a door-to-door salesman can double the number of sales he makes during a day by doubling the number of customers he calls on (assuming that he continues to give an adequate sales pitch to each customer). Compare this to an interval schedule in which reinforcement is mostly time contingent. For example, on an FI 1-minute schedule, no more than 50 reinforcers can be earned in a 50-minute session. Under such circumstances, responding at a high rate throughout each interval does not pay off and is essentially a waste of energy. Instead, it makes more sense to respond in a way that will simply maximize the possibility of attaining the reinforcer soon after it becomes available. On an FI schedule, this means responding at a gradually increasing rate as the interval draws to a close; on a VI schedule, this means responding at a moderate, steady pace throughout the interval.

It can also be seen that fixed schedules (FR and FI) tend to produce post-reinforcement pauses, whereas variable schedules (VR and VI) do not. On a variable schedule, there is often the possibility of a relatively immediate reinforcer, even if one has just attained a reinforcer, which tempts one to immediately resume responding. By comparison, on a fixed schedule, attaining one reinforcer means that the next reinforcer is necessarily some distance away. On an FR schedule, this results in a short post-reinforcement pause before grinding out another set of responses; on an FI schedule, the post-reinforcement pause is followed by a gradually increasing rate of response as the interval draws to a close and the reinforcer becomes imminent.

Which of these workers is on a ratio schedule of reinforcement?

QUICK QUIZ F

1. In general, (ratio/interval) schedules tend to produce a high rate of response. This is because the reinforcer in such schedules is entirely r__________ contingent, meaning that the rapidity with which responses are emitted (does/does not) affect how soon the reinforcer is obtained.
2. On __________ schedules, the reinforcer is largely time contingent, meaning that the rapidity with which responses are emitted has (little/considerable) effect on how soon the reinforcer is obtained.
3. In general, (variable/fixed) schedules produce little or no post-reinforcement pausing because such schedules often provide the possibility of relatively i__________ reinforcement, even if one has just obtained a reinforcer.
4. In general, __________ schedules produce post-reinforcement pauses because obtaining one reinforcer means that the next reinforcer is necessarily quite (distant/near).

Other Simple Schedules of Reinforcement

Duration Schedules On a duration schedule, reinforcement is contingent on performing a behavior continuously throughout a period of time. On a ***fixed duration (FD) schedule***, the behavior must be performed continuously for a fixed, predictable period of time. For example, the rat must run in the wheel for 60 seconds to earn one pellet of food (an FD 60-sec schedule). Likewise, Julie may decide that her son can watch television each evening only after he completes 2 hours of studying (an FD 2-hr schedule).

On a ***variable duration (VD) schedule***, the behavior must be performed continuously for a varying, unpredictable period of time. For example, the rat must run in the wheel for an average of 60 seconds to earn one pellet of food, with the required time varying between 1 second and 120 seconds on any particular trial (a VD 60-sec schedule). And Julie may decide to reinforce her son's studying with cookies and other treats at varying points in time that happen to average out to about one treat every 30 minutes (a VD 30-min schedule). *(Question: How do FD and VD schedules differ from FI and VI schedules)?*

Although duration schedules are sometimes useful in modifying certain human behaviors, such as studying, they are in some ways rather imprecise compared to the four basic schedules discussed earlier. With FR schedules, for example, one knows precisely what was done to achieve the reinforcer, namely, a certain number of responses. On an FD schedule, however, what constitutes "continuous performance of behavior" during the interval could vary widely. With respect to wheel running, for example, a "lazy" rat could dawdle along at barely a walk, while an "energetic" rat might rotate the wheel at a tremendous pace. Both would receive the reinforcer. Similarly, Julie's son might read only a few pages during his 2-hour study session or charge through several chapters; in either case, he would receive the reinforcer of being allowed to watch television. Remember too, from Chapter 6, how reinforcing the mere performance of an activity with no regard to level of performance can undermine a person's intrinsic interest in that activity. This danger obviously applies to duration schedules; one therefore needs to be cautious in their use. Nevertheless, many successful writers write according to an FD schedule of reinforcement (i.e., they write for a fixed amount of time each day), although there are also some who write according to an FR schedule—that is, they strive to complete a certain number of words or pages each day (Currey, 2013; Silvia, 2007). An informal survey of your fellow students will likely show that they too vary in the extent to which they study for time or to accomplish a certain amount of work (e.g., to finish a chapter), something you may wish to explore in optimizing your own study behavior.

Response-Rate Schedules As we have seen, different types of intermittent schedules produce different rates of response (i.e., they have different *schedule effects*). These different rates are essentially by-products of the schedule. However, in a ***response-rate schedule***, reinforcement is directly contingent upon the organism's rate of response. Let's examine three types of response-rate schedules.

In ***differential reinforcement of high rates (DRH)***, reinforcement is contingent upon emitting *at least* a certain number of responses in a certain period of time—or, more generally, reinforcement is provided for responding at a fast rate. The term *differential reinforcement* means simply that one type of response is reinforced while another is not. In a DRH schedule, reinforcement is provided for a high rate of response and not for a low rate. For example, a rat might receive a food pellet only if it emits at least 30 lever presses within a period of a minute. Similarly, a worker on an assembly line may be told that she can keep her job only if she assembles a minimum of 20 carburetors per hour. By requiring so many responses in a short period of time, DRH schedules ensure a high rate of responding. Athletic events such as running and swimming are prime examples of DRH schedules in that winning is directly contingent on a rapid series of responses.

In ***differential reinforcement of low rates (DRL)***, a minimum amount of time must pass between each response before the reinforcer will be delivered—or, more generally, reinforcement is provided for responding at a slow rate. For example, a rat might receive a food pellet only if it waits at least 10 seconds between lever presses. So how is this different from an FI 10-sec schedule? Remember that on an FI schedule, responses that occur during the interval have no effect; on a DRL schedule, however, responses that occur during the interval do have an effect—an adverse effect in that they *prevent* reinforcement from occurring. In other words, responding during the interval must *not* occur in order for a response following the interval to produce a reinforcer.

Human examples of DRL schedules consist of situations in which a person is required to perform an action slowly. For example, a parent might praise a child for brushing her teeth slowly or completing her homework slowly, given that going too fast generally results in sloppy performance. Once the quality of performance improves, reinforcement can then be made contingent on responding at a normal speed.

In ***differential reinforcement of paced responding (DRP)***, reinforcement is contingent upon emitting a series of responses at a set rate—or, more generally, reinforcement is provided for responding neither too fast nor too slow. For example, a rat might receive a food pellet if it emits 10 consecutive responses, with each response separated by an interval of no less than 1.5 and no more than 2.5 seconds. Similarly, musical activities, such as playing in a band or dancing to music, require that the relevant actions be performed at a specific pace. People who are very good at this are said to have a good sense of timing or rhythm. Further examples of DRP schedules can be found in noncompetitive swimming or running. People often perform these activities at a pace that is fast enough to ensure benefits to health and a feeling of well-being, yet not so fast as to result in exhaustion and possible injury. In fact, even competitive swimmers and runners, especially those who compete over long distances, will often set a specific pace throughout much of the race. Doing so ensures that they have sufficient energy at the end for a last-minute sprint (DRH) to the finish line, thereby maximizing their chances of clocking a good time.

QUICK QUIZ G

1. On a (VD/VI) schedule, reinforcement is contingent upon responding continuously for a varying period of time; on an (FI/FD) schedule, reinforcement is contingent upon the first response after a fixed period of time.
2. As Tessa sits quietly in the doctor's office, her mother occasionally gives her a hug as a reward. As a result, Tessa is more likely to sit quietly on future visits to the doctor. This is an example of a(n) ______________ ______________ schedule of reinforcement.
3. In practicing the slow-motion exercise known as tai chi, Tung noticed that the more slowly he moved, the more thoroughly his muscles relaxed. This is an example of

d_____ reinforcement of _____ _____ behavior (abbreviated _____).

4. In a video game, the faster you destroy all the targets, the more bonus points you obtain. This is an example of _____ reinforcement of _____ _____ behavior (abbreviated _____).

5. Frank discovers that he feels better if he jogs at a nice, even rhythm that is neither too fast nor too slow. This is an example of _____ reinforcement of _____ behavior (abbreviated _____).

Noncontingent Schedules On a ***noncontingent schedule of reinforcement***, the reinforcer is delivered *independently* of any response. In other words, a response is not required for the reinforcer to be obtained. Such schedules are also called *response-independent schedules*. There are two types of noncontingent schedules: fixed time and variable time.

On a ***fixed time (FT) schedule***, the reinforcer is delivered following a fixed, predictable period of time, regardless of the organism's behavior. For example, on a fixed time 30-second (FT 30-sec) schedule, a pigeon receives access to food every 30 seconds regardless of its behavior. Likewise, many people receive Christmas gifts each year, independently of whether they have been naughty or nice—an FT 1-year schedule. FT schedules therefore involve the delivery of a "free" reinforcer following a predictable period of time.

On a ***variable time (VT) schedule***, the reinforcer is delivered following a varying, unpredictable period of time, regardless of the organism's behavior. For example, on a variable time 30-second (VT 30-sec) schedule, a pigeon receives access to food after an average interval of 30 seconds, with the actual interval on any particular trial ranging from, say, 1 second to 60 seconds. Similarly, you may coincidentally run into an old friend about every 3 months on average (a VT 3-month schedule). VT schedules therefore involve the delivery of a free reinforcer following an unpredictable period of time. (*Question: How do FT and VT schedules differ from FI and VI schedules*)?

QUICK QUIZ H

1. On a non_____ schedule of reinforcement, a response is not required to obtain a reinforcer. Such a schedule is also called a r_____-i_____ schedule of reinforcement.

2. Every morning at 7:00 A.M., a robin perches outside Marilyn's bedroom window and begins singing. Given that Marilyn very much enjoys the robin's song, this is an example of a _____ _____ 24-hour schedule of reinforcement (abbreviated _____).

3. For farmers, rainfall is an example of a noncontingent reinforcer that is typically delivered on a _____ _____ schedule (abbreviated _____).

Noncontingent reinforcement may account for some forms of superstitious behavior. In the first investigation of this possibility, Skinner (1948b) presented pigeons with food every 15 seconds (FT 15-sec) regardless of their behavior. Although you might think that such free reinforcers would have little effect on the pigeons' behavior (other than encouraging them to stay close to the feeder), quite the opposite occurred. Six of the eight pigeons began to display ritualistic patterns of behavior. For example, one bird began turning counterclockwise circles, while another repeatedly thrust its head into an upper corner of the chamber. Two other pigeons displayed a swaying pendulum motion of the head and body. Skinner believed these behaviors developed because they had been accidentally reinforced by the coincidental presentation of food. For example, if a pigeon just happened to turn a counterclockwise circle before food delivery, that behavior would be accidentally reinforced and increase in frequency. This would increase the likelihood of the same behavior occurring the next time food was delivered, which would further strengthen it. The eventual result would be a well-established pattern of turning circles, as though turning circles somehow caused the food to appear.

Some researchers have argued that Skinner's evidence for superstitious behavior in the pigeon may not be as clear-cut as he believed. They claim that at least some of the ritualistic behaviors he observed may have consisted of innate tendencies, almost like fidgeting behaviors, that are often elicited during a period of waiting (Staddon & Simmelhag, 1971). These tendencies, which are discussed in Chapter 12, are known as *adjunctive behaviors*. Nevertheless, other experiments have replicated the effect of noncontingent reinforcement on the development of superstitious behavior. Ono (1987), for example, placed students in a booth that contained three levers and a counter. The students were told that "if you do something, you may get points on the counter" (p. 263). They were also told to get as many points as possible. In reality, the points were delivered on either an FT or VT schedule, so the students' behavior actually had no effect on point delivery. Nevertheless, most students developed at least temporary patterns of superstitious lever pulling; that is, they pulled the lever as though it were effective in producing points. Interestingly, one student started with lever pulling but then coincidentally received a point after simply touching the counter. This led to a superstitious pattern of climbing on the counter and touching different parts of the apparatus, apparently in the belief that this action produced the points. She then jumped off the apparatus at just the time that she received another point, which led to a superstitious pattern of repeatedly jumping in the air and touching the ceiling! After several minutes of this, she finally quit, apparently as a result of fatigue.

Professional athletes and gamblers are particularly prone to the development of superstitions, some of which may evolve in the manner that Skinner suggests. Under constant threat of losing their position to an eager newcomer, professional athletes are constantly on the lookout for anything that might enhance their performance. As a result, unusual events that precede a fine performance, such as humming a certain tune or wearing an unusual article of clothing, may be quickly identified and then deliberately reproduced in the hopes of reproducing that performance. Gamblers display even stronger tendencies toward the development of superstitions, probably because the activity in which they are engaged is even more uncertain in its outcome. Bingo players, for example, commonly carry lucky pendants, stuffed animals, or pieces of jewelry to each game, and they are often adamant (almost pathologically so) about obtaining cards that contain certain patterns or are drawn from the top or bottom of the stack. Many of these rituals probably evolved because they were at one time associated with a big win.

Herrnstein (1966) noted that superstitious behaviors can sometimes develop as by-products of contingent reinforcement for some other behavior. For example, a businessman might believe it is important to impress customers with a firm handshake, when in fact it is merely the handshake, and not the firmness of the handshake, that is the critical factor. (Unfortunately, such a superstition could have serious consequences if the businessman then attempts to branch out into the Asian market, where a firm handshake is often regarded as a sign of disrespect.) Similarly, some managers might come to believe that "pushing the panic button" is an effective way to deal with crises, simply because it is usually followed by a successful outcome. What they fail to realize is that a low-key approach might have been equally if not more effective—and certainly a lot less stressful.

Question: Although Skinner's (1948b) original demonstration of superstitious behavior involved the use of a fixed time schedule, you might wish to consider whether superstitious behavior in humans is more likely to develop under a fixed or variable time schedule. To answer this, think about the types of situations in which you are particularly likely to find superstitious behavior in humans. Is it in situations that involve predictable events or unpredictable events? Obviously, it is unpredictable events, such as games of chance, performance in sports, hunting and fishing ("Jana's lucky lure"), and so forth. In this sense, at least from a human perspective, superstitious behavior can be seen as an attempt to make an unpredictable situation more predictable.

QUICK QUIZ I

1. When noncontingent reinforcement happens to follow a particular behavior, that behavior may (increase/decrease) in strength. Such behavior is referred to as s__________ behavior.
2. Herrnstein (1966) noted that superstitious behaviors can sometimes develop as a by-product of (contingent/noncontingent) reinforcement for some other behavior.
3. As shown by the kinds of situations in which superstitious behaviors develop in humans, such behaviors seem most likely to develop on a(n) (VT/FT) schedule of reinforcement.

What happens if a noncontingent schedule of reinforcement is superimposed on a regular, contingent schedule of reinforcement? What if, for example, a pigeon responding on a VI schedule of food reinforcement also receives extra reinforcers for free? Will the pigeon's rate of response on the VI schedule increase or decrease? In fact, the pigeon's rate of response on the noncontingent schedule will decrease (Rachlin & Baum,

1972). Just as people on welfare might sometimes become less inclined to look for work, the pigeon that receives free reinforcers will work less vigorously for contingent reinforcers. Suggestive evidence of this effect can even be found among professional athletes. One study, conducted several years ago, found that major league pitchers who had signed long-term contracts showed a significant decline in number of innings pitched relative to pitchers who only signed a 1-year contract (O'Brien, Figlerski, Howard, & Caggiano, 1981). Insofar as a long-term contract or a guaranteed purse (as in boxing) virtually guarantees a hefty salary regardless of performance, these results are consistent with the possibility that athletic performance might sometimes decline when the money earned is no longer contingent on level of performance.

At this point, you might be thinking that noncontingent reinforcement is all bad, given that it leads to superstitious behavior in some situations and to poor performance in others. In fact, noncontingent reinforcement is sometimes quite beneficial. More specifically, it can be an effective means for reducing the frequency of maladaptive behaviors. For example, children who act out often do so to obtain attention. If, however, they are given a sufficient amount of attention on a noncontingent basis, they will no longer have to act out to obtain it. Noncontingent reinforcement has even been shown to reduce the frequency of self-injurious behavior. Such behavior, which can consist of head-banging or biting chunks of flesh out of one's arm, is sometimes displayed by people who suffer from certain types of developmental disorders, and can be notoriously difficult to treat. In some of these cases, the behavior appears to be maintained by the attention it elicits from caretakers. Research has shown, however, that if the caretakers provide the individual with plenty of attention on a noncontingent basis, then the frequency of their self-injurious behavior may be greatly reduced (e.g., Hagopian, Fisher, & Legacy, 1994). In a sense, they no longer have to injure themselves to receive attention because they are now receiving lots of attention for free.

The beneficial effects of noncontingent reinforcement can also be seen as providing empirical support for the value of what Carl Rogers (1959), the famous humanistic psychologist, called "unconditional positive regard." Unconditional positive regard refers to the love, respect, and acceptance that one receives from significant others, regardless of one's behavior. Rogers assumed that such regard is a necessary precondition for the development of a healthy personality. From a behavioral perspective, unconditional positive regard can be viewed as a form of noncontingent social reinforcement, which can indeed have beneficial effects. In fact, it seems likely that proper child rearing requires healthy doses of both noncontingent reinforcement, which gives the child a secure base from which to explore the world and take risks, and contingent reinforcement, which helps to shape the child's behavior in appropriate ways, maximize skill development, and prevent the development of passivity. Thus, Abraham Maslow (1971), another famous humanistic psychologist, argued that child rearing should be neither too restrictive nor too lenient, which in behavioral terms can be taken to imply that the social reinforcement children receive should be neither excessively contingent nor excessively noncontingent.

QUICK QUIZ J

1. During the time that a rat is responding for food on a VR 100 schedule, we begin delivering additional food on a VT 60-second schedule. As a result, the rate of response on the VR schedule is likely to (increase/decrease/remain unchanged).
2. A child who is often hugged during the course of the day, regardless of what he is doing, is in humanistic terms receiving unconditional positive regard. In behavioral terms, he is receiving a form of non__________ social reinforcement. As a result, this child may be (more/less) likely to act out in order to receive attention.

Complex Schedules of Reinforcement

All of the schedules previously described are relatively simple in that there is only one basic requirement. On the other hand, a ***complex schedule*** consists of a combination of two or more simple schedules. There are a wide variety of such schedules, three of which are described here. Two other types of complex schedules—multiple schedules and concurrent schedules—are discussed in later chapters.

Conjunctive Schedules A ***conjunctive schedule*** is a type of complex schedule in which the requirements of two or more simple schedules must be met before a reinforcer is delivered. For example, on a conjunctive FI 2-minute FR 100 schedule, reinforcement is contingent upon completing 100 lever presses plus at least one lever press following a 2-minute interval. Many of the contingencies that we encounter in everyday life are examples of conjunctive schedules. The wages you earn on a job are contingent upon working a certain number of hours each week *and* doing a sufficient amount of work so that you will not be fired. Likewise, Jon's fiancée might have chosen to marry him because he is kind *and* humorous *and* interesting *and* drives a Porsche. With any one of these components missing, she would have paid little attention to him.

Adjusting Schedules In an ***adjusting schedule***, the response requirement changes as a function of the organism's performance while responding for the previous reinforcer. For example, on an FR 100 schedule, if the rat completes all 100 responses within a 5-minute interval, we then increase the requirement to 110 responses (FR 110). In other words, because the rat has performed so well, we expect even better performance in the future.

In a similar fashion, when Tara displayed excellent ability in mastering her violin lessons, she and her parents decided to increase the amount she had to learn each week. And when Lily's high school students performed poorly on their exams, she gradually decreased the amount of material they had to learn each week. (It is, of course, in this manner that standards in school become gradually lowered, often to the detriment of the students.)

The process of shaping involves an adjusting schedule insofar as the criterion for reinforcement is raised depending on the animal's performance. As soon as the rat has learned to stand near the lever to get food, the criterion is raised to touching the lever, placing a paw on the lever, and so forth. The requirement for reinforcement changes as soon as the rat has successfully met the previous requirement.

QUICK QUIZ K

1. A(n) ____________ schedule is one that consists of a combination of two or more simple schedules.
2. In a(n) ____________ schedule, the response requirement changes as a function of the organism's performance while responding for the previous reinforcer. In a(n) ____________ schedule, the requirements of two or more simple schedules must be met before the reinforcer is delivered.
3. To the extent that a gymnast is trying to improve his performance, he is likely on a(n) ____________ schedule of reinforcement; to the extent that his performance is judged according to both the form and quickness of his moves, he is on a(n) ____________ schedule.

Chained Schedules A ***chained schedule*** consists of a sequence of two or more simple schedules, each of which has its own S^D and the last of which results in a terminal reinforcer. In other words, the person or animal must work through a series of component schedules to obtain the sought-after reinforcer. A chained schedule differs from a conjunctive schedule in that the two component schedules must be completed in a particular order, which is not required in a conjunctive schedule.

As an example of a chained schedule, a pigeon in a standard operant conditioning chamber is presented with a VR 20 schedule on a green key, followed by an FI 10-sec schedule on a red key, which then leads to the terminal reinforcer of food. Thus, an average of 20 responses on the green key will result in a change in key color to red, following which the first response on the red key after a 10-second interval will be reinforced by food. The food is the terminal reinforcer that supports the entire chain. This chain can be diagrammed as follows:

	VR 20		FI 10-sec	
Green key:	***Peck*** →	**Red key:**	***Peck*** →	**Food**
S^D	R	S^R/S^D	R	S^R

Note that the presentation of the red key is both a secondary reinforcer for completing the preceding VR 20 schedule and an S^D for responding on the subsequent FI 10-sec schedule. Note, too, that this is an example of a *two-link chain*, with the VR 20 schedule constituting the first, or initial, link and the FI 10-sec schedule constituting the second, or terminal, link. By adding yet another schedule to the start of the chain, we can create a three-link chain, for example:

VI 30-sec		VR 20		FI 10-sec		
White key:	***Peck*** →	**Green key:**	***Peck*** →	**Red key:**	***Peck*** →	**Food**
S^D	R	S^R/S^D	R	S^R/S^D	R	S^R

In this case, both the green and red keys function as secondary reinforcers that help maintain behavior throughout the chain.

QUICK QUIZ L

1. A chained schedule consists of a sequence of two or more simple schedules, each of which has its own ____________ and the last of which results in a t__________ r__________.
2. Within a chain, completion of each of the early links ends in a (primary/secondary) reinforcer, which also functions as the ____________ for the next link of the chain.

Once pigeons learn which schedule is associated with which key, they generally show the appropriate response patterns for those schedules. In the preceding example, this would be a moderate, steady rate of response on the white key, a high rate of response on the green key, and a scalloped pattern of responding on the red key. Nevertheless, responding tends to be somewhat weaker in the earlier links of a chain than in the later links. This can be seen most clearly when each link consists of the same schedule. For example, Kelleher and Fry (1962) presented pigeons with a three-link chained schedule with each link consisting of an FI 60-sec schedule:

FI 60-sec		FI 60-sec		FI 60-sec		
White key:	***Peck*** →	**Green key:**	***Peck*** →	**Red key:**	***Peck*** →	**Food**
S^D	R	S^R/S^D	R	S^R/S^D	R	S^R

The pigeons displayed very long pauses and a slow rate of response on the white key compared to the other two keys. The greatest amount of responding occurred on the red key.

Why would the earlier links of the chain be associated with weaker responding? One way of looking at it is that in the later links, the terminal reinforcer is more immediate and hence more influential, while in the early links, the terminal reinforcer is more distant and hence less influential (remember that delayed reinforcement is less effective than immediate reinforcement). Another way of looking at it is that the secondary reinforcers supporting behavior in the early links are less directly associated with food and are therefore relatively weak (e.g., the green key is associated with food only indirectly through its association with the red key). From this perspective, a chained schedule can be seen as the operant equivalent of higher-order classical conditioning—in which, for example, a tone (CS_1) associated with food (US) elicits less salivation than the food does, and a light (CS_2) associated with the tone elicits less salivation than the tone does. Similarly, in the example of the chained schedule, the red key associated with the food is a less powerful reinforcer than the food, and the green key associated with the red key is a less powerful reinforcer than the red key. (If you find that you can no longer remember the concept of higher-order classical conditioning, you should go back and review it.)

The difference in response strength between the early and later links in a chain is representative of a more general behavioral principle known as the goal gradient effect. The ***goal gradient effect*** is an increase in the strength and/or efficiency of responding as one draws near to the goal. For example, rats running through a maze to obtain food tend to run faster and make fewer wrong turns as they near the goal box (Hull, 1932). Similarly, a student writing an essay is likely to take shorter breaks and work more intensely as she nears the end. Dolphin trainers are well aware of the goal gradient effect. Dolphins who are trained to perform long chains of behaviors have a tendency to drift toward "sloppy" performance during the early parts of the chain, and trainers have to be vigilant to ensure that the dolphin's behavior is not reinforced when this occurs (Pryor, 1975). (Perhaps the most profound example of a goal gradient, however, is that shown by people who desperately need to urinate and become speed demons as they near the washroom.)

An efficient way to establish responding on a chained schedule is to train the final link first and the initial link last, a process known as *backward chaining*. Using the pigeon example, the pigeon would first be trained to respond on the red key to obtain food. This will establish the red key as a secondary reinforcer through its association with food. The presentation of the red key can then be used to reinforce responding on the green key. Once this is established, the presentation of the green key can be used to reinforce responding on the white key.

In these examples, each link in the chain required the same type of behavior, namely, key pecking. It is also possible to create behavior chains in which each link consists of a different behavior. For example, a rat might have to climb over a barrier and then run through a tunnel to obtain food. This can be diagrammed as follows:

Barrier: ***Climb over barrier*** **→ Tunnel:** ***Run through tunnel*** **→ Food**
S^D R S^R/S^D R S^R

Note that the sight of the tunnel is both a secondary reinforcer for climbing over the barrier and a discriminative stimulus for then running through the tunnel.

As with the previous examples, backward chaining would be the best way to train this sequence of behaviors. Thus, the rat would first be trained to run through the tunnel for food. Once this is established, it would be taught to climb over the barrier to get to the tunnel, with the sight of the tunnel acting as a secondary reinforcer. In this manner, very long chains of behavior can be established. In one reported example, a rat was trained to go up a ladder, cross a platform, climb a rope, cross a bridge, get into a little elevator

FIGURE 7.2 Through shaping and chaining, animals can be taught to display some surprising behaviors.

Ross Anania/Media Bakery

© Keystone/Hulton Archive/Getty Images

box, release the pulley holding the box, lower the box "paw over paw" to the floor, and then press a button to obtain the food (Pryor, 1975). Of course, each of these behaviors also had to be shaped (through reinforcement of successive approximations to the target behavior). Shaping and chaining are thus the basic means by which circus and marine animals are trained to perform some remarkable feats (see Figure 7.2).

Most human endeavors involve response chains, some of which are very long. The act of reading this chapter, for example, consists of reading section after section, until the terminal reinforcer of completing the entire chapter has been attained. Completing each section serves as both a secondary reinforcer for having read that section as well as an S^D for reading the next section. Reading the chapter is in turn part of a much larger chain of behaviors that includes attending lectures, taking notes, and studying, the terminal reinforcer for which is passing the course. Fortunately, backward chaining is not required for the development of such chains, because language enables us to describe to one another the required sequence of behaviors (such as by providing a course syllabus). In other words, for humans, response chains are often established through instructions.

Unfortunately, in the case of very long chains, such as completing a course, the terminal reinforcer is often extremely distant, with the result that behavior is easily disrupted during the early part of the chain (remember the goal gradient principle). This is yet another reason for why it is much easier to be a diligent student the night before the midterm than during the first week of the semester. Can anything be done to alleviate this problem? One possibility is to make the completion of each link in the chain more salient (i.e., more noticeable), thereby enhancing its value as a secondary reinforcer. Novelists, for example, need to write hundreds, or even thousands, of pages before the terminal reinforcer of a completed book is attained. To keep themselves on track, some novelists keep detailed records of their progress, such as charting the number of words written each day as well as the exact dates on which chapters were started and completed (Wallace & Pear, 1977). These records outline their achievements, thereby providing a much-needed source of secondary reinforcement throughout the process. Similarly, students sometimes keep detailed records of the number of hours studied or pages read. They might also compile a "to-do" list of assignments and then cross off each item as it is completed. Crossing off an item provides a clear record that a task has been accomplished and also functions as a secondary reinforcer that helps motivate us (Lakein, 1973). In fact, it can be so reinforcing that some people will actually add a task to a to-do list *after* they have completed it, simply to have the pleasure of crossing it off!

QUICK QUIZ M

1. Responding tends to be weaker in the (earlier/later) links of a chain. This is an example of the g________ g________ effect, in which the strength or efficiency of responding (increases/decreases) as the organism approaches the goal.
2. An efficient way to train a complex chain, especially in animals, is through b________ chaining, in which the (first/last) link of the chain is trained first. However, this type of procedure usually is not required with verbally proficient humans, with whom behavior chains can be quickly established through the use of ins________.
3. One suggestion for enhancing our behavior in the early part of a long response chain is to make the completion of each link more (salient/gradual), thereby enhancing its value as a s________ reinforcer.

Theories of Reinforcement

In this section, we briefly discuss some major theories of reinforcement. We begin with Clark Hull's early drive reduction view of reinforcement. This is followed by a brief description of a highly influential approach known as the Premack principle. This principle is of immense practical importance, and it has helped revolutionize the manner in which the process of reinforcement is now conceptualized. In fact, two other theoretical approaches that we discuss—the response deprivation hypothesis and the bliss point approach—can be viewed as outgrowths of the Premack principle.

Drive Reduction Theory

An early approach to understanding reinforcement, and one that was strongly championed by Hull (1943), is drive reduction theory. In ***drive reduction theory***, an event is reinforcing to the extent that it is associated with a reduction in some type of physiological drive. Thus, food deprivation produces a "hunger drive," which then propels the animal to seek out food. When food is obtained, the hunger drive is reduced. At the same time, the behavior that preceded this drive reduction, and led to the food, is automatically strengthened. In very simple terms (in actuality, the theory is more complex than this), if a hungry rat in a maze turns left just before it finds food in the goal box, the act of turning left in the maze will be automatically strengthened by the subsequent reduction in hunger.

We touched upon this theory in Chapter 6 when we noted that primary reinforcers are often those events that seem to reduce a physiological need. From this perspective, secondary reinforcers are events that have become reinforcers because they have been associated, either directly or indirectly, with a primary reinforcer and, hence, with some type of drive reduction. Thus, a person enjoys collecting cookbooks because cooking is associated with eating food, which in turn has been associated with a reduction in hunger. According to Hull, all reinforcers are associated, either directly or indirectly, with some type of drive reduction.

In Chapter 6, we noted that a major problem with this physiological view of reinforcement is that some reinforcers do not seem to be associated with drive reduction. A rat will press a lever to obtain access to a running wheel, a chimpanzee will press a button so that it can obtain a peek into another room, and teenagers will spend considerable amounts of money to be exposed to earsplitting levels of rock music. It is difficult to see how such events are associated with a reduction in some type of physiological need. Instead, it seems as though the motivation for such behavior exists more in the nature of the reinforcing stimulus than in the state of the organism.

Incentive motivation is motivation that is derived from some property of the reinforcer, as opposed to an internal drive state. Playing a video game for the fun of it, attending a concert because you enjoy the music, and working to earn enough money to buy a Porsche are examples of behaviors that are motivated by incentives. Even events that seem to be clearly associated with drive reduction can be strongly affected by incentive factors. For example, going to a restaurant for a meal might be largely driven by hunger; however, the fact that you prefer a restaurant that serves hot, spicy food is an example of incentive motivation. The spiciness of the food plays no role in the reduction of hunger; it is simply a form of sensory stimulation that you find highly reinforcing.

In conclusion, most theorists no longer believe that drive reduction theory can offer a comprehensive account of reinforcement, and this approach has now been largely abandoned. Some recent approaches have instead emphasized observable behavior patterns as opposed to hypothetical internal processes in their explanation of the reinforcement process. A major step in this direction was the Premack principle.

QUICK QUIZ N

1. According to drive reduction theory, an event is reinforcing if it is associated with a reduction in some type of p__________ drive.
2. According to this theory, a s__________ reinforcer is one that has been associated, directly or indirectly, with a p__________ reinforcer.
3. A major problem with drive reduction theory is that __________ __________.
4. The motivation that is derived from some property of the reinforcer is called __________ motivation.
5. Research has shown that hungry rats will perform more effectively in a T-maze when the reinforcer for a correct response (right turn versus left turn) consists of several small pellets as opposed to one large pellet (Capaldi, Miller, & Alptekin, 1989). The fact that several small bites of food are a more effective reinforcer than one large bite is consistent with the notion of (drive reduction/incentive motivation).

The Premack Principle

Remember how Skinner defined reinforcers (and punishers) by their effect on behavior? This unfortunately presents us with a problem. In the real world, it would be nice to know ahead of time whether a certain event can function as a reinforcer. One way to do this, of course, would be to take something the person or animal seems to like and use that as a reinforcer. But it is not always easy to determine what a person or animal likes. Moreover, events that we might believe should be liked might not actually function as reinforcers. To a 5-year-old boy, a kiss from his mother is great if he needs comforting, but not when he is trying to show off to his friends. Fortunately, the Premack principle provides a more objective way to determine whether something can be used as a reinforcer (Premack, 1965).

The Premack principle is based on the notion that reinforcers can often be viewed as behaviors rather than stimuli. For example, rather than saying that lever pressing was reinforced by *food* (a stimulus), we could say that lever pressing was reinforced by the act of *eating food* (a behavior). Similarly, rather than saying that playing appropriately was reinforced by *television*, we could instead say that it was reinforced by *watching television*. When we view reinforcers in this manner—as behaviors rather than stimuli—then the process of reinforcement can be conceptualized as a sequence of two behaviors: (1) the behavior that is being reinforced, followed by (2) the behavior that is the reinforcer. Moreover, by comparing the probability or frequency of two behaviors, we can determine whether one can be used as a reinforcer for the other.

More specifically, the ***Premack principle*** states that a high-probability behavior can be used to reinforce a low-probability behavior. For example, when a rat is hungry, eating food has a higher likelihood of occurrence than running in a wheel. This means that eating food, which is the high-probability behavior (HPB), can be used to reinforce the target behavior of running in a wheel, which is the low-probability behavior (LPB). In other words, the rat will run in the wheel to obtain access to the food:

Target behavior **Consequence**
Running in a wheel **(LPB)** → **Eating food (HPB)**
R $\mathbf{S^R}$

On the other hand, if the rat is not hungry, then eating food is less likely to occur than running in a wheel. In this case, running in a wheel can be used as a reinforcer for the target behavior of eating food. In other words, the rat will eat to obtain access to the wheel.

Target behavior **Consequence**
Eating food **(LPB)** → **Running in a wheel (HPB)**
R $\mathbf{S^R}$

By focusing on the relative probabilities (or relative frequencies) of behaviors, the Premack principle allows us to quickly identify potential reinforcers. If Kaily spends only a few minutes each morning doing chores, but at least an hour reading comic books, then the opportunity to read comic books (a higher-probability behavior) can be used to reinforce doing chores (a lower-probability behavior).

Do chores → **Read comic books**
R $\mathbf{S^R}$

In fact, if you want an easy way to remember the Premack principle, just think of Grandma's rule: First you work (a low-probability behavior), then you play (a high-probability behavior).

The Premack principle has proven to be very useful in applied settings. For example, a person with autism who spends many hours each day rocking back and forth might be very unresponsive to consequences that are normally reinforcing for others, such as receiving praise. The Premack principle, however, suggests that the opportunity to rock back and forth can be used as an effective reinforcer for another behavior that we might wish to strengthen, such as interacting with others. Thus, the Premack principle is a handy principle to keep in mind when confronted by a situation in which normal reinforcers seem to have little effect.

The Premack principle can also be useful for students. A common recommendation is that students should reward themselves (present a reinforcer to themselves) each time they study rather than, say, play computer games. Some students, however, will complain that they just can't think of a good reward in such situations. But the Premack principle provides a solution; if studying is a low-probability behavior and playing computer games is a high-probability behavior, then it should be possible to use gaming as a reward for studying (although, as noted earlier, there are certain complexities involved in this type of "self-reinforcement" procedure that will be discussed in Chapter 10).

QUICK QUIZ O

1. The Premack principle proposes that reinforcers can often be viewed as ____________ rather than stimuli. For example, rather than saying that the rat's lever pressing was reinforced with food, we could say that it was reinforced with ____________ food.
2. The Premack principle states that a(n) ____________-____________ behavior can be used as a reinforcer for a(n) ____________-____________ behavior.
3. According to the Premack principle, if you crack your knuckles 3 times per hour and burp 20 times per hour, then the opportunity to ____________ can probably be used as a reinforcer for ____________.
4. If you drink five soda pops each day and only one glass of orange juice, then the opportunity to drink ____________ can likely be used as a reinforcer for drinking ____________.
5. If "*Chew bubble gum* → Play video games" is a diagram of a reinforcement procedure based on the Premack principle, then chewing bubble gum must be a (lower/higher)-probability behavior than playing video games.
6. Similar to the Premack principle, in Grandma's rule, first you (work/play), which is a (LPB/HPB), and then you (work/play), which is a (LPB/HPB).

Response Deprivation Hypothesis

The Premack principle requires us to know the relative probabilities of two behaviors before we can judge whether one will be an effective reinforcer for the other. But what if we have information on only one behavior? Is there any way that we can tell whether that behavior can function as a reinforcer before actually trying it out?

The ***response deprivation hypothesis*** states that a behavior can serve as a reinforcer when (1) access to the behavior is restricted and (2) its frequency thereby falls below its preferred level of occurrence (Timberlake & Allison, 1974). The preferred level of an activity is its baseline level of occurrence when the animal can freely engage in that activity. For example, imagine that a rat typically runs for 1 hour a day whenever it has free access to a running wheel. This 1 hour per day is the rat's preferred level of running. If the rat is then allowed free access to the wheel for only 15 minutes per day, it will be unable to reach this preferred level and will be in a state of deprivation with regard to running. According to the response deprivation hypothesis, the rat will now be willing to work (e.g., press a lever) to obtain additional time on the wheel.

Lever press → **Running in a wheel**
R **S^R**

The response deprivation approach also provides a general explanation for why contingencies of reinforcement are effective. Contingencies of reinforcement are effective to the extent that they create a condition in which the organism is confronted with the possibility of a certain response falling below its baseline level. Take Kaily, who enjoys reading comic books each day. If we establish a contingency in which she has to do her chores before reading comic books, her baseline level of free comic book reading will drop to zero. She will therefore be willing to do chores to maintain her preferred level of comic book time.

Do chores → **Read comic books**
R **S^R^**

You will notice that the diagram given here is the same as that given for the Premack principle, and in fact both approaches will often lead to the same type of contingency being established. But the interpretation of why it works is different. In this case, reading comic books is a reinforcer simply because the contingency threatens to push free comic book reading to below its preferred rate of occurrence. The relative probabilities of the two behaviors are irrelevant, meaning that it does not matter if the probability of reading comic books at the outset is higher or lower than the probability of doing chores. Even if Kaily is a workaholic who spends much of her time doing chores anyway, we could get her to do yet more chores by threatening to reduce her comic book time. The only thing that matters is whether comic book reading is in danger of falling below its preferred level if the contingency is not met. Thus, the response deprivation hypothesis is applicable to a wider range of conditions than the Premack principle. (Question 4 in the following Quick Quiz may help clarify this.)

To help distinguish between the Premack principle and the response deprivation hypothesis, ask yourself whether the main point seems to be the frequency of one behavior relative to another (in which case the Premack principle is applicable) or the frequency of one behavior relative to its preferred level (in which case the response deprivation hypothesis is applicable).

QUICK QUIZ P

1. According to the response deprivation hypothesis, a response can serve as a reinforcer if free access to the response is (provided/restricted) and its frequency then falls (above/below) its baseline level of occurrence.
2. If a child normally watches 4 hours of television per night, we can make television watching a reinforcer if we restrict free access to the television to (more/less) than 4 hours per night.
3. The response deprivation hypothesis differs from the Premack principle in that we need only know the baseline frequency of the (reinforced/reinforcing) behavior.
4. Kaily typically watches television for 4 hours per day and reads comic books for 1 hour per day. You then set up a contingency whereby Kaily must watch

4.5 hours of television each day in order to have access to her comic books. According to the Premack principle, this will likely be an (effective/ineffective) contingency. According to the response deprivation hypothesis, this will likely be an (effective/ineffective) contingency.

Behavioral Bliss Point Approach

The response deprivation hypothesis assumes there is an optimal level of behavior that an organism strives to maintain. This same assumption can be made for the manner in which an organism distributes its behavior between two or more activities. According to the ***behavioral bliss point approach***, an organism with free access to alternative activities will distribute its behavior in such a way as to maximize overall reinforcement (Allison, 1983). For example, a rat that can freely choose between running in a wheel and exploring a maze might spend 1 hour per day running in the wheel and 2 hours exploring the maze. This distribution of behavior represents the optimal reinforcement available from those two activities—that is, the *behavioral bliss point*—for that particular rat.

Note that this optimal distribution of behavior is based on the notion that each activity is freely available. When activities are not freely available—as when the two activities are intertwined in a contingency of reinforcement—then the optimal distribution may become unattainable. Imagine, for example, that a contingency is created in which the rat has to run in the wheel for 60 seconds to obtain 30 seconds of access to the maze:

Wheel running **(60 seconds) → Maze exploration (30 seconds)**
R **S^R**

It will now be impossible for the rat to reach its behavioral bliss point for these two activities. When they are freely available, the rat prefers twice as much maze exploration (2 hours) as wheel running (1 hour). But our contingency forces the rat to engage in twice as much wheel running as maze exploration. To obtain the preferred 2 hours of maze exploration, the rat would have to engage in 4 hours of running, which is far beyond its preferred level for that activity. Thus, it will be impossible for the rat to attain its behavioral bliss point for those activities.

A reasonable assumption as to what will happen in such circumstances is that the rat will compromise by distributing its activities in such a way as to draw as near as possible to its behavioral bliss point. For instance, it might choose to run a total of 2 hours per day to obtain 1 hour of maze exploration. This is not as enjoyable as the preferred distribution of 1 hour of running and 2 hours of maze exploration; but, given the contingencies, it will have to do. Likewise, most of us are forced to spend several more hours working and several fewer hours enjoying the finer things in life than we would if we were independently wealthy and could freely do whatever we want. The behavioral bliss point for our varied activities is essentially unattainable. Instead, faced with certain contingencies that must be met in order to survive, we distribute our activities in such a way as to draw as near to the bliss point as possible.

The behavioral bliss point approach assumes that organisms attempt to distribute their behavior so as to maximize overall reinforcement. This, of course, is a very rational way to behave. In Chapter 10, you will encounter an alternative theory, known as melioration theory, which maintains that organisms, including people, are not that rational and that various processes often entice the organism away from maximization. Note, too, that none of the theories discussed in this chapter take account of an animal's innate tendencies toward certain patterns of behavior, which may affect how easily certain behaviors can be trained. In Chapter 12, you will encounter a theory that does take account of such tendencies.

QUICK QUIZ Q

1. According to the behavioral bliss point approach, an organism that (is forced to/can freely) engage in alternative activities will distribute its behavior in such a way as to (optimize/balance) the available reinforcement.
2. Contingencies of reinforcement often (disrupt/enhance) the distribution of behavior such that it is (easy/impossible) to obtain the optimal amount of reinforcement.
3. Given this state of affairs, the organism will distribute its activities to get as (near to/far from) the bliss point as possible.

ADVICE FOR THE LOVELORN

Dear Dr. Dee,

I recently began dating a classmate. We get along really well at school, so it seemed like we would be a perfect match. Unfortunately, once we started dating, our relationship seemed to lose a lot of its energy, and our lives seemed a lot less satisfying. Someone suggested that we must each have an unconscious fear of commitment. What do you think?

Less Than Blissful

ADVICE FOR THE LOVELORN

Dear Less,

I suppose it is possible that you have an unconscious fear of commitment—if there is such a thing as an unconscious fear of commitment. On the other hand, it may be that the amount of time you spend interacting with one another at school is actually the optimal amount of time given the various reinforcers available in your relationship. Spending additional time together (which also means spending less time on alternative activities) has, for each of you, resulted in a distribution of behavior that is further removed from your behavioral bliss point. Obviously, a good relationship should move you toward your bliss point, not away from it. Try being just friends-at-school again, and see if that restores some of the satisfaction in your relationship.

Behaviorally yours,

Dr. Dee

SUMMARY

A schedule of reinforcement is the response requirement that must be met to obtain a reinforcer. Different types of schedules produce different patterns of responding, which are known as schedule effects.

In a continuous schedule of reinforcement, each response is reinforced. In an intermittent schedule of reinforcement, only some responses are reinforced. There are four basic intermittent schedules. On a fixed ratio schedule, a fixed number of responses is required for reinforcement, while on a variable ratio schedule, a varying number of responses is required. Both schedules produce a high rate of response, with the fixed ratio schedule also producing a post-reinforcement pause. On a fixed interval schedule, the first response after a fixed period of time is reinforced, while on a variable interval schedule, the first response after a varying period of time is reinforced. The former produces a scalloped pattern of responding, whereas the latter produces a moderate, steady pattern of responding.

On a fixed duration schedule, reinforcement is contingent upon responding continuously for a fixed, predictable period of time; on a variable duration schedule, reinforcement is contingent upon responding continuously for a varying, unpredictable period of time. Response-rate schedules specifically reinforce the rate of response. For example, on a DRH schedule, reinforcement is contingent on a high rate of response, whereas on a DRL schedule, it is contingent on a low rate of response. On a DRP schedule, reinforcement is contingent on a particular rate of response—neither too fast nor too slow. By contrast, on a noncontingent schedule of reinforcement, the reinforcer is delivered following a certain period of time regardless of the organism's behavior. The time period can either be fixed (a fixed time schedule) or varied (a variable time schedule). Noncontingent schedules sometimes result in the development of superstitious behavior.

A complex schedule consists of two or more simple schedules. In a conjunctive schedule, the requirements of two or more simple schedules must be met before a reinforcer is delivered; in an adjusting schedule, the response requirement changes as a function of the organism's performance while responding for the previous reinforcer. On a chained schedule, reinforcement is contingent upon meeting the requirements of two or more successive schedules, each with its own discriminative stimulus. Responding tends to become stronger and/or more efficient toward the end of the chain, which is an instance of the goal gradient effect. Behavior chains are often best established by training the last link first and the first link last.

According to drive reduction theory, an event is reinforcing if it is associated with a reduction in some type of internal physiological drive. However, some behaviors seem motivated more by the external consequence (known as incentive motivation) than by an internal drive state. The Premack principle assumes that high-probability behaviors can be used as reinforcers for low-probability behaviors. The response deprivation hypothesis states that a behavior can be used as a reinforcer if access to the behavior is restricted so that its frequency falls below its baseline rate of occurrence. The behavioral bliss point approach assumes that organisms distribute their behavior in such a manner as to maximize their overall reinforcement.

SUGGESTED READINGS

Ferster, C. B., & Skinner, B. F. (1957). *Schedules of reinforcement*. New York: Appleton-Century-Crofts. The seminal book on schedule effects. Not a book for light reading, but glancing through it will give you a sense of the history of behavior analysis and what real schedule effects look like.

Herrnstein, R. J. (1966). Superstition: A corollary of the principle of operant conditioning. In W. K. Honig (Ed.), *Operant behavior: Areas of research and application*. New York: Appleton-Century-Crofts. A discussion of the behavioral approach to superstitious behavior. The discussion of human superstitions at the end of the article would be of most interest to undergraduates.

Timberlake, W., & Farmer-Dougan, V. A. (1991). Reinforcement in applied settings: Figuring out ahead of time what will work. *Psychological Bulletin, 110*, 379–391. Reviews the Premack principle and the response deprivation approach to reinforcement and its usefulness in applied settings.

STUDY QUESTIONS

1. What is a schedule of reinforcement? Distinguish between continuous and intermittent schedules of reinforcement.
2. Name and define the four basic intermittent schedules and describe (or graph) the typical response pattern produced by each.
3. Name and define two types of duration schedules and two types of noncontingent schedules. How do they differ from FI and VI schedules of reinforcement?
4. Name and define three types of response-rate schedules. Give an example of each.
5. What is a conjunctive schedule, and what is an adjusting schedule? Give an example of each. In what way does shaping involve the use of an adjusting schedule?
6. What is a chained schedule? Diagram and label an example of a chained schedule. How does a chained schedule differ from a conjunctive schedule?
7. What type of reinforcer serves to maintain behavior throughout the early links in a chained schedule? What is the best way to establish responding on a chained schedule in animals? What is the relationship between the goal gradient effect and a chained schedule of reinforcement?
8. Describe the drive reduction theory of reinforcement. What is a major difficulty with this theory? What is incentive motivation?
9. Outline the Premack principle. Outline the response deprivation hypothesis. Illustrate the difference between the two using the example of a child (who dreams of being a rock star) being allowed to practice guitar as a reinforcer for practicing piano.
10. Describe the behavioral bliss point approach to reinforcement. Illustrate your answer with the example of a contingency in which a child must practice piano for 2 hours before being allowed to practice guitar for 1 hour.

CONCEPT REVIEW

adjusting schedule. A schedule in which the response requirement changes as a function of the organism's performance while responding for the previous reinforcer.

behavioral bliss point approach. The theory that an organism with free access to alternative activities will distribute its behavior in such a way as to maximize overall reinforcement.

chained schedule. A schedule consisting of a sequence of two or more simple schedules, each with its own S^D and the last of which results in a terminal reinforcer.

complex schedule. A schedule consisting of a combination of two or more simple schedules.

conjunctive schedule. A type of complex schedule in which the requirements of two or more simple schedules must be met before a reinforcer is delivered.

continuous reinforcement schedule. A schedule in which each specified response is reinforced.

differential reinforcement of high rates (DRH). A schedule in which reinforcement is contingent upon emitting at least a certain number of responses in a certain period of time—or, more generally, reinforcement is provided for responding at a fast rate.

differential reinforcement of low rates (DRL). A schedule in which a minimum amount of time must pass between each response before the reinforcer will be delivered—or, more generally, reinforcement is provided for responding at a slow rate.

differential reinforcement of paced responding (DRP). A schedule in which reinforcement is contingent upon emitting a series of responses at a set rate—or, more generally, reinforcement is provided for responding neither too fast nor too slow.

drive reduction theory. According to this theory, an event is reinforcing to the extent that it is associated with a reduction in some type of physiological drive.

fixed duration (FD) schedule. A schedule in which reinforcement is contingent upon continuous performance of a behavior for a fixed, predictable period of time.

fixed interval (FI) schedule. A schedule in which reinforcement is contingent upon the first response after a fixed, predictable period of time.

fixed ratio (FR) schedule. A schedule in which reinforcement is contingent upon a fixed, predictable number of responses.

fixed time (FT) schedule. A schedule in which the reinforcer is delivered following a fixed, predictable period of time, regardless of the organism's behavior.

goal gradient effect. An increase in the strength and/or efficiency of responding as one draws near to the goal.

incentive motivation. Motivation derived from some property of the reinforcer, as opposed to an internal drive state.

intermittent (or partial) reinforcement schedule. A schedule in which only some responses are reinforced.

noncontingent schedule of reinforcement. A schedule in which the reinforcer is delivered independently of any response. Also known as a *response-independent schedule*.

Premack principle. The notion that a high-probability behavior can be used to reinforce a low-probability behavior.

ratio strain. A disruption in responding due to an overly demanding response requirement.

response deprivation hypothesis. The notion that a behavior can serve as a reinforcer when (1) access to the behavior is restricted and (2) its frequency thereby falls below its preferred level of occurrence.

response-rate schedule. A schedule in which reinforcement is directly contingent upon the organism's rate of response.

schedule of reinforcement. The response requirement that must be met to obtain reinforcement.

variable duration (VD) schedule. A schedule in which reinforcement is contingent upon continuous performance of a behavior for a varying, unpredictable period of time.

variable interval (VI) schedule. A schedule in which reinforcement is contingent upon the first response after a varying, unpredictable period of time.

variable ratio (VR) schedule. A schedule in which reinforcement is contingent upon a varying, unpredictable number of responses.

variable time (VT) schedule. A schedule in which the reinforcer is delivered following a varying, unpredictable period of time, regardless of the organism's behavior.

CHAPTER TEST

21. On a ____________ schedule, reinforcement is contingent upon the first response *during* a varying period of time. (A) fixed interval, (B) variable time, (C) fixed time, (D) variable interval, (E) none of the preceding.
6. On a __fixed ratio__ schedule (abbreviated __FR__), reinforcement is contingent upon a fixed, predictable number of responses. This produces a __high__ rate of response often accompanied by a __postreinforcement pause__
17. On a (use the abbreviations) __DRL__ schedule, a minimum amount of time must pass between each response before the reinforcer will be delivered. On a __DRH__ schedule, reinforcement is contingent upon emitting at least a certain number of responses in a certain period of time. On a __DRP__ schedule, reinforcement is contingent on emitting a series of responses at a specific rate.
10. If Jason is extremely persistent in asking Neem out for a date, she will occasionally accept his invitation. Of the four basic schedules, Jason's behavior of asking Neem for a date is most likely on a __variable__ __ratio__ schedule of reinforcement.
36. Russ is so impressed with how quickly his Betta learned to swim in a circle that he keeps doubling the number of circles it has to perform in order to receive a reinforcer. This is an example of a(n) __adjusting__ schedule of reinforcement (one that is particularly likely to suffer from r__atio__ s__train__).
8. On a ____________ schedule, a response *must not* occur until 20 seconds have elapsed since the last reinforcer. (A) VI 20-sec, (B) VT 20-sec, (C) FT 20-sec, (D) FI 20-sec, (E) none of the preceding.
28. Post-reinforcement pauses are most likely to occur on which two types of simple intermittent schedules? __fixed interval__ and __fixed ratio__.

16. On response rate schedules, reinforcement is contingent upon the rate of response.
31. Shawna often goes for a walk through the woods, but she rarely does yard work. According to the Premack Principle walking through the woods could be used as a(n) reinforcer for yard work.
5. On a(n) fixed interval schedule (abbreviated FI), reinforcement is contingent upon the first response *after* a fixed period of time. This produces a(n) scalloped pattern of responding.
13. A(n) fixed ratio schedule generally produces a high rate of response with a short pause following the attainment of each reinforcer. In general, the higher the requirement, the (longer/shorter) the pause.
29. On a(n) ________ schedule, a response cannot be reinforced until after 20 seconds have elapsed since the last reinforcer. (A) VI 20-sec, (B) VT 20-sec, (C) FT 20-sec, (D) FI 20-sec, (E) none of the preceding.
37. Ahmed's daily routine consists of swimming without rest for 30 minutes, following which he takes a break. This most closely resembles a(n) fixed duration schedule of reinforcement.
3. If a dog receives a treat each time it begs for one, its begging is being maintained on a(n) continuous schedule of reinforcement. If it only sometimes receives a treat when it begs for one, its begging is being maintained on a(n) intermittent schedule of reinforcement.
27. Dersu often carried a lucky charm with him when he went out hunting. This is because the appearance of game was often on a (use the abbreviation) VT schedule of reinforcement.
32. Gina often goes for a walk through the woods, and even more often she does yard work. According to the response deprivation hypothesis, walking through the woods could still be used as a reinforcer for yard work given that one restricts the frequency of walking to below its baseline level.
26. On a fixed interval schedule, reinforcement is contingent upon the first response ________ a fixed period of time. (A) during, (B) before, (C) after, (D) none of the preceding.
9. Neem accepts Jason's invitation for a date only when she has "nothing better to do." Of the four basic intermittent schedules, Jason's behavior of asking Neem for a date is best described as being on a(n) variable interval schedule of reinforcement.
38. When Deanna screams continuously, her mother occasionally pays attention to her. This is most likely an example of a(n) VD schedule of reinforcement.
30. Drinking a soda to quench your thirst is an example of drive reduction; drinking a soda because you love its tangy sweetness is an example of incentive motivation.
4. On a(n) variable ratio schedule (abbreviated VR), reinforcement is contingent upon a varying, unpredictable number of responses.

This generally produces a(n) ______________ rate of response (with/without) a post-reinforcement pause.

24. A pigeon pecks a green key on a VI 60-sec schedule, which results in the insertion of a foot-treadle into the chamber. The pigeon then presses the treadle 10 times, following which it receives food. To train this chain of behaviors, one should start with ______________.
11. Neem accepts Jason's invitation for a date only when he has just been paid his monthly salary. Of the four simple schedules, the contingency governing Jason's behavior of asking Neem for a date seems most similar to a(n) ______________ schedule of reinforcement.
35. "If I'm not a success in every aspect of my life, my family will reject me." This is a severe example of a(n) ______________ schedule of reinforcement.
25. Dagoni works for longer and longer periods of time and takes fewer and fewer breaks as his project nears completion. This is an example of the ______________ effect.
18. On a(n) ______________ schedule of reinforcement, the reinforcer is delivered independently of any response.
7. On a(n) ______________ schedule (abbreviated ______________), reinforcement is contingent upon the first response after a varying interval of time. This produces a ______________ rate of response (with/without) a post-reinforcement pause.
15. Gambling is often maintained by a(n) ______________ schedule of reinforcement.
20. On a(n) ______________ schedule (abbreviated ______________), the reinforcer is delivered following a varying period of time.
33. Anna ideally likes to exercise for 1 hour each morning, followed by a 30-minute sauna, in turn followed by a half hour of drinking coffee and reading the newspaper. Unfortunately, due to other commitments, she actually spends 45 minutes exercising, followed by a 15-minute sauna, and a half hour drinking coffee and reading the paper. According to the ______________ approach, Anna's ideal schedule provides the ______________ amount of reinforcement that can be obtained from those activities, while her actual schedule represents her attempt to draw as near to the ______________ point as possible.
1. A(n) ______________ is the response requirement that must be met to obtain reinforcement.
22. A(n) ______________ schedule is a sequence of two or more component schedules, each of which has its own ______________ stimulus and the last of which results in a(n) ______________ reinforcer.
34. The abbreviation DRL refers to ______________ reinforcement of ______________ rate behavior.
14. As noted in the opening scenario to this chapter, Mandy found that she had to work very hard to entice Alvin to pay attention to her. It is quite

likely that her behavior was on a(n) __________ schedule of reinforcement. As a result, she began experiencing periods of time where she simply gave up and stopped trying. Eventually, she stopped seeing him altogether. When her sister asked why, Mandy, having just read this chapter, replied, "__________ __________."

2. Different response requirements have different effects on behavior. For example, ratio schedules tend to produce (higher/lower) rates of behavior than interval schedules. Likewise, fixed schedules tend to produce __________ whereas variable schedules often do not. Such differences in response patterns are known as __________.
23. A pigeon pecks a green key on a VR 9 schedule, then a red key on an FI 20-sec, following which it receives food. The reinforcer for pecking the green key is the presentation of the __________, which is a(n) __________ reinforcer.
12. Eddy finds that he has to thump his old television set exactly twice before the picture will clear up. His behavior of thumping the television set is on a (be specific and use the abbreviation) __________ schedule of reinforcement.
19. On a(n) __________ schedule (abbreviated __________), the reinforcer is delivered following a fixed interval of time, regardless of the organism's behavior.

ANSWERS TO CHAPTER TEST

1. schedule of reinforcement (reinforcement schedule)
2. higher; post-reinforcement pauses; schedule effects
3. continuous (CRF or FR1); intermittent
4. variable ratio; VR; high; without
5. fixed interval; FI; scalloped
6. fixed ratio; FR; high; post-reinforcement pause
7. variable interval; VI; moderate; without
8. E
9. variable interval
10. variable ratio
11. fixed interval (or FI 1-month)
12. FR 2
13. fixed ratio; longer
14. variable ratio; ratio strain
15. variable ratio
16. response rate (DRL, DRH, and DRP)
17. DRL; DRH; DRP
18. noncontingent (or response-independent)
19. fixed time; FT
20. variable time; VT
21. E
22. chained; discriminative; terminal
23. red key; secondary
24. treadle pressing
25. goal gradient
26. C
27. VT
28. fixed interval and fixed ratio
29. D
30. drive; incentive
31. Premack principle; reinforcer
32. response deprivation hypothesis; below; baseline
33. behavioral bliss point; optimal (maximum); bliss
34. differential; low
35. conjunctive
36. adjusting; ratio strain
37. fixed duration (or FD 30-min)
38. VD

CHAPTER 8

EXTINCTION AND STIMULUS CONTROL

CHAPTER OUTLINE

Poppea gained access to Nero, and established her ascendancy. First she used flirtatious wiles, pretending to be unable to resist her passion for Nero's looks. Then, as the emperor fell in love with her, she became haughty, and if he kept her for more than two nights she insisted that she was married and could not give up her marriage.

TACITUS, *THE ANNALS OF IMPERIAL ROME*

Extinction

In the past few chapters, we have concentrated on strengthening operant behavior through the process of reinforcement. However, as previously noted, a behavior that has been strengthened through reinforcement can also be weakened through extinction. To reiterate, ***extinction*** is the nonreinforcement of a previously reinforced response, the result of which is a decrease in the strength of that response. As with classical conditioning, the term *extinction* refers to both a procedure and a process. The *procedure* of extinction is the nonreinforcement of a previously reinforced response; the *process* of extinction is the resultant decrease in response strength.

Take, for example, a situation in which a rat has learned to press a lever for food:

Lever press → **Food**
R $\mathbf{S^R}$

If lever pressing is no longer followed by food:

Lever press → **No food**
R —

then the frequency of lever pressing will decline. The act of withholding food delivery following a lever press is the procedure of extinction, and the resultant decline in responding is the process of extinction. If lever pressing ceases entirely, the response is said to have been *extinguished*; if it has not yet ceased entirely, then the response has been only *partially extinguished*. Similarly, consider a child who has learned to whine to obtain candy:

Whining → **Candy**
R $\mathbf{S^R}$

If whining no longer produces candy:

Whining → **No candy**
R —

the frequency of whining will decline. The procedure of extinction is the nondelivery of candy following the behavior, and the process of extinction is the resultant decline in the behavior. If the whining is completely eliminated, then it has been extinguished. If whining still occurs, but at a lower frequency, then it has been partially extinguished.

An important, but often neglected, aspect of applying an extinction procedure is to ensure that the consequence being withheld is in fact the reinforcer that is maintaining the behavior. You might believe that the consequence of candy is reinforcing a child's tendency to whine, when in fact it is the accompanying attention from the parent. If this is the case, and the parent continues to provide attention for whining (for example, by arguing with the child each time he or she whines), then withholding the candy might have little or no effect on the behavior. Conversely, some people make the blanket assumption that children often misbehave in order to get attention and equate the procedure of extinction with simply ignoring the occurrence of a behavior. But there are many reasons why a child might misbehave, and gaining attention is only one possibility. Hence, determining the actual reinforcer that is maintaining a behavior is a critical first step in extinguishing a behavior.

QUICK QUIZ A

1. Extinction is the ____________ of a previously ____________ response, the result of which is a(n) ____________ in the strength of that response.
2. Whenever Jana's friend Karla phoned late in the evening, she would invariably complain about her coworkers, to which Jana would listen attentively. But as these phone calls became more and more frequent, Jana wondered if she was reinforcing Karla's behavior of phoning and complaining; so she decided to screen her late-evening calls and not answer any such calls from Karla. Eventually, Karla stopped phoning at that time, and they resumed a normal friendship that excluded lengthy complaints over the phone. Jana used the (procedure/process) of extinction when she stopped answering Karla's late-evening calls, while the ____________ of extinction is the eventual cessation of such calls.
3. In carrying out an extinction procedure, an important first step is to ensure that the consequence being withdrawn is in fact the ____________ for the behavior.

Side Effects of Extinction

When an extinction procedure is implemented, it is often accompanied by certain side effects. It is important to be aware of these side effects because they can mislead one into believing that an extinction procedure is not having an effect when in fact it is.

1. **Extinction Burst.** The implementation of an extinction procedure does not always result in an immediate decrease in responding. Instead, one often finds an ***extinction burst***, a temporary increase in the frequency and intensity of responding when extinction is first implemented.

Suppose, for example, that we reinforce every fourth lever press by a rat (an FR 4 schedule of reinforcement). When extinction is implemented, the rat will initially react by pressing the lever both more rapidly and more forcefully. The rat's behavior is analogous to our behavior when we plug money into a candy machine, press the button, and receive nothing in return. We do not just give up and walk away. Instead, we press the button several times in a row, often with increasing amounts of force. Our behavior toward the machine shows the same increase in frequency and intensity that characterizes an extinction burst.

2. **Increase in Variability.** An extinction procedure can also result in an increase in the variability of a behavior (Antonitis, 1951). For example, a rat whose lever pressing no longer produces food might vary the manner in which it presses the lever. If the rat typically pressed the lever with its right paw, it might now try pressing it with its left paw. As well, if the rat usually pressed the lever in the center, it might now press it more to one side or the other. Similarly, when confronted by a candy machine that has just stolen our money, we will likely vary the manner in which we push the button, such as holding it down for a second before releasing it. And we will almost certainly try pressing other buttons on the machine to see if we can at least obtain a different selection.[1]
3. **Emotional Behavior.** Extinction is often accompanied by emotional behavior (Zeiler, 1971). The hungry pigeon that suddenly finds that key pecking no longer produces food soon becomes agitated (as evidenced, for example, by quick jerky movements and wing flapping). Likewise, people often become upset when confronted by a candy machine that does not deliver the goods. Such emotional responses are what we typically refer to as *frustration*.
4. **Aggression.** One type of emotional behavior that is particularly common during an extinction procedure is aggression. In fact, extinction procedures have been used to study aggressive behavior in animals. For example, research has shown that a pigeon whose key pecking for food is placed on extinction will reliably attack another pigeon (or model of a pigeon) that happens to be nearby (Azrin, Hutchinson, & Hake, 1966). Extinction-induced aggression (also called *frustration-induced aggression*) is also common in humans. People often become angry with those who block them from obtaining an important goal. For that matter, even uncooperative vending machines are sometimes attacked.
5. **Resurgence.** A rather unusual side effect of extinction is ***resurgence***, the reappearance during extinction of other behaviors that had once been

[1]Although we have treated them separately in this text, the increase in response variability during extinction is sometimes regarded as one aspect of an extinction burst. In other words, an extinction burst can be defined as an increase in the rate, intensity, and variability of responding following the implementation of an extinction procedure.

effective in obtaining reinforcement (Epstein, 1985). Hull (1934), for example, trained rats to first run a 20-foot pattern through a maze to obtain food, then a 40-foot pattern. When all running was then placed on extinction, the rats initially persisted with the 40-foot pattern, then returned to the 20-foot pattern before quitting. It was as though they were attempting to make the food reappear by repeating a pattern that had earlier been effective. Resurgence resembles the psychoanalytic concept of *regression*, which is the reappearance of immature behavior in reaction to frustration or conflict. Thus, a husband faced with a wife who largely ignores him might begin spending increasing amounts of time at his parents' house. Faced with the lack of reinforcement in his marriage, he returns to a setting that once provided a rich source of reinforcement.

6. **Depression.** Extinction can also lead to depressive-like symptoms. For example, Klinger, Barta, and Kemble (1974) had rats run down an alleyway for food and then immediately followed this with an assessment of the rats' activity level in an open field test. Thus, each session consisted of two phases: (1) running down an alleyway for food, followed by (2) placement in an open area that the rats could freely explore. When extinction was implemented on the alleyway task, activity in the open field test first increased to above normal (a sort of generalized extinction burst), then decreased to below normal, followed by a return to normal (see Figure 8.1).

Klinger et al. (1974) noted that low activity is a common symptom of depression; moreover, depression is often associated with loss of reinforcement (Lewinsohn, 1974). For example, if someone dies, the people for whom that individual was a major source of reinforcement are essentially experiencing extinction, and they will likely become depressed for a period of time. And one symptom of such depression is a low level of activity. The fact that a similar process occurs in rats suggests that a temporary period of depression (as evidenced by a decrease in activity) following the loss of a major reinforcer should be regarded as a normal aspect of disengagement from that reinforcer (Klinger, 1975).

These side effects of extinction can obviously be an impediment to successfully implementing an extinction procedure. Note, too, that these side effects can be inadvertently strengthened if one suddenly gives in and provides the subject with the sought-after reinforcer. Imagine, for example, that Bobbie has learned that by begging at the supermarket he can usually entice his mother into buying him some candy. One day, however, Bobbie's mother decides to withhold the candy, with the result that he becomes very loud and persistent (an extinction burst) as well as emotionally upset and aggressive. If Bobbie's mother now gives in and buys him some candy, what type of behavior has she reinforced? Obviously not the behavior of being polite and well mannered in the supermarket. In this way, parents sometimes

FIGURE 8.1 Changes in rats' activity level in an open field test as a function of extinction on a preceding straight-alley maze task. (*Source*: Adapted with kind permission from Springer Science + Business Media: *Animal Learning and Behavior,*" Cyclic activity changes during extinction in rats: A potential model of depression," 2, 1974, pp. 313–316, by E. Klinger, S. G. Barta, E. D. Kemble, copyright © 1974 by the Psychonomic Society.

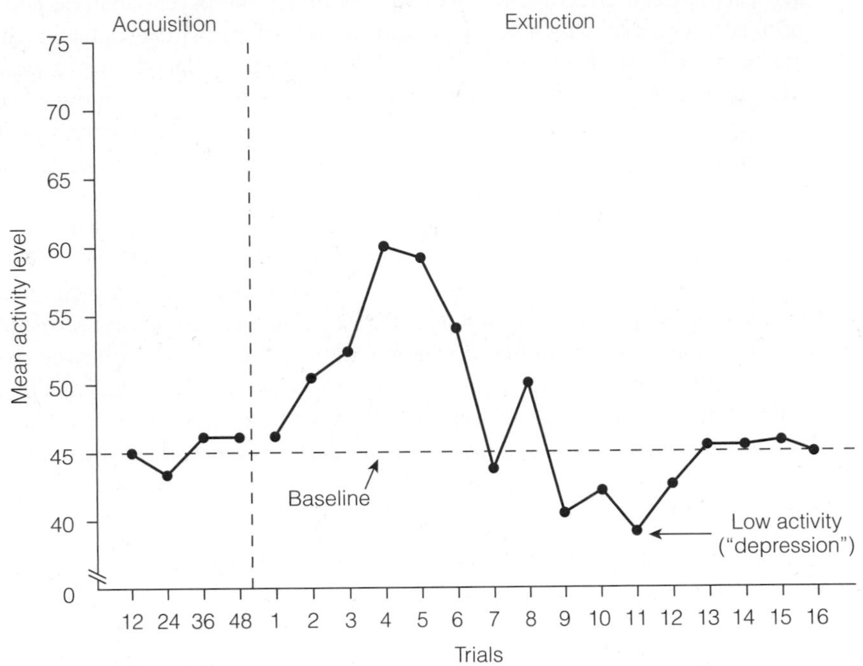

inadvertently train their children to throw severe temper tantrums, a tendency that could have serious consequences if maintained later in life. After all, what the media calls "road rage"—or "air rage" when passengers become belligerent on airline flights—might, in many cases, simply be an adult version of a temper tantrum, a behavior pattern that was inadvertently established in childhood.

QUICK QUIZ B

1. Krissy asked her father to buy her a toy, as he usually did, when they were out shopping. Unfortunately, Krissy's father had spent all of his money on building supplies and told her that he had nothing left for a toy. The first thing that might happen is that Krissy will (increase/decrease) the frequency with which she asks for a toy and will ask for a toy with a (louder/softer) voice. This process is known as an e_xtinction_ b_urst_.

2. Krissy is also likely to ask for the toy in many different ways, because extinction often results in an increase in the v<u>ariability</u> of a behavior.
3. Krissy might also begin showing a lot of em<u>otimal</u> behavior, including ag<u>gression</u>.
4. When her father still refuses to buy her a toy, Krissy suddenly asks her dad to pick her up and carry her, something she has not asked for since she was much smaller. This could be an example of r<u>esurgence</u>, or what psychoanalysts call r<u>egression</u>.
5. On the trip home, Krissy, who never did get a toy, sat silently and sullenly stared out the window. This is not surprising, because extinction is sometimes followed by a temporary period of d<u>epression</u>.

ADVICE FOR THE LOVELORN

Dear Dr. Dee,

Why is it that I act so weird whenever I break up with a guy? One day I am intent on reestablishing the relationship, the next day I am so angry I don't ever want to see him again. Then I usually get all depressed and lie around in bed for days on end.

What a Rollercoaster

Dear What,

Sounds like extinction to me. The loss of a relationship is the loss of a major reinforcer in your life. You therefore go through many of the side effects that accompany extinction. You experience an extinction burst ("intent on reestablishing the relationship"), become angry ("don't ever want to see the guy again"), and eventually get depressed.

Solution: Extinction effects are a normal part of life, so don't expect that you shouldn't feel something. But you might be able to moderate your feelings a bit so they are not quite so painful. In particular, stay active as much as possible and seek out alternative sources of reinforcement. And try to avoid lying in bed for days on end, as this will only further reduce the reinforcement in your life. In fact, lying in bed for days on end will make just about anyone depressed, regardless of his or her relationship status!

Behaviorally yours,

Dr. Dee

FIGURE 8.2 Two hypothetical extinction curves. Following an initial period of reinforcement at the start of the session, the extinction procedure is implemented. This results in a brief extinction burst, followed by a decline in responding. The decline is more gradual in the top example than in the bottom example and hence illustrates greater resistance to extinction.

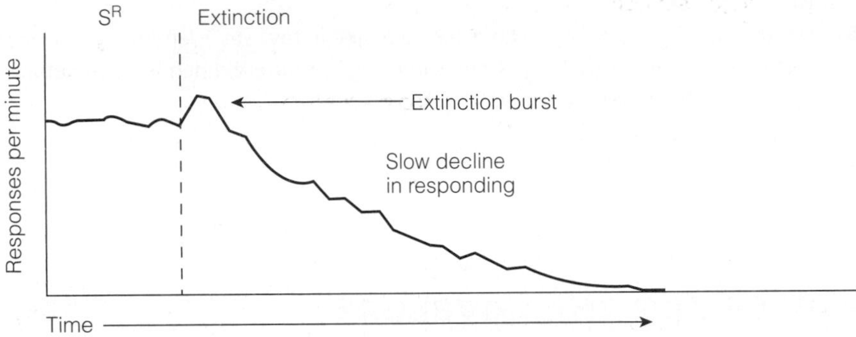

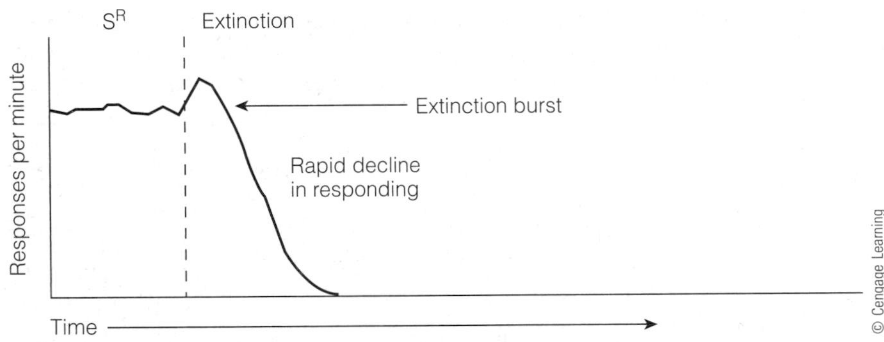

Resistance to Extinction

Resistance to extinction is the extent to which responding persists after an extinction procedure has been implemented. A response that is very persistent is said to have high resistance to extinction, while a response that disappears quickly is said to have low resistance to extinction (see Figure 8.2). For example, a dog that continues to beg for food at the dinner table for 20 minutes after everyone has stopped feeding it is displaying much higher resistance to extinction than does a dog that stops begging after 5 minutes.

Resistance to extinction can be affected by a number of factors, including the following:

Schedule of Reinforcement The schedule of reinforcement is the most important factor influencing resistance to extinction. According to the ***partial reinforcement effect***, behavior that has been maintained on an intermittent (partial) schedule of reinforcement will extinguish more slowly than behavior that has been maintained on a continuous schedule. Thus, lever pressing that has been reinforced on an FR 10 schedule will take longer to extinguish than lever pressing that has been reinforced on a CRF (FR 1) schedule. Similarly, lever pressing that has been reinforced on an FR 100 schedule will take longer to extinguish than lever pressing that has been reinforced on an FR 10 schedule. Resistance to extinction is particularly strong when behavior has been maintained on a variable ratio (VR) schedule (G. S. Reynolds, 1975); thus, a VR 20 schedule will produce greater resistance to extinction than an FR 20 schedule.

One way of thinking about the partial reinforcement effect is that the less frequent the reinforcer, the longer it takes the person or animal to "discover" that reinforcement is no longer available (Mowrer & Jones, 1945). It obviously takes much longer for a rat to discover that reinforcement is no longer available when it has been receiving reinforcement on, say, a VR 100 schedule than on a CRF schedule. A less mentalistic interpretation is that there is a much greater contrast between a CRF schedule and extinction than between a VR 100 schedule and extinction. On a VR 100 schedule, the rat has learned to emit many responses in the absence of reinforcement; hence, it is more persistent in its responding when an extinction procedure is implemented (E. J. Capaldi, 1966).

The partial reinforcement effect helps account for certain types of annoying or maladaptive behaviors that are difficult to eliminate. Dogs that beg for food are often extremely persistent. Paradoxically, as mentioned earlier, this is sometimes the result of previously unsuccessful attempts at extinction. Imagine, for example, that all family members agree to stop feeding the dog at the dinner table. If one person nevertheless slips the dog a morsel when it is making a particularly big fuss, the begging will become both more intense and more persistent. This means that the next attempt at extinction will be even more difficult.

Of course, the partial reinforcement effect also suggests a possible solution to this problem. If behavior that has been continuously reinforced is less resistant to extinction, then it might help to first spend several days reinforcing each instance of begging. Then, when extinction is implemented, the dog's tendency to beg might extinguish more rapidly (Lerman & Iwata, 1996).

History of Reinforcement In general, the more reinforcers an individual has received for a behavior, the greater the resistance to extinction. Lever pressing will extinguish more rapidly if a rat has previously earned only 10 reinforcers for lever pressing than if it has earned 100 reinforcers. Likewise, a child who has only recently picked up the habit of whining for candy should stop relatively quickly when the behavior is placed on extinction, as opposed to a child who has been at it for several months. From a practical perspective, this means it is much easier to extinguish an unwanted behavior, such as whining for candy, when it first becomes evident (hence the saying, "nip it in the bud"). There is, however, a limit in the extent to which further reinforcers will produce increased resistance to extinction. Furomoto (1971), for example, found that resistance to extinction for key pecking in pigeons reached its maximum after about 1,000 reinforcers.

Magnitude of the Reinforcer The magnitude of the reinforcer can also affect resistance to extinction. For example, large-magnitude reinforcers sometimes result in greater resistance to extinction than small-magnitude reinforcers. Thus, lever pressing might take longer to extinguish following a training period in which each reinforcer consisted of a large pellet of food than if the reinforcer were a small pellet of food. Lever pressing might also take longer to extinguish if the reinforcer was a highly preferred food item than if it were a less-preferred food item. From a practical perspective, this means that a dog's behavior of begging at the dinner table might extinguish more easily if you first spend several days feeding it small bites of less-preferred morsels (Lerman & Iwata, 1996). Unfortunately, one problem with this strategy is that the effect of reinforcer magnitude on resistance to extinction is not entirely consistent. In fact, researchers sometimes find that smaller reinforcers result in greater resistance to extinction (e.g., Ellis, 1962).

Degree of Deprivation Not surprisingly, the degree to which an organism is deprived of a reinforcer also affects resistance to extinction. In general, the greater the level of deprivation, the greater the resistance to extinction (Perin, 1942). A rat that is only slightly hungry will cease lever pressing more quickly than a rat that is very hungry. This suggests yet another strategy for extinguishing a dog's tendency to beg at the table: Feed the dog before the meal.

Previous Experience with Extinction When sessions of extinction are alternated with sessions of reinforcement, the greater the number of exposures to extinction, the quicker the behavior will extinguish during subsequent exposures (Bullock & Smith, 1953). For example, if a rat experiences several sessions of extinction randomly interspersed with several sessions of reinforcement, it will eventually learn to stop lever pressing soon after the start of an extinction session. The rat has learned that if it has not received reinforcement soon after the start of a session, then it is likely that no reinforcement will be forthcoming for the remainder of the session. Similarly, a child might learn that if he does not receive candy within the first 10 minutes of whining at the supermarket, he might as well give up for the day. It also leads to the prediction that people who have been through relationship breakups on numerous occasions will more quickly get over such breakups and move on to a new relationship.

Distinctive Signal for Extinction Extinction is facilitated when there is a distinctive stimulus that signals the onset of extinction. As briefly noted in Chapter 6, such a stimulus is called a *discriminative stimulus for extinction* and is more fully discussed later in this chapter.

QUICK QUIZ C

1. R__________ to __________ is the extent to which responding persists after an extinction procedure is implemented.
2. According to the p__________ r__________ effect, responses that have been maintained on an intermittent schedule will show (more/less) resistance to extinction than responses that have been reinforced on a continuous schedule.
3. Among the four basic intermittent schedules, the (use the abbreviation) __________ schedule is particularly likely to produce strong resistance to extinction.
4. In general, a behavior that has been reinforced many times is likely to be (much easier/more difficult) to extinguish.
5. Resistance to extinction is generally greater when the behavior that is being extinguished has been reinforced with a (high/low)-magnitude reinforcer, though the opposite effect has also been found.
6. In general, there is a(n) (direct/inverse) relationship between resistance to extinction and the organism's level of deprivation for the reinforcer.
7. Previous experience with extinction, as well as a distinctive signal for extinction, tends to produce a(n) (increase/decrease) in resistance to extinction.

Spontaneous Recovery

Although extinction is a reliable process for weakening a behavior, it would be a mistake to assume that once a response has been extinguished, it has been permanently eliminated. As with extinction of a classically conditioned response, extinction of an operant response is often followed by *spontaneous recovery* (Skinner, 1938). As you will recall, ***spontaneous recovery*** is the reappearance of an extinguished response following a rest period after extinction. Suppose, for example, that we extinguish a rat's behavior of lever pressing. The next day, when we place the rat back in the experimental chamber, it will probably commence lever pressing again. It is almost as though it has forgotten that lever pressing no longer produces food. Nevertheless, the behavior will likely be weaker than it was at the start of the extinction phase the day before, and will extinguish more quickly given that we continue to withhold reinforcement. Similarly, on the third day, we might again find some recovery of lever pressing, but it will be even weaker than the day before and will extinguish even more quickly. This process might repeat itself several times, with each recovery being weaker and more readily extinguished than the previous one. Following several extinction sessions, we will eventually reach the point at which spontaneous recovery does not occur (apart from a few tentative lever presses every once in a while), and the behavior will have essentially been eliminated (see Figure 8.3). Likewise, a

FIGURE 8.3 Graph of hypothetical data illustrating spontaneous recovery across repeated sessions of extinction.

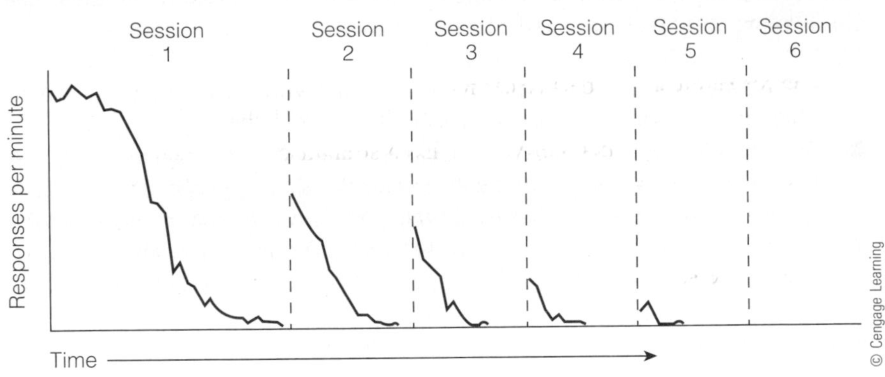

child's tendency to throw tantrums in the supermarket to obtain candy might require several visits to the supermarket during which a tantrum does not produce candy before the behavior is fully eliminated. In short, when applying an extinction procedure, you have to be persistent.

Skinner (1950) proposed that spontaneous recovery may be a function of discriminative stimuli (S^Ds) associated with the start of the session. For an experimental rat, the experience of being taken from the home cage, weighed, and placed in an operant chamber is itself a signal for the availability of food. ("Oh, goody, I'm being weighed. That means I'll soon be able to earn some food by lever pressing.") Only after repeated exposure to these events without receiving food does the rat at last stop emitting the learned behavior. Similarly, for the child who has learned to throw tantrums in the supermarket to receive candy, entering the supermarket is itself an S^D for the availability of candy. The child will require repeated exposure to the sequence of entering the supermarket, throwing a tantrum, and not receiving candy before this cue becomes ineffective.

QUICK QUIZ D

1. S__________ is the reappearance of an extinguished response at a later point in time.
2. In general, each time this occurs, the behavior is (weaker/stronger) than before and extinguishes (more/less) readily.
3. Skinner believed that this phenomenon is a function of __________ that are uniquely associated with the start of the session.

Differential Reinforcement of Other Behavior

The process of extinction can be greatly enhanced by both extinguishing the target behavior *and* reinforcing the occurrence of a replacement behavior. This procedure is known as ***differential reinforcement of other behavior (DRO)***, which is the reinforcement of any behavior other than the target behavior that is being extinguished. DRO procedures tend to be more effective than simple extinction procedures because the target behavior is weakened both by the lack of reinforcement for that behavior and by the reinforcement of alternative behaviors that come to replace it. Hence, it is easier to extinguish a child's habit of whining for candy at a supermarket if you not only withdraw the reinforcement for whining but also explicitly reinforce alternative behaviors, especially the behavior of being well-mannered.[2] Unlike a straight extinction procedure, in a DRO procedure the child is not being deprived of reinforcement within that setting; this will thereby reduce or eliminate possible side effects normally resulting from extinction. Note that the reinforcement for well-mannered behavior can include the very candy for which the child has been whining. He can therefore still obtain candy, but only if he exhibits an appropriate pattern of behavior. (The candy, of course, can then be gradually phased out—or replaced by a healthier treat—as the appropriate behavior becomes firmly established.)

A particularly useful type of differential reinforcement procedure is called *functional communication training* (or *differential reinforcement of functional communication*). Many unwanted behaviors occur because the child is attempting to attain an important reinforcer, such as attention, but is doing so inappropriately. If the child is instead taught to communicate his or her need for the reinforcer in a socially appropriate manner ("Gee Mom, I'm really bored. Can you help me find something interesting to do?"), then the frequency of inappropriate behaviors (such as misbehaving to get mom's attention) is likely to decrease. So in functional communication training, the behavior of clearly and appropriately communicating one's desires is differentially reinforced (e.g., Durand, 1990).

As noted, differential reinforcement procedures can reduce many of the unwanted side effects of extinction, such as frustration and aggression. As a general rule, therefore, whenever one attempts to extinguish an unwanted behavior, one should also provide plenty of reinforcement for more appropriate behavior (Miltenberger, 2012).

QUICK QUIZ E

1. The procedure of reinforcing all behaviors except the particular target behavior that you wish to extinguish is known as d__________ r__________ of o__________ behavior (abbreviated __________).
2. Giving a dog a treat whenever it does something other than jump up on visitors as they enter the house is an example of a (use the abbreviation) __________ procedure.
3. The above procedure tends to (strengthen/reduce) many of the side effects of extinction, such as an ex__________ bu__________.

---

[2]A precise type of DRO procedure in which the "other behavior" is specifically incompatible with the target behavior is *differential reinforcement of incompatible behavior (DRI)*. Thus, paying attention to a child if he is doing something other than fighting with his little sister is a basic DRO procedure, while paying attention to him only when he is interacting in a friendly manner with his little sister is a DRI procedure.

And Furthermore

Extinction of Bedtime Tantrums in Young Children

A common difficulty faced by many parents is training children to go to bed at night without fussing or throwing a tantrum. The problem often arises because parents pay attention to a child who is throwing a tantrum and getting out of bed, thereby inadvertently reinforcing the very behavior that is annoying them. Of course, the obvious solution to this problem is for the parents to place the child's tantrums on extinction by leaving the child alone in his or her room until he or she finally falls asleep. Research has in fact shown this to be a highly effective procedure. Rickert and Johnson (1988), for example, randomly assigned children to either a systematic ignoring condition (extinction), scheduled awakenings throughout the night (to comfort the child), or a control condition in which parents carried on as normal. In the systematic ignoring condition, the parents were told to initially check on their child's safety when the child made a fuss and then ignore all further cries. Results revealed that children who underwent the extinction procedure experienced considerably greater improvement in their sleep patterns than the children in the other two conditions.

Thus, extinction seems to be an effective treatment for this type of problem. Unfortunately, it suffers from a major drawback. Many parents find it impossible to totally ignore their children's persistent heartfelt pleas during the night, especially during the initial stages of treatment when such pleas are likely to be magnified in both intensity and duration (the typical extinction burst). As a result, "graduated extinction procedures" have been devised that are more acceptable to parents and less upsetting to the child. Adams and Rickert (1989), for example, instructed parents to wait for a predetermined period of time, based on what they felt was an acceptable duration, before responding to the child's calls. The parents were also instructed to comfort the child for only 15 seconds or less. Combined with a consistent bedtime routine, this less-stringent procedure was quite effective in helping many parents, and children, finally get a good night's sleep (see Mindell, 1999, for a review).

Stimulus Control

As previously noted, when a behavior has been consistently reinforced in the presence of a certain stimulus, that stimulus will begin to affect the probability of the behavior. This stimulus, known as a discriminative stimulus (S^D), does not automatically elicit the behavior in the manner of a CS eliciting a reflex in a cause-and-effect manner; rather, it merely signals the availability of reinforcement, thereby increasing the probability that the behavior will occur. The S^D therefore does not "elicit" behavior in the manner that a CS does; rather, it simply increases the likelihood of the behavior occurring—which some behaviorists indicate by saying that the S^D "evokes" the behavior (e.g., Miltenberger, 2012). Thus, while a tone (CS) associated with food is said to "elicit" the response of salivation, a light (S^D) that signals the availability of food for lever pressing is said to "evoke" the response of lever pressing. Such behavior is then said to be under ***stimulus control***, which means that the presence of the discriminative stimulus reliably affects the probability of the behavior (or reliably "evokes" the behavior).

For example, if a 2000-Hz tone signals that lever pressing will lead to food:

2000-Hz Tone: *Lever press* → Food
S^D R S^R

and the rat thus learns to press the lever only in the presence of the tone, the behavior of lever pressing is then said to be under stimulus control. Similarly, the sound of a ringing telephone has strong stimulus control over whether people will pick it up and say hello. People never answer phones that are not ringing and almost always answer phones that are ringing. Here are some other examples of stimulus control (with the S^D italicized):

- At *red lights*, we stop; at *green lights*, we proceed.
- If *someone smiles at us*, we smile at them.
- In an *elevator* we stand facing the front rather than the back.
- When we hear an *ambulance siren behind us*, we pull our car over to the side of the road and stop or slow down.
- When you *receive a text message on your cell phone*, you automatically read it (despite promising yourself that you wouldn't look at your cell phone while studying).
- When the *professor begins lecturing*, students cease talking among themselves.[3]

In this section, we will look more closely at discriminative stimuli and their effects on behavior. Note that some of the principles discussed, such as stimulus generalization, represent operant versions of principles discussed in earlier chapters on classical conditioning.

Stimulus Generalization and Discrimination

In our discussion of classical conditioning, we noted that stimuli that are similar to a CS can also elicit a CR, by a process known as *stimulus generalization*. A similar process occurs in operant conditioning. In operant conditioning, ***stimulus generalization*** is the tendency for an operant response to be emitted in the presence of a stimulus that is similar to an S^D. In general, the more similar the stimulus, the stronger the response. Take, for example, a rat that has learned to press a lever for food whenever it hears a 2000-Hz tone. If we then present the rat with a series of tones that vary in pitch, we will find that it also presses the lever in the presence of these other tones, particularly in the presence of a tone that is similar to the original S^D.

[3]Some of these examples also represent a special type of stimulus control known as an instructional control ("Do not drive through red lights, or you will get a ticket!"). The concept of instructional control is discussed in the section on rule-governed behavior in Chapter 11.

Thus, the rat will display a higher rate of lever pressing in the presence of an 1800- or 2200-Hz tone, both of which are more similar to the original S^D, than in the presence of a 1200- or 2800-Hz tone, which are less similar.

This tendency to generalize across different stimuli can be depicted in a ***generalization gradient***, which depicts the strength of responding in the presence of stimuli that are similar to the S^D and that vary along a continuum. As shown in Figure 8.4, gradients can vary in their degree of steepness. A relatively steep gradient indicates that rate of responding drops sharply as

FIGURE 8.4 Two hypothetical generalization gradients depicting rate of lever pressing in the presence of tones that vary in pitch between 1200 and 2800 Hz ("Hertz" is the number of sound waves per second generated by a sound source). In both examples, tones that are more similar to the original S^D (a 2000-Hz tone) are associated with stronger responding. However, generalization is much greater in the bottom gradient, which is relatively flat, than in the top gradient, which is relatively steep.

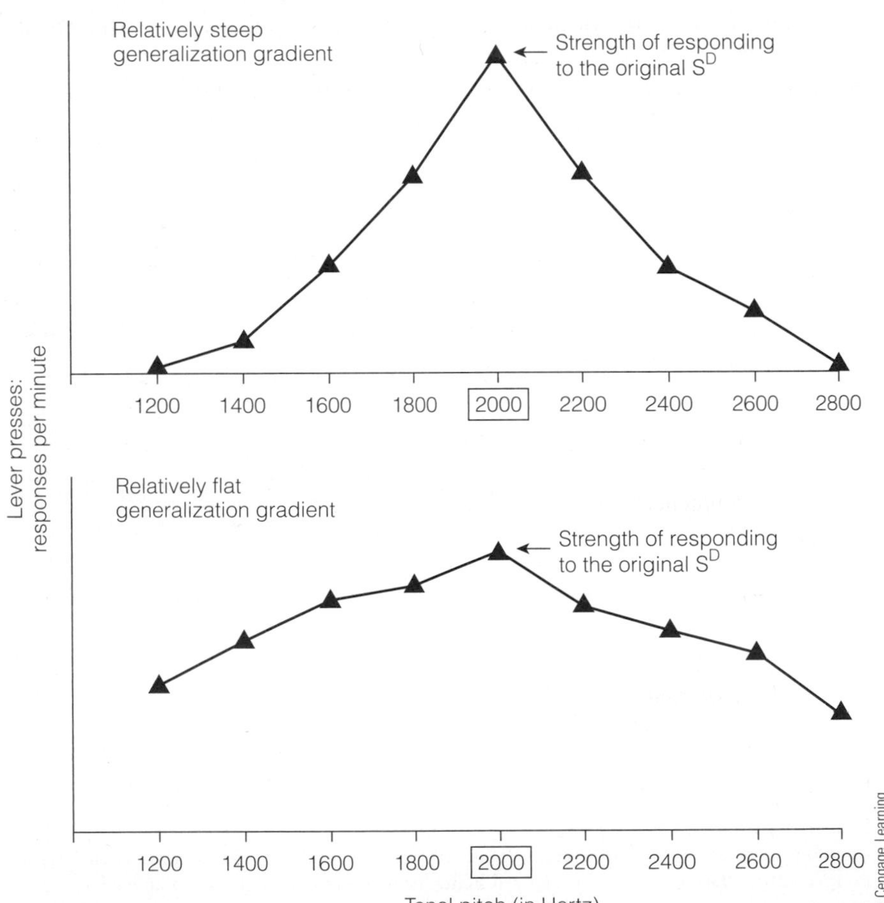

the stimuli become increasingly different from the S^D, while a relatively flat gradient indicates that responding drops gradually as the stimuli become increasingly different from the S^D. In other words, a flat gradient indicates more generalization, while a steep gradient indicates less generalization.[4]

As in classical conditioning, the opposite of stimulus generalization in operant conditioning is ***stimulus discrimination***, the tendency for an operant response to be emitted more in the presence of one stimulus than another. More generalization means less discrimination, and less generalization means more discrimination. Thus, a steep gradient indicates weak generalization and strong discrimination, whereas a flat gradient indicates strong generalization and weak discrimination.

QUICK QUIZ F

1. A behavior is said to be under strong s__________ c__________ when it is highly likely to occur in the presence of a certain stimulus.
2. In operant conditioning, the term s__________ g__________ refers to the tendency for a response to be emitted in the presence of stimuli that are similar to the original __________. The opposite process, called s__________ d__________, refers to the tendency for the response to be emitted more in the presence of one stimulus than another.
3. In general, stimuli that are (more/less) similar produce stronger generalization.
4. A g__________ gr__________ indicates the strength of responding to stimuli that vary along a continuum.
5. In a graph that depicts a g__________ g__________, a relatively flat line indicates more __________ and less __________. A relatively steep graph indicates more __________ and less __________.
6. When Jonathan looked at his watch and noticed that it was 12:30 P.M., he decided that it was time for lunch. Jonathan's eating behavior appears to be under strong s__________ c__________.
7. Jonathan always goes for lunch around 12:30, with the range being somewhere between 12:25 and 12:35 P.M. The generalization gradient for this behavior across various points in time would therefore be much (steeper/flatter) than if the range was between 12:00 and 1:00. This indicates a pattern of strong (discrimination/generalization) and weak __________ for Jonathan's lunch-going behavior across different points in time.

Discrimination training, as applied to operant conditioning, involves reinforcement of responding in the presence of one stimulus (the S^D) and not another stimulus. As noted in Chapter 6, the latter is called a *discriminative stimulus for extinction* (S^{Δ}), which is a stimulus that signals the absence of reinforcement. For example, if we wish to train a rat to discriminate between a

[4]Generalization gradients are also used to indicate the extent of stimulus generalization in classical conditioning. Imagine, for example, that the 2000-Hz tone in Figure 8.4 is a CS that has been associated with food and now elicits a conditioned salivary response. A steep generalization gradient would indicate weak generalization of the CR across tones, while a flat gradient would indicate strong generalization of the CR across tones.

2000-Hz tone and a 1200-Hz tone, we would present the two tones in random order. Whenever the 2000-Hz tone sounds, a lever press produces food; whenever the 1200-Hz tone sounds, a lever press does *not* produce food.

2000-Hz Tone: Lever press → Food
S^D R S^R
1200-Hz Tone: Lever press → No food
S^Δ R —

After repeated exposure to these contingencies, the rat will soon learn to press the lever in the presence of the 2000-Hz tone and not in the presence of the 1200-Hz tone. We can then say that the rat's behavior of lever pressing is under strong stimulus control.

In similar fashion, if the manager where you work complies with your requests for a day off only when he appears to be in a good mood and does not comply when he appears to be in a bad mood, you learn to make requests only when he is in a good mood. The manager's appearance exerts strong stimulus control over the probability of your making a request. In this sense, one characteristic of people who have good social skills is that they can make fine discriminations between social cues—such as facial expression and body posture—which enables them to maximize the amount of social reinforcement (and minimize the amount of social punishment) obtained during their exchanges with others. Likewise, college roommates are more likely to live in harmony to the extent that they learn to discriminate between each other's social cues and modify their actions appropriately.

The ability to discriminate can also be tested using a matching-to-sample procedure in which an animal is first shown a sample stimulus and then is required to select that stimulus out of a group of alternative stimuli. The extent to which the animal is able to select the correct stimulus is regarded as an indicator of its ability to discriminate between the two stimuli.

QUICK QUIZ G

1. In a discrimination training procedure, responses that occur in the presence of the (use the symbol) ______ are reinforced, while those that occur in the presence of the ______ are not reinforced. This latter stimulus is called a d______ s______ for e______.
2. An "Open for Business" sign is a(n) (use the abbreviation) ______ for entering the store and making a purchase, while a "Closed for Business" sign is a(n) ______ for attempting such behavior.

The Peak Shift Effect

An unusual effect often produced by discrimination training is the peak shift effect. According to the ***peak shift effect***, the peak of a generalization gradient following discrimination training will shift from the S^D to a stimulus that is further removed from the S^Δ (Hanson, 1959). This constitutes an

FIGURE 8.5 Illustration of a peak shift effect following discrimination training. Prior to discrimination training (top panel), the gradient is relatively flat. Following discrimination training (bottom panel), in which a 1200-Hz tone has been established as an S^{Δ}, the strongest response occurs not in the presence of the S^{D} (the 2000-Hz tone), but in the presence of a stimulus further removed from the S^{Δ}. The gradient in the bottom panel therefore illustrates the peak shift effect.

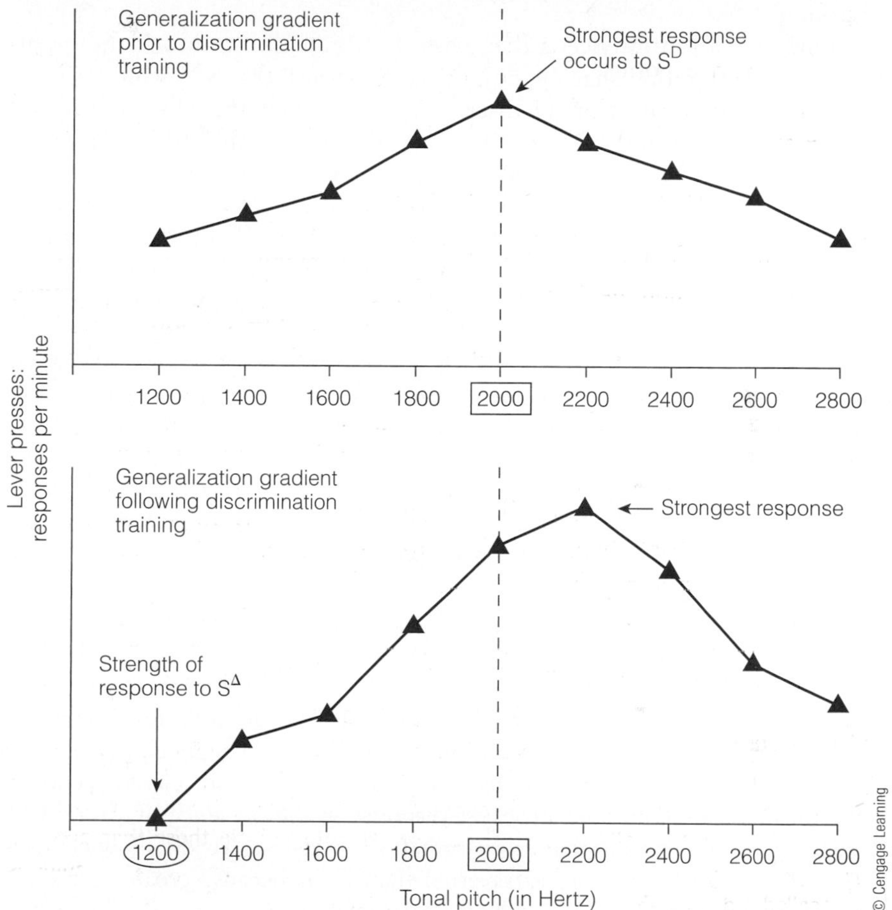

exception to the general principle that the strongest response in a generalization gradient occurs in the presence of the original S^{D}.

Suppose, for example, that we first train a rat to press a lever in the presence of a 2000-Hz tone. We then conduct a test for generalization across a range of tones varying in pitch between 1200 and 2800 Hz, and we find a generalization gradient like that shown in the top panel of Figure 8.5. We then submit the rat to a discrimination training procedure in which we reinforce lever pressing in the presence of a 2000-Hz tone (S^{D}) and not in the presence of a 1200-Hz tone (S^{Δ}). When this has been successfully accomplished (the rat responds only in the presence of the 2000-Hz tone and not in the presence of the 1200-Hz tone), we again test for generalization across a range of tones. What we are likely to find with this rat is a generalization gradient something like that depicted in the bottom panel of Figure 8.5. Look carefully at this gradient. How does it differ from the gradient in the top portion of the figure, which represents generalization in the absence of discrimination training?

One obvious difference is that, with discrimination training, the gradient drops off more sharply on the side toward the S^{Δ}, which simply means that this rat strongly discriminates between the S^{Δ} and the S^{D}. But what is the other difference between the two graphs? Before discrimination training (the top panel), the strongest response occurs to the S^{D} (the 2000-Hz tone). Following discrimination training (the bottom panel), the strongest response shifts away from the S^{D} to a stimulus that lies in a direction opposite to the S^{Δ} (in this case, it shifts to a 2200-Hz tone). This shift in the peak of the generalization gradient is the peak shift effect.

Perhaps a fanciful example will help clarify the peak shift effect. Suppose that Mr. Shallow identifies women entirely on the basis of how extraverted versus introverted they are. Jackie, with whom he had a very boring relationship, was an introvert (an S^{Δ}), while Dana, with whom he had a wonderfully exciting relationship, was an extravert (an S^{D}). He then moves to a new city and begins touring the singles bars seeking a new mate. According to the peak shift effect, he will likely seek out a woman who is even more extraverted than Dana.

One explanation for the peak shift effect is that during discrimination training, subjects respond in terms of the relative, rather than the absolute values, of stimuli (Kohler, 1918/1939). Thus, according to this interpretation, the rat does not learn merely that a 2000-Hz tone indicates food and a 1200-Hz tone indicates no food; rather, it learns that a higher-pitched tone indicates food and a lower-pitched tone indicates no food. Given a choice, the rat therefore emits the strongest response in the presence of a tone that has an even higher pitch than the original S^{D}. Likewise, Mr. Shallow chooses a woman who is even more extraverted than Dana because greater extraversion has been associated with a better relationship.

Another explanation for the peak shift effect is that, despite discrimination training, the S^{D} is still somewhat similar to the S^{Δ} and has acquired some of its negative properties (Spence, 1937). From this perspective, the 2000-Hz tone (the S^{D}) is somewhat similar to the 1200-Hz tone (the S^{Δ}), making the 2000-Hz tone slightly less attractive than it would have been if the S^{Δ} had never been trained. Thus, a tone that has a slightly higher pitch than 2000 Hz, and is thereby less similar to the 1200-Hz tone, will result in the highest rate of responding. Likewise, Mr. Shallow seeks a woman who is very extraverted because he is attempting to find a woman who is even more dissimilar from Jackie, with whom he had such a poor relationship.[5]

QUICK QUIZ H

1. In the peak shift effect, the peak of a generalization gradient, following d__________ t__________, shifts away from the __________ to a stimulus that is further removed from the __________.
2. If an orange key light is trained as an S^D in a key pecking task with pigeons, and the pigeons are then exposed to other key colors ranging from yellow on one end of the continuum to red on the other (with orange in the middle), then the peak of the generalization gradient will likely be to a (yellowish-orange/orange/orange-reddish) key light.
3. If a pigeon undergoes discrimination training in which a yellow key light is explicitly established as an S^{Δ} and an orange key light is explicitly established as the S^D, the strongest response in the generalization gradient will likely be to a (yellowish-orange/orange/orange-reddish) key light. This effect is known as the __________ __________ effect.

Multiple Schedules and Behavioral Contrast

Stimulus control is often studied using a type of complex schedule known as a multiple schedule. A ***multiple schedule*** consists of two or more independent schedules presented in sequence, each resulting in reinforcement and each having a distinctive S^D. For example, a pigeon might first be presented with a red key that signals an FI 30-sec schedule, completion of which results in food. The key light then changes to green, which signals a VI 30-sec schedule, completion of which also results in food. These two schedules can be presented in either random or alternating order, or for set periods of time (such as 2 minutes on the red FI 30-sec schedule followed by 2 minutes on the green VI 30-sec schedule followed by another 2 minutes on the red FI 30-sec schedule, etc.). The following schematic shows the two schedules presented in alternating order:

FI 30-sec   **VI 30-sec**
Red key: Key peck → Food/Green key: Key peck → Food/Red key:. . . etc.
S^D R S^R S^D R S^R S^D

Note that a multiple schedule differs from a chained schedule in that a chained schedule requires that all of the component schedules be completed before the sought-after reinforcer is delivered. For example, on a *chain* FI 30-sec VI 30-sec schedule, both the FI and VI components must be completed to obtain food. On a *multiple* FI 30-sec VI 30-sec schedule, however, completion of each component schedule results in food.

[5] The peak shift effect is also found in classical conditioning following discrimination training between a CS+ and a CS−. For example, if the CS+ for a CR of salivation was a 2000-Hz tone and the CS− was a 1200-Hz tone, what would the peak shift effect consist of?

On a multiple schedule, stimulus control is demonstrated when the subject responds differently in the presence of the S^Ds associated with the different schedules. For example, with sufficient experience on a multiple FI 30-sec VI 30-sec schedule, a pigeon will likely show a scalloped pattern of responding on the red key signaling the FI component, and a moderate, steady pattern of responding on the green key signaling the VI component. The pigeon's response pattern on each key color will be the appropriate pattern for the schedule of reinforcement that is in effect on that key.

QUICK QUIZ I

1. On a m______________ schedule, two or more schedules are presented (sequentially/simultaneously), with each resulting in a ______________ and having its own distinctive ______________.
2. This type of schedule differs from a chained schedule in that a ______________ is provided after each component schedule is completed.
3. On a multiple VI 50-sec VR 50 schedule, we are likely to find a high rate of response on the (VI/VR/both) schedule.

An interesting phenomenon that can be investigated using multiple schedules is behavioral contrast. ***Behavioral contrast*** occurs when a change in the rate of *reinforcement* on one component of a multiple schedule produces an opposite change in the rate of *response* on another component (G. S. Reynolds, 1961). In other words, as the rate of reinforcement on one component changes in one direction, the rate of response on the other component changes in the opposite direction.

There are two basic contrast effects: positive and negative. In a ***negative contrast effect***, an increase in the rate of *reinforcement* on one component produces a decrease in the rate of *response* on the other component. Suppose, for example, that a pigeon first receives several sessions of exposure to a multiple VI 60-sec VI 60-sec schedule:

VI 60-sec **VI 60-sec**
Red key: Key peck → Food/Green key: Key peck → Food/etc.

Because both schedules are the same, the pigeon responds equally on both the red key and the green key. Following this, the VI 60-sec component on the red key is changed to VI 30-sec, which provides a higher rate of reinforcement (on average, two reinforcers per minute as opposed to one reinforcer per minute):

VI 30-sec **VI 60-sec**
Red key: Key peck → Food/Green key: Key peck → Food/etc.

With more reinforcement now available on the red key, the pigeon will decrease its rate of response on the green key, which is associated with the unchanged VI 60-sec component. Simply put, because the first component in the sequence is now more attractive, the second component seems relatively less attractive. The situation is analogous to a woman whose husband has suddenly become much more affectionate and caring at home; as a result, she spends less time flirting with other men at work. The men at work seem relatively less attractive compared to her Romeo at home.

In a ***positive contrast effect***, a decrease in rate of *reinforcement* on one component results in an increase in rate of *response* on the other component. If, for example, on a multiple VI 60-sec VI 60-sec schedule:

VI 60-sec VI 60-sec
Red key: Key peck → Food/Green key: Key peck → Food/etc.

the first VI 60-sec component is suddenly changed to VI 120-sec:

***VI 120-sec* VI 60-sec**
Red key: Key peck → Food/Green key: Key peck → Food/etc.

the pigeon will increase its rate of response on the unchanged VI 60-sec component. As one component becomes less attractive (changing from VI 60-sec to VI 120-sec), the unchanged component becomes relatively more attractive. The situation is analogous to the woman whose husband has become less caring and affectionate at home; as a result, she spends more time flirting with other men at work. The men at work seem relatively more attractive compared to the dud she has at home.

Positive contrast effects are also evident when the change in one component of the multiple schedule involves not a decrease in the amount of reinforcement but implementation of a punisher, such as a mild electric shock. As the one alternative suddenly becomes punishing, the remaining alternative, which is still reinforcing, is viewed as even more attractive (Brethower & Reynolds, 1962). This might explain what happens in some volatile relationships in which couples report strong overall feelings of affection for each other (Gottman, 1994). The intermittent periods of aversiveness seem to heighten the couple's appreciation of each other during periods of affection. Such relationships can therefore thrive, *given* that the positive aspects of the relationship significantly outweigh the negative aspects.[6]

---

[6]Similar contrast effects occur when there is a shift in the magnitude of a reinforcer (Crespi, 1942). For example, rats that experience a sudden switch from receiving a small amount of food for running down an alleyway to receiving a large amount of food for running down the alleyway will run faster for the large amount (a positive contrast effect) than if they had always received the large amount. And those that are shifted from a large amount of food to a small amount will run slower (a negative contrast effect).

Warning

Remember that with positive and negative contrast, we are concerned with how changing the rate of reinforcement on the first component of a multiple schedule affects the rate of responding on the second component. The rate of responding will, of course, also change on the first component because the schedule of reinforcement on that component has changed, but that is not surprising. What is surprising is the change in response rate on the second component, even though the schedule of reinforcement in that component has remained the same. Thus, it is the change in response rate on the second component that is the focus of concern in behavioral contrast.

QUICK QUIZ J

1. In (positive/negative) behavioral contrast, an increase in (responding/reinforcement) on one alternative results in a(n) (increase/decrease) in (responding/reinforcement) on the other alternative.
2. In __________ behavioral contrast, a decrease in reinforcement on one alternative results in a(n) __________ in __________ on the other alternative.
3. A pigeon that experiences a shift from a multiple FR 10 VI 60-sec schedule to a multiple FR 100 VI 60-sec schedule will likely (increase/decrease) its responding on the VI 60-sec component. This is an example of a __________ contrast effect.
4. When Levin (a lonely bachelor in Tolstoy's novel *Anna Karenina*) proposed to the beautiful young Kitty, she rejected him. Levin was devastated and decided to devote the rest of his life to his work. Kitty, in turn, was subsequently rejected by the handsome young military officer, Vronsky, whom she had mistakenly assumed was intent on marrying her. Kitty was devastated and deeply regretted having turned down Levin, whom she now perceived to be a fine man. A year later, they encountered each other at a social gathering. Relative to individuals who have not experienced such hardships in establishing a relationship, we would expect their affection for each other to be much (deeper/shallower) than normal. Of the two types of contrast effects you have just learned about this, this example is most similar to a __________ contrast effect.

An additional type of contrast effect is ***anticipatory contrast***, in which the rate of response varies inversely with an upcoming ("anticipated") change in the rate of reinforcement (B. A. Williams, 1981). For example, Pliskoff (1963) found that pigeons increased their rate of responding for reinforcement when they were presented with a stimulus signaling that extinction was imminent. In other words, faced with the impending loss of reinforcement, the pigeons responded all the more vigorously for reinforcement while it was still available.

Anticipatory contrast seems analogous to what many of us have experienced—that things we are about to lose often seem to increase in value. For example, Lindsay views her relationship with Bryce as rather dull and uninteresting until she learns that Bryce might be romantically interested in another woman. Faced with the possibility that she might lose him, she now becomes intensely interested in him. Unfortunately, some people may use anticipatory contrast as a deliberate tactic to strengthen a partner's feelings of attachment. Read again the anecdote at the beginning of this chapter about Poppea's relationship with the Roman emperor Nero. In behavioral terms, Poppea first established herself as an effective reinforcer for Nero; then, to further increase her value, she intermittently threatened to withdraw herself from his company. In anticipation of possibly losing her, Nero became even more attached.

The occurrence of these contrast effects indicates that behaviors should not be viewed in isolation. Consequences for behavior in one setting can greatly affect the strength of behavior in another setting. Consider, for example, a young girl who is increasingly neglected at home, perhaps because her parents are going through a divorce. She might try to compensate for this circumstance by seeking more attention at school (a positive contrast effect), perhaps to the point of misbehaving. Although the parents might blame the school for her misbehavior, she is in fact reacting to the lack of reinforcement at home. Thus, to borrow a concept from humanistic psychology, behavior needs to be viewed in a holistic manner, with the recognition that behavior in one setting can be influenced by contingencies operating in other settings.

QUICK QUIZ K

1. An increase in the rate of responding for an available reinforcer when faced with the possibility of losing it in the near future is known as __________ contrast.
2. If Jackie hears her mother say that it is getting close to her bedtime, she is likely to become (more/less) __________ involved in the computer game she is playing.
3. Vronsky (a character in Tolstoy's *Anna Karenina*) falls deeply in love with Anna, who is the wife of another man. For several months, they carry on a passionate affair. When Anna, however, finally leaves her husband to be with him, Vronsky finds that he soon becomes bored with their relationship. The fact that his feelings for Anna were much stronger when their relationship was more precarious is in keeping with the __________ contrast effect.

Fading and Errorless Discrimination Learning

While discrimination training is an effective way for establishing stimulus control, it has its limitations. For example, during the process of learning to discriminate an S^D from an S^Δ, the subject will initially make several "mistakes" by responding in the presence of the S^Δ. Because such responses do

And Furthermore

St. Neots Margin

The anticipatory contrast effect described by Pliskoff (1963) reflects the pigeon's reaction to a potential difficulty—namely, the impending loss of a reinforcer. According to British writer Colin Wilson (1972), such difficulties may provide our lives with a sense of meaning when more pleasant stimuli have failed. Wilson's description of how he discovered this concept provides an interesting illustration.

> In 1954, I was hitch-hiking to Peterborough on a hot Saturday afternoon. I felt listless, bored and resentful: I didn't want to go to Peterborough—it was a kind of business trip—and I didn't particularly long to be back in London either. There was hardly any traffic on the road, but eventually I got a lift. Within ten minutes, there was an odd noise in the engine of the lorry. The driver said: 'I'm afraid something's gone wrong—I'll have to drop you off at the next garage.' I was too listless to care. I walked on, and eventually a second lorry stopped for me. Then occurred the absurd coincidence. After ten minutes or so, there was a knocking noise from *his* gearbox. When he said: 'It sounds as if something's gone wrong,' I thought: 'Oh *no!*' and then caught myself thinking it, and thought: 'That's the first definite reaction I've experienced today.' We drove on slowly—he was anxious to get to Peterborough, *and by this time, so was I.* He found that if he dropped speed to just under twenty miles an hour, the knocking noise stopped; as soon as he exceeded it, it started again. We both listened intently for any resumption of the trouble. Finally, as we were passing through a town called St. Neots, he said: 'Well, I think if we stay at this speed, we should make it.' And I felt a surge of delight. Then I thought: 'This is absurd. My situation hasn't *improved* since I got into the lorry—in fact, it has got worse, since he is now crawling along. All that has happened is that an inconvenience has been threatened and then the threat withdrawn. And suddenly, my boredom and indifference have vanished.' I formulated then the notion that there is a borderland or threshold of the mind that can be stimulated by pain or inconvenience, but not pleasure. (p. 27)

Wilson labeled the concept *St. Neots margin* after the town they were driving through at the time. He proposes that such difficulties create "meaning" by forcing us to concentrate, and that the absence of such concentration makes life dull and uninteresting. But we can also view these difficulties as a type of contrast effect in which we are in danger of losing a reinforcer. As a result, we respond more vigorously for the reinforcer and value it more highly.

Contrast effects may therefore provide our lives with a sense of meaning that might otherwise be missing. Wilson describes, for example, how the writer Sartre claimed that he never felt so free as during the war when, as a member of the French Resistance, he was in constant danger of being arrested. In danger of losing his freedom, he truly appreciated his freedom. Consider too Balderston's (1924) play, *A Morality Play for the Leisured Class*, which recounts the story of a man who dies and finds himself in the afterlife. When a shining presence tells him that he can have any pleasure he desires by merely wishing it, he is overjoyed and fully indulges himself. He soon discovers, however, that things quickly lose their value when they are so easily attained. Facing an eternity of profound boredom (in which contrast effects are completely absent), he finally exclaims that he would rather be in hell—at which point the presence asks: "And wherever do you think you *are*, sir?"

not result in reinforcement, the subject may become frustrated and display a great deal of emotional behavior. It would be helpful, therefore, if there was a method of discrimination training that minimized these effects.

Errorless discrimination training is a gradual training procedure that minimizes the number of errors (i.e., nonreinforced responses to the S^{Δ}) and reduces many of the adverse effects associated with discrimination training. It involves two aspects: (1) The S^{Δ} is introduced early in training, soon after the animal has learned to respond appropriately to the S^{D}, and (2) the S^{Δ} is presented in weak form to begin with and then gradually strengthened. This process of gradually altering the intensity of a stimulus is known as ***fading***. (For example, one can *fade in* music by presenting it faintly to begin with and gradually turning up the volume, or *fade out* music by presenting it loudly to begin with and gradually turning down the volume.)

Terrace (1963a) used errorless discrimination training to establish a red-green discrimination in pigeons. The pigeons were first trained to peck a red key on a VI 60-sec schedule of reinforcement. As soon as this behavior was established, occasional 5-second periods of extinction were presented in which the key light was switched off. Since pigeons tend not to peck a dark key, the dark key was easily established as an effective S^{Δ} for not responding. The VI period and the extinction period were then gradually lengthened until they each lasted 3 minutes. Following this, the dark key was illuminated with a faint greenish hue that was slowly intensified. As the green key color was faded in (as an S^{Δ}) and gradually replaced the dark key, the pigeons emitted almost no responses toward it; that is, they made almost no errors. By comparison, pigeons that were exposed to a dark key that was suddenly replaced by a brightly lit green key made numerous responses on it before finally discriminating it from the red S^{D} key. The pigeons exposed to the errorless procedure also showed few of the adverse side effects of discrimination training, such as emotional behavior.

Errorless procedures can also be used to transfer control from one type of stimulus to another. For example, Terrace (1963b) first trained pigeons to discriminate between a red key as the S^{D} and a green key as the S^{Δ}. He then gradually faded in a vertical line (the new S^{D}) on the red key and a horizontal line (the new S^{Δ}) on the green key, while at the same time fading out the colors. Eventually, the pigeons were pecking a colorless key that had a vertical line and not pecking a colorless key that had a horizontal line. With virtually no errors, stimulus control for pecking had been transferred from key color (red versus green) to line orientation (vertical versus horizontal).

Errorless discrimination training may have practical applications. For example, Haupt, Van Kirk, and Terraciano (1975) used an errorless procedure to enhance the learning of basic arithmetic skills. In their study, a 9-year-old girl who had a history of difficulties in basic arithmetic was given a series of addition problems using a standard drill procedure and a series of subtraction problems using an errorless procedure. The standard drill procedure for the addition problems consisted of presenting the problems on flash cards in which the answers were initially covered. If the child did not know the answer, the answer was uncovered and shown to her. The errorless procedure for the subtraction problems was similar except that the answer on each flash card was initially left exposed to view and then, over successive presentations, gradually blocked out by adding successive sheets of cellophane. The correct answer was thus initially available as a prompt for the correct answer and then gradually faded out. During a subsequent test, the girl made significantly fewer errors on the subtraction problems, for which the errorless procedure had been used, than on the addition problems, for which the standard drill procedure had been used.

Although errorless discrimination training might seem like the perfect answer to many unresolved problems in education, it has some serious drawbacks. Discriminations that have been established through errorless training are more difficult to modify at a later time. For example, Marsh and Johnson (1968) taught pigeons to discriminate between two key colors in which one color was the S^D and the other the S^{Δ}. Pigeons that had been taught to discriminate using an errorless procedure experienced extreme difficulty learning a new discrimination in which the meaning of the key colors was reversed (i.e., the color that had previously been the S^{Δ} now became the S^D, and vice versa). In contrast, pigeons that had learned the original discrimination in the normal error-filled way handled the reversal quite handily. Thus, although normal discrimination training has more adverse side effects compared to errorless discrimination training, it also results in greater flexibility when what is learned has to be modified later. For this reason, errorless procedures may be most useful in rote learning of basic facts, such as arithmetic and spelling, in which the substance of what is learned is unlikely to change. With material that requires greater flexibility, however, such as that typically found in most college-level courses, errorless learning might be a significant impediment (Pierce & Epling, 1999).[7]

QUICK QUIZ L

1. In e__________ discrimination training, the S^{Δ} is presented (early/later) in the training procedure, and at very (weak/strong) intensity to begin with.
2. This type of discrimination training is likely to produce (more/less) emotional behavior compared to the standard form of discrimination training.
3. This type of discrimination training is also likely to produce behavior patterns that are (easy/difficult) to modify at a later point in time.
4. Gradually altering the intensity of a stimulus is called fa__________.

Stimulus Control: Additional Applications

There are many ways in which stimulus control can be used to manage behavior. Perhaps the most impressive use of stimulus control is by animal

[7]This accords with the more general finding, briefly mentioned in Chapter 1, that experiencing a certain amount of difficulty during the learning process can enhance long-term retention and understanding (Schmidt & Bjork, 1992).

trainers, especially those who train animals for public performance. Dolphin trainers, for example, use a mere whistle or gesture to set off a dazzling display of leaps and twirls. Indeed, the control is so precise that the dolphins often seem like robots, an impression that probably contributes to the growing opposition to such shows. Not only has the animal been removed from its natural environment, it now appears to be a slave to the trainer's every whim. (Karen Pryor, 1999, however, contends that the reality is quite different, with such training—especially that which involves positive reinforcement—being much more a two-way process of communication than brute force control.)

A particularly useful form of stimulus control for animal management is *targeting*. In targeting, one trains an animal to approach and touch a particular object, as in training a dog to touch the end of a stick with its nose. Targeting is a key aspect of teaching dolphins to make their impressive leaps. The dolphin first receives reinforcement for touching a target stick with its snout, following which the stick is raised higher and higher, enticing the dolphin to leap higher and higher to touch it. Targeting is commonly used to manage animals in zoos. By simply moving the target stick, zookeepers can lead the animals from one cage to another or position them precisely for medical examinations. Animals can also be taught to target a point of light from a laser beam, which then allows the handler to send the animal to a spot some distance away. This can be a useful procedure for directing search-and-rescue dogs in disaster areas that are difficult for the handler to traverse (Pryor, 1999; see also "From TB to Landmines: Animals to the Rescue" in the And Furthermore box).

Stimulus control can also be used to eliminate certain types of problem behaviors in animals. Pryor (1999), for example, describes how she once experienced considerable difficulty in training a dolphin to wear suction cups over its eyes (as part of an intended demonstration of the dolphin's ability to swim solely by sonar). Although the cups did not hurt, the dolphin refused to wear them and would cleverly sink to the bottom of the pool for several minutes whenever it saw Pryor approaching with the cups. Initially stumped, Pryor finally hit on the idea of reinforcing the behavior of sinking by giving the dolphin a fish whenever it did so (which, she reports, seemed to greatly surprise the dolphin). Soon, the dolphin was sinking at high frequency to earn fish, at which point Pryor began to reinforce the behavior only after a cue had been presented. In short order, the dolphin was sinking only on cue, meaning that the behavior was now under strong stimulus control. Pryor found that she was then able to reintroduce the suction cups and place them on the dolphin without difficulty. In the absence of the cue for sinking, the dolphin no longer had a tendency to sink to avoid the cups. In similar fashion, a dog that has been trained to bark on cue may be less likely to bark at other times. In short, by putting a behavior "on cue," the behavior is less likely to occur in the absence of the cue.

And Furthermore

From TB to Landmines: Animals to the Rescue

Search-and-rescue dogs are an excellent example of discrimination training with animals that has had considerable benefit for humans. Dogs have a keen sense of hearing and smell, which have proven useful for a variety of tasks, from hunting to search-and-rescue to drug detection. A particularly important manner in which dogs are being used these days is for landmine detection (McLean, 2003). Landmines are an extreme hazard in former war zones, with large numbers of civilians being maimed or killed each year. Considerable effort is needed just to detect the mines, which is where the superior olfactory abilities of dogs have proven useful.

In an interesting twist, giant African pouched rats are now also being trained for landmine detection (Poling, Weetjens, Cox, Beyene, & Sully, 2010). These rats have several advantages over dogs: (1) they are less expensive and easier to maintain, (2) they do not get attached to their handlers like dogs will and hence can be assigned to different handlers, and (3) the rats are so light that they can step on mines without setting them off. But training rats (and dogs) for this task can be very difficult, requiring a highly accurate form of discrimination that will reliably generalize across different settings. Landmine detection is, after all, an area of work in which "almost perfect" can be a disaster, and behavior analysts have an important role to play in devising optimal training procedures (Jones, 2011).

An even more unique setting in which discrimination training of animals may prove useful is the cancer clinic. Interest began in 1989 with a letter to the medical journal *The Lancet* that described a woman whose dog alerted her to the presence of a malignant tumor:

> The patient first became aware of the lesion because her dog . . . would constantly sniff at it. The dog . . . showed no interest in the other moles on the patient's body but frequently spent several minutes a day sniffing intently at the lesion, even through the patient's trousers. As a consequence, the patient became increasingly suspicious. This ritual continued for several months and culminated in the dog trying to bite off the lesion when the patient wore shorts. This prompted the patient to seek further medical attention [at which point the malignancy was discovered and removed]. (Williams & Pembroke, 1989, p. 734).

Similar reports followed, including one in which a dog detected a malignant mole that had been incorrectly assessed by a doctor as nonmalignant (Church & Williams, 2001). Although anecdotal, these reports strongly suggested that dogs have the ability to discriminate cancerous from noncancerous lesions, which led researchers to wonder if dogs could be systematically trained to detect cancers. Several such studies have now been conducted, and results have been encouraging (Moser & McCulloch, 2010). Giant African pouched rats are also getting in on the action, only in this case with detection of tuberculosis by sniffing samples of patients' sputum (Poling, Weetjens, Cox, Beyene, Durgin, & Mahoney, 2011).

But what about the behavior analyst's favorite animal, the pigeon? Well, pigeons do have excellent vision, and behavior analysts have tried to make use of this ability. In

WWII, Skinner proposed using pigeons housed in the nose cone of a missile to visually guide the missile to a military target. He was in fact able to demonstrate that pigeons were capable of performing this task; but the military was unenthusiastic about it and the project was dropped. Similarly, in the 1970s, an attempt was made to train pigeons for search-and-rescue missions at sea (Azar, 2002). Housed in a transparent bubble below a helicopter, the pigeons responded to the sight of tiny objects in the seascape by pecking at response keys that guided the pilot to the target. The pigeons were reportedly 93% accurate—the flight crews were only 38% accurate—but the program was nevertheless cancelled when the need for budget cuts arose. As with Skinner's missile project, it seems that the "laugh factor" may have also played a role; it was difficult for people to take these pigeon projects seriously. Likewise, Verhave (1966) trained pigeons as "assembly line workers" to detect defective drug capsules for a drug manufacturer. The pigeons were 99% accurate after only one week of training, but the drug company never followed through on the project, one reason being publicity concerns that might arise from using pigeons as "quality control inspectors."

Stimulus control is also an important aspect of human behavior, though we sometimes overlook it as a simple means for facilitating certain aspects of our behavior. Consider Stephanie, who promises herself that she will take vitamins each evening but so often forgets to do so that she eventually gives up. All she really needs to do is create a salient cue for taking vitamins, such as placing the vitamin bottle beside the alarm clock that she sets each evening. Likewise, the person who remembers to take her umbrella is the person who sets it beside the door when she hears on the news that it might soon be raining.

Stimulus control procedures are also the treatment of choice for *sleep-onset insomnia*, in which people have difficulty falling asleep. For example, Bootzin, Epstein, and Wood (1991) recommend the following procedure:

1. Go to bed only when you are sleepy.
2. Use the bed only for sleeping (or sex). Do not lie in bed to read, study, or watch television.
3. If you cannot fall asleep within 10 to 20 minutes, get out of bed and go to another room. Go back to bed only when you feel sleepy.
4. Repeat the above rule as often as necessary. This rule should also be applied if you are unable to fall asleep after a middle-of-the-night awakening.
5. Use your alarm to get up at the same time each morning, regardless of how you slept the night before.
6. Do not take naps during the day.

The obvious goal of the program is to make lying in bed a strong cue for sleeping. Research has shown this to be an effective program, with many people reporting considerable improvement in their sleep habits both immediately following the program and at long-term follow-up (Lichstein & Riedel, 1994).

QUICK QUIZ M

1. Training a rhinoceros to touch the end of a stick with its nose is an example of a behavior management technique called t______________.
2. Jaclyn's cat has a terrible habit of jumping up on the kitchen counter whenever she is preparing food. How might Jaclyn use a stimulus control procedure to eliminate this behavior? ____
____.

Study Tip: Stimulus control is also useful for creating an effective study environment. As we previously noted in Chapter 4, many students study best in an environment in which distractions (cues for behavior other than studying) are kept to a minimum (e.g., Heffernan & Richards, 1981; Plant, Ericsson, Hill, & Asberg, 2005). Students can also benefit from the use of a dedicated study environment, such as a particular desk, in which the cues are strongly associated with studying. As a result, the mere act of placing oneself in the environment can almost automatically evoke the tendency to study (Skinner, 1987; Steel, 2010). Of course, this type of stimulus control cannot be established overnight. Sitting at a desk for 3 hours trying to study but daydreaming instead will only associate the desk with daydreaming. Better to begin with short, high-quality study periods and then gradually progress to longer study periods (although, as the *Calvin and Hobbes* cartoon suggests, not too gradually).

A classic example of such a procedure was reported by Fox (1962). In the initial experiment, the students were instructed to schedule a 1-hour study period per day and to spend at least part of that hour studying their most difficult course. They were also told to conduct that studying only in a particular setting, to have only their study materials with them in that setting, and not to be in that setting on other occasions. They were also told that if they became bored or started to daydream, they were to complete just a bit more studying and then leave the setting. Finally, any studying done outside the special 1-hour period had to be done elsewhere. Initially, none of the students could study throughout the 1-hour period, but they gradually built up the ability to do so. A similar procedure was then carried out for each of their other courses, with the result that students were eventually studying each course for 1 hour per day. This

Calvin and Hobbes by Bill Watterson

program—which also involved instruction in other academic skills—resulted in considerable improvement in students' grades.

In a second experiment, graduate students who were only infrequently practicing a required foreign language were provided a special setting to use for practice. They were also told to practice each day in that setting for at least 10 minutes, but for no more than 1 hour. This procedure, which combines stimulus control with the just-get-started tactic discussed in Chapter 7, proved to be highly effective, with all of the students soon engaging in high-quality practice for the full hour each day. Although this study leaves much to be desired from a scientific perspective (what are some of the ways in which it is only a weak demonstration of the effectiveness of these procedures?), you may find it interesting to experiment with using similar procedures to enhance your own studying. (See also "Edwin Guthrie: Stimulus Control for the Practical Person" in the And Furthermore box for an additional study tip.)

And Furthermore

Edwin Guthrie: Stimulus Control for the Practical Person

Edwin Guthrie (1886–1959) was a famous learning theorist who strongly emphasized the role of stimulus control. This is because, from his perspective, all learning is a function of one basic principle: If a behavior occurs in the presence of certain stimuli, then the presence of those stimuli will automatically evoke the behavior (Guthrie, 1952). In other words, Guthrie's theory is an extreme version of an S-R theory.

Guthrie's theory makes a startlingly blunt prediction about behavior. Whatever you did the last time you were in a certain setting is exactly what you will do the next time you are in that setting. Suppose, for example, that the last time you walked down a certain hallway, you entered the first doorway to the right. Guthrie's theory predicts that the next time you walk down that hallway, you will again enter the first doorway to the right, *given that all the stimuli are the same as when you last walked down that hallway.* Of course, this last part is the catch. The stimuli that precede a behavior—and this can include both internal and external stimuli—are never exactly the same from one occasion to the next. Instead, they are only more or less similar, with the result that a behavior is only more or less likely to be repeated. Note also that the consequences of the behavior—for example, perhaps you entered the first doorway to the right because it leads to the cafeteria where you bought coffee—do not enter into the equation. Guthrie viewed consequences as having only an indirect effect on behavior, though his explanation for how this works is too complex to delve into here.

Guthrie himself did little research, and the research that was done provided only equivocal support for his theory. As a result, it receives little attention from modern-day researchers. Nonetheless, Guthrie's approach still has its adherents and is still considered a major theory of learning (Hergenhahn, 2009). Perhaps one reason for its enduring attraction is the simplicity of the theory (scientists often find a parsimonious explanation quite attractive, possibly because they so often have to deal with complexities). Another reason is the engaging practicality of the theory.

One of Guthrie's most cited examples is that of a young girl who each day threw her coat on the floor when she arrived home and was each day scolded by her mother (Guthrie, 1952). On the surface, we might speculate that the girl repeated the behavior because it was reinforced by the attention she received from her mother. From Guthrie's perspective, however, the mother's reaction had little effect on the behavior. Rather, the stimuli that the girl encountered when she entered the house had become so strongly connected to the response of throwing the coat on the floor that this response automatically occurred each time she entered. To solve the problem, the mother began to insist that the child pick up her coat, go back outside, and then practice the behavior of entering the house and hanging up the coat. The stimuli present when the girl entered the house then became associated with the act of hanging up the coat rather than throwing it on the floor, and the new behavior supplanted the old.

Another example is that of a student who was having difficulty studying because she was continually distracted by the sound of a neighbor's radio (Guthrie, 1952). Instead of trying to force herself to study, the student read mystery stories. The stories were so interesting that she was able to read them without being distracted by the sound of the radio. Within a week, the behavior of concentrating while reading had become so firmly attached to that setting that she was then able to switch back to her study materials and concentrate well despite the radio.

This last example implies that students who have difficulty concentrating might sometimes do well to study something interesting before they study something boring. Starting with interesting material might establish a strong level of concentration that will then carry over to the less interesting material. This, of course, seems to contradict Grandma's rule—or the Premack principle, if you will—which contends that you should work before you play (applied to studying, this suggests that you should start with less interesting material and finish off with more interesting material). Guthrie, by contrast, seems to suggest that it might sometimes be useful to play before you work.

SUMMARY

Extinction is the nonreinforcement of a previously reinforced response, the result of which is a decrease in the strength of that response. Implementation of an extinction procedure is often followed by an extinction burst, which is a temporary increase in the rate and intensity of a behavior. Extinction is also followed by an increase in the variability of behavior and in emotional behavior, especially aggression. Extinction can also be accompanied by resurgence—the sudden appearance of a different behavior that had previously been reinforced—and depression.

Resistance to extinction is the extent to which responding persists during extinction. According to the partial reinforcement effect, an intermittent schedule of reinforcement, especially a VR schedule, produces greater resistance to extinction than a continuous schedule. Resistance is also affected by the number of times the behavior has been reinforced, the magnitude of the reinforcers that have been used, and the extent to which the animal has been deprived of the reinforcer. Previous experience with extinction tends to lower resistance to extinction, as does the presence of a discriminative stimulus for extinction (known as an S^{Δ}).

Spontaneous recovery is the reappearance of an extinguished response following a rest period after extinction. With repeated sessions of extinction, however, the amount of recovery gradually diminishes. The process of extinction can be facilitated through differential reinforcement of other behaviors.

A behavior is said to be under stimulus control when the presence of an S^D reliably affects the likelihood of a behavior. The tendency to respond to stimuli similar to the S^D is called stimulus generalization; the tendency not to respond to such stimuli is stimulus discrimination. A graph that indicates the degree of generalization to similar stimuli is a generalization gradient. A flat gradient indicates strong generalization; a steep gradient indicates weak generalization. The peak shift effect is the tendency, following discrimination training, for the peak of a generalization gradient to shift to one side of the S^D, to a point that is further removed from the S^{Δ}.

A multiple schedule consists of two or more schedules presented in sequence, each resulting in reinforcement and each having a distinctive S^D. Multiple schedules are used to study contrast effects. In a negative contrast effect, an increase in reinforcement on one component of a multiple schedule produces a decrease in responding on the other component. In a positive contrast effect, a decrease in the reinforcement on one component produces an increase in responding on the other component. In anticipatory contrast, the rate of response varies inversely with an upcoming ("anticipated") change in the rate of reinforcement.

Errorless discrimination training is a procedure that minimizes the number of errors and reduces many of the side effects associated with discrimination training. It involves presenting the S^{Δ} early in training, beginning in weak form and then gradually strengthening it (known as a fading procedure). A drawback to errorless discrimination training is that behavior acquired in this fashion is later more difficult to modify.

Stimulus control procedures have been applied to a number of behavior problems, ranging from managing animals in zoos to facilitating the act of studying to treating insomnia.

SUGGESTED READINGS

Guthrie, E. R. (1952). *The psychology of learning* (Rev. ed.). New York: Harper & Row. (Original work published in 1935.) Guthrie's very readable book outlines his provocatively simple theory of learning, backed up by plenty of down-home practical examples.

Lerman, D. C., & Iwata, B. A. (1996). Developing a technology for the use of operant extinction in clinical settings: An examination of basic and applied research. *Journal of Applied Behavior Analysis*, *29*, 345–382. A nice overview of the use of extinction in applied settings.

Mindell, J. A. (1999). Empirically supported treatments in pediatric psychology: Bedtime refusal and night wakings in young children. *Journal of Pediatric Psychology*, *24*, 465–481. Sleepless parents, or those who do not wish to become sleepless parents, will likely appreciate this overview of various methods for getting children to stay in bed at night.

STUDY QUESTIONS

1. Define extinction as it applies to operant conditioning. What are six side effects of extinction, and which of these side effects is likely to create the most difficulty in trying to carry out extinction?
2. What is resistance to extinction? What is the partial reinforcement effect? Which schedule of reinforcement is likely to produce the highest resistance to extinction?
3. What are four factors other than the schedule of reinforcement that can affect resistance to extinction?
4. What is spontaneous recovery, and how is it affected by successive sessions of extinction?
5. Define a DRO procedure. Why is a DRO procedure often more effective than a straight extinction procedure in eliminating a behavior?
6. Define stimulus control. What are stimulus generalization and stimulus discrimination *as they occur in operant conditioning*? Diagram an example of a discrimination training procedure (be sure to include the appropriate abbreviations for each component).
7. What is a generalization gradient? How does the shape of the gradient reflect the degree of generalization? With the use of a graph, describe what a peak shift effect consists of.
8. Diagram an example of a multiple schedule that involves the response of lever pressing, FR 20 and VI 30-sec schedules of reinforcement, and the stimuli of tone and light. Be sure to include the appropriate label for each component (S^D, etc.). How does this differ from a chained schedule?
9. Define positive contrast, negative contrast, and anticipatory contrast, and give an example of each.
10. Describe errorless discrimination training and the two basic aspects of this procedure. What is a major drawback of such training?
11. How might a bird owner use stimulus control to eliminate a parrot's tendency to squawk for long periods of time? How might a novelist use stimulus control to facilitate the act of writing?

CONCEPT REVIEW

anticipatory contrast. The process whereby the rate of response varies inversely with an upcoming ("anticipated") change in the rate of reinforcement.

behavioral contrast. A change in the rate of *reinforcement* on one component of a multiple schedule produces an opposite change in the rate of *response* on another component.

differential reinforcement of other behavior (DRO). Reinforcement of any behavior other than a target behavior that is being extinguished.

discrimination training. As applied to operant conditioning, the differential reinforcement of responding in the presence of one stimulus (the S^D) and not another.

errorless discrimination training. A discrimination training procedure that minimizes the number of errors (i.e., nonreinforced responses to the S^{Δ}) and reduces many of the adverse effects associated with discrimination training.

extinction. The nonreinforcement of a previously reinforced response, the result of which is a decrease in the strength of that response.

extinction burst. A temporary increase in the frequency and intensity of responding when extinction is first implemented.

fading. The process of gradually altering the intensity of a stimulus.

generalization gradient. A measure of the strength of responding in the presence of stimuli that are similar to the S^D and vary along a continuum.

multiple schedule. A complex schedule consisting of two or more independent schedules presented in sequence, each resulting in reinforcement and each having a distinctive S^D.

negative contrast effect. An increase in the rate of *reinforcement* on one component of a multiple schedule produces a decrease in the rate of *response* on the other component.

partial reinforcement effect. The process whereby behavior that has been maintained on an intermittent (partial) schedule of reinforcement extinguishes more slowly than behavior that has been maintained on a continuous schedule.

peak shift effect. Following discrimination training, the peak of a generalization gradient will shift from the S^D to a stimulus that is further removed from the S^{Δ}.

positive contrast effect. A decrease in rate of reinforcement on one component of a multiple schedule produces an increase in the rate of response on the other component.

resistance to extinction. The extent to which responding persists after an extinction procedure has been implemented.

resurgence. The reappearance during extinction of other behaviors that had once been effective in obtaining reinforcement.

spontaneous recovery. The reappearance of an extinguished response following a rest period after extinction.

stimulus control. A situation in which the presence of a discriminative stimulus reliably affects the probability of a behavior.

stimulus discrimination. In operant conditioning, the tendency for an operant response to be emitted more in the presence of one stimulus than another.

stimulus generalization. In operant conditioning, the tendency for an operant response to be emitted in the presence of a stimulus that is similar to an S^D.

CHAPTER TEST

16. When Asha's parents won the lottery and bought her lots of neat playthings, she became (less/more) interested in school. This is an example of a(n) ________ contrast effect.

4. When Erin was babysitting Lucie, it took hours before Lucie would stop pestering her for a treat (Erin had been instructed to stop giving her treats). The next time Erin babysits Lucie, Lucie will (probably/probably not) resume asking for a treat. This can be considered an example of an extinction effect known as ________. This may be occurring in this case because the entry of a babysitter into the house is, for Lucie, a(n) ________ stimulus indicating that a treat will soon become available.

10. Lucie is ecstatic when Tamsen is her babysitter, and completely indifferent when Natasha is her babysitter. This is because Tamsen tends to give her treats, but Natasha does not. Thus, Tamsen is a(n) (give the abbreviation) ________ for the availability of treats, while Natasha is a(n) ________.

27. More persistent is to less persistent as (high/low) resistance to extinction is to ________ resistance to extinction.

15. When Trish's friend Laura spread some nasty rumors about her, Trish stopped talking to her. Laura did not understand the reason for Trish's silence and initially (increased/decreased) the frequency with which she attempted to talk to Laura. From the perspective of this being an extinction process, Laura's behavior can be seen as an example of a(n) ________.

9. Right after Gina was stung by a hornet, she was as likely to run away from houseflies as from hornets, which is an example of stimulus ________. One year later, we find that Gina runs away from hornets but not houseflies, which is an example of stimulus ________.

19. Lana finds that the children in her class are extremely unruly. To solve this problem, she announces that whenever she is holding up a flag, the children can run around and do whatever they want. Then, periodically throughout the day, she holds up the flag for a few minutes and lets the children run around like crazy. She also finds that when the flag is not

being held up, the children are now relatively (quiet/noisy), insofar as the behavior of running around is now under __________.

5. When Charlene took her daughter, Lucie, to the store, it took hours before Lucie would stop making a fuss and pestering her for a treat. Charlene could likely have speeded up this process through the use of a(n) (give the abbreviation) __________ procedure.

11. When Mehgan lived in Vancouver, she dated Mike, who was quite uneducated, and David, who was moderately educated. She had a boring time with Mike and a great time with David. She then moved to Dallas and set her sights on meeting someone new. According to the __________ effect, we would expect her to be most interested in meeting someone (as educated as/more educated than) David.

21. In behavioral __________, a change in the rate of __________ on one component of a multiple schedule is followed by a(n) (similar/opposite) change in the rate of __________ on the other component.

7. On a generalization gradient, the strongest response typically occurs to the __________.

13. The nonreinforcement of a previously reinforced response defines the __________ of extinction, while the resultant decrease in the strength of that response defines the __________ of extinction.

3. A dog whose begging for food has been reinforced 200 times is likely to show greater __________ to extinction than a dog whose begging has been reinforced only 10 times.

20. When Trish's friend Laura spread some nasty rumors about her, Trish stopped talking to her. Laura tried different ways to get Trish to talk to her: phoning her, e-mailing, writing letters, and sending messages through mutual friends. The many ways in which Laura attempted to interact with Trish are indicative of an effect that often accompanies extinction, which is an increase in the v__________ of a behavior.

25. While teaching his daughter the letters of the alphabet, Vern would say each letter as he showed it to her and then encourage her to repeat what he said. He then began to say the letters more and more softly, with the result that she eventually said them on her own without any prompt from him. This can be seen as an example of __________ discrimination learning. One problem with this type of method is that the learning that results from this procedure tends to be (inflexible/too flexible).

22. When Trish's friend Laura spread some nasty rumors about her, Trish stopped talking to her. Laura tried very hard to get Trish to talk to her. She also became emotionally (upset/distant), which included becoming __________ with Trish.

2. When visiting a foreign resort last summer, you frequently encountered a group of children in the street who were trying to sell souvenirs. Although you always rejected their sales pitches, they were incredibly persistent. Chances are that this persistence results because their

behavior of selling merchandise is on a(n) __________ schedule of reinforcement. Another factor would be that the children seemed quite poor; hence, they were relatively __________ of the sought-after reinforcer.

8. A __________ indicates the strength of responding in the presence of stimuli that are similar to the __________ and that vary along a __________.

23. When Tamara first moved to the city, she went out each evening and had a great time. One evening at a nightclub, however, she had a frightening experience that really turned her off the club scene. Interestingly, she subsequently became (more/less) interested in other activities, including her job. This may be an example of a(n) __________ contrast effect.

14. The first step in carrying out an extinction procedure is to identify the __________ that is maintaining the behavior.

18. When Trish's friend Laura spread some nasty rumors about her, Trish stopped talking to her. Laura tried to get Trish to talk to her but quickly gave up. Laura's behavior of trying to interact with Trish seems to have (low/high) resistance to extinction.

24. Ahmed found school only slightly interesting. Unfortunately, his lack of studying led to some very poor marks one semester, with the result that he faced the threat of being forced to withdraw for a year. Based on what you have learned in this chapter, throughout the rest of the semester, Ahmed probably became (more/less) interested in his academic studies. This can be seen as an example of a(n) __________ contrast effect.

12. A multiple schedule consists of two or more independent schedules presented (simultaneously/sequentially), each resulting in a(n) __________ and each having a distinctive __________.

1. When Trish's friend Laura spread some nasty rumors about her, Trish stopped talking to her. Laura tried hard to get Trish to talk to her. She even asked Trish if she would like to go to the local video arcade, which had been one of their favorite activities when they first became friends. This may be an example of an extinction effect known as __________.

17. Yan lives in a very crowded city, so he trains his little boy to stay in close contact with his right hand whenever they are walking in a crowd. This is similar to a behavior management technique known as __________ that is used to guide animals.

6. When the commander yells "Charge!" all of his troops climb out of the trench and start running toward the enemy. The behavior of these troops is obviously under strong __________ control.

26. When Trish's best friend Laura spread some nasty rumors about her, Trish stopped talking to her. Laura tried very hard to get Trish to talk to her. When Trish refused, Laura eventually became __________, one symptom of which was a relatively (low/high) level of activity.

ANSWERS TO CHAPTER TEST

1. resurgence
2. intermittent (VR); deprived
3. resistance
4. probably; spontaneous recovery; discriminative
5. DRO
6. stimulus
7. S^D
8. generalization gradient; S^D; continuum
9. generalization; discrimination
10. S^D; S^Δ
11. peak shift; more educated than
12. sequentially; reinforcer; S^D
13. procedure; process
14. reinforcer
15. increased; extinction burst
16. less; negative
17. targeting
18. low
19. quiet; stimulus control
20. variability
21. contrast; reinforcement; opposite; response
22. upset; angry (or aggressive)
23. more; positive
24. more; anticipatory
25. errorless; inflexible
26. depressed; low
27. high; low

CHAPTER 9

ESCAPE, AVOIDANCE, AND PUNISHMENT

CHAPTER OUTLINE

James informed Misha, his new girlfriend, that he was once married to a woman who had been diagnosed with depression. He explained that she had stopped working, moped around the house all day, and would often break down and start crying. Despite his best efforts to be supportive, they finally got a divorce. Misha felt a lot of sympathy for James, who was obviously a very caring fellow. After several months, though, she noticed that she herself was becoming depressed. Although James was often quite affectionate, he would also become angry with her or, worse yet, grow coldly silent for no apparent reason. He also had a tendency to contradict her whenever she offered her opinion on some matter, and he took special pains to point out her mistakes (because, he said, he loved her so much that he wanted to be honest with her). Misha then learned that James's former wife had made a remarkable recovery soon after their divorce.

This chapter explores the effects of aversive consequences on behavior. We begin by examining the role of negative reinforcement in the development of escape and avoidance behaviors. As you will see, this process plays a critical role in the development and maintenance of phobic and obsessive-compulsive disorders in humans. We follow this with a discussion of punishment, in which the presentation or withdrawal of consequences serves to suppress a behavior. We discuss some of the undesirable side effects of punishment as well as some of the ways in which punishment can be effective. The chapter concludes with a discussion of the harmful effects of noncontingent punishment, in which the punishing stimulus is delivered independently of the individual's behavior.

Escape and Avoidance

As you will recall from Chapter 6, negative reinforcement consists of the removal of an aversive stimulus following a response, which then leads to an increase in the strength of that response. For example, if we wave our hands at a bothersome wasp and the wasp flies away, we will likely repeat that action with the next wasp that annoys us. Negative reinforcement is associated with two types of behavior: (1) *escape behavior*, in which performance of the behavior terminates the aversive stimulus, and (2) *avoidance behavior*, in which performance of the behavior prevents the aversive stimulus from occurring. Thus, we escape from the rain when we run indoors after it has started; we avoid the rain when we head indoors before it has started.

Typically, one first learns to escape from an aversive stimulus and then to avoid it. This process can be demonstrated using a *shuttle avoidance procedure*, in which an animal has to shuttle back and forth in a box to avoid an aversive stimulus. In a typical procedure, a rat is placed in a chamber divided by a low barrier. A stimulus of some sort, such as a light, is presented for, say, 10 seconds, followed by a mild electric shock. The rat can escape the shock by climbing over the barrier to the other side of the compartment, as it will quickly learn to do whenever it feels a shock (see top panel of Figure 9.1). Technically speaking, at this early point in the process, the presence of a shock is a discriminative stimulus that sets the occasion for (or evokes) the escape behavior of crossing the barrier. Crossing the barrier is then negatively reinforced by the removal of shock:

Shock: ***Cross barrier*** **→ Removal of shock**
S^D **R** **S^R**

Now, remember that the shock is preceded by the presentation of a light, which is essentially a warning signal that a shock is about to occur. As the rat learns to associate the light with the shock, it will begin crossing the barrier whenever the light is presented and before the shock begins (see bottom panel of Figure 9.1). The light is now a discriminative stimulus for the avoidance response of crossing the barrier.

Light: ***Cross barrier*** **→ Avoidance of shock**
S^D **R** **S^R**

FIGURE 9.1 Escape and avoidance in a shuttle avoidance task. As shown in the top panel, the animal first learns to escape from the shock by climbing over the barrier whenever a shock occurs. Later, as it learns that the light predicts the occurrence of shock, it climbs over the barrier whenever the light appears, thereby avoiding the shock (as shown in the bottom panel). (*Source*: Nairne, 2000.)

In similar fashion, we might first learn to escape from an upsetting conversation with a racist acquaintance by inventing an excuse for leaving. After a few experiences, however, we might begin actively avoiding that individual before any encounter. By doing so, we avoid having to endure any exposure to that person's racist views.

QUICK QUIZ A

1. Behavior that terminates an aversive stimulus is called __________ behavior, whereas behavior that prevents an aversive stimulus from occurring is called __________ behavior.
2. Typically, one first learns to __________ from an aversive stimulus, and then to __________ it.
3. Julio initially takes vitamin C whenever he has a cold, in the hope that it will shorten the duration of his symptoms. Feeling that this is effective, he begins taking it daily in the hope that it will keep him from getting a cold. Julio initially took the vitamin C to (avoid/escape) the symptoms of a cold; he later took it to __________ the symptoms of a cold.
4. In the shuttle avoidance procedure described previously, the rat first learns to __________ from the shock, with the __________ acting as the S^D for the behavior. The rat later learns to __________ the shock, with the __________ acting as the S^D for the behavior.

Two-Process Theory of Avoidance

Researchers have generally shown more interest in studying avoidance behavior than escape behavior. This is because, from a theoretical perspective, escape behavior is relatively easy to understand. For example, when escaping from shock by climbing over a barrier, the rat moves from a clearly aversive situation to a nonaversive situation. But the motivation underlying avoidance behavior is less apparent. When climbing over a barrier to avoid shock, the rat seems to be moving from one nonaversive situation (no shock) to another nonaversive situation (no shock). How can a lack of change function as a reinforcer?

An early attempt to explain avoidance behavior was the *two-process theory of avoidance* (also known as the *two-factor theory of avoidance*) proposed by Mowrer (1947, 1960). According to this theory, two processes are involved in learning an avoidance response. The first process is classical conditioning of a fear response to a CS. For example, in the shuttle avoidance procedure described previously, the light that precedes the shock becomes a CS that elicits a conditioned fear reaction:

Light: Shock → *Fear*
NS US UR

Light → *Fear*
CS CR

Once this conditioned fear has been established, it then forms the basis of an operant conditioning procedure. If the CS generates a conditioned fear response, then moving away from the CS should result in a reduction of fear. This reduction of fear should in turn serve as a negative reinforcer for the response that produced it. In our experimental example, presentation of the light elicits a conditioned fear response, while climbing over the barrier produces a reduction in fear that serves as a negative reinforcer for that behavior.

Light: ***Climb over barrier*** **→ Reduction in fear**
S^D R S^R

Thus, Mowrer's ***two-process theory of avoidance*** proposes that avoidance behavior is the result of two distinct processes: (1) classical conditioning, in which a fear response comes to be elicited by a CS, and (2) operant conditioning, in which moving away from the CS is negatively reinforced by a reduction in fear.

QUICK QUIZ B

1. It is relatively easy to understand the process underlying (escape/avoidance) conditioning because the organism moves from a(n) ____________ situation to a non____________ situation. By contrast, it is more difficult to understand ____________ conditioning because the organism moves from a(n) ____________ situation to another ____________ situation.
2. According to Mowrer, avoidance is the result of two distinct processes: (1) Classical conditioning of a fear response, and (2) operant conditioning in which an avoidance response is negatively reinforced by a reduction in fear.

Mowrer's two-process theory generated an enormous amount of research, with researchers soon discovering several difficulties with it. One problem was that avoidance responses are often extremely persistent. R. L. Solomon, Kamin, and Wynne (1953), for example, found that dogs would continue to jump a barrier to avoid shock for hundreds of trials even though the shock apparatus had been disconnected and avoidance was no longer necessary. One dog, for example, made more than 600 avoidance responses before the experimenters finally gave up and put a stop to the session.

On the surface, it seems as though two-process theory cannot account for such persistence. If the animal repeatedly encounters the CS in the absence of the US, then fear of the CS should eventually extinguish—meaning that the animal should eventually stop jumping over the barrier. But it seemed as though the behavior would not extinguish. Why not?

A possible answer to this question is provided by a modification of two-process theory known as the *anxiety conservation hypothesis* (R. L. Solomon & Wynne, 1954). According to this approach, avoidance responses usually occur so quickly that there is insufficient exposure to the CS for the conditioned fear to fully extinguish—that is, a good deal of the conditioned fear is conserved because exposures to the CS are too brief for extinction to take place.[1] For this reason, avoidance responses can be extremely persistent. In addition, supporters of two-process theory have pointed out that avoidance responses are not as persistent as sometimes claimed (Levis, 1989). If one continues to expose the animal to the aversive CS, extinction will often eventually occur given that there are no further pairings of the CS with the US. Thus, the fact that avoidance responses are extremely persistent might not be as damaging a criticism of two-process theory as was first assumed.

Researchers, however, also discovered a second, more serious difficulty with two-process theory. They found that, after repeated avoidance trials, animals appeared to show no evidence of fear but continued to make the avoidance response anyway (R. L. Solomon & Wynne, 1953). In other words, once the animals had become adept at making the avoidance response, they seemed to become almost nonchalant and relaxed while carrying it out. This constituted a major problem for two-process theory: If the animals are no longer afraid of the CS, how can avoidance of the CS be negatively reinforced by a reduction in fear?

This was a pretty damaging criticism, and for a while it looked as though two-process theory was pretty much on the ropes. Levis (1989), however, has argued that although animals in avoidance experiments may become significantly *less* fearful with experience, there is no evidence that they become completely nonfearful. In fact, evidence suggests that if an animal completely loses its fear of the aversive CS, then, just as two-process theory predicts, the avoidance response ceases to occur. But as long as some fear remains, the avoidance response continues, suggesting that fear reduction is still functioning as a negative reinforcer for the behavior (Levis & Boyd, 1979).

Other theories have also been proposed to account for avoidance behavior. According to *one-process theory*, for example, the act of avoidance is negatively reinforced simply by the lower rate of aversive stimulation with which it is associated (Herrnstein, 1969; Herrnstein & Hineline, 1966). Thus, the rat in a shuttle avoidance task persistently climbs over the barrier when the light comes on because this action results in a decreased rate of shock, and not because it results in decreased feelings of fear. The attractive aspect of this theory is that it does away with any reference to an internal state of fear, the existence of which has to be inferred. The overall reduction in aversive stimulation that accompanies avoidance is regarded as a sufficient explanation for the behavior. (See Domjan, 2015, for an overview of different theories of avoidance.)

The debate over which processes underlie avoidance behavior will likely continue for some time. At the very least, avoidance behavior is turning out to be more complicated than researchers originally suspected. Fortunately,

---

[1]According to Eysenck's (1968) theory of incubation (discussed in Chapter 5), such brief exposures might also strengthen a conditioned fear response, which would further counteract the process of extinction.

the knowledge gained from all this theorizing and research is proving to have practical application, particularly in the analysis and treatment of anxiety disorders, a topic to which we turn next.

QUICK QUIZ C

1. One apparent problem with two-process theory is that, even after hundreds of trials, the avoidance response does not seem to ______________.
2. However, according to the anx______________ c______________ hypothesis, avoidance responses usually occur so (quickly/slowly) that exposures to the (CS/US) are too (long/brief) for ______________ to take place.
3. A second problem with Mowrer's theory is that after sufficient experience with avoiding the aversive CS, the animals no longer show any ______________, yet they continue to make the avoidance response. Levis, however, contends that such animals are nevertheless still (slightly/strongly) fearful, otherwise the avoidance response would extinguish.
4. According to the one-process theory of avoidance, the avoidance response is negatively reinforced by a reduction in overall rate of av______________ stimulation, as opposed to a reduction in ______________.

Avoidance Conditioning and Phobias

In Chapter 5, we noted that the basis of many phobias is the development of a classically conditioned fear response, which then fails to extinguish because the individual avoids the feared stimulus. At that time, we focused on the classical conditioning aspect of a phobia. Let us now examine the role of avoidance learning in phobic development.

As noted, avoidance learning appears to be a fundamental process in the development and maintenance of phobic behavior. This is no doubt one reason for the intense interest researchers have shown in studying avoidance. Indeed, demonstrations of avoidance learning in laboratory rats have often been regarded as applicable to phobic conditioning in humans. But is avoidance conditioning in the laboratory a true analogue of human phobic conditioning? Does a rat avoid shock in a shuttle avoidance procedure in the same manner that a person avoids dogs after being bitten? In fact, some have argued that there are considerable differences between avoidance conditioning in an experimental setting and human phobic conditioning.

Mineka (1985), for example, has claimed that there are limitations in applying models of experimental avoidance to human phobias. For example, *experimental avoidance in animals seems to condition less readily than phobic avoidance in humans.* Experimental avoidance typically requires at least a few pairings of the CS and the US (e.g., light and shock) before avoidance has been reliably established, and even then is usually less than 100% certain. For example, in a shuttle avoidance task, the rat will occasionally be tardy in climbing over the barrier, with the result that it sometimes receives a shock. By contrast, human phobias often require only a single, brief conditioning trial to produce avoidance that is both strong and persistent. It might take only a single dog attack for a person to develop a dog phobia, and they will consistently avoid dogs thereafter.

QUICK QUIZ D

1. According to Mineka, a limitation of applying experimental models of avoidance to phobias is that experimental avoidance conditions (more/less) readily than does phobic avoidance.
2. Experimental avoidance often requires (one/a few) conditioning trial(s), while phobic avoidance usually requires ______________ conditioning trial(s); additionally, (experimental/phobic) avoidance is less than 100% certain.

In response to Mineka's (1985) concerns about the applicability of experimental avoidance conditioning to human phobias, Stampfl (1987) proposed that an adequate experimental analogue of a human phobia would, among other things, require the reliable establishment of a fear response with only a single, brief pairing of the CS and US and the occurrence of avoidance on 100% of trials. Stampfl acknowledged that when using these criteria the typical avoidance-conditioning procedure is an inadequate analogue of human phobic conditioning. He then devised an experimental procedure that produced avoidance conditioning that met these criteria.

Stampfl's (1987) procedure focuses on the fact that people with phobias typically make the avoidance response early in the chain of events leading up to the feared stimulus. For example, a person with an elevator phobia will plan his day well ahead of time so that he will not be faced with any pressure to take an elevator. He may, for example, arrange an appointment with a dentist whose office is on the main floor of an office building. This type of planning is important because not doing so could result in a direct encounter with a phobic stimulus, which in turn could greatly increase the cost involved in avoiding it (such as by having to climb the stairs to get to a dentist's office on the 23rd floor). Thus, *the phobic individual learns to make the avoidance response early in the chain of events so as to minimize the effort of avoiding.*

The opportunity to make an early avoidance response is typically absent from most experimental avoidance procedures. Stampfl, however, designed an apparatus that provided just such an opportunity. As depicted in Figure 9.2, the apparatus consisted of an alleyway that was 5 feet in length and contained a dark compartment at one end. Each rat was first allowed to explore the alleyway at its leisure, during which time it came to strongly prefer the black compartment (rats generally prefer the dark). The rat was then given a foot shock while in the black compartment, at which point it fled to the far end of the alleyway. Three minutes later, a conveyor belt was turned on that began to slowly carry the rat toward the dark compartment. During this first trial, most rats waited until they reached the black sidewall area of the apparatus before running back to the far end. When they did run back to the far end, they broke a photobeam that stopped

FIGURE 9.2 Illustration of a 5-foot automated alleyway similar to the one used by Stampfl (1987).

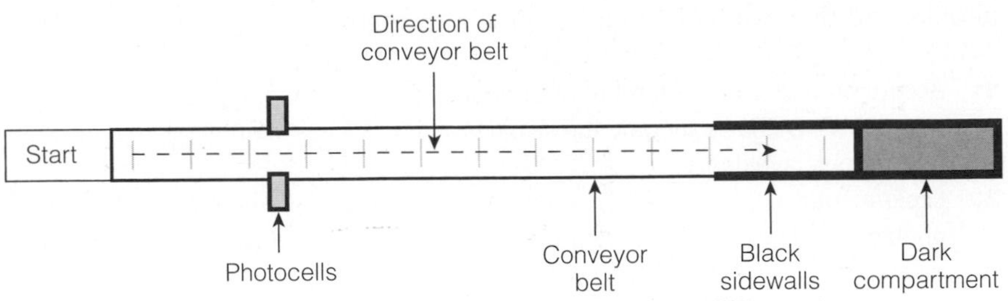

the conveyor belt for a 3-minute period. The conveyor belt then started up again, and the procedure was repeated. This initial session lasted 2 hours. During the second session, the response requirement for stopping the conveyor belt was increased from FR 1 to FR 10 (i.e., the rat had to run back and cross the photobeam 10 times before the conveyor belt would stop).

Stampfl (1987) found that the rats soon learned to run back to the safe area immediately after the conveyor belt started up. In other words, rather than waiting until they reached the black sidewalls before running back, they began running back after traveling only a short distance. In this manner, they were able to minimize the effort involved in breaking the photobeam and stopping the belt. Moreover, under these circumstances, the rats completely avoided entering the black compartment on more than 1,000 consecutive trials, thereby consistently avoiding the aversive CS that was associated with shock. Furthermore, this persistent avoidance response resulted from only a single brief exposure to shock.

In summary, Stampfl's results seem to confirm that a critical factor in the maintenance of phobic behavior is that the avoidance response occurs early in the sequence of events leading up to the phobic stimulus, thereby minimizing the effort involved in avoiding the stimulus. Such early responding greatly reduces the extent to which the avoidance response can be extinguished, because the individual experiences little or no exposure to the aversive CS. In terms of the anxiety conservation hypothesis discussed earlier, exposure to the aversive stimulus is so minimal that the avoidance response is extremely resistant to extinction. It is therefore not surprising that phobic behaviors are often extremely persistent.

QUICK QUIZ E

1. A critical aspect of Stampfl's experimental analogue of phobic conditioning is that the avoidance response can occur (early/late) in the sequence of events leading up to the feared CS, thereby (maximizing/minimizing) the amount of effort involved in making the response.
2. This results in (little/considerable) exposure to the feared CS, thereby greatly (increasing/reducing) the likelihood that the fear response will e____________.

Avoidance Conditioning and Obsessive-Compulsive Disorder

Phobia is one type of disorder in which avoidance conditioning plays a critical role. Another is *obsessive-compulsive disorder* (OCD), a disorder characterized by persistent thoughts, impulses, or images (called obsessions), and repetitive, stereotyped actions (called compulsions) that are carried out in response to the obsessions. For example, a person might have an *obsessive* worry about contacting germs; this leads to a *compulsive* tendency to take a shower and clean the house many times each day. Or a person might have an obsessive worry about whether she locked her apartment door when she left that morning, which leads to a compulsive pattern of returning to the apartment several times a day to check it. Note that the person recognizes that the compulsive behavior is clearly excessive but nevertheless feels compelled to perform the action. (Interestingly, cleaning and checking are the two most common forms of compulsive behavior.)

OCD was once considered a particularly difficult disorder to treat. This changed when clinicians began analyzing OCD in terms of avoidance conditioning, especially Mowrer's two-process theory (Rachman & Hodgson, 1980). The applicability of this theory to OCD lies in the fact that obsessions and compulsions have opposite effects on anxiety. In general, *obsessions are associated with an increase in anxiety, whereas compulsions are associated with a decrease in anxiety*. For example, a person who has a contamination fear and is a compulsive cleaner usually experiences an increase in anxiety after exposure to situations in which "contamination" might have occurred, such as when taking out the garbage. Garbage elicits such strong anxiety that any part of the body that has touched garbage also elicits anxiety. Taking a shower, however, results in the removal of this anxiety. From the perspective of two-process theory, the feeling of anxiety is a classically conditioned response elicited by contact with the garbage, while showering is an operant response that is negatively reinforced by a reduction in anxiety.

The role of avoidance in OCD is virtually the same as in phobic behavior, except that OCD typically involves an active avoidance response while phobic behavior typically involves a passive avoidance response. That is, a person with OCD will generally *do* something in order to reduce anxiety (such as showering), while a person with a phobia will generally *not do* something in order to reduce anxiety (such as not go near a dog). Nevertheless, individuals with OCD can also utilize passive avoidance responses (e.g., by avoiding garbage whenever possible) such that some of their behavior patterns can also be characterized as phobic.

Two-process theory helped clarify our understanding of OCD and led to the development of the first effective treatment for the disorder. If a compulsive behavior pattern (such as excessive washing) is maintained by avoidance of an anxiety-arousing event (such as contact with germs), then preventing the avoidance response from occurring should result in the eventual extinction of anxiety. This treatment method is known as ***exposure and response prevention (ERP)***, a method of treating OCD that involves prolonged exposure to the anxiety-arousing event while not engaging in the compulsive behavior pattern that reduces the anxiety (e.g., Steketee & Foa, 1985). As with recent versions of exposure-based treatments for phobic behavior, ERP combines the graduated exposure of systematic desensitization with the prolonged exposure of flooding therapy. For example, a compulsive cleaner might be required to first touch objects associated with slight anxiety (such as door handles and hand rails), then objects associated with moderate anxiety (such as garbage cans and dogs), and finally objects associated with intense anxiety (such as dead birds and dog excrement). These graduated exposures are first carried out imaginally—given that the person has good imagery ability—and then *in vivo*—given that live exposure to the anxiety-arousing event is practical. The exposures are also relatively long, often 90 minutes or more, to ensure sufficient time for the anxiety to begin to extinguish. In addition to scheduled treatment sessions, the client is told to practice exposures at home. The client is also told not to perform any compulsive behavior patterns; for example, a compulsive washer might be instructed to avoid all nonessential showers except for one 10-minute shower every 5 days! Once the obsessive-compulsive pattern has been successfully eliminated, normal patterns of behavior are then reestablished (Steketee & Foa, 1985).

Although Mowrer's two-process theory has proven quite useful in enhancing our understanding and treatment of OCD, it does not provide an entirely adequate explanation for it (Steketee & Foa, 1985). For example, people with OCD are usually unable to recall any particular conditioning event that could account for the obsessional anxiety response. People who have a contamination fear, for example, typically do not recall, say, falling into a cesspool before the onset of the fear. On the other hand, onset of OCD does often coincide with a period of stress. One possibility, therefore, is that stress sensitizes certain individuals in such a way that normal concerns, such as those about cleanliness and safety, become greatly exaggerated. Thus, just as the process of selective sensitization might lead to the development of a phobia (as discussed in Chapter 5), so too it might lead to the development of OCD. Furthermore, just as genetic factors may predispose some people to develop a phobia (also discussed in Chapter 5), so too some people might have a genetic predisposition toward developing OCD (Billet, Richter, & Kennedy, 1998).

On a more cognitive level, people with OCD often hold the irrational belief that they should be in complete control of their thoughts—failing to realize that intrusive thoughts are not uncommon and that most people simply ignore them. In other words, they fail to realize that some thoughts are essentially respondents (reflexes) that are automatically elicited by certain stimuli, and that it is futile to try to control such thoughts. People with OCD also have a tendency to feel personally responsible for events that are highly improbable. They therefore carry out various safety actions, such as rechecking doors and stoves, that other people would not bother with (Salkovskis, 1998). Given the involvement of cognitive factors in OCD, attempts have been made to combine ERP with cognitive ther-

"I THINK I WAS BETTER OFF WHEN I WAS OBSESSIVE-COMPULSIVE."

apy on the assumption that directly modifying these false belief systems might enhance treatment. However, the specific efficacy of these cognitive interventions has not yet been firmly established, and ERP by itself remains the treatment of choice for OCD (Foa, Franklin, & Kozak, 1998; Tolin & Steketee, 2007).

QUICK QUIZ F

1. Janice continually worries that her alarm clock might not be set, and that she will wake up late for class. She therefore checks the alarm clock about 20 times each night before finally falling asleep. The persistent thoughts about the alarm clock not being set are classified as a(n) (compulsion/obsession) while the frequent checking of the clock is classified as a(n) ______________.
2. In general, (compulsions/obsessions) are associated with an increase in anxiety, whereas ______________ are associated with a decrease in anxiety.
3. From the perspective of two-process theory, this decrease in anxiety likely functions as a n______________ r______________ for the compulsive behavior.
4. Exposure and response prevention (ERP) therapy for OCD involves prolonged exposure to anxiety-arousing events while (engaging/not engaging) in the (obsessive/compulsive) behavior that serves to reduce the anxiety.
5. ERP is similar to systematic desensitization in that exposure to the anxiety-provoking event is usually (gradual/sudden). It is similar to flooding therapy in that exposure to the anxiety-provoking event is (brief/prolonged).

6. People with OCD are usually (able/unable) to recall a particular conditioning event that was the cause of the obsessional anxiety response. The disorder often arises, however, during times of s____________. This suggests that a process of s____________ may exacerbate normal concerns about cleanliness and safety.
7. People with OCD fail to realize that intrusive thoughts are (common/uncommon) and that such thoughts are often (controllable/uncontrollable). They also (take/fail to take) responsibility for highly (probable/improbable) events.
8. Some evidence suggests that cognitive interventions for OCD, when combined with ERP, provide (much/little) additional benefit.

And Furthermore

Approach-Avoidance Conflict (or "I Can't Believe I Volunteered for This!")

Given that avoidance behaviors can be so strong and persistent, you might wonder how it is that we sometimes commit ourselves to events that we later wish we had avoided. Why does Jan, for example, regularly agree to meet an old high school acquaintance for dinner when they have completely separate lives and almost nothing to talk about it (though Jan's acquaintance seems blissfully unaware of it).

These situations typically involve what is known as an *approach-avoidance conflict*, involving events that are in some ways rewarding and in some ways punishing, that is, the events have both appetitive and aversive aspects to them (Dollard & Miller, 1950). The critical factor governing this conflict is the manner in which distance affects the value of these different consequences. If you recall from Chapter 6, immediacy has a strong effect on the value of a reward, with immediate rewards typically being much stronger than delayed rewards. As it turns out, immediacy can have an even more powerful effect on punishers, with immediate punishers being far stronger than delayed punishers.

What this means is that when an event is still some distance away (in either time or space), the rewarding aspects of the event may outweigh the aversive aspects of the event. For this reason, agreeing to get up early on a Saturday morning to help a friend of a friend shingle his house can seem like a great idea when the event is still a week away. After all, you typically enjoy helping others and you need the exercise anyway. As time passes, however, the aversive aspects of an event may increase to the point of becoming considerably stronger than the rewarding aspects. Thus, on Saturday morning, you can't believe you ever made such a foolish promise; the aversive aspects of dragging yourself out of bed to do hours of free labor for a virtual stranger now greatly outweigh any rewards associated with it.

This pattern of behavior has been demonstrated in rats (see Dollard & Miller, 1950). Rats are first trained to run down an alleyway to obtain food in a goal box. On one trial, however, they also receive a shock in the goal box, as a result of which, on the next trial, they will very likely run partway to the goal and then stop. In the start box, the possibility of obtaining food outweighs the possibility of a shock and the rats are motivated to run forward; but as they near the goal box, the possibility of receiving a shock now becomes dominant. In other words, far from the goal, the appetitive aspects outweigh the aversive aspects; near to the goal, the aversive aspects outweigh the appetitive aspects.

This process may also account for why some couples repeatedly break up and then get back together again. They originally broke up because the aversive aspects of the relationship were beginning to outweigh the rewarding aspects. After breaking up, however—in which case they are now more "distant" from each other—the rewarding aspects of the relationship come to the fore. They think more often about the good times they had together and begin to lament ever having broken up. But if they get back together again, the aversive aspects now become salient, and they then break up again. Some couples can spend years vacillating back and forth through this cycle. Fortunately, the extent to which a relationship is rewarding versus punishing is, for various reasons, always shifting about, as a result of which the relationship usually resolves itself one way or the other.

Punishment

Escape and avoidance conditioning involves the strengthening of a behavior through the removal of an aversive stimulus. By contrast, punishment involves the weakening of a behavior through the application of an aversive stimulus or the removal of an appetitive stimulus. In this section, we discuss various types of punishment, as well various concerns about the application of punishment. We also briefly describe various theories of punishment.

Types of Punishment

Let us begin by reviewing the basic distinction between positive and negative punishment. *Positive punishment consists of the presentation of a certain event following a response, which then leads to a decrease in the future strength of that response.* In simple everyday terms, the behavior results in the delivery of something the person or animal hates, so the subject is less likely to behave that way in the future. Receiving a spanking for swearing and being reprimanded for talking back to the boss are both examples of positive punishment (given that these consequences result in a subsequent decrease in the frequency of these behaviors).

By contrast, negative punishment consists of the removal of a certain event following a response, which then leads to a decrease in the future strength of that response. In everyday terms, the behavior results in the removal of something the person or animal likes, so the subject is less likely to behave that way in the future. A loss of employment for being obnoxious and a loss of dessert for complaining at the dinner table are both examples of negative punishment (again, given that the consequence results in a subsequent decrease in such behavior). Note that the events being removed are pleasant events that can typically serve as positive reinforcers; thus, negative punishment can also be defined as the loss of a positive reinforcer (a pleasant event) following a response.

There are two basic types of negative punishment: time-out and response cost. ***Time-out*** involves the loss of access to positive reinforcers for a brief period of time following the occurrence of a problem behavior. Time-out has become popular with modern-day parents, who frequently attempt to punish a child's misbehavior by sending the child to the bedroom or by making her sit in a corner for several minutes. Unfortunately, time-out procedures are often poorly applied, with the result that they have little effect on the problem behavior. For example, time-out is likely to be ineffective if the time-out setting is actually more reinforcing than the setting from which the child was removed. In fact, sending a child to her room for acting out at the dinner table might reinforce rather than punish the behavior of acting out if the child dislikes sitting at the dinner table. Another problem is that parents often use time-outs that are too long. The purpose of time-out is not to get the child "out of your hair" for a period of time but to facilitate the development of more appropriate behaviors. Those appropriate behaviors need to be reinforced, which cannot be done if the child is sitting in her room for hours on end. Time-out periods should therefore be quite brief, especially for young children. In fact, a time-out period as short as a minute may be all that is required to effectively suppress the unwanted behavior, especially if one immediately sets out to reinforce more appropriate behaviors as soon as the child is returned to the normal setting (Miltenberger, 2012).

The other type of negative punishment is ***response cost***, which is the removal of a specific reinforcer following the occurrence of a problem behavior. Receiving a fine (which involves the loss of money) for speeding or taking a child's toys away for playing aggressively are examples of response cost. An advantage of a response cost procedure is that one can easily adjust the severity of the punishment to suit the behavior being punished. Slight aggression with a younger sibling could result in the loss of dessert, while more severe aggression could result in the loss of dessert as well as the opportunity to watch television that evening. A drawback to response cost, however, is that you must clearly identify a reinforcer that, if removed, will have an impact on behavior. It therefore requires a more careful analysis of the situation than a time-out procedure does. (See Miltenberger, 2012, for a more complete discussion of time-out and response cost procedures.)

Note that negative punishment is quite different from extinction, even though both involve the removal of reinforcers and both result in a decrease in the strength of a behavior. In the case of extinction, a behavior that used to produce a reinforcer no longer does, and the person therefore stops performing the behavior. If Jason used to receive cookies as a result of whining, but he no longer receives cookies by whining, then he will eventually stop whining. In the case of negative punishment, however, performing the behavior results in the loss of a reinforcer that the person would otherwise possess. Imagine, for example, that Jason has already received some cookies but then starts whining for a soda pop. If each time he whines, one of his cookies is taken away, then he is likely to stop whining. Thus, to distinguish between extinction and negative punishment, ask yourself whether the behavior grows weaker because *performing the behavior no longer leads to something* (in which case, the process is *extinction*) or because *performing the behavior leads to the removal of something that you would otherwise possess* (in which case the process is *negative punishment*).

QUICK QUIZ G

1. When the cat sat at your feet and meowed annoyingly during breakfast one morning, you sprayed it with water. As a result, the cat did not come near the table or meow the next time you sat down for a meal. The consequence for the cat's meowing consisted of the (presentation/removal) of a stimulus, and the cat's behavior subsequently (decreased/increased) in frequency. Therefore, this is an example of ______________ ______________.
2. Negative punishment involves the (presentation/removal) of a stimulus following a response that subsequently results in a(n) (increase/decrease) in the likelihood of that response occurring again.
3. When Bobbi threw a temper tantrum, her mother turned off the television program that Bobbi was watching. Bobbi's mother is applying a (response cost/time-out) procedure.
4. When Bobbi threw a temper tantrum, Bobbi's mother made her sit in the corner for a minute. Bobbi's mother is applying a (response cost/time-out) procedure.
5. A(n) (advantage/disadvantage) of a time-out procedure is that one (does/does not) have to clearly identify a specific reinforcer before implementing the procedure. A(n) (advantage/disadvantage) of a response cost procedure is that one (can/cannot) easily modify the severity of the punishment to suit the behavior.
6. When Val began whining, her mother immediately stopped playing with her and left the room. Val quickly stopped whining. This is an example of (extinction/negative punishment).
7. Val's mother used to play with Val whenever she whined but then stopped doing so. As a result, Val's whining soon ceased. This is an example of (extinction/negative punishment).
8. If the frequency of a behavior decreases because performing the behavior no longer leads to something, the process involved is (extinction/negative punishment). If the frequency of a behavior decreases because performing the behavior leads to the removal of something, the process involved is (extinction/negative punishment).

Punishment can also be differentiated in other ways. For example, just as one can distinguish between intrinsic and extrinsic reinforcement, one can distinguish between intrinsic and extrinsic punishment. ***Intrinsic punishment*** is punishment that is an inherent aspect of the behavior being punished. In other words, the activity itself is punishing, such that the person performing the behavior is now less likely to repeat it. Doing push-ups is intrinsically punishing if you stop doing push-ups in the future because of the effort involved. ***Extrinsic punishment*** is punishment that is not an inherent aspect of the behavior being punished, but simply follows the behavior. In other words, the activity is followed by a separate event that serves to punish the activity. Being chastised after lighting up a cigarette ("Are you still indulging in that filthy habit?") is extrinsically punishing if it subsequently reduces how frequently you smoke.

One can also distinguish between primary and secondary punishers. A ***primary (or unconditioned) punisher*** is an event that is innately punishing. Loosely speaking, these are events that we are born to dislike. Electric shock, intense heat, and loud noise are examples of primary punishers. A ***secondary (or conditioned) punisher*** is an event that has become punishing because it has in the past been associated with some other punisher. For example, if shock is an effective punisher, then a tone that has been paired with shock in a classical conditioning procedure:

Tone: Shock → *Fear*
NS US UR

Tone → *Fear*
CS CR

will become a conditioned aversive stimulus that can then be used as a secondary punisher. For example, presentation of the tone could now be used to punish wheel running:

Running in a wheel **→ Tone**
R $\mathbf{S^P}$

Human behavior is often under the control of secondary punishers. A traffic ticket might effectively punish our tendency to speed, and an icy stare from our partner might effectively punish our tendency to drink too much at a party. Both the fine and the stare are punishing because they have been associated with other types of aversive events: loss of money in the one case and heated arguments in the other.

A special type of secondary punisher is a ***generalized (or generalized secondary) punisher***, which is an event that has become punishing because it has in the past been associated with many other punishers. The icy stare is probably best categorized as a generalized punisher because disapproving looks have no doubt been associated with numerous unpleasant events such as reprimands as a child, marital arguments as an adult, and disciplinary action during one's stint in the army.

QUICK QUIZ H

1. Exercising to the point of exhaustion is for many people likely to be an (extrinsically/intrinsically) punishing event.
2. The bad taste of rotting food will likely, for most people, function as a (primary/secondary) punisher, while being taken to a restaurant that has served such food will function as a ____________ punisher.
3. Looking at an old photo album reminds you of your loneliness as a child, the loss of a favorite pet, and a childhood friend who died. As a result, you stop looking at it. The old photo album can be classified as a g ____________ punisher.

Problems with the Use of Punishment

Although many people believe that behaviorists promote the use of punishment, behaviorists in fact have a general bias against it. This bias results from several problems that are associated with punishment (e.g., Newsom, Favell, & Rincover, 1983; Van Houten, 1983):

1. *Punishment of maladaptive behavior doesn't directly strengthen the occurrence of adaptive behavior*, which is what one typically hopes to achieve. Punishing the act of playing aggressively with other children will not automatically result in the child playing more cooperatively.
2. *Punishing one behavior may simply result in a generalized suppression of other behaviors.* A child who has been punished for playing aggressively will not necessarily begin playing more cooperatively; she might instead simply stop playing with other children, which is not at all what was intended.
3. *The person delivering the punishment could become an S^D for punishment, with the result that the unwanted behavior is selectively suppressed only when that person is present.* The child, for example, might come to view the father as a discriminative stimulus for punishment and therefore continue to misbehave when the father is absent. The child has thus learned not to get caught misbehaving, rather than not to misbehave.
4. *Punishment might simply teach the individual to avoid the person who delivered the punishment.* A child who is severely punished by her father might begin minimizing the time she spends with her father. This would obviously be less than ideal, especially if the father has much to offer the child.
5. *Punishment is likely to elicit a strong emotional response.* This is especially the case with the use of positive punishment, such as spanking or yelling, which is likely to result in crying or other displays of distress. These strong emotional responses are not only unpleasant but will also interfere with any subsequent attempt to teach the child more appropriate behavior. A child who is crying uncontrollably is not in an ideal state for learning anything new, such as how to play appropriately.
6. *Punishment can sometimes elicit an aggressive reaction.* Earlier in this text, we mentioned how a painful stimulus, such as electric shock, can elicit attack behavior in rats. Humans can also react with anger when subjected to aversive stimulation. This anger can be directed toward the individual responsible for the aversive event or, if there are inhibitions about doing so, can be directed toward a substitute target. Thus, a child who is severely punished for being noisy might not aggress toward the parent who spanked her but instead aggress toward her younger sibling when the parents have left the room.
7. *The use of punishment, through the process of modeling, could teach the person that punishment is an acceptable means of controlling behavior.* As a

result, children whose behavior is being controlled through the use of punishment may themselves begin punishing others to control the behavior of others.

8. *Because punishment often has an immediate effect in stopping an unwanted behavior, the use of punishment is often strongly reinforced.* If hitting one's children has the immediate effect of getting them to stop making noise (an immediate negative reinforcer), then the behavior of hitting them has been strongly reinforced. The use of punishment can therefore be quite seductive, enticing the parent to use it more and more frequently, possibly to the point of becoming abusive.

QUICK QUIZ I

1. Punishment, especially (positive/negative) punishment, can often elicit a strong e____________ reaction. This reaction might include ____________ that, if not directed toward the punisher, might be directed toward a substitute target.
2. Punishment of an inappropriate behavior (will/will not) directly strengthen the occurrence of an appropriate behavior. It might even result in a g____________ suppression of behavior.
3. The use of punishment could, through the process of m____________, teach the recipient that punishment is an acceptable means for modifying a person's behavior. Yelling at your dog for chewing your slippers might teach the dog to avoid ____________ rather than the slippers. Yelling at your dog for chewing your slippers might also teach your dog not to chew the slippers only when ____________.
4. If punishment has an i____________ effect in getting someone to stop annoying us, this result can then act as a strong n____________ r____________ for using punishment in the future.

Study Tip: Punishment may also play a role in the tendency to procrastinate. For example, Robert Boice (e.g., 1989, 1996) has conducted detailed analyses of the work habits of faculty members, distinguishing those who are productive writers from those who are not (the writing of articles and books arguably being one of the most challenging tasks professors face). A major finding was that productive faculty tended to engage in short, consistent writing sessions spread throughout the week, while nonproductive faculty tended to engage in intermittent "binge" episodes of writing spread far apart—that is, they frequently procrastinated, and then, when they did write, they wrote intensively for long periods of time. Although the procrastinators believed that long, intense writing sessions were necessary to be productive, Boice concluded that binge writing itself was part of the problem. However invigorated one might feel during an intense session of writing—and procrastinators often reported this—this pattern of work is so effortful that one soon starts to avoid it. In essence, *binge writing sessions are sufficiently aversive that they punish the act of writing.* This can then set up (as discussed earlier in this chapter) an approach-avoidance conflict in which a professor may have the best of intentions to work on the writing each day or week but continually find last-minute excuses to avoid doing so.

Based on these results, Boice devised workshops to help professors overcome their tendency to procrastinate. A major component of these workshops is to learn to write in brief daily sessions, perhaps only 30 minutes per day at first, with the act of stopping on time considered as important as starting on time. The goal is to break the tendency to engage in binge writing sessions and to begin to experience writing as less aversive and more enjoyable. Combined with other tactics, such as establishing a balanced lifestyle, arranging a comfortable (nonaversive) writing environment, and seeking out mentors for feedback, these workshops have proven to be very effective in helping many faculty members become more productive.

Although Boice's advice is directed toward faculty, it has obvious implications for students. Students should seriously consider the benefits of engaging in shorter, more consistent study sessions throughout the semester (though, for most students, a certain amount of cramming around deadline dates and exam time is probably unavoidable). Consider too that if you study just one extra hour per weekday in, say, the first 8 weeks of the semester—during which time many students do only minimal studying—this will add up to 40 extra hours of studying. This is a whopping amount of studying, especially if it is high-quality studying, and would very likely have a significant impact on your grades. You should also consider systematically breaking up long study sessions into a series of brief sessions with frequent breaks for rest and recuperation. (In this regard, some people find it useful to use a timer to strengthen the amount of stimulus control over the behavior. One example of this, widely discussed on the Internet, is the "Pomodoro Technique": e.g., http://en.wikipedia.org/wiki/Pomodoro_Technique).[2]

[2]Another excellent (and very readable) book on how to become a more productive writer is *How to Write a Lot: A Practical Guide to Productive Academic Writing* by Paul J. Silvia (2007). Silvia is himself a psychologist, and the book is directed specifically toward psychology faculty and students. Silvia does a particularly good job of demolishing the typical excuses for not writing, such as needing to "find time" to write (nice try, but time is not lost and does not need finding; you need to *schedule time* for writing just like you schedule time for work and for school). The book is also written from an explicitly behavioral perspective, with practical advice on such things as the importance of establishing clear goals, the usefulness of tracking one's progress, and the benefits of self-reinforcement.

Benefits and the Effective Use of Punishment

For the reasons outlined previously, most behaviorists tend to avoid or minimize the use of punishment. Nevertheless, there may be some circumstances in which punishment is judged appropriate, such as in quickly suppressing a potentially dangerous behavior in a young child (e.g., stopping a child from jabbing at another child's face with a sharpened pencil). This is especially the case given that alternative interventions, such as extinction and reinforcement of other behaviors, often take considerable time to have an effect. In addition to quickly suppressing a particular behavior pattern, punishment can also have some beneficial side effects (e.g., Newsom et al., 1983; Van Houten, 1983):

1. *Punishment can sometimes lead to an increase in social behavior.* For example, a young child who has been scolded for playing aggressively with

his sister may become more affectionate toward his sister when the time-out period has ended. Thus, although punishment does not directly teach more appropriate behaviors, such behaviors may sometimes arise as a side effect. Why would such increases in social behavior occur? One possibility is that punishment may activate an innate tendency in humans to become more sociable in an effort to restore one's relationship with others.

2. *Paradoxically, punishment sometimes results in an improvement in mood, such as less crying.* This is the opposite of what one would usually expect, which is that punishment would lead to more emotional behavior, not less. In some cases, however, it may be that the child was misbehaving because he or she was in some way agitated; in such cases, the punishment might distract the child and disrupt the agitation.
3. *Punishment can increase attention to the environment,* as shown by increased eye contact and interest in ongoing activities. Shouting at a child, for example, might motivate the child to become more vigilant. This can be especially valuable with children who tend to pay little attention to what is happening around them.

In summary, under some circumstances, the application of punishment may be justified and beneficial. If punishment is used, however, the following requirements should be met to maximize the possibility that it will be effective.

1. *As much as possible, punishment should be immediate rather than delayed.* Unfortunately, in the real world, delayed punishment is often the rule rather than the exception. A child's misbehavior is frequently discovered only several minutes or hours after its occurrence, and the delivery of a reprimand following such a long delay may have little effect. This is particularly the case with very young children and animals who, because they are unable to understand explanations, are unlikely to associate the punishment with the unwanted behavior. For example, yelling at a dog for making a mess on the carpet several hours after the incident has occurred will probably only upset the animal and do little to prevent future mishaps.
2. *At least at the outset, punishment should consistently follow each occurrence of the unwanted behavior.* Punishment tends to be less effective in suppressing a behavior when only some instances of the unwanted behavior are punished. In other words, unlike intermittent reinforcement, which has a strong effect on behavior, intermittent punishment tends to have a weak effect on behavior. Nevertheless, once the behavior has been effectively suppressed through consistent punishment, then intermittent punishment may be sufficient to maintain the suppression, especially if nonpunished occurrences of the maladaptive behavior are not being intermittently reinforced (Clark, Rowbury, Baer, & Baer, 1973).
3. *Punishment should be intense enough from the outset to suppress the target behavior* (though—and this is the tricky part—not so intense as to be

unnecessarily abusive). If one begins with a very mild punisher that is ineffective, and then gradually increases the intensity, it might require a very intense punisher to eventually suppress the unwanted behavior. For example, N. E. Miller (1960) presented rats with a very mild shock whenever they entered an alleyway, and then gradually increased the intensity of the shock until the rats eventually ceased entering the alleyway. He found that the behavior ceased only with high levels of shock, far beyond what would normally have been required to suppress such a behavior. Likewise, a father who initially uses a very mild reprimand to try to get his daughter to stop teasing the dog, and then gradually increases the severity of the reprimand, might eventually have to deliver a very severe reprimand or worse before she will comply. But if the father had started with a moderately severe reprimand, the daughter might have immediately complied, thereby saving the two of them (as well as the dog) a lot of grief. By starting with such a mild intervention and then gradually increasing its severity, the father essentially allowed the daughter to adapt to the punishing stimulus.

4. *Negative punishment is generally preferable to positive punishment.* Negative punishment procedures, such as time-out and response cost, are generally less likely to produce many of the harmful side effects associated with punishment as opposed to positive punishment procedures such as spanking and yelling. Negative punishment can, nevertheless, become abusive, such as when children are forced to endure extremely long time-out periods or are exposed to severe response cost procedures, such as removal of sufficient food.
5. *With individuals who have language capacity, punishment is more effective when accompanied by an explanation.* A possible reason for this is that an explanation will help clarify the exact behavior that is being punished, thereby making it easier for the child to avoid punishment in the future. This accords with the more general recommendation that children should be given frequent feedback about their behavior, both good and bad, because this will greatly facilitate the children's attempts to learn appropriate behavior (Craig, Kermis, & Digdon, 1998).
6. *Punishment of inappropriate behavior should be combined with positive reinforcement for appropriate behavior.* This is perhaps the most important rule. As with extinction, punishment of unwanted behavior will be more effective if it is combined with differential reinforcement for other behavior, especially behavior that is incompatible with the target behavior. As the appropriate behavior is strengthened, it will come to supplant the inappropriate behavior. Thus, applying a time-out period to a child for playing inappropriately might have little effect if the child's behavior of playing appropriately has not been adequately reinforced. Time-out periods should, therefore, be followed by abundant reinforcement for appropriate behavior. In fact, differential reinforcement of appropriate behavior (which might include

functional communication training as discussed in Chapter 8) should always be considered the primary tool for eliminating unwanted behaviors. (For a complete discussion of issues involved in the punishment of human behavior, see Axelrod & Apsche, 1983.)

QUICK QUIZ J

1. Beneficial side effects of punishment include increases in s__________ behavior, improvements in m__________, and increased a__________ to the environment.
2. With verbally proficient humans, punishment tends to be more effective when it is accompanied by an e__________.
3. In general, when implementing a punishment procedure, one should begin with a punisher of sufficient i__________ to suppress the behavior.
4. Unlike reinforcement, punishment tends to have a stronger impact on behavior if delivered (consistently/intermittently).
5. In general, when attempting to punish a maladaptive behavior, one should also attempt to __________ more adaptive behavior.
6. If punishment is to be used, it should be im__________, since d__________ punishment tends to be relatively ineffective.
7. In general, (positive/negative) punishment is preferred insofar as it is likely to have (more/fewer) side effects.

Theories of Punishment

Although a good deal of research has gone into investigating the effectiveness of punishment, less attention has been paid to developing and testing various theories of punishment. We will nevertheless briefly consider three theoretical approaches to punishment.

Conditioned Suppression Theory This theory is based on early work by Skinner (1938). He found that although punishment can quickly suppress a behavior, the behavior often quickly recovers when the punishment is withdrawn. What Skinner (1953) assumed was happening was that punishment generates an emotional response that tends to suppress any ongoing appetitive behavior. Crudely put, when the rat is shocked for pressing a lever that produces food, it becomes so upset that it loses interest in the food and therefore does not press the lever to obtain it. If, however, the shock is withdrawn, the rat resumes lever pressing as soon as it calms down enough for its interest in food to be revived. By analogy, if Tyler no longer teases his sister after being scolded for doing so, it is simply because he is too upset to pay much attention to his sister. Thus, the ***conditioned suppression theory of punishment*** assumes that punishment does not weaken a behavior but instead produces an emotional response that interferes with the occurrence of the behavior.

The temporary effect that Skinner (1938) found when he attempted to punish a rat's behavior led him to conclude that punishment is an ineffective means for producing a lasting change in behavior. Skinner's experiment, however, utilized a relatively weak form of punishment: a device that slapped the rat on the paw when it attempted to press a lever. Subsequent research revealed that more intense forms of punishment, such as strong electric shocks, are capable of suppressing behavior for much longer periods of time (Azrin & Holz, 1966).

Avoidance Theory of Punishment According to the ***avoidance theory of punishment***, punishment actually involves a type of avoidance conditioning in which the avoidance response consists of any behavior other than the behavior being punished (e.g., Dinsmoor, 1954). In other words, just as the behavior of jumping over a barrier is strengthened by shock avoidance in a shuttle avoidance situation, so too is the behavior of doing "anything other than lever pressing" reinforced by shock avoidance in a punishment-of-lever-pressing situation. Thus, in carrying out the following punishment procedure:

Lever press → **Shock**
R $\quad$ $\mathbf{S^P}$

one is actually carrying out the following avoidance conditioning procedure:

Any behavior other than lever pressing → **No Shock**
R $\quad$ $\mathbf{S^R}$

in which any behavior other than lever pressing is negatively reinforced by the absence of shock (e.g., Dinsmoor, 1954). Similarly, according to this theory, Tyler no longer teases his sister after being scolded for doing so because any behavior he carries out other than teasing his sister is negatively reinforced by the absence of a scolding. If correct, this means that punishment procedures are actually a form of negative reinforcement.

As with conditioned suppression theory, the avoidance theory of punishment assumes that punishment does not directly weaken a behavior. It simply replaces the punished behavior with an avoidance response of some sort. A disadvantage of this theory, however, is that it carries with it all of the theoretical difficulties associated with avoidance conditioning, some of which we discussed earlier in this chapter.

The Premack Approach to Punishment As you will recall from Chapter 7, the Premack principle holds that a high-probability behavior (HPB) can be used to reinforce a low-probability behavior (LPB). As it turns out, the opposite can be applied to punishment. According to the ***Premack principle of punishment***, an LPB can be used to punish an HPB (Premack, 1971a).

Take, for example, a rat that is both hungry and tuckered out from exercising. The rat in this condition is much more likely to eat food (an

HPB) than to run in a wheel (an LPB). In terms of the Premack principle of reinforcement, this means that the behavior of eating can be used as a reinforcer for the behavior of running in a wheel:

Running in a wheel (LPB) → **Eating food (HPB)**
R S^R

Conversely, according to the Premack principle of punishment, one can also use running in a wheel to punish the behavior of eating:

Eating food (HPB) → **Running in a wheel (LPB)**
R S^P

If eating food is followed by the consequence of being forced to run in a motorized wheel, the rat will be less likely to eat than if this consequence did not exist. To bring this point home, imagine how much easier it would be for a person who hates exercising to stick to a diet if he were forced to run a mile each time he ate something not on the diet.

Note that this approach implicitly assumes that punishment is the opposite of reinforcement: If reinforcement strengthens behavior, then punishment weakens behavior. In this sense, it differs from the previous two theories in that it views punishment as the mirror opposite of reinforcement. (See Domjan, 2015, for an extended discussion of theories of punishment.)

QUICK QUIZ K

1. According to the conditioned suppression theory of punishment, the application of punishment does not directly w__________ a behavior; instead, it produces an em__________ reaction that tends to interfere with ongoing behavior.
2. This theory was based on evidence by Skinner that punishment tends to produce a (temporary/permanent) effect. This effect, however, probably results from using relatively (strong/weak) forms of punishment.
3. According to the __________ theory of punishment, a rat stops lever pressing when lever pressing is followed by shock because the occurrence of any behavior other than lever pressing is n__________ r__________ by the nonoccurrence of shock.
4. According to the punishment version of the Premack principle, the occurrence of a __________-__________ behavior can be used to punish the occurrence of a __________-__________ behavior. This means that if Sally rarely washes dishes and often bites her nails, then the behavior of __________ __________ can be used to punish the occurrence of __________ __________.
5. According to the Premack principle, if running (an HPB) is followed by push-ups (an LPB), then running should (decrease/increase) in frequency, which is an instance of (reinforcement/punishment). If push-ups (LPB) are followed by running (HPB), then the push-ups should __________ in frequency, which is an instance of __________.

Noncontingent Punishment

In the typical escape/avoidance procedure, the aversive stimulus is controllable in the sense that the animal is able to make a response that significantly reduces its effect. Likewise, in a punishment procedure, the animal has some semblance of control because if it does not make the response, then it will not be punished. In both cases, some type of contingency exists. But what if such a contingency were absent? What if the aversive event was essentially uncontrollable (and even unpredictable), such that whatever you do, you are unable to influence your exposure to that event? In the same manner that noncontingent reinforcement has some unique effects on behavior (as discussed in Chapter 7), so too does noncontingent punishment. Let us examine some of these effects.

Learned Helplessness

Consider the following experiment by Seligman and Maier (1967). The experiment began with an initial phase in which dogs were suspended in a harness and exposed to one of three conditions. In an *inescapable-shock condition*, the dogs received a series of shocks but were unable to do anything about them. In an *escapable-shock condition*, the dogs received shocks but were able to terminate each shock by pressing a panel with their snout. Each dog in this condition was also *yoked to* (paired up with) a dog in the first condition, such that when it turned off the shock for itself, it also turned off the shock for its partner dog in the other condition. Thus, the only difference between these two dogs was that the dog in the escapable-shock condition had control over the shocks while the dog in the inescapable-shock condition did not. Finally, some dogs were in a *no-shock control condition*: These dogs were never shocked and simply waited out the session suspended in the harness.

In the next phase of the experiment, all of the dogs were exposed to a shuttle avoidance procedure in which the task was to learn to avoid shock by jumping over a barrier, each shock being preceded by a 10-second period of darkness. The dogs exposed to the no-shock control condition in the initial phase of the experiment soon learned to avoid the shock by jumping over the barrier during the period of darkness. The dogs exposed to the escapable-shock condition also learned the avoidance task quickly. The dogs from the inescapable-shock condition, however, behaved quite differently. When shocked, many of them initially ran around in great distress but then lay on the floor and whimpered. They made no effort to escape the shock. Even stranger, the few dogs that did by chance jump over the barrier, successfully escaping the shock, seemed unable to learn from this experience and failed to repeat it on the next trial. In summary, the prior exposure to inescapable shock seemed to impair the dogs' ability to learn to escape shock when escape later became possible. This phenomenon is known as ***learned helplessness***, a decrement in learning ability that results from repeated exposure to uncontrollable aversive events.

Seligman and Maier (1967) theorized that the dogs became helpless because they had learned during exposure to inescapable shock that any attempt to escape was useless—in other words, that there was a *lack of contingency* between making a response and achieving a certain outcome. As a result, when confronted with shock in a new situation, they simply gave up. Other researchers, however, have proposed alternative explanations. For example, one theory suggests that animals exposed to inescapable aversive stimulation are distressed, and because of this distress they have difficulty attending to the relationship between behavior and its outcomes. Evidence for this theory includes the fact that if animals are given a very salient feedback stimulus whenever they make a successful escape response, such as by sounding a loud bell, the learned helplessness effect may disappear and the animals may once more learn such tasks effectively (Maier, Jackson, & Tomie, 1987).

Learned helplessness may account for certain difficulties experienced by humans. For example, Dweck and Reppucci (1973) found that children who attempted to answer unsolvable problems later had considerable difficulty answering solvable problems. This suggests that children who have difficulty passing math exams in school, possibly because of poor teaching, might grow up to become "math-anxious" individuals who quickly give up when confronted by any sort of math problem. Learned helplessness may even be implicated in certain forms of depression (Seligman, 1975). People who suffer a series of uncontrollable aversive events—loss of a job, physical illness, divorce, and so on—may become extremely passive and despondent. Like animals exposed to inescapable shock, they show little interest in improving their lot in life. (See also the opening vignette to this chapter.)

Fortunately, researchers have discovered a way to eliminate learned helplessness. The helpless animal will eventually recover its ability to escape on its own if it is repeatedly forced to escape the aversive stimulus—for example, if it is repeatedly dragged from the shock side of the chamber to the no-shock side (Seligman & Maier, 1967; Seligman, Rosellini, & Kozak, 1975). In similar fashion, behavioral treatments for depression often involve encouraging the patient to accomplish a graded series of tasks, starting with relatively minor tasks, such as writing a letter, and progressing to more difficult tasks, such as seeking a new job (Seligman, 1975).

Research has also suggested a means for preventing the development of learned helplessness. Experiments have revealed that prior exposure to escapable shock often immunizes an animal against becoming helpless when it is later exposed to inescapable shock (Seligman et al., 1975); the animal will persist in trying to escape the shock rather than give up. This suggests that a history of successfully overcoming minor adversities might immunize a person against depression when the person is later confronted by more serious difficulties. As a tree is strengthened by exposure to winds strong enough to bend but not break its limbs, so too individuals seem to be strengthened by exposure to manageable amounts of misfortune.

QUICK QUIZ L

1. The original experiments on learned ____________ revealed that dogs that had first been exposed to inescapable shock had (no difficulty/difficulty) learning an escape response when later exposed to (escapable/inescapable) shock.
2. It seemed as though these dogs had learned that there (is/is not) a contingency between their behavior and the offset of shock.
3. This effect can be overcome by (forcing/enticing) the dogs to make an escape response. As well, dogs that have had previous exposure to escapable shock are (more/less) susceptible to becoming helpless when later exposed to inescapable shock.
4. Learned helplessness may account for various difficulties in humans, including the clinical disorder known as d____________.

Masserman's Experimental Neurosis

As you may recall, experimental neurosis is an *experimentally produced disorder in which animals exposed to unpredictable events develop neurotic-like symptoms.* We first encountered this phenomenon in our discussion of Pavlov's work on discrimination training in dogs (see Chapter 4). He and his colleagues discovered that dogs that had difficulty discriminating which cues predicted the delivery of food seemed to experience a nervous breakdown. Pavlov hypothesized that human neuroses might likewise develop as a result of exposure to unpredictable events.

A variation on Pavlov's procedure, involving the use of aversive rather than appetitive stimuli, was developed by Masserman (1943). He found that cats that experienced unpredictable electric shocks or blasts of air while eating often developed a pattern of neurotic-like symptoms. For example, normally quiet cats became restless and agitated, and normally active cats became withdrawn and passive—sometimes even to the point of becoming rigidly immobile (a symptom known as catalepsy). The cats also developed phobic responses to cues associated with feeding (since feeding had become associated with shock), as well as unusual "counterphobic" responses (e.g., a cat might run to the goal box, stick its head inside the box, and then simply stare at the experimenter—as though to say, "let's get it over with"). It generally took only two or three presentations of the aversive stimulus to elicit these symptoms, which might then last several months.

More recent work (but with rats, not cats) has shown that many of these symptoms are similar to those found in posttraumatic stress disorder (PTSD) in humans (e.g., Foa, Zinbarg, & Rothbaum, 1992). PTSD is a disorder that results from exposure to unpredictable life-threatening events, such as tornadoes, physical and sexual assaults, and battlefield experiences. Symptoms include sleep difficulties, exaggerated startle response, intrusive recollections about the trauma, and nightmares. As well, victims often demonstrate fear and avoidance of trauma-associated stimuli (phobias), as well as a general numbing of responsiveness (e.g., a restricted range of emotions). Although the subjective symptoms of PTSD, such as intrusive recollections, are impossible to replicate in animals (we have no idea what animals are actually thinking), many of the overt symptoms, such as phobic behavior, agitation, and passivity, are similar to those shown by animals subjected to noncontingent, unpredictable aversive stimulation.

Experimental neurosis is therefore proving to be a useful means for investigating the development of traumatic symptoms. For instance, as a general rule, traumatic symptoms are more easily induced in animals when the aversive stimulus is delivered in an environment that the animal has long associated with safety or some type of appetitive event. For example, unpredictable shocks delivered in a setting in which the animal typically eats food are especially likely to induce neurotic symptoms (Masserman, 1943). This suggests, for example, that symptoms of PTSD are more likely to arise when a person is unexpectedly attacked in the safety of his or her own home as opposed to a strange or dangerous area of town. The person who is attacked at home generalizes the experience and perceives the world as a dangerous, unpredictable place, with the result that he or she thereafter remains constantly vigilant (Foa et al., 1992).

You may be wondering how Masserman's experimental neurosis procedure differs from learned helplessness. The basic difference is that the typical learned helplessness procedure involves repeated exposure to aversive events that are predictable but uncontrollable. It is equivalent to being beaten up every day at 8:00 A.M. At first you try to escape from the beating, but eventually you give up any hope of escape. Masserman's experimental neurosis, on the other hand, involves infrequent but unpredictable exposure to aversive events. It is analogous to being unexpectedly dragged off every once in a while and beaten. The result is constant hypervigilance and an array of psychological and behavioral symptoms. But note that unpredictability also implies uncontrollability, so there is considerable overlap between the symptoms produced by learned helplessness and those produced by Masserman's experimental neurosis procedure (Foa et al., 1992).

QUICK QUIZ M

1. Experimental neurosis occurs when animals exposed to un____________ events develop neurotic-like symptoms.
2. In these situations, normally (quiet/active) cats became restless and agitated, whereas normally (quiet/active) cats became withdrawn and passive.
3. When food was paired with unpredictable shock, the cats also developed p____________ and counter____________ responses to the food.
4. Evidence suggests that neurotic symptoms are more likely to develop when the traumatic event occurs in an environment that a person generally regards as (safe/dangerous).
5. Learned helplessness results from repeated exposure to aversive events that are un____________; experimental neurosis results from exposure to events that are un____________.

ADVICE FOR THE LOVELORN

Dear Dr. Dee,

I am in a relationship that is starting to depress me, though most of what is happening is quite subtle. For example, when I'm really excited about something, my partner will usually act quite disinterested. Similarly, when I suggest doing something that I believe will be fun, she usually turns it down and suggests something else. She also gets snippy with me (or worse yet, gives me the silent treatment) at the most unexpected moments.

I have tried talking to her about it, but she says that I am overreacting and then points to how affectionate she usually is (which is true).

So Am I Overreacting?

Dear So,

It sounds like you are in a relationship where much of your behavior is being subtly punished, some of it on a noncontingent basis. Thus, you are starting to perceive that whatever you do makes little difference. So it is not surprising that you are becoming depressed. You need to calmly point out to your partner the damaging effects of what she is doing, and the extent to which it is making you depressed.

First, however, you might wish to examine your own behavior to see if you are doing something to reinforce this pattern of behavior in your partner. Relationship problems are usually a two-way street, with neither party solely responsible for the difficulty. For example, perhaps you acquiesce to your partner's wishes so often that you are essentially rewarding her for behaving this way. If that is the case, you may need to become a bit more assertive about your wishes. In fact, it could well be that she would be much happier if you were more assertive and your relationship with each other was more balanced.

Behaviorally yours,

Dr. Dee

And Furthermore

Dissociative Identity Disorder: A Behavioral Perspective

Some clinicians believe that the most severe disorder produced by trauma is dissociative identity disorder (DID; formerly called multiple personality disorder). The essential characteristic of this disorder is two or more personality states (or alter personalities) that repeatedly take control of behavior. Patients also suffer from extensive amnesia, with some personalities often unaware of the existence of other personalities. For example, in the classic case of Eve White (portrayed in the 1957 movie *The Three Faces of Eve*), the original personality of Eve White was reportedly unaware of an alter personality named Eve Black. Eve Black, however, was fully aware of Eve White and enjoyed making life difficult for her (Thigpen & Cleckley, 1957). The concept of DID is, however, extremely controversial.

Behaviorists have traditionally viewed multiple personalities as distinct patterns of behavior (both overt and covert) that have arisen in response to distinctly different contingencies of reinforcement (Skinner, 1953). This reasoning has been carried a step further in the *posttraumatic model* of DID, which assumes that DID usually results from childhood trauma (e.g., Ross, 1997). According to this model, an abused child can more easily cope with everyday life by usually forgetting about the abusive incidents and by pretending that the abuse is happening to someone else. In behavioral terms, this self-deception can be conceptualized as a type of covert avoidance response—"Nothing bad is happening to me"—that is negatively reinforced by a reduction in anxiety. As a result, the child learns to compartmentalize the distressing experience into a separate personality pattern that has its own dispositions and memories (Kohlenberg & Tsai, 1991). This style of coping may become so habitual that it eventually results in the formation of dozens, or even hundreds, of separate personality states.

Others, however, have argued that DID is usually not the result of trauma but instead the result of suggestive influence (Lilienfeld et al., 1999; Spanos, 1996). According to this *sociocognitive model* (which can also be conceptualized as a cognitive-behavioral model), the patient's displays of alter personalities have been inadvertently shaped through processes of social reinforcement and observational learning. Supportive evidence for this model includes the following:

- The first clear observations of alter personalities are often obtained following exposure to a therapist who communicates to the patient that displays of alter personalities will be considered appropriate (and hence socially reinforced)—such as by asking the patient "if there is another thought process, part of the mind, part, person or force" within or who wishes to communicate with the therapist (e.g., Braun, 1980, p. 213).
- The number of alter personalities displayed by patients usually increases as therapy progresses, as does the patients' ability to quickly switch from one alter to another (Ross, 1997). This suggests that a process of shaping may be involved.
- The number of DID cases rose sharply following dramatic presentations of the disorder to the public during the 1970s and 1980s, such as the case of Sybil, which became a best-selling book (Schreiber, 1973) and a popular movie. This suggests that observational learning may have played a role in the increased prevalence of the disorder.

Direct evidence for the role of behavioral processes in DID was reported by Kohlenberg (1973). He found that, by manipulating the amount of reinforcement a patient received for displaying one of three alter personalities, he was able to manipulate the amount of time a particular personality was displayed. He then devised a successful treatment program that included reinforcing displays of the personality that acted normally and ignoring displays of other personalities.

Supporters of the posttraumatic model (e.g., Gleaves, 1996; Ross, 1997; Ross & Norton, 1989) and the sociocognitive model (e.g., Lilienfeld et al., 1999; Powell & Gee, 1999; Spanos, 1994, 1996) have each presented a series of arguments and counterarguments in support of their positions. The result has been some movement toward a middle ground. Ross (1997), for example, acknowledged that at least some cases of DID have been artificially induced in therapy, while Lilienfeld et al. (1999) acknowledged that a tendency toward developing DID-type symptoms might sometimes be the result of trauma. Likewise, Phelps (2000) has presented a behavioral account of DID, arguing that, although alter personalities could conceivably arise from a history of childhood trauma, therapists might also inadvertently strengthen displays of alter personalities through processes of social reinforcement.

SUMMARY

Negative reinforcement plays an important role in the development of escape and avoidance behaviors. A typical procedure for studying escape and avoidance is a shuttle avoidance task. In it, the rat first learns to escape shock by climbing over a barrier whenever it feels a shock; it then learns to avoid shock by climbing over the barrier in the presence of a cue that predicts shock delivery.

According to Mowrer's two-process theory, avoidance behavior results from: (1) classical conditioning, in which a fear response comes to be elicited by a CS, and (2) operant conditioning, in which moving away from the CS is negatively reinforced by a reduction in fear. One criticism of this theory is that the avoidance response is extremely persistent, even when the aversive US is no longer presented. According to the anxiety conservation hypothesis, however, avoidance occurs so quickly that there is insufficient exposure to the CS for extinction of the fear response to take place. A second criticism of the two-process theory is that once the animals become accustomed to making the avoidance response, they no longer seem fearful of the CS; hence, it seems that reduction in fear cannot serve as a negative reinforcer for avoidance. One answer to this criticism is that, although the animals may be significantly less fearful, they may still be slightly fearful.

Avoidance conditioning in animals differs in certain ways from phobic conditioning in humans. For example, the conditioning occurs more readily in humans, usually requiring only a single trial to produce extremely persistent avoidance. Stampfl, however, showed that phobic-like avoidance could be achieved in rats by providing them with the opportunity to make the avoidance response early in the chain of events leading up to the CS, thereby minimizing the amount of effort involved.

Avoidance conditioning plays a role in obsessive-compulsive disorders. Obsessions produce an increase in anxiety that is then reduced by carrying out the compulsive behavior pattern. Treatment procedures have been developed involving prolonged exposure to the anxiety-arousing event without engaging in the compulsive behavior pattern, thereby allowing the anxiety to be extinguished.

Positive punishment involves the presentation of an aversive stimulus, whereas negative punishment involves the removal of an appetitive stimulus. Two common forms of negative punishment are time-out, which involves the removal of access to all reinforcers, and response cost, which involves the removal of a specific reinforcer. Intrinsic punishment is punishment that is an integral aspect of the behavior being punished (i.e., the behavior itself is punishing), whereas extrinsic punishment is punishment that is not an integral aspect of the behavior being punished. A primary punisher is one that is naturally punishing, and a secondary punisher is an event that is punishing because it has been associated with some other punisher. A generalized punisher has been associated with many other punishers.

There are several problems with the use of punishment, including a general suppression of behavior, avoidance of the person carrying out the punishment, elicitation of strong emotional responses, and an increase in aggressive behavior. Nevertheless, beneficial side effects can also occur, such as improvements in social behavior, mood, and attention. Punishment is more effective if delivered immediately, consistently, and at sufficient intensity to suppress the behavior. It also helps if punishment is accompanied by an explanation and if it is combined with positive reinforcement for appropriate behavior.

According to the conditioned suppression theory of punishment, punishment suppresses a behavior because it produces an emotional response that interferes with the behavior. According to the avoidance theory of punishment, punishment is a type of avoidance conditioning in which the avoidance response consists of doing anything other than the behavior that is being punished. The Premack principle, as applied to punishment, proposes that low-probability behaviors can be used as punishers for high-probability behaviors.

Learned helplessness is a decrement in learning ability following exposure to inescapable aversive stimulation. Learned helplessness can be overcome by repeatedly forcing the animal to make the avoidance response, and can be prevented by providing an animal with prior exposure to escapable aversive stimulation. In Masserman's experimental neurosis procedure, animals are exposed to unpredictable aversive stimulation. This produces symptoms that are similar to those experienced by people who have developed posttraumatic stress disorder.

SUGGESTED READINGS

Newsom, C., Favell, J., & Rincover, A. (1983). The side effects of punishment. In S. Axelrod & J. Apsche (Eds.), *The effects of punishment on human behavior*. New York: Academic Press. A nice overview of the harmful, as well as beneficial, side effects of punishment.

Spanos, N. P. (1996). *Multiple identities & false memories: A sociocognitive perspective.* Washington, DC: American Psychological Association.

Lilienfeld, S. O., Kirsch, I., Sarbin, T. R., Lynn, S. J., Chaves, J. F., Ganaway, G. K., & Powell, R. A. (1999). Dissociative identity disorder and the sociocognitive model: Recalling the lessons of the past. *Psychological Bulletin, 125*, 507–523. This article and Spanos's book together constitute a comprehensive presentation of the sociocognitive (or cognitive-behavioral) perspective on multiple personality disorder.

Sidman, M. (1989). *Coercion and its fallout.* Boston: Authors Cooperative. A strong indictment by a major behaviorist of the use of punishment to control human behavior.

STUDY QUESTIONS

1. Distinguish between escape and avoidance behavior, and describe the evolution of these behaviors in a shuttle avoidance procedure. How does Mowrer's two-process theory account for avoidance behavior?
2. What are two criticisms of Mowrer's two-process theory of avoidance? How have these criticisms been answered?
3. In what ways is experimental avoidance conditioning different from human phobic conditioning? According to Stampfl, what is a critical factor in the development and maintenance of phobic behavior that is often missing from experimental demonstrations of avoidance?
4. How can the two-process theory of avoidance account for obsessive-compulsive disorder?
5. Distinguish between time-out and response cost procedures, and between extrinsic punishment and intrinsic punishment. Give an example of each.
6. What is the distinction between a primary punisher and a secondary punisher? What is a generalized punisher? Provide clear examples of each.
7. Briefly outline the problems listed concerning the use of punishment.
8. What is the major advantage of punishment over extinction? What are three beneficial side effects of punishment?
9. Briefly outline the characteristics of effective punishment.

10. Describe the conditioned suppression theory of punishment, the avoidance theory of punishment, and the Premack approach to punishment.
11. Describe the basic experimental procedure (with control group) that was first used to demonstrate learned helplessness in dogs and the outcome that was observed. How can learned helplessness in dogs be eliminated? How can dogs be immunized against the development of learned helplessness?
12. Describe Masserman's procedure for inducing experimental neurosis in cats, and list some of the symptoms he observed. How does experimental neurosis differ from learned helplessness and how is it similar?

CONCEPT REVIEW

avoidance theory of punishment. The theory that punishment involves a type of avoidance conditioning in which the avoidance response consists of any behavior other than the behavior being punished.

conditioned suppression theory of punishment. The theory that punishment does not weaken a behavior, but instead produces an emotional response that interferes with the occurrence of the behavior.

exposure and response prevention (ERP). A method of treating obsessive-compulsive behavior that involves prolonged exposure to anxiety-arousing events while not engaging in the compulsive behavior pattern that reduces the anxiety.

extrinsic punishment. Punishment that is not an inherent aspect of the behavior being punished but that simply follows the behavior.

generalized (or generalized secondary) punisher. An event that has become punishing because it has in the past been associated with many other punishers.

intrinsic punishment. Punishment that is an inherent aspect of the behavior being punished, that is, the behavior itself is punishing.

learned helplessness. A decrement in learning ability that results from repeated exposure to uncontrollable aversive events.

Premack principle of punishment. A low-probability behavior (LPB) can be used to punish a high-probability behavior (HPB).

primary (or unconditioned) punisher. Any event that is innately punishing.

response cost. A form of negative punishment involving the removal of a specific reinforcer following the occurrence of a behavior.

secondary (or conditioned) punisher. An event that has become punishing because it has in the past been associated with some other punisher.

time-out. A form of negative punishment involving the loss of access to positive reinforcers for a brief period of time following the occurrence of a problem behavior.

two-process theory of avoidance. The theory that avoidance behavior is the result of two distinct processes: (1) classical conditioning, in which a fear response comes to be elicited by a CS, and (2) operant conditioning, in which moving away from the CS is negatively reinforced by a reduction in fear.

CHAPTER TEST

11. According to Mowrer, the two processes that underlie avoidance behavior are: (1) c___________ conditioning, in which a(n) ___________ response comes to be elicited by a CS, and (2) ___________ conditioning, in which moving away from the CS is ___________ reinforced by a reduction in ___________.
3. According to the ___________ theory of punishment, if a rat is shocked for lever pressing, then any behavior other than ___________ will be___________ reinforced by the nonoccurrence of shock.
27. If a father punishes his son for being aggressive with his playmates, the son may learn not to be aggressive only when the father is ___________.
8. Otto woke up one night to find an intruder standing over him in his bedroom. When the intruder saw that Otto was awake, he stabbed him and fled. Boyd was walking through a strange part of town one night when he too was stabbed. In keeping with certain research findings on experimental ___________, the person most likely to suffer symptoms of PTSD is ___________.
14. One criticism of Mowrer's two-process theory is that animals continue to make the avoidance response even though they no longer seem to be ___________ of the CS. One reply to this criticism is that although the animals may become significantly less ___________ of the CS, they do not in fact become completely ___________.
20. A person who checks her apartment door dozens of times each night to make sure that it is locked probably experiences a(n) ___________ in anxiety when she thinks about whether the door is locked and a(n) ___________ in anxiety when she checks it. This then acts as a ___________ reinforcer for the behavior of checking.
15. According to the ___________theory of avoidance, I avoid bees simply because I am then less likely to be stung and not because I feel a reduction in fear.
9. Obert did not want to go to school one morning and so pretended that he was ill. Sure enough, his mother fell for the trick and let him stay home that day. Thereafter, Obert often pretended that he was ill so that he did not have to go to school. Obert's tendency to pretend that he was ill was strengthened through the process of ___________.
28. One problem with spanking a child for spilling food is that the spanking will likely elicit a strong ___________ response that will temporarily

prevent the child from eating appropriately. The child may also become ___________ as a result of the spanking, which might later be directed to his little brother or sister. He might also learn that an effective means of controlling others is through the use of ___________.

19. Mowrer's two-process theory seems highly applicable to obsessive-compulsive disorder in that the occurrence of an obsessive thought is associated with a(n) ___________ in anxiety, while performance of a compulsive behavior is associated with a(n) ___________ in anxiety.
2. Skinner concluded that punishment generates a conditioned ___________ reaction that then suppresses any appetitive behavior, and that the appetitive behavior (will/will not) quickly recover once the punishment is withdrawn. Later research showed that this may be because Skinner had used a relatively (strong/weak) form of punishment in his research.
13. One criticism of Mowrer's two-process theory is that an avoidance response often does not seem to ___________, even after hundreds of trials. According to the ___________ hypothesis, however, this is because exposures to the aversive stimulus are too brief for ___________ to take place.
4. According to the Premack principle, if Rick smokes a lot and rarely vacuums, then ___________ can serve as an effective punisher for ___________.
22. Losing your wallet by being careless is an example of a (negative/positive) punisher, while getting a shock by being careless is an example of a ___________ punisher (assuming in each case that the behavior of carelessness subsequently ___________ in frequency).
12. According to Mowrer, I go out of my way to avoid bees because behaving this way has been (positively/negatively) (reinforced/punished) by a(n) ___________ in fear.
29. One problem with spanking a child for being noisy is that this will likely have a(n) ___________ effect in suppressing the behavior, which then serves as a strong reinforcer for the use of spanking on future occasions.
25. If you spank a dog for making a mess on the carpet, the dog might learn to avoid ___________ rather than avoid making a mess on the carpet.
10. The theoretical difficulty with avoidance behavior, as opposed to escape behavior, is that the individual is moving from one (aversive/nonaversive) situation to another, and it is difficult to see how a (change/lack of change) can serve as a reinforcer.
31. The beneficial side effects of punishment can include increases in s___________ behavior, improvements in m___________, and increased a___________ to the environment.
21. One difference between OCD and a phobia is that a phobia usually involves a(n) (passive/active) avoidance response, while OCD usually involves a(n) ___________ avoidance response.

7. Pietro is having great difficulty sleeping, is easily startled, and has developed various phobias. Pietro's symptoms are similar to those shown by Masserman's cats that were exposed to ___________ aversive stimulation. This set of symptoms in experimental animals is known as experimental ___________; in humans, it is known as ___________ disorder.
16. Experiments with animals have shown that an effective way to overcome learned helplessness is to present a salient stimulus (like a loud noise) each time an escape response (occurs/fails to occur).
1. For children who are old enough to understand language, punishment should always be combined with a(n) ___________.
23. Making a child sit in a corner for being too noisy is an example of a(n) ___________ procedure, while turning off the television set when the child is too noisy is an example of a(n) ___________ procedure.
5. When Renee was in elementary school, she was cruelly teased by a classmate each recess. The teachers ignored her pleas for help, as did her other classmates. Seligman would predict that, as time passes, Renee is likely to (decrease/increase) her efforts to stop the teasing. In other words, she will begin to suffer from learned ___________. She may also become clinically ___________.
17. According to Mineka, there are limitations in the extent to which experimental demonstrations of avoidance are analogous to human phobias. For example, in an experimental demonstration of avoidance that involves a tone and an aversive air blast, the rat will likely require (one/more than one) conditioning trial. By comparison, a bee phobia in humans typically requires ___________ conditioning trial. As well, the rat's avoidance behavior is likely to be (more/less) consistent than the avoidance behavior in a bee phobia.
26. One problem with spanking a child for being noisy while playing with his friends is that he might not only stop being noisy but also stop ___________.
30. A parent who wishes to punish her little girl for playing too roughly with the cat would do well to impose the punishing consequence ___________ after the occurrence of the unwanted behavior and, at least initially, on a(n) (consistent/unpredictable) basis. The parent should also ___________ the behavior of playing appropriately with the cat.
6. According to learned helplessness research, Clint is (more/less) likely to become depressed following a bitter divorce if his own parents divorced when he was a child and he later recovered from the experience.
24. Hugh got injured at work while goofing around, and as a result he became less likely to goof around. Eduardo got reprimanded by the boss for goofing around, and he also became less likely to goof around. Getting injured is a (primary/secondary) punisher for the behavior of goofing around, while getting reprimanded is a ___________ punisher.

18. Stampfl demonstrated that a critical factor in phobic conditioning is the possibility of making a(n) (early/late) avoidance response, thereby minimizing the amount of __________ involved in avoiding the feared event.

ANSWERS TO CHAPTER TEST

1. explanation
2. emotional; will; weak
3. avoidance; lever pressing; negatively
4. vacuuming; smoking
5. decrease; helplessness; depressed
6. less
7. unpredictable; neurosis; posttraumatic stress
8. neurosis; Otto
9. negative reinforcement
10. nonaversive; lack of change
11. classical; fear; operant; negatively; fear
12. negatively; reinforced; reduction
13. extinguish; anxiety conservation; extinction
14. fearful; fearful; nonfearful
15. one-process
16. occurs
17. more than one; one; less
18. early; effort
19. increase; decrease
20. increase; decrease; negative
21. passive; active
22. negative; positive; decreases
23. time-out; response cost
24. primary; secondary (or generalized secondary)
25. you
26. playing with his friends
27. present (or nearby)
28. emotional; aggressive (angry); punishment
29. immediate
30. immediately; consistent; positively reinforce
31. social; mood; attention

CHAPTER 10

CHOICE, MATCHING, AND SELF-CONTROL

CHAPTER OUTLINE

Mark was becoming quite frustrated by Jan's insistence that they were spending too much time together. He told her that if two people truly love each other, they should want to spend as much time together as possible. Jan countered that she did love him but that spending too much time together was making their relationship dull and boring. For her, life was more fulfilling when she interacted with a variety of people each day.

Operant conditioning in the real world is rarely a matter of being offered only one source of reinforcement. Instead, individuals typically choose between alternative sources of reinforcement. In this chapter, we examine some of the principles by which such choices are made—especially the principle of matching, which stipulates that the amount of behavior directed toward an alternative is often proportional to the amount of reinforcement we receive from that alternative. We also examine the types of choices involved when people attempt to exert "self-control" over their behavior.

Choice and Matching

Concurrent Schedules

In operant conditioning experiments, investigations of choice behavior often make use of a type of complex schedule known as a concurrent schedule. A ***concurrent schedule of reinforcement*** consists of the simultaneous presentation of two or more independent schedules, each leading to a reinforcer. The organism is thus allowed a choice between responding on one schedule versus the other.

For example, a pigeon may be given a choice between responding on a red key that is associated with a VR 20 schedule of reinforcement and a green key that is associated with a VR 50 schedule of reinforcement (see Figure 10.1). We can diagram this situation as follows:

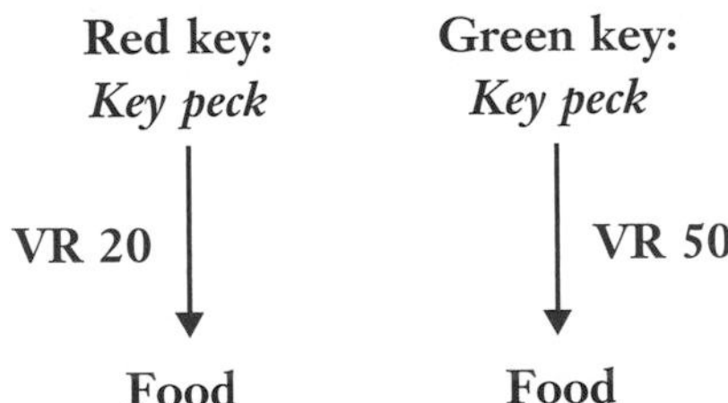

Which alternative would you choose? If you think of this situation as analogous to choosing between two slot machines, one of which pays off after an average of 20 quarters are plugged in and the other of which pays off after an average of 50 quarters are plugged in, the choice becomes easy. You would pick the better-paying machine, that is, the one that requires an average of

FIGURE 10.1 Illustration of a two-key operant procedure in which two schedules of reinforcement are simultaneously available, in this case, a VR 20 schedule on the red key and a VR 50 schedule on the green key. The two schedules thus form the two components of a *concurrent VR 20 VR 50* schedule of reinforcement. (*Source*: Domjan, 2003.)

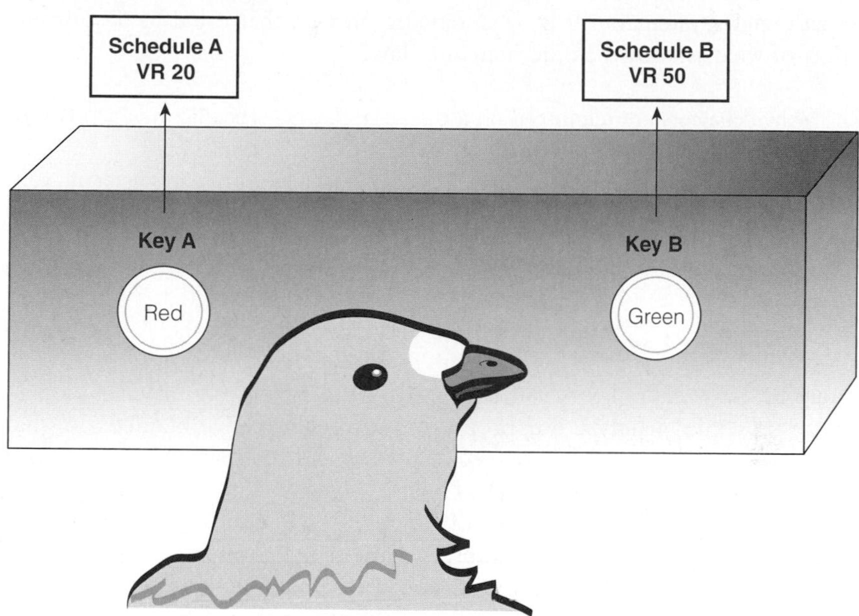

only 20 quarters to produce a win (if you can fight off everyone else who wants that machine). Similarly, the pigeon will come to develop an exclusive preference for the VR 20 alternative (Herrnstein & Loveland, 1975).

Choice between concurrent VR schedules is easy because an exclusive preference for the richer alternative clearly provides the better payoff. But what about concurrent VI schedules? What if, for example, a pigeon is presented with a concurrent VI 30-sec VI 60-sec schedule?

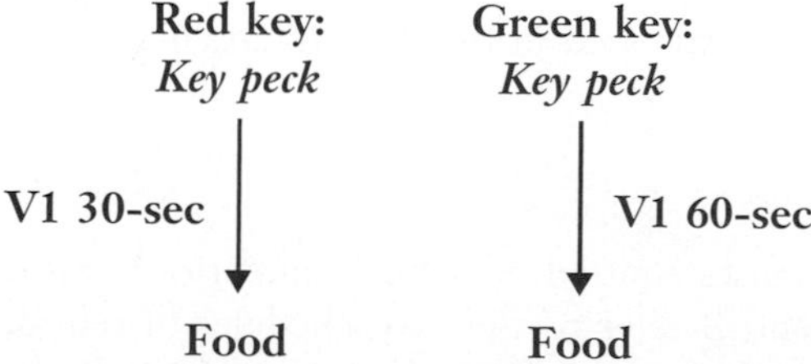

Remember that on VI schedules, reinforcers become available at unpredictable points in time (and any responses before that point will not result in reinforcement). Given this unpredictability, will the bird just randomly distribute its responses between the two alternatives, hoping to catch the reinforcers on each alternative as they become available (just as in trying to phone two friends at home, you might repeatedly dial each number in random order hoping to catch each person soon after he or she arrives home)? Herrnstein (1961) carried out just such an experiment using various schedule values and found that the pigeon's behavior under such circumstances is actually quite systematic. It is so systematic, in fact, that it led to the formulation of what is known as the matching law.

QUICK QUIZ A

1. Many behaviors are reinforced on a c__________ schedule in which two or more schedules of reinforcement are s__________ available.
2. In a choice between a VR 25 and a VR 75 schedule of reinforcement, your best strategy would be to choose the __________ schedule (100/50/25)% of the time.

The Matching Law

The ***matching law*** holds that the proportion of responses emitted on a particular schedule matches the proportion of reinforcers obtained on that schedule (note that it is *proportion* of responses and reinforcers and not *number* of responses and reinforcers). Thus, a pigeon will emit approximately twice as many responses on the VI 30-sec schedule as on the VI 60-sec schedule because the rate of reinforcement on the former will be twice as great as on the latter (an average of two reinforcers per minute on the VI 30-sec schedule versus one reinforcer per minute on the VI 60-sec schedule). Similarly, a pigeon will emit three times as many responses on a VI 10-sec schedule as it will on a VI 30-sec schedule because the VI 10-sec schedule provides three times the rate of reinforcement (an average of six reinforcers per minute on the VI 10-sec schedule versus two per minute on the VI 30-sec schedule). *The matching law therefore predicts a consistent relationship between the proportion of reinforcers obtained on a certain alternative and the proportion of responses emitted on that alternative.* If a pigeon earns 10% of its reinforcers on an alternative, then it will emit 10% of its responses on that alternative; if it earns 60% of its reinforcers on an alternative, then it will emit 60% of its responses on it.

The matching law can also be expressed in the form of an equation:

$$\frac{R_A}{R_A + R_B} = \frac{S^R{}_A}{S^R{}_A + S^R{}_B}$$

where R is the number of responses emitted, S^R is the number of reinforcers earned, and the subscripts A and B refer to the two schedules of reinforcement. Thus, R_A is the number of responses emitted on schedule A, R_B is the number of responses emitted on schedule B, $S^R{}_A$ is the number of reinforcers earned on schedule A, and $S^R{}_B$ is the number of reinforcers earned on schedule B. Therefore, the term to the left of the equal sign:

$$\frac{R_A}{R_A + R_B}$$

indicates the proportion of responses emitted on schedule A. It is the number of responses emitted on schedule A divided by the total number emitted on both schedules. The term to the right of the equal sign:

$$\frac{S^R{}_A}{S^R{}_A + S^R{}_B}$$

indicates the proportion of reinforcers earned on schedule A. It is the number of reinforcers earned on schedule A divided by the total number earned on both schedules.

To illustrate how the equation works, let us look at some hypothetical data from an experiment involving a choice between a VI 30-sec and a VI 60-sec schedule. If the pigeon picks up most or all of the reinforcers available on each alternative in a 1-hour session, it should obtain about twice as many reinforcers on the VI 30-sec schedule as on the VI 60-sec. Imagine that this is essentially what happens: Our hypothetical pigeon obtains 119 reinforcers on the VI 30-sec schedule and 58 reinforcers (about half as many) on the VI 60-sec schedule. Plugging these values into the right-hand term of the equation, we get

$$\frac{S^R_{VI\ 30\text{-}s}}{S^R_{VI\ 30\text{-}s} + S^R_{VI\ 60\text{-}s}} = \frac{119}{119 + 58} = \frac{119}{177} = .67$$

which means that the proportion of reinforcers obtained from the VI 30-sec schedule is .67. In other words, 67% (about 2/3) of the reinforcers acquired during the session are obtained from the VI 30-sec schedule, and 33% (about 1/3) are obtained from the VI 60-sec schedule (meaning that twice as many reinforcers are obtained from the VI 30-sec schedule). As for responses, imagine that our hypothetical pigeon emits 2,800 responses on the VI 30-sec schedule and 1,450 responses on the VI 60-sec schedule. Plugging these values into the left-hand term of the equation, we get

$$\frac{R_{VI\ 30\text{-}s}}{R_{VI\ 30\text{-}s} + R_{VI\ 60\text{-}s}} = \frac{2800}{2800 + 1450} = \frac{2800}{4250} = .66$$

Thus, the proportion of responses emitted on the VI 30-sec schedule is .66. In other words, 66% of the responses are emitted on the VI 30-sec schedule (and 34% are emitted on the VI 60-sec schedule). In keeping with the matching law, this figure closely matches the proportion of reinforcement obtained on the VI 30-sec schedule (.67). In other words, the proportion of responses emitted on the VI 30-sec schedule approximately matches the proportion of reinforcers earned on it. (For results from Herrnstein's [1961] original matching experiment in which pigeons chose between several different combinations of schedules, see Figure 10.2.)

Matching appears to be a basic principle of choice behavior, applicable to a variety of situations and species. For example, Houston (1986) investigated

FIGURE 10.2 Experimental results depicting the proportion of responses emitted by two pigeons on key A. Different combinations of schedules were offered on key A versus key B across the different conditions of the experiment, with the schedule values ranging from VI 90-sec to VI 540-sec to extinction (no reinforcers available). As the schedule combinations changed and the proportion of reinforcers earned on key A increased from approximately .1 to 1.0, the proportion of responses emitted on key A increased in similar fashion. (*Source*: Adapted from "Relative and absolute strength of response as a function of frequency of reinforcement," by R. J. Herrnstein, 1961, *Journal of Experimental Analysis of Behavior*, *4*, pp. 267–272. Copyright © 1961 by the Society for the Experimental Analysis of Behavior, Inc. Reprinted with permission.)

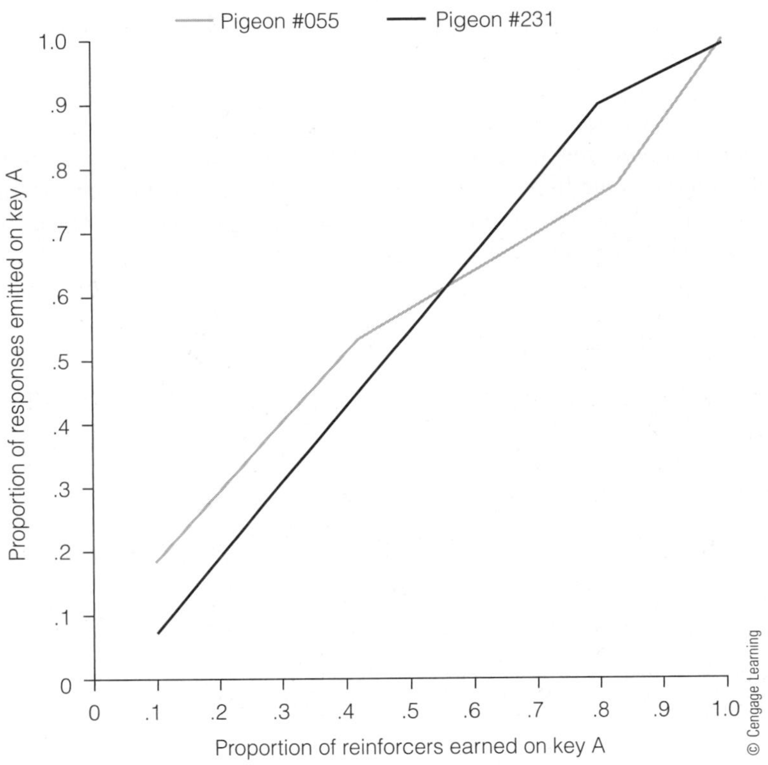

the extent to which the pied wagtail, an insectivorous bird in Britain, distributed its foraging behavior between two separate patches of food: (1) a stretch of territory along the banks of the Thames River, which the territorial owner defended from other wagtails (and only some birds owned territories), and (2) an open meadow that any wagtail could visit and feed upon as part of the flock. Those birds that owned territories tended to walk circular routes within their territories, feeding off insects that were regularly washed up by the river. If, however, food along the river was scarce, the owner could fly over to the meadow and feed with the flock. (In a sense, finding nothing to eat at home, the bird had the option of eating out at the local restaurant.) Houston found that the proportion of time a bird spent in one food patch versus the other (its own territory versus the public meadow) approximately matched the proportion of food it obtained in that patch.

Matching is also applicable to human social behavior. For example, in a group situation, we must choose between directing our conversation to one person or another, each of whom provides a different rate of reinforcement (in the form of comments or acknowledgments). In one investigation, Conger and Killeen (1974) asked student volunteers to participate with three other students in a discussion session on drug abuse. Each volunteer was unaware that the other members of the group were actually confederates of the experimenter. During the discussion session, while the volunteer was talking, two of the confederates sat on either side and intermittently expressed approval in response to whatever the volunteer happened to be saying at that time. The experimenters systematically varied the frequency of verbal approvals delivered by each of these confederates. They found that the relative amount of time the volunteer looked at each confederate matched the relative frequency of verbal approval delivered by that confederate. If one confederate delivered twice as many approvals as the other confederate, then that confederate was looked at twice as often. In general, these results suggest that the principle of matching may underlie various aspects of human social interaction.

QUICK QUIZ B

1. According to the matching law, the (number/proportion) of ________ on an alternative matches the (number/proportion) of ________ obtained on that alternative.
2. On a concurrent VI 60-sec VI 120-sec schedule, the pigeon should emit about (half/twice) as many responses on the VI 60-sec alternative as opposed to the VI 120-sec alternative.
3. If a pigeon emits 1,100 responses on key A and 3,100 responses on key B, then the proportion of responses on key A is ________. If the pigeon also earned 32 reinforcers on key A and 85 reinforcers on key B, then the proportion of reinforcers earned on key A is ________. This pigeon (did/did not) approximately match pr________ of r________ to pr________ of r________ obtained.

Deviations from Matching

Although matching provides a good description of behavior in many choice situations, exceptions have been noted. In general, there are three types of exceptions, or deviations, from matching (Baum, 1974, 1979). The first deviation, which is quite common, is called undermatching. In ***undermatching***, the proportion of responses on the richer schedule versus the poorer schedule is less different than would be predicted by matching (to remember this, think of *under*matching as *less* different). For example, the matching law predicts that the proportion of responses should be .67 on the richer VI 30-sec schedule and .33 on the poorer VI 60-sec schedule. If we instead find proportions of .60 and .40, respectively, then undermatching has occurred. There is less of a difference in responding between the richer and poorer schedules than would be predicted by matching.

Undermatching can occur when there is little cost for switching from one schedule to another. For example, in our previous description of a hypothetical matching experiment, we actually left out an important aspect of the procedure. Whenever the pigeon switches from one key to another, the act of doing so initiates a slight delay of, say, 2 seconds during which no response will be effective in producing a reinforcer, even if a reinforcer happens to be available at that time. It is as though, when the pigeon switches from one key to another, the first peck on the new key is simply a statement of intent that says, "I now want to try this key," following which there is a 2-second delay before any peck can actually earn a reinforcer. This delay feature is called a *changeover delay* or COD.

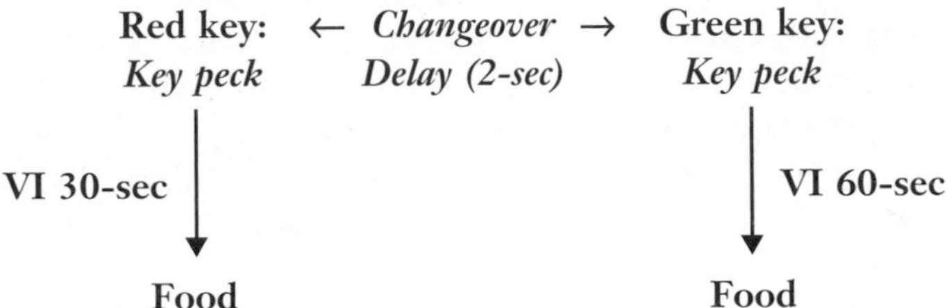

Without a COD, a pigeon will simply alternate pecks back and forth on each key, catching each reinforcer as soon as it becomes available. Only when a slight cost for switching is added to the situation does the pigeon spend more time on the richer alternative.

The COD can be thought of as the experimental equivalent of a foraging situation in which the animal has to travel a certain distance between food patches. If two food patches are extremely close together (say, each patch is separated by only a narrow stream), then undermatching is likely to occur. The animal will simply move back and forth from one side to another, looking for prey, even if one side is generally a much richer area in which to hunt. If, however, the two patches are more widely separated (say, the stream is somewhat broad), then the animal is more likely to match the amount of time it spends on one side of the stream to the number of prey that it obtains on that side. It will spend proportionately more time on the rich side of the stream, and less time on the poor side of the stream.

A second deviation from matching is called overmatching. In ***overmatching***, the proportion of responses on the richer schedule versus the poorer schedule is more different than would be predicted by matching (to remember this, think of *over*matching as *more* different). For example, the matching law predicts that the proportion of responses should be .67 on the richer VI 30-sec schedule and .33 on the poorer VI 60-sec schedule. If we instead find proportions of .80 and .20, respectively, then overmatching has occurred. There is more of a difference in responding between the richer and poorer schedules than would be predicted by matching.

Overmatching can occur when the cost of moving from one alternative to another is very high. For example, Baum (1974) found that overmatching occurred when a pigeon had to walk around a partition and climb across a wooden hurdle to switch from one response key to another. The pigeon switched less often and spent more time on the richer alternative than the matching law would predict. Similarly, a predator that has to cross a deep, fast-moving stream to move from one food patch to another might make the trip only infrequently and spend considerably more time in the richer food patch than predicted by matching.

QUICK QUIZ C

1. When the difference in the proportion of responding on richer versus poorer alternatives is greater than would be predicted by matching, we say that ____________ has occurred.
2. When the difference in the proportion of responding on richer versus poorer alternatives is less than would be predicted by matching, we say that ____________ has occurred.
3. In experimental studies of matching, the act of switching from one alternative to another results in a c____________ d____________: a short period of time that must pass before any response can produce a reinforcer.
4. This experimental procedure seems analogous to f____________ situations in which an animal has to t____________ a certain d____________ from one food patch to another.
5. In general, food patches that are separated by a very great distance will produce ____________matching, while food patches that are separated by a very short distance will produce ____________matching.

The final deviation from matching is called bias. ***Bias from matching*** occurs when one response alternative attracts a higher proportion of responses than would be predicted by matching, regardless of whether that alternative contains the richer or poorer schedule of reinforcement. For example, suppose that our two schedules are VI 30-sec and VI 60-sec, and that we alternate which schedule is associated with a red key versus green key. The matching law predicts that the proportion of responses on the red key should be .67 when the richer VI 30-sec schedule is presented on it, and .33 when the poorer VI 60-sec schedule is presented on it. But if the proportions instead turned out to be .77 when the VI 30-sec schedule is presented on it and .43 when the VI 60-sec schedule is presented on it, then bias has occurred (see Table 10.1). The pigeon is emitting 10% more responses on the red key than predicted by matching, both when it is the richer alternative and when it is the poorer alternative. (Of course, this also means that the pigeon is emitting 10% fewer responses on the green key.) In a sense, the pigeon seems to like red more than green and therefore expends extra effort on the red key over and above the amount of responding dictated by the schedule of reinforcement. Similarly, in a conversation with a group of individuals, Erin might spend additional time directing her conversation toward Jason, whom she finds very attractive. For example, on one day, he provides

TABLE 10.1 Hypothetical results indicating bias from matching. More responses are emitted on the red key, both when it is the richer alternative (VI 30-sec) and when it is the poorer alternative (VI 60-sec), than would be predicted by matching. (Of course, this also means that fewer responses are emitted on the green key than would be predicted by matching.)

CONDITION A (RICHER SCHEDULE ON RED KEY)	PREDICTED	OBTAINED
Red key: VI 30-sec	.67	.77
Green key: VI 60-sec	.33	.23
CONDITION B (POORER SCHEDULE ON RED KEY)		
Red key: VI 60-sec	.33	.43
Green key: VI 30-sec	.67	.57

72% of the reinforcers during a conversation, but she looks at him 84% of the time; on another day, he provides only 23% of the reinforcers, but she looks at him 36% of the time. In each case, she looks at him more than would be predicted by matching. His attractiveness is an additional factor, over and above the amount of conversational reinforcement he offers, that influences how much she looks at him.

Bias can be a precise way to measure preference. For example, on a concurrent VI 60-sec VI 60-sec schedule, the pigeon should respond equally on the two alternatives. But what if each alternative leads to a different reinforcer, perhaps wheat on one side and buckwheat on the other? Under these circumstances, the extent to which the pigeon biases its responding toward the schedule leading to wheat indicates the extent of the pigeon's preference for wheat. In fact, Miller (1976) carried out just such an experiment and found that pigeons preferred wheat over buckwheat by a ratio of about 1.4 to 1.0. If we think of key pecks as equivalent to how much money pigeons would be willing to spend for one alternative versus the other, then the pigeons were willing to spend $1.40 on a bag of wheat compared to only $1.00 for a bag of buckwheat. Bias in matching can, therefore, be used to indicate degree of preference for different reinforcers.

In summary, undermatching occurs when the difference in responding between the richer and poorer schedules is less than predicted by matching. Overmatching occurs when the difference in responding between the richer and poorer schedules is more than predicted by matching. And bias occurs when one response alternative receives more responses than predicted by matching regardless of whether it contains the richer or poorer schedule.

Each of these deviations has been incorporated into more complex versions of the matching law (Baum, 1974).

As with the phenomenon of behavioral contrast (discussed in Chapter 8), the matching law reminds us that operant behavior should often be viewed in context. The amount of behavior directed toward an alternative is a function of the amount of reinforcement available on that alternative as well as the amount of reinforcement available on other alternatives. This notion has important implications for everyday behavior. For example, although a child might spend little time reading, this does not mean that reading is not a reinforcing activity for that child. If other highly reinforcing activities, such as computer games and television, happen to be simultaneously available, reading may be losing out simply because it provides less reinforcement (especially immediate reinforcement) than those other activities. Thus, a simple but effective way to motivate the child to read might be to limit the amount of time those other activities are available. In the absence of such alternatives, the child might naturally gravitate toward reading as a source of reinforcement.

QUICK QUIZ D

1. When greater responding is shown for a particular response alternative than would be predicted by matching regardless of the amount of reinforcement obtained from that alternative, we say that the organism has a b__________ for that alternative.
2. Food patches that differ in the type of prey found within them may produce the type of deviation from matching known as __________.
3. When a bear obtains 70% of its food from a nearby stream, it spends 80% of its time at the stream; when it obtains 30% of its food from the stream, it spends 25% of its time at the stream. When a cougar obtains 20% of its food in a particular canyon, it spends 35% of its time in that canyon; when it obtains 65% of its food from that canyon, it spends 80% of its time in the canyon. Among the three types of deviation from matching, the bear shows evidence of __________ while the cougar shows evidence of __________.

Matching and Melioration

The matching law describes how behavior is distributed across various alternatives in a choice situation. It does not, however, explain why this pattern of distribution occurs. You might think that it occurs simply because it somehow maximizes one's overall level of reinforcement, a proposition known as *maximization (or optimization) theory* (e.g., Rachlin, 1978). An alternative explanation, however, is called melioration theory (to *meliorate* means "to make better"). According to ***melioration theory***, the distribution of behavior in a choice situation shifts toward those alternatives that have higher value regardless of the long-term effect on the overall amount of reinforcement (Herrnstein, 1990). For example, suppose that when a pigeon is first confronted with a concurrent VI 30-sec VI 60-sec schedule, it emits an equal

And Furthermore

Basketball and the Matching Law

In an interesting application of the matching law to sports activities, Vollmer and Bourret (2000) examined the allocation of 2- versus 3-point shots made by male and female basketball players at a major university. The question of interest was whether the players would match the proportion of shots taken from the 3-point range to the proportion of reinforcers (baskets) they obtained from that range. The researchers found that such matching did indeed occur (particularly when the matching equation was altered somewhat to account for the greater value of 3-point shots). In other words, if a certain player obtained about 35% of his or her points from the 3-point range, then about 35% of his or her shots tended to occur from that range. The authors speculated that this ability to match the proportion of shots attempted from a certain range to the proportion of points obtained from that range may be a distinguishing characteristic of player excellence. One author, for example, described how he casually observed a local street game in which 3-point shots were frequently attempted even though they were almost never successful. In other words, it seemed that less skillful players did not display the same tendency to match that the university players had displayed (this was a top-ranked university, by the way). In fact, subsequent research (e.g., Alferink, Critchfield, & Hitt, 2009) has confirmed that the matching law (with some deviations) is a good predictor of basketball shot selection by more successful players at both the college and professional level.

You may have noticed that this type of matching suggests that basketball shots are reinforced on a VI schedule, which contradicts the typical notion that shot-making in such activities is reinforced on a VR schedule (with rate of reinforcement largely dependent on the number of shots attempted). Vollmer and Bourret (2000), however, suggest that basketball shots may in fact be reinforced on a combination (conjunctive) VR-VI schedule, with reinforcement dependent both on the number of shots attempted (the VR component) and on defensive lapses by the opposition that occur at unpredictable points in time (the VI component). (See also Reed, Critchfield, & Martens, 2006, and Stilling & Critchfield, 2010, for an application of the matching law to play selection in National Football League games.)

number of responses on both alternatives. The responses emitted on the VI 30-sec schedule will result in twice as many reinforcers as those emitted on the VI 60-sec schedule. Thus, in terms of benefits (reinforcers obtained) versus costs (responses made), the VI 30-sec schedule will have a much higher value than the VI 60-sec schedule, because the bird will have obtained twice as many reinforcers on the VI 30-sec schedule for the same amount of work. This will make the VI 30-sec schedule a very attractive alternative to the pigeon, with the result that the pigeon will be tempted in subsequent sessions to shift more and more of its behavior in that direction. This shifting, however, will cease at the point of matching, because that is the point at which the two alternatives have about equal value. The pigeon will still be earning twice as many reinforcers on the VI 30-sec schedule, but in doing so it will be expending twice as many responses on that alternative. Thus, the cost of each alternative (in responses made) will now match the benefits obtained from that alternative (in reinforcers earned). Melioration in this situation is thus a sort of leveling-out process, in which behavior shifts until the two alternatives have about equal value in terms of costs versus benefits.

At this point, you might be thinking that melioration is rather trivial. Why would an animal or person not shift behavior toward the higher valued alternative? The problem is that this tendency to move toward the higher valued alternative can sometimes result in a substantial reduction in the total amount of reinforcement obtained. There are three ways in which this can occur.

First, an alternative may not require as much responding as one is distributing toward it to obtain all of the available reinforcers. Consider, for example, a pigeon that is presented with a concurrent VR 100 VI 30-sec schedule (note that the first alternative is a VR schedule). On the VR 100 alternative, 100 responses on average will result in a reinforcer, while on the VI 30-sec alternative, the first response after an average interval of 30 seconds will result in a reinforcer. What is the pigeon's best strategy in this situation?

The best strategy is for the pigeon to spend most of its time on the VR schedule in which the number of reinforcers obtained is directly tied to the number of responses made, and then briefly switch to the VI alternative about every 30 seconds or so to pick up any reinforcer that might have become available on that alternative. This strategy will maximize the amount of reinforcement obtained. In reality, pigeons tend to match the amount of time spent on the VI schedule to the number of reinforcers earned on that schedule, thereby spending more time on the VI schedule and less time on the VR schedule than they should (Herrnstein & Heyman, 1979). Thus, if a pigeon happens to obtain 60% of its reinforcers from the VI 30-sec schedule, it will spend 60% of its time responding on the VI 30-sec schedule and only 40% of its time responding on the VR 100 schedule—a distribution of behavior that greatly reduces the overall amount of reinforcement than could have been obtained during the session. Hence, the pigeon's tendency to match (meliorate) has the effect of producing an overall level of reinforcement that is suboptimal.

In similar fashion, Henry, a salesman with a large manufacturing company, might spend too much time courting clients who are relatively easy sells (in reality, he only needs to call on such clients once a month to make a sale), and too little time courting retailers who are relatively difficult sells (who need to be intensively courted before a sale can be made). If Henry shifted some of his time away from the easy clients and toward the difficult clients, he might experience almost no loss of business from the former and a substantial gain in business from the latter. Unfortunately, because the rich schedule of reinforcement provided by the easy clients is very attractive to him, he continues to spend too much time with his easy clients and too little time with his difficult clients.

As another example, consider the manner in which many students distribute study time between the courses they are taking. Students often spend the most time studying for their most enjoyable course and the least time studying for their least enjoyable course. Yet the least enjoyable course is probably the one on which students should spend the most time studying. The result is that they spend the least time studying those courses that require the most work.

QUICK QUIZ E

1. According to ____________ theory, the distribution of behavior in a choice situation shifts toward that alternative that has a (lower/higher) value. This shifting will cease at the point where the two outcomes are (approximately equal/maximally different) in terms of costs versus benefits.
2. A rat faced with a concurrent VR 60 VI 80-sec schedule will spend more time on the ____________ schedule than necessary to pick up all of the available reinforcers on that schedule. This result is consistent with ____________ theory but contradicts what is known as m____________ (or op____________) theory.
3. Shona spends a lot of time cleaning her apartment, which she quite enjoys, and little time studying, which she does not enjoy. Chances are that this distribution of behavior, which results from the tendency to ____________, (will/will not) maximize the amount of reinforcement in her life.

A second problem with melioration is that overindulgence in a highly reinforcing alternative can often result in long-term habituation to that alternative, thus reducing its value as a reinforcer. Suppose, for example, that you suddenly become so rich that you can eat as much as you want of whatever you want. Before becoming rich, you rarely ate lobster, which you absolutely loved. Now, with your newfound wealth, you begin eating lobster almost every day. The problem is that if you eat lobster this frequently, you will likely become habituated to it, such that, although still enjoyable, it is no longer the heavenly treat that it once was. For this reason, many people fondly remember those times in their lives when they had limited resources and had to struggle a bit to get by. The overall amount of reinforcement they experienced at that time, when highly valued items such as lobster could be experienced in only small quantities and truly enjoyed, actually may have been much greater than it is now. (Long-term habituation is also part of the problem experienced by the central character in the story discussed in the And Furthermore box on St. Neots Margin in Chapter 8, who found himself in the afterlife and was granted any desire he wished.)[1]

This same process can be a contributing factor to the development of substance abuse. If drinking in a bar is a highly enjoyable activity, you might begin shifting more and more of your behavior in that direction. Eventually, you will be spending so much time in the bar that the overall amount of reinforcement

---

[1]See also the chapter entitled "What Is Wrong With Daily Life in the Western World?" in Skinner (1987). Skinner does not use the term *melioration*, but many of the examples he provides can be interpreted as examples of this process.

ADVICE FOR THE LOVELORN

Dear Dr. Dee,

My boyfriend spends almost all his time with me, which I find depressing. I try to tell him that I need some breathing space, but he seems to think that if I truly loved him, I would want to be with him always. What is your opinion on this?

Smothered

Dear Smothered,

Sounds as if your love relationship may have fallen prey to the damaging effects of melioration. Although some people believe that being in love with someone means wanting to be with that person always, the reality is that too much togetherness may result in a severe case of habituation. Add to this the possibility that the two individuals involved are also spending much less time interacting with other people, and it could well be that the overall amount of reinforcement in their lives is actually less than it was before they met. This suggests that some relationships might improve if the couple spent a bit less time together and worked a bit harder at maintaining other sources of social reinforcement (given that this does not become a cheap excuse for having an affair!). So, behaviorally speaking, I agree with you.

Behaviorally yours,

Dr. Dee

in your life is substantially reduced—both because drinking is no longer as enjoyable as when you drank less frequently, and because you are now in the bar so much that you are missing out on reinforcers from other, non-alcohol-related activities. You may in fact be fully aware that your alcohol-oriented life is not very satisfying (in fact, such awareness is a defining characteristic of an addiction), yet find it very difficult to break free and reject the pleasure of heading to the bar for another evening of positive reinforcement.

Many of the previous examples can also be seen as instances of a *third, more general problem, which is that melioration is often the result of behavior being too strongly governed by immediate consequences as opposed to delayed consequences.* The immediate reinforcement available from studying more enjoyable courses tempts one away from working on less enjoyable courses and maximizing one's overall grade point average at the end of the term (a delayed reinforcer). And the immediate reinforcement available from going to the bar each evening tempts one away from moderating one's drinking and eventually establishing a more healthy and satisfying lifestyle (a delayed reinforcer). The difficulties that arise from the strong preference for immediate reinforcers over delayed reinforcers are described more fully in the following section.

QUICK QUIZ F

1. One problem with melioration is that this tendency may result in (over/under) indulgence of a favored reinforcer with the result that we may experience long-term h_____________ to it. This means that our enjoyment of life may be greatest when we (do/do not) have all that we desire.
2. Another problem is that melioration can result in too much time being spent on those alternatives that provide relatively i_____________ reinforcement and not enough time on those that provide d_____________ reinforcement.

Self-Control

In our discussion of melioration, we noted that people often engage in suboptimal patterns of behavior. Moreover, although people realize that these patterns are suboptimal, they seem unable to change them. They decide to quit smoking but do not persist more than a day; they are determined to go for a run each morning but cannot get out of bed to do so; they resolve to study each evening but spend most evenings either watching television or socializing. In short, they know what to do, but they do not do it. To use the common vernacular, they lack self-control.

Why people have such difficulty controlling their behavior has long been a matter of conjecture. Plato maintained that people engage in actions that are not in their best interest because of a lack of education, and that once they realize that it is to their benefit to behave appropriately, they will do so. Aristotle disagreed, however, noting that individuals often behave in ways that they clearly recognize as counterproductive. Many people, at least in this culture, would probably agree with Aristotle. They would probably also contend that self-control seems to require a certain mental faculty called willpower. A person who behaves wisely and resists temptations is said to have a lot of willpower, whereas a person who behaves poorly and yields to temptations is said to have little willpower. But is the concept of willpower, as used in this manner, really an explanation? Or is it one of those false explanations based on circular reasoning?

> *"Sam quit smoking. He must have a lot of willpower."*
> "How do you know he has a lot of willpower?"
> *"Well, he quit smoking, didn't he?"*

The term *willpower*, used in this way, merely describes what Sam did—that he was able to quit smoking. It does not explain why he was able to quit smoking. For this reason, telling someone that they need to use more willpower to quit smoking is usually a pointless exercise. They would love to have more willpower—if only someone would tell them what it is and where to get it.

In the remainder of this chapter, we discuss some behavioral approaches to self-control. These approaches generally reject the traditional concept of willpower and instead focus on the relationship between behavior and its outcomes. We begin with Skinner's rudimentary analysis of self-control.

Skinner on Self-Control

Skinner (1953) viewed self-control, or "self-management," not as an issue of willpower but as an issue involving conflicting outcomes. For example, drinking alcohol can lead to both positive outcomes (e.g., increased confidence and feelings of relaxation) and negative outcomes (e.g., a hangover along with that idiotic tattoo you found on your arm the next morning). Skinner also proposed that managing this conflict involves two types of responses: a *controlling response* that serves to alter the frequency of a *controlled response*. Suppose, for example, that to control the amount of money you spend, you leave your credit card and most of your money at home when heading out one evening. The act of leaving the card and money at home is the controlling response, while the amount you subsequently spend is the controlled response. By emitting the one response, you affect the other.

Skinner (1953) listed several types of controlling responses, some of which are described here.

Physical Restraint With this type of controlling response, you physically manipulate the environment to prevent the occurrence of some problem behavior. Leaving money at home so you will spend less during the evening is one example; loaning your television set to a friend for the rest of the semester so you will be more likely to study than watch television is another.

Depriving and Satiating Another tactic for controlling your behavior is to utilize the motivating operations of deprivation and satiation to alter the extent to which a certain event can act as a reinforcer. If you are attempting to diet, for example, you might do well to shop for groceries immediately *after* a meal. If you are satiated, as opposed to hungry, during your shopping trip, you may be less tempted to purchase fattening items such as cookies and ice cream.

Doing Something Else To prevent yourself from engaging in certain behaviors, it is sometimes helpful to perform an alternate behavior. Thus, people who are trying to quit smoking sometimes find it helpful to chew gum, and people who are trying to diet sometimes find it helpful to sip tea or sugar-free sodas.

Self-Reinforcement and Self-Punishment A self-control tactic that might seem obvious from a behavioral standpoint is to simply reinforce your own behavior. Although Skinner suggested that this might work, he also noted a certain difficulty with it. In the typical operant conditioning paradigm, the reinforcer is delivered only when the appropriate response is emitted. The rat must press the lever to receive food, the child must clean his room to receive a cookie, and the student must study and perform well on an exam to receive a high mark. In the case of self-reinforcement, however, this contingency is much weaker. You might promise yourself that you will have a pizza after completing 3 hours of studying, but what is to stop you from *not* studying and having the pizza anyway? To use Martin and Pear's (1999) terminology, what is to stop you from "*short-circuiting*" the contingency and immediately consuming the reward without performing the intended behavior?

A similar problem exists with the use of self-punishment. You might promise yourself that you will do 20 push-ups following each cigarette smoked, but what is to stop you from smoking a cigarette anyway and not bothering with the push-ups? Note too that if you do perform the push-ups, it might punish not only the act of smoking but also the act of carrying through on your promise to punish yourself. As a result, you will be less likely to do the push-ups the next time you have a smoke. In fact, research has shown that people who attempt to use self-punishment often fail to deliver the consequences to themselves (Worthington, 1979).

Thus, self-reinforcement and self-punishment may not function in the same manner as normal reinforcement and punishment (Catania, 1975). Rachlin (1974), for example, has proposed that self-reinforcement might simply make the completion of an intended behavior more *salient*, thereby enhancing its value as a secondary reinforcer. For example, eating a pizza after 3 hours of studying might simply be the equivalent of setting off fireworks and sounding the trumpets for a job well done. There is also some evidence that, for many people, self-delivered consequences are more effective when the person perceives that other people are aware of the contingency, suggesting that the social consequences for attaining or not attaining

the intended goal are often an important aspect of *self*-reinforcement and *self*-punishment procedures (Hayes et al., 1985).

Despite these concerns, Bandura (1976) and others maintain that self-delivered consequences can function in much the same manner as externally delivered consequences, given that the individual has been properly socialized to adhere to self-set standards and to feel guilty for violating such standards. It is also the case that many people do make use of self-reinforcement and self-punishment procedures in trying to control their behavior. Heffernan and Richards (1981), for example, found that 75% of students who had successfully improved their study habits reported using self-reinforcement—which, if you don't already do this yourself, you should seriously consider experimenting with. Conversely, Gary Player, a famous golfer from the Nicklaus-Palmer era, is a staunch believer in the value of self-punishment for maintaining a disciplined lifestyle—such as by forcing himself to do an extra 200 sit-ups (over and above the normal 800!) after a game in which he has let himself become irritable (Kossoff, 1999). Self-delivered contingencies are, therefore, a recommended component of many self-management programs (Watson & Tharp, 2014).

QUICK QUIZ G

1. Behavioral approaches largely (accept/reject) the concept of willpower as an explanation for self-control.

2. Skinner analyzed self-control from the perspective of a ____________ response that alters the frequency of a subsequent response that is known as the ____________ response.

3. Suppose you post a reminder on your refrigerator about a long-distance phone call you should make this weekend. Posting the reminder is the ____________ response, while making the call on the weekend is the ____________ response.

4. Folding your arms to keep from chewing your nails is an example of the use of p____________ r____________ to control your behavior.

5. A problem with the use of self-reinforcement is that we may be tempted to consume the ____________ without engaging in the behavior. This problem is known as s____________-____________ the contingency.

6. This can also be a problem in the use of s____________-p____________, in which case we may engage in the behavior and not p____________ ourselves.

7. Some people believe that self-reinforcement is really a way of making the completion of a behavior (more/less) salient, thereby enhancing its value as a s____________ reinforcer.

8. There is also some evidence that self-reinforcement is more effective when others (know/do not know) about the contingency that we have arranged for ourselves.

9. Bandura believes that self-reinforcement and self-punishment can work for people who are likely to feel g____________ if they violate standards that they have set for themselves.

And Furthermore

B. F. Skinner: The Master of Self-Control

It is ironic that B. F. Skinner, the staunch determinist, was in fact very much an expert in the art of self-control. Of course, from his perspective, he was merely exerting effective control over the environmental variables that determined his behavior. Although he maintained that the ultimate cause of our behavior lies in our genes and in the environment, he admitted that "to a considerable extent an individual does appear to shape his own destiny" (Skinner, 1953, p. 228). As it turns out, Skinner proved to be his own best example in this regard.

In behavioral terms, Skinner engineered his environment to be as effective and reinforcing as possible, particularly with respect to his academic work. In Chapter 8, for example, we mentioned how he recommended creating an environment devoted specifically to writing, thereby establishing strong stimulus control over that activity. In addition to this, Skinner (1987) wrote so regularly, at the same time each day, that it seemed to generate a kind of circadian rhythm. Evidence of this occurred when, upon traveling to a different time zone, he would experience the urge to engage in "verbal behavior" at his regular writing time back home! Moreover, in true behaviorist fashion (what is good for the pigeon is good for the behaviorist), Skinner carefully monitored the amount of time he wrote each day and plotted it on a cumulative record. He recognized that the most important factor in being productive was consistency. As he put it:

> Suppose you are at your desk two hours a day and produce on average 50 words an hour. That is not much, but it is about 35,000 words a year, and a book every two or three years. I have found this to be reinforcing enough. (Skinner, 1987, p. 138)

Although many people equate self-control with living a rigid and disciplined lifestyle, it was quite the opposite in Skinner's case. After he had once overworked himself to the point where he began to experience symptoms of angina, he resolved to lead a more relaxed and stress-free existence. He restricted his writing activities to a few hours each morning and devoted the rest of the day to less taxing activities, including watching football on television, listening to music, and reading mystery novels (R. Epstein, 1997). For Skinner, relaxation was not only enjoyable but also a critical factor in being an effective academic. In a paper entitled, *How to Discover What You Have to Say: A Talk to Students*, he described it thus:

> Imagine that you are to play a piano tomorrow night with a symphony orchestra. What will you do between now and then? You will get to bed early for a good night's rest. Tomorrow morning you may practice a little but not too much. During the day, you will eat lightly, take a nap, and in other ways try to put yourself in the best possible condition for your performance in the evening. Thinking effectively about a complex set of circumstances is more demanding than playing a piano, yet how often do you prepare yourself to do so in a similar way? (Skinner 1987, p. 133)

In a sense, Skinner very much lived his behaviorism. Just as Freud spent a few minutes each day analyzing his dreams, Skinner spent a few minutes each day analyzing the variables that controlled his behavior (R. Epstein, 1997). To all appearances, it was a successful endeavor. As former student Robert Epstein put it, "Fred was the most creative, most productive, and happiest person I have ever known. I cannot prove that his exceptional self-management skills were the cause, but I have no doubt whatsoever that they were" (p. 564).

Study Tip: Obviously, many of the study tips offered in previous chapters revolve around the issue of self-control. This chapter, in addition to offering further tips for studying, also offers some theoretical frameworks within which to conceptualize the self-management tactics being suggested. For now, however, let's consider more carefully the emphasis Skinner placed on balance and relaxation in his life and his suggestion that students do likewise. Contrary to what many students believe, one does not have to suffer through endless hours of tedious studying to excel in one's courses. In fact, proficient students generally report that an important aspect of being academically successful is to lead a balanced life with plenty of opportunity for rest and relaxation (Bouvier & Powell, 2008). Thus, it can be just as important for students to schedule sufficient amounts of recreation in their lives as it is to schedule sufficient amounts of studying. It is also important for students to pay close attention to the three pillars of a healthy lifestyle: adequate sleep, regular exercise, and healthy eating patterns (bearing in mind that, in each case, what is optimal for you may be different from what is optimal for someone else). Allowing these behaviors to deteriorate—as so often happens in undergraduates, especially those who, for the first time, are living away from home—can significantly undermine one's ability to learn and study. Fortunately, these behaviors are as amenable to tactics of behavior self-management as the act of studying is. And to the extent that you learn to properly manage these behaviors, you will not only enhance your chances of academic success, but also your chances of having a truly fulfilling life, both at college and beyond. It is no exaggeration to say that the extent to which you learn to effectively manage these behaviors—as difficult and challenging as that might sometimes be—could be among the most important things you learn in college.

Self-Control as a Temporal Issue

Skinner recognized that self-control issues involve choice between conflicting consequences, but others have emphasized that a frequent, critical aspect of this conflict is that one is choosing between alternatives that differ in the extent to which the consequences are immediate versus delayed (e.g., Rachlin, 1974). As noted earlier, immediate consequences are generally more powerful than delayed consequences, a fact that can readily lead to suboptimal choices. Take, for example, a student who can either go out for the evening and have a good time (which is a relatively immediate or "smaller sooner reward") or study in the hopes of achieving an excellent grade (which is a relatively delayed or "larger later reward"). In a straight choice between having a fun evening and an excellent grade, she would clearly choose the excellent grade. But the fun evening is immediately available and hence powerful, and she will be sorely tempted to indulge herself in an evening's entertainment. Similarly, a pigeon who must choose between pecking a green key that leads to an immediate 2 seconds of access to grain (a smaller sooner reward) or pecking a red key that leads to a 10-second delay followed by 6 seconds of access to grain (a larger later reward) may strongly prefer the small, immediate reward. Thus, *from a temporal perspective, lack of self-control arises from the fact that our behavior is more heavily influenced by immediate consequences than by delayed consequences.*

Self-control can also involve choice between a smaller sooner punisher and a larger later punisher—only in this instance it is selection of the smaller sooner alternative that is most beneficial. In deciding whether to go to the dentist, for example, we choose between enduring a small amount of discomfort in the near future (from minor dental treatment) and risking a large amount of discomfort in the distant future (from an infected tooth). Unfortunately, the prospect of experiencing discomfort in the near future (from a visit to the dentist) might exert such strong control over our behavior that we avoid going to the dentist, with the result that we suffer much greater discomfort later. Likewise, a rat given a choice between accepting a small shock immediately or receiving a strong shock 10-seconds from now might choose the latter, with the result that it experiences a considerably stronger shock than it had to.

Of course, in many self-control situations, the full set of controlling consequences is a bit more complicated than a simple choice between two rewards or two punishers. Choosing not to smoke, for example, leads to both a smaller sooner punisher in the form of withdrawal symptoms and a larger later reward in the form of improved health, whereas continuing to smoke leads to a smaller sooner reward in the form of a nicotine high and a larger later punisher in the form of deteriorating health. Note, too, that later consequences are usually less certain than sooner consequences. There is no guarantee that you will become sick and die an early death if you continue to smoke (though you would be foolish to chance it), nor is there any guarantee that you will become radiantly healthy if you quit smoking (you might, after all, catch some disease that is not related to smoking). You can, however, be pretty certain that your next cigarette will be enjoyable, and that if you quit smoking you will soon experience withdrawal symptoms. Thus, delayed consequences often suffer from a sort of double whammy: Their value is weakened both because they are delayed and because they are less certain. Add to this the especially powerful effects of immediate punishers (as noted in the Chapter 9 discussion of approach-avoidance conflict), and it is easy to understand how delayed consequences, such as one's health status 10 years from now, can have such weak effects on behavior compared to immediate consequences (see Table 10.2).

TABLE 10.2 Full set of immediate and delayed consequences for the alternatives of quitting smoking versus continuing to smoke.

	IMMEDIATE CONSEQUENCE (CERTAIN)	DELAYED CONSEQUENCE (UNCERTAIN)
Quitting smoking	Withdrawal symptoms	Improvement in health
Continuing to smoke	Nicotine high	Deterioration in health

Self-control issues in the real world therefore often involve a rather complex set of contingencies (e.g., Brigham, 1978). To investigate this issue, however, researchers have typically focused on relatively simple choices, most commonly a choice between a smaller sooner reward and a larger later reward. The task of choosing between such alternatives is known as a *delay of gratification* task because the person or animal must forgo the smaller sooner reward (i.e., the subject has to "delay gratification") to obtain the larger later reward. Thus, in such tasks, ***self-control*** consists of choosing a larger later reward over a smaller sooner reward; the opposite of self-control, known as ***impulsiveness***, consists of choosing a smaller sooner reward over a larger later reward.

QUICK QUIZ H

1. From a temporal perspective, self-control problems arise from the extent to which we are more heavily influenced by (immediate/delayed) consequences.
2. Self-control is shown by choice of a (smaller sooner/larger later) reward over a ____________ reward. It can also be shown by choice of a (smaller sooner/larger later) punisher over a ____________ punisher.
3. With respect to choice between rewards, the opposite of self-control is called i____________, which is demonstrated by choice of a (smaller sooner/larger later) reward over a ____________ reward.
4. An additional problem in self-control situations is that the delayed consequences tend to be (more/less) certain than the immediate consequences.
5. Outline the full set of consequences involved in choosing between studying and not studying:

	Immediate	*Delayed*
Studying		
Not studying		

Mischel's Delay of Gratification Paradigm

Some of the earliest systematic research using a delay-of-gratification procedure was carried out by the social learning theorist Walter Mischel (e.g., 1966, 1974, 2014). In a typical experiment, a child was led into a room that contained two items (such as pretzels and marshmallows), one of which was clearly preferred. The child was told that he or she could attain the preferred item by simply waiting for the experimenter to return. If the child wished, however, the experimenter could be summoned by sounding a signal, at which point the child received only the smaller, non-preferred item. The question of interest was to see what sorts of strategies children might use to wait out the delay period and obtain the larger reward.

Researchers who conducted such studies quickly noted that the extent to which children avoided attending to a reward had a significant effect on their resistance to temptation. For example, one strategy employed by many children was to simply avert their eyes from the promised rewards or cover their eyes with their hands. Many children also adopted Skinner's tactic of "doing something else," such as talking or singing to themselves or inventing games. Children were also better able to wait out the delay period when the rewards were not present as opposed to when they were present. Thus, resistance to temptation was greatly enhanced by not attending to the tempting reward.

Later research revealed that the manner in which children thought about the rewards also made a difference. Children who were instructed to focus on the abstract properties of the rewards, such as viewing pretzels as tiny logs or marshmallows as clouds, did better than children who focused on the rewards as concrete objects (i.e., seeing pretzels for what they are). Note that these strategies are quite different from what one might suppose should happen from a "positive thinking" perspective, which usually recommends keeping one's attention firmly fixed on the desired outcome. In these studies, children who focused on the desired outcome, and conceptualized it as a desired outcome, generally became impulsive and were unable to wait long enough to receive the larger later reward.

An interesting aspect of this research is the follow-up evaluations conducted on children who participated in some of the earliest studies. For example, the children who, in the original study (at 4 years of age), had devised tactics that enabled them to wait for the preferred reward were, at 17 years of age, more "cognitively and socially competent"—meaning that they could cope well with frustrations, were academically proficient, and got along well with their peers (Shoda, Mischel, & Peake, 1990). This suggests that one's ability to devise appropriate tactics to delay gratification is a basic skill that can enhance many areas of one's life. (See Mischel, 2014, for an engaging first-person account of this research and updated information on the individuals who participated.)

QUICK QUIZ I

1. Children who are (most/least) successful at a delay of gratification task generally keep their attention firmly fixed on the desired treat.
2. While waiting for dessert, Housam imagines that the Jell-O looks like wobbly chunks of glass. By contrast, Ruby views the Jell-O as, well, Jell-O. Between the two of them, ____________ is less likely to get into trouble by eating the Jell-O before being told that it is okay to do so. This is because delay of gratification can be enhanced by thinking about the desired reward in ab____________ rather than c____________ terms.

The Ainslie–Rachlin Model of Self-Control

While the Mischel studies focused on the processes involved in resisting an immediately available temptation, the Ainslie–Rachlin model of self-control focuses on the fact that preference between smaller sooner and larger later rewards can shift over time (Ainslie, 1975; Rachlin, 1974). For example, have you ever promised yourself in the morning that you would study all afternoon, only to find yourself spending the afternoon socializing with friends? In the morning, you clearly preferred studying over socializing that afternoon; but when the afternoon actually arrived, you preferred socializing over studying. In other words, you experienced a reversal of preference as time passed and the smaller sooner reward (socializing) became imminent. The Ainslie–Rachlin model provides an explanation for this reversal of preference and suggests ways to minimize its occurrence and facilitate attainment of the larger later reward.

The Ainslie–Rachlin model is based on the assumption that the value of a reward is a "hyperbolic" function of its delay. In simple terms, what this means is that the delay curve for a reward—which describes the relationship between reward value and time delay—is upwardly scalloped (similar to an FI scallop), with decreasing delays producing larger and larger increments in value. In other words, the value of a reward increases more and more sharply as delay decreases and attainment of the reward becomes imminent (see Figure 10.3).

For example, think about a young child who has been promised a birthday party. When the party is still 3 weeks away, it is likely to be worth very little to him. Three weeks is a long time for a young child, and if you ask him if he would rather have the birthday party in 3 weeks or a chocolate bar right now, he just might prefer the chocolate bar. In other words, a birthday party at 3 weeks' delay is worth less than one chocolate bar available immediately. A week later, with the birthday party still 2 weeks away, you might

FIGURE 10.3 Graph indicating relationship between reward value and delay. Moving from left to right along the horizontal axis represents passage of time, with reward delivery drawing ever nearer. As delay decreases (reward draws near), reward value increases slowly at first and then more and more sharply as the reward becomes imminent.

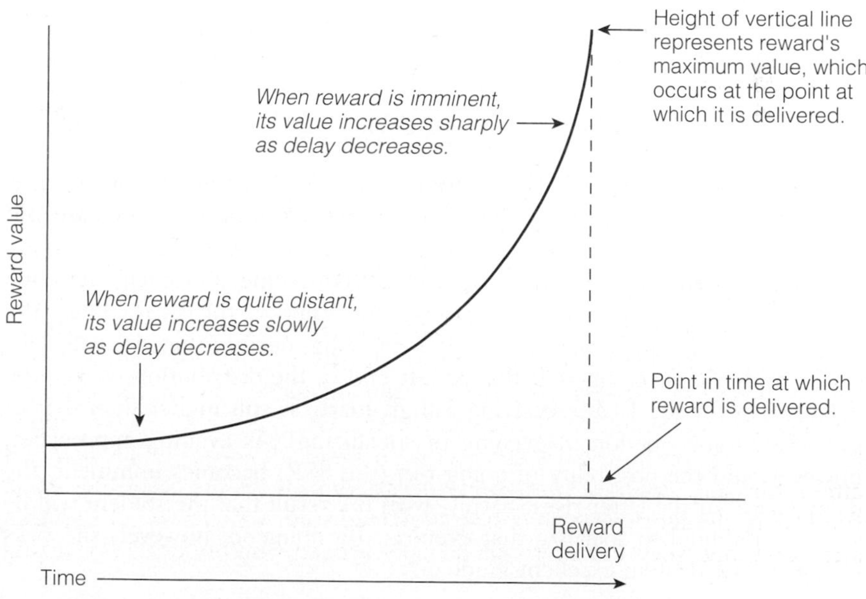

find that little has changed and that he would still be willing to trade the birthday party for the chocolate bar. The value of the birthday party at 2 weeks' delay has increased little, if at all, compared to its value the previous week. When the party is 1 week away, however, you might find that the value of the party has increased significantly and that you would now have to offer him two or three chocolate bars before he would agree to cancel the party. And by the time another week has passed and the day of the birthday party has arrived, he may be so excited that he would reject a year's worth of chocolate bars in order to have that party. The value of the party increased sharply as it became imminent.

Much of the experimental evidence for such upwardly scalloped delay functions is derived from research with rats and pigeons, for whom delays of even a few seconds have significant effects on preference. A hungry pigeon, for example, might show weak preference for a reinforcer that is delayed by 15 seconds, slightly stronger preference for one that is delayed by 10 seconds, moderately stronger preference for one that is delayed by 5 seconds, and very strong preference for one that is available immediately (0 seconds delay). The value of the reward increased only slightly between 15 and 10 seconds, moderately between 10 and 5 seconds, and greatly between 5 and 0 seconds. The delay curve for this pigeon would therefore be only slightly sloped between 15 and 10 seconds, moderately sloped between 10 and 5 seconds, and steeply sloped between 5 and 0 seconds, which is similar to the delay curve shown in Figure 10.3.

QUICK QUIZ J

1. The Ainslie–Rachlin model is based on the finding that as a reward becomes imminent, its value increases more and more (slowly/sharply), yielding a "delay curve" (or delay function) that is upwardly sc____________.
2. I offer to give people a thousand dollars. People are told that they will receive the thousand dollars in either 3 months, 2 months, 1 month, or immediately. Between which conditions are we likely to find the largest difference in level of excitement about receiving the money (3 months vs. 2 months/2 months vs. 1 month/1 month vs. immediately)? Between which conditions would we find the second largest difference in level of excitement? ____________________.

The manner in which delay functions account for preference reversal is shown in Figure 10.4. At an early point in time, when both rewards are still distant, the larger later reward (LLR) is clearly preferred. As time passes, however, and the smaller sooner reward (SSR) becomes imminent, its value increases sharply and comes to outweigh the value of the LLR. Thus, the student who, when she wakes up in the morning, decides that she will definitely study that evening is at the far left end of the distribution, where the delay curve for the LLR (receiving a high mark) is still higher than that of the SSR (going out for an evening of socializing). As evening approaches, however, and the possibility of going out (the SSR) becomes imminent, the delay curve for the latter rises sharply, with the result that the student will be strongly tempted to socialize that evening. By doing so, however, she risks losing the LLR of an excellent grade.

FIGURE 10.4 Graph indicating relative values of a smaller sooner reward (SSR) and a larger later reward (LLR) as time passes. At an early point in time, before the SSR becomes imminent, its value is less than the value of the LLR. As time passes, however, and the SSR becomes imminent, its value increases sharply and comes to outweigh the value of the LLR.

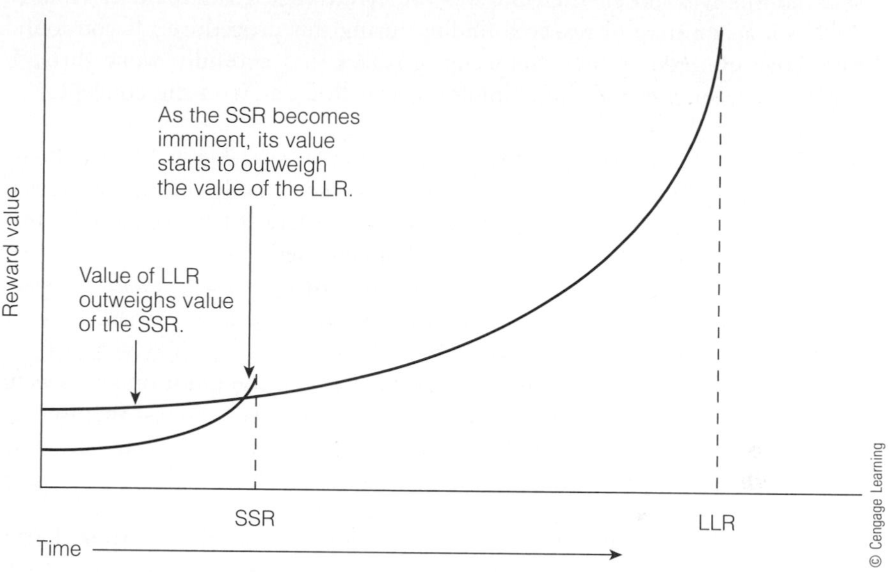

Such preference reversals have been demonstrated experimentally with pigeons. Green, Fisher, Perlow, and Sherman (1981) presented pigeons with a choice between two schedules of reinforcement. In one condition, a peck on the red key resulted in a 20-sec delay followed by 2-sec access to grain (the SSR), while a peck on the green key resulted in a 24-sec delay followed by 6-sec access to grain (the LLR). In this circumstance the pigeons strongly preferred the LLR; they selected it in more than 80% of the trials. In another condition, a peck on the red key resulted in a 2-sec delay followed by 2-sec access to grain, while a peck on the green key resulted in a 6-sec delay followed by 6-sec access to grain. This latter condition is similar to the first condition in that the LLR still occurs 4 seconds later than the SSR, but it is different in that both alternatives are now much closer. Under this circumstance the pigeons strongly preferred the SSR, which was almost immediately available. Thus, just as the Ainslie–Rachlin model predicts, when the SSR reward was imminent, its value outweighed the value of the LLR. But when both the SSR and the LLR were further away, the pigeons strongly preferred the LLR. As the delay values changed, the pigeons displayed a reversal of preference between the two alternatives.

Human subjects making hypothetical choices have also demonstrated preference reversals. In one study by Ainslie and Haendel (1983), most participants said that they would prefer to receive a $100 certified check that can be cashed immediately to a $200 certified check that can be cashed in 2 years. However, when the delays for both alternatives were increased by 6 years—a $100 check that can be cashed in 6 years versus a $200 check that can be cashed in 8 years—subjects preferred the $200 alternative. Thus, with both alternatives quite distant, the LLR was preferred; with both alternatives closer, the SSR was preferred. (See Critchfield & Kollins, 2001, for a summary of research findings using this procedure.) If you found the above examples rather confusing, go back and carefully work through them. If you understand the examples, you will understand the concept.

QUICK QUIZ K

1. If confronted by a choice between one food pellet available in 10 seconds and two food pellets available in 15 seconds, a rat would likely choose the (former/latter). But if 9 seconds were allowed to pass before the rat could make that choice, then it would likely choose the (former/latter).
2. In the above example, as the (smaller sooner/larger later) reward becomes imminent, its value comes to outweigh the value of the other reward.

Given that this type of preference reversal occurs, the question arises as to whether anything can be done about it. Two alternatives suggest themselves: (1) raise the value of the LLR at early points in time and (2) lower the value of the SSR when it becomes imminent.

Changing the Shape of the Delay Function for the Larger Later Reward The basic reason preference reversal occurs is because the LLR has low value at long delays; that is, its delay curve is deeply scalloped. If the delay curve were less deeply scalloped—meaning that the value of the LLR did not decline so drastically as a function of delay—then it would stand a better chance of outweighing any temptations that crop up along the way. This type of situation is illustrated in Figure 10.5.

Herrnstein (1981) suggested several variables that can affect the shape of a delay function. For example, *there appear to be innate differences in impulsivity between species.* Delays of only a few seconds can make a huge difference for rats and pigeons, but make little or no difference for humans, whose behavior is often directed toward consequences that will be delivered hours, days, or even years in the future. (As noted earlier, humans' ability to use language to represent distant events may play a critical role in this behavior.) Thus, delay functions for humans are generally less deeply scalloped than they are for other animals.

There may be individual differences, with some individuals being more impulsive than others. For example, people with antisocial personality disorder, which may have a strong genetic basis, are generally very impulsive (Kaplan, Sadock, & Grebb, 1994). Such individuals presumably have deeply scalloped delay functions. Less extreme differences no doubt exist among normal individuals in the population. Some people may have an inborn temperament that predisposes them toward displaying the necessary patience to achieve long-term outcomes, whereas others have a temperament that predisposes them toward being rather impulsive.

FIGURE 10.5 Graph indicating relative values of a smaller sooner reward (SSR) and a larger later reward (LLR) in which the delay function for the LLR is less deeply scalloped (somewhat flatter). Under such conditions, the value of the LLR will remain higher than the value of the SSR even as the SSR becomes imminent.

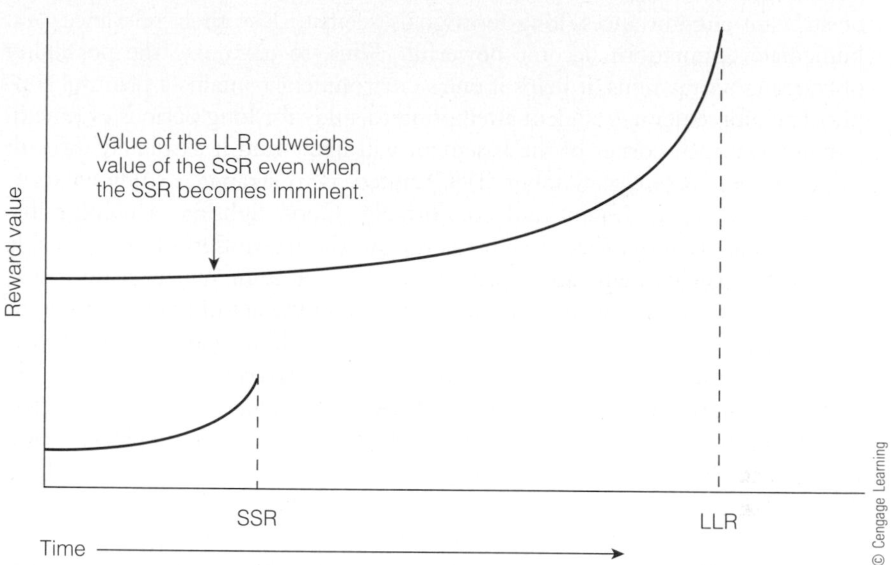

People generally become less impulsive as they grow older. Although young children find it difficult to resist having a cookie before dinner, most adults are quite capable of doing so (well, at least more often than when they were kids). In fact, an increased ability to resist temptation and pursue long-term goals is considered a hallmark of maturity.

People generally become less impulsive after repeated experience with responding for delayed rewards. As children grow older, caretakers require them to display more and more patience—such as by forcing them to wait until after dinner to have a dessert—thereby gradually shaping their ability to delay gratification. Interestingly, in a scene from Skinner's (1948a) novel, *Walden II*, which depicts a utopian community designed around behavioral principles, children are described as waiting in front of their meals for a short time before eating. With successive meals, the waiting period was gradually lengthened. Although such a procedure might sound frightfully authoritarian, it is probably not much different from what most parents carry out less formally as they expect their children to gradually display more and more patience as they grow older. Interestingly, the efficacy of Skinner's approach has been demonstrated experimentally. Research has shown that both pigeons (Mazur & Logue, 1978) and children (Newman & Kanfer, 1976) demonstrate an increased ability to resist the temptation of a smaller sooner reward after being exposed to large rewards that are systematically delayed for longer and longer periods of time.

The availability of other sources of reinforcement may also serve to reduce impulsiveness. Many people find that they are more impulsive during periods characterized by an overall lack of reinforcement. For example, Kimberly experiences a strong urge to resume smoking after she loses her job, and Mike begins drinking heavily after his girlfriend leaves him. Under depressing or stressful circumstances, long-term goals seem to lose their relevance, and immediate temptations become powerful. Thus, to maximize the possibility of resisting temptations, it helps if one's environment contains a plentiful supply of reinforcement. A student attempting to study for long periods of time in a dingy, cramped corner of the basement will likely find it extremely difficult to persist. Far better, as Skinner (1987) noted, is to arrange a study environment that is both pleasant and comfortable. Good lighting, a comfortable chair, and a well-organized desk (to eliminate the frustration of being unable to find things)—perhaps accompanied by some pleasant music in the background and a cup of coffee to sip on—will enable the act of studying to compete more effectively with such temptations as watching television or playing computer games. Self-reinforcement procedures may also play a role here, in that they ensure that the person intermittently engages in some pleasant activities while attempting to complete a difficult task, for example by playing computer games for 15 minutes following every 2 hours of studying (the trick, of course, being to keep the game playing to only 15 minutes).

Finally, as noted in our discussion of behavior chains (Chapter 7), *we can more easily maintain responding for a distant goal by setting up an explicit series of subgoals.* The successful completion of each subgoal provides a salient form of secondary reinforcement that helps maintain progress toward the larger later reward. Additionally, because the secondary reinforcement from the completion of a subgoal is relatively immediate, it can compete more effectively with temptations that crop up along the way. Note, however, that for most people, subgoals that are relatively precise will be more effective than subgoals that are relatively vague (see Study Tip in Chapter 11).

QUICK QUIZ L

1. One strategy for increasing self-control is to make the delay function (or delay curve) for the larger later reward (more/less) deeply scalloped.
2. The delay functions for a pigeon will likely be (more/less) deeply scalloped than those for a human, which means that the pigeon is relatively (less/more) impulsive.
3. The delay functions for a 6-year-old child will likely be (more/less) deeply scalloped than those for a 15-year-old, meaning that the 15-year-old is relatively (more/less) impulsive.
4. Exposure to gradually increasing delays seems to make the delay function (more/less) deeply scalloped.
5. A person is likely to be (more/less) impulsive in a pleasant environment as opposed to an unpleasant environment.
6. From the perspective of the Ainslie–Rachlin model, the setting up and attainment of a subgoal related to a delayed reward serves to (raise/lower) the delay function for that reward at early points in time, making it (more/less) deeply scalloped.

Making a Commitment Response Flattening out the delay gradient for the larger later reward (making it less deeply scalloped) is perhaps the ideal answer to problems of self-control. It seems unlikely, however, that this tactic will always be successful. For a person who smokes, the immediate reinforcement to be derived from having a cigarette (both positive reinforcement in the form of a nicotine high and negative reinforcement in the form of avoiding withdrawal symptoms) is likely to be a powerful temptation. In such circumstances, the exercise of self-control might be facilitated through the use of a "commitment response" (Rachlin, 1974, 1991). A ***commitment response*** (also known as a *precommitment response*) is an action carried out at an early point in time that serves either to eliminate or greatly reduce the value of an upcoming temptation.

As an example of a commitment response, consider a student who, in the morning, decides that she definitely needs to study that evening. At this early point in time, the value of studying to ensure a good mark outweighs the value of alternate activities, such as going out with friends or watching television. Through experience, however, the student has learned that these early-morning preferences mean little when evening rolls around and more immediate reinforcement from other activities becomes available. To ensure that she studies tonight, she knows that she has to somehow eliminate ahead of time the various temptations that will arise. Thus, that morning, she gives her younger brother $20 and instructs him to keep it if she fails to study that evening. By making this monetary commitment, she has essentially locked herself into studying. As illustrated in Figure 10.6, the aversive consequence that would result from not studying (her obnoxious brother having a good time at her expense) has so reduced the value of any alternate activity that it no longer effectively competes with the value of studying and the larger later reward of obtaining a good mark.

Behavioral contracting, in which a person formally arranges to attain certain rewards for resisting temptation or receive certain punishers for yielding to temptation, essentially operates on this principle. The contract is negotiated with the therapist at an early point in time, before encountering the temptation. The contingencies outlined in the contract serve to reduce the attractiveness of the tempting alternative. Of course, in some circumstances, it might even be possible to completely eliminate the tempting alternative. A graduate student who is spending too much time watching television rather than working on his thesis—an unfortunately all too common difficulty—might solve the problem by giving his television to a friend for the rest of the semester.

Although the use of a commitment strategy might be seen as one that requires a certain amount of intelligence and foresight, experiments have shown that even pigeons can learn to make commitment responses. Rachlin and Green (1972) presented pigeons with a choice between a smaller sooner food reward and a larger later food reward. The pigeons invariably chose the SSR over the LLR. The pigeons were then given the option, several seconds before being presented with this choice, of pecking another key that would eliminate the SSR as one of the choices and leave the LLR as the only

FIGURE 10.6 Effect of a commitment strategy on preference between a smaller sooner reward (SSR) and a larger later reward (LLR). The commitment response needs to be made before the SSR becomes imminent. It will be effective to the extent that it reduces the value of the SSR, even when it is imminent, to below the value of the LLR.

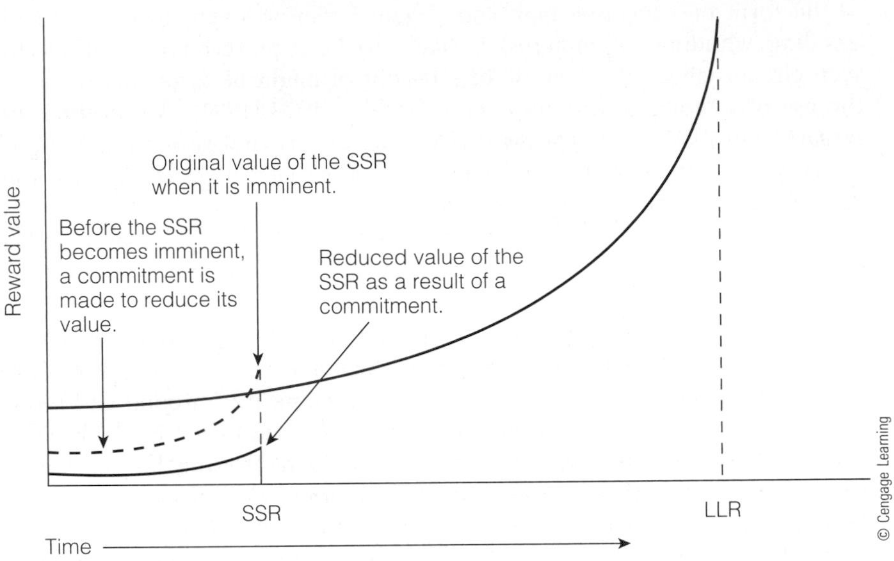

alternative. Some of the pigeons learned to select this option, thereby essentially removing the temptation ahead of time. The pigeons did the equivalent of giving away the television set in the morning so that, when evening came around, they would be more likely to study.[2]

QUICK QUIZ M

1. A ____________ response is designed to either eliminate or reduce the value of an upcoming temptation.
2. Such a response is most likely to be carried out at a(n) (early/later) point in time when the temptation is quite (near/distant).
3. Gary would love to go running each evening but always feels so tired after work that he just plumps down in his favorite chair when he gets home and has a glass of wine. If Gary wishes to make a commitment to go running, such as arranging to go running with a neighbor, he is most likely to make this commitment (the day before/immediately before) the run is supposed to take place.

[2]Given the variety of items and services that can be purchased online these days, it should come as no surprise to learn that behavior contracting services are also available online. The first such service, called *stickK*, was founded by two economists, Dean Karlan and Ian Ayres, who came up with the idea after successfully implementing a behavior contract with each other to lose weight. The engaging story of their weight loss program can be found at the service's Web site: http://www.stickK.com. *Beeminder* is yet another online behavior contracting service. It may be of particular interest to students in that it includes the option of first trying it out with just a verbal commitment and without actually having to commit money: https://www.beeminder.com/.

The Small-But-Cumulative Effects Model

The basic delay of gratification paradigm, which both Mischel's early research and the original Ainslie–Rachlin model are built upon, involves a simple choice between a single SSR and a single LLR. This is, however, an extreme simplification of the full set of contingencies that we often face when trying to control our behavior. As mentioned earlier, many situations involve choosing between a combination of rewarding and punishing outcomes that vary not only in their value and delay but also in the certainty with which they are likely to occur. More importantly, in relation to the issue of certainty, many of the most difficult self-control issues cannot be resolved by a single choice; rather, they require an ongoing (often never-ending) series of choices, with any single choice having relatively little effect. Thus, according to this ***small-but-cumulative effects model***, each individual choice on a self-control task has only a small but cumulative effect on our likelihood of obtaining the desired long-term outcome (e.g., Malott, 1989; see also Ainslie, 2001, and Rachlin, 2000).

Imagine, for example, that you have been following a program of healthy eating, but you then find yourself choosing between a restaurant's world-famous Greaze-Burger and their far healthier, but much less appetizing, Tofu Salad Supreme. In terms of achieving the larger later reward of good health, the choice might seem obvious. But is it obvious? That one Greaze-Burger, *by itself*, is unlikely to make any difference in your quest to become healthy; in the same way, a single Tofu Salad Supreme will not, by itself, make you healthy. It is only by repeatedly selecting tofu salads over Greaze-Burgers that you will realize any significant, long-term effects on your health. So it is relatively easy, on any particular occasion, to talk yourself into making an exception to your healthy eating plan: "Hey, it's been a tough day, so why not indulge just this once?" The problem, of course, is that this same logic applies each time you encounter a tasty treat. Each single treat that you encounter will not, in and of itself, significantly affect your health. But to the extent that you are thereby seduced into frequently consuming those treats (and we very often are), you undermine the possibility of achieving good health.

This small-but-cumulative effects approach can be incorporated into the basic Ainslie–Rachlin model that we discussed earlier. The fact that each single choice of a smaller sooner reward has such little effect in the long run helps allow its value, when it becomes imminent, to rise above the value of the larger later reward. After all, would you really be tempted to eat a Greaze-Burger if you knew that one burger would, like a slow-acting poison, give you a heart attack in 20 or 30 years? Would you really smoke a cigarette if you knew that one cigarette would someday give you cancer? And would you really watch TV tonight rather than study if you knew that not studying tonight would, with certainty, result in failing the course? Not likely. It is only because that one burger, one cigarette, or one TV night is unlikely, by itself, to result in such punishing outcomes that its value can rise so sharply when it becomes imminent.

Thus, in many situations, each choice of an SSR versus LLR has only a small but cumulative effect on the outcome, which helps explain why self-control is, for many of us, such a difficult task. Fortunately, the small-but-cumulative effects model also suggests ways to improve self-control. One is to make salient the fact that individual choices are not isolated events, but rather parts of a whole. This may be one of the reasons why self-monitoring can by itself have beneficial effects on behavior; tracking the behavior on an ongoing basis forces us to view the behavior from a holistic perspective. The small-but-cumulative-effects model also clarifies the importance of having a plan in place to handle occasional lapses (a relapse prevention plan), given that we will very likely be faced with an ongoing series of highly seductive temptations that we may not always be able to resist (e.g., Marlatt & Gordon, 1985; Watson & Tharp, 2014). This model also indicates the importance of establishing rules that clearly distinguish between acceptable and unacceptable behaviors, since the actual point when an impulsive behavior becomes harmful is often not clear. For some people or in some circumstances, the effective rule might be total abstinence from a tempting event. For example, the Alcoholics Anonymous rule of never consuming alcohol seems to be an effective boundary for some people who have been addicted to alcohol. For other people or in other circumstances, however, it may be that total abstinence is too severe and one might do better to occasionally indulge oneself within clearly specified limits. For example, for many students, a flexible study plan that allows for some level of indulgence or interruptions may be more effective than a highly rigid plan that is difficult to maintain (see Ainslie, 2001).

We will return again to the issue of self-control, and especially the importance of establishing clear rules for our behavior, when we discuss rule-governed behavior in Chapter 11.

QUICK QUIZ N

1. According to the __________ model, self-control is a difficult task because each temptation has only a __________ but __________ effect on our likelihood of obtaining the long-term goal.
2. This model highlights the potential usefulness of establishing clear r__________ for distinguishing between acceptable and unacceptable behaviors, since the point at which impulsive behavior becomes harmful (is/is not) clear.

And Furthermore

Self-Control: How Sweet It Is! Or Is It?

Although the emphasis in this chapter has been on behavioral approaches to self-control, which largely ignore internal constructs such as willpower, there are other approaches to self-control that do emphasize such constructs. For example, according to the *limited resource model* of self-control (also referred to as the *strength* or *ego-depletion* model), self-regulatory behaviors are fueled by a type of limited internal energy (Baumeister, Bratslavsky, Muraven, & Tice, 1998). A key proposition of the model is that this internal resource—which is what most people would call "willpower"—is depleted by tasks that require mental or emotional effort, such as studying, solving puzzles, or resisting a temptation. This in turn results in a decrease in our ability to self-regulate, as indicated by a significant reduction in performance on subsequent tasks or by an increased likelihood of impulsive behavior. For example, in one study (Gailliot et al., 2007), participants in the "ego-depletion" condition were asked to watch a short video with instructions to focus only on a woman's face and not look at the words appearing at the bottom of the screen (which many participants would find difficult to do). Participants in a control group were simply told to watch the video. Participants in both groups were then given a Stroop test, which is a test of attentional ability. As predicted by the model, those who had been exposed to the ego-depletion task performed significantly worse on the Stroop test compared to those in the control group. Self-regulation, from this perspective, is therefore like a muscle that can become temporarily fatigued through intense use (but which can also be strengthened through repeated efforts).

Interestingly, Baumeister and his colleagues also identified glucose ("blood sugar") as playing a critical role in these effects (Gailliot et al., 2007). They reported that ego-depleting tasks significantly reduced blood glucose levels, and that the usual decrement in performance following such tasks could be reversed by giving participants a sugary solution to drink. These results suggest that glucose is the underlying factor that fuels a person's willpower and self-control.

The strength model of self-regulation has proven to be highly popular. Perhaps this is because it resonates so well with cherished notions of willpower and self-determination. Recently, though, evolutionary psychologist Robert Kurzban (2010a, 2010b) has challenged the model, arguing that it is based on outdated and simplistic notions about how the brain operates. For example, the idea that the brain burns up large amounts of glucose when engaged in cognitively effortful activity has been shown to be false; in reality, such activities require miniscule amounts of energy, making it extremely unlikely that cognitive processing would be significantly affected by the kinds of brief "ego-depletion" tasks often used. The ego-depletion model has also been challenged by Job and colleagues, who found that the effects of an ego-depleting task on subsequent performance (Job, Dweck, & Walton, 2010), and the effects of ingesting glucose on restoring performance (Job, Walton, Bernecker, & Dweck, 2013), were critically dependent on participants' belief that willpower is a limited resource. Of interest to students, they also found that students who did *not* believe in the limited resource model of self-control coped better with a heavy course load than did students who did believe in the limited resource model (Job, Walton, Bernecker, & Dweck, 2015). This suggests that holding the belief that self-control is a limited resource could actually undermine one's self-control.

Although the validity of the limited resource model is being called into question—with self-control being nowhere near as fragile as the original model proposed—it has drawn attention to some important notions. As noted earlier, Skinner carefully restricted the amount of writing he did on any particular day so as to ensure that he was well rested for his next writing session (R. Epstein, 1997). He recognized that he functioned

(*continued*)

best by limiting the amount of effortful writing he did, and by constraining that writing to particular times. But he did not feel the need to speculate about the existence of a limited, internal resource to account for it. He was content to stick to what he could observe, both internally and externally, and what he could manipulate, such as the chair he sat on (ensuring that it was comfortable), the room he wrote in (ensuring that it was efficiently laid out), and the amount of sleep he obtained (by placing a "sleeping cubicle" nearby). Skinner appears to have led a highly productive and satisfying life, and anyone wishing to do likewise would do well to pay close attention to his emphasis on behavior and environment. But this doesn't mean that nonbehavioral models of self-control, such as the limited resource model, might not also lead to some unique insights. (We will revisit the issue of willpower, and how it might be accounted for from a more behavioral perspective, toward the end of Chapter 11.)

SUMMARY

On a concurrent schedule of reinforcement, the subject responds on two or more independent schedules of reinforcement that are simultaneously available. Choice behavior in such situations often obeys the matching law, which predicts that the proportion of responses emitted on an alternative will match the proportion of reinforcers received on that alternative. The matching law has been shown to have real-world applicability, ranging from predicting communication patterns in humans to foraging behavior in animals.

Researchers have also discovered certain deviations from matching. In undermatching, the difference in proportion of responses on the richer versus poorer schedules is less than predicted by matching. In overmatching, the difference in proportion of responses on the richer versus poorer schedules is greater than predicted by matching. Bias from matching occurs when one alternative receives more responses than would be predicted by matching, both when it contains the poorer schedule and when it contains the richer schedule.

According to melioration theory, matching results from the subject's tendency to shift behavior toward a better-paying alternative. This tendency can sometimes reduce the overall amount of reinforcement. For example, more behavior may be directed to a better-paying alternative than is needed to obtain the available reinforcers. And overindulgence in a highly reinforcing alternative can result in long-term habituation to that alternative. Melioration also results in a tendency to be overly attracted to immediate reinforcers.

Skinner viewed self-control as involving a choice between conflicting outcomes. He believed that self-control is facilitated by emitting a controlling response that alters the probability of a controlled response. Specific techniques of self-control include such tactics as physical self-restraint, self-deprivation, and self-reinforcement. A major problem with the latter is that one can easily short-circuit such self-directed consequences.

Others have noted that self-control involves a choice between immediate outcomes, which are relatively powerful, and delayed outcomes, which are relatively weak. From this perspective, self-control can be defined as choosing a larger later reward (LLR) over a smaller sooner reward (SSR), while impulsiveness can be defined as choosing an SSR over an LLR.

Research has shown that children who resist temptation in a delay of gratification task tend to distract themselves from the tempting reward. As well, children can better resist temptation when they think of the reward in abstract rather than concrete terms. Follow-up research revealed that children who were successful in delaying gratification were, years later, more academically and socially successful.

The Ainslie–Rachlin model of self-control is based on the assumption that the delay function for a reward is often deeply scalloped, so that its value increases sharply as it becomes imminent. This explains why preferences for LLRs and SSRs tend to shift over time. When both rewards are far away, the value of the LLR outweighs the value of the SSR. As the SSR becomes imminent, however, its value rises sharply, possibly exceeding the value of the LLR at that time.

Thus, one means for facilitating self-control is flattening the delay function for the LLR so that its value remains fairly high even at long delays. Factors that may affect the shape of a delay function include biological variables (including differences between species and between individuals within a species), age, experience with responding for delayed rewards, the presence of other sources of reinforcement, and the attainment of subgoals. Another means for facilitating self-control is by making a commitment to the LLR at an early point in time, before the SSR becomes imminent. A commitment response is a response that serves to reduce the value of the SSR when it becomes imminent.

According to the small-but-cumulative effects model, each individual choice on a self-control task has a small but cumulative effect on our likelihood of obtaining the desired long-term outcome. It is largely because of this factor that we are frequently tempted to make an exception to a self-control program insofar as each individual temptation has only an insignificant effect on our long-term goal. It is for this reason that clear boundaries between acceptable versus unacceptable behavior and relapse prevention programs are so important.

SUGGESTED READINGS

Epstein, R. (1997). Skinner as self-manager. *Journal of Applied Behavior Analysis*, *30*, 545–568. An interesting discussion of Skinner's use of behavioral techniques to manage his own behavior.

Herrnstein, R. J. (1997). *The matching law: Papers in psychology and economics.* Cambridge, MA: Harvard University Press. For the serious student who wishes to acquire a more in-depth understanding of matching, melioration, and the behavioral approach to economics.

Watson, D. L., & Tharp, R. G. (2014). *Self-directed behavior: Self-modification for personal adjustment* (10th ed.). Belmont, CA: Wadsworth Cengage Learning. A good source book on various tactics of self-control for a wide range of everyday behavior problems.

STUDY QUESTIONS

1. What is a concurrent schedule? Diagram an example of a concurrent schedule that might be used in an operant conditioning experiment with pigeons. What is the likely pattern of behavior on a concurrent VR 20 VR 60 schedule of reinforcement, and why is this the case?
2. Define the matching law and give the matching equation. Using the equation, show what the matching law predicts concerning the distribution of behavior displayed on a concurrent VI 10-sec VI 30-sec schedule of reinforcement. (Hint: What is the expected distribution of reinforcers on this schedule?)
3. What is a changeover delay (COD)? In what sense is a COD similar to a foraging situation with animals?
4. What is overmatching versus undermatching? Give an example of over-matching and undermatching (with hypothetical proportions) that might occur on a concurrent VI 20-sec VI 30-sec schedule (which means that you must first work out the expected proportions with these schedules).
5. What is bias from matching? Give an example of bias (with hypothetical proportions) that might occur on a concurrent VI 15-sec VI 60-sec schedule, and response alternatives consisting of a green key and a blue key.
6. Describe melioration theory. Briefly describe three ways, with examples, in which the tendency to meliorate can reduce the overall level of reinforcement.
7. What is the distinction between controlled response and controlling response? What is the major difficulty with the use of self-reinforcement and self-punishment?
8. What are the definitions of self-control and impulsiveness within the context of a delay of gratification task? Describe some of the strategies children use to facilitate success in a delay of gratification task.
9. With the help of a graph, describe how the Ainslie–Rachlin model accounts for preference reversal between a smaller sooner reward and a larger later reward.
10. List four variables that can affect the shape of the delay function and hence the extent to which a person or animal is likely to display self-control.
11. With the help of a graph, describe how a commitment response can be used to facilitate self-control.
12. Describe the small-but-cumulative effects model of self-control and impulsiveness. Explain how this accounts for the difficulty people often have in studying on a regular basis and in following an exercise program.

CONCEPT REVIEW

bias from matching. A deviation from matching in which one response alternative attracts a higher proportion of responses than would be predicted by matching, regardless of whether that alternative contains the richer or poorer schedule.

commitment response. An action carried out at an early point in time that serves to either eliminate or reduce the value of an upcoming temptation. Also called a *precommitment response*.

concurrent schedule of reinforcement. A complex schedule consisting of the simultaneous presentation of two or more independent schedules, each leading to a reinforcer.

impulsiveness. With respect to choice between two rewards, selecting a smaller sooner reward over a larger later reward.

matching law. The principle that the *proportion* of responses emitted on a particular schedule matches the *proportion* of reinforcers obtained on that schedule.

melioration theory. A theory of matching that holds that the distribution of behavior in a choice situation shifts toward those alternatives that have higher value regardless of the long-term effect on overall amount of reinforcement.

overmatching. A deviation from matching in which the proportion of responses on the richer schedule versus poorer schedule is more different than would be predicted by matching.

self-control. With respect to choice between two rewards, selecting a larger later reward over a smaller sooner reward.

small-but-cumulative effects model. A model of self-control in which each individual choice between a smaller sooner and larger later reward has only a small but cumulative effect on our likelihood of obtaining the desired outcome.

undermatching. A deviation from matching in which the proportion of responses on the richer schedule versus poorer schedule is less different than would be predicted by matching.

CHAPTER TEST

12. According to the ___________ law, if 25% of reinforcers are obtained on one of two simultaneously available schedules, then ___________ of responses are likely to be emitted on that schedule.
6. The Ainslie–Rachlin model is based on the assumption that the value of a reward increases more and more sharply as delay ___________ and attainment of the reward becomes ___________.
17. The matching law predicts that on a concurrent VI 15-sec VI 60-sec schedule, ___________% of responses should be emitted on the VI 15-sec schedule and ___________% on the VI 60-sec schedule. In

reality, the pigeon emits 65% on the VI 15-sec schedule and 35% on the VI 60-sec schedule. This is an example of ___________ matching.

9. A(n) ___________ schedule of reinforcement consists of the simultaneous presentation of two or more independent schedules, each of which leads to a(n) ___________.
13. The ___________ law holds that the ___________ of responses emitted on a particular schedule will match the ___________ of reinforcers obtained on that schedule.
31. Hoa sometimes feels well and sometimes feels sick. If feeling healthy is a form of reinforcement, we would expect Hoa to be most impulsive when she is feeling (healthy/sick).
20. The matching law predicts that on a concurrent VI 10-sec VI 30-sec schedule, ___________% of responses should be emitted on the VI 30-sec schedule and ___________% on the VI 10-sec schedule. In reality, you obtain 15% on the VI 30-sec schedule and 85% on the VI 10-sec schedule. This is an example of ___________ matching.
3. From a temporal perspective, lack of self-control arises from the fact that our behavior is more heavily influenced by ___________ consequences as opposed to ___________ consequences.
18. When the cost of switching between schedules is quite high, then ___________ matching is likely to occur. When the cost of switching is extremely low, then ___________ matching is likely to occur.
30. Exposure to rewards that are presented at gradually increasing delays is likely to result in a(n) (increase/decrease) in impulsiveness, which also means that the reward delay curve for these individuals has become (more/less) deeply scalloped.
1. You always eat a full meal before going shopping, so that you will not be tempted (through hunger) to buy those chocolate cookies you are addicted to. From the perspective of self-control, Skinner would refer to the act of eating the meal as the ___________ response and the subsequent decreased tendency to buy cookies as the ___________ response.
27. In general, melioration is often the result of behavior being too strongly governed by ___________ consequences as opposed to ___________ consequences.
10. Given a choice between a VR 100 schedule and a VR 40 schedule of reinforcement, a rat is likely to show (exclusive/partial) preference for the ___________ schedule.
35. Given a choice between a VI 60-sec schedule and a VI 20-sec schedule, a pigeon is likely to emit ___________% of its responses to the VI 20-sec alternative.
23. According to ___________ theory, the distribution of behavior in a choice situation shifts toward those alternatives that have ___________ value regardless of the effect on the overall amount of reinforcement.

14. Given a choice between a VI 40-sec schedule and a VI 20-sec schedule, a rat is likely to emit ___________% of its responses to the VI 40-sec alternative.

5. From a behavioral perspective, self-control consists of preference for a(n) ___________ reward over a(n) ___________ reward, while the opposite of self-control, known as ___________, consists of preference for a(n) ___________ reward over a(n) ___________ reward.

26. As soon as Mario retired, he moved to Florida and went for walks on the beach every day. Unfortunately, although going for walks continued to be his most enjoyable activity, it soon became less enjoyable than it used to be. This appears to be an example of how the tendency to ___________ can result in long-term ___________.

33. A commitment response is most likely to be made at a(n) (early/later) point in time before the (smaller sooner/larger later) reward becomes imminent.

16. As Sal and his wife converse with the neighbor one evening, Sal is three times more responsive to the neighbor's comments than his wife is. Research evidence suggests that the neighbor will direct his conversation toward Sal, as opposed to his wife, (three times as often/exclusively).

28. In general, humans have a (more/less) deeply scalloped delay function than chickens. As well, a person who is very impulsive is likely to have a (more/less) deeply scalloped delay function than a person who is very patient.

7. In keeping with the Ainslie–Rachlin model of self-control, I am most likely to choose $50 over $100 when the choice is between: (A) $50 now versus $100 a year from now, or (B) $50 a year from now versus $100 two years from now. The answer is alternative ___________, which means that I tend to become impulsive when the smaller sooner reward is (imminent/delayed).

11. According to the matching law, the proportion of ___________ emitted on a certain schedule will roughly equal the proportion of ___________ obtained on that schedule.

4. To the extent that Romano gets up early to study for his math test next week, as opposed to lying in bed an extra hour, he is displaying self-___________. To the extent that he chooses to lie in bed, he is displaying ___________.

19. As Sal and his wife converse with the neighbor one day, Sal is three times more responsive to the neighbor's comments than his wife is. The neighbor, however, looks at Sal's wife about as often as he looks at Sal. During the next day's conversation, Sal's wife is three times more responsive to the neighbor's comments than Sal is. This time the neighbor looks at Sal's wife five times as often as he looks at Sal. This appears to be an example of the deviation from matching known as ___________, which also suggests that the neighbor finds Sal's wife ___________.

32. Maria announces to her parents that she is going to study all weekend, knowing that they will severely chastise her if she does not live up to

her promise. Given that Maria hates being chastised by her parents, her announcement can be seen as a(n) ________ response that will lower the value of any alternate activity that might interfere with studying during the weekend.

21. You tend to shop at two favorite clothing stores, Madison's Fine Fashions and Mike's Grubbies. Over time, you have learned that Mike's is twice as likely to have something in stock that you wish to buy. If the two stores are side by side, then you are likely to visit Mike's (twice/equally) as often as Madison's. This is an example of ________ matching.
8. According to the Ainslie–Rachlin model, one way to enhance self-control would be to raise the delay curve for the (smaller sooner/larger later) reward.
24. On a concurrent VR 50 VI 30-sec schedule, a pigeon is likely to ________ the number of responses emitted on each schedule to the number of reinforcers obtained. By doing so, it (will/will not) maximize the amount of reinforcement it obtains during the session. Such results support the ________ theory of matching.
25. Professor Huynh spends a lot of time reading articles, which she enjoys, but little time in the lab doing research, which she does not enjoy. Insofar as she needs to do research to maintain her position at the university, this appears to be an example of how ________ can lead to suboptimal patterns of behavior.
2. You decide to do your housework each evening at 7:00 P.M., and then reward yourself with 1 hour of playing your favorite computer game. A major problem with this kind of self-reinforcement procedure is that you might ________________________.
This problem is known as ________ the contingency.
34. The ________ effects model of self-control helps emphasize the importance of establishing rules that clearly distinguish between acceptable and unacceptable behavior. It also makes clear the importance of having a(n) ________ prevention plan to cope with situations in which we might violate our self-control program.
22. You tend to shop at two favorite clothing stores, Madison's Fine Fashions and Mike's Grubbies. Over time, you have learned that Mike's is twice as likely to have something in stock that you wish to buy. If the two stores are separated by a long and difficult drive, then you are likely to demonstrate ________ matching in your visits to Mike's versus Madison's, which means that you are (twice/more than twice) as likely to visit Mike's than Madison's.
15. According to the ________ effects model, a student will often have difficulty studying on a particular night because the consequences for not studying that one night are (aversively significant/largely insignificant).
29. In general, as people grow from childhood into adulthood, their delay curves will likely become (more/less) deeply scalloped.

ANSWERS TO CHAPTER TEST

1. controlling; controlled
2. play the game and not do the housework; short-circuiting
3. immediate; delayed
4. control; impulsiveness
5. larger later; smaller sooner; impulsiveness; smaller sooner; larger later
6. decreases; imminent
7. A; imminent
8. larger later
9. concurrent; reinforcer
10. exclusive; VR 40
11. responses; reinforcers
12. matching; 25%
13. matching; proportion; proportion
14. 33%
15. small-but-cumulative; largely insignificant
16. three times as often
17. 80%; 20%; under
18. over; under
19. bias; attractive
20. 25%; 75%; over
21. equally; under
22. over; more than twice
23. melioration; higher
24. match; will not; melioration
25. melioration
26. meliorate; habituation
27. immediate; delayed
28. less; more
29. less
30. decrease; less
31. sick
32. commitment ("controlling" would also be correct)
33. early; smaller sooner
34. small-but-cumulative; relapse
35. 75%

CHAPTER 11

OBSERVATIONAL LEARNING AND RULE-GOVERNED BEHAVIOR

CHAPTER OUTLINE

"I don't care what Dr. Dee says!" Gina shouted in exasperation when Steve again pronounced judgment on some aspect of their relationship. "I am starting to wish you had never enrolled in that stupid course. Why don't you just listen to what I'm saying rather than act like 'Mr. Behaviorist' all the time?"

Much of this text has been concerned with basic processes of conditioning in which new patterns of behavior are acquired through direct exposure to the relevant events. Ming fears dogs because she was once bitten by a dog, and Kyle goes to a particular restaurant because in the past he received good food there. However, not all behavior patterns are acquired this directly. Some people acquire a fear of dogs without ever being attacked by a dog, or they eagerly head off to a restaurant despite never having been there before. Such behaviors have somehow been acquired in the absence of any direct exposure to the relevant events.

In this chapter, we focus on two processes that allow us to alter behavior patterns through indirect means. We begin with observational learning (a process that was touched on in previous chapters), which plays a strong role in human learning but is also found in animals. We follow that with a discussion of how we use language to generate rules (or instructions) to control behavior, including the implications of "rule-governed behavior" for understanding and enhancing self-control.

Observational or Social Learning

Do you remember your first day of school? If so, you probably remember being a little afraid and unsure about what to do when you first arrived—where to stand, who to talk to, even where to go to the bathroom. After a while, though, it all became much clearer because you could watch what other people did and follow them. This type of learning is called *observational learning*.

In ***observational learning***, the behavior of a *model* is witnessed by an *observer* and the observer's behavior is subsequently changed. Because observational learning is essentially a social process, and humans are social beings, we can quickly acquire new behavior patterns in this way (Bandura, 1986). In fact, observational learning is often referred to as *social learning* and, as discussed in Chapter 1, constitutes a significant aspect of Bandura's social learning theory. There is considerable evidence that people can improve their performance on many tasks, including sports, simply by watching others perform (e.g., Blandin, Lhuisset, & Proteau, 1999; Shea, Wright, Wulf, & Whitacre, 2000). In fact, this type of learning can occur without our even being aware that our behavior has been influenced in this way. For example, we may see television commercials showing attractive people modeling new, even undesirable, behaviors such as driving too fast in a new car. This subtle form of modeling might then affect our behavior when we find ourselves in a similar situation. Conversely, models need not be aware that their behavior is being observed, which means that we do not have to "teach'" someone for them to learn from us. This is another reason the term *social learning* is often used. Being in a social situation can change behavior, even if no one in the group realizes it.

Observational learning can be involved in both classical and operant conditioning. We begin, however, with two rudimentary forms of social influence, known as *contagious behavior* and *stimulus enhancement*, that are often confused with more sophisticated forms of observational learning.

Contagious Behavior and Stimulus Enhancement

Contagious behavior is a more-or-less instinctive or reflexive behavior triggered by the occurrence of the same behavior in another individual. For example, suppose you and your friends are sitting around a table in the library, studying for a quiz. You start to yawn. One by one, each of your classmates also yawns. Not a good sign for how your study session will progress, but it is an excellent example of contagious behavior.

Although yawning is one of the best-documented examples of contagious behavior in humans (see Provine, 1996, for a review), other behaviors in both humans and other animals are potentially contagious. All it takes to get a flock of ducks off and flying is one startled duck. The rest flee even if they do not detect any real threat. Fear responses of all kinds are quite contagious, which makes good adaptive sense. In a dangerous environment, you are more likely to survive and reproduce if you flee when you notice that someone else is fleeing, as opposed to taking the time to look around and ask a lot of questions such as "Hey Burt, why are you running from that bear?"

Behaviors that are important for social interaction and bonding are also often contagious. Have you ever noticed that you rarely laugh when you are alone? Even when watching a funny movie or reading a humorous novel (which, as media, could be considered quasi-social events), we laugh more in the presence of others than when we are by ourselves (Provine, 1996). Television producers know this, so they include laugh tracks or live (laughing) audiences in most comedy programs. Most of us have had the experience of starting to laugh with a friend and being unable to stop. Even when the laughing dies down, and even if you don't remember why you started in the first place, if the other person chuckles just a bit it will set you off for another bout of side-splitting laughter. A powerful example of this type of emotional contagion can be seen in a case documented in Tanganyika, from a boarding school for 12- to 18-year-old girls (Rankin & Philip, 1963). The girls one day began to laugh uncontrollably, which subsequently spread through the entire district. Officials even had to temporarily close the school in order to contain the "epidemic"!

Orienting responses can also be contagious. Not only do we orient ourselves toward stimuli we have just sensed (like a sudden noise or movement in our peripheral visual field), but we also orient ourselves in the direction that *others* have oriented. For example, infants as young as 4 months of age will follow the gaze of others (Farroni, Johnson, Brockbank, & Simion, 2000), and adults will do likewise. To test this response, simply have a conversation with someone, and then shift your gaze over his or her shoulder and widen your eyes a bit. See how quickly the other person turns to look. Interestingly, this effect also occurs across species. If you have a pet, you may have found yourself orienting in the direction of your pet's gaze, and becoming frustrated when you did not see anything! Because dogs and cats have somewhat different perceptual systems than humans, they can often hear, see, or smell things that we cannot detect. *(Question: Can you think of an evolutionary explanation for why orienting should be contagious, even across species?)*

Another rudimentary form of social influence, which is related to contagious orienting, is ***stimulus enhancement***, in which the probability of a behavior is changed because an individual's attention is drawn to a particular item or location by the behavior of another individual. For example, imagine that you are sitting in a waiting room, reading a magazine, when a father and his daughter walk in. The girl emits a giggle of delight, so you look up and see that she is running toward a large bowl of candy in the corner that you had not previously noticed. Five minutes later, you help yourself to some candy. You do so, however, not because she took some candy (which as you will see would be an example of observational learning of an operant response), but simply because her behavior made you aware of the candy.

Stimulus enhancement is particularly effective for increasing the probability of a behavior associated with eating, drinking, or mating (although it can also be effective for other behaviors). These behaviors often have strong instinctive components; and in the presence of the appropriate triggers, the behaviors are highly likely to occur. Stimulus enhancement simply allows the triggers to be noticed. In the example of the candy, once your attention is directed toward the candy, the incentive value of the candy is sufficient to lead to its consumption whether or not the little girl actually took some candy (e.g., her father might have actually stopped her from having candy, but you would have taken some of it anyway).

A wide variety of cues can lead to stimulus enhancement. Animals will often use scent marking at food sites. When a conspecific (another animal of the same species) comes across the scent mark, that scent is sufficient to cause the animal to pay close attention to the location and find the food. The behavior of the model could happen hours or even days before the observer arrived, but the resulting stimulus enhancement of the location of food was a result of an observer utilizing a social cue to direct its behavior. Stimulus enhancement effects can also be generated by using learned symbols. One of the authors recalls an incident from her undergraduate days, when a classmate put up large orange arrow signs in the hallway pointing toward an

FIGURE 11.1 Young children learn many behaviors through observation. (Unfortunately for parents, this particular behavior pattern occurs much less readily when children reach their teens.)

Steve Mason/Getty Images

empty classroom where he waited. Within an hour, more than a dozen students and two professors wandered into the empty classroom to ask what was happening there. (It would likely be no surprise to you that the classmate was also a psychology major.)

Behavioral contagion and stimulus enhancement are clearly examples of social influence. But it can be argued that they are at best rudimentary forms of social influence in that they may result in only a momentary change in behavior (though subsequent processes, like being rewarded by candy for going to the candy bowl, could result in a more lasting change). More substantial forms of learning occur when observation of a model is involved in classical and operant conditioning (see Figure 11.1).

Observational Learning in Classical Conditioning

As mentioned earlier, observational learning is often involved in the development of classically conditioned responses. In such cases, the stimuli involved are usually *emotional* in nature. For example, imagine a young child walking into a daycare center. She sees other children laughing and smiling while playing with a new toy. The smiles and laughter of the other children can act as stimuli that elicit similar emotional responses in the observer. Such emotions, called ***vicarious emotional responses***, are classically conditioned emotional responses that result from seeing those emotional responses exhibited by others. This type of conditioning is therefore called *vicarious emotional conditioning*.

Vicarious emotional conditioning can take place in two ways. First, as noted in Chapter 5, expressions of fear in others may act as unconditioned stimuli (USs) that elicit the emotion of fear in ourselves (Mineka, 1987). In other words, because we quickly need to learn which events are dangerous, we may have an inherited tendency to react fearfully whenever we see someone else looking fearful. For example, a young child could learn to fear jellyfish in the following way:

Jellyfish: Look of fear in others → *Fear in oneself*
NS US UR
Jellyfish → *Fear in oneself*
CS CR

The more traditional way of viewing the process of vicarious emotional conditioning, however, is to construe it as a form of higher-order conditioning. In this case, the emotional reactions of others serve as conditioned stimuli (CSs) rather than USs. For example, because fearful looks in others are often associated with frightening events, they come to serve as CSs for the emotion of fear in ourselves:

Look of fear in others: Frightening events → *Fear in oneself*
NS_1 US UR
Look of fear in others → *Fear in oneself*
CS_1 CR

This look of fear in others can now function as a CS in the higher-order conditioning of a fear response to a previously neutral stimulus (NS), such as a jellyfish:

Jellyfish: Look of fear in others → *Fear in oneself*
NS_2 CS_1 CR
Jellyfish → *Fear in oneself*
CS_2 CR

Thus, with respect to fear conditioning, the look of fear in others may function as either a US or a CS. Of course, it is also possible that both processes are involved, and they may even combine to produce a stronger fear reaction. Higher-order conditioning no doubt plays a major role in the conditioning of other, subtler emotions. For example, because smiles are usually associated with pleasurable events—such as when a smiling mother feeds a baby—they quickly become conditioned to elicit pleasurable emotions. In diagram form:

Smiles in others: Pleasurable events → *Pleasant emotions in oneself*
NS_1 US UR
Smiles in others → *Pleasant emotions in oneself*
CS_1 CR

As a result, through observing others' reactions to a novel event, we may now acquire the same type of emotional response through a process of higher-order conditioning:

Raw oysters: Smiles in others → *Pleasant emotions in oneself*
NS_2 CS_1 CR
Raw oysters → *Pleasant emotions in oneself*
CS_2 CR

Needless to say, vicarious emotional responses, once acquired, can motivate other types of new behavior patterns (e.g., Eisenberg, McCreath, & Ahn, 1988; Gold, Fultz, Burke, & Prisco, 1992). After watching happy children playing with a toy, the observing child may be eager to play with the toy herself. And once we have seen someone else react fearfully to a particular type of spider, we may go out of our way to avoid any encounter with that type of spider (Mineka & Cook, 1993). Also, as noted in Chapter 4, many advertisers use emotional conditioning to influence our view of their products. When we see a television family reunited by a long-distance phone call, with tears of joy flowing freely, the vicarious emotions elicited by the joy of the models can cause us to associate the phone company with that emotion. Thus, the phone company becomes a positive CS, and the likelihood of our subscribing to its service increases. (See "It's an Acquired Taste ..." in the And Furthermore box.)

QUICK QUIZ A

1. In observational learning, the person performing a behavior is the m__________; the person watching the behavior is the o__________.
2. From a classical conditioning perspective, smiles, giggles, and laughs are CSs that can elicit v__________ e__________ r__________ in observers.
3. In fear conditioning, the expressions of fear in other people may function as (CSs/USs/both CSs and USs) that elicit the same emotional response in ourselves.
4. David watches a television infomercial about a new product guaranteed to promote weight loss. The audience members are smiling, laughing, and enthusiastic in their praise for the product. Later, David decides that he will buy the product, even though he initially viewed it with skepticism. David's buying decision is probably motivated by v__________ e__________ conditioning that occurred during exposure to the infomercial.

Observational Learning in Operant Conditioning

Just as the observation of a model can influence the development of classically conditioned responses, it can also influence the development of operant responses. Descriptions of this process traditionally emphasize the distinction between *acquisition* and *performance* of a behavior. For example, you may have watched your parents driving a car for years, and you may have thereby *acquired* most of the basic information needed to drive the car—how to start it, how to shift gears, how to use the signal lights, and so on. However,

And Furthermore

It's An Acquired Taste ...

In this chapter, we describe some of the ways we learn from those around us. One area of social learning that has been studied extensively is how we learn to eat and drink. Of course, eating and drinking are behaviors that occur very naturally, so we do not have to learn to eat and drink, but we do seem to learn *what* to eat and drink. Across the world, there are dramatic differences in flavor preferences, foods that are considered edible, and various practices associated with preparing and consuming food. Many North Americans, for example, have a hard time imagining how someone would enjoy the flavor and texture of various bugs, how it would feel to sit down to a dinner of dog or horse, or why anyone would eat something like haggis.

Much social learning about food and flavor preference is related to stimulus enhancement and social referencing, through which individuals (especially young children) attend to those things that others are attending to, and look to others for emotional cues about how to behave. If your niece is watching you eat a slice of pizza and sees the expression of pure joy on your face, she will be inclined to try the pizza as well. In general, children tend to eat the foods that are eaten around them, and these culturally or socially mediated preferences are strengthened over time, even for flavors that are very strong (see Rozin, Fischler, Imada, Sarubin, & Wrzesniewski, 1999, for a cross-cultural comparison of food preferences and attitudes).

In addition to food preferences, there is evidence for socially learned preferences for alcohol. In humans, it has been demonstrated that children like the smell of alcohol if they have been raised by parents who drink heavily (Mennella & Garcia, 2000). In fact, exposure to alcohol early in life is a risk factor for alcohol use by adolescents (Streissguth, Barr, Bookstein, Samson, & Olson, 1999). This socially mediated preference for alcohol can even be found in animals. Rats that are raised with alcohol available, but that do not observe alcohol consumption by their mother or foster mother, drink little alcohol when they are adolescents. In fact, most laboratory rats will not drink plain alcohol when it is available unless the concentration is very low. However, if they observe their mother or foster mother drinking alcohol, those young rats will drink twice as much alcohol when they are adolescents (Honey & Galef, 2003; Honey, Varley, & Galef, 2004). This type of social learning is fairly powerful and long lasting. With only a week of exposure and a delay of one month before having an opportunity to drink alcohol, young rats will still demonstrate an enhanced preference for alcohol (Honey & Galef, 2004). In fact, Hunt and Hallmark (2001) found that even as little as 30 minutes of exposure to an adolescent (rather than adult) rat can also lead to alcohol use.

We do not usually think of alcohol as an "odd" thing to consume; but alcohol is actually a relatively unpalatable substance, especially without the addition of various sugars and flavorings. Most people and animals initially dislike the flavor and smell of high concentrations of alcohol. However, once the rewarding, intoxicating aspects of alcohol have been experienced, it becomes more enjoyable. Observational learning is one way to enhance the likelihood that someone will try alcohol in the first place, which can then lead to a preference for alcohol and the possibility of alcohol abuse.

(*continued*)

So here is something to think about: If we acquire all sorts of complex behaviors through social learning, is it not likely that we also learn *how* to drink from those around us? And just as some individuals might be learning maladaptive patterns of drinking from their families or peers, might others be learning to drink in a controlled or "responsible" way? Certainly there are multiple factors involved in the development of uncontrolled drinking, including genetic predisposition and one's ability to delay gratification as well as processes of social learning. But the next time you are in a bar or at some social event where alcohol is served, take a moment to watch the people around you and consider the roles of emotional contagion, stimulus enhancement, and observational learning in the drinking behavior you observe.

until you reached legal driving age, you were not permitted to translate that acquired knowledge into the actual *performance* of driving.

Acquisition Acquisition of an operant response (or, for that matter, a classically conditioned response) through observational learning first requires that the observer pay attention to the behavior of the model. After all, you cannot learn from someone unless you actually watch what that person does. So, what makes us attend to a model?

First, we are very sensitive to the *consequences of the model's behavior*. If a model's behavior is reinforced, an observer is more likely to attend to the behavior. For example, if you see a television commercial featuring a husband receiving lavish praise and affection for sending flowers to his wife, you are likely to learn that sending flowers may result in positive reinforcement.

A second factor that influences attention is whether the *observer receives reinforcement for the behavior of attending to a model* (e.g., Pepperberg & Sherman, 2000). Teaching is often based on this principle. Teachers demonstrate desired behaviors—something as basic as reading or as complex as writing a college essay—and reinforce their students' attention to their demonstrations. They may also use various techniques for drawing attention to their behaviors, including prompting ("Look here. See what I'm doing?") and physical modeling ("Hold the football like this, with one hand behind the other"). Teachers then provide verbal reinforcers when students pay attention ("Good!"). Reinforcing observer attention in these ways can greatly increase the amount of knowledge that an observer can acquire from a model.

A third determinant of whether we attend to a model depends on *whether the observer has sufficient skills to benefit from the modeling*. For example, if a model plays "Chopsticks" on the piano, even a musically inexperienced observer may be able to pick up the tune quickly and, with appropriate help, play it herself. However, if a model plays a complex Beethoven sonata, the observer may give up all hope of ever being able to play the piano. If you play computer or video games, you have probably felt this way. Watching expert players can be a humbling experience and may keep observers from trying the games themselves. Modeling works only when observers have the skills necessary to learn the behavior.

Finally, *the personal characteristics of a model can strongly influence the extent to which we will attend to their behavior*. We are much more likely to attend to models who resemble us—for example, if they are roughly the same age, dress similarly, and have similar interests (e.g., Bussey & Bandura, 1984; Dowling, 1984). We also attend to models we respect or admire, or who are noted authorities in that realm of activity. If the coach of your junior hockey team is a former NHL player and teammate of Wayne Gretzky's, you pay much more attention to what he tells you than if he is the local high school football coach who got pushed into coaching hockey because no one else is available.

Of course, you can acquire information about a behavior without ever translating that information into performance. Television exposes viewers to thousands of hours of violent scenes, yet only a few people ever "act out" those violent behaviors. How we move from knowledge to performance is the topic of the next section.

QUICK QUIZ B

1. You may watch cooking shows on television and learn how to perform complex culinary feats. Translating that knowledge into a gourmet meal is the difference between learning and p__________.
2. An important aspect of gaining information about a modeled behavior is the extent to which we att__________ to the model.
3. Teachers often directly reinforce the behavior of paying __________, sometimes accompanied by the use of pr__________, such as "Look at what I'm doing."
4. The average person is unlikely to pay much attention to the precise moves of a grand master in chess simply because the average person does not have the sk__________ to benefit from that type of modeling.
5. You are more likely to pay attention to a model whose behavior is (reinforced/not reinforced), who is (similar/dissimilar) to you, who is (admired/hated), and who is a noted au__________ in that activity.

Performance How does observational learning translate into behavior? As you might expect, it involves those familiar processes of reinforcement and punishment (e.g., Carroll & Bandura, 1987). Reinforcement and punishment work to modify our behavior in modeling situations in three ways. First, *we are more likely (or less likely) to perform a modeled behavior when we have observed the modeled behavior being reinforced (or punished)* (e.g., Bandura & McDonald, 1994; G. R. Fouts & Click, 1979). The effect of such consequences on our behavior is technically known as *vicarious reinforcement (or vicarious punishment)*. For example, when a model is seen using a fragrance that appears to attract members of the opposite sex to her like flies to honey, that increases the likelihood that an observer will try that fragrance herself (assuming she desires the same effect!). And if you watch a comedian telling a joke that gets a big laugh, you may repeat that same joke to your friends. Conversely, if you see a comedian tell a joke that bombs, you are not likely to repeat it.

A second factor that influences performance is the consequence for the observer of performing the modeled behavior. *We are more (or less) likely to perform a modeled behavior when we ourselves will experience reinforcement (or punishment) for performing that behavior.* If you tell the same joke that got the comedian a big laugh and your friends love it, then you will continue to tell it; if you tell the joke and everyone frowns, then you probably will not tell it again. In general, the reinforcement or punishment of the observer's behavior ultimately determines whether a modeled behavior will be performed (e.g., Weiss, Suckow, & Rakestraw, 1999).

A third factor that influences our performance is *our own history of reinforcement or punishment for performing modeled behaviors.* Throughout our lives, we learn when it is appropriate to perform modeled behaviors as well as who is an appropriate model. Chances are that behavior modeled after that of teachers, coaches, and parents has been explicitly reinforced while behavior modeled after that of less exemplary individuals has been explicitly punished ("Don't be like that awful boy next door!"). As well, performance of a modeled behavior can be *differentially reinforced* in different contexts. The performance of some modeled behaviors—such as smoking or swearing—may be reinforced in the presence of your close friends but punished in the presence of your parents. Thus, over the years we gradually learn, through our own unique history of reinforcement and punishment, when it is appropriate to perform behaviors that have been modeled by others. (See also the discussion of *generalized imitation* in the next section.)

QUICK QUIZ C

1. Not only are you more likely to att__________ to a model's behavior if you see the model's behavior reinforced, you are also more likely to p__________ that behavior.
2. A second factor that influences whether we will perform a modeled behavior is the c__________ we receive for performing the behavior.
3. A third factor that influences our performance of a modeled behavior is our h__________ of r__________ for performing modeled behaviors.
4. When you repeat an off-color joke to your friends, they laugh heartily; but when you tell the same joke to your parents, you are met with frowns. Due to dif__________ reinforcement, you soon learn to tell such jokes only when you are with your friends.

Imitation

Imitation is a term that is often used interchangeably with observational learning. ***True imitation***, however, is a form of observational learning that involves the close duplication of a novel behavior (or sequence of behaviors). For example, imagine that Chelsea is standing in a line outside an exclusive club when she sees a woman walk to the front of the line and begin flirting with the doorman. The doorman allows the woman to enter without standing in line. Chelsea gets out of line, walks up to the doorman, and also begins flirting with him. If she flirts in a different way from the other woman (using her own "flirting style"), this would be an example of observational learning but not true imitation. But if she flirts in virtually the same way as the other woman, which also happens to be quite different from the way Chelsea normally flirts (so it is a novel behavior pattern for her), then we would say that true imitation has taken place.

Children have a strong tendency to imitate the behaviors of those around them, hence the popularity of games like "Simon Says." Interestingly, operant conditioning appears to play a major role in the development of this ability. In the earliest study along these lines, Baer and Sherman (1964) reinforced children's behavior of imitating certain behavior patterns that were displayed by a puppet. The researchers found that this process resulted in an increase not only in the frequency of the behaviors that had been reinforced but also in the frequency of other behaviors that had been displayed by the model but for which the children had never received reinforcement. In other words, the children had acquired a generalized tendency to imitate the model.

Generalized imitation is therefore the tendency to imitate a new modeled behavior with no specific reinforcement for doing so. This process has considerable real-world application. Applied behavior analysts make use of it when working with children who are developmentally delayed or have autism and who are often deficient in their ability to learn through observation (e.g., Baer, Peterson, & Sherman, 1967; Lovaas, 1987; Lynch, 1998). By deliberately reinforcing the imitation of some behaviors, therapists can produce in these children a generalized tendency to imitate, which then greatly facilitates subsequent training.

Can Animals Imitate? Although it is clear that humans are capable of true imitation, there has been considerable debate over the extent to which animals are capable of it (e.g., Galef, 1988; Tomasello, 1996). This is actually an old issue; early animal behaviorists and learning theorists, like Romanes (1884), Morgan (1900), and Thorndike (1911), debated whether animals could "intentionally" imitate (which could be construed as indicative of higher-level cognitive functioning) or whether any appearance of imitation was due to some lower-level, perhaps instinctive, mechanism. Now the controversy has again arisen, with a wealth of experimental studies examining the issue.

Most of these studies have examined the ability of animals, usually monkeys and apes, to solve novel problems such as how to obtain food locked away in a box. In a typical experiment, the animals watch a model perform a complex series of behaviors—such as getting a key, opening a lock, pulling a lever, and then using a stick to pull food out of a hole that has now been revealed in the side of the box. The observer animal is then given a chance to try opening the box. If the animal can imitate, it should be able to duplicate the actions performed by the model to obtain the food. What often happens, though, is that the animals do not copy the actions of the model exactly—they may pull the lever, for example, but not use the key; or they may turn the box over and shake it to remove the food rather than use the stick (e.g., Call, 1999; Call & Tomasello, 1995; Nagel, Olguin, & Tomasello, 1993; Whiten, 1998).

Further, when animals do show evidence of imitation in these types of studies, it is often not clear that the effects of stimulus enhancement and other potential confounds have been ruled out. For example, Chesler (1969) demonstrated that kittens more quickly learned to press a lever for food if they had observed their mothers pressing a lever than if they had observed a strange female cat pressing the lever. Although this study has been widely cited as providing evidence of imitation, Galef (1988) points out that the study might simply demonstrate that mothers are better stimulus enhancers than strangers are. Kittens may pay more attention to their mother than to a stranger, and attend to any item that she manipulates. Thus, simple stimulus enhancement could result in a duplication of behavior that looks a lot like imitation. Due to these kinds of difficulties, some researchers have suggested that nonhuman animals are incapable of true imitation (e.g., Tomasello, 1996).

Other researchers, however, have argued that sufficient evidence now exists, gathered from well-controlled studies, to indicate that at least some animals (especially birds and great apes) are capable of true imitation (see Zentall, 2006, for a review). For example, in a study by Nguyen, Klein, and Zentall (2005), demonstrator pigeons were trained either to peck at or step on a treadle and then push a screen either to the left or to the right to obtain food. Observer pigeons were significantly more likely to demonstrate the sequence they had observed (e.g., treadle step and screen push right) as opposed to a sequence they had not observed (treadle peck and screen push left).

It has also been argued that past research on this issue has sometimes utilized inappropriate criteria for judging imitative ability in animals. Horowitz (2003), for example, replicated a study using a task that had previously revealed greater evidence of true imitation in children than in chimpanzees, except that Horowitz also gave the task to human adults. He found that the adults' level of imitation was more similar to that of the chimpanzees than the children's was! In other words, both human adults and chimpanzees displayed more flexible behavior patterns in solving the problem—as compared to the children, who had a stronger tendency simply to do what the model had demonstrated. The lower rate of imitation that had been shown by chimpanzees compared to the children in the previous study therefore seems like a poor basis for drawing inferences about their lack of imitative ability, insofar as one can hardly argue that human adults are also incapable of true imitation.

Finally, researchers have uncovered some impressive anecdotal evidence of true imitation. Russon and Galdikas (1993, 1995) observed orangutans living with humans in a camp designed to reintroduce the animals to the wild. They found that the orangutans regularly copied the complex actions of the humans with whom they interacted, including learning to hang hammocks, build bridges, and use boats. In one case, an orangutan even learned how to start a fire—something that the researchers did not expect and certainly did not demonstrate on purpose! (See "Can Animals Teach?" in the And Furthermore box.)

And Furthermore

Can Animals Teach?

We have so far discussed whether animals can learn by observing a model. An even more interesting question, perhaps, is whether animals can "deliberately" act as models for teaching another animal. This is not an easy question to answer, because people usually assume that teaching requires a "conscious intention" to demonstrate, or transfer knowledge from one individual to another, which is obviously difficult to assess in nonhuman animals. For example, consider an ape that seems to be calling her offspring's attention toward her tool use. By simply observing her actions, we may find it difficult to determine if she is trying to teach her young to use a tool to get food or simply trying to get food while at the same time keeping her offspring nearby. If her offspring do learn to use the same tool in the same way, were they intentionally taught by the mother? Or did the offspring simply pick up the behavior on their own through observational learning or stimulus enhancement?

As with true imitation, some researchers have argued that teaching is a behavior performed only by humans (King, 1991). They contend that evidence that does suggest teaching by animals is often anecdotal and subject to *anthropomorphism* (assuming human motives or characteristics when observing animal behavior). Nevertheless, evidence has been gathered suggesting that at least some nonhuman animals, especially chimpanzees (Boesch, 1991) and bonobos (once known as "pygmy chimpanzees"), do behave as teachers. A few anecdotes in particular are difficult to ignore. For example:

> At the Georgia State University Language Research Center in Atlanta, a bonobo called Kanzi has been trained to communicate with people. He has become a bonobo celebrity, known for his fabulous understanding of spoken English. Realizing that some of his fellow apes do not have the same training, Kanzi occasionally adopts the role of teacher. He once sat next to Tamuli, a younger sister who has had minimal exposure to human speech, while a researcher tried to get Tamuli to respond to simple verbal requests; the untrained bonobo didn't respond. As the researcher addressed Tamuli, it was Kanzi who began to act out the meanings. When Tamuli was asked to groom Kanzi, he took her hand and placed it under his chin, squeezing it between his chin and chest. In this position, Kanzi stared into Tamuli's eyes with what people interpreted as a questioning gaze. When Kanzi repeated the action, the young female rested her fingers on his chest as if wondering what to do. (de Waal, 2005, pp. 6–7)

In the quote, you may have noticed several assumptions, which may or may not be warranted, that were made about Kanzi's and Tamuli's motives. On the other hand, the behaviors Kanzi displayed are the types of behaviors that, with humans, we often use to

(*continued*)

Kanzi with his trainer, Sue Savage-Rumbaugh.

Laurentiu Garofeanu/Barcroft Media/Landov

infer the existence of an "intention." It is difficult, therefore, to witness a behavior like this and not have the impression that Kanzi is making a human-like attempt at teaching. But it should also be noted that Kanzi is unique among bonobos in his demonstrated language and problem-solving abilities, and he may have skills that are not typical of other apes. (You will read more about language learning in animals in Chapter 13.)

QUICK QUIZ D

1. If a young gorilla learns to gather tasty wild ginger plants by watching his mother forage, we can say that he has demonstrated o__________ learning.
2. Copying a new behavior to achieve a particular result is (true imitation/stimulus enhancement); having one's attention drawn to a particular place or thing is (true imitation/stimulus enhancement).
3. Jessica has just purchased a new computer and is trying to learn how to access the Internet. She asks her friend Jill to show her how to do it. Jill performs a complicated series of clicks and keystrokes, and Jessica watches closely. If Jessica then connects to the Internet on her own using the same actions as Jill, Jessica's behavior is best described as an example of (true imitation/stimulus enhancement).

4. Joe has also purchased a new computer and is trying to access the Internet. He watches his friend Daryl as he accesses the Internet and notices that he uses a couple of applications to do so. Joe opens those applications himself and then plays around with the settings until he figures it out. Joe's behavior is best described as an example of (true imitation/stimulus enhancement).

Social Learning and Aggression

Bandura is well known for his studies on aggression, and he is particularly famous for what are now known as the "Bobo doll studies" (e.g., Bandura, 1965). In those studies, children observed adult models behaving aggressively toward a Bobo doll (an inflatable toy doll that pops back up when pushed over). The children were then tested to determine whether they also had learned to behave aggressively. The research involved various types of models, various forms of demonstrated aggression, and children of varying ages. In these studies, Bandura found some *striking* evidence concerning the social learning of aggression (pun intended).

First, children who observed a model behaving aggressively toward the Bobo doll and other targets tended to replicate the same behaviors when they were allowed into the same room that the model had previously occupied (Bandura, Ross, & Ross, 1961; Bandura, Ross, & Ross, 1963; Bandura, 1965). By *replicate*, we do not just mean that the children demonstrated an increase in general aggression (although that also occurred). The children in Bandura's studies were very precise in some of their aggressive behavior, performing many of the same movements toward the same targets, using the same weapons, and uttering the same hostile statements. In other words, these children demonstrated true imitation of the model's aggressive behavior.

The children were also influenced by the consequences that the model experienced while behaving aggressively. Although simply witnessing the aggressive adult often resulted in aggressive behavior, the effect was even

Two images from Albert Bandura's famous Bobo doll study. The image on the left is from the film of the aggressive adult model that was shown to the children (the Bobo doll has bounced into the air from the force of the attack). The image on the right shows one of the children later attacking the Bobo doll.

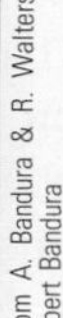

Courtesy of Albert Bandura

stronger if the child had observed reinforcement of the adult's aggression. Likewise, children who had observed the models' aggressive behavior being punished were somewhat *less likely* to reproduce the behaviors spontaneously. However, if the researchers then offered the children incentives to behave aggressively, the level of aggression went back up; the children showed that they had in fact learned the behaviors well (Bandura, 1965).

In a related study, children watched a televised fight in the presence of an adult male. The adult watched the film with the children and responded approvingly, disapprovingly, or made no comment. Children who had heard the disapproving comments produced far fewer aggressive behaviors upon testing compared to the other two groups—*but only when the disapproving adult was present*. In the absence of the disapproving adult, these children exhibited an increase in aggression (Hicks, 1968).

QUICK QUIZ E

1. The aggressive behavior of children in Bandura's studies was so similar to the model's behavior that it can be considered as an example of t__________ i__________.
2. Watching a model demonstrate violent behavior has been shown to lead to an (increase/decrease) in violence by observers; observing the reinforcement of violent behavior further (increased/decreased) the amount of violence displayed by observers.
3. Although children in Bandura's study exhibited somewhat less violent behavior if the model's behavior had been p__________, their levels of violence increased again if they were later offered a(n) __________ for behaving violently.

Social Learning and Media Violence: From Bobo Doll to Grand Theft Auto In his research, Bandura found that filmed violence was as effective as live violence for inducing violent behavior in observers (Bandura, Ross, & Ross, 1963). Although this research was conducted before the extreme proliferation of mass media in the late twentieth century, these preliminary findings foreshadowed the concerns of modern researchers who examine the impact of violent media on the behavior of children and adolescents.

Children have always had opportunities to learn about violence, by observing violence at home and in the community. Children are often exposed to warfare and are sometimes even trained as soldiers. Social learning of violence by children is therefore nothing new, but the constant availability of aggressive or violent models is new and pervasive. Between 1950, when approximately 9% of American homes contained a television, and 2000, when virtually all North American families owned a television (Federal Trade Commission, 2000), there has been a substantial change in children's exposure to violent media. In addition to television, which is an essentially passive medium (one simply watches it), children are increasingly exposed to violent or aggressive video games that allow for a high degree of interaction and participation. Indeed, when looking at the hyperrealistic violent games now available—including the Grand Theft Auto™ series of games that depict violent criminal behavior such as theft, murder, and rape—it's hard to believe that in the 1980s, some parents complained that Pac-Man was too violent because Pac-Man went around eating the other characters!

Longitudinal studies and prospective studies are especially useful for isolating critical factors in violent behavior. Eron and his colleagues have studied a large sample of boys from 1960 until the present day. They have found that the amount of violent media viewed in childhood is significantly correlated with aggressive and antisocial behavior 10 years later, even after controlling for variables such as initial aggressiveness, social class, and education (Eron, Huesmann, Lefkowitz, & Walder, 1972). This early viewing of violence, and early aggression, has also been shown to be significantly related to adult criminality (Huesmann, 1986), although the relationship is weaker. More recently, Johnson and his colleagues have summarized the results of a 17-year study, in which they determined that the amount of television watched in childhood is positively correlated with amount of aggressive or violent behavior toward others (Johnson, Cohen, Kasen, & Brook, 2007). Although Johnson's team found a bidirectional relationship between viewing violence and aggressive behavior (in which those who are aggressive also tend to seek out violent media), the effect of violent media on later aggressive behavior was still robust.

Are there sex differences in the effects of media violence? Most studies find that males are more likely to express the effects of exposure to violent video games. C. A. Anderson and Dill (2000) report that male video-game players have a more hostile view of the world than do females, and some longitudinal studies suggest that males are more aggressive than females after exposure to violent media (Eron et al., 1972; Huesmann, Moise-Titus, Podolski, & Eron, 2003; Lefkowitz, Eron, Walder, & Huesmann, 1977). This conforms to results described by Bandura (1965) in his early Bobo doll studies. For example, he found that boys tended to produce more spontaneous acts of aggression than girls did. He also found that girls inhibited their aggression to a greater degree if the model had been punished. Once an incentive was provided for reproducing the aggressive acts, however, the sex differences disappeared. It appears therefore that girls learn violence as well as boys do, but girls have a greater tendency to inhibit violence unless there is an incentive for violence. Girls will also demonstrate a higher frequency of aggressive acts when the aggressive model is female as opposed to male (see review by Bandura, 1973). Since most violent models in the media and on computer games are male, this could account for some of the sex differences that we observe.

One troubling possibility is that, although exposure to violent media does not predispose females toward behaving aggressively as much as it does males, it might make females more vulnerable to being *victims* of aggression. Desensitization to violence may allow females to feel that violence and aggression are normal aspects of life, which could lead them to enter violent relationships. This may be related to the fact that, whereas most models of violent behavior are male, a high proportion of victims are female. Thus, in the same way that exposure to spousal violence in childhood increases the likelihood of becoming a victim of spousal abuse in adulthood (Ehrensaft et al., 2003), it is possible that females who watch violent media are more likely to become victims of violence.

Given all the evidence for the damaging effects of media violence, from both experimental and correlational studies, why do we rarely see this evidence clearly reported in the newspapers and other aspects of the popular press? Bushman and Anderson (2001) have proposed several reasons for why this is the case. For one thing, media sources are often interlinked. Thus, if the film or television industry wants to promote (or suppress) a particular viewpoint, they are likely to have connections at the level of newspapers and magazines that enable them to do so. Media outlets also tend to take a "balanced" approach to the topic of media violence by frequently including comments from researchers who believe that the effects of media violence have been overstated. On the surface, this appears to be a fair approach, since both sides of the debate are given equal representation. However, insofar as the vast majority of researchers agree that media violence is dangerous, then the "equal airtime" given to the few naysayers tends to mislead the public into believing that the evidence linking media violence and aggression is much weaker than it is. Finally, researchers themselves have not been forceful enough in presenting their findings to the public. For example, media executives have sometimes argued that the correlations between media violence and aggression are so small as to be of little real significance, whereas in fact they are almost as high as the correlations between cigarette smoking and lung cancer—and they are higher than the correlations between passive smoking and lung cancer, exposure to asbestos and laryngeal cancer, and condom use and sexually transmitted HIV! No one argues that these correlations are so small as to be of little real significance.

The comparison to lung cancer is particularly instructive. Smoking is an important cause of lung cancer—but it is not the only cause, and many people who smoke will never get lung cancer. On average, however, the risk of developing lung cancer if you are a smoker is substantially higher than if you are a nonsmoker. The same logic holds true for the effects of media violence on violent behavior. Watching violent TV is not the only contributing factor to personal violence, and many individuals who watch violent films or play violent computer games will never demonstrate an increase in violent behavior. But some individuals will demonstrate an increase in violent behavior. Furthermore, it requires only a few such individuals to significantly impact whole communities and even entire nations, as shown by as the Columbine High School shootings and the Boston Marathon bombings. As noted earlier, the possibility also exists that exposure to media violence can increase the likelihood of someone becoming a victim of violence. Therefore, although further research is warranted, it appears that media violence is very likely a significant contributor to violence in society.

QUICK QUIZ F

1. Longitudinal studies have shown that exposure to violent media is (strongly/weakly) correlated with ag__________ and anti__________ behavior.
2. One troubling aspect of sex differences in response to media violence is that while (males/females) are more likely to become violent as a result of such exposure, (males/females) may be more likely to become __________ of violence.

3. The problem with the media giving equal airtime to those who are (convinced/skeptical) about the effects of media violence on violent behavior is that the public is then misled into thinking that the evidence for such effects is (stronger/weaker) than it actually is.

Rule-Governed Behavior

Observational learning is one way in which we can learn appropriate behavior prior to directly experiencing the contingencies that actually control that behavior. Another means by which we can indirectly learn a behavior is through the use of language, which greatly enhances our ability to interact with one another and to adapt to the world around us. A prime example of this is the manner in which language allows us to influence each other, and ourselves, through the presentation of rules. (See also "The Analysis of Verbal Behavior" in the And Furthermore box.)

And Furthermore

The Analysis of Verbal Behavior

Although many people view behavior analysis as being unconcerned with uniquely human forms of behavior—hence the tendency by behavior analysts to conduct research with rats and pigeons—Skinner in fact had a strong interest in language or, more precisely, what he called *verbal behavior.* He considered this type of behavior to be of special importance in humans, but also assumed that it is governed by many of the same principles that govern other behavior (Skinner, 1957).

From a behavior analytic perspective, *verbal behavior* is behavior that involves language and results in a consequence. It can be spoken, written, or gestural, and it requires both a speaker and a listener—although these can sometimes be the same individual, as when we talk to ourselves. In general, the speaker emits the behavior and the listener provides the consequence. As with operant behavior in general, verbal behavior is strengthened through reinforcement and weakened through punishment or extinction. Thus, whereas language is typically analyzed in terms of its structure (e.g., subject, object, verb), verbal behavior is analyzed in terms of its function. This is not to say, however, that a genetic predisposition to learn language might not play a role in determining the structure of language—which was the crux of Chomsky's (1959) critique of Skinner's analysis of verbal behavior (but see MacCorquodale [1970] and Palmer [2006] for rebuttals). But even if a genetic predisposition does play a role, the ways in which we use language are nevertheless strongly determined by its consequences.

For example, in Skinner's analysis, a *mand* (as in "demand") is verbal behavior that requests or seeks something that the speaker wants or needs. "Please pass the donuts" and "Where is the broom?" are examples of mands, with receiving the requested action or item being the effective reinforcer. Note that the form of the mand is determined by

(*continued*)

the motivation that lies behind it, as in requesting donuts when we are hungry and trying to obtain a broom when we've spilled salt on the floor. Conversely, a *tact* (as in "contacting" something) is verbal behavior that labels or identifies an environmental event, such as when you say, "That is a Chevrolet" or "I am eating a sandwich." In this case, the form of the behavior is determined by the object or event being identified (which is essentially the S^D for the event), and the effective consequence is typically some type of social reinforcement—as occurs when you correctly respond to a question someone has asked (e.g., "What type of car is that?"). Needless to say, to mand and tact correctly are among the first aspects of verbal behavior that young children learn, and are critical in determining their ability to interact effectively with the world around them. Another type of verbal behavior young children need to learn is rule-governed behavior, which is discussed in the remainder of this chapter.

Definitions and Characteristics

A ***rule*** can be defined as a verbal description of a contingency. In other words, it is a statement telling us that in a certain setting, if we perform a certain behavior, then a certain consequence will follow: "If you drive through a red light, you will get a ticket"; "If you study diligently throughout the semester, you will get a good grade"; and "If you are pleasant to others, they will be pleasant to you" are all examples of rules. Likewise, the course syllabus you receive at the start of a course is a set of rules about what you need to do to pass the course, and a guidebook to Paris is a set of rules about how best to find and enjoy the sites of Paris. Behavior that has been generated through exposure to rules, such as doing what the course outline tells you to do or touring Paris in the manner suggested by the guidebook, is known as ***rule-governed behavior*** (Skinner, 1969).

In its purest form, a rule is simply a statement about a contingency; it does not say anything about how we should respond with respect to that contingency. If it does say something about how we should respond, then it can also be called an *instruction* (Malott, Malott, & Trojan, 2000). Thus, "If you drive through a red light, you will get a ticket" is simply a rule, whereas "Don't drive through a red light, or you will get a ticket" (or "Don't drive through a red light!" in which case the consequence is implied) is an instruction. In this discussion, however, we will use the terms *rule* and *instruction* interchangeably given that many of the rules that concern us are offered in the form of instructions. (See Baldwin & Baldwin, 1998, for a further discussion of the different types of rules.)

Rules (or instructions) are extremely useful for rapidly establishing appropriate patterns of behavior. As with observational learning, we can learn how to behave effectively in a certain setting before we have any direct experience with the contingencies operating in that setting. We do not have to repeatedly drive through red lights to find out what happens if we do, and we do not have to fail a course repeatedly to figure out how to pass the course. We simply have to follow the rules that we have been given in order to behave effectively in those settings.

To illustrate the effectiveness of using rules to modify behavior, consider the task of teaching a rat to press a lever for food whenever it hears a tone. First, you have to shape the behavior of lever pressing by reinforcing closer and closer approximations to it. Then, once lever pressing is well established, you reinforce lever presses that occur only in the presence of a tone and not those that occur in the absence of the tone. Eventually, the rat learns to press the lever only when the tone is sounding. Now consider the task of teaching a person to press a button to earn money whenever a light is turned on (a common task in operant conditioning experiments with humans). All you have to do is sit the person down in front of the panel and provide the following instructions: "Whenever the light is on, you can earn money by pressing this button." Instantly, you have a button-pushing, money-earning human on your hands. What may require several hours of training with a rat requires only a few seconds of instruction with a verbally proficient human.

Learning to follow rules is so beneficial and important that parents devote considerable time to training this ability in young children. When Billie, for example, complies with his mother's request to pick up his toys, his mother praises him for doing so. Billie soon learns that people are pleased when he complies with their instructions, and he is therefore more likely to comply in the future. Billie later learns that following instructions can also be useful for completing a task. When, for example, he ignores the instructions that accompany a model airplane kit, he makes a complete mess of things; when he follows the instructions, he produces a great-looking model. Billie therefore learns that good things happen when he follows instructions; consequently, he acquires a generalized tendency to follow instructions. Of course, if bad things had happened when Billie followed instructions, or if good things happened when he did not follow instructions, he might instead have acquired a generalized tendency not to follow instructions and to be noncompliant. Thus, the extent to which we follow instructions—as well as the specific instructions we choose to follow—depends largely on the consequences we have received for following instructions (Baldwin & Baldwin, 1998).

QUICK QUIZ G

1. A rule can be defined as a v___________ d___________ of a c___________.

2. Behavior that is generated through exposure to rules is known as r___________-g___________ behavior.

3. A rule that also indicates how you *should* behave with respect to a contingency is called an i___________.

4. Rules are extremely useful in that they allow us to learn about appropriate patterns of behavior in a setting (with/without) direct exposure to the contingencies operating in that setting.

5. Children learn to follow instructions because they are often (praised/ignored) for following instructions. As well, they learn that following instructions is usually a (good/poor) way to actually accomplish a task.

6. The result is that most children acquire a (generalized/localized) tendency to follow instructions.
7. In general, the extent to which we follow instructions—as well as the specific instructions we choose to follow—depends largely on the c__________ we have received for following instructions.

Some Disadvantages of Rule-Governed Behavior

As you can see, rules can be very useful. Unfortunately, they also have their drawbacks. One drawback is that rule-governed behavior is often less efficient than behavior that has been directly shaped by natural contingencies. For example, no matter how many books you read on how to play golf, you will undoubtedly be a poor golfer unless you devote considerable time to actually playing and practicing the game (see Figure 11.2). Instructions can

FIGURE 11.2 Although golf lessons are a great way to get started in the game, the rules learned are, at best, general pointers that must then be modified through the actual experience of hitting the ball and seeing where it goes.

A good example of how the inflexible application of rules can get in the way of organizational efficiency.

give us only a rudimentary knowledge of how to play, and while this may be useful for getting started or for modifying certain aspects of an established game, nothing can replace the actual experience of hitting a golf ball and seeing where it goes (Baldwin & Baldwin, 1998).

A second drawback of rule-governed behavior is that such behavior is sometimes surprisingly insensitive to the actual contingencies of reinforcement operating in a particular setting. This phenomenon has been demonstrated experimentally. For example, when human participants are told they can earn money by pressing a button, they will indeed begin pressing the button. Their button pressing may not, however, be very efficient given the schedule of reinforcement that is in effect. For instance, on an FI schedule of reinforcement, human subjects often do not display the scalloped pattern of responding that is typical of FI performance in rats and pigeons. Some subjects, for example, respond rapidly throughout the interval, as though continuous, rapid responding is necessary to produce the reinforcer (Lowe, 1979). Focusing only upon the rule they have been given—"Push the button to earn money"—they never slow down enough to realize that such a high rate of response is unnecessary.[1] (See also Bentall, Lowe, & Beasty, 1985; Lowe, Beasty, & Bentall, 1983).

Likewise, a person who is taught to swing a golf club a certain way may persist with that swing for several years despite the fact that it is inappropriate for her build and level of flexibility. Because she is locked into the notion that she must follow the instructions she has been given, her golf game may

[1]The first author of this text directly experienced this phenomenon when, as a graduate student, he was conducting just such a button-pushing study. Because each session in the study lasted a couple of hours (and because the task was excruciatingly boring), subjects were given 10-minute breaks at regular intervals throughout each session. One subject, however, began spending almost all of her breaks in the washroom. Asked if she was not feeling well, she explained that she was going to the washroom to run her arm under cold water to reduce the pain. As it turns out, having been told that pushing buttons would produce money, she assumed that faster button pushing produced more money. She therefore pushed the button at a blistering pace throughout each session, so much so that her arm muscles had begun to cramp. In fact, the money was being delivered on variable interval (VI) schedules of reinforcement, and she could have earned the full amount each session with a quite leisurely rate of response.

never evolve to a more effective level. Similarly, a veteran businessman who has acquired a set of rules about how best to conduct business may have difficulty modifying his business practices to compete effectively in the new global economy. As the world of business changes, his old rules, highly effective in the old economy, are now an impediment. Thus, although rules are often extremely beneficial, we do well to recognize that they have their limitations and often require modification according to the particular circumstances in which we find ourselves. (See also "Psychopathology, Psychotherapy, and Rule-Governed Behavior" in the And Furthermore box.)

QUICK QUIZ H

1. One difficulty is that rule-governed behavior is often (less/more) efficient than behavior that has been shaped by natural c__________.
2. Another difficulty is that rule-governed behavior is sometimes surprisingly ins__________ to the actual contingencies of reinforcement.
3. As an example of the above, experimental subjects who are told to press a button to earn money sometimes display a (scalloped pattern/high rate) of responding on an FI schedule of reinforcement, which is (the same as/different from) the type of responding typically shown on such schedules by animals.

And Furthermore

Psychopathology, Psychotherapy, and Rule-Governed Behavior

The fact that rule-governed behavior is sometimes insensitive to the actual contingencies has important implications, not only for everyday activities such as learning golf or conducting business, but also for understanding various forms of psychopathology. The starting point for this notion was the aforementioned finding that human subjects in operant conditioning experiments who are given instructions (rules) to "press the button" often behave in ways that are highly inefficient. This led to speculation that rule-governed behavior in general might often be insensitive to the actual contingencies, which in turn suggested that this insensitivity might even account for some forms of psychopathology. The outcome of this line of reasoning was an innovative form of therapy known as *Acceptance and Commitment Therapy* (or ACT; Hayes, Strosahl, & Wilson, 1999).

The basic rationale that underlies ACT is that human verbal behavior has both advantages and disadvantages. Just as language allows us to reminisce about the past and plan for tomorrow, so too it allows us to relive painful experiences and catastrophize about the future. Thus, our ability to use language can sometimes be a serious drawback. (By comparison, your friendly neighborhood tree squirrel, with virtually no language, lives almost entirely in the present and seems largely immune to the many forms of neurosis that plague humans.)

More specifically, according to Hayes et al. (1999), the culture that we live in engrains within us a particular set of rules about our psychological difficulties. These include:

- Psychological problems are indicated by unpleasant feelings, thoughts, bodily sensations, etc.

- These unpleasant experiences are "signals" that we have some type of deficiency (e.g., a lack of confidence) that needs to change for us to become healthy.
- This can be achieved by understanding or modifying the factors that caused the difficulty (e.g., "working through" our thoughts and feelings about a difficult childhood that resulted in low self-confidence).

In short, we must somehow get rid of our negative thoughts and feelings in order to live a satisfying life.

The main difficulty with these rules and the ways in which we try to deal them is that they are largely ineffective. For example, some symptoms are reflexive in nature and have been classically conditioned through exposure to upsetting experiences. Hence, attempting to alleviate the symptoms by deliberately suppressing them, as many people try to do, is unlikely to be effective. Thus, the basic goal in ACT is to enable clients to see the futility of their usual strategies for handling their symptoms. Through a diverse array of therapeutic techniques, clients are encouraged to "give up the struggle" and to "lean forward" into their symptoms. Once they learn to accept their thoughts and feelings as they are, they can then commit themselves to carrying out personally valued activities. This process by itself may result in a certain degree of symptom alleviation, insofar as clients will no longer be avoiding the events that elicit their symptoms (thereby allowing extinction to take place). More importantly, though, clients will come to understand that unpleasant thoughts and feelings are a normal part of everyday life, and that eliminating these events is not a prerequisite for engaging in appropriate and worthwhile behavior. (For examples of the therapeutic techniques used, see Hayes et al., 1999; see also Waltz & Hayes, 2010, for a recent overview of ACT.)

ACT is not the only type of therapy that preaches the benefits of focusing on behavior and accepting one's thoughts and feelings. Two other behaviorally oriented forms of therapy, *dialectical behavior therapy* (Linehan, 1993) and *functional analytic psychotherapy* (Kohlenberg & Tsai, 1991), also include aspects of acceptance, as does an older Japanese form of therapy, known as *Morita therapy.* Morita therapists, in particular, view psychological difficulties as arising from living a feeling-centered rather than behavior-centered lifestyle. Similar to ACT, clients in Morita therapy are taught to accept their feelings, to know their purpose, and to do what needs to be done. They learn that feelings are largely uncontrollable while actions are controllable, and that they must place greater emphasis on the latter if they wish to lead a satisfying life (see Reynolds, 1984, for a readable introduction to this style of therapy).

Personal Rules in Self-Regulation

Although rules have their drawbacks, their advantages obviously outweigh their disadvantages. For this reason, we use rules not only to influence the behavior of others but also to influence our own behavior. In other words, we often give ourselves instructions as to how we should behave: "I should study in the library rather than at home, because it is much quieter in the library"; "I should work out each day if I want to remain fit and healthy"; and "If I am polite to others, they will be polite to me." Such statements can be called ***personal rules (or self-instructions)***, which can be defined as

ADVICE FOR THE LOVELORN

Dear Dr. Dee,

My boyfriend and I very much enjoy reading your columns. Unfortunately, Steve (my boyfriend) has begun using the ideas in these columns to analyze each and every aspect of our relationship. I know he means well, but it is starting to drive me nuts. Furthermore, I think his conclusions about our relationship are usually dead wrong. What is your opinion on this?

Going Nutty

Dear Going,

At the start of this book, we explicitly warned against taking these columns too seriously. For one thing, the advice given is usually quite speculative; it is not grounded in scientific research, nor is it based on a careful assessment of the relationship being discussed (which, in any case, is just a fictional relationship). Thus, our purpose in presenting these columns is simply to give students a sense of the *potential* ways in which behavioral principles *might* be applicable to some important aspects of human behavior.

It is also important to recognize that each relationship is unique, meaning there's no guarantee that advice that is appropriate for one relationship is relevant to another relationship. In fact, you can think of such advice as a rule for how to improve your relationship—and the act of following that advice as a form of rule-governed behavior. As we discuss in this chapter, such rules may not accurately reflect the actual contingencies that are in effect, and the person following the rule may become insensitive to the actual contingencies. This may be what has happened in your boyfriend's case. He seems to have concluded that the advice given in these columns is relevant to your own situation, which it might not be.

Tell him to lighten up a bit, pay less attention to what's being said in these advice columns (or, for that matter, anyone else's advice column), and pay more attention to what's going on in your relationship. And if you do need advice, there is often nothing better than some plain old common sense from one's close friends and family. These people often have a better understanding of the type of person you are and the actual contingencies surrounding your relationship than any advice columnist could ever have.

Behaviorally yours,

Dr. Dee

verbal descriptions of contingencies that we present to ourselves to influence our behavior (Ainslie, 1992).

Many of the personal rules that we use to regulate our behavior exert their effect as a function of "say–do correspondence." ***Say–do correspondence*** occurs when there is a close match between what we say we are going to do and what we actually do at a later time. If I say that I will go running at 4:00 in the afternoon and then actually go running at that time, my statement of what I intend to do matches the actual behavior that I later perform. As with rule-governed behavior in general, parents play a critical role in the development of this correspondence. If Billie promises that he will put his toys away when he is finished playing with them, and later he does put his toys away, his parents are quite pleased and praise him for carrying through on his promise. But when he does not carry through on his promise, they are annoyed. To the extent that Billie's parents apply these consequences consistently, Billie will likely grow up to display a strong level of say–do correspondence. He will become known as a reliable individual who can be trusted to carry through on his promises to others. Not only that, he may concurrently develop an ability to carry through on his promises to himself, which means that he will be able to use such promises as personal rules to guide his own behavior (Guevremont, Osnes, & Stokes, 1986).

Although personal rules can be useful in helping us manage our behavior, not all personal rules are equally effective. Ainslie (1986), for example, has proposed that personal rules are most effective when they establish a "bright boundary" between acceptable and unacceptable patterns of behavior. A bright boundary is a strategic concept stating that military leaders should make use of clearly specified landmarks, such as rivers, streams, or roads, to mark the limits of their territory. Such boundaries are easier to defend because they allow one to clearly determine when the enemy has intruded into one's territory. Similarly, in trying to carry through on rules for our own behavior, we are more likely to succeed when the rule specifically sets out the conditions under which it has been obeyed or violated. This is related to the notion, discussed in Chapter 10, that each choice in a self-control situation often has only a small but cumulative effect upon the overall outcome. Each sugary soda that we drink will not, by itself, undermine our efforts at attaining good health; rather, it is only the repeated consumption of sodas that undermines our health. If we wish to occasionally indulge in such treats, it might help to clearly specify the level at which we will do so, since there is no natural boundary indicating the point at which further indulgence will significantly undermine our health.

The importance of clear, specific rules on behavior has been empirically supported. For example, participants who specified when and where they would take a vitamin supplement were significantly more consistent in taking the supplement than were those who merely intended to take the supplement (Sheeran & Orbell, 1999). Likewise, patients who specified when, where, and how they would make a cervical cancer screening appointment were more likely to obtain such screening than were those who had not made such plans (Sheeran & Orbell, 2000). More recently, Luszczynska, Sobczyk, and Abraham (2007) asked a group of Weight Watchers participants to formulate specific food and exercise plans for each day throughout the week (e.g., "This is my plan concerning the consumption of sweets for the next 7 days. I plan to eat … [listing type and amount of sweets] at … [indicating time at which it would be eaten] at … [indicating place at which it would be eaten]"). The participants also made specific relapse prevention plans for how they would cope with temptations that might arise ("If someone offers me my favorite unhealthy food, then I will …"). Compared to a control group of Weight Watchers participants who did not formulate such plans, those who did lost twice as much weight during a 2-month period.

Thus, the act of clearly specifying when, where, and how a goal is to be accomplished can significantly affect the probability of accomplishing that goal. Gollwitzer (1999) refers to such when-where-and-how statements as *implementation intentions*. However, to be more consistent with Ainslie's (1992) terminology, they could also be called ***personal process rules***: personal rules that indicate the specific process by which a task is to be accomplished. And a possible reason such rules are effective is that they establish a bright boundary between actions that conform to the rule and those that do not. (See also Schmitt, 2001, for a discussion of the issues involved in establishing instructional control over behavior that needs to occur at a later point in time.)

QUICK QUIZ I

1. A p__________ rule is a description of a contingency that we verbalize to ourselves to influence our own behavior.
2. A close match between what we say we are going to do and what we actually do at a later point in time is called a __________-__________ c__________.
3. People who have been trained to display a high level of __________ -__________ correspondence can (more/less) effectively use personal rules (or self-instructions) to influence their behavior.
4. P__________ p__________ rules indicate the specific process by which a task is to be carried out. The formulation of such rules tends to (increase/decrease) the likelihood that the task will be accomplished. Such rules have also been called im__________ i__________.

And Furthermore

Say–Do Correspondence and Willpower

Using personal rules to regulate one's behavior represents a form of say–do correspondence. Moreover, to the extent that one displays a strong level of say–do correspondence, such personal rules might even function as a type of *commitment response*. As you may recall from Chapter 10, a commitment response is any response made at an early point in time that so reduces the value of a smaller sooner reward that it no longer serves as a temptation when it becomes imminent. One is therefore able to ignore the temptation and carry on working toward a larger later reward. Thus, handing your sister $10 with the understanding that she will return it only if you have completed a certain amount of studying that evening will reduce the value of any non-study activity to a level where you will in fact be quite likely to study (because any activity that interferes with studying will be associated with the loss of $10). Perhaps, however, people who display a strong level of say–do correspondence do not require such artificial consequences to control their behavior; perhaps for them the mere act of promising to do something is by itself a sufficient form of commitment.

To what extent can self-promises serve as a strong form of commitment? Consider the following passage from a letter quoted by William James (1907) in his classic article, "The Energies of Men":

> My device [Prince Pueckler-Muskau writes to his wife] is this: I give my word of honour most solemnly to myself to do or to leave undone this or that. I am of course extremely cautious in the use of this expedient, but when once the word is given, even though I afterwards think I have been precipitate or mistaken, I hold it to be perfectly irrevocable, whatever inconveniences I foresee likely to result. If I were capable of breaking my word after such mature consideration, I should lose all respect for myself —and what man of sense would not prefer death to such an alternative? (p. 16)

The prince describes how, once he has vowed to perform or not perform an activity, he feels duty bound to carry out this vow. As a result, he is able to use this device to accomplish tasks that would otherwise be very difficult. He is also extremely careful in using this device, recognizing that its potency lies in the fact that he *always* keeps his word in such matters. In other words, a major consequence motivating adherence to his verbal commitments is that he always keeps these commitments, and to the extent that he does so they will remain a valuable tool (see also Ainslie, 1992). Note, too, how the prince pronounces these verbal commitments in a "most solemn" manner, thereby establishing a *bright boundary* between statements of intention that must be fulfilled ("I swear most solemnly that I shall complete this project by the weekend") and more ordinary statements of intention, which do not represent a commitment ("I should really try to complete this project by the weekend").

Another example of the power of verbal commitments can be found in the life of Mohandas K. (Mahatma) Gandhi, the famous statesman who led India to independence and whose philosophy of passive resistance strongly influenced Martin Luther King Jr. In his autobiography (1927/1957), Gandhi reveals that he made frequent use of verbal commitments to control his behavior and that the effectiveness of these commitments lay partly in the fact that breaking a commitment produced within him a tremendous feeling of guilt. At one point, for example, he was severely ill and was strongly urged by his doctors to drink milk (as a needed source of protein). As a committed vegetarian, he refused, maintaining that he would rather die than break his vow never to eat animal products. Only when his advisors pointed out to him that he had probably been thinking of cow's milk when he made his vow and not goat's milk did he acquiesce and drink goat's milk. He recovered from his illness but

The great Indian statesman, Mahatma Gandhi, displayed a considerable degree of "say–do correspondence" during his illustrious life.

(*continued*)

nevertheless felt considerable guilt over violating the spirit, if not the precise intention, of the vow he had made.

The strength of Gandhi's verbal commitments is also illustrated by the effect of his vow to remain sexually abstinent (despite being married). Before making the vow—and believing that it should be possible to practice abstinence without a vow—he had found the task extremely difficult. Making the vow, however, immediately resolved these difficulties. As he later wrote:

> As I look back on the twenty years of the vow, I am filled with pleasure and wonderment. The more or less successful practice of self-control had been going on since 1901. But the freedom and joy that came to me after taking the vow had never been experienced before 1906. Before the vow I had been open to being overcome by temptation at any moment. Now the vow was a sure shield against temptation. (Gandhi, 1927/1957, p. 208)

Gandhi's description indicates that the vow was such a strong form of commitment that it essentially eliminated the temptation to engage in sexual intercourse, thereby removing any sense of conflict.

You may remember how, in our discussion of self-control in Chapter 10, we questioned whether the concept of willpower was useful, noting that it was often no more than a descriptive term for the fact that a person had in fact been able to resist a temptation. But one way in which it might be useful is when it refers to an individual's ability to make use of a verbal commitment—derived in turn from a history of training in strong say-do correspondence—to exert control over his or her behavior. Thus, some individuals may indeed have a considerable amount of self-control (or willpower) in the sense of doing what they say they are going to do. In support of this possibility, research has shown that say-do correspondence is a major predictor of procrastination in students, with students who report doing what they say they are going to do being much less likely to procrastinate in their studies (Howell, Watson, Powell, & Buro, 2006).

Finally, what about those of us who wish we could more often carry through on our verbal commitments? Although we may not be capable of acquiring the same ability as Gandhi, most of us would probably agree that we are too often lacking in our level of say-do correspondence. In this regard, we might do well to close with yet another passage from William James (1890/1983), who wrote often on the concept of will (bracketed comments are ours):

> As a final practical maxim, relative to these habits of the will, we may, then, offer something like this: *Keep the faculty of effort alive in you by a little gratuitous effort every day.* That is, be systematically ascetic or heroic in little unnecessary points, do every day or two something for no other reason than that you would rather not do it [*and because you promised yourself you would do it*], so that when the hour of dire need draws nigh, it may find you not unnerved and untrained to stand the test. Asceticism of this sort is like the insurance which a man pays on his house and goods. The tax does him no good at the time, and possibly may never bring him a return. But if the fire *does* come, his having paid it will be his salvation from ruin. So with the man who has daily inured himself to habits of concentrated attention, energetic volition, and self-denial in unnecessary things. He will stand like a tower when everything rocks around him, and when his softer fellow-mortals are winnowed like chaff in the blast (p. 130; see also Barrett, 1931, and Assagioli, 1974; see Oaten and Cheng, 2006, for evidence concerning the extent to which repeated practice at self-control on one task can generalize to other tasks).

Study Tip: Needless to say, the importance of personal process rules (or implementation intentions) has considerable relevance for studying. For example, the statement, "I will study this evening," is so vaguely worded that one is at high risk of delaying the act of studying until it is too late to study. The point at which the rule has been violated is not easily determined until we have, in a sense, been overrun and lost the battle. By contrast, the statement, "I will study from 7:00 P.M. to 9:00 P.M. this evening," is so specific that any violation of the rule—for example, it is now 7:10 P.M. and we are still watching television—will be readily apparent.

The importance of specificity also applies to longer-range plans for studying. Gollwitzer and Brandstätter (1997) asked college students to name two projects they intended to complete during Christmas break, one of which would be easy to accomplish (e.g., go skating) and the other of which would be difficult to accomplish (e.g., complete an English assignment). Students were also asked if they had made a decision about when and where the activity would be carried out. Following the Christmas break, the same students were asked if they had completed the project. For activities that were easy to implement, about 80% of the students said they had indeed completed them. With such easy projects, it seemed to make little difference if the students had also decided upon a time and place for implementing them. For difficult projects, however, students who had decided when and where their project would be carried out were significantly more likely to have completed it compared to those who had not made such a decision.

That said, one occasionally encounters students who seem to function well without setting specific times and places for their studying. The writer recalls one student who did try scheduling specific times and reported that it made her decidedly *less* efficient. But it turns out that she already had a rule that was, for her, highly effective—and that was to study at odd times during the day when she wasn't otherwise occupied, which she did religiously. By comparison, planning precise times for her studying significantly *lowered* the amount of studying she did. This is a good example of how, whatever the research findings might be, one should never assume that those findings are necessarily optimal for you.

SUMMARY

In observational learning, an observer's behavior is altered as a result of observing a model's behavior. Two simple forms of observational influence are contagious behavior and stimulus enhancement. In the classical conditioning aspect of observational learning, the emotional cues exhibited by a model serve as CSs that elicit conditioned responses, called vicarious emotional responses, in an observer. The operant conditioning aspect of observational learning concerns the manner in which a model's operant behavior is translated into the behavior of an observer. First, the observer must acquire information from the model. Such acquisition depends on the consequences of the model's behavior, the personal characteristics of the model, whether the observer is capable of understanding and duplicating the modeled behavior, and whether the observer is explicitly reinforced for attending to the modeled behavior. Translating acquired knowledge into performance in turn depends on whether the observer's performance of the behavior is reinforced or punished.

Animals also learn by observation. However, unlike humans, many animal species appear to be unable to truly imitate the actions of another individual. Apparent examples of imitation can often be explained as examples of stimulus enhancement, which involves directing an animal's attention to a particular place or object, thereby making it more likely that the animal will approach that place or object. There is evidence, however, of true imitation in some species, and perhaps even intentional teaching.

Although much of social learning is beneficial and positive, social learning of violent behavior is more controversial, especially in the context of exposure to violence through mass media and interactive games. Bandura (1965) initially warned of the power of social learning of violent behavior in his classic "Bobo doll studies." More recent correlational and experimental evidence suggests that exposure to media violence increases the likelihood that a person will behave violently or become a victim of violence.

A rule is a verbal description of a contingency, and behavior that is generated as a result of such rules is known as rule-governed behavior. A rule that also includes information about how we should behave in a setting is an instruction. Rules are highly adaptive in that they allow us to learn about contingencies without having to directly experience those contingencies. Parents spend considerable effort training their children to follow rules, and children learn that following rules not only leads to praise but also facilitates accomplishing a task.

Nevertheless, rules have their drawbacks. First, rule-governed behavior is often less efficient than behavior that has been shaped by actual contingencies. Second, rule-governed behavior is sometimes surprisingly insensitive to contingencies. A personal rule (or self-instruction) is a description of a contingency that we verbalize to ourselves to influence our own behavior. The use of personal rules to regulate behavior is dependent on training in say–do correspondence, which occurs when there is a close match between what we say we are going to do and what we actually do at a later time. Personal rules tend to be most effective when they are stated in such a way that there is a clear distinction (a bright boundary) between when the rule has been followed and when it has not. In support of this, researchers have shown that specifying personal process rules (or implementation intentions) indicating the specific manner in which a project is to be carried out increases the likelihood that the project will be accomplished.

SUGGESTED READINGS

Bushman, B. J., & Anderson, C. A. (2001). Media violence and the American public: Scientific facts versus media misinformation. *American Psychologist*, *56*, 477–489. An interesting presentation of just how strong the evidence is for the harmful effects of media violence on viewers, and how this finding has remained hidden from the general public.

Malott, R. W., & Suarez, E. A. T. (2004). *Principles of behavior* (5th ed.). Upper Saddle River, NJ: Pearson. See Chapter 24, "A Theory of Rule-Governed Behavior," for a readable discussion of how behaviors that are directed toward delayed consequences, such as studying to obtain a good mark on an exam, are largely the result of instructional control. The authors theorize that, in such instances, the occurrence of guilt and anxiety for not following instructions—and the avoidance of guilt and anxiety by following instructions—may be the effective consequence that actually motivates the behavior.

STUDY QUESTIONS

1. What is observational learning? Define contagious behavior and stimulus enhancement and give an example of each.
2. What are vicarious emotional responses? Diagram, with appropriate abbreviations, the higher-order conditioning process by which a smile can become a conditioned stimulus for pleasant emotions.
3. List three features that determine whether an observer will attend to a model's behavior. List three ways in which acquisition of information through observation can translate into performance of the behavior.
4. What is true imitation? Describe evidence indicating that some animals are capable of true imitation.
5. Describe Bandura's Bobo doll studies, including some of the sex differences that were found. Why has evidence about the relationship between violent media and violent behavior been underestimated or ignored?
6. Define the terms *rule* and *rule-governed behavior*. How do instructions differ from rules?
7. What is the main advantage of rule-governed behavior over contingency-shaped behavior? What are two disadvantages of rule-governed behavior?
8. What is a personal rule? What is say–do correspondence, and how is it related to the effectiveness of personal rules for controlling behavior?
9. What is a personal process rule (or implementation intention)? Explain how the concept of a "bright-boundary" is related to the effectiveness of such rules?

CONCEPT REVIEW

contagious behavior. A more-or-less instinctive or reflexive behavior triggered by the occurrence of the same behavior in another individual.

generalized imitation. The tendency to imitate a new modeled behavior in the absence of any specific reinforcement for doing so.

observational learning. The process whereby the behavior of a model is witnessed by an observer, and the observer's behavior is subsequently changed.

personal process rule. A personal rule that indicates the specific process by which a task is to be accomplished. (Also called an *implementation intention*.)

personal rule (or self-instruction). A verbal description of a contingency that we present to ourselves to influence our behavior.

rule. A verbal description of a contingency.

rule-governed behavior. Behavior that has been generated through exposure to rules.

say–do correspondence. A close match between what we say we are going to do and what we actually do at a later time.

stimulus enhancement. Directing attention to a particular place or object, making it more likely that the observer will approach that place or object.

true imitation. Duplicating a novel behavior (or sequence of behaviors) to achieve a specific goal.

vicarious emotional response. A classically conditioned emotional response resulting from seeing that emotional response exhibited by others.

CHAPTER TEST

11. Many animal species, when shown a sequence of actions designed to extract food from a locked box, (do/do not) duplicate the sequence exactly. This suggests that few species exhibit true ________.
1. Improving your golf game by watching a video of an excellent golf player is a form of ________ learning.
25. At the start of each day, Victoria carefully plans out her studying for the day, writing down what she will study as well as when and where she will study. Although she is not always successful in fulfilling these plans, she usually accomplishes most of what she sets out to do. Her success is likely due to the fact that she is making use of personal ________ rules that establish a(n) ________ boundary between acceptable and unacceptable patterns of behavior.
6. If Claire observes her friend David laughing while enjoying a game of table tennis, she is (more/less) likely to try the game herself. If Claire observes David frowning while he struggles over a math problem, she is (more/less) likely to tackle the problem herself.
19. A rule that includes information about how we *should* respond is called a(n) ________.
26. "I should sit straight if I wish to prevent back problems." This is an example of a(n) ________ rule (or self-________).
12. If a dog sees another dog eating at a particular location, it is more likely to visit that location later. This is an example of ________.
5. The stimuli involved in the classical conditioning aspect of observational learning are often (emotional/rational) in nature.

10. Tina tells herself each day that she will study, but she rarely succeeds in doing so. This illustrates a lack of ________ correspondence, which also means that, in general, she may have difficulty using ________ rules to control her behavior.
3. Smiling, yawning, laughing, and orienting when others do so are all examples of ________.
20. A big advantage of rules is that one (has to/does not have to) directly experience a set of contingencies to behave appropriately with respect to those contingencies.
14. Bandura demonstrated that children who observed violent models were (more/less) likely to behave violently themselves. Further, the behavior of the observers was so (similar/dissimilar) to that of the models, it could be considered as examples of ________.
2. Observational learning can be involved in both ________ and ________ conditioning.
16. Longitudinal studies have demonstrated that exposure to violent media is (significantly/nonsignificantly) associated with violent behavior and criminality in observers.
22. Joel is very noncompliant. Chances are that he has received reinforcement for (following/not following) instructions and/or punishment for (following/not following) instructions.
13. Directing a person's or animal's attention to an object or place is called ________; duplicating the actions of a model to obtain a goal is called ________.
23. When Salima's mom became ill with a neurological disorder, Salima was, for several years, assigned the task of giving her a daily massage to loosen up her muscles. By contrast, Byron has taken several massage workshops. Interestingly, Byron is less skillful at massage than Salima, which may reflect the fact that ________ behavior is sometimes less efficient than behavior that has been shaped through direct exposure to the natural ________.
17. Exposure to violent media may increase observers' violent behavior; it may also make some observers more likely to become ________ of violence, especially (males/females).
4. Contagion of orienting responses is closely related to the process of s________ e________.
8. After training her daughter to imitate the manner in which she eats food with a knife and fork, Ashley noticed her daughter spontaneously imitating the manner in which Ashley uses a spoon to eat soup. This is an example of a process known as ________.
18. A(n) ________ can be defined as a verbal description of a contingency, while ________ behavior is the behavior that is generated by such verbal descriptions.

15. Bandura determined that children were affected both by live violence and __________ violence. Thus, Bandura was the first to demonstrate the potential influence of the mass m__________ on violent behavior.
21. Children receive reinforcement for following instructions, both by their caretakers and by the fact that instructions can help them accomplish a task. As a result, most children acquire a (generalized/specific) tendency to follow instructions.
9. If a juvenile rat watches its mother eat a novel food, like chocolate chips, the young rat is (more/less/neither more nor less) likely to try the chocolate chips.
24. Kent read somewhere that women are very attracted to a man who acts strong and dominant. Despite his efforts to appear strong and dominant, he is eventually dumped by every woman he meets. He nevertheless assumes that there must be something wrong with these women and persists in cultivating his heroic image. Kent's problem may reflect the fact that __________ behavior is sometimes surprisingly insensitive to the actual contingencies of reinforcement.
7. If a model receives reinforcement for performing a behavior, an observer is (more/less) likely to perform the same behavior; if a model receives punishment for performing a behavior, an observer is (more/less) likely to perform the same behavior.

ANSWERS TO CHAPTER TEST

1. observational
2. classical; operant
3. contagious behaviors
4. stimulus enhancement
5. emotional
6. more; less
7. more; less
8. generalized imitation
9. more
10. say–do; personal
11. do not; imitation
12. stimulus enhancement
13. stimulus enhancement; true imitation
14. more; similar; true imitation
15. filmed; media
16. significantly
17. victims; females
18. rule; rule-governed
19. instruction
20. does not have to
21. generalized
22. not following; following
23. rule-governed; contingencies
24. rule-governed
25. process; bright
26. personal; instruction

CHAPTER 12

BIOLOGICAL DISPOSITIONS IN LEARNING

CHAPTER OUTLINE

Ken was worried about his girlfriend, Chantal, who had lost a lot of weight in recent months. Nevertheless, Chantal maintained that she was still overweight and needed to lose a few more pounds. Ken had heard that anorexia is characterized by a distorted body image, in which people deny how thin they are. He wondered if Chantal was suffering from this type of denial. He had also heard that anorexia often results from growing up in an overcontrolling family—though on the surface, it seemed like her family was pretty nice.

Other than his concerns about her weight, Ken thought Chantal was terrific. He particularly loved the fact that she shared his enthusiasm for long-distance running. In fact, she was more addicted to running than he was.

By this time, you probably realize that the basic principles of conditioning have a surprising degree of generality and apply to a wide range of species and behaviors. But you may also recall how, at certain points in this text, we have noted some limitations in this regard. For example, people more readily learn to be afraid of events that have some type of evolutionary association with danger, such as snakes and spiders, than they do of modern-day events, such as cars and toasters. It is possible then that we have inherited a biological tendency to learn certain types of fears more readily than others. This innate tendency for an organism to more easily learn certain types of behaviors or to associate certain types of events with each other is known as **preparedness**. In this chapter, we further explore the role of biological preparedness in conditioning, as well as the manner in which such preparedness seems to produce an overlap between processes of classical conditioning and operant conditioning.

Preparedness and Conditioning

Preparedness in Classical Conditioning

Fear conditioning is one form of classical conditioning in which preparedness seems to play an important role. You may remember, for example, that *backward conditioning*, in which the US precedes the NS, typically produces little if any conditioning. Thus, if the rat first receives a shock and then hears a tone:

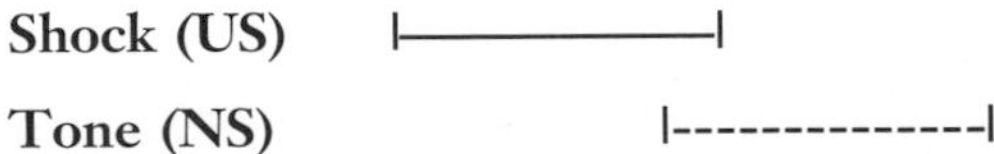

it typically will not learn to fear the tone. However, under some circumstances, backward conditioning can be achieved, such as when the NS is a "biologically relevant" stimulus for fear (Keith-Lucas & Guttman, 1975). For example, if we use the sight of a snake as the NS:

Shock (US) |———————|

Snake (NS) |———————|

then backward conditioning might occur even though the shock came first. Thus, backward conditioning works with the snake but not the tone. As previously noted, some researchers (e.g., Seligman, 1971) have proposed that many species of animals (including people) have an inherited predisposition to fear certain types of events. From this perspective, rats have an inherited predisposition to fear snakes, because snakes have constituted a significant threat to rats throughout their evolutionary history. This predisposition is so strong that even if the snake is presented after the shock, the fear elicited by the shock still becomes associated with the snake. (Needless to say, such predispositions would also facilitate conditioning using a delayed, trace, or simultaneous procedure.)

Another example of the role of preparedness is ***taste aversion conditioning***, a form of classical conditioning in which a food item that has been paired with gastrointestinal illness becomes a conditioned aversive stimulus. Simply put, an animal that becomes sick after ingesting a food item associates the food with the illness and subsequently finds it distasteful.

Conditioned taste aversions are quite common. In one survey 65% of undergraduates reported developing a taste aversion at some point in their lives (Logue, Ophir, & Strauss, 1981). Interestingly, and perhaps not surprisingly, many of these aversions involved an alcoholic drink of some sort. Most taste aversions are quite rational because the person believes that the food or drink item was actually the cause of the illness. In some cases, however, the person knows that the item did not cause the illness and that the illness was instead caused by some other factor (such as the flu) with which the food or drink was only coincidentally associated. Nevertheless, the person still finds the item highly aversive—a convincing testament to the strength of this type of conditioning.

In a typical experiment on taste aversion conditioning, rats are first given some type of preferred food or drink to ingest, such as sweet-tasting (saccharin-flavored) water. The animal is then made to feel sick, either by injecting a nausea-inducing drug directly into the gut or through exposure to X-ray irradiation. After the rat recovers, it is given a choice of either sweet water or normal water. Although a rat typically prefers sweet water over normal water, it now strongly prefers the normal water. This indicates that the sweet water has become an aversive conditioned stimulus (CS) through its association with illness. This procedure can be diagrammed as follows:

Sweet water: X-ray irradiation → ***Nausea***
NS US UR

Sweet water → ***Nausea*** (as indicated by avoidance of the sweet water)
CS CR

Taste aversion conditioning involves many of the same processes found in other forms of classical conditioning (Schafe & Bernstein, 1996). For example, *stimulus generalization* often occurs when food items that taste similar to the aversive item are also perceived as aversive. Thus, a conditioned aversion to one type of fish might generalize to other types of fish. A conditioned taste aversion can also be *extinguished* if the aversive food item is repeatedly ingested without further illness. As well, *overshadowing* can occur in that we are more likely to develop an aversion to a stronger-tasting food item, such as onions, than to a milder-tasting item, such as potatoes, that was consumed at the same meal. And the presence of a food item that already has aversive associations can *block* the development of aversive associations to other food items. If you have already acquired a taste aversion to peas, but force yourself to eat them anyway, and then get sick because of some spoiled fish that was served at the same meal, you will probably *not* develop an aversion to the fish. The presence of the peas (already a CS for nausea) will likely block any conditioning occurring to the fish.

Of particular importance in taste aversion conditioning is the phenomenon of *latent inhibition*. We are more likely to associate a relatively novel item, such as an unusual liqueur, with sickness than we would a more familiar item such as beer (Kalat, 1974). Latent inhibition helps explain why it is often difficult to poison a rat. When a rat encounters a novel food item, such as rat bait, it will most likely eat only a small amount of the item before moving on to other, more familiar items. If the rat later becomes ill, it will associate the illness with the novel item rather than with any of the familiar items. The rat also has a high probability of recovering from the illness because it will have eaten only a small amount of the poisoned item.[1]

QUICK QUIZ A

1. The term p____________ refers to an innate tendency for an organism to more easily learn certain types of behaviors or to associate certain types of events with each other.
2. Taste aversion conditioning is a type of cl____________ conditioning in which a food item that has been paired with gastrointestinal illness becomes a c____________ av____________ stimulus.
3. After recovering from a bad case of the flu, Robbie could not bring himself to eat oatmeal, which he had tried to eat during his illness. In all likelihood, Robbie has developed a t____________ a____________ to the oatmeal.
4. Robbie now dislikes other types of porridge as well, which appears to be an example of s____________ g____________.

[1]This tendency to be wary of new food items, which is also present in humans and is especially strong in children, is known as *dietary neophobia* (a *neophobia* is a fear of something new). Neophobia is particularly important for rats, which are physically incapable of vomiting in order to purge toxins from the stomach. More generally, neophobia is an especially adaptive tendency for small animals and the young of most species because the dose-response relationships for many toxins are body-weight dependent. Simply put, small animals are more susceptible to food poisoning than large animals and have therefore evolved to be especially wary of food poisoning.

5. Robbie's aversion to porridge would likely ex____________ if he repeatedly ate it without experiencing any further illness.

6. According to the o____________ effect, the strongest-tasting item in a meal is most likely to become associated with a subsequent illness. As well, a food item that was previously associated with illness will b____________ the development of aversive associations to other items in a meal.

7. In keeping with the process of la____________ in____________, Robbie would have been less likely to develop a taste aversion to oatmeal porridge if he had frequently eaten oatmeal before his illness.

Although taste aversion conditioning is in many ways similar to other forms of classical conditioning, there are also major differences.

1. *The Formation of Associations Over Long Delays.* In most classical conditioning procedures, the neutral stimulus (NS) and unconditioned stimulus (US) must occur in close temporal proximity, separated by no more than a few seconds. By contrast, taste aversions can develop when food items are consumed several hours before the sickness develops. For example, Etscorn and Stephens (1973) found that rats could develop taste aversions to flavored water that had been ingested up to 24 hours before they were injected with an illness-inducing drug. The ability to associate food with illness after lengthy periods of time is highly adaptive in that poisonous substances often have a delayed effect. If animals were unable to form such delayed associations, they would be at great risk of repeatedly consuming a poisonous food item and eventually perishing.
2. *One-Trial Conditioning.* Strong conditioned taste aversions can usually be achieved with only a single pairing of food with illness, particularly when the food item is novel (Riley & Clarke, 1977). One-trial conditioning sometimes occurs in other forms of conditioning, especially fear conditioning, but not as consistently as it does in taste aversion conditioning. As with the ability to form associations over long delays, one-trial conditioning of taste aversions is highly adaptive insofar as it minimizes the possibility of a repeat, possibly fatal, experience with a poisonous substance.
3. *Specificity of Associations.* When you feel nauseous following a meal, do you associate the nausea with that episode of *American Idol* you are watching (even though, given the quality of some of the singing, that might seem appropriate), or with the meal? Fortunately for the broadcast network, you are more likely to associate the nausea with the meal. Similarly, the rat that receives an injection of a nausea-inducing drug several hours after drinking a sweet water solution does not associate the illness with the injection; it instead associates the illness with the sweet water. In other words, there seems to be a strong, inherited tendency to associate a gastrointestinal illness with food or drink rather than with any other kind of item (Garcia & Koelling, 1966). This type of preparedness is sometimes referred to as ***CS-US relevance***, an

innate tendency to more readily associate certain types of stimuli with each other.

An excellent example of the role of CS-US relevance in taste aversion conditioning was provided by Garcia and Koelling (1966) in their initial demonstration of this type of conditioning. In this experiment, the rats initially drank sweet water that was paired with a light and a noise (each time they licked the water tube, they heard a click and saw a light flash). This compound stimulus can therefore be described as "bright, noisy, sweet water." After consuming the water, some of the rats received a slight foot shock that elicited a fear reaction, while other rats received a dose of X-ray irradiation that made them nauseous. Finally, all of the rats were given a choice between two water bottles, one containing only "bright, noisy" water (i.e., regular water combined with a light and a click) and the other containing only sweet water. Can you guess the results?

The rats that had been made nauseous by the X-ray irradiation avoided the sweet water and drank the bright, noisy water, which is consistent with the basic notion that nausea is more readily associated with taste than with other kinds of stimuli.

Conditioning trial:
Bright, noisy, sweet water: X-ray irradiation → *Nausea*
NS US UR

Test trial:
Sweet water → *Nausea*
CS CR
Bright, noisy water → No nausea
NS —

But what about the rats that received a foot shock? It turns out that they avoided the bright, noisy water but not the sweet water. In other words, they developed a fear of the noise and lights that had been combined with the water, but not the taste, and were therefore quite willing to drink the sweet water.

Conditioning trial:
Bright, noisy, sweet water: Foot shock → *Fear*
NS US UR

Test trial:
Bright, noisy water → *Fear*
CS CR
Sweet water → No fear
NS —

Thus, not only do rats have a predisposition to readily associate nausea with taste, they also have a predisposition to associate tactually painful events with visual and auditory stimuli. This makes sense from an evolutionary perspective in that tactile pain is more likely to result from something "out there" that a rat can see and hear, whereas nausea is more likely to result from something that a rat ingests and can be tasted. Thus, for a rat to evolve in such a way that it could readily make such associations would facilitate its survival.

Further evidence for the role of biological dispositions in taste aversion conditioning has been revealed by comparative research on inter-species differences in the types of stimuli that can be associated. In one experiment, both quail and rats drank dark blue, sour-tasting water before being made ill (Wilcoxon, Dragoin, & Kral, 1971). The animals were then given a choice between dark blue water and sour-tasting water. As expected, the rats naturally avoided the sour-tasting water and strongly preferred the dark blue water. They associated the taste of the water with the nausea. The quail, however, were more likely to avoid the dark blue water than the sour-tasting water. This suggests that quail, which are daytime feeders and rely heavily on vision for identifying food, are more disposed to associate the visual aspects (rather than the taste aspects) of food with nausea. Rats, however, being nighttime feeders, rely more heavily on taste (and smell) than vision and are therefore generally disposed to associate the taste (and smell) aspects of food with nausea. (This is not to say that rats cannot learn to associate the visual aspects of food with nausea. They can, but additional conditioning trials are required to form such associations.)

In addition to between-species differences, there are often sex differences in taste aversion learning, which can be related to differences in sensory and perceptual processing. In humans, females are better than males at detecting odors and discriminating among odors. Because of this ability, women are more reactive to odors associated with the experience of nausea and are more prone to developing taste aversions (Chambers, Yuan, Brownson, & Wang, 1997). As well, most women report that their sense of smell and taste is enhanced during the early stages of pregnancy, which often leads to the development of taste aversions (Nordin, Broman, Olafsson, & Wulff, 2004). Although experiencing these kinds of symptoms during early pregnancy might seem counterproductive, it is actually an adaptive mechanism. Fetal organ systems are developing during the first few months of pregnancy and are highly vulnerable to damage by toxins at this stage. A dislike of certain foods (especially bitter foods) and a propensity to taste aversions might prevent a woman from ingesting foods that contain dangerous bacteria (bitterness can indicate the presence of bacteria).

It should be noted that research on taste aversion conditioning has practical applications. For example, cancer patients sometimes develop aversions to food items that have been inadvertently associated with the nausea resulting from chemotherapy (Bernstein, 1991). Because cancer patients often suffer from severe weight loss anyway, the development of taste aversions that lead to avoidance of certain food items could be serious. Fortunately, research has suggested ways to minimize this problem. One way is to serve meals that consist of highly familiar foods. In keeping with the latent inhibition effect, familiar foods will be less likely to become associated with nausea. Along the same lines, the patient can be served a highly novel, yet trivial, food item just before a chemotherapy session. This novel item will then be associated with the nausea, preventing the development of taste aversions to other, more essential food items. For example, in one study, children about to undergo chemotherapy were given coconut- or root-beer-flavored candies following a regular meal. Compared to children who had not been given these candies, the children in the study later developed fewer aversions to their regular food items (Broberg & Bernstein, 1987). The nausea from the chemotherapy had become associated with the unusual candies rather than regular food items.

Taste aversion conditioning also has implications for wildlife management. For example, if coyotes are given ground mutton (wrapped in sheep skin) that has been laced with a nausea-inducing chemical, they will subsequently refuse to attack sheep (Gustavson, Garcia, Hankins, & Rusiniak, 1974). Insofar as attacks upon livestock are not only costly to ranchers but also a major impediment in efforts to protect certain predators from extinction, taste aversion conditioning would seem to be a potential solution to the problem. For example, if you seed an area with nausea-inducing packets of mutton or beef, you might soon have a pack of wolves that avoid livestock like the plague. Unfortunately, early field tests by wildlife officials in the United States were largely unsuccessful—the predators continued to prey upon livestock—as a result of which interest in the procedure soon dwindled. Some researchers, however, claim that the conditioning procedures used in these early tests were badly confounded, with cues being left on the meat packets that allowed the predators to discriminate "treated" meat from untreated meat. As a result, the predators learned to avoid the treated meat packets but continued to hunt livestock. However, renewed efforts are now underway to once again implement such programs, but this time with a greater focus on proper controls (Dingfelder, 2010). (See also "Predation Politics: The Sad Story of Wolves, Conditioned Taste Aversion, and the Wildlife Management Hierarchy" at http://www.conditionedtasteaversion.net/ for one researcher's perspective on the extent to which taste aversion conditioning has been neglected in wildlife management.)

QUICK QUIZ B

1. Distinctive features of taste aversion conditioning, compared to other types of classical conditioning, include the fact that the associations can be formed over (short/long) delays, typically require (one/several) pairing(s) of the NS and US, and (are/are not) specific to certain types of stimuli.
2. In the classic experiment by Garcia and Koelling, the rats that had been made ill avoided the (sweet water/bright, noisy water), while the rats that had been shocked avoided the ____________ water.
3. In the experiment on taste aversions in quail and rats, the rats avoided the (blue/sour) water, while the quail avoided the ____________ water.
4. To counter the possibility that chemotherapy-induced nausea will result in the development of taste aversions, patients should be fed meals that consist mostly

of (familiar/unfamiliar) foods. As well, just before the chemotherapy session, they can be given some trivial type of (familiar/unfamiliar) food item, which will attract most of the aversive associations.

5. According to the concept of ____________ ____________, certain types of stimuli are more easily associated with each other.

Preparedness in Operant Conditioning

Biological preparedness also seems to play a role in some forms of operant conditioning. For example, Stevenson-Hinde (1973) found that the sound of recorded chaffinch songs (chaffinches are a type of bird) was an effective reinforcer for training chaffinches to perch in a certain spot, but not for training them to key-peck. Conversely, food was an effective reinforcer for training them to key-peck but not for training them to perch in a certain spot. Chaffinches seem to be biologically prepared to associate perching in a certain spot with the consequence of hearing songs, and to associate pecking with the consequence of obtaining food.

In a similar manner, rats will more readily learn to press a lever to obtain food pellets than to avoid shock (Bolles, 1970). But they readily learn to freeze or run to avoid shock. Once more, the explanation for these differences may reside in the animals' evolutionary history. Rats have evolved dexterous forepaws that are often used for eating; thus, pressing a lever for food is not far removed from the type of food-gathering behavior they display in the natural environment. However, avoiding painful events is, for a rat, more

And Furthermore

Conditioned Food Preferences

Just as conditioning processes sometimes make foods aversive, such processes can also make foods more appetitive. For example, a powerful way to increase our preference for a disliked food is to mix it with some food item or sweetener that we strongly prefer. This may be how some people grow to like black coffee: They first drink it with cream and sugar and then gradually eliminate the extra ingredients as the taste of the coffee itself becomes pleasurable. Similarly, in one study, college students developed increased preference for broccoli or cauliflower after eating it a few times with sugar (E. D. Capaldi, 1996). Unfortunately, few parents use such a method to improve their children's eating habits, possibly because they perceive sugar to be unhealthy and do not realize that the sugar can later be withdrawn (Casey & Rozin, 1989). Instead, parents often try to entice their children to eat a disliked food by offering dessert as a reward—a strategy that easily backfires in that the contrast between the disliked food and the subsequent dessert might result in the former becoming even more disliked. (See E. D. Capaldi, 1996, for other ways in which food preferences can be conditioned.)

naturally related to the response of freezing or running than it is to manipulating objects with its forepaws.

Biological dispositions for certain types of avoidance responses have also been found in pigeons. Bedford and Anger (cited in Bolles, 1979) found that pigeons will quickly learn to fly from one perch to another to avoid shock, but they will not learn to peck a response key to avoid shock. As with rats, the typical behavior pigeons use when fleeing danger provides an explanation: Flying is the usual way a pigeon escapes danger, while pecking is not. Thus pigeons, like rats, seem predisposed to learn certain types of avoidance responses more readily than others.

It may have occurred to you from the preceding examples that preparedness seems to play a particularly strong role in avoidance behavior. This observation has led Bolles (1970, 1979) to propose that some avoidance responses are actually not operants (in the sense of being controlled by their consequences) but are instead elicited behaviors (that are controlled by the stimuli that precede them). More specifically, he contends that aversive stimulation elicits a *species-specific defense reaction* (SSDR), which in the natural environment is often effective in countering danger. For this reason, a rat easily learns to run or freeze to avoid painful stimulation, simply because running and freezing are behaviors that are naturally *elicited* in dangerous situations. Indeed, a rat's tendency to freeze is so strong that it will sometimes freeze even when doing so results in a shock rather than avoids it. (Humans also have a tendency to freeze when feeling threatened, even when it is counterproductive to do so—such as when giving a speech to a large audience or being ordered about by a gunman.)

QUICK QUIZ C

1. Chaffinches easily learn to associate (perching/pecking) with the consequence of hearing a song and ____________ with the consequence of obtaining food.
2. Rats are biologically prepared to learn to avoid a painful stimulus by (lever pressing/running), while pigeons are biologically prepared to learn to avoid a painful stimulus by (pecking/flying).
3. According to Bolles, these types of avoidance responses are s____________-s____________ defense reactions (abbreviated ____________) that are naturally e____________ by the aversive stimulus.

Operant–Respondent Interactions

Bolles's concept of the SSDR is one example of how it is sometimes difficult to distinguish between operant behaviors and respondent (or elicited) behaviors. In this section, we discuss two further examples of the overlap between operants and respondents: instinctive drift and sign tracking.

Instinctive Drift

It was once assumed that an animal could be trained to perform just about any behavior it was physically capable of performing. Indeed, considering the remarkable array of behaviors that animals can be trained to display, this assumption does not seem unreasonable. There are, however, limits to such training, as two of Skinner's students discovered in the course of training animals for show business.

Marian and Keller Breland were former students of Skinner's who decided to put their knowledge of operant conditioning to commercial use. They established a business of training animals to perform unusual behaviors for television commercials and movies. In this endeavor, they were usually quite successful. Occasionally, however, they encountered some rather interesting limitations in what certain animals could be taught (Breland & Breland, 1961). For example, they once attempted to train a pig to deposit a wooden coin in a piggy bank. Using processes of shaping and chaining, the training initially proceeded quite smoothly. As time passed, however, a strange thing began to happen. The pig no longer simply deposited the coin in the bank, but started tossing the coin in the air and then rooting at it on the ground. Eventually, the tossing and rooting became so frequent that the coin never made its way to the bank. The Brelands also attempted to use a raccoon for this trick, but here too they ran into difficulties. As training progressed, the raccoon began rubbing the coin back and forth in its paws rather than dropping it into the bank. This stereotyped action sequence eventually became so dominant that this attempt too had to be abandoned.

Although these results were originally regarded as a strange anomaly and a serious blow to the generality of operant conditioning, it is now recognized that they merely represented situations in which a classically conditioned, fixed action pattern had gradually emerged to interfere with the operant behavior that was being shaped. With both the pig and the raccoon, the coin had become so strongly associated with food that it began to elicit species-specific behavior patterns associated with feeding. In the case of the pig, this meant that the coin was subjected to the type of rooting behavior pigs often display when feeding. In the case of the raccoon, the coin was repeatedly rubbed and washed in the way raccoons normally rub and wash their food (often shellfish). In both cases, the coin had become a conditioned stimulus (CS) that elicited a conditioned response (CR) in the form of a food-related, fixed action pattern.

Thus, in the case of the pig, the Brelands intended this:

Coin: ***Deposit coin in bank*** **→ Food**
S^D R S^R

which is an operant conditioning procedure. Initially, this worked quite well, but as the coin became more and more strongly associated with food, what happened instead was this:

Coin: Food → ***Rooting***
NS US UR
Coin → ***Rooting***
CS CR

which is a classical conditioning procedure. And as the classically conditioned response increased in strength, it eventually overrode the operantly conditioned response of depositing the coin in the bank. Thus, ***instinctive drift*** is an instance of classical conditioning in which a genetically based, fixed action pattern gradually emerges and displaces the behavior that is being operantly conditioned.

QUICK QUIZ D

1. In the experiment with the raccoon, the coin became a (CS/S^D) that elicited a (R/CR/UR) of washing and rubbing.
2. This phenomenon is known as i__________ d__________, in which a f__________ a__________ pattern displaces the op__________ behavior that is being shaped.

Sign Tracking

Pavlov once reported that one of his dogs, during a classical conditioning experiment, approached a light that had signaled the delivery of food and licked it (Pavlov, 1941). It seemed as though the light not only signaled food but had acquired some of its appetitive properties. Little attention was paid to this finding, however, until recently. This phenomenon is now known as sign tracking.

In ***sign tracking***, an organism approaches a stimulus that signals the presentation of an appetitive event (Tomie, Brooks, & Zito, 1989). The approach behavior seems very much like an operant behavior because it appears to be quite goal directed, yet the procedure that produces it is more closely akin to classical conditioning. Thus, sign tracking is yet another way in which classical and operant conditioning appear to overlap.

Take, for example, a hungry dog that has been trained to sit on a mat to receive food presented in a dish at the far side of the room. Suppose, too, that a light is presented just before the food, such that this light becomes a cue for food delivery (see Figure 12.1). A couple of things are liable to happen because of this arrangement. One is that the dog will probably start salivating whenever the light is presented. Through classical conditioning, the light will have become a CS for the conditioned response of salivation. But that is not all that will happen. Logically, when the light appears (which is a signal for food delivery), the dog should immediately walk over to the food dish and wait for the food. What happens instead is that the dog *walks over to the light* and starts displaying food-related behaviors toward it, such as licking it or even barking at it as though soliciting food from it. These behaviors are of course entirely unnecessary and have no effect on whether the food will appear. It seems as though the light has become so strongly associated with food that it is now a CS that elicits innate food-related behavior patterns (see Jenkins, Barrera, Ireland, & Woodside, 1978, for a description of a similar experiment).

Sign tracking has also been found in pigeons, and in fact it helps to account for the ease with which pigeons learn to peck a response key for food. Brown

FIGURE 12.1 Experimental setting for a sign-tracking experiment. The dog first learns to sit on the mat to receive food. A light is then presented before each food delivery.

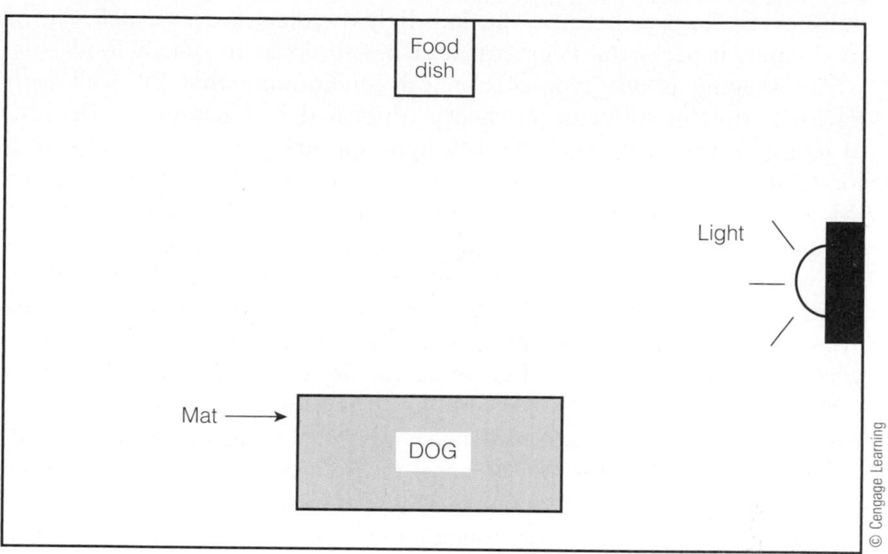

and Jenkins (1968) presented pigeons with a key light for 8 seconds followed by the *noncontingent* delivery of food. Although the pigeons did not have to peck the key to obtain the food, they soon began doing so anyway. It was as though the pigeons automatically pecked the key, simply because it was associated with food. The pecking therefore seemed to be an elicited response, with the key light functioning as a CS through its association with food:

Key light: Food → *Peck*
NS US UR
Key light: → *Peck*
CS CR

This procedure is known as ***autoshaping***, a type of sign tracking in which a pigeon comes to automatically peck at a key because the key light has been associated with the noncontingent (response-independent) delivery of food. Rather than trying to deliberately shape the behavior of key pecking, the researcher merely has to put the pigeon in the chamber, program the equipment to present light and food in the appropriate order, and presto, within an hour or so, out pops a key-pecking pigeon. Once the pecking response has been established this way, the food can then be made *contingent* upon pecking (i.e., food appears only when the key has been pecked), at which point the pecking begins functioning as an operant:

Key light: *Peck* → Food
S^D R S^R

Thus, a behavior that starts off as an elicited behavior (controlled by the stimulus that precedes it) becomes transformed into an operant behavior (controlled mostly by its consequence). In other words, the pigeon initially pecks the key because the key light predicts the free delivery of food; later, it pecks the key because it has to do so to obtain food.

Autoshaping is one type of classical conditioning that fits well with Pavlov's stimulus-substitution theory (discussed in Chapter 5). Because of its association with food, the key light appears to become a substitute for food, with the bird attempting to consume it. Further evidence for this stimulus-substitution interpretation comes from an experiment that compared autoshaped key pecks toward a key light signaling water delivery versus a key light signaling food delivery (Jenkins & Moore, 1973). When the bird pecked a key associated with water, it did so with its eyes open and its beak almost closed—the standard pattern of behavior when pigeons drink water. But when the bird pecked a key associated with food delivery, it did so with its eyes closed and its beak open, which is the standard pattern of behavior when a pigeon pecks at food. (The eyes are closed possibly because, in the natural environment, pecking at food sometimes results in dust or pebbles being thrown upward.) In other words, it seemed as though the bird was attempting to drink the key that was associated with water and eat the key that was associated with food.

Autoshaping procedures have powerful effects on behavior. For example, pigeons will peck a key associated with food even when doing so *prevents* the delivery of food (Williams & Williams, 1969). In other words, although the contingency requires the pigeons to refrain from pecking to actually obtain the food (they should simply wait for the food when the key light appears), they will nevertheless compulsively peck at the key. The key light exerts such strong control over the behavior that it essentially overrides the negative punishment (loss of food) associated with pecking. This phenomenon, in which sign tracking persists despite the resultant loss of a reinforcer, is known as *negative automaintenance*.

QUICK QUIZ E

1. In s__________ t__________, an organism approaches a stimulus that signals the availability of food. In such circumstances, the stimulus is best defined as a(n) (CS/US/S^D), while the approach behavior is best defined as a(n) (CR/UR/operant).
2. In au__________, a pigeon will begin to peck a lit response key that is presented for 8 seconds before the non__________ delivery of food. The peck in this situation appears to be functioning as a(n) (elicited/operant) behavior. Later, when a peck is required for the food to be delivered, the peck becomes a(n) __________ behavior.
3. In n__________ aut__________, pigeons will peck a lit response key that signals food delivery even when the act of pecking (prevents/facilitates) the delivery of food.

ADVICE FOR THE LOVELORN

Dear Dr. Dee,

My old girlfriend, to whom I was very attached, recently moved away. I am now trying to get over her, but I still find myself going to our favorite restaurant, our favorite beach, and so on. Why do I torture myself like this?

What a Birdbrain

Dear Birdbrain,

Think of your behavior as similar to sign tracking. Your girlfriend was a powerful appetitive stimulus, with the result that you now approach stimuli that have been strongly associated with her. In fact (and somewhat in keeping with your signature), researchers have found similar behavior patterns in Japanese quail. Burns and Domjan (1996) found that if they lowered a block of wood into a chamber just before opening a door that allowed access to a female quail, male quail had a strong tendency to approach and stand near the block of wood rather than near the door. The block of wood had become a CS that elicited what was essentially a sexual sign-tracking response. In similar fashion, we may have a tendency to approach settings that are strongly associated with a person with whom we have had an intimate relationship. In any event, your "birdbrained" tendency to approach these settings should eventually extinguish.

Behaviorally yours,

Dr. Dee

Adjunctive Behavior

Instinctive drift and sign tracking represent two types of anomalous (unexpected) behavior patterns that can develop during an operant conditioning procedure. Yet another type of anomaly is adjunctive behavior. ***Adjunctive behavior*** is an excessive pattern of behavior that emerges as a by-product of an intermittent schedule of reinforcement for some other behavior. In other words, as one behavior is being strengthened through intermittent reinforcement, another quite different behavior emerges as a side effect of that procedure. Adjunctive behavior is sometimes referred to as *schedule-induced behavior*, and the two terms will be used interchangeably in this discussion.

Basic Procedure and Defining Characteristics

Falk (1961) was the first person to systematically investigate adjunctive behavior in animals. He found that when rats were trained to press a lever for food on an intermittent schedule of reinforcement, they also began drinking excessive amounts of water. During a 3-hour session, the rats drank almost three-and-a-half times the amount they would normally drink in an entire day. (To get a handle on this, imagine that a person who typically drinks 8 glasses of water a day instead drinks 28 glasses of water in a 3-hour period!) In fact, some of the rats drank up to half their body weight in water. These numbers are all the more remarkable because the rats were food deprived, not water deprived, and food deprivation typically produces a decrease, not an increase, in water intake. This pattern of excessive drinking—called *schedule-induced polydipsia* (polydipsia means "excessive thirst")—developed quite rapidly, usually beginning in the first session and becoming firmly established by the second session.

Studies of adjunctive behavior typically employ fixed interval (FI) or fixed time (FT) schedules of reinforcement (Falk, 1971). On such schedules, the delivery of each reinforcer is followed by a period of time during which another reinforcer is not available. It is during such *interreinforcement intervals* that adjunctive behavior occurs. For example, when schedule-induced polydipsia is generated by exposure to an FI schedule of food reinforcement, the rat usually drinks during the post-reinforcement pause that is typical of such schedules. Thus, a short period of time during which there is a low probability or zero probability of reinforcement seems to be a critical factor in the development of adjunctive behavior.

Researchers soon discovered that schedule-induced polydipsia could be generated in other species, including mice, pigeons, and chimpanzees. They also discovered that it was possible to generate other types of adjunctive behaviors, such as chewing on wood shavings, licking at an air stream (presumably because of the sensory stimulation it provides), and aggression. In the latter case, it was found that pigeons exposed to an FI or FT schedule of food delivery soon began attacking a nearby target pigeon—or, more commonly, a picture or stuffed model of a pigeon—following each reinforcer (e.g., Flory & Ellis, 1973). Unlike extinction-induced aggression, which often grows weaker over time, this type of schedule-induced aggression tends to remain strong and persistent. (See Falk, 1971, 1977, and Staddon, 1977, for overviews of the findings on adjunctive behavior.)

Researchers also found that adjunctive behavior could be generated using reinforcers other than food delivery. For example, rats were found to eat excessive amounts of food (i.e., they engaged in schedule-induced eating) when exposed to an intermittent schedule of electrical stimulation to the pleasure centers in the brain (J. F. Wilson & Cantor, 1987). Thus, rather than using food as a reinforcer to produce some other type of adjunctive behavior, these researchers used electrical stimulation of the pleasure centers as a reinforcer to produce an adjunctive pattern of eating. Interestingly, these rats gained considerable weight due to their compulsive tendency to snack between reinforcers, suggesting that schedule-induced eating may play a role in the development of obesity.

QUICK QUIZ F

1. Adjunctive behavior is an excessive pattern of behavior that emerges as a ____________ effect of a(n) ____________ schedule of reinforcement for (the same/a different) behavior.
2. Adjunctive behavior is also referred to as s____________-i____________ behavior.
3. An excessive pattern of drinking that is produced by exposure to an intermittent schedule of food reinforcement is called s____________-____________ p____________.
4. Studies of adjunctive behavior typically use (fixed interval/variable interval) or (fixed time/variable time) schedules of food reinforcement. This is because adjunctive behavior tends to occur during a period of time in which there is a (high/low) probability of reinforcement.

According to Falk (1971, 1977), adjunctive behavior has several distinguishing features. These include the following:

1. As previously noted, *adjunctive behavior typically occurs in the period immediately following consumption of an intermittent reinforcer*. For example, in schedule-induced polydipsia, the rat will quickly eat each food pellet as soon as it is delivered and then immediately move over to the drinking tube for a quick bout of drinking. The start of the interval between food pellets, therefore, tends to be dominated by drinking. The end of the interval, however, as the next pellet becomes imminent, tends to be dominated by food-related behaviors, such as lever pressing for the food (Staddon, 1977).
2. *Adjunctive behavior is affected by the level of deprivation for the scheduled reinforcer. The greater the level of deprivation for the reinforcer, the stronger the adjunctive behavior that emerges as a by-product*. For example, with schedule-induced polydipsia, greater food deprivation not only produces a higher rate of lever pressing for food pellets, it also produces a higher rate of drinking between food pellets.
3. *Adjunctive behaviors can function as reinforcers for other behaviors*. This is in keeping with the Premack principle, which holds that high-probability behaviors can often serve as effective reinforcers for low-probability behaviors. Thus, with schedule-induced polydipsia, the rat will not only press a lever to obtain access to food pellets but, during the interval between food pellets, it will also press a lever to gain access to water so that it can engage in adjunctive drinking.
4. *There is an optimal interval between reinforcers for the development of adjunctive behavior*. For example, rats may engage in little drinking with an

interreinforcement interval of 30 seconds between food pellets, progressively more drinking as the interval is lengthened to 120 seconds (2 minutes), and then progressively less drinking as the interval is lengthened beyond that. At an interreinforcement interval of 300 seconds, one again finds little drinking. The optimal interreinforcement intervals for several other types of adjunctive behaviors tend to be similar, often in the range of 1 to 3 minutes.

QUICK QUIZ G

1. Adjunctive behavior tends to occur (just before/just after) delivery of a reinforcer.
2. As the deprivation level for the scheduled reinforcer increases, the strength of the adjunctive behavior associated with it tends to (increase/decrease).
3. The opportunity to engage in an adjunctive behavior can serve as a (reinforcer/punisher) for some other behavior. This is in keeping with the P___________ principle, in which (high/low)-probability behavior can serve as a reinforcer for (high/low)-probability behavior.
4. The optimal interreinforcement interval for the production of adjunctive behavior is often in the range of (a few seconds/a few minutes/several minutes).

Adjunctive Behavior in Humans

The preceding discussion probably has you wondering about the extent to which adjunctive behaviors occur in humans. Extreme polydipsia occasionally occurs in humans; for example, psychiatric patients sometimes compulsively ingest large amounts of fluids (which can be dangerous insofar as it upsets the balance of electrolytes in the body). But it is not clear how this relates to schedule-induced polydipsia in rats (Wallace & Singer, 1976). On an anecdotal level, however, Falk (1977) has noted that a diverse range of human behaviors, from nail biting and talkativeness to snacking and coffee drinking, are commonly associated with periods of enforced waiting. Falk (1998) also noted that drug and alcohol abuse is frequently found in environments that provide sparse levels of economic and social reinforcement, suggesting that adjunctive processes (in addition to the physiological effects of the drug) contribute to the development of drug and alcohol abuse. This is supported by the fact that schedule-induced polydipsia has been used to induce rats to drink excessive amounts of water containing alcohol or other drugs. In other words, schedule-induced polydipsia can be used to create an animal analogue of drug and alcohol abuse (Falk, 1993; Riley & Wetherington, 1989).

On an experimental level, humans have shown adjunctive-type behavior patterns that are similar to, though not as extreme as, those found in animals. For example, Doyle and Samson (1988) found that human subjects exposed to FI schedules of monetary reinforcement for game playing displayed an increased tendency to drink water following each reinforcer. Similar to schedule-induced polydipsia in animals, the length of the interval between reinforcers was an important variable, with nearly twice as much drinking occurring on an FI 90-sec schedule as on an FI 30-sec schedule.

Experimental evidence for adjunctive drug use in humans has also been obtained. Cherek (1982) found high rates of cigarette smoking when monetary payment for button pushing was presented on an FI 120-sec schedule as opposed to FI 30-sec, 60-sec, or 240-sec schedules. And Doyle and Samson (1988) found high rates of beer sipping when monetary payment for playing a game was presented on an FI 90-sec schedule as opposed to an FI 30-sec schedule. In both cases, the drug-related behavior (smoking or beer sipping) was most likely to occur during the period immediately following delivery of the reinforcer, which is consistent with the notion that it was functioning as an adjunctive behavior. Studies such as these support the notion that adjunctive processes may play a role in the development of substance abuse in humans. Especially in the early phases of an addiction, adjunctive processes may encourage an individual to frequently consume an addictive substance, with the result that the person eventually becomes addicted to it (Falk, 1998).

QUICK QUIZ H

1. Evidence that humans engage in adjunctive behavior includes the fact that studies of adjunctive-type behavior patterns in human subjects usually (find/do not find) an optimal time interval between reinforcers for producing such behaviors.
2. Certain behavior patterns in humans, such as smoking and nail biting, are often associated with periods of (extreme activity/enforced waiting), which (agrees with/contradicts) the notion that these may be adjunctive behaviors.
3. It has also been noted that alcohol and drug abuse is most likely to develop in environments in which economic and social reinforcers are (frequently/infrequently) available, which (agrees with/contradicts) the notion that these may be adjunctive behaviors.
4. Adjunctive processes may play a particularly important role in the development of an addiction during its (early/later) stages.

Adjunctive Behavior as Displacement Activity

Why would a tendency to develop adjunctive behaviors ever have evolved? What purpose do such activities serve, especially given how self-destructive they sometimes are? For example, it requires a considerable amount of energy for a rat to process and excrete the huge amounts of water ingested during a session of schedule-induced polydipsia. And drug and alcohol abuse is decidedly counterproductive for both rats and humans.

In this regard, Falk (1977) has proposed that adjunctive behaviors represent a type of ***displacement activity***, an apparently irrelevant activity sometimes displayed by animals when confronted by conflict or thwarted from attaining a goal. For example, a bird that is unable to reach an insect hidden between some rocks might begin pecking at nearby twigs. This behavior seems completely unrelated to the goal of capturing the insect, which led early investigators to propose that displacement activities like this serve simply as a means of releasing pent-up energy (Tinbergen, 1951).

In contrast to this energy release model, Falk (1977) proposes that displacement activities serve two purposes. First, they provide for a more diversified range of behaviors in a particular setting, and a diverse range of behavior is often beneficial. Consider, for example, a bird that has a tendency to peck at twigs while waiting for an insect to emerge from its hiding place. By doing so, the bird may uncover another source of food or may even stumble upon using a twig as a tool for rooting out the insect. In fact, some species of birds do use twigs to root out insects—an evolved pattern of behavior that may have begun as a displacement activity. In similar fashion, an employee who grows restless and busies herself with some paperwork while waiting for an important phone call is apt to be a more productive employee than one who simply stares at the phone until the phone call arrives.

A second benefit of displacement activities is that they help the animal remain in a situation where a significant reinforcer might eventually become available. Periods of little or no reinforcement can be aversive—as any student knows when buckling down to study a boring subject matter—and anything that can alleviate the aversiveness of these intervals will heighten the probability of attaining the delayed reinforcer. Thus, pecking the ground gives the bird "something to do" while waiting for an insect to emerge from its hiding place, just as whittling a stick allows a hunter to patiently wait for a moose, and munching on licorice enables a student to sit still and study patiently throughout a study session.

Adjunctive behavior can therefore be seen as a natural tendency to do something else while waiting for a reinforcer. To the extent that it enhances the individual's ability to wait out the delay period, it thus constitutes a sort of built-in self-control device. This is a paradoxical notion in that adjunctive behaviors, such as smoking and drinking, are usually the kinds of behaviors that are viewed as impulsive (Tomie, 1996). But this depends on the specific consequence one is referring to. Smoking is an impulsive behavior in terms of providing short-term pleasure at the risk of one's long-term health, but it can also enhance self-control in the sense of helping an individual work long hours to obtain a promotion. For this reason, students often find it difficult to quit smoking during the academic year. Quitting smoking not only results in the temporary onset of withdrawal symptoms, it also undermines the student's ability to study for long periods of time. Congruent with this notion, it has been shown that people who successfully overcome an addiction (such as alcoholism) are more likely to seek out a replacement for the addictive activity (such as coffee drinking) than those who are not successful in overcoming their addiction (Brown, Stetson, & Beatty, 1989). The moral of the story is that adjunctive behaviors sometimes serve a purpose, and we might do well to acknowledge that purpose and find other ways to fulfill it.[2]

QUICK QUIZ I

1. According to Falk, adjunctive behavior may be a type of d____________ activity, which is an irrelevant activity displayed by animals when confronted by c____________ or when they are (able/unable) to achieve a goal.
2. One benefit of such activities is that it is often useful to engage in (just one type/a diverse range) of behavior(s) in a situation.
3. The second benefit derived from such activities is that they may facilitate (moving away from/remaining near) a potential reinforcer.
4. To the extent that adjunctive activities facilitate waiting for, or working toward, a(n) (immediate/delayed) reinforcer, such activities may (facilitate/impede) efforts at self-control.

Study Tip: To the extent that adjunctive behaviors may facilitate self-control, they may also help explain why many students like to sip on a drink (like coffee) or munch on snacks while studying. Although the items chosen typically contain caffeine or simple carbohydrates that may act as a stimulant and increase attention, and are also pleasurable activities that provide a source of immediate reinforcement as one works toward the distant goal of passing the course, these activities may also serve as adjunctive behaviors in the sense of enabling one to remain in a situation in which reinforcers are relatively sparse. In keeping with this possibility, it is not unusual to encounter students who claim to sip only plain water while studying *even when they are not thirsty.* The mere activity of sipping water seems sufficient to keep them on task. Thus, finding a suitable adjunctive behavior to engage in while studying—preferably something that will not adversely impact one's health—may be yet another tool one can use to facilitate "hitting the books" on a consistent basis.

Activity Anorexia

One type of behavior that can be generated as an adjunctive behavior is wheel running. When exposed to an intermittent schedule of food reinforcement for lever pressing, rats will run in a wheel for several seconds during the interval between reinforcers (Levitsky & Collier, 1968). A related type of procedure, however, produces even more extreme running. Known as

[2]Sigmund Freud was famous for his ability to work long hours, which is often attributed to his "self-discipline." Yet this self-discipline seems to have been at least partially dependent on the availability of an adjunctive activity in the form of smoking. He once complained that if he could not smoke, he could not work. Unfortunately, his 20-cigars-a-day habit resulted in cancer of the jaw, from which he eventually died (Gay, 1988).

activity anorexia, it has important implications for people who are undertaking a diet and exercise program to lose weight.[3]

Basic Procedure and Defining Characteristics

The procedure for creating activity anorexia is as follows: If rats are allowed to access food for only a single, say, 1.5-hour meal period each day, and if they have access to a running wheel during the 22.5-hour interval between meals, they will begin to spend increasing amounts of time running during that interval. Not only that, the more they run, the less they eat, and the less they eat, the more they run. In other words, a sort of negative feedback cycle develops in which the two behavioral tendencies, increased running and decreased eating, reciprocally strengthen each other. Within a week or so, the rats are running enormous distances—up to 20,000 revolutions of the wheel per day (equivalent to about 12 miles!)—and eating nothing. If the process is allowed to continue (for humane reasons, the experiment is usually terminated before this), the rats will become completely emaciated and die (e.g., Routtenberg & Kuznesof, 1967).

Thus, ***activity anorexia*** is an abnormally high level of activity and low level of food intake generated by exposure to a time restricted schedule of feeding (Epling & Pierce, 1991). It is important to note that rats that are given restricted access to food, but with *no* wheel available, do just fine—they easily ingest enough food during the 1.5-hour meal period to maintain body weight. Rats that have access to a wheel, but without food restriction, also do fine—they display only moderate levels of running and no tendency toward self-starvation. It is the combination of food restriction and the opportunity to run that is so devastating.

QUICK QUIZ J

1. The basic procedure for the development of ac__________ an__________ in rats is the presentation of (one/several) meal period(s) each day along with access to a running wheel during the (meal/between-meal) period.
2. This can be defined as an abnormally (low/high) level of activity and a (low/high) level of food intake generated by exposure to a t__________-r__________ schedule of feeding.

Comparisons with Anorexia Nervosa

Activity anorexia was first investigated by Routtenberg and Kuznesof (1967). Two other researchers, Epling and Pierce (e.g., 1988), later noted

[3]Activity anorexia is considered by some researchers to be a type of adjunctive or schedule-induced behavior (e.g., Falk, 1994), and by other researchers to be a separate class of behaviors involving distinctly different processes (e.g., Beneke, Schulte, & Vander Tuig, 1995). For purposes of this discussion, we will adopt the latter position.

its similarity to *anorexia nervosa* in humans. Anorexia nervosa is a psychiatric disorder in which patients refuse to eat adequate amounts of food and as a result lose extreme amounts of weight. People with this disorder often require hospitalization; of those who do become hospitalized, more than 10% eventually die from the disorder or from complications associated with it (such as from a disruption of the body's electrolyte balance; American Psychiatric Association, *Diagnostic and Statistical Manual IV*, 2000).

Epling and Pierce (1991) contend that there are several similarities between activity anorexia in rats and anorexia nervosa in humans. For example, just as activity anorexia in rats can be precipitated by imposing a restricted schedule of feeding, so too anorexia nervosa in humans usually begins when the person deliberately undertakes a diet to lose weight. Even more significant, anorexia in humans, as with anorexia in rats, is often accompanied by very high levels of activity (Davis, Katzman, & Kirsh, 1999; Katz, 1996). This may consist of a deliberate exercise program designed to facilitate weight loss, or it may be displayed as a severe sort of restlessness. Although clinicians have typically regarded such high activity as a secondary characteristic of the disorder (e.g., Bruch, 1978), Epling and Pierce (1996) suggest that it is more fundamental than that. Thus, as with activity anorexia in rats, many cases of anorexia nervosa in humans might result from the combined effects of a stringent diet and high activity levels.

The importance of high activity levels in the development of anorexia nervosa is supported by several lines of evidence. First, even in humans who do not have anorexia, a sudden increase in activity is often followed by a decrease in food intake, and a decrease in food intake is often followed by an increase in activity (Epling & Pierce, 1996). Second, individuals who engage in high levels of activity appear to be at high risk for anorexia. For example, ballet dancers, who are under constant pressure to remain thin and are extremely active, show a higher incidence of the disorder than do fashion models who are under pressure only to remain thin (Garner & Garfinkel, 1980). Likewise, a surprising number of athletes develop symptoms of anorexia (Katz, 1986; Wheeler, 1996) or an "overtraining syndrome" that bears many similarities to anorexia (Yates, 1996).

In addition to high activity levels, there are other interesting parallels between anorexia in rats and humans. For example, just as anorexia nervosa in humans is more common among adolescents (APA, 2000), activity anorexia is more easily induced in adolescent rats than in older rats (Woods & Routtenberg, 1971). Another similarity concerns the manner in which people with anorexia approach food. Although they eat little, they nevertheless remain interested in food (Bruch, 1978). For example, they often enjoy preparing food for others. As well, when they do eat, they often spend considerable time arranging the food on their plates, cutting it into pieces, and slowly savoring each bite. Anecdotal evidence suggests that anorexic rats might sometimes behave similarly (D. P. Boer, 2000, personal communication). Although the rats eat little or no food during each meal period, they do spend considerable time shredding the food with their teeth and spitting it out. In other words, like humans, rats seem to remain quite interested in food, even if they are not eating it.

Thus, activity anorexia in rats appears to be a rather close analogue of anorexia nervosa in humans. As with most analogues, however, the similarity is less than perfect. For example, the rat with anorexia is physically restricted from accessing food except during the meal period, whereas the person with anorexia is on a self-imposed diet with food still freely available. Epling and Pierce (1991) argue, however, that the free availability of food may be more apparent than real. Just as the researcher physically restricts the rat's supply of food, societal pressures to become thin may psychologically restrict a person's access to food. Women, of course, are more commonly subjected to such pressures, which probably contributes to the greater frequency of anorexia in women than in men. But medical biases probably also play a role; thin females are readily labeled "anorexic," but thin males are, well, thin.

A more substantial difference between humans and rats is that anorexia in humans is often accompanied by bulimia: a tendency to binge on food and then purge oneself by vomiting or taking laxatives. In fact, psychiatrists distinguish between two types of anorexia: the *restricting type*, which is characterized by simple food restriction, and the *binge-eating/purging type*, in which dieting is combined with episodes of binging and purging (APA, 2000). Of course, anorexic rats do not binge and purge; indeed, it would be difficult for them to do so because rats are physically incapable of vomiting. Thus, activity anorexia in rats is most relevant to the restricting type of anorexia in humans. And, in fact, the restricting type of anorexia is most strongly associated with high activity levels (Katz, 1996).

QUICK QUIZ K

1. As with the development of activity anorexia in rats, most instances of human anorexia begin with the person undertaking a d__________. As well, humans with anorexia tend to display (high/low) levels of activity.
2. A sharp increase in activity is often associated with a(n) (decrease/increase) in food intake, which in turn can result in a(n) (decrease/increase) in activity.
3. Anecdotal evidence suggests that, as with anorexia in humans, rats suffering from activity anorexia are often quite (interested/uninterested) in food.
4. Similar to anorexia nervosa in humans, activity anorexia in rats is more easily induced in (adolescent/adult) rats.
5. Activity anorexia in rats is most similar to the r__________ type of anorexia in humans rather than the b__________/p__________ type of anorexia.

Underlying Mechanisms

Given the self-destructive nature of activity anorexia, what are the mechanisms underlying it? On a neurophysiological level, the processes involved are complex, involving several classes of hormones and neurotransmitters (Guisinger, 2003). Endorphins, for example, are a class of morphine-like substances in the brain that have been implicated in pain reduction. They have also been implicated in the feeling of pleasure that sometimes accompanies prolonged exercise, which is commonly known as "runner's high" (Wheeler, 1996). Significantly, drugs that block the effect of endorphins will temporarily lower the rate of wheel running in food-deprived rats (Boer, Epling, Pierce, & Russell, 1990).

Such evidence suggests that both activity anorexia in rats and anorexia nervosa in humans might be maintained by what is essentially an addiction to an endorphin high (Marrazzi & Luby, 1986). In support of this notion, patients with anorexia often report that the experience of anorexia is quite similar to a drug-induced high. To quote three patients: "One feels intoxicated, literally how I think alcoholism works" (Bruch, 1978, p. 73); "being hungry has the same effect as a drug, and you feel outside your body" (p. 118); and perhaps most disturbing, "I enjoy having this disease and I want it" (p. 2).

From an evolutionary perspective, it has been suggested that a tendency toward activity anorexia might have survival value (Epling & Pierce, 1988; Guisinger, 2003). An animal that becomes highly active when food supplies are scarce is more likely to travel great distances and encounter new food supplies. Under extreme circumstances, the animal might even do well to ignore small amounts of food encountered along the way—the gathering of which could be costly in terms of time and energy spent relative to the amount of energy gained—and cease traveling only when an adequate food supply has been reached. In support of this notion, research has shown that activity anorexia can often be halted by suddenly providing access to a continuous supply of food (Epling & Pierce, 1991). When confronted with a plentiful food source, the rats cease running and begin eating. Evolutionary pressures may also contribute to the increased incidence of anorexia in women. When placed on a calorie-restricted diet, female rats demonstrate increases in both activity level and learning ability more so than male rats, which may represent an evolutionarily based tendency that enables females to compete effectively for resources in times of food scarcity (Marten et al., 2007).

QUICK QUIZ L

1. E__________ are a class of morphine-like substances in the brain that are associated with p__________ reduction. These substances have been implicated in the feeling of pl__________ that is sometimes experienced following prolonged exercise, and which (is/is not) also reported by patients with anorexia.
2. This finding suggests that both activity anorexia in rats and anorexia nervosa in humans may be maintained by a(n) __________ high.
3. From an evolutionary perspective, increased activity in response to decreased food intake could (interfere with/facilitate) contacting a new food supply.
4. This evolutionary perspective is supported by evidence that the activity anorexia cycle can be broken by suddenly providing (intermittent/continuous) access to food.

Clinical Implications

The activity anorexia model has several clinical implications. From a treatment perspective, the model suggests that behavioral treatments for anorexia nervosa should focus as much on establishing normal patterns of activity as they do on establishing normal patterns of eating. As well, research into the biochemistry underlying this phenomenon could facilitate the development of drugs for treating anorexia. For example, it may be possible to develop long-lasting endorphin blockers that will effectively reduce the feelings of pleasure that help maintain the anorexic process.

The activity anorexia model also has implications for prevention. First and foremost, people should be warned that combining a stringent exercise program with severe dieting places them at risk for developing this disorder. The model thus calls into question those disciplines that traditionally combine dieting with intense activity. As already noted, one such discipline is ballet; another is amateur wrestling. Wrestlers are traditionally expected to lose several pounds before competition so as to compete in the lightest weight category possible. Many of the physical and psychological changes accompanying this process are similar to those found in anorexia nervosa—an indication that these athletes are at risk for developing symptoms of the disorder (Symbaluk, 1996).

The activity anorexia model also suggests that people who are dieting and may be susceptible to anorexia should eat several small meals per day as opposed to a single large meal, insofar as rats do not become anorexic when the 1.5-hour meal period is broken up into several shorter meal periods (Epling & Pierce, 1991). As well, people who are attempting to increase their exercise levels should do so slowly, because rats that become anorexic display the greatest reduction in food intake following a sharp increase in activity (Pierce & Epling, 1996). (Interestingly, the sharp increase in activity also has been shown to be most clearly associated with appetite suppression in humans.) And, finally, dieters should ensure that their meals are nutritionally well balanced. Research has shown that activity anorexia is more easily induced in rats that are on a low-protein diet as opposed to a normal diet (Beneke & Vander Tuig, 1996).

Of course, further research is needed to confirm the usefulness of these suggestions for preventing anorexia nervosa in humans. What is clear, however, is that a combination of severe dieting and exercise can have serious consequences and should not be undertaken lightly.

QUICK QUIZ M

1. The activity anorexia model suggests that therapists should focus as much on establishing normal a______________ levels as they presently do on establishing normal eating patterns.
2. Suggestions for minimizing the risk of anorexia in humans who may be susceptible to the disorder include eating (several/one) meal(s) per day, increasing exercise levels (rapidly/slowly), and eating a diet that is (imbalanced/well balanced).

And Furthermore

The Healthy Side of the Diet–Activity Connection

We have so far discussed the negative aspect of the connection between food restriction and activity. There is also a positive side to this connection. Boer (1990) found that by adjusting the *amount of food* eaten by the rats, as opposed to the *length of the meal period*, he could precisely control the amount of wheel running. For example, rats that were given 15 grams of food once per day developed the typical activity anorexia cycle (see also Morse et al., 1995), whereas rats that were given 18 grams of food displayed only a moderate level of running (5–6 miles per day) with no tendency toward self-starvation. These rats were also quite healthy. Interestingly, the same effect was found using rats that had a genetic predisposition toward obesity (J. C. Russell et al., 1989). Raised on a regime of diet and exercise, these "genetically fat" rats remained incredibly lean and fit—an impressive demonstration of the healthy effects of a healthy lifestyle, even in subjects whose genetics are working against them.

It is also worth repeating that, as noted in Chapter 2, food restriction is currently the most reliable means known for slowing the aging process, at least in nonhuman animals. Lest the reader imagine, however, that this might be a good excuse for eating like a person with anorexia and quickly losing a lot of weight, the health-enhancing effects of low-calorie diets demand regular meals composed of highly nutritious foods—a far cry from the "two carrots and a cookie" diet of many people with anorexia. (See also Rothschild, Hoddy, Jambazian, & Varady, 2014, for a recent overview of the effects of time-restricted feeding on health status.)

Behavior Systems Theory

As seen throughout this chapter, biological dispositions appear to play a strong role in many aspects of conditioning. Needless to say, this evidence has led several researchers to propose various theories to explain these findings. The most comprehensive of these is behavior systems theory (e.g., Timberlake, 1993; Timberlake & Lucas, 1989). According to ***behavior systems theory***, an animal's behavior is organized into certain innate systems (such as feeding, mating, and avoiding predators), with each system becoming activated in relevant situations. (The theory is actually more complex than this, but a simplified version will suffice for now.) To use the analogy of computers, it is as though the brain contains several software programs for handling commonly encountered situations. Some of the responses generated by these programs may be very rigid, in the form of a reflex or fixed action pattern, while others may be more flexible and sensitive to the consequences of the response. Different systems may also overlap such that a response that is typically associated with one system may sometimes be instigated by another system.

As an example, let us consider the *feeding system* in the rat. When a rat is hungry, it becomes predisposed to engage in food-related behaviors, such as salivating, chewing, food handling (with its paws), searching for food, and so on. Thus, during a period of hunger, all of these behaviors become primed, meaning that they can easily be set in motion by particular cues. For example, in a situation in which the delivery and consumption of food is imminent, behaviors such as salivating and food handling will be activated. But if food is very distant, a general search pattern may be activated which might include running and exploring.

Interestingly, this theory helps explain the types of experimental procedures that have evolved to study learning in animals. It is no accident that the favorite methods for studying learning in rats have been maze running and lever pressing. These methods have become widely adopted because they work so well, and they work so well because they match the types of behaviors that rats are naturally predisposed to display in food-related situations. Thus, rats are great at running through mazes because they have evolved to run along narrow, enclosed spaces—such as through tunnels in a burrow—to find food. Similarly, rats have evolved dexterous forepaws that they use to pick up food and manipulate it. Therefore, manipulating something with their forepaws, such as pressing a lever, is for them a natural response associated with feeding.

Behavior systems theory also provides an explanation for many of the unusual behavior patterns described in this chapter. For example, consider a sign-tracking experiment in which dogs approach a light that predicts food and begin to beg and whine as though they are soliciting food from it. Dogs are pack animals for which feeding is a social event, and subordinate animals often have to solicit food from the dominant leader who controls that food. Thus, the feeding situation that was set up in these experiments, in which a light strongly predicted the delivery of food, essentially elicited this social component of the dog's feeding system.

Although behavior systems theory assigns an important role to innate patterns of behavior, it assigns an equally important role to the environmental cues that determine which behavior will be activated. An illustration can be found in sign-tracking studies with rats. Timberlake and Grant (1975) devised a chamber in which a *stimulus rat* could be mechanically inserted and withdrawn (see Figure 12.2). When the stimulus rat was inserted just before the delivery of food, thus becoming a CS for food, the participant rat would approach the stimulus rat and engage in various forms of social behavior, including sniffing the mouth, pawing, and grooming. This behavior pattern becomes understandable when we consider that rats have evolved to pay close attention to what other rats are eating and will even steal food from the mouths of other rats. The stimulus rat that predicted the delivery of food therefore seemed to elicit this social component of the feeding system in the participant rat. By contrast, a wooden block that predicted the delivery of food did not elicit social contact, with the participant rat merely orienting toward it. Likewise, in a different study, a rolling marble that predicted food delivery elicited a pattern of clawing, grasping, and gnawing, as though the rat was attempting to capture and consume the marble

FIGURE 12.2 Illustration of the apparatus used by Timberlake and Grant (1975). The stimulus rat became a CS when it was inserted on a movable platform into the experimental chamber just before the delivery of food.

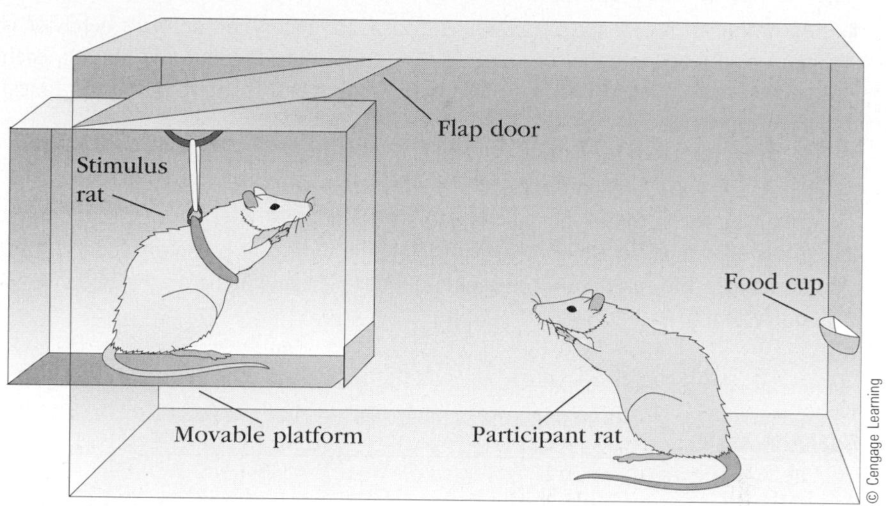

(Timberlake, 1983). Presumably, the moving marble activated the predatory component of the rat's feeding system, such as would naturally be activated by a small, moving insect (rats often hunt and devour insects). Such predatory behavior was not elicited, however, when the moving marble predicted the delivery of water.

The extent to which behavior systems theory can provide a comprehensive explanation for animal behavior has yet to be determined. According to Mazur (2002), neither does this theory undermine the importance of basic principles of conditioning, such as reinforcement and punishment, as powerful factors in learning and behavior. Behavior systems theory does, however, remind us of the need to pay attention to an animal's innate tendencies when attempting to modify its behavior. For example, the dog that habitually nips at your hand when you attempt to touch its food is not simply displaying a behavior that has been negatively reinforced by the removal of your hand. Rather, it might also indicate that the dog has assumed a position of dominance within the household, a naturally evolved pattern of behavior that is highly adaptive within a pack but rather a nuisance among humans. In a sense, the dog's tendency to be food aggressive reflects both the social component of its feeding system as well as the feeding component of its social system. Thus, a comprehensive attempt to modify this behavior might need to include strategies for signaling to the dog its subordinate status within the family—such as feeding the dog by hand rather than providing free food throughout the day (thereby clearly indicating to the dog that humans control the food supply).

Fortunately, just as shaping is becoming a well-established technique among pet owners, so too is an appreciation of the need to understand a pet's innate tendencies (e.g., Coren, 1994; McConnell, 2003).

QUICK QUIZ N

1. According to b____________ s____________ theory, an animal's behavior is organized into a number of s____________, such as feeding and mating, each consisting of a set of relevant responses that can be activated (at certain times/in certain settings).
2. In terms of this theory, Bolles's notion of sp____________-sp____________ d____________ reactions (SSDR) is concerned with responses that would be driven by the defense-against-predators system.
3. In the sign-tracking experiment with dogs, the light that predicted food seemed to activate the (predatory/consummatory/social) component of the dog's feeding system.

SUMMARY

Animals appear to be biologically prepared to learn some things more readily than others. For example, in taste aversion conditioning, a food item that has been paired with nausea quickly becomes conditioned as an aversive CS. This type of conditioning is similar to other forms of classical conditioning in that processes such as stimulus generalization, extinction, and overshadowing can be found. It differs from other forms of classical conditioning in that strong associations can be formed over long delays and require only a single conditioning trial. As well, the nausea is specifically associated with a food item rather than some other stimulus.

Examples of preparedness in operant conditioning include how easily food can be used to reinforce pecking but not perching in chaffinches, while the sound of a chaffinch song can be used to reinforce perching but not pecking. As well, rats more easily learn to run or freeze to escape shock than press a lever to escape shock. The latter example suggests that many escape behaviors may be species-specific defense reactions elicited by the aversive stimulus.

Instinctive drift is a genetically based, fixed action pattern that gradually emerges to displace a behavior that is being operantly conditioned. Sign tracking is a tendency to approach (and perhaps make contact with) a stimulus that signals the presentation of an appetitive event. In both cases, the behavior superficially appears to be a goal-directed operant behavior, yet the procedures that produce it suggest it is actually an elicited (or respondent) behavior.

Adjunctive behavior, also known as schedule-induced behavior, is an excessive pattern of behavior that emerges as a by-product of an intermittent schedule of reinforcement. In schedule-induced polydipsia, for example, rats drink extreme amounts of water during the interval between food reinforcers that are delivered on an FI or FT schedule. Adjunctive behavior typically occurs in the period immediately following the delivery of the scheduled reinforcer, varies directly with the level of deprivation for the scheduled reinforcer, and can function as a reinforcer for another behavior. For many adjunctive behaviors, there is also an optimal interreinforcement interval. Examples of possible adjunctive behaviors in humans include smoking cigarettes, drinking alcohol, and using drugs. Adjunctive behavior may be a type of displacement activity that functions to ensure a diverse range of activities in a setting and to facilitate waiting for a delayed reinforcer.

Activity anorexia is a pattern of excessive activity and low food intake in animals as a result of exposure to a restricted food supply. It bears many similarities to certain forms of anorexia nervosa in humans, which is characterized by severe dieting and high activity levels. Evidence suggests that activity anorexia in animals as well as anorexia nervosa in humans may be maintained by an endorphin high that accompanies the process. From an evolutionary perspective, a tendency toward activity anorexia might induce an animal to travel long distances, thereby increasing the likelihood of encountering a new food supply. Clinical implications that have grown out of this research include the possibility of developing long-lasting endorphin blockers that could break the anorexic cycle. These findings also suggest that people should be cautious about combining a stringent diet with severe exercise.

According to behavior systems theory, an animal's behavior is organized into several motivational systems. Each of these systems encompasses a set of relevant responses; and in turn, each response can be activated by situational cues. This theory accounts for some unusual behavior patterns, such as sign tracking. It may also account for the particular tasks that researchers have used to study animal learning.

SUGGESTED READINGS

Garcia, J. (1981). Tilting at the paper mills of academe. *American Psychologist*, *36*, 149–158. Garcia's engaging account of the difficulties he encountered in attempting to publish his early results on taste aversion conditioning simply because they violated certain assumptions of classical conditioning that were widely held at that time.

Epling, W. F., & Pierce, W. D. (1991). *Solving the anorexia puzzle: A scientific approach*. Toronto, Canada: Hogrefe & Huber. Epling and Pierce's overview of activity anorexia and its applicability to understanding anorexia nervosa in humans.

Coren, S. (1994). *The intelligence of dogs: A guide to the thoughts, emotions, and inner lives of our canine companions.* New York: Free Press. A fun and interesting guide for helping us better understand our canine companions, particularly from the perspective of their innate predispositions.

STUDY QUESTIONS

1. Define preparedness and CS-US relevance. Diagram the results of the study by Garcia and Koelling (1966) that illustrates the role of biological preparedness in classical conditioning.
2. What is taste aversion conditioning? Outline three ways in which taste aversion conditioning differs from most other forms of classical conditioning.
3. What are some examples of the role of preparedness in operant conditioning?
4. What is instinctive drift? What is sign tracking? Describe (or diagram) an example of each.
5. Define autoshaping and describe the procedure used to produce it. Describe the food versus water study with pigeons that seems particularly supportive of a stimulus-substitution interpretation of autoshaping.
6. Define adjunctive behavior. What is schedule-induced polydipsia, and what is the precise procedure for experimentally inducing it in rats?
7. What are four characteristics of adjunctive behaviors?
8. What are displacement activities, and what are two benefits that may be derived from such activities?
9. Define activity anorexia. List three similarities (other than high activity and low food intake) between activity anorexia in rats and anorexia nervosa in humans.
10. Briefly describe the evolutionary explanation for the occurrence of activity anorexia. What type of chemical substance in the brain seems to play a role in the development of anorexia?
11. List two implications for treatment and four implications for prevention that have grown out of research into activity anorexia.
12. Define behavior systems theory. Describe the results of sign-tracking studies in rats that highlight the importance of environmental cues.

CONCEPT REVIEW

activity anorexia. An abnormally high level of activity and low level of food intake generated by exposure to a time-restricted schedule of feeding.

adjunctive behavior. An excessive pattern of behavior that emerges as a by-product of an intermittent schedule of reinforcement for some other behavior.

autoshaping. A type of sign tracking in which a pigeon comes to automatically peck at a response key because the key light has been associated with the response-independent delivery of food.

behavior systems theory. A theory proposing that an animal's behavior is organized into certain systems or categories (such as feeding, mating, and avoiding predators), with each category containing a set of relevant responses that can become activated in certain situations.

CS-US relevance. An innate tendency to easily associate certain types of stimuli with each other.

displacement activity. An apparently irrelevant activity sometimes displayed by animals when confronted by conflict or thwarted from attaining a goal.

instinctive drift. An instance of classical conditioning in which a genetically based, fixed action pattern gradually emerges and displaces a behavior that is being operantly conditioned.

preparedness. An innate tendency for an organism to more easily learn certain types of behaviors or to associate certain types of events with each other.

sign tracking. A type of elicited behavior in which an organism approaches a stimulus that signals the presentation of an appetitive event.

taste aversion conditioning. A form of classical conditioning in which a food item that has been paired with gastrointestinal illness becomes a conditioned aversive stimulus.

CHAPTER TEST

9. To prevent the development of anorexia nervosa, humans who want to diet but may be susceptible to anorexia might do well to eat (several small/one large) meal(s) per day. And if they are exercising, they should increase the level of exercise (quickly/slowly).
20. Taste aversion conditioning differs from most other forms of classical conditioning in that strong associations can be formed over ____________ delays and in (many/a single) trial(s).
2. According to the phenomenon of negative ____________, a pigeon will compulsively peck at a key light that precedes the delivery of food even though the key peck (prevents/results in) the delivery of food.
28. Displacement activities, including certain types of adjunctive behaviors, may serve as a type of self-____________ device in that they facilitate the act of waiting for a ____________ reinforcer.
11. In general, a pigeon that is (more/less) food deprived will display a greater tendency to engage in schedule-induced aggression.
1. When a key light is presented just before the noncontingent delivery of food, the pigeon will begin pecking at the key. This phenomenon is known as ____________.
24. When a pig receives reinforcement for carrying a napkin from one table to another, it eventually starts dropping it and rooting at it on the ground. This is an example of a phenomenon known as ____________ in which a ____________ pattern gradually emerges and replaces the operant behavior that one is attempting to condition.
4. An excessive pattern of behavior that emerges as a by-product of an intermittent schedule of reinforcement for some other behavior is called ____________ behavior.

12. In schedule-induced polydipsia, a rat likely (will/will not) learn to press a lever to gain access to a (drinking tube/running wheel) during the interval between food pellets.
19. Angie became sick to her stomach when she and her new boyfriend, Gerald, were on their way home after dining at an exotic restaurant. Fortunately for (Gerald/the restaurant), Angie is most likely to form an aversion to (Gerald/the food).
33. According to ___________ ___________ theory, behaviors related to mating would constitute a system of behavior, and spreading one's tail feathers to attract a female would constitute a relevant response within that system.
26. A(n) ___________ activity is a (highly relevant/seemingly irrelevant) activity sometimes displayed by animals when confronted by conflict or blocked from attaining a goal.
16. Following a turkey dinner in which, for the first time, Paul also tasted some caviar, he became quite nauseous. As a result, he may acquire a conditioned ___________, most likely to the (turkey/caviar).
31. Activity anorexia is more easily induced among relatively (young/old) rats, which is (similar to/different from) the pattern found with humans who suffer from anorexia.
8. Whenever a person combines a stringent exercise program with a severe diet, he or she may be at risk for developing symptoms of ___________.
13. For the development of adjunctive behaviors, the optimal interval between the delivery of reinforcers is often about (2/6/9) minutes.
22. My canary likes the sound of my whistling. Research suggests that my whistling will be a more effective reinforcer if I am attempting to train the bird to (perch in a certain spot/peck at the floor).
29. An abnormally high level of activity and low level of food intake generated by restricted access to food is called ___________.
6. From an evolutionary perspective, a tendency toward activity anorexia could (increase/decrease) the likelihood of the animal encountering a new food supply. Indirect evidence for this includes the fact that the activity anorexia cycle can often be (stopped/greatly enhanced) by suddenly presenting the animal with a continuous supply of food.
18. When Selma was eating oatmeal porridge one morning, she broke a tooth on a small pebble that accidentally had been mixed in with it. The next morning, after eating some bran flakes, she became terribly ill. If she develops aversions as a result of these experiences, chances are that they will be an aversion to the (look/taste) of oatmeal and the ___________ of bran flakes.
10. Adjunctive behavior tends to develop when a behavior is being reinforced on a(n) ___________ or ___________ schedule of reinforcement, with

the optimal interval often being in the range of ________ minutes. Adjunctive behavior is most likely to occur in the interval immediately (following/preceding) the presentation of each reinforcer.

23. When a rat is shocked, it easily learns to run to the other side of the chamber to escape. According to Bolles, this is because the running is actually a(n) (operant/respondent) that is (elicited/negatively reinforced) by the (application/removal) of shock.
7. The activity anorexia model suggests that behavioral treatments for anorexia nervosa should focus as much on establishing normal patterns of ________ as they do on establishing normal patterns of eating.
14. The tendency for many people to smoke while waiting in traffic can be viewed as an example of a(n) ________ behavior in humans.
3. Adjunctive behavior is also known as ________ behavior.
27. One advantage of displacement activities is that they allow for a more (diverse/focused) pattern of behavior, which is often advantageous.
32. In behavior systems theory, behavior is organized into a number of (innate/learned) systems, which are then activated by relevant ________.
21. An innate tendency to more readily associate certain types of stimuli with each other is a type of preparedness that is known as ________.
17. Taste aversion conditioning occurs less readily to (familiar/unfamiliar) food items, which is an example of ________ in classical conditioning. This type of conditioning also occurs most readily to the (strongest/mildest)-tasting item in the meal, which is an example of the ________ effect in classical conditioning.
5. A class of brain chemicals that may play a particularly important role in the development of anorexia in both rats and humans is ________. Evidence for this includes the fact that people suffering from anorexia often report that the feeling that accompanies the disorder is quite (unpleasant/pleasant).
25. A behavior pattern in which an organism approaches a stimulus that signals the presentation of an appetitive event is known as ________.
30. As with the development of anorexia in rats, many cases of anorexia in humans might be the result of the combined effects of ________ restriction and high ________ levels.
15. Despite getting a shock when he plugged in his toaster one day, Antonio feels only slight anxiety when using it. On the other hand, he is deathly afraid of spiders, ever since one jumped on him when he tried to swat it. The difference in how easily Antonio learned to fear these two events seems to be an illustration of the effect of ________ on conditioning.

ANSWERS TO CHAPTER TEST

1. autoshaping
2. automaintenance; prevents
3. schedule-induced
4. adjunctive (or schedule-induced)
5. endorphins; pleasant
6. increase; stopped
7. activity
8. anorexia nervosa
9. several small; slowly
10. FT; FI; 1-3; following
11. more
12. will; drinking tube
13. 2
14. adjunctive
15. preparedness
16. taste aversion; caviar
17. familiar; latent inhibition; strongest; overshadowing
18. look; taste
19. Gerald; the food
20. long; a single
21. CS-US relevance
22. perch in a certain spot
23. respondent; elicited; application
24. instinctive drift; fixed action
25. sign tracking
26. displacement; seemingly irrelevant
27. diverse
28. control; delayed
29. activity anorexia
30. food; activity
31. young; similar to
32. innate; cues (or situations)
33. behavior systems

Chapter 13

COMPARATIVE COGNITION

CHAPTER OUTLINE

Kary was very excited when her parents gave her a lovebird to keep her company while away at college. She named him Oscar, and what a great little guy he turned out to be. Mind you, he has been acting a little strange lately. He squawked like crazy when her new boyfriend dropped by the other night, which completely spoiled the mood. He also has a weird tendency to throw up on her sometimes. She wonders if he's in some way allergic to her.

What Is Comparative Cognition?

As you learned in the last chapter, there are many species-specific differences in learning, with certain types of learning often dependent on a particular genetic predisposition. In this chapter, we will explore this topic in more detail by examining evidence from the field of research known as comparative cognition. ***Comparative cognition*** is the study of information processing across a variety of species, including humans. As noted in Chapter 1, comparative cognition is becoming an increasingly popular research area among many behaviorists these days, with research being conducted on such topics as memory, categorization, decision making, problem solving, and even complex processes like language use and deception. The term "comparative" refers to the practice of comparing such abilities across species to determine whether their skills are similar or different. This area is sometimes also called "cognitive behaviorism" or "animal cognition," but many researchers prefer the term "comparative cognition" because it recognizes that comparison is key to understanding a species' abilities. It also acknowledges that even when we study the cognitive abilities of just one species, we are often comparing that species to our own.[1]

Within comparative psychology, *Tinbergen's "four questions"* or *"four levels of analysis"* (Tinbergen, 1963) are traditionally used to categorize research findings (see Figure 13.1). The first two questions deal with the *ultimate cause* of a trait, which refers to *the reasons for which that trait evolved within a species*, while the last two questions deal with the *proximate cause* of a trait, which refers to *the more immediate causes for the expression of that trait in an individual* ("proximate" means nearer or more immediate). Listed below are Tinbergen's four questions, with the example of taste aversion learning included to help illustrate their meaning.

[1]As mentioned in Chapter 1, not all behaviorists agree with the growing popularity of cognitive explanations of behavior. They contend that noncognitive interpretations are in many cases equally viable. Such debates can be quite complicated, and hence are beyond the scope of this textbook. This chapter, being about comparative cognition, will be written from a cognitive perspective—but this is not to deny that some interesting arguments can be made for a noncognitive interpretation of certain findings.

FIGURE 13.1 Tinbergen's four "questions" (or levels of analysis)

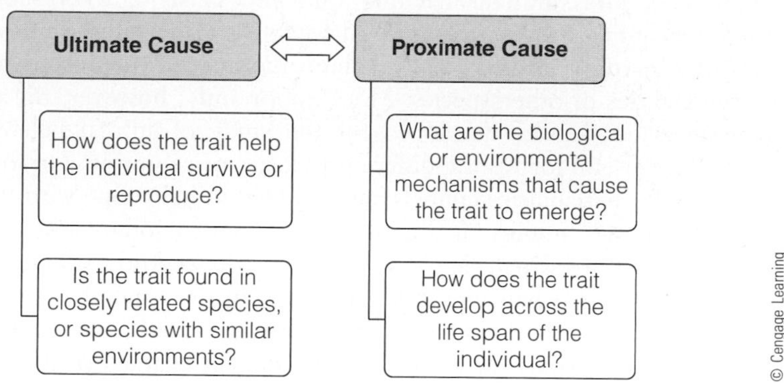

Ultimate Cause (relating to the evolution of a trait within a species):

1) *What purpose does this trait serve for survival or reproduction?*
Example: One-trial taste aversion learning allows an organism to avoid poisonous food. This would lead to an enhanced rate of survival and reproductive success for members of that species.
2) *How is this trait distributed across species?*
Example: Taste aversions are quickly learned in most species with a varied (and therefore risky) diet. Rats (that are unable to vomit when ill) learn it especially quickly. This suggests that individual species acquire taste aversions in ways that are adaptive for their ecological niches.

Proximate Cause (relating to the expression of the trait within an individual):

3) *What biological and environmental events lead to the expression of this trait in an individual?*
Example: On a biological level, taste aversion learning appears to depend on having a functioning amygdala (Reilly & Bornovalova, 2005). On an environmental level, there must also be a conditioning experience in which a flavor was followed by nausea or illness.
4) *How does this trait emerge or change during an individual's development?*
Example: Taste aversion learning begins around the time of weaning in mammalian species (Gubernick & Alberts, 1984) and can persist for years.

While any given study may examine only one of these questions at a time, you will generally find researchers working at each level of analysis. As you progress through this chapter, you may find it useful to think about these four questions for each study that is described.

You might also be wondering why comparative psychology has become so popular in recent years. Obviously, many people find animal behavior fascinating, as indicated by the many television stations and programs devoted to this topic. But why the fascination? One suggestion is known as the ***biophilia***

hypothesis (Wilson, 1984), which is that humans have an inherited predisposition to be drawn to nature, including other animals (biophilia means "love of nature"). Thus, humans may find it innately satisfying to do such things as keep pets, go to zoos, and hang bird feeders outside their windows. Simple curiosity by itself may also play a role in the interest many researchers have in the abilities of other species. More importantly, however, the techniques that behaviorists have developed for the study of animal behavior are in many ways useful for testing different theories of cognition and for uncovering the different abilities animals have evolved to help cope with their world. As you will see, studies such as these have led to some rather remarkable findings, many of which demonstrate how little we know about the animals that surround us. That said, it is also important to remember that comparative researchers are, in keeping with Thorndike's (1911) concerns about the dangers of *anthropomorphism* (attributing human characteristics to animals), careful to operationalize their variables in ways that can readily be replicated and to define behavior in ways that can be precisely measured.

Finally, you may remember from Chapter 2 how experiments in this area often utilize comparative designs to compare the abilities of different species. (If you no longer remember what a comparative design involves, you should quickly go back and review it.) Be aware, however, that the comparative psychologists, biologists, and primatologists (researchers who study primates) who work in this area also use a variety of other methods to test their hypotheses. Thus, in this chapter, you will find examples of correlational studies, observational studies, and case studies, as well as various types of experimental research, including comparative designs.

QUICK QUIZ A

1. Comparative cognition is the study of inf__________ pr__________ across a variety of species.
2. Tinbergen's "four questions" are related to the ul__________ cause of a trait and the pr__________ cause of a trait.
3. Humans have a tendency to be interested in animals and nature. According to the b__________ hypothesis, this is an inh__________ tendency.

Memory in Animals

How to Study Animal Memory

Memory processes in animals have been an important area of study in comparative cognition, and one that might seem to present a rather unique challenge. With humans, we closely identify memory with various kinds of verbal behavior. For example, your professor will likely assess your memory for the material you are now studying by giving you a quiz or an exam at some future time when you will be required to verbally respond (in writing) to various verbal stimuli (questions). Animals, however, do not have such verbal ability, so how then can we study their memory?

In answering this question, we need to consider that the act of remembering is, to a large extent, a matter of stimulus discrimination. For example, on a multiple-choice test, each question presents a series of statements (verbal stimuli), but only one of them corresponds to material that you studied earlier. To the extent that the material is well remembered, you will be able to discriminate the correct statement from the other alternatives. If the material is not well remembered—an all too common occurrence, unfortunately—you could very well end up selecting a wrong alternative.

In studying animal memory, similar procedures are used; that is, at one time the animal is shown a certain stimulus and is then, at a later time, required to identify that stimulus in order to receive a reinforcer. One procedure often used in these types of studies is called delayed matching-to-sample. In ***delayed matching-to-sample***, the animal is first shown a sample stimulus and then, following a delay, is required to select that stimulus out of a set of alternative stimuli. The extent to which the animal is able to select the correct stimulus is regarded as an indicator of its ability to remember that stimulus.

An example of a delayed matching-to-sample task for pigeons is shown in Figure 13.2. The chamber contains three response keys. In the basic procedure, the two side keys are initially dark while a sample stimulus, such as a triangle, is shown on the center key. When the pigeon pecks this sample (or target) stimulus—note that a response is required at this point to ensure that the pigeon has noticed the stimulus—a delay period is entered in which all three keys are dark. Following the delay period, a test period is entered in which the center key is dark and the two side keys are illuminated, one with a triangle and the other with a square. Pecking the triangle (which "matches the sample") is immediately reinforced with food, while pecking the square simply instigates a time-out period followed by the presentation of another trial. Thus, to earn food, the pigeon must select the correct alternative by remembering the sample stimulus that it was shown before the delay.

Using this procedure, one can investigate memory processes in pigeons by systematically altering various aspects of the procedure, such as the similarity of the stimuli during the test phase, the length of time the sample stimulus is presented, the length of the delay period, and the extent to which the delay period includes the presentation of other stimuli that could potentially interfere with the pigeon's memory for the sample stimulus. A particularly interesting capacity that has been investigated in this way is called *directed forgetting*. Directed forgetting occurs when you have been told to forget something—such as when your math professor makes a mistake in a calculation and tells you to forget what she just wrote on the board (assuming that you understood what she was writing in the first place)—and as a result, you do indeed have poorer memory for that material than you would have had without the instruction to forget it. Figure 13.3 shows an example of a directed forgetting procedure for pigeons. The sample stimulus is presented as usual. During the delay period, however, the pigeon is shown either an O on the center key, which indicates that it must remember the sample stimulus, or an X, which

FIGURE 13.2 The series of events in a delayed matching-to-sample task. The pigeon is first required to peck at the sample stimulus, which initiates a delay interval in which all keys are dark. Following the delay, a test phase occurs in which pecking at the stimulus that matches the sample results in food. The position of the correct stimulus randomly alternates across trials between the right and left keys; the sample stimulus randomly alternates between a square and a triangle.

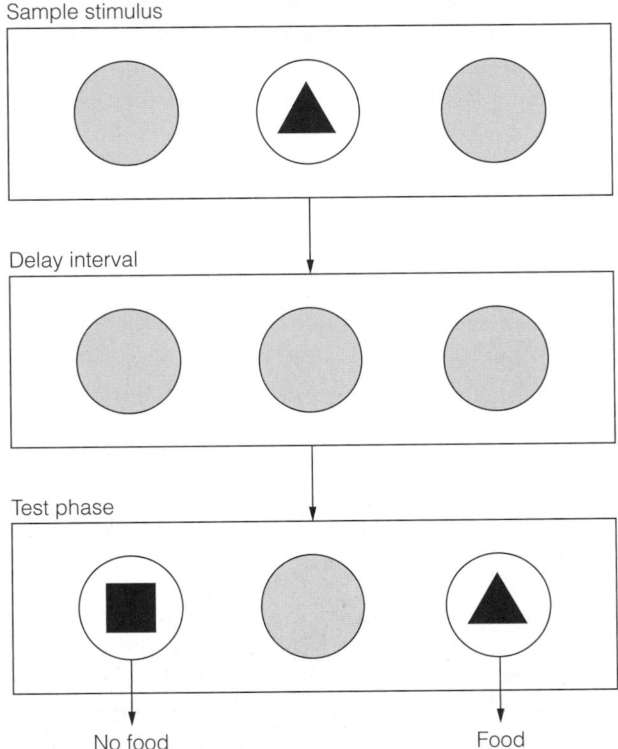

indicates that it can forget the sample stimulus because the trial will be starting over again. In essence, the O tells the pigeon that everything is okay and that the test phase will be occurring as usual, whereas the X tells the pigeon something like, "Whoops, made a mistake; we'll be starting over again, so you may as well forget what you've just been shown."

The question, therefore, is whether pigeons are actually less likely to remember the sample stimulus when they have been shown the X (the forget cue) as opposed to the O (the remember cue). The way to test this is to occasionally fool the pigeon by presenting the X and then proceeding to the test phase anyway (sort of like an evil professor who later tests you on lecture material that she explicitly said would not be on the exam). When this is done, it turns out that pigeons do in fact perform worse in the test phase following the forget cue than they do following the remember cue. In other words,

FIGURE 13.3 A delayed matching-to-sample procedure for investigating directed forgetting. During a *remember trial*, the O (the "remember" stimulus) during the delay interval indicates that a test phase will be occurring as usual. During a *forget trial*, the X (the "forget" stimulus) during the delay interval indicates that a test phase will not occur and that the sample stimulus can be forgotten. Forget trials, however, occasionally end with a test phase.

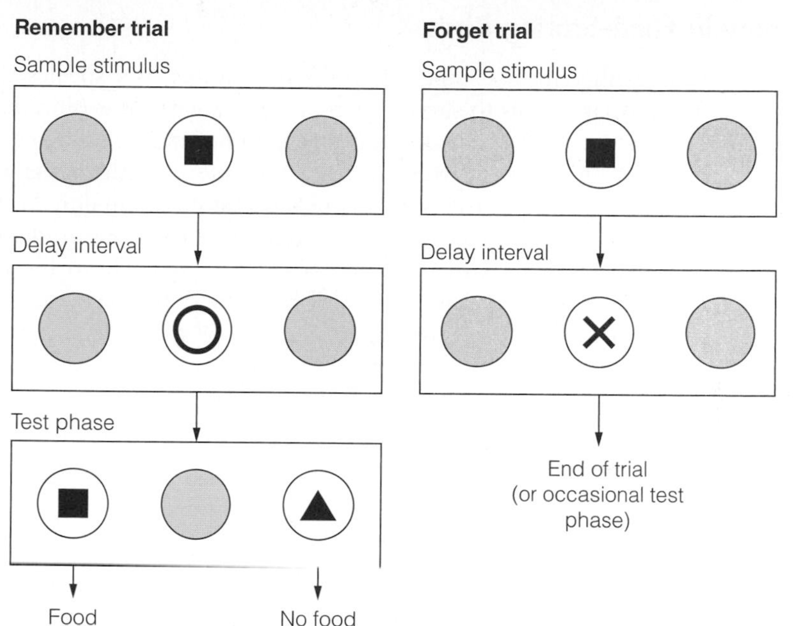

when the pigeons are "told" that they need not remember a particular stimulus, they do in fact display poorer memory for that stimulus in the future (e.g., Maki & Hegvik, 1980; see also Kaiser, Sherburne, & Zentall, 1997).

Directed forgetting is only one of the phenomena that comparative psychologists have investigated in birds and is in a sense a demonstration of the potential similarities between birds and humans in the types of memory processes we exhibit. As you will see in the next section, a good deal of effort has also gone into demonstrating the kinds of differences that can occur in memory processes between species.

QUICK QUIZ B

1. Memory is often a matter of s__________ d__________ in which one is first exposed to a stimulus and is then required to respond to that stimulus at a later time.
2. A useful procedure for studying memory is a d__________ __________-to-s__________ task. In it, the animal is first shown a s__________ stimulus and then, following a de__________, is required to select that stimulus out of a set of alternative stimuli.

3. In a directed forgetting task, the pigeon is shown a cue during the ____________ period, which signals whether the s____________ stimulus should be remembered or forgotten.
4. On directed forgetting tasks, pigeons are (less/more) likely to select the correct stimulus following exposure to the forget cue.

Memory in Food-Storing Birds

As you may remember from Chapter 1, traits or features of a species that allow members of that species to survive or reproduce are called evolutionary adaptations. Different species have different adaptations because each species occupies its own niche in the environment. For example, a moth that is well camouflaged in its environment is well adapted to that environment. Moths without a camouflaged appearance are more likely to be eaten by predators, whereas moths that blend in with trees or grasses are less likely to be seen and eaten. Camouflaged moths, therefore, will have the opportunity to leave behind more offspring that carry the same genes, and subsequent generations will have more moths with the genes for camouflage and fewer moths without those genes. Predation is, in this case, the selective pressure that leads to the evolution of camouflage in our moth. This is an example of how a physical trait can evolve. But what about a cognitive trait like memory?

If you live in a location where the seasons change dramatically, then you have likely seen a variety of ways that bird species survive a harsh winter when food is difficult to find. Many bird species, like geese and ducks, migrate from colder areas to warmer areas in order to be able to access food and open water. Such species have therefore evolved rather impressive spatial navigation abilities (Mettke-Hofmann & Greenberg, 2005). Likewise, some birds are predators, and have evolved keen vision and hearing abilities to facilitate hunting during all seasons of the year (Tucker, 2000). But many non-predators that don't migrate have a different solution; they store food in the fall that they retrieve over the winter. For example, Clark's nutcrackers and black-capped chickadees can store thousands of food items across hundreds of locations, and will retrieve most of them through the course of the winter (Shettleworth, 2010; Sherry & Hoshooley, 2009). For those of us who have difficulty remembering where we left our car keys, this is an incredible feat of memory! However, in order to test whether this ability is specific to these birds, rather than an ability that all birds have but only some birds make use of, it is necessary to bring both food-storing and non-storing birds into the lab for controlled tests of their memory abilities.

In a comparison of four species of corvids (Clark's nutcrackers, pinyon jays, scrub jays, and Mexican jays) that differ in their reliance on food storing, the Clark's nutcracker significantly outperformed the other three species in tests of retrieval accuracy (Balda & Kamil, 2006). This isn't surprising given that the Clark's nutcracker lives in a harsh, mountainous environment and only survives if it can successfully retrieve its food caches in the winter. Interestingly, the Clark's nutcracker was also better at learning certain types of mazes and at other tests of spatial memory, suggesting that this is a generalized ability as opposed to one that is highly specific to one particular setting.

In another study, Brodbeck and Shettleworth (1995) compared the memory ability of black-capped chickadees (a food-storing species) to that of dark-eyed juncos (a non-storing species) using a modified delayed matching-to-sample task. In one condition, during training, each bird was presented with, say, a blue stimulus on the left and a red stimulus on the right, with the blue stimulus on the left being the target stimulus (i.e., selecting it led to food). This means that there were two cues that could be used to indicate the correct target: color (blue) and position (left). Following training, however, the bird was suddenly presented with a blue stimulus on the right (opposite side to training) and a green stimulus on the left (different color from training). The question of interest was, which stimulus would the chickadee versus the junco now select as the target? If you think about it, birds that are prone to remembering *location* should choose the green stimulus on the left, because even though it is the wrong color (it isn't blue), it is in the correct location (on the left). However, birds that are prone to remembering *visual features* of a stimulus should choose the blue stimulus on the right because it has the correct visual appearance (blue) even though it is in the wrong location (right). Now think about food-storing birds, like chickadees, and what features of a stimulus would be more important to them. Would it be more adaptive for them to remember what the tree looks like or where the tree is? Trees aren't likely to move, but they are likely to change in appearance as a result of losing leaves and being covered in snow. This means that chickadees would do best to remember where things are, and should therefore be more likely to choose the stimulus that is in the correct location—and this is precisely what they did. While juncos showed little preference for color or location in this task, chickadees showed a strong preference for location.

What is it about food-storing birds that lead them to preferentially recall the *location* of an item rather than some other feature? Is it a result of social learning or an innate tendency? In terms of biological factors, it has been discovered that the size of the hippocampus (an area of the brain strongly implicated in spatial memory) is positively correlated with the amount of food storing that a species does (Pravosudov, 2009) as well as with the amount of practice that any individual within that species has had (Clayton, 2001). Thus, food-storing species of birds have a larger hippocampus than non-storing species, and individual birds with more food-storing experience have a larger hippocampus than those with less storing experience. In fact, chickadees actually grow new hippocampal neurons in fall, when it is time to start storing food for winter. Neurons also continue to be recruited throughout the winter, or die off quickly if they are not activated by appropriate experience (Sherry & Hoshooley, 2007). Thus, much like other arguments regarding the relative contributions of nurture and nature, experience and biology, the answer is that there is an interaction between the two factors.

The important thing to take away from all this is that similar species can have different abilities if they are subjected to different environmental demands; as well, different species can have similar abilities if they are subjected to similar environmental demands. Thus, chickadees and juncos are similar species, but only chickadees need to store food in the winter, and they are the ones with a strong tendency to remember location. Conversely, chickadees and nutcrackers are quite different species, yet they both have excellent spatial memory because both are food-storing species for whom location is critical. From an evolutionary perspective, the memory abilities of food-storing birds have been selected for because those individuals that were better able to retrieve food caches—and learn to retrieve caches as a result of experience—left behind more offspring, and those offspring inherited that ability.

QUICK QUIZ C

1. When comparing Clark's nutcrackers to other corvids, the nutcracker has better (spatial/temporal) memory, which is important for food storing.
2. In a test comparing chickadees to juncos, it was found that chickadees, who store food, pay more attention to the (location/color) of an item.
3. The hi____________ is an area of the brain that is important for spatial memory, and food-storing birds tend to have (greater/lesser) volume in this area.

Can Animals Count?

The Case of Clever Hans

Imagine that you've left four cookies sitting on a plate in the living room while you walk to the kitchen to get a drink. When you come back, would you notice if there were only three cookies left on the plate? Unless there is something very wrong with your human brain, you would likely perceive the difference immediately. This ability is known as ***numerosity***, which is an understanding of quantity. But what about other animals? Are they too capable of numerosity, or could you safely steal a cookie from them?

In the late 1800s, a German horse named Hans became a sensation when it was demonstrated that he could correctly answer mathematical questions by tapping his hoof on the ground. His owner was a math teacher who trained Hans in much the same way that he would teach young children to count and do simple arithmetic, only instead of answering verbally Hans was trained to respond by tapping. He could answer questions that involved adding and subtracting, as well as more complex operations such as fractions. He could even keep track of dates on a calendar. For example, if he were asked "Today is the 5th and it is a Wednesday, so what will the date be on

Friday?" then Hans would tap the ground seven times to indicate that Friday would be the 7th. Pretty impressive, isn't it? The German Board of Education even set up a commission of scientists (appropriately named "the Hans Commission") to investigate whether there was some trickery involved. But they ruled that Hans was answering questions legitimately with no obvious cues from his trainer. In operant conditioning terms, the commission believed that Hans had learned to do the following:

Question posed: ***Tap out the correct answer*** **→ Earn a tasty treat**
S^D R S^R

Despite the commission's conclusion, a psychologist named Oskar Pfungst remained skeptical. A few years later, he systematically reassessed Hans's abilities and determined that Hans was not quite as clever as he seemed. He found that Hans could not answer questions correctly if (1) he could not see the person asking the question or (2) the person asking the question did not know the answer to the question (Pfungst, 1911). Pfungst discovered that Hans was instead attending to subtle changes in the posture and facial features of the questioner, which would almost always change when Hans reached the correct number of taps. For example, if Hans was posed the question, "What is 5 plus 5?", he would simply begin tapping. In turn, the questioner would begin counting the taps, and when Hans reached the correct answer of 10, would almost invariably, on an unconscious level, alter some aspect of his features, such as by slightly dipping his head. In other words, Hans had simply learned to begin tapping on the ground until certain aspects of the questioner's features changed. Of course, this by itself was an impressive ability for a horse. But it was also clear that what Hans was doing was not arithmetic, but rather exhibiting a very subtle form of stimulus discrimination. Essentially, from an operant conditioning perspective, what Hans had really learned was the following chain of behaviors:

Question posed: ***Tap ground*** **→ Subtle change in appearance of questioner**
S^D R S^R/S^D

Stop tapping **→ Tasty treat**
R S^R

The case of Clever Hans provided an important lesson for researchers studying animal intelligence and cognition. It clearly indicated the need to have certain controls in place for differentiating a sophisticated "cognitive" skill like counting from more basic types of learned behavior. For example, it is often necessary to have experimenters that are *blind* to the purpose of the experiment or to the "expected" behavior of the animal in order to ensure that they are not somehow biasing or guiding the behavior. Unfortunately, another outcome of the Clever Hans case was that some people took it as

Clever Hans only *appeared* to be capable of incredible feats of intellect.
(*Source*: From http://www.skepdic.com/cleverhans)

evidence that only humans have numerical ability. But is that the case? As you will see, research has revealed that a variety of other species can in fact process information about numbers.

Beyond Clever Hans: Evidence for Numerical Ability in Animals

Otto Koehler was an early psychologist who was interested in animal intelligence. In order to test whether animals could count, he trained several species of birds, such as parrots, that were known for their "intelligence" to differentiate between numerical values (Koehler, 1951). For this he used a direct *matching-to-sample* task, similar to that described earlier, but without any delay between the presentation of the sample stimulus and the test stimuli. Whereas a delayed matching-to-sample task is used to test memory, a direct matching-to-sample task can be used for testing categorization. For example, a parrot might be shown a sample card with three dots on it along with two other cards that also have dots on them, one of which matched the number of dots on the sample. The parrot had to choose the *matching* card, such as by flipping it over, in order to earn the reinforcer. An important aspect of this procedure is that the dots could be of varying sizes and orientations, so the bird could not simply choose a card that was a replica of the sample. For example, the sample card might have two large dots and one small dot laid out in a line, whereas the correct response card could have three small dots organized in a triangle pattern. It was the *number* of dots that mattered and not their size or orientation. As it turns out, Koehler's research revealed that birds were particularly good at this task so long as the numbers remained relatively small. Some birds could match numbers as large as six or seven, but most failed beyond that point. Results like this therefore indicate that some animals can respond to stimuli in terms of their quantity and that they can differentiate quantity from volume or size.

Another type of procedure used to investigate numerical abilities in animals is borrowed from developmental studies with human infants, and hence allows for a direct comparison of animals' abilities with infants' abilities. Using a bucket with a false bottom, a researcher places items (grapes, toys, or some other valued commodity) into a bucket one at a time while the subject (animal or human infant) watches. In some trials, each item remains in the visible portion of the bucket, while in other trials items are hidden in the false bottom. The subject is then given the opportunity to look into the bucket and retrieve the items. In the "visible" trials, the subject will find the exact number of items that had been placed in the bucket. In the "hidden" trials, the subject will find a number of items that is fewer than what it had seen being placed in the bucket. The independent variable is the amount of time the subject spends searching for items when allowed to retrieve the items from the bucket. Human infants even under one year of age will continue searching after retrieving one item if they saw two items go into the bucket. They will also keep searching if they retrieve two items after seeing three items go into the bucket. Once the quantity of items gets beyond three, however, they don't seem to keep track (Feigenson & Carey, 2003).

How does this skill compare to that of other species? As it turns out, several species demonstrate a similar ability. Mongoose lemurs, for example, will keep searching after retrieving one item if they witnessed two or more items being placed in the bucket. They can also distinguish between larger quantities, but only in a proportional sense. They can distinguish that two is more than one (as evidenced by their search time if they only find one) and that four is more than two, but they are not as good at distinguishing that three is more than two (finding two items, they may not bother searching for the third one) or that eight is more than six. This is the case even though the absolute difference between, say, eight and six is actually larger than the difference between two and one and is equal to the difference between four and two. What does this tell us about lemurs' ability to understand quantity? They don't seem to do it in terms of counting or absolute quantity, but rather in terms of proportion. (Two is readily distinguished from four because two is 50% less than four, but six is not readily distinguished from eight because six is only 25% less than eight. Thus, they can distinguish a large proportional difference but not a small proportional difference.) Interestingly, this same species of lemur will also continue to search after retrieving a whole grape if they saw two half grapes placed into the bucket. This suggests they are tracking the number of food items as opposed to the volume of food items (Lewis, Jaffe, & Brannon, 2005).

Thus, a variety of studies with nonhuman species have provided evidence of numerosity in animals. Primates have been repeatedly tested for this skill, and all have demonstrated some capacity for distinguishing among small numbers. Larger numbers, however, seem to be well understood only by older humans (Shettleworth, 2010).

QUICK QUIZ D

1. The case of Clever Hans reminds us that it is often important to have testers who are (blind to/aware of) the conditions or expectations of the test.
2. Koehler used a direct m____________-to-s____________ task in order to determine whether parrots could match cards with different numbers of items on them.
3. Results from Koehler's studies indicate that some birds can distinguish q____________ from vo____________ or si____________.
4. Using a bucket with a false bottom, researchers have determined that human infants will (continue/not continue) to search if three items were placed in the bucket but only two items can be seen.
5. Using the same bucket task, lemurs seem to track differences between placed versus found items based on (proportion/absolute quantity).
6. A variety of species are capable of distinguishing between (large/small) numbers.

And Furthermore

When "Bird Brains" Outperform People

It's easy to assume that humans are cognitively superior to other species. Humans may not have wings, claws, or pretty stripes, but we do have wonderfully large brains! There are times, however, when our highly specialized intellect fails us, and other species beat us in complex tasks.

In an old TV game show called *Let's Make a Deal*, contestants were asked to choose between three doors. Behind each door was a prize. One prize was valuable, such as a trip or a large sum of cash, whereas the other two were far less valuable (e.g., an old donkey or a month's supply of toilet paper). After the choice had been made, the host would open, not the chosen door, but one of the unchosen doors to reveal a worthless prize behind it. The contestant would then have the option of A) sticking with the original choice or B) switching to the other remaining door. What choice would you make?

If you are like most people, you would probably stay with your original choice because you would perceive that you started with a 1/3 probability of having chosen correctly (one of the three doors has a valuable prize behind it) and now that one door has been removed, the probability that you chose correctly has increased to 1/2. Thus, you may as well stay with your original choice. Another way of looking at it is that between the two remaining doors, there is now a 50% chance that you have chosen the valuable prize, so whether you switch or don't switch, the probability will remain the same.

Well, it turns out that you are wrong! In this logic problem (which is now known as the *Monty Hall dilemma*, after the host of the TV show), there is a higher probability of winning if you *switch* after one of the doors has been eliminated! The reason is as follows. When you start out, there is a 1/3 probability that you chose correctly and 2/3 probability that you chose incorrectly. The 2/3 probability of being wrong *does not change* when one of the options is removed. So 2/3 of the time, sticking with your original choice will result in a loss. (If you are still confused by it, don't worry; even some mathematicians are fooled by this problem [Vos Savant, 1990]. For further explanations, just search the Web for the *Monty Hall dilemma*.)

So how do pigeons do on a task like this? After playing this game several times (for food, rather than trips and cash), they begin to show evidence of *matching* and *overmatching* as described in Chapter 10. In other words, pigeons will match, or overmatch, the proportion of times they switch according to the proportion of times switching has led to reinforcement. Because switching alternatives on this task leads to reinforcement two-thirds of the time, then pigeons will choose to switch two-thirds of the time (or, in the case of overmatching, more than that). This means that pigeons perform significantly better on this task than do humans who, with their wondrous brainpower, tend not to switch even after repeated trials (Herbranson & Schroeder, 2010)!

So why are humans so terrible at this task? One way of looking at it is that humans are using "classical probability" by looking at the problem and trying to calculate the likelihood that the prize is behind a given door. Thus, humans look ahead and attempt to rationally (if incorrectly) predict the probability of a certain outcome given the alternatives available. Most of the time, that would be a good strategy, but not in situations like this in which the outcome is tricky. Pigeons, however, appear to utilize "empirical probability," in which choices are made based on prior experience with a task (Herbranson & Schroeder, 2010). (It is as though they are asking themselves, what happened the last 10 times that I stayed versus the last 10 times that I switched?) Thus, while clever humans are trying to reason things out, independent of their experience, the pigeons are simply reacting on the basis of their experience. And in the same way that rule-governed learning is sometimes inferior to learning based on the actual contingencies of reinforcement (as discussed in Chapter 11), so too statistical reasoning is sometimes inferior.

But why don't human subjects learn to override this tendency when they are given repeated experiences with the task (which is an advantage the game-show participants never had)? It appears that humans have a strong bias toward trying to predict certain types of outcomes and basing their behavior on that prediction. It should be noted that children outperform adults on this task, so this appears to be a bias that develops as one grows older (DeNeys, 2006). On top of this, because of the one-third trials where our choice to stay turns out to be correct, we may to use this as evidence that our non-switching strategy is correct. In a sense, we are intermittently reinforced for non-switching, with instances of success being more salient than instances of failure. From a cognitive perspective, this is known as *confirmation bias*, in which we notice evidence that supports our strategy and ignore evidence that contradicts it, even though the contradictory evidence occurs more frequently than supportive evidence.

Of course, another way of looking at it is that people sometimes think they're a lot more clever than they are!

Category Learning and Relational Decisions

If various animals can determine how many items are in a group, can they also determine whether those items *belong together* or not? Learning a category involves being able to generalize and discriminate, two features of learning that are found across species. The procedures used to determine whether animals can learn to categorize are very similar to those used in studying basic processes of discrimination and generalization as outlined in earlier chapters. In other words, animals are subjected to a discrimination training procedure and then tested on the extent to which the learned response subsequently generalizes to other stimuli.

To start with a simple example, Herrnstein (1979) used standard discrimination training to get pigeons to categorize "trees" by presenting 40 pictures that contained trees and 40 pictures that did not contain trees. The birds earned reinforcement for pecking at a "tree" picture (an S^D), but not for pecking at a "non-tree" picture (an S^Δ). Not surprisingly, pigeons learned to discriminate trees from non-trees and would only peck at the tree photos. The next step in the process was to determine whether pigeons could generalize this training to novel pictures. As it turns out, the birds were very likely to peck at novel tree pictures, and very unlikely to peck at novel non-tree pictures. This demonstrates that pigeons can learn to group similar items together and then apply the "category" of *tree* to items they haven't seen before.

A more complicated ability involves organizing items or individuals in terms of how they relate to one another. For example, if you know that your friend is dating someone, then you know it would be risky to try flirting with that person. You understand that there is a social connection between those two people that affects the way you interact with them. It would also be useful to understand other social hierarchies that exist in your world. If you know that Helen is Richard's boss, and Stephen is Helen's boss, then you can infer that Stephen is more powerful than Richard. This second example requires a skill known as ***transitive inference***: a form of reasoning in which the relationship between two objects can be inferred by knowing the relationship of each to a third object. To use an abstract example, if $A > B$ and $B > C$, then $A > C$ (where $>$ means "greater than"). Humans seem particularly good at this type of reasoning. Other species may also be capable of this type of reasoning, but it seems to depend on the type of social structure that exists for the species.

Looking again at lemurs, some species live in large social groups with clear dominance hierarchies while other species of lemurs live in small groups without a rigid hierarchy. It is theorized that living in a society, with all its rules and relationships, leads to an evolution of cognitive skills that would facilitate living socially. You can imagine how dangerous it would be if you were unable to identify the dominant individuals (or the bullies, or the friendly people) in your group. Thus, it is predicted that social species should be better at understanding things like hierarchies and hence at making transitive inferences.

In order to test this hypothesis, MacLean, Merritt, and Brannon (2008) trained two groups of lemurs on a transitive inference task. One group consisted of ring-tailed lemurs, who are very social and live in large groups with a rigid social hierarchy. The second group consisted of mongoose lemurs, who are less social and live in small unstructured groups.

During training, the animals were presented a series of trials in which two images (such as an image of *wavy lines* paired with an image of a *person*, or an image of a *star* paired with an image of *dots*) were simultaneously presented on a touch screen (see Figure 13.4). For each pair of items, one of the images was "higher ranked," which meant that selecting it resulted in reinforcement (it was an S^D), and the other item was "lower ranked," which meant that selecting it did not result in reinforcement (it was an S^Δ). But whether the item was higher ranked or lower ranked depended

FIGURE 13.4 Researcher Elizabeth Brannon with one of the lemurs working on a touch screen computer. (*Source*: Retrieved from: http://brannonlab.org.s84504.gridserver.com/wp-content/uploads/2010/06/Liz-with-Ringtail.jpg)

on which other image it was paired with. For example (going back to the use of letters, which will be easier to follow), when images B and C were presented together, then selecting image B was reinforced (which we will indicate as B > C), whereas when images C and D were presented together, then selecting item C was reinforced (C > D). Training therefore consisted of having the lemurs learn the relative rankings of images within each of a number of pairs, such as: A > B, B > C, C > D, D > E, and E > F. During the actual training sessions, each image was randomly presented on either the left or right side of the screen, regardless of whether it was higher ranked on that occasion or lower ranked, to prevent the animal from learning to select on the basis of location rather than image. As it turns out, both types of lemurs learned this task quite readily, and selected the higher ranked image the majority of the time.

Following training, a test phase was conducted in which the lemurs were given 30 recall trials of familiar adjacent pairs (e.g., C and D, the same as during training) and 6 trials of novel, previously nonadjacent pairs (e.g., B and D, which were never paired during training). The question was whether, when presented with the novel pairings, the lemurs would transfer their understanding of the relative rankings to the novel pair. For example, would they transfer B's rank over C, and C's rank over D, into a choice of B over D? In fact, the ring-tailed lemurs (the social ones) performed quite well on this task and were able to use their previous training to make inferences about relationships among new pairs of items. Moreover, the farther apart the novel items were on the scale (e.g., B and F as opposed to B and D), the greater the accuracy that the ring-tailed lemurs displayed. The mongoose lemurs, on the other hand, responded at around chance level for all novel pairs. But when the researchers repeated this experiment using a correction procedure (all subjects were given more feedback on their performance and more systematic training about the hierarchy), both groups performed equally well. This suggests that both species are capable of learning the task, but that ring-tailed lemurs learn it more readily, with less explicit instruction. This supports the hypothesis that social hierarchy is an evolutionary pressure that enhances the acquisition of this type of skill (MacLean, Merritt, & Brannon, 2008).

QUICK QUIZ E

1. Herrnstein (1979) trained pigeons to peck at pictures of trees, and not at non-trees. This is a discr__________ tr__________ procedure.

2. Herrnstein's study revealed that pigeons could g__________ their discrimination to novel pictures of trees, which suggests that they had learned the c__________ of tree.

3. Trevor is taller than Leah, and Leah is taller than Jeff. If you know that Trevor is taller than Jeff, then you have successfully made a tr__________ in__________. Species of lemurs with rigid social hierarchies are (more/less) skilled at this task than the less social species.

Concepts of Tools, Self, and Others

Making and Using Tools

One piece of evidence that an animal has higher cognitive abilities is tool use. Using an item in a manipulative way demonstrates that the individual understands the relationship between objects and their effects. For example, imagine that you've dropped your keys into a tight spot that you can't reach. If you get a wire hanger and bend it so that you can use it to hook your keys and drag them out, then you have shown that you understand how to manipulate the environment to have a desired effect. You have solved a problem by utilizing a separate piece of equipment. Humans are great problem-solvers and tool-users, but a number of other species are capable of such skills also.

The simplest form of tool use involves the use of an existing item. For example, a sea otter will use rocks to crack open the shells of mussels or crabs (Hall & Schaller, 1964). Use of rocks to open nuts, shellfish, or eggs is also common among primates as well as some birds (Fragaszy, Izar, Visalberghi, Ottoni, & De Oliveira, 2004; Shettleworth, 2010). Chimpanzees are known to use twigs to "fish" for termites by sticking the twigs into a termite mound. The termites swarm the invading tool, and then the chimp can withdraw the twig and slide a whole troupe of termites into her mouth at once (Sanz & Morgan, 2007). Chimps also use twigs to dip honey out of beehives (Boesch & Boesch, 1990), marrow out of bones, and water out of puddles (Sanz & Morgan, 2007). Sometimes tools are used for protection or for comfort. Chimpanzees have been observed laying down vegetation just to sit on and using leaves to cover their heads from the rain. They will also use leaves to clean wounds or wipe their faces (Sanz & Morgan, 2007). Bonobos (formerly named "pygmy chimpanzees" because they are so similar to chimps it was thought they were the same species) will sometimes use leaves and branches to cover their nests during bad weather (Kano, 1982), and dolphins will cover their snouts with sponges in order to prevent injury while hunting (Smolker, Richards, Connor, Mann, & Berggren, 1997).

Will just any rock or twig be sufficient for the task? For some species there doesn't appear to be a great deal of selectivity, but others are very picky. For example, black-breasted buzzards (Aumann, 1990) and Egyptian vultures (Thouless, Fanshawe, & Bertram, 1989) have been shown to prefer a particular weight and size of stone when selecting stones to crack open the eggs of other birds. New Caledonian crows also tend to be choosy about their tools, such as a twig they will use to fetch food out of a hole. In laboratory studies, crows will preferentially select tools that are long enough to reach a desired item, and some will select the appropriate tool even if it must be retrieved from another room (Chappell & Kacelnik, 2002). Tool use by itself seems to indicate a certain amount of intelligence and planning, but selectivity in tool use suggests a more sophisticated understanding of cause and effect.

QUICK QUIZ F

1. Tool use by a species is evidence of understanding relationships between objects and their (cause/effect).
2. The simplest form of tool is a(n) (existing/familiar) item like a stick or a rock.
3. Buzzards and vultures show (no/some) preference for the weight of rocks they use to crack open eggs. This is evidence of (more/less) cognitive complexity than simple tool use.

Further evidence of planning is found among species that keep tools for more than one use. Saving or carrying a tool when there is no immediate need for it implies that the animal has the capacity to *expect* a future need for the tool. This prospective and proactive behavior is typical of chimpanzees, bonobos, and orangutans, all of whom can maintain a variety of tools for a variety of tasks (Mulcahy & Call, 2006). Some non-primates will also save tools for another time. For example, a sea otter will often keep a rock that has been previously used to crack open crustaceans, even when it is not currently feeding (Hall & Schaller, 1964). One of the most striking examples of saving an item for later use comes from an animal that one might not have expected to be capable of such foresight. Veined octopuses have been filmed using and transporting coconut shells, which they use as portable shelters and hiding places (Finn, Tregenza, & Norman, 2009; videos of this can be found on the Web by doing a search for *octopus* and *coconut shell*). If you watch the video, you'll see that carrying your shelter around is not an easy task! The octopus finds a shell, wraps its tentacles around it, and then "walks" with the shell tucked up under its body. When it encounters a predator, it then drops the shell and climbs underneath. One octopus was filmed using two half-shells and combining them to create a closed unit. But this is not the only example of clever behavior by octopuses. For example, at the Sea Star Aquarium in Germany, one problematic octopus is known for throwing rocks to smash glass, juggling the hermit crabs in its enclosure, and repeatedly short-circuiting a light by squirting a stream of water into the fixture (*Otto the octopus wreaks havoc*, 2008). Although this is anecdotal evidence, any animal that is rumored to juggle its cage-mates deserves further study!

Beyond tool use and tool carrying, it would seem to require even greater cognitive complexity to combine tools or to modify existing materials in order to create a new tool. The species that demonstrate this level of intelligence are very few indeed. Not surprisingly, though, chimpanzees have demonstrated this kind of ability. The chimpanzees of the Goualougo Triangle in the Congo use two or more types of sticks in order to fish for termites. One type of stick is harvested from a tree that produces straight, rigid twigs with smooth sides. These sticks are gathered and taken to the foraging site, which may be more than 100 meters away. There, the sticks are broken to a particular length and the chimps sharpen the ends by chewing them. Once modified, the sticks are used to poke holes into termite mounds. Next, another type of tool is inserted into the mound to actually gather the termites. These have been harvested from a different type of plant, with long flexible stalks and fibers that can be frayed to create a brush-like effect that the termites will stick to (Sanz & Morgan, 2007). As you can see, this is a multistep process that requires harvesting of two different types of plants, at different points in time, and at locations that are not necessarily near the spot where they are modified or used. The chimpanzees that are successful at termite fishing in this way do seem capable of a rather sophisticated level of planning.

Where does the ability to use or create tools come from? Like many complex skills, animals can learn to use tools through observation and social interaction. For example, in the Taï Forest in western Africa, chimpanzees use stone tools to crack coula nuts that are steadied or braced in tree trunks or other rocks. This hammer-and-anvil technique allows the chimp to focus a lot of force on a precise area, cracking the hard outer shell of the nut without pulverizing the softer seeds inside. It is a delicate task, and it takes up to seven years to master the skill. Very young chimps sit and watch the nutcrackers work, and they don't start using the nut-cracking tools until around three years of age. After that, practice makes perfect (with a bit of additional facilitation from role models), but the learning is slow (Boesch & Boesch-Achermann, 2000).

Although social learning may be the primary way in which animals acquire many of their tool-using skills, there may also be a certain amount of insight or innovation involved. In the laboratory and in the field, crows and chimpanzees have demonstrated novel use of implements, novel modification of implements over time, and even modification of implements that have not previously been encountered (Yamamoto, Yamakoshi, Humle, & Matsuzawa, 2008; Weir, Chappell, & Kacelnik, 2002). This suggests an ability to go beyond what one has been socially taught, and it is possible that tool use often involves both insight and social learning. (See Figure 13.5.)

FIGURE 13.5 Betty the crow, who became famous for her discovery of how to fashion a tool to retrieve a "food bucket" from a "well." In the photo at left, Betty has just finished bending a wire into the shape of a hook. She then inserts the wire into the well to hook the handle of the bucket and retrieve it (Weir, Chappell, & Kacelnik, 2002, p. 981). Videos of Betty's performance can readily be found by searching the Web for Betty the crow. (*Source*: Retrieved from http://users.ox.ac.uk/~kgroup/tools/crow_photos.shtml)

Oxford University – Dept. of Zoology

QUICK QUIZ G

1. Saving a tool for later use is common among (mammals/primates), but (is sometimes/is not) seen among other animals.
2. Chimps have also shown the ability to (create/modify/both create and modify) tools.
3. It appears that chimps learn to crack nuts through a long, gradual process of so___________ le___________.
4. In order for tool use to start, researchers have speculated that there may be some form of (insight/innate ability) involved when an item is used in a new way for the first time.

Theory of Mind

The creation, modification, retention, and use of tools demonstrates that a variety of species, including primates, birds, marine mammals, and even invertebrates, can evolve the cognitive capacity to understand cause and effect, and to plan ahead in order to manipulate the environment. Could these animals also have other abilities that we typically consider to be "uniquely human"? What about the ability to understand the minds of others, and use that information to achieve different types of goals? ***Theory of mind*** is the tendency to attribute mental states to other individuals (Premack & Woodruff, 1978). This means seeing oneself as separate from others, and recognizing that the content of another's mind is different from one's own. If you have a theory of mind, then you can understand that someone else has information you don't (so you can ask questions of them), or that someone lacks information that you have (so you can conceal or share that information). As adult humans, we often take this ability for granted. We can ponder our own thoughts, and how others perceive us. We can share juicy gossip or lie about an upcoming surprise party. As discussed previously, however, the need to avoid anthropomorphism necessitates the use of very strict tests and cautious interpretation in assessing this kind of ability in animals.

QUICK QUIZ H

1. Camilla sees a spider near her sister Rory. Camilla knows that Rory is afraid of spiders, so she intentionally steps on the spider before Rory sees it. This intentional behavior suggests that Camilla has a th___________ of m___________.
2. Sharing or concealing information requires you to understand that you are (separate from/the same as) others, and that the content of your mind is (the same as/different from) others'.

Self-Awareness and Differentiating Self From Others

One of the key features of a mind that can understand other minds is called ***self-awareness***: the ability to see oneself as separate from others. It's difficult for a human to imagine what it must be like to not recognize oneself in the mirror or to not feel separate from others, but it seems as though many species do not have that ability. A classic test of self-awareness is known as the *mark and mirror task*. This test was developed independently by Gordon Gallup (1970), an animal behaviorist, and Beulah Amsterdam (1972), a clinical child psychologist. Both researchers were interested in the emergence of self-recognition and self-exploration that young primates (including humans) demonstrate when they have access to their own reflection. It was clear to both researchers that young apes and toddlers were interested in mirrors, but were they using mirrors in the same way? Were they seeing *themselves* or just an image?

Although different versions of the mark and mirror task have been used, the key features of the task are as follows: First, the subject is marked on the face with a noticeable bit of odorless paint or makeup. It is important that the subject not be aware of the mark when it is applied. Generally the mark is applied surreptitiously during another habitual activity, like when a mother cleans her child's face or when a zoo handler is petting the face of a young chimp during a daily interaction. Next, the subject is given access to a mirror, and the subject's behavior is coded for his or her reaction to the image in the mirror. Evidence of self-recognition includes the subject touching the mark on its face while looking in the mirror, and other uses of the mirror to explore its body. For example, chimps will use the mirror to look at their teeth or get a very close look at their bottoms! Evidence of a lack of self-recognition includes reacting to the image as if it were another individual. In chimps this usually means aggression or fear. In infants, it may mean pointing to the image and saying "baby!" (if that is how the infant normally interacts with other infants). When both chimpanzees and human infants are tested in similar ways, it is clear that both species demonstrate self-recognition before the age of three years. Humans generally pass the test by around 24 months, and many chimpanzees pass the test by 28 months of age (Bard, Todd, Bernier, Love, & Leavens, 2006). Other species that pass the mark and mirror task include dolphins (Reiss & Marino, 2001), magpies (Prior, Schwartz, & Güntürkün, 2008), and elephants (Plotnik, de Waal, & Reiss, 2006), as well as great apes like bonobos, orangutans, gibbons, and gorillas (e.g., Heschl & Fuchsbichler, 2009). It has even been demonstrated in pigeons, though it took a considerable amount of training before it became evident (Epstein, Lanza, & Skinner, 1981).[2] Interestingly, even in

[2]Not surprisingly, Epstein, Lanza, and Skinner (1981) interpreted these results as indicating that a cognitive interpretation of such constructs as "self-awareness" is unwarranted, and that researchers should instead focus on discovering the contingencies of reinforcement that lead a person or animal to display the type of behavior patterns that we interpret as self-awareness. Others, however, have argued that no pigeon has ever been found to spontaneously use a mirror for self-exploration, nor has any pigeon ever passed the mark and mirror task without explicit training (de Waal, 2008). Videos of the pigeon and self-awareness study can be found on the Web by searching for such keywords as *Epstein*, *Skinner*, *pigeons*, and *cognition*. The full video also includes a fascinating demonstration of training a pigeon to solve the classic "box-and-banana" problem that was famously used by Kohler (1959) to test for the occurrence of "insight" in chimpanzees (which Skinner and Epstein also argue is unwarranted).

species where self-recognition has been documented, it is not necessarily displayed by all members of the group. It appears that there is considerable variance within a species in terms of these cognitive abilities (Shettleworth, 2010).

QUICK QUIZ I

1. The mark and mirror task is a classic test of s____________-aw____________ that has been used with a variety of species including humans.
2. Aside from primates, other species that show evidence of self-awareness include do____________, el____________, and mag____________.
3. There is considerable (variability/consistency) within a species for many high-level cognitive abilities. This means that (all/not all) individuals within a species will show evidence of such abilities.

Once you have the ability to see yourself as separate from others, what thoughts emerge from that ability? Can you then use information in different ways? (Or, to put it rather confusingly, do you know that they know that you know what they know?) In an attempt to determine whether children and other animal species can "understand the contents of another mind," researchers have used tasks where certain information is provided to the subject and then the subject is questioned or observed to see if that information is used to correctly infer what another individual knows. In the *false belief task*, children are told a story using props. For example, a researcher might tell the following story to a child: "Sally was playing with her teddy bear. Then it was time for dinner. Sally put her bear away in her toy box [here, the researcher would place the teddy bear into the toy box] and she went downstairs to eat. While she was gone, Sally's brother Billy came in and played with the teddy bear. Billy put the teddy bear under the bed [here, the researcher would place the bear under the toy bed]. When Sally came back into the room, where do you think she looked for her teddy bear?" Children under the age of about four years typically say that Sally will look under the bed. This is where the bear is, and this is where the subject knows the bear to be. Children over the age of four typically respond that Sally will look in the box, because that's where Sally left it and she didn't know that the bear had been moved (see Baron-Cohen, Tager-Flusberg, & Cohen, 2000). This is an excellent task for verbal children, who can tell you where to look and also explain their choices. But how could you test for this sort of ability in other species?

Chimpanzees live within a dominance hierarchy, and tend to be very competitive for food. If two chimps want the same food item, and one is more dominant than the other, then the dominant individual always takes the food or injures the lower-ranking chimp if there is conflict. Brian Hare and his colleagues used this situation to create a test that would determine whether low-ranking chimps could avoid punishment and still obtain food by inferring what a dominant chimp knows (Hare, Call, & Tomasello, 2001). Two bananas were placed inside an enclosure. A dominant chimp

FIGURE 13.6 In the *hidden banana task*, the subordinate chimp on the right can see both bananas, while the dominant chimp on the left is unable to see the banana on the other side of the barrier. If the subordinate chimp can infer what the dominant chimp can see, then, to minimize conflict, it should choose the hidden banana. (Although both bananas are placed closer to the dominant chimp, the subordinate chimp will be given a head start into the enclosure.) (*Source*: Reprinted with permission from Shettleworth, S. J., *Cognition, Evolution, and Behavior.* Figure 12.13 on page 444. Copyright © 2010 by Oxford University Press.)

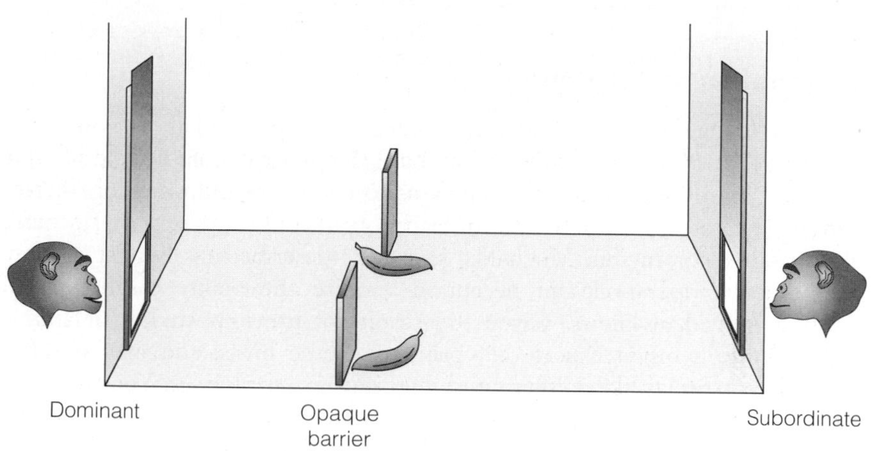

could see into the enclosure from one end, and the subordinate chimp could see into the enclosure from the opposite end. The chimps could see each other, and, if they were to take the perspective of the other, should also be able to know what the other is capable of seeing. One banana was placed in an area where it could clearly be seen by both chimps, but a second banana was placed behind a barrier where it could *only* be seen by the subordinate chimp. This *hidden banana* was put behind the barrier while the subordinate chimp was watching, but the dominant chimp was not watching. This meant that the subordinate chimp could potentially retrieve the "hidden" banana without conflict, because the dominant chimp would be unaware of its presence (see Figure 13.6). But were the subordinate chimps actually capable of inferring what the dominant chimp did or did not know? In this and other variations of the task, subordinate chimps preferentially went for the hidden banana. This demonstrates that they were able to use information about what could be known by the dominant chimp to their advantage (Hare et al., 2001). Similar research has revealed that other species, including jays, ravens, and baboons, also act as if they are inferring the knowledge of another individual (Shettleworth, 2010).

QUICK QUIZ J

1. The (false/correct) b__________ task is used to determine whether a child can use information correctly to infer what someone else would know.
2. Julie knows that someone placed Billy's teddy bear in a box, but Billy doesn't know. When asked where Billy would look, Julie says he will look in the box. Julie is likely (older/younger) than 4 years of age.
3. Using the "hidden banana" task, it has been demonstrated that subordinate chimps (can/cannot) use information about what dominant chimps know to make safe decisions in a competitive task.

Cooperation and Deception

If I have unique information about a potential resource and about your abilities, there are two key ways that I could use that information. I could provide you with information that would allow us to cooperate and work together to acquire the resource, or I could mislead you in some way so that I acquire the resource for myself. Much like the tasks described in the last section, intentional cooperation and deception require the ability to infer what another individual knows. Given the results of previous studies of animal cognition, you might expect that primates, some birds, and maybe a few other social species like dolphins and dogs have these abilities. You would be correct!

Many species appear to cooperate in hunting, caring for infants, alarm calling, and other social activities. These examples of mutual action for mutual benefit are interesting, but because the behaviors are often acquired gradually over long periods of time, after considerable exposure to a variety of experiences, they are not necessarily evidence that animals are cooperating "intentionally" or with an "understanding" of how their actions affect other individuals (Shettleworth, 2010). However, animals that appear to have a theory of mind are sometimes able to cooperate in laboratory settings on novel tasks that require coordinated actions. One such task is the *rope task*, in which a rope is strung loosely through hooks attached to a board. On the board is food. If both animals pull the rope at the same time, the board will be pulled toward the animals' enclosure and they will get the food. But if only one animal pulls the rope, then the rope will simply slide through the hooks and detach itself from the board. One animal then has a rope, but no food.

So how do chimps fare in a cooperative task? Not well. Despite their intelligence at solving many other problems, chimpanzees are so competitive with one another that they seem to have a difficult time cooperating. In situations where they do cooperate, it is usually two individuals that have a history of sharing food (like a mother and daughter) or a pair comprised of one dominant individual and one subordinate (with the dominant one taking the entire prize most of the time) (Melis, Hare, & Tomasello, 2006). Bonobos, however, tend to do very well at this task. Chimps and bonobos are closely related, but bonobos tend to be less aggressive and more cooperative than chimps (Rilling et al., 2011). Bonobos engage in cooperative feeding, are very tolerant of one another, and will coordinate their actions by paying close attention to what their task partners are doing (Hare, Melis, Woods, Hastings, & Wrangham, 2007). Other species that tend to do well on the rope task include carnivores that are tolerant of one another, like spotted hyenas (Drea & Carter, 2009) and rooks, a bird species similar to ravens (Seed, Clayton, & Emory, 2008). As more species are tested using these sorts of procedures, we will likely find more evidence of animal cooperation. However, it is not expected to be a particularly widespread ability.

If cooperation is rare, then what about *deception*? When we use the term deception in this context, we are referring to either concealment of information or the presentation of misinformation. There are other, simpler forms of deception in the wild, including the use of camouflage or evasion of predators, but those forms of deception are more mechanistic processes for which a theory of mind is unnecessary. For the purpose of making inferences about animal cognition, the type of deception described here requires more "thought."

Not surprisingly, chimps are capable of deceiving one another and also of deceiving humans. In one laboratory task, chimps were shown two containers, one of which contained a food reward. In some cases, chimps would interact with a *cooperative* trainer; if the chimp pointed to the container that held food, the trainer would retrieve the food and share it. In other cases the chimps would interact with an *uncooperative* trainer; if the chimp pointed to the container that held food, the trainer would retrieve the food and eat all of it himself. Chimps in this latter condition initially learned to share no information. In fact, they would turn their backs on the trainer and refuse to take part in the task at all (but they would still cooperate with the cooperative trainer). Eventually, though, after many trials, some of the chimps learned to point toward the empty container when interacting with the uncooperative trainer. This misinformation was only provided to the uncooperative trainer, which suggests those chimps were selectively providing misinformation to the uncooperative trainer (Woodruff & Premack, 1979).

Other, more complex examples of misinformation come from observations in the field and in large social groups of animals. Frans de Waal (1986) observed a chimp that limped for a week after a violent encounter with a rival, but only limped when the rival was watching! In another example, a low-ranking male would make an alarm call, which led other more dominant males to go investigate. Once the other males had left the area, the first male would take the opportunity to copulate with females, unharassed by the more dominant males. Although this appears to be an example of a clever ruse, it is important to remember that such reports are anecdotal, with the behaviors occurring in uncontrolled situations. It remains possible that the alarm call was not an actual misdirection, and the low-ranking male simply took advantage of the absence of the dominant males. Then again, it could be as clever as it appears.

QUICK QUIZ K

1. Intentional cooperation or deception requires a th____________ of m____________.
2. In the rope task, two animals must (cooperate/compete) by pulling at the same time in order to get food.
3. Bonobos are (more/less) successful in cooperative tasks than chimps, which is likely related to bonobos being (more/less) competitive over food.
4. Chimps can learn to point toward an empty container when interacting with an (ethical/unethical) trainer. This is evidence that chimps are (capable/incapable) of deception.
5. There is a great deal of (experimental/anecdotal) evidence of misinformation among chimpanzees, but further (observation/controlled testing) is necessary to determine whether this behavior represents intelligence.

Language

Since you have managed to make it this far in this book, it is a pretty safe bet that you understand language, and not only *written* language but *spoken* language and *symbolic* language—like road signs, gestures, and "body language"—as well. Language has often been used as the defining feature of human beings—the thing that makes our species unique. We use language, whether written, spoken, or symbolic, to communicate everything—meaning, motives, feelings, and beliefs. In fact, it is difficult to imagine how humans could exist without language.

If language is so basic to the human condition, you may wonder why we even discuss a topic like language in a textbook on learning. After all, many people believe language is not learned like other behaviors but rather is largely innate (e.g., Chomsky, 1988; Pinker, 1994). According to this view, humans are born with a "black box" that helps them to quickly acquire language, an ability not shared by other species. However, as you've likely noticed from earlier comparisons among species in this chapter, there is a continuity of cognitive ability across species. If this continuity applies to numerosity, categorization, and even self-awareness, it follows that we might also see examples of language capacity in other species. Is it possible, then, that animals can use language? This is a topic that behaviorists and ethologists have spent considerable effort attempting to answer, and in this section we summarize some of what they have discovered.

In order to discuss whether animals can use language, we must first define what we mean by language and distinguish it from the more general category of "communication." There is no question that animal species communicate with one another. ***Communication*** is the process of sending and receiving a signal of some sort. When a dog growls and another dog backs down, it can be said that the dogs have communicated with each other. When a female baboon's bottom swells and turns bright red, a male baboon notices this signal and will attempt to mate with her. She has communicated her receptivity, and his behavior changed as a result. Communication does not need to be intentional (the baboon does not intentionally grow a large red bottom), and there is no need to invoke much cognitive function in order to explain the changes in behavior that result from these types of communication. There are a number of species-specific signals like this that elicit largely innate patterns of behavior.

Communication signals are often species-specific.

Most animal behaviorists agree that ***language*** is a special category of communication which has some key features—symbols, syntax, and semantics—that distinguish it from other forms of communication (Fitch, 2005). Each of these features is described below.

1. *Symbols* In human language, we use discrete units of meaning to communicate with one another. Those units may be spoken words, specific gestures (as in sign language), an image (think of the shape of a stop sign or the simple figures used to indicate the men's and women's washrooms), or words written on a page. A ***symbol*** is therefore a cue that is used to represent an experience or object that you can then share with someone else. An interesting thing about human language is that we can make up new symbols and change the meaning of existing symbols.

Think of a word like "e-mail" that didn't exist 30 years ago. Similarly, the word "web" has been modified to refer not only to a structure made by spiders, but also to the Internet. This ability to associate arbitrary symbols with objects or events is known as ***reference***, and it is considered an important characteristic of symbols used in language.

2. *Syntax* Another important aspect of language is ***syntax***: the system of grammatical rules by which symbols are arranged. Think about the word "e-mail" again. I can use it in a sentence as a noun ("I just checked my e-mail") or as a verb ("I'll e-mail you a copy of that file as soon as I get back to my office"). If I reordered the words in one of those sentences, then it would change or lose meaning ("E-mail just I checked my"). Understanding these rules, and using them to combine symbols, allows us to have an unlimited ability to communicate about things and ideas.
3. *Semantics* A critical aspect of language is ***semantics***, which is the meaning associated with symbols. It is this meaning that allows us to refer to things that aren't currently visible or tangible. For example, you might talk about your friend who is out of the country or you might talk about an idea, like "truth," that has no real physical form. You can also talk about things that you subjectively experience but others are unable to perceive within you, like your emotions or thoughts about the future.

When we look at other species, we can see that they all communicate in some way. But in order for that communication to be called language, it must meet the standards that we use to define human language. This system of standards allows us to communicate with others *intentionally and with great specificity*. Of course, to be fair, not all human communication satisfies the criteria for language either. We respond to all sorts of cues in other people that don't involve symbols, syntax, or semantics. The communication system known as "body language" isn't really language at all, by these standards. If I bring my eyebrows together, cross my arms in front of my chest, and purse my lips together, then I can signal my emotional state to you without using arbitrary symbols. I may change your behavior and you may even have an awareness of my state of mind, but you don't actually know what I'm thinking about. On the other hand, if I were to say to you "I'm really frustrated with this project I'm working on, and I need you to turn down the music so that I can concentrate," then you are able to use all the information contained in my use of language to understand why I'm scowling, and also what you should do next. I was able to *intentionally* provide you with *specific information* that you can use. So language is special and provides strong evidence of the complexity of human cognition.

There are, however, many examples of animal species that have evolved fascinating communication systems of their own. Vervet monkeys are small primates that live in Africa. Unfortunately for vervets, they are preyed upon by a wide variety of other species, including snakes, leopards, and eagles, each of which attacks the monkeys in a different way. Vervets are constantly on guard against predators, and their system of communication incorporates alarm calls. When one vervet makes an alarm call as a result of spotting a predator, other vervets pay close attention and will often hide or escape the area. Alarm calling is not unique to vervets; many other animal species use alarm calls too. What *is* rather unique is that vervets have different calls for different predator types, and the different calls elicit different behavioral responses from the rest of the group. Thus, if a vervet monkey spots an eagle flying overhead, she sounds the "eagle" alarm, and the other vervets all dive for cover in the dense underbrush of the forest. If one of the monkeys sees a leopard, a different call is given, and the monkeys climb into the nearest tall tree (Seyfarth, Cheney, & Marler, 1980). This communication system (which seems extremely logical to us language-using humans) is very special, because it illustrates that animals can use a sound to symbolically refer to an object that exists in the world. As previously mentioned, this ability to associate arbitrary symbols with objects or events is called *reference*, and it is one of the important features of any language (e.g., Savage-Rumbaugh, 1993; Fitch, 2005). We take reference for granted because human languages are based on the idea that a combination of arbitrary sounds can stand for actual objects. Both "apple" (in English) and "pomme" (in French) refer to the tasty round object found on trees. As it turns out, some animals, such as vervets, also seem capable of the referential use of symbols.

Does the existence of reference in animal communication mean that animals are using symbols in the same way that humans are? If I were to hear someone yell "snake!", not only would my behavior change (like a vervet, I might stand up tall and look around my feet), but I might also generate a covert image of a snake. But we have no way of knowing if vervets generate covert images of what they are responding to. It does, however, seem that young vervets learn alarm calls through a process of social learning. Infant vervets are initially startled by the alarm calls but do not behave in a manner that suggests they "understand" the calls; later, through exposure to the behavior of their mothers and other adults, they come to behave in a manner similar to the adults (Seyfarth & Cheney, 1986). The various alarm calls therefore act as discriminative stimuli in the observational learning and operant conditioning of particular behaviors: "eagle" calls signal that looking to the air or hiding under cover is appropriate; "leopard" calls signal that jumping into a tree is appropriate; and "snake" calls signal that standing up tall and scanning the grasses is warranted. But the fact that alarm calls clearly *influence* the behavior of other animals doesn't mean that there is any identifiable *information* or *intent* contained in the signal itself (Rendall, Owren, & Ryan, 2009). (See the And Furthermore section, "A Border Collie Is Worth a Thousand Words," for a remarkable example of the referential understanding of words by a dog.)

QUICK QUIZ L

1. The process of sending and receiving s____________ is known as c____________.
2. Shelly sees a door that has a sign on it with a stick figure wearing a skirt. She knows that this is a women's washroom because the picture is a s____________ that many people use and understand.
3. The phrase "the dog bit the man" differs in s____________ from the phrase "the man bit the dog."
4. If you change the word "happy" to "unhappy," you have altered the se____________ content.
5. The alarm calls of vervet monkeys, which (vary/do not vary) according to predator, provide evidence that they are (capable/not capable) of (reference/syntax).

And Furthermore

A Border Collie Is Worth a Thousand Words

If you have a dog, then you know that dogs learn to associate particular words with actions or objects. Hearing the command to "sit" is usually a strong discriminative stimulus for the behavior of sitting. Likewise, many dogs learn the names of the people around them and the items they regularly play with. It's fairly straightforward to train a dog to fetch a leash or a particular toy. Anecdotally, one of your authors needs to spell the word "WALK" when talking to other people at home if she doesn't want her dog to start barking and spinning in circles near the front door. How many words can a dog learn? To what extent can dogs learn words the way that people do, as symbols that represent other things?

Two researchers, John Pilley and Alliston Reid (2010), raised a female border collie named Chaser from the age of eight weeks. She was trained four to five hours per day on a variety of obedience tasks, herding skills that are typical for border collies, and word learning. This training continued for three years. This bright young dog learned the names for over 1,000 toys and other items, in addition to a wide variety of commands and names for people. This performance is quite impressive, but Pilley and Reid did more than just determine Chaser's vocabulary. Using very controlled and systematic testing, they determined that Chaser's "verbal" abilities were evidence that a dog could learn the difference between nouns (toys) and verbs (commands), that she understood the words rather than merely responding to some subtle cue by the trainer, and that she could learn to categorize her toys based on particular features. They also demonstrated that Chaser could learn new words through a process of "exclusion." This means that if she was asked to retrieve an unknown item with a name she had never heard before, she could correctly select that item if it were placed among items she already knew. When tested two years after her official verbal training ended, Chaser still demonstrated nearly perfect retention of names and commands that hadn't been recently practiced. That's impressive!

Before you decide to tackle this sort of training with your own puppy, keep in mind that border collies are known for their ability to learn and follow commands and their attention to auditory cues even when distractions are present. This is what makes them excellent herding dogs, prized for their quick learning and responsiveness. Border collies and other dogs on the upper end of the canine intelligence spectrum (Coren, 1994) are ideal for this sort of study, but may not represent the word-learning abilities of all dogs.

Chaser in action. (*Source*: From http://newsfeed.time.com/2011/01/05/chaser-the-border-collie-the-smartest-dog-in-the-world/)

Manuela Hartling/Reuters

Can Animals "Talk"?

Now that we know a few important characteristics of language (symbols, syntax, and semantics), let's go back to our original question: Can animals use language? This question has intrigued people for generations. After all, who has not wished that a pet dog or cat could talk and wondered what the pet might say if it could? The most comprehensive research programs aimed at this question have attempted to teach animals a human-like language. Unlike Dr. Doolittle, who talked *to* the animals, many researchers have tried to teach the animals to talk to *us*.

The best-known research on language learning in animals involves our closest relatives, the great apes, including chimpanzees, gorillas, orangutans, and bonobos. The great apes share many characteristics in common with humans, from anatomy, blood chemistry, and DNA all the way to social behavior and cognitive skills (e.g., Begun, 1999). Because chimpanzees in particular are closely related to humans, the early experiments in this area focused on them. The first attempts to teach chimps language were based on the assumption that wild chimpanzees did not use language simply because they had no motivation to do so. It was assumed that, with proper training, chimpanzees could learn and use human language. The first researchers, therefore, tried to train chimps to speak by raising infant chimps in a home environment similar to that in which infant children are reared (e.g., Hayes & Hayes, 1951; Kellogg & Kellogg, 1933). Such studies are called *cross-fostering* experiments because the chimpanzees were raised in human foster homes. This research received considerable public interest, and one of the chimps, named Viki, became quite a celebrity. However, even though the chimpanzees thrived in the home environment, they never learned to talk. In fact, Viki only learned to produce four words: cup, up, mama, and papa. Watching old films of Viki, it is obvious that "speaking" is not something that chimps do naturally. Viki had to tortuously manipulate her mouth with her hand to produce those four short words.

Sign Language Experiments

Although chimps lacked the vocal apparatus to produce comprehensible speech, language experiments with chimpanzees eventually revealed that they might be capable of producing and understanding other forms of language. Thus, the next approach was to teach chimpanzees a different kind of language, one that relied on gestures instead of spoken words. In the wild, chimpanzees do communicate with each other using gestures—pointing, arm waving, and so on—so it seemed logical to assume that they might be able to learn a language that relied on hand gestures such as American Sign Language (ASL). Sign languages have been used by deaf people for many years, and there are many such languages. ASL has existed for more than 100 years and is commonly used in North America. Contrary to popular belief, sign languages are not simply "finger spelling" of English words. They are complex, rich languages that share all the important features of any language, including reference and grammar. Each signed "word" can convey different meanings, depending on the inflection, and some words can represent entire phrases. Sign languages are also learned in the same way that spoken languages are learned, through modeling, correction by adults, and learning the rules of grammar.

Experimenters conducted cross-fostering studies on chimps' ability to learn ASL in a natural home environment, thereby simulating the way human children learn language. This meant that the chimps were not taught by rote memorization or language drills but learned in day-to-day activities in a family group. Of course, the prospect of raising chimps like humans was a daunting one. The researchers had to devote years of their lives to the project, because language acquisition is a long-term effort. The researchers also had to become fluent in ASL and to only use signs, not spoken English, in the presence of their foster "children." The first ASL cross-fostering study was named Project Washoe, after Washoe County in Reno, Nevada. An infant chimp named Washoe was raised by two scientists, Beatrix and Allen Gardner (e.g., Gardner & Gardner, 1969). Following Washoe, other chimps were cross-fostered to replicate the findings of Project Washoe (and to give Washoe someone to "talk" to) (Gardner, Gardner, & Van Cantfort, 1989).

The researchers discovered that the best way to teach apes sign language is to use modeling—demonstrating the sign while performing the action that the sign refers to, such as signing "open" while opening a door. They also used a technique called *molding*, which involves placing the ape's hands in the correct signing position and associating that position with the object being "talked" about. Using these techniques, most ASL-trained chimps ended up with vocabularies of well over 100 signs. Both these procedures worked better than standard operant conditioning, which paired food reward with correct signing. The researchers found that rewarding each sign with food resulted in a very automatic or "reflexive" type of behavior that was oriented to the food reward. This process seems somewhat similar to the process of undermining intrinsic motivation through extrinsic rewards, which was briefly discussed in Chapter 6. Food rewards seemed to focus the chimps on producing the signs rather than on communicating with the researchers. Interestingly, though, Washoe (like other language-trained chimpanzees) often signed spontaneously, even when she was alone, which suggests that the signing behavior was rewarding in and of itself.

Strictly controlled tests of language use were performed with many of the chimpanzees trained in sign language (e.g., Fouts, 1973). All the chimps seemed to pass the test of *reference*, that is, they could all use the arbitrary ASL signs to refer to objects and could easily categorize novel objects using signs. For example, if Washoe was shown a photo of a kitten that she had never seen before, she immediately emitted the (correct) sign for "cat." Whether the ASL-trained chimps exhibited the other features of language —syntax and semantics—is much less clear. There is some evidence that Washoe did follow the grammatical rules of ASL. She responded to questions such as "What is that?" with, for example, "That apple" rather than simply "Apple" (Gardner & Gardner, 1975). However, there is only anecdotal evidence that Washoe and other language-trained chimps used signs in novel contexts or produced novel signs for unfamiliar objects. Further, ASL is not a rigid language. The syntax (or ordering of words) is relatively loose, so ASL speakers are not required to follow strict sequences of words. It is therefore extremely difficult to systematically assess chimpanzees' use of language when the language is a fluid, gestural language like ASL.

QUICK QUIZ M

1. Early attempts to teach chimpanzees to speak (succeeded/did not succeed) because chimps (have/do not have) the verbal apparatus to produce speech.
2. Later studies examined whether chimpanzees could learn a symbolic, gestural language called A__________ S__________ L__________.
3. In c__________-f__________ experiments, apes are raised in human environments.

4. Researchers found that (shaping/modeling) was the easiest way to teach sign language to the chimpanzees. They also found mol_____________, which involves physically placing the ape's hands in the correct position, to be an effective method.
5. Rewarding correct signs with food tended to produce (automatic/deliberate)-type behavior that provided (strong/little) evidence of actually communicating with the researchers.
6. Almost all apes that have been trained in ASL can demonstrate (reference/grammar).

Artificial Language Experiments

To get around the difficulties posed by the sign language cross-fostering studies, the next series of experiments designed to assess language learning in animals were conducted in laboratory situations using artificially constructed languages. These languages did not consist of spoken words or physical gestures; rather, they consisted of visual symbols, either plastic tokens placed on a magnetic board (Premack, 1971b; 1976) or symbols on a computer keyboard (Rumbaugh, 1977; Savage-Rumbaugh, McDonald, Sevcik, Hopkins, & Rubert, 1986). The chimps that participated in these experiments were not raised in human-like environments and did not interact with their caretakers in the same way that Washoe and the other ASL-trained chimps did. They lived in laboratories, and they conversed via the artificial language. A typical sentence in one of these languages—called "Yerkish" after the Yerkes Primate Research Center where it was created—is ? WHAT NAME OF THIS. You may notice that Yerkish grammar is *not* the same as English grammar. The question mark is placed at the beginning of the sentence and there are words missing. Nonetheless, it has its own grammar and is a language. The chimps that learned Yerkish could respond to questions and also ask for objects (e.g., PLEASE MACHINE GIVE BANANA). Although this type of language may seem restricted compared to ASL—and indeed it is, with a much smaller vocabulary and very rigid grammatical rules—it is constructed that way purposefully. The idea was to discover, once and for all, whether chimps could learn and use all the basic features of language. Also, the artificial and highly controlled surroundings made systematic assessment relatively easy. Everything the chimps "said" was displayed and recorded by a computer, so the way the chimps were using language was much clearer than in the ASL studies.

Unfortunately, the artificial language experiments did not give the unequivocal answers that scientists were hoping for. The chimps in these experiments, like the ones in the ASL studies, did appear to use symbols to represent or categorize objects, so they seemed to have the ability to *reference* objects. However, whether the chimps had mastered the artificial *grammar* was less clear. Most of the chimps' sentences were of the form PLEASE MACHINE GIVE "X" (where "X" was usually a preferred food item, such as apples, bananas, or M&M candies). It can be argued that learning to produce a sequence of symbols like PLEASE MACHINE GIVE X is not the same as learning the underlying rules governing language production. In fact, pigeons can be readily trained to peck a sequence of four symbols to receive a food reward (Terrace, 1985), and very few people would say that those pigeons had learned language. It is clear, though, that the chimps in the artificial language experiments generally did not have much to talk about except obtaining food, so perhaps this type of study was not a fair test of their language ability after all. And although recent studies of ape language ability claim to have produced stronger evidence of language capacity (e.g., Benson, Greaves, O'Donnell, & Taglialatela, 2002; Savage-Rumbaugh, Shanker, & Taylor, 1998), some language specialists remain unimpressed (e.g., Anderson, 2006).

Taking the results of the cross-fostering ASL studies and the artificial language experiments together, it is difficult to draw a firm conclusion. Chimpanzees definitely can learn to use symbols to refer to objects, but they just as definitely do not use those symbols in the same way that adult humans do (Terrace, 1979; Terrace, Petitio, Sanders, & Bever, 1979). But how do other animals fare in this regard?

QUICK QUIZ N

1. Studies of animals' ability to use symbolic languages created by researchers in a laboratory setting are known as (artificial/cross-fostering) language experiments.
2. These studies allowed researchers to systematically assess the language abilities of chimpanzees in a (more/less) controlled setting than was the case with the sign language cross-fostering studies.
3. One of the first artificial languages created was called (Yerda/Yerkish).
4. Results of the artificial language experiments strongly suggest that many of the chimpanzees mastered (reference/grammar), but there is less evidence that they mastered (reference/grammar).

Although the language studies with chimpanzees received the most public attention, other researchers have focused on training language in other species, ranging from parrots (Pepperberg, 1999) to gorillas (Patterson & Linden, 1981) to dolphins (Herman, Pack, & Morrel-Samuels, 1993). That list of species might seem completely random to you, but in fact, animals that have been language-trained share some important features. First, they have relatively large, complex brains, which makes it likely that they have the cognitive capacity to represent concepts. Second, they are usually species that are extremely social. Social species, such as humans, generally evolve more complicated communication abilities simply because they have more neighbors to "talk" to and about. Dolphins are a good example of that because they have both large brains and a social system in which they regularly interact with members of their own and other species. In fact, although dolphins are far removed from primates in an evolutionary sense, they are often thought of as similar to primates in terms of cognitive abilities. (The alleged "mystical" qualities of dolphin-human interactions that have been reported also added to their cachet as potential language users.)

For almost 30 years, Louis Herman and his colleagues studied the cognitive abilities of dolphins and whales, and trained dolphins to use symbolic languages (e.g., Herman, Richards, & Wolz, 1984). Two dolphins were each trained with a different artificial language. One dolphin, called Akeakamai, learned a gestural language, similar to ASL. The other dolphin, called Phoenix, learned a computer-generated language of acoustic signals, similar to Yerkish. Both dolphins "worked" on their language training in large tanks at the University of Hawaii (nice work if you can get it!). Although the languages are limited to describing things that the dolphins can see and do underwater, it is clear that the animals learned a vocabulary of symbols—ball, pipe, surfboard, spit, fetch, bottom, and so on—that *refer* to objects and actions (Herman & Forestell, 1985; Shyan & Herman, 1987). It is also clear that the dolphins understood rudimentary *grammatical* rules. For example, when given a sentence like FRISBEE FETCH BASKET, Phoenix would take the Frisbee and put it in the basket. When the sentence was given in the opposite order—BASKET FETCH FRISBEE—she would take the basket to the Frisbee. Both dolphins also showed very accurate performance on novel sentences, using new "words" (e.g., Herman, Kuczaj, & Holder, 1993; Herman, Morrel-Samuels, & Pack, 1990). Interestingly, California sea lions, another sea mammal species, have also learned symbolic gestures and can respond accurately to three-word sentences like those used with the dolphins (Schusterman & Gisiner, 1988).[3]

So, back to our original question: Can animals use language? As you now know, this is not a simple question, and it certainly does not have a simple answer. It depends on how you define language, and whom you ask. Some animal species are clearly capable of learning some aspects of language and of using symbols in a variety of situations. Teaching animals to use language has also expanded the types of questions researchers are asking about the way animals think. Although we may never be able to sit down with a chimpanzee and have a deep discussion about the meaning of life, we have been able to study complex phenomena such as concept discrimination and categorization (Savage-Rumbaugh, Rumbaugh, Smith, & Lawson, 1980) and logical reasoning (Premack & Woodruff, 1978), which are very difficult to study without "words" of some kind.

The evidence that animals are capable of some of the cognitive skills necessary for language production suggests that, much like for other complex cognitive skills, there is a continuum of abilities, and that different species with different social and physical environments have evolved specialized ways of dealing with those environments. Perhaps one day we will understand the extent of dolphin or bonobo communication and we will discover a language ability that humans lack, because it is an ability that is specific to the selective pressures faced by that species. It is unlikely that we will stumble across that skill by accident, because as humans we have a tendency to compare all other

---

[3]Akeakamai died in 2003, but she has been immortalized as a character in a science fiction novel, and in a number of videos for National Geographic and other nature programs. She even has her own Wikipedia page!

species to ourselves when it comes to cognitive abilities and we don't imagine things that are beyond our experience. Just like it is difficult to imagine how a dolphin can use sonar to "see" items that are hidden behind a barrier (Pack & Herman, 1995), it is also difficult to imagine a type of language that humans couldn't understand or use. Although this is merely a "what if" sort of thought, it is possible that we underestimate the abilities of some species due to a combination of necessary scientific skepticism and a bit of human self-centeredness. Fortunately, scientists will continue to investigate the various aspects of animal cognition and will no doubt discover further similarities and differences among species in their manner of communication. (See also "Alex Speaks" in the And Furthermore box.)

QUICK QUIZ O

1. Dolphins, gorillas, and parrots are all (social/solitary) species that have relatively (complex/simple) brains, which makes them good candidates for studying language acquisition.
2. Dolphins have been taught to communicate acoustically as well as gesturally, which is evidence that they may be able to use (simple/symbolic) language.
3. BALL FETCH BASKET means the opposite of BASKET FETCH BALL to language-trained dolphins. This suggests that, unlike many of the language-trained chimps, these dolphins can understand the gr__________ rules of a language.

And Furthermore

Alex Speaks

You know that someone is a celebrity when his death is announced on international news broadcasts, including CNN and the BBC, and obituaries are published in the *New York Times*, the *Economist*, and a variety of other high-level publications. Alex was that kind of celebrity, and when he died at age 31, his death was mourned by the people who loved him as well as by scientists around the world. His last words were "You be good. I love you." It might therefore surprise you to learn that Alex was a grey parrot, but not just any grey parrot. He was the focus of a 30-year research project conducted by Irene Pepperberg to determine whether a parrot could learn to speak. His name is actually an acronym for the study: Avian Learning Experiment.

Grey parrots are great mimics, capable of reproducing a wide variety of sounds. Unlike apes, whose vocal apparatus is not suited to the production of human words, parrots can make most of the sounds associated with human speech and have a reputation for repeating phrases they have heard. Alex was purchased in a pet store when he was about a year old, and began his language training right away. Dr. Pepperberg used a training method known as the model-rival technique. This method uses a competitor for the subject being trained, and that competitor also acts as a model for the behavior to be learned. If Alex was learning to name colors, the trainer would hold up a color stimulus and ask, "What color is it?" The competitor (usually a student in the lab) would

(*continued*)

Alex demonstrating his cognitive abilities. (*Source*: From the *New York Times*, http://www.nytimes.com/2007/09/10/science/10cnd-parrot.html)

Juniors Bildarchiv/Alamy

answer the question correctly and be rewarded with a treat like an almond or a piece of banana. Gradually, Alex learned to name colors, learned the names of items, and also learned the words for numbers (Pepperberg, 2009).

When he died, Alex knew over 150 words, including 50 names for items, their colors, sizes, and other descriptors. Further, he used the words in new ways to describe novel items that he had never encountered. His word for the newly introduced "apple" was "bannerry," which was likely a combination of "banana" and "cherry," two fruits that were familiar (Pepperberg, 2007). If you search online for videos of Alex speaking, you'll see just how clear his speech was and how easy it was to communicate with him.

Was Alex using language? He certainly used words in a referential sense, as a result of the operant and social learning that he experienced. He also responded as though he understood the meaning, or semantic content, of speech. He also demonstrated the ability to create new words and refer to items that were not present. What Alex could not do was to understand the grammar associated with language, including the use of verb tenses or many changes in syntax. Thus, according to the definition of language provided earlier in the chapter, Alex could not be described as truly using language. Dr. Pepperberg is therefore careful to describe his skills as communication using human words (Pepperberg, 2009).

Even more impressive than Alex's verbal skills are the other skills that he displayed because of this verbal ability. For example, when shown an array of blue and green items including blocks, keys, and toy cars, Alex could respond correctly to the question "How many green blocks?" This question requires Alex to count the number of items that are in two different categories. He couldn't just count the green items, and he couldn't just count the blocks. He had to count only the green blocks (Pepperberg, 1992). This sort of understanding of overlapping categories, as well as numerosity, would have been difficult to test without using language cues.

Alex died young (grey parrots can live to be 50) and likely did not reach his full potential. There are other birds being trained by Pepperberg's lab, and it is hoped that further studies will reveal the extent of parrot intelligence.

ADVICE FOR THE LOVELORN

Dear Dr. Dee,

My pet bird Oscar has been behaving strangely! He's a lovebird, and I think he's taking his name a little too seriously. Ever since I got him, he has been very attached to me, but recently this attachment has gotten a bit out of control. He's behaving like a possessive boyfriend. He needs to be near me at all times and gets very noisy and angry when I leave or when I'm too close to another person. One day while I was sitting outside on the patio, he pecked constantly at the window and made all sorts of noise until I came inside. What is really annoying is that when I finally let him perch on my lap or shoulder, he throws up on me! What's that all about? I know that you usually deal with all-human relationships, but could you please give me some insight about my love-struck lovebird?

Oscar's Obsession

Dear Obsession,

You're in luck, because I know a thing or two about relationships in a variety of species! The lovebird is known for bonding with a single monogamous mate and forming a strong attachment. If another bird isn't available, then they do tend to act out their affections on their human companions. As for the vomit, that's actually a sign of his commitment to you, because male lovebirds regurgitate food to feed their mates that stay on the nest!

You might consider getting Oscar another bird to bond with. It could be a girlfriend from his own species, or another parrot-type bird that can tolerate the aggressive wooing that lovebirds tend to display. If getting another bird isn't an option, then you should consider using some extinction techniques to reduce his possessive behaviors. If you give in to his demands, then you'll just strengthen his needy behavior!

You should also realize that, although animals do show evidence of emotions, the experience of "love" that Oscar is feeling may not be at all the same thing that humans experience. There is much that we don't understand about animal emotion, even though it seems clear that there are similarities in basic emotions across species. Fear, contentment, anger, and even affection seem common in so many animals that it would be foolish to assume that animals don't "feel." We just can't be sure that they feel things in the same way that we do. So you should let poor Oscar down gently, and try to remember that his bird brain (and heart) functions somewhat differently than yours!

Behaviorally yours,

Dr. Dee

SUMMARY

Comparative cognition is the study of information processing in a variety of animal species, including humans. Research in animal memory often utilizes tasks developed by behaviorists to study discrimination and generalization. A typical procedure for studying memory in animals is a delayed matching-to-sample task, in which a subject receives reinforcement for selecting the correct match to a sample stimulus it had previously seen. As evidence of evolutionary adaptation, food-storing birds have better spatial memory than non-storing birds, and rely more on location cues than visual cues.

Numerosity is an understanding of quantity. The horse Clever Hans appeared to have an understanding of quantity, but it was later shown that he was actually responding to subtle cues inadvertently displayed by the questioner. Better controlled tests of numerosity have revealed that some species of birds can discriminate different numbers of items. Using a bucket task, lemurs have been shown to respond similarly to human infants in that they continue to search when they have seen more items placed in the bucket than are later found. In doing so, lemurs seem to be responding to differences in the proportion of items, as opposed to differences in the absolute number of items, that were placed versus found.

Evidence that animals can categorize stimuli includes pigeons that have been trained to discriminate photos of trees from photos of non-trees and then generalize this concept to new photos. Certain social species seem capable of transitive inference; for example, if a ring-tailed lemur earns a reinforcer for selecting A over B and for selecting B over C, then when A and C are presented together, it is likely to select A.

The use of tools requires that animals understand that objects have effects and can be manipulated. Examples include chimps that use twigs, rocks, and other items from their environment as tools for foraging and for comfort. Octopuses, vultures, otters, and crows also use tools. At a more advanced level, some species have demonstrated selectivity about which items to use, and can even retain, combine, and modify objects for tool use.

A theory of mind is the ability to infer the existence of mental states in others. A step in this direction is self-awareness, which is recognizing oneself as separate from others. Using a mark and mirror task, self-awareness is generally shown by human infants at 24 months of age and by chimps at 28 months of age. Other species that demonstrate self-awareness include dolphins, magpies, and elephants. The "hidden banana" task has revealed that chimps are capable of inferring what a dominant chimp knows and can then use that information to retrieve food in a way that will avoid conflict. A theory of mind is also necessary for intentional cooperation and deception. Apes and certain social carnivores have been shown to cooperate on the rope task, and apes have been shown to intentionally deceive.

Defining features of language include symbols, syntax, and semantics. The ability to use arbitrary symbols is known as reference. Research programs have attempted to teach animals, mostly chimpanzees, a human-like language.

The first studies attempted, unsuccessfully, to teach chimps to speak. Later studies focused on teaching them to use gestural (sign) language. The chimps learned to use dozens of signs, although systematic assessment of their abilities was difficult. Later studies were conducted in better controlled settings with artificially constructed languages. The chimpanzees participating in these experiments readily used the symbols to refer to food items and behaviors, but evidence of grammatical ability was less clear. Other species have likewise demonstrated referential use of symbols and, in the case of dolphins, a rudimentary understanding of grammar. In general, however, only the referential use of symbols has been consistently found among a small number of animal species.

SUGGESTED READINGS

Boesch, C., and Boesch-Achermann, H. (2000). *The chimpanzees of the Taï Forest: Behavioural ecology and evolution.* Oxford: Oxford University Press. An exploration of tool use by chimpanzees, as well as the social learning and social behavior of a particular group of chimps.

de Waal, F. B. M. (2005). *Our inner ape.* New York: Riverhead Books. In this book, de Waal explains the differences between chimpanzees and bonobos, and describes the social behaviors and skills of these great apes.

Rendall, D., Owren, M. J., & Ryan, M. J. (2009). What do animal signals mean? *Animal Behavior*, *78*, 233–240. A summary of the literature on animal communication, it explains what we know and don't know about whether animals are capable of actual language use.

STUDY QUESTIONS

1. Define the term *comparative cognition.* Outline Tinbergen's four questions that are used to categorize research findings. Be sure to include the distinction between ultimate causes and proximate causes.
2. What is the biophilia hypothesis? What is anthropomorphism, and how do comparative researchers guard against it?
3. Using a diagram, describe the delayed matching-to-sample procedure used to study memory in pigeons.
4. What are two research findings that are indicative of evolutionary adaptation in the memory abilities of food-storing birds?
5. Briefly describe the case of Clever Hans and its eventual outcome. Describe a research study in which animals were shown to display numerosity.
6. Define transitive inference. Briefly describe a research study in which transitive inference was displayed by animals. Outline Herrnstein's (1979) experimental demonstration of concept learning in the pigeon.
7. What is the simplest form of tool use in animals (and give an example)? What are two examples of more sophisticated tool use in animals?

8. What is a theory of mind? Define self-awareness and describe how it is commonly assessed in chimps and children.
9. Describe the hidden banana task used with chimps to assess their ability to infer the thoughts of others, and the results that have been obtained.
10. Describe some experimental tasks used for assessing cooperation and deception in animals, and the results that have been obtained.
11. Define communication. Describe three distinctive features of language as well as the concept of reference?
12. Distinguish between ASL and artificial language studies. What was the reasoning behind trying to teach animals each of these types of language?
13. What have been the general findings regarding attempted demonstrations of language learning in chimps and in dolphins? What is the overall conclusion regarding language learning in animals?

CONCEPT REVIEW

biophilia hypothesis. The inherited predisposition in humans to be drawn to or bond with nature, including other animals.
communication. The process of sending and receiving a signal of some sort.
comparative cognition. The study of information processing across a variety of species.
delayed matching-to-sample. A memory task in which the animal is first shown a sample stimulus and then, following a delay, is required to select that stimulus out of a group of alternative stimuli.
language. A special category of communication which has key features—symbols, syntax, and semantics—that distinguish it from other forms of communication.
numerosity. An understanding of quantity.
reference. The ability to associate arbitrary symbols with objects or events.
self-awareness. The ability to perceive oneself as separate from others.
semantics. The meaning associated with symbols.
symbol. A cue that is used to represent some experience or object that you can then share with someone else.
syntax. The system of grammatical rules by which symbols are arranged.
theory of mind. The tendency to attribute mental states to other individuals.
transitive inference. A form of reasoning in which the relationship between two objects can be inferred by knowing the relationship of each to a third object.

CHAPTER TEST

22. The mark and mirror task is used to assess the capacity for s____________.
9. Although Clever Hans appeared to know how to count and do arithmetic, further testing revealed that he was actually responding to ________________________________.

16. Highly social species are (better/worse) at transitive inference tasks when compared to less social species.
4. A pigeon is shown a circle in a center key and then 10 seconds later must choose between a circle and a square on two side keys. Pecking at the circle will earn the pigeon a reinforcer. This is known as a delayed ______________ task.
25. Bonobos outperform chimpanzees on tasks that require (cooperation/deception); this is likely because bonobos tend to be much (more/less) competitive than chimps.
31. Research has shown that chimps are capable of the ______________ aspect of language but not necessarily the proper use of ______________.
20. Chimpanzees' hammer-and-anvil technique of cracking nuts takes (several years/a few days) to master and appears to be mostly the result of (insight/social learning).
1. The study of information processing across a variety of species is most commonly referred to as ______________ cognition.
23. Human infants tend to show evidence of self-awareness by about (12/24/36) months of age; chimpanzees tend to show a similar ability (A) never, (B) at a slightly older age, (C) at a much older age.
27. If a bird avoids an area because it heard the territorial call of another bird, this is evidence that the birds are capable of (communication/language/both).
14. A rat learns to press a lever each time some type of piano music is played, but not when some type of trumpet music is played. This is an example of (A) transitive inference, (B) category learning, (C) numerosity, (D) reference.
29. If a vervet monkey gives the eagle call, then the other vervets will dive for cover, but if the leopard call is given, then the others will jump up into the trees. Thus, vervets seem capable of using the ______________ aspect of language in their communications.
28. If the phrase "hand on the snack" becomes "snack on the hand," then both the ______________ and the ______________ aspects of the sentence have changed.
2. If you are studying the brain mechanisms associated with learning, then you are focused on the (proximate/ultimate) cause of a trait; if you are examining how learning allows a species to survive or reproduce, then you are focused on the (proximate/ultimate) cause of a trait.
19. Chimpanzees (are/are not) capable of creating new tools by modifying objects and combining objects.
5. In a directed forgetting task with pigeons, subjects tend to (recall/not recall) a stimulus that had been followed by a "forget" cue.
30. Chaser the border collie has learned to identify by name more than (10/100/1,000) different toys.

8. In a direct matching-to-sample task in which the sample varies in both location and color, chickadees are most likely to match according to (location/color/either) and juncos are most likely to match according to (location/color/either). This is in keeping with the fact that chickadees, but not juncos, ____________ for the winter.
21. The ability to intentionally cooperate or deceive another individual is considered to be evidence that the animal has a(n) ____________.
6. Migrating birds have excellent navigation abilities, which help them to survive their long journeys. Their navigation abilities are an example of a(n) ____________ adaptation.
12. Numerosity is an understanding of ____________.
11. A pigeon is shown a star in a center key and must later choose between a circle and a star presented at the same time on two side keys. Pecking at the star will earn the pigeon a reinforcer. This is an example of a ____________ task.
24. The "hidden banana" task indicates roughly the same ability in chimps as does the ____________ belief task in verbal human children, which means that both chimps and children have a ____________.
15. Tracy asked Elaine for advice about a problem with her boss, Chris. Elaine recommended that she speak to Maggie, because Maggie is Chris's boss. Elaine has used her understanding of ____________ inference to determine what advice to give.
10. After learning to discriminate the color green and also to discriminate the shape of a block, Alex the parrot was able to correctly answer a question like "How many green blocks?" when shown a number of objects of different colors and shapes. Thus, with the use of words, he was able to demonstrate that he understood the concept of (categorization/numerosity/both).
18. A delayed matching-to-sample task is often used as a test of (memory/ability to categorize).
3. Eli watched his new kitten pounce on a toy. He thought, "She must be practicing hunting because she knows it will make her better at it when she's an adult." This statement reveals Eli's tendency toward ____________, which is something that animal researchers should avoid.
26. A mongoose lemur watches as you place a number of grapes inside a bucket. When it searches the bucket, it finds one less grape than you originally placed in the bucket. It is most likely to search for the missing grape if you originally placed (3/5) grapes in the bucket. This is because their perception of changes in quantity appears to be based on (proportional differences/absolute differences).
13. To solve problems associated with the likelihood of an event, humans tend to use (classical/empirical) probability, which is based on (experience/reasoning), while pigeons seem to use ____________ probability, which is based on ____________. This results in better performance by (pigeons/humans) in the Monty Hall dilemma.

7. When we compare food-storing birds to non-storing birds, food-storing birds appear to have better __________ memory. On a neurological level, they also have a larger __________.
17. While bird-watching, Brian observed a crow use a twig to pry open a fast-food container that someone had left lying in the park. The crow's use of the twig is considered an example of __________.

ANSWERS TO CHAPTER TEST

1. comparative
2. proximate; ultimate
3. anthropomorphism
4. matching-to-sample
5. not recall
6. evolutionary
7. spatial; hippocampus
8. location; either; store food
9. changes in features (or cues) inadvertently emitted by the questioner
10. both
11. delayed matching-to-sample
12. quantity
13. classical; reasoning; empirical; experience; pigeons
14. B
15. transitive
16. better
17. tool use
18. memory
19. are
20. several years; social learning
21. theory of mind
22. self-awareness
23. 24; B
24. false; theory of mind
25. cooperation; less
26. 3; proportional differences
27. communication
28. syntax; semantic
29. reference
30. 1,000
31. reference; grammar (or syntax)

Appendix

A BRIEF GUIDE TO BEHAVIOR SELF-MANAGEMENT

Problems in self-management (or self-control) underlie many of the difficulties students face in college. Such difficulties often involve choosing between behaviors that lead to conflicting outcomes, one of which has high value but is delayed (which in this text is called a *larger later reward* [LLR]) and the other of which has low value but is relatively immediate (which is called a *smaller sooner reward* [SSR]). Should you study this evening, which will help you obtain good grades and maximize your chances of getting into law school (an LLR), or should you watch television, which will be immediately enjoyable (an SSR) but won't do a thing for your grades? Should you go for a run, which will help you become fit and healthy (an LLR), or head to the pub for an evening of entertainment (an SSR)? A person who frequently chooses SSRs over LLRs is said to be "impulsive," while a person who frequently chooses LLRs over SSRs is said to have "willpower" or exhibit "self-control." SSRs are, of course, what we typically call temptations, and they can be a major impediment to achieving our goals in life.

In general, successfully managing this dilemma involves one or both of the following:

- *Increase the frequency of desirable behavior*—that is, the behavior that leads to the LLR (studying, exercising), which may be effortful or unpleasant in the short run but will be beneficial in the long run (high grades, good health).
- *Decrease the frequency of undesirable behavior*—that is, the SSR (watching television, going to the pub), which is easy and pleasant in the short run but may be harmful in the long run (low grades, poor health).

In this appendix, we briefly outline some basic strategies that may assist you in handling this dilemma. We begin, however, with some general guidelines to provide a framework for the strategies that follow. (See Chapter 10 for an extended discussion of various factors and processes that may underlie issues of self-control. Note as well that because some students may be reading this appendix prior to having read the textbook, the following discussion is, at times, somewhat less technical than what is found in the text.)

General Guidelines for Effective Self-Management

1. *Don't rely on willpower.* Many people assume they can overcome temptations by gritting their teeth and "making up their mind" to do the right thing. Although this might occasionally work (for reasons described in Chapter 11), the reality is that, for most of us, it often has little or no effect on our behavior. Many a smoker has sworn off cigarettes forever—"This time for sure!"—only to find himself buying another pack a few days later.
2. *Emphasize overt (external) behaviors over covert (internal) behaviors.* Similar to the above, many people assume that the key to controlling their

behavior is to focus on their thoughts (e.g., negative versus positive thoughts) and emotions (e.g., feelings of anxiety versus calmness). Although this might sometimes be helpful, we often do better to focus on overt behaviors. Overt behaviors tend to be less nebulous and therefore easier to track and manage than internal behaviors. And even when the focus is clearly on an internal behavior (e.g., reducing feelings of anxiety), the things you actually do to change that behavior will often involve changes in overt behavior (e.g., posting reminders and arranging rewards for consistently meditating or practicing techniques of relaxation).

3. *Be proactive rather than reactive.* Because temptations are difficult to resist when they become imminent, effective self-control usually involves doing something *ahead of time* to prevent us from succumbing to the temptation when it arises. For many of us, it's too late to ponder how best to handle our cookie cravings when a cookie is staring us in the face, or make a rational choice between going for a run versus ordering pizza at the end of a long, hard day.
4. *Alter the environment to alter your behavior.* The things you do ahead of time to manage your behavior should typically include altering some aspect of your environment. This might be anything from rearranging the desk at which you study (the present arrangement being more strongly associated with playing computer games all evening than studying) to rewarding yourself with a pizza for going for a run (see, you get to have your pizza after all). Most of the examples listed for each of the following strategies involve altering some aspect of the environment.

Basic Strategies of Behavior Self-Management

Following is a brief list of strategies and tactics that have proven helpful in behavior self-management. Note that the examples provided represent only a small subset of the options available. Be aware as well that some of the tactics can be classified under more than one strategy; creating subgoals, for example, can be both a strong cue for what needs to be done as well as a potential reinforcer (as an indicator of progress) once that subgoal has been accomplished.

1. *Self-monitoring*
   An important first step in behavior self-management is to track the occurrence of the "target behavior" you wish to change. This will not only give you an accurate picture of where the behavior is at prior to your intervention (the baseline phase) and during your intervention (the treatment phase), it can also by itself lead to a positive change in behavior. During the baseline phase, one should ideally also do a *functional assessment* of the behavior, which involves carefully tracking the

antecedents (e.g., cues) that precede the behavior and the consequences that follow the behavior. You may discover, for example, that your study sessions in the library are disrupted by friends more often than you realized, which has obvious implications for where you should be studying. That said, conducting a full functional assessment of a behavior can sometimes be quite effortful such that a person ends up abandoning the program before even getting to the intervention stage. In such circumstances, one may do better to pare down the amount of information being collected to a more manageable level. Further information on conducting a full functional assessment, as well as sample recording sheets you can use for such an assessment, can be found in Miltenberger (2012) and in Watson and Tharp (2014).

2. *Manipulating the antecedent cues to the behavior*
   This often involves altering the environmental cues (S^Ds) that precede the target behavior and thereby facilitate its occurrence (i.e., they exert "stimulus control" over the behavior). Two basic strategies are:

   a) *Increase the cues for desirable behavior.* For example, as noted in Chapter 11, specific plans for when we study or exercise each week (written down in a day planner that we frequently check) will, for many people, effectively increase the likelihood of those behaviors. Another possibility is to essentially "habitize" a behavior by repeatedly practicing that behavior in the presence of certain cues. If you only study and do nothing else at your desk or you consistently meditate after turning off the alarm each morning, then those cues (sitting at your desk and turning off the alarm) may become effective "triggers" for the occurrence of those behaviors. The behavior has essentially become a "habit" such that little effort is now required for its performance in those situations.
   b) *Reduce the cues for undesirable behavior.* Not surprisingly, we are less likely to snack if there are no snacks in sight, and we are less likely to check our cell phone for messages if the phone is out of sight. A variation on this strategy is to *narrow the cues for undesirable behavior*, allowing the behavior to occur only in specific circumstances. For example, allowing yourself to smoke only when you are sitting on a chair in your garage may be a useful first step in cutting out smoking altogether.

3. *Manipulating the response effort for a behavior*
   In this case, you increase or decrease the occurrence of a behavior by making it more easy or less easy to perform. The two options are:

   a) *Decrease the response effort for desirable behavior.* If you find that you rarely go for a workout at the gym, which is a considerable distance away, then consider the possibility of exercising at home instead. Even slight reductions in response effort can sometimes be effective. Having one's running gear already laid out and ready to put on when you get up in the morning might significantly enhance the likelihood of going for a run in the morning.

b) *Increase the response effort for undesirable behavior.* If you're addicted to checking your smartphone for messages while studying (and the writer has had students who reported just that), then try placing the smartphone in another part of the house that you have to get up to go to (which the students found surprisingly effective).

4. *Changing the level of motivation*

   This strategy involves procedures that alter how motivated we are to perform the target behavior (referred to in the text as "motivating operations"). Once again there are two options:

   a) *Increase motivation for desirable behavior.* Learning how to cook healthy meals that are highly appetizing might significantly increase the frequency with which you eat such meals. And reading anecdotes about people who have greatly improved their health by adopting a certain diet might increase your motivation to adopt a similar diet (hence, the popularity of the many blogs that present such anecdotes).
   b) *Decrease motivation for undesirable behavior.* A common trick used by dieters is to eat just prior to grocery shopping; one is then less likely to buy fattening foods such as ice cream and cookies . And the writer once knew someone who overcame his addiction to a video game by forcing himself to play it continuously until he was absolutely sick of it (which is known as a "satiation procedure").

5. *Manipulating the consequences for the behavior*

   A critical aspect of achieving a long-term goal (LLR) is to somehow arrange for more immediate consequences along the way. Basic tactics to consider are:

   a) *Create and accomplish subgoals.* Accomplishing a major task almost always involves dividing the task up into a series of subgoals. These subgoals not only serve as cues for our behavior, the successful completion of each also serves as a reward for our behavior. In fact, just making a to-do list of all the tasks that need to be accomplished and then crossing off each item as it is completed is, for some people, a highly satisfying activity.
   b) *Self-reinforce (or self-reward) desirable behavior.* Here, we are mainly referring to artificial rewards that don't naturally follow from the behavior but will hopefully strengthen the behavior anyway. Watching a favorite television show after completing a certain amount of studying and meeting a friend for coffee after each workout are examples of self-reinforcement. Although, as noted in the text, self-reinforcement is a weak type of contingency—nothing prevents you from taking the reward without performing the behavior—it is nevertheless a simple intervention that many people find helpful.

c) *Self-punish undesirable behavior.* Throwing away a $5 bill each time you swear and forcing yourself to do push-ups each time you bite your nails are examples of self-punishment. Self-punishment is even more problematic than self-reinforcement because of a strong tendency by most people to not carry out the punishment. That said, one sometimes encounters people for whom it seems to be effective.

d) *Make a commitment response.* As defined in Chapter 10, a commitment response is an action carried out ahead of time that reliably eliminates or reduces the value of an upcoming temptation. It often involves placing control of the consequences in the hands of another person. Commitments can vary in strength from relatively mild, such as posting your self-monitoring sheet on the refrigerator door so your roommates can see how much studying you've done (and will tease you if you slack off), to very strong, such as when people sign a behavior contract that commits them to losing significant amounts of money if they fail to do what they agreed to do.

6. *Altering the target behavior*
The main concern here is whether you've chosen the right target behavior. If you have difficulty running on a consistent basis, you might wish to consider if running is the right exercise for you (as opposed to, say, cycling or swimming). Likewise, if regular snacking throughout the day seems to increase your feelings of hunger—even though it is supposed to do the opposite—then consider the possibility that you're an individual for whom frequent snacking is counterproductive. Additionally, *rather than focus on eliminating an undesirable behavior, it is sometimes better to focus on strengthening an alternative behavior that will replace it.* In fact, this is the main tactic used in treating nervous habits such as nail biting and teeth grinding. More detailed information about such "habit reversal procedures" can be found in Miltenberger (2012).

Additional Thoughts

In Chapter 11, we discuss the extent to which human behavior is often influenced by rules or instructions. In this regard, a self-management program is essentially a set of personal rules that you adopt in an attempt to modify your behavior. People who are successful at self-management have, to some extent, created an effective set of rules that work for them. The following are a few rules (or "meta-rules," if you will) that you may wish to consider in devising your own program.

- *Keep it simple.* Although it often helps to implement more than one self-change tactic at a time (e.g., you implement both precise planning and self-rewards to facilitate studying), self-management programs can sometimes become so complicated that just carrying out the program is itself a major exercise in self-management! As noted earlier, this especially applies to self-monitoring, where trying to record large amounts of information can become so effortful that you don't even make it past the baseline stage.

- *Keep it reasonable.* It is very common for people to try to do too much too quickly when attempting to change their behavior. Severe diets and heavy workouts make for good television programs, but in the absence of coaches and camera crews to keep you on track, such programs are usually a recipe for failure. A more modest plan—such as, in the case of exercise, completing just a few sit-ups and push-ups each morning—is far more likely to be successful, which then creates a foundation for gradually building up to a more substantial workout. In fact, add to this program the option of doing a bit extra whenever you feel like it, and you might be surprised at the amount of exercise you soon find yourself doing (in keeping with the "just-get-started" tactic discussed in the text).
- *Beware the "abstinence violation effect."* Many people regard a self-management program as a "do-or-die" affair, such that if they fail to fully adhere to the program, they may as well abandon it. (This is particularly common when people attempt to abstain from addictive behaviors, like smoking; hence the name of the effect.) Most of us do far better, however, to regard self-management as a work in progress, one that involves both successes and failures, and where occasional lapses are expected and even prepared for. In fact, the most critical issue in behavior self-management is not whether you violate the program but what you do *after* you violate the program. Do you abandon the program, or do you (with appropriate adjustments) "get back on the wagon"?
- *Self-experiment.* Following from the above, the main key to effective self-management is to adopt an experimental attitude in which controlling one's behavior is perceived to be less a problem to fret over than a puzzle to be solved. As with any experiment, it necessitates gathering information, testing possible solutions, assessing their effects, and altering one's plans accordingly. And this need not be a dire enterprise. As Robert Epstein (1997) wrote of B. F. Skinner:

  > Fred's use of self-management techniques was easy and natural for him. In no way did it smack of the "tyranny" of the self-control training of *Walden Two* [Skinner's 1948 novel]. It was like a game that he played, a puzzle to be solved, and he enjoyed the process as much as the results. (p. 559)

See also Miltenberger (2012) and Watson and Tharp (2014) for additional information on conducting a self-management program and the types of behaviors to which it can be applied.

Glossary

abolishing operation. A procedure that decreases the appetitiveness or aversiveness of a stimulus.

acquisition. The process of developing and strengthening a conditioned response through repeated pairings of an NS (or CS) with a US.

activity anorexia. An abnormally high level of activity and low level of food intake generated by exposure to a time-restricted schedule of feeding.

adjunctive behavior. An excessive pattern of behavior that emerges as a by-product of an intermittent schedule of reinforcement for some other behavior.

adjusting schedule. A schedule in which the response requirement changes as a function of the organism's performance while responding to the previous reinforcer.

anticipatory contrast. The process whereby the rate of response varies inversely with an upcoming ("anticipated") change in the rate of reinforcement.

appetitive conditioning. Conditioning procedure in which the US is an appetitive event (one that an organism approaches or seeks out).

appetitive stimulus. An event that an organism will seek out.

applied behavior analysis. A technology of behavior in which basic principles of behavior are applied to real-world issues.

autoshaping. A type of sign tracking in which a pigeon comes to automatically peck at a response key because the key light has been associated with the response-independent delivery of food.

aversion therapy. A form of behavior therapy that attempts to reduce the attractiveness of a desired event by associating it with an aversive stimulus.

aversive conditioning. Conditioning procedure in which the US is an aversive event (one that an organism avoids).

aversive stimulus. An event that an organism will avoid.

avoidance behavior. Behavior that occurs before the aversive stimulus is presented and thereby prevents its delivery.

avoidance theory of punishment. The theory that punishment involves a type of avoidance conditioning in which the avoidance response consists of any behavior other than the behavior being punished.

backward conditioning. Conditioning procedure in which the onset of the NS follows the onset of the US.

baseline. The normal frequency of a behavior prior to an intervention.

behavior. Any activity of an organism that can be observed or somehow measured.

behavior analysis (or experimental analysis of behavior). The behavioral science that grew out of Skinner's philosophy of radical behaviorism.

behavior systems theory. A theory proposing that an animal's behavior is organized into certain systems or categories (such as feeding, mating, and avoiding predators), with each category containing a set of relevant responses that can become activated in certain situations.

behavioral bliss point approach. The theory that an organism with free access to alternative activities will distribute its behavior in such a way as to maximize overall reinforcement.

behavioral contrast. A change in the rate of *reinforcement* on one component of a multiple schedule produces an opposite change in the rate of *response* on another component.

behaviorism. A natural science approach to psychology that traditionally focuses on the study of environmental influences on observable behavior.

bias from matching. A deviation from matching in which one response alternative attracts a higher proportion of responses than would be predicted by matching, regardless of whether that alternative contains the richer versus poorer schedule.

biophilia hypothesis. The inherited predisposition in humans to be drawn to or bond with nature, including other animals.

blocking. The phenomenon whereby the presence of an established CS interferes with conditioning of a new CS.

British empiricism. A philosophical school of thought that maintains that almost all knowledge is a function of experience.

chained schedule. A schedule consisting of a sequence of two or more simple schedules, each with its own S^D and the last of which results in a terminal reinforcer.

changing-criterion design. A type of single-subject design in which the effect of the treatment is demonstrated by how closely the behavior matches a criterion that is systematically altered.

classical conditioning. A process whereby a stimulus comes to elicit a response because it has been paired with (or associated with) another stimulus. Also known as *Pavlovian conditioning* or *respondent conditioning*.

cognitive behaviorism. A brand of behaviorism that utilizes intervening variables, usually in the form of hypothesized cognitive processes, to help explain behavior. Sometimes called "purposive behaviorism." (As noted in Chapter 13, to the extent that it focuses upon research with nonhuman animals, it is also referred to as *animal cognition* or, more commonly, *comparative cognition*.)

cognitive map. The mental representation of one's spatial surroundings.

commitment response. An action carried out at an early point in time that serves to either eliminate or reduce the value of an upcoming temptation. Also called a *precommitment response*.

communication. The process of sending and receiving a signal of some sort.

comparative cognition. The study of information processing across a variety of species.

comparative design. A type of group design in which different species constitute one of the independent variables.

compensatory-response model. A model of conditioning in which a CS that has been repeatedly associated with the primary response (a-process) to a US will eventually come to elicit a compensatory response (b-process).

complex schedule. A schedule consisting of a combination of two or more simple schedules.

compound stimulus. A complex stimulus that consists of the simultaneous presentation of two or more individual stimuli.

concurrent schedule of reinforcement. A complex schedule consisting of the simultaneous presentation of two or more independent schedules, each leading to a reinforcer.

conditioned response (CR). The response, often similar to the unconditioned response, that is elicited by the conditioned stimulus.

conditioned stimulus (CS). Any stimulus that, although initially neutral, comes to elicit a response because it has been associated with (paired with) an unconditioned stimulus.

conditioned suppression theory of punishment. The theory that punishment does not weaken a behavior, but instead produces an emotional response that interferes with the occurrence of the behavior.

conjunctive schedule. A type of complex schedule in which the requirements of two or more simple schedules must be met before a reinforcer is delivered.

contagious behavior. A more-or-less instinctive or reflexive behavior triggered by the occurrence of the same behavior in another individual.

contingency. A predictive relationship between two events such that the occurrence of one event predicts the probable occurrence of the other.

continuous reinforcement schedule. A schedule in which each specified response is reinforced.

contrived reinforcers. Reinforcers that have been deliberately arranged to modify a behavior; they are not a typical consequence of the behavior in that setting. Also called *artificial reinforcers.*

control group design. A type of group design in which, at its simplest, subjects are randomly assigned to either an experimental (or treatment) group or a control group.

counterconditioning. The procedure whereby a CS that elicits one type of response is associated with an event that elicits an incompatible response.

countercontrol. The deliberate manipulation of environmental events to alter their impact on our behavior.

covert behavior. Behavior that can be subjectively perceived only by the person performing the behavior. Thoughts and feelings are covert behaviors. Also known as *private behaviors or private events.*

CS-US relevance. An innate tendency to easily associate certain types of stimuli with each other.

cumulative recorder. A device that records total number of responses over time and provides a graphic depiction of the rate of response.

delayed conditioning. Conditioning procedure in which the onset of the NS precedes the onset of the US, and the two stimuli overlap.

delayed matching-to-sample. A memory task in which the animal is first shown a sample stimulus and then, following a delay, is required to select that stimulus out of a group of alternative stimuli.

dependent variable. That aspect of an experiment that is allowed to freely vary to determine if it is affected by changes in the independent variable.

descriptive research. Research that focuses on describing the behavior and the circumstances within which it occurs.

differential reinforcement of high rates (DRH). A schedule in which reinforcement is contingent upon emitting at least a certain number of responses in a certain period of time—or, more generally, reinforcement is provided for responding at a fast rate.

differential reinforcement of low rates (DRL). A schedule in which a minimum amount of time must pass between each response before the reinforcer will be delivered—or, more generally, reinforcement is provided for responding at a slow rate.

differential reinforcement of other behavior (DRO). Reinforcement of any behavior other than a target behavior that is being extinguished.

differential reinforcement of paced responding (DRP). A schedule in which reinforcement is contingent upon emitting a series of responses at a set rate—or, more generally, reinforcement is provided for responding neither too fast nor too slow.

discrimination training. As applied to operant conditioning, the differential reinforcement of responding in the presence of one stimulus (the S^D) and not another.

discriminative stimulus (S^D). A stimulus in the presence of which responses are reinforced and in the absence of which they are not reinforced, that is, a stimulus that signals the availability of reinforcement.

discriminative stimulus for extinction (S^Δ). A stimulus that signals the absence of reinforcement.

discriminative stimulus for punishment (S^{Dp}). A stimulus that signals that a response will be punished.

dishabituation. The reappearance of a habituated response to a stimulus following the presentation of another, seemingly irrelevant novel stimulus.

disinhibition. The sudden recovery of a conditioned response during an extinction procedure when a novel stimulus is introduced.

displacement activity. An apparently irrelevant activity sometimes displayed by animals when confronted by conflict or thwarted from attaining a goal.

drive reduction theory. According to this theory, an event is reinforcing to the extent that it is associated with a reduction in some type of physiological drive.

duration. The total amount of time that an individual repeatedly or continuously performs a certain behavior.

elicited behavior. Behavior that is drawn out (elicited) by a preceding stimulus. Also known as *respondent behavior*.

empiricism. In psychology, the assumption that behavior patterns are mostly learned rather than inherited. Also known as the *nurture* perspective (or, more rarely, as *nurturism*).

errorless discrimination training. A discrimination training procedure that minimizes the number of errors (i.e., nonreinforced responses to the S^Δ) and reduces many of the adverse effects associated with discrimination training.

escape behavior. A behavior that results in the termination of an aversive stimulus.

establishing operation. A procedure that increases the appetitiveness or aversiveness of a stimulus.

evolutionary adaptation. An inherited trait (physical or behavioral) that has been shaped through natural selection.

excitatory conditioning. Conditioning procedure in which the NS is associated with the *presentation* of a US.

experimental neurosis. An experimentally produced disorder in which animals exposed to unpredictable events develop neurotic-like symptoms.

experimental research. A research method in which one or more independent variables are systematically varied to determine their effect on a dependent variable.

exposure and response prevention (ERP). A method of treating obsessive-compulsive behavior that involves prolonged exposure to anxiety-arousing events while not engaging in the compulsive behavior pattern that reduces the anxiety.

extinction (in classical conditioning). The process whereby a conditioned response can be weakened or eliminated when the CS is repeatedly presented in the absence of the US; also, the procedure whereby this happens, namely, the repeated presentation of the CS in the absence of the US.

extinction (in operant conditioning). The weakening of a behavior through the nonreinforcement of a previously reinforced behavior.

extinction burst. A temporary increase in the frequency and intensity of responding when extinction is first implemented.

extrinsic punishment. Punishment that is not an inherent aspect of the behavior being punished but that simply follows the behavior.

extrinsic reinforcement. The reinforcement provided by a consequence that is external to the behavior, that is, an extrinsic reinforcer.

factorial design. A type of group design in which one examines the effects of two or more independent variables (or factors) across groups of subjects.

fading. The process of gradually altering the intensity of a stimulus.

fixed action pattern. A fixed sequence of responses elicited by a specific stimulus.

fixed duration (FD) schedule. A schedule in which reinforcement is contingent upon continuous performance of a behavior for a fixed, predictable period of time.

fixed interval (FI) schedule. A schedule in which reinforcement is contingent upon the first response after a fixed, predictable period of time.

fixed ratio (FR) schedule. A schedule in which reinforcement is contingent upon a fixed, predictable number of responses.

fixed time (FT) schedule. A schedule in which the reinforcer is delivered following a fixed, predictable period of time, regardless of the organism's behavior.

flexion response. The automatic response of jerking one's hand or foot away from a hot or sharp object.

flooding therapy. A behavioral treatment for phobias that involves prolonged exposure to a feared stimulus, thereby providing maximal opportunity for the conditioned fear response to be extinguished.

functional relationship. The relationship between changes in an independent variable and changes in a dependent variable; a cause-and-effect relationship.

functionalism. An approach to psychology that proposes that the mind evolved to help us adapt to the world around us and that the focus of psychology should be the study of those adaptive processes.

generalization gradient. A measure of the strength of responding in the presence of stimuli that are similar to the S^D (or CS) and vary along a continuum.

generalized imitation. The tendency to imitate a new modeled behavior in the absence of any specific reinforcement for doing so.

generalized punisher. An event that has become punishing because it has in the past been associated with many other punishers. Also called a *generalized secondary punisher*.

generalized reinforcer. A type of secondary reinforcer that has been associated with several other reinforcers. Also called a *generalized secondary reinforcer*.

goal gradient effect. An increase in the strength and/or efficiency of responding as one draws near to the goal.

group design. A type of experimental research in which one manipulates one or more independent variables across groups of subjects.

habituation. A decrease in the strength of an elicited behavior following repeated presentations of the eliciting stimulus.

higher-order conditioning. The process whereby a neutral stimulus that is associated with a CS (rather than a US) also becomes a CS.

impulsiveness. With respect to choice between two rewards, selecting a smaller sooner reward over a larger later reward.

incentive motivation. Motivation derived from some property of the reinforcer, as opposed to an internal drive state.

incubation. The strengthening of a conditioned fear response as a result of brief exposures to the aversive CS.

independent variable. That aspect of an experiment that is made to systematically vary across the different conditions in an experiment.

inhibitory conditioning. Conditioning procedure in which the NS is associated with the *absence* or *removal* of a US.

instinctive drift. An instance of classical conditioning in which a genetically based, fixed action pattern gradually emerges and displaces a behavior that is being operantly conditioned.

intensity. The force or magnitude of a behavior.

intermittent (or partial) reinforcement schedule. A schedule in which only some responses are reinforced.

interval recording. The measurement of whether or not a behavior occurs within a series of continuous intervals. (The number of times that the behavior occurs within each interval is irrelevant.)

intrinsic punishment. Punishment that is an inherent aspect of the behavior being punished, that is, the behavior itself is punishing.

intrinsic reinforcement. Reinforcement provided by the mere act of performing the behavior, that is, the behavior itself is reinforcing.

introspection. The attempt to accurately describe one's conscious thoughts, emotions, and sensory experiences.

language. A special category of communication which has key features—symbols, syntax, and semantics—that distinguish it from other forms of communication.

latency. The length of time required for a behavior to begin.

latent inhibition. The phenomenon whereby a familiar stimulus is more difficult to condition as a CS than is an unfamiliar (novel) stimulus.

latent learning. Learning that occurs in the absence of any observable demonstration of learning and only becomes apparent at a later time.

law of contiguity. A law of association holding that events that occur in close proximity to each other in time or space are readily associated with each other.

law of contrast. A law of association holding that events that are opposite from each other are readily associated with each other.

law of effect. As stated by Thorndike, the proposition that behaviors that lead to a satisfying state of affairs are strengthened or "stamped in," while behaviors that lead to an unsatisfying or annoying state of affairs are weakened or "stamped out."

law of frequency. A law of association holding that the more frequently two items occur together, the more strongly they are associated with each other.

law of similarity. A law of association holding that events that are similar to each other are readily associated with each other.

learned helplessness. A decrement in learning ability that results from repeated exposure to uncontrollable aversive events.

learning. A relatively permanent change in behavior that results from some type of experience.

matching law. The principle that the *proportion* of responses emitted on a particular schedule matches the *proportion* of reinforcers obtained on that schedule.

melioration theory. A theory of matching that holds that the distribution of behavior in a choice situation shifts toward those alternatives that have higher value regardless of the long-term effect on overall amount of reinforcement.

methodological behaviorism. A brand of behaviorism that asserts that, for methodological reasons, psychologists should study only those behaviors that can be directly observed.

mind–body dualism. Descartes' philosophical assumption that some human behaviors are bodily reflexes that are automatically elicited by external stimulation, while other behaviors are freely chosen.

motivating operation. A procedure that affects the appetitiveness or aversiveness of a stimulus. (There are two types: establishing operations and abolishing operations.)

multiple-baseline design. A type of single-subject design in which a treatment is instituted at successive points in time for two or more persons, settings, or behaviors.

multiple schedule. A complex schedule consisting of two or more independent schedules presented in sequence, each resulting in reinforcement and each having a distinctive S^D.

nativism. The assumption that a person's characteristics are largely inborn. Also known as the *nature* perspective.

natural reinforcers. Reinforcers that are naturally provided for a certain behavior; they are a typical consequence of the behavior within that setting.

natural selection. The evolutionary principle according to which organisms that are better able to adapt to environmental pressures are more likely to reproduce and pass along those adaptive characteristics than those that cannot adapt.

naturalistic observation. A descriptive research approach that involves the systematic observation and recording of behavior in its natural environment.

negative contrast effect. An increase in the rate of *reinforcement* on one component of a multiple schedule produces a decrease in the rate of *response* on the other component.

negative punishment. The removal of a stimulus (one that is usually considered pleasant or rewarding) following a response, which then leads to a decrease in the future strength of that response.

negative reinforcement. The removal of a stimulus (one that is usually considered unpleasant or aversive) following a response, which then leads to an increase in the future strength of that response.

neobehaviorism. A brand of behaviorism that utilizes intervening variables, in the form of hypothesized physiological processes, to help explain behavior.

noncontingent schedule of reinforcement. A schedule in which the reinforcer is delivered independently of any response. Also known as a response-independent schedule.

numerosity. An understanding of quantity.

observational learning. The process whereby the behavior of a model is witnessed by an observer, and the observer's behavior is subsequently changed.

occasion setting. A procedure in which a stimulus (known as an occasion setter) signals whether a CS is likely to be followed by a US and thereby controls whether the CS will elicit a CR.

operant behavior. A class of emitted responses that result in certain consequences; these consequences, in turn, affect the future probability (strength) of those responses.

operant conditioning. A type of learning in which the future probability (strength) of a behavior is affected by its consequences.

opponent-process theory. A theory proposing that an emotional event elicits two competing processes: (1) an a-process (or primary process) that is directly elicited by the event, and (2) a b-process (or opponent process) that is elicited by the a-process and serves to counteract the a-process.

orienting response. The automatic positioning of oneself to facilitate attending to a stimulus.

overexpectation effect. The decrease in the conditioned response that occurs when two separately conditioned CSs are combined into a compound stimulus for further pairings with the US.

overmatching. A deviation from matching in which the proportion of responses on the richer schedule versus poorer schedule is more different than would be predicted by matching.

overshadowing. The phenomenon whereby the more salient member of a compound stimulus is more readily conditioned as a CS and thereby interferes with conditioning of the less salient member.

overt behavior. Behavior that can potentially be observed by an individual other than the one performing the behavior.

partial reinforcement effect. The process whereby behavior that has been maintained on an intermittent (partial) schedule of reinforcement extinguishes more slowly than behavior that has been maintained on a continuous schedule.

peak shift effect. Following discrimination training, the peak of a generalization gradient will shift from the S^D to a stimulus that is further removed from the S^Δ.

personal process rule. A personal rule that indicates the specific process by which a task is to be accomplished. (Also called an *implementation intention.*)

personal rule (or self-instruction). A verbal description of a contingency that we present to ourselves to influence our behavior.

positive contrast effect. A decrease in rate of reinforcement on one component of a multiple schedule produces an increase in the rate of response on the other component.

positive punishment. The presentation of a stimulus (one that is usually considered unpleasant or aversive) following a response, which then leads to a decrease in the future strength of that response.

positive reinforcement. The presentation of a stimulus (one that is usually considered pleasant or rewarding) following a response, which then leads to an increase in the future strength of that response.

Premack principle. The notion that a high-probability behavior can be used to reinforce a low-probability behavior.

Premack principle of punishment. The notion that a low-probability behavior (LPB) can be used to punish a high-probability behavior (HPB).

preparatory-response theory. A theory of classical conditioning that proposes that the purpose of the CR is to prepare the organism for the presentation of the US.

preparedness. An innate tendency for an organism to more easily learn certain types of behaviors or to associate certain types of events with each other.

primary (or unconditioned) punisher. Any event that is innately punishing.

primary (or unconditioned) reinforcer. An event that is innately reinforcing.

pseudoconditioning. A situation in which an elicited response that appears to be a CR is actually the result of sensitization rather than conditioning.

punisher. An event that (1) follows a behavior and (2) decreases the future probability of that behavior.

radical behaviorism. A brand of behaviorism that emphasizes the influence of the environment on overt behavior, rejects the use of internal events to explain behavior, and views thoughts and feelings as behaviors that themselves need to be explained.

rate of response. The frequency with which a response occurs in a certain period of time.

ratio strain. A disruption in responding due to an overly demanding response requirement.

reciprocal determinism. The assumption that environmental events, observable behavior, and "person variables" (including internal events) reciprocally influence each other.

reciprocal inhibition. The process whereby the occurrence of a response is inhibited by the occurrence of an incompatible response.

reference. The ability to associate arbitrary symbols with objects or events.

reflex. A relatively simple, involuntary response to a stimulus.

reflex arc. A neural structure that underlies many reflexes and consists of a sensory neuron, an interneuron, and a motor neuron.

reinforcer. An event that (1) follows a behavior and (2) increases the future probability of that behavior.

Rescorla-Wagner theory. A theory of classical conditioning that proposes that a given US can support only so much conditioning and that this amount of conditioning must be distributed among the various CSs.

resistance to extinction. The extent to which responding persists after an extinction procedure has been implemented.

response. A particular instance of a behavior.

response cost. A form of negative punishment involving the removal of a specific reinforcer following the occurrence of a behavior.

response deprivation hypothesis. The notion that a behavior can serve as a reinforcer when (1) access to the behavior is restricted and (2) its frequency thereby falls below its preferred level of occurrence.

response-rate schedule. A schedule in which reinforcement is directly contingent upon the organism's rate of response.

resurgence. The reappearance during extinction of other behaviors that had once been effective in obtaining reinforcement.

reversal design. A type of single-subject design that involves repeated alternations between a baseline period and a treatment period.

rule. A verbal description of a contingency.

rule-governed behavior. Behavior that has been generated through exposure to rules.

say–do correspondence. A close match between what we say we are going to do and what we actually do at a later time.

schedule of reinforcement. The response requirement that must be met to obtain reinforcement.

secondary (or conditioned) punisher. An event that is punishing because it has been associated with some other punisher.

secondary (or conditioned) reinforcer. An event that is reinforcing because it has been associated with some other reinforcer.

selective sensitization. An increase in one's reactivity to a potentially fearful stimulus following exposure to an unrelated stressful event.

self-awareness. The ability to perceive oneself as separate from others.

self-control. With respect to choice between two rewards, selecting a larger later reward over a smaller sooner reward.

semantic generalization. The generalization of a conditioned response to verbal stimuli that are similar in meaning to the CS.

semantics. The meaning associated with symbols.

sensitization. An increase in the strength of an elicited response following repeated presentations of the eliciting stimulus.

sensory preconditioning. When one stimulus is conditioned as a CS, another stimulus with which it was previously associated can also become a CS.

shaping. The gradual creation of new behavior through reinforcement of successive approximations to that behavior.

sign stimulus (or releaser). A specific stimulus that elicits a fixed action pattern.

sign tracking. A type of elicited behavior in which an organism approaches a stimulus that signals the presentation of an appetitive event.

simple-comparison design. A type of single-subject design in which behavior in a baseline condition is compared to behavior in a subsequent treatment condition.

simultaneous conditioning. Conditioning procedure in which the onset of the NS and the onset of the US are simultaneous.

single-subject design. A research design that requires only one or a few subjects in order to conduct an entire experiment. (Also known as *single-case* or *small-n* designs.)

small-but-cumulative effects model. A model of self-control in which each individual choice between a smaller sooner and larger later reward has only a small but cumulative effect on our likelihood of obtaining the desired outcome.

social learning theory. A brand of behaviorism that strongly emphasizes the importance of observational learning and cognitive variables in explaining human behavior. Also known as "cognitive social learning theory" or "social-cognitive theory."

spatial contiguity. The extent to which events are situated close to each other in space.

speed. The length of time required to perform a complete episode of a behavior from start to finish.

spontaneous recovery (in classical conditioning). The reappearance of a conditioned response to a CS following a rest period after extinction has occurred.

spontaneous recovery (in operant conditioning). The reappearance of an operant response following a rest period after extinction has occurred.

S-R theory (or stimulus-response theory). The theory that learning involves the establishment of a connection between a specific stimulus (S) and a specific response (R).

startle response. A defensive reaction to a sudden, unexpected stimulus, which involves automatic tightening of skeletal muscles and various hormonal and visceral changes.

stimulus. Any event that can potentially influence behavior. (The plural for stimulus is *stimuli*.)
stimulus control. A situation in which the presence of a discriminative stimulus reliably affects the probability of a behavior.
stimulus discrimination. In classical conditioning, the tendency for a response to be elicited more by one stimulus than another; in operant conditioning, the tendency for an operant response to be emitted more in the presence of one stimulus than another.
stimulus enhancement. Directing attention to a particular place or object, making it more likely that the observer will approach that place or object.
stimulus generalization. In classical conditioning, the tendency for a CR to occur in the presence of a stimulus that is similar to the CS; in operant conditioning, the tendency for an operant response to be emitted in the presence of a stimulus that is similar to an S^D.
stimulus-substitution theory. A theory of classical conditioning that proposes that the CS acts as a substitute for the US.
structuralism. An approach to psychology that assumes that it is possible to determine the structure of the mind by identifying the basic elements that compose it.
symbol. A cue that is used to represent some experience or object that you can then share with someone else.
syntax. The system of grammatical rules by which symbols are arranged.
systematic desensitization. A behavioral treatment for phobias that involves pairing relaxation with a succession of stimuli that elicit increasing levels of fear.
taste aversion conditioning. A form of classical conditioning in which a food item that has been paired with gastrointestinal illness becomes a conditioned aversive stimulus.
temperament. An individual's level of emotional reactivity that, to a large extent, is genetically determined.
temporal conditioning. A form of classical conditioning in which the CS is the passage of time.
temporal contiguity. The extent to which events occur close together in time.
theory of mind. The tendency to attribute mental states to other individuals.
three-term contingency. The relationship between a discriminative stimulus, an operant behavior, and a consequence (reinforcer or punisher).
time-out. A form of negative punishment involving the loss of access to positive reinforcers for a brief period of time following the occurrence of a problem behavior.
time-sample recording. The measurement of whether or not a behavior occurs within a series of discontinuous intervals. (The number of times that it occurs within each interval is irrelevant.)
topography. The physical form of a behavior.
trace conditioning. Conditioning procedure in which the onset and offset of the NS precede the onset of the US.
transitive inference. A form of reasoning in which the relationship between two objects can be inferred by knowing the relationship of each to a third object.
true imitation. Duplicating a novel behavior (or sequence of behaviors) to achieve a specific goal.
two-process theory of avoidance. The theory that avoidance behavior is the result of two distinct processes: (1) classical conditioning, in which a fear response

comes to be elicited by a CS, and (2) operant conditioning, in which moving away from the CS is negatively reinforced by a reduction in fear.

unconditioned response (UR). The response that is naturally (without prior learning) elicited by the unconditioned stimulus.

unconditioned stimulus (US). A stimulus that naturally (without prior learning) elicits a response.

undermatching. A deviation from matching in which the proportion of responses on the richer schedule versus poorer schedule is less different than would be predicted by matching.

US revaluation. A process that involves the postconditioning presentation of the US at a different level of intensity, thereby altering the strength of response to the previously conditioned CS.

variable. A characteristic of a person, place, or thing that can change (vary) over time or from one situation to another.

variable duration (VD) schedule. A schedule in which reinforcement is contingent upon continuous performance of a behavior for a varying, unpredictable period of time.

variable interval (VI) schedule. A schedule in which reinforcement is contingent upon the first response after a varying, unpredictable period of time.

variable ratio (VR) schedule. A schedule in which reinforcement is contingent upon a varying, unpredictable number of responses.

variable time (VT) schedule. A schedule in which the reinforcer is delivered following a varying, unpredictable period of time, regardless of the organism's behavior.

vicarious emotional response. A classically conditioned emotional response resulting from seeing that emotional response exhibited by others.

References

Adams, L. A., & Rickert, V. I. (1989). Reducing bedtime tantrums: Comparison between positive routines and graduated extinction. *Pediatrics*, *84*, 585–588.

Ader, R. (2003). Conditioned immunomodulation: Research needs and directions. *Brain, Behavior, and Immunity*, *17*, 51–57.

Ader, R., & Cohen, N. (1975). Behaviorally conditioned immunosuppression. *Psychosomatic Medicine*, *37*, 333–340.

Ainslie, G. (1975). Specious reward: A behavioral theory of impulsiveness and impulse control. *Psychological Bulletin*, *82*, 463–496.

Ainslie, G. (1986). Beyond microeconomics: Conflict among interests in a multiple self as a determinant of value. In J. Elster (Ed.), *The multiple self*. Cambridge, UK: Cambridge University Press.

Ainslie, G. (1992). *Picoeconomics: The strategic intervention of successive motivational states within the person*. Cambridge, UK: Cambridge University Press.

Ainslie, G. (2001). *The breakdown of will*. Cambridge, UK: Cambridge University Press.

Ainslie, G., & Haendel, V. (1983). The motives of the will. In E. Gottheil, A. T. McLellan, & K. Druley (Eds.), *Etiologic aspects of alcohol and drug abuse*. Springfield, IL: Charles C. Thomas.

Alferink, L. A., Critchfield, T. S., & Hitt, J. L. (2009). Generality of the matching law as a descriptor of shot selection in basketball. *Journal of Applied Behavior Analysis*, *42*, 595–608.

Allison, J. (1983). *Behavioral economics*. New York, NY: Praeger.

Amabile, T. M., Hennessey, B. A., & Grossman, B. S. (1986). Social influences on creativity: The effects of contracted-for reward. *Journal of Personality and Social Psychology*, *50*, 14–23.

American Psychiatric Association. (2000). *Diagnostic and statistical manual of mental disorders* (4th ed., text revision). Washington, DC: Author.

Amsterdam, B. (1972). Mirror self-image reactions before age two. *Developmental Psychobiology*, *5*, 297–305.

Anderson, C. A., & Dill, K. E. (2000). Video games and aggressive thoughts, feelings, and behavior in the laboratory and in life. *Journal of Personality and Social Psychology*, *78*, 772–790.

Anderson, C. M., Hawkins, R. P., Freeman, K. A., & Scotti, J. R. (2000). Private events: Do they belong in a science of human behavior? *The Behavior Analyst*, *23*, 1–10.

Anderson, S. R. (2006). *Doctor Doolittle's delusion: Animals and the uniqueness of human language*. New Haven, CT: Yale University Press.

Antonitis, J. J. (1951). Response variability in the white rat during conditioning, extinction, and reconditioning. *Journal of Experimental Psychology*, *42*, 273–281.

Assagioli, R. (1974). *The act of will*. New York, NY: Penguin.

Aumann, T. (1990). Use of stones by the Black-breasted Buzzard. *Hamirostra melanosternon* to gain access to egg contents for food. *Emu*, *90*, 141–144.

Axelrod, S., & Apsche, J. (Eds.). (1983). *The effects of punishment on human behavior*. New York, NY: Academic Press.

Axelrod, S., Hall, R. V., Weiss, L., & Rohrer, S. (1974). Use of self-imposed contingencies to reduce the frequency of smoking behavior. In M. J. Mahoney & C. E. Carlson (Eds.), *Self-control:Power to the person*. Monterey, CA: Brooks/Cole.

Azar, B. (2002, October). Pigeons as baggage screeners, rats as rescuers. *Monitor on Psychology, 33*(9), 42.

Azrin, N. H., & Holz, W. C. (1966). Punishment. In W. K. Honig (Ed.), *Operant behavior: Areas of research and application*. New York, NY: Appleton.

Azrin, N. H., Hutchinson, R. R., & Hake, D. F. (1966). Extinction-induced aggression. *Journal of the Experimental Analysis of Behavior, 9*, 191–204.

Baeninger, R., & Ulm, R. R. (1969). Overcoming the effects of prior punishment on inter-species aggression in the rat. *Journal of Comparative and Physiological Psychology, 69*, 628–635.

Baer, D. M., Peterson, R. F., & Sherman, J. A. (1967). The development of imitation by reinforcing behavioral similarity to a model. *Journal of the Experimental Analysis of Behavior, 10*, 405–416.

Baer, D. M., & Sherman, J. A. (1964). Reinforcement control of generalized imitation in young children. *Journal of Experimental Child Psychology, 1*, 37–49.

Baker, T. B., & Cannon, D. S. (1979). Taste aversion therapy with alcoholics: Techniques and evidence of a conditioned response. *Behaviour Research and Therapy, 17*, 229–242.

Balda, R. P., & Kamil, A. C. (2006). Linking life zones, life history traits, ecology, and spatial cognition in four allopatric southwestern seed caching corvids. In M. F. Brown & R. G. Cook (Eds.), *Animal spatial cognition: Comparative, neural, and computational approaches*. Retrieved from http://www.pigeon.psy.tufts.edu/asc/balda/

Balderston, J. L. (1924). *A morality play for the leisured class*. New York, NY: Appleton.

Baldwin, J. D., & Baldwin, J. I. (1998). *Behavior principles in everyday life* (3rd ed.). Upper Saddle River, NJ: Prentice-Hall.

Bandura, A. (1965). Influence of models' reinforcement contingencies on the acquisition of imitative response. *Journal of Personality and Social Psychology, 1*, 589–595.

Bandura, A. (1973). *Aggression: A social learning analysis*. Englewood Cliffs, NJ: Prentice-Hall.

Bandura, A. (1975). Effecting change through participant modeling. In J. D. Krumboltz & C. E. Thoresen (Eds.), *Counseling methods*. New York, NY: Holt, Rinehart & Winston.

Bandura, A. (1976). Self-reinforcement: Theoretical and methodological considerations. *Behaviorism, 4*, 135–155.

Bandura, A. (1977). *Social learning theory*. Englewood Cliffs, NJ: Prentice-Hall.

Bandura, A. (1986). *Social foundations of thought and action: A social cognitive theory*. Upper Saddle River, NJ: Prentice-Hall.

Bandura, A. (1997). *Self-efficacy: The exercise of self-control.* New York, NY: W. H. Freeman.

Bandura, A., Blanchard, E. B., & Ritter, B. (1969). The relative efficacy of desensitization and modeling approaches for inducing behavioral, affective, and attitudinal changes. *Journal of Personality and Social Psychology, 13*, 173–199.

Bandura, A., & McDonald, F. J. (1994). Influence of social reinforcement and the behavior of models in shaping children's moral judgments. In B. Puka (Ed.),

Defining perspectives in moral development. Moral development: A compendium (Vol. 1). New York, NY: Garland.

Bandura, A., Ross, D., & Ross, S. A. (1961). Transmission of aggression through imitation of aggressive models. *Journal of Abnormal and Social Psychology*, *63*, 575–582.

Bandura, A., Ross, D., & Ross, S. A. (1963). Imitation of film-mediated aggressive models. *Journal of Abnormal and Social Psychology*, *66*, 3–11.

Bard, K. A., Todd, B. K., Bernier, C., Love, J., & Leavens, D. A. (2006). Self-awareness in human and chimpanzee infants: What is measured and what is meant by the mark and mirror test? *Infancy*, *9*, 191–219.

Barlow, D. H. (1988). *Anxiety and its disorders: The nature and treatment of anxiety and panic*. New York, NY: Guilford.

Baron-Cohen, S., Tager-Flusberg, H., & Cohen, D. (Eds.). (2000). *Understanding other minds: Perspectives from developmental cognitive neuroscience*. Oxford, England: Oxford University Press.

Barrett, B. (1931). *The strength of will and how to develop it*. New York, NY: R. R. Smith.

Bartlett, T. (2014, June 2). The search for psychology's lost boy. *Chronicle of Higher Education*. Retrieved from http://chronicle.com/article/The-Search-for-Psychologys/146747/

Baum, W. M. (1974). On two types of deviation from the matching law: Bias and undermatching. *Journal of the Experimental Analysis of Behavior*, *22*, 231–242.

Baum, W. M. (1979). Matching, undermatching, and overmatching in studies of choice. *Journal of the Experimental Analysis of Behavior*, *32*, 269–281.

Baumeister, R. F., Bratslavsky, E., Muraven, M., & Tice, D. M. (1998). Ego depletion: Is the active self a limited resource? *Journal of Personality and Social Psychology*, *74*, 1252–1265.

Beck, H. P., Levinson, S., & Irons, G. (2009). Finding Little Albert: A journey to John B. Watson's infant laboratory. *American Psychologist*, *64*, 605–614.

Begun, D. R. (1999). Hominid family values: Morphological and molecular data on relations among the great apes and humans. In S. T. Parker, R. W. Mitchell, & H. L. Miles (Eds.), *The mentalities of gorillas and orangutans: Comparative perspectives*. Cambridge, UK: Cambridge University Press.

Beneke, W. M., Schulte, S. E., & Vander Tuig, J. G. (1995). An analysis of excessive running in the development of activity anorexia. *Physiology and Behavior*, *58*, 451–457.

Beneke, W. M., & Vander Tuig, J. G. (1996). Effects of dietary protein and food restriction on voluntary running of rats living in activity wheels. In W. F. Epling & W. D. Pierce (Eds.), *Activity anorexia: Theory, research, and treatment*. Mahwah, NJ: Erlbaum.

Benjamin L. T., Jr., Whitaker, J. L., Ramsey, R. M., & Zeve, D. R. (2007). John B. Watson's alleged sex research: An appraisal of the evidence. *American Psychologist*, *62*, 131–139.

Bennett, R. H., & Samson, H. H. (1991). Ethanol-related cues and behavioral tolerance to ethanol in humans. *Psychological Record*, *41*, 429–437.

Benson, J., Greaves, W., O'Donnell, M., & Taglialatela, J. (2002). Evidence for symbolic language processing in a Bonobo (*Pan paniscus*). *Journal of Consciousness Studies*, *9*, 33–56.

Bentall, R. P., Lowe, C. F., & Beasty, A. (1985). The role of verbal behavior in human learning: II. Developmental differences. *Journal of the Experimental Analysis of Behavior*, *43*, 165–180.

Bernstein, I. L. (1991). Aversion conditioning in response to cancer and cancer treatment. *Clinical Psychology Review*, *11*, 185–191.

Billet, E. A., Richter, M. A., & Kennedy, J. L. (1998). Genetics of obsessive-compulsive disorder. In R. P. Swinson, M. M. Antony, S. Rachman, & M. A. Richter (Eds.), *Obsessive-compulsive disorder: Theory, research, and treatment*. New York, NY: Guilford.

Binder, C. (1996). Behavioral fluency: Evolution of a new paradigm. *The Behavior Analyst*, *19*, 163–197.

Bjork, D. W. (1993). *B. F. Skinner: A life*. New York, NY: Basic Books.

Blandin, Y., Lhuisset, L., & Proteau, L. (1999). Cognitive processes underlying observational learning of motor skills. *Quarterly Journal of Experimental Psychology: Human Experimental Psychology*, *52A*, 957–979.

Boer, D. P. (1990). Determinants of excessive running in activity-anorexia. *Dissertation Abstracts International*, *50*(11-B), 5351.

Boer, D. P., Epling, W. F., Pierce, W. D., & Russell, J. C. (1990). Suppression of food deprivation-induced high-rate wheel running in rats. *Physiology and Behavior*, *48*, 339–342.

Boesch, C. (1991). Teaching among wild chimpanzees. *Animal Behaviour*, *41*, 530–532.

Boesch, C., & Boesch, H. (1990). Tool use and tool making in wild chimpanzees. *Folia Primatologica*, *54*, 86–99.

Boesch, C., & Boesch-Achermann, H. (2000). *The chimpanzees of the Taï Forest: Behavioural ecology and evolution*. Oxford, England: Oxford University Press.

Boice, R. (1989). Procrastination, business and bingeing. *Behaviour Research and Therapy*, *27*, 605–611.

Boice, R. (1996). *Procrastination and blocking: A novel, practical approach*. Westport, CT: Praeger.

Bolles, R. C. (1970). Species-specific defense reactions and avoidance learning. *Psychological Review*, *77*, 32–48.

Bolles, R. C. (1979). *Learning theory* (2nd ed.). New York, NY: Holt, Rinehart & Winston.

Bootzin, R. R., Epstein, D., & Wood, J. M. (1991). Stimulus control instructions. In P. J. Hauri (Ed.), *Case studies in insomnia*. New York, NY: Plenum Press.

Bouvier, K. A., & Powell, R. A. (2008, June). *A driven versus balanced approach to studying: The importance of rest and recuperation in academic performance*. Poster presented at the Annual Convention of the Canadian Psychological Association, Halifax, Nova Scotia.

Bovbjerg, D. H., Redd, W. H., Maier, L. A., Holland, J. C., Lesko L. M., Niedzwiecki, ... Hakes, T. B. (1990). Anticipatory immune suppression and nausea in women receiving cyclic chemotherapy for ovarian cancer. *Journal of Consulting and Clinical Psychology*, *58*, 153–157.

Braun, B. G. (1980). Hypnosis for multiple personalities. In H. J. Wain (Ed.), *Clinical hypnosis in medicine*. Chicago, IL: Yearbook Medical.

Breland, K., & Breland, M. (1961). The misbehavior of organisms. *American Psychologist*, *16*, 681–684.

Brethower, D. M., & Reynolds, G. S. (1962). A facilitative effect of punishment on unpunished responding. *Journal of the Experimental Analysis of Behavior*, *5*, 191–199.

Brigham, T. A. (1978). Self-control. In A. C. Catania & T. A. Brigham (Eds.), *Handbook of applied behavior analysis*. New York, NY: Irvington.

Broberg, D. J., & Bernstein, I. L. (1987). Candy as a scapegoat in the prevention of food aversions in children receiving chemotherapy. *Cancer*, *60*, 2344–2347.

Brodbeck, D. R., & Shettleworth, S. J. (1995). Matching location and color of a compound stimulus: Comparison of a food-storing and a non-storing bird species. *Journal of Experimental Psychology: Animal Behavior Processes*, *21*, 64–77.

Brogden, W. J. (1939). Sensory pre-conditioning. *Journal of Experimental Psychology*, *25*, 323–332.

Brown, P. L., & Jenkins, H. M. (1968). Autoshaping of the pigeon's key-peck. *Journal of the Experimental Analysis of Behavior*, *11*, 1–8.

Brown, S. A., Stetson, B. A., & Beatty, P. A. (1989). Cognitive and behavioral features of adolescent coping in high-risk drinking situations. *Addictive Behaviors*, *14*, 43–52.

Bruch, H. (1978). *The golden cage: The enigma of anorexia nervosa*. Cambridge, MA: Harvard University Press.

Buckley, K. W. (1989). *Mechanical man: John Broadus Watson and the beginnings of behaviorism*. New York, NY: Guilford.

Bullock, D. H., & Smith, W. C. (1953). An effect of repeated conditioning-extinction upon operant strength. *Journal of Experimental Psychology*, *46*, 349–352.

Burns, M., & Domjan, M. (1996). Sign tracking versus goal tracking in the sexual conditioning of male Japanese quail *(Coturnix japonica)*. *Journal of Experimental Psychology: Animal Behavior Processes*, *22*, 297–306.

Bushman, B. J., & Anderson, C. A. (2001). Media violence and the American public: Scientific facts versus media misinformation. *American Psychologist*, *56*, 477–489.

Buske-Kirschbaum, A., Kirschbaum, C., Stierle, H., Jabaij, L., & Hellhammer, D. (1994). Conditioned manipulation of natural killer (NK) cells in humans using a discriminative learning protocol. *Biological Psychology*, *38*, 143–155.

Bussey, K., & Bandura, A. (1984). Influence of gender constancy and social power on sex-linked modeling. *Journal of Personality and Social Psychology*, *47*, 1292–1302.

Byrne, D., & Clore, G. L. (1970). A reinforcement model of evaluative responses. *Personality: An International Journal*, *1*, 103–128.

Call, J. (1999). Levels of imitation and cognitive mechanisms in orangutans. In S. T. Parker, R. W. Mitchell, & H. L. Miles (Eds.), *The mentalities of gorillas and orangutans: Comparative perspectives*. Cambridge, UK: Cambridge University Press.

Call, J., & Tomasello, M. (1995). The use of social information in the problem-solving of orangutans *(Pongo pygmaeus)* and human children *(Homo sapiens)*. *Journal of Comparative Psychology*, *109*, 308–320.

Cameron, J. (2001). Negative effects of reward on intrinsic motivation—A limited phenomenon: Comment on Deci, Koestner, and Ryan (2001). *Review of Educational Research*, *71*, 29–42.

Cameron, J., & Pierce, W. D. (1994). Reinforcement, reward, and intrinsic motivation: A meta-analysis. *Review of Educational Research*, *64*, 363–423.

Cameron, J., & Pierce, W. D. (2002). *Rewards and intrinsic motivation: Resolving the controversy*. Westport, CT: Bergin & Garvey.

Cameron, J., Pierce, W. D., Banko, K. M., & Gear, M. (2005). Achievement-based rewards and intrinsic motivation: A test for cognitive mediators. *Journal of Educational Psychology*, *97*, 641–655.

Capaldi, E. D. (1996). Conditioned food preferences. In E. D. Capaldi (Ed.), *Why we eat what we eat: The psychology of eating*. Washington, DC: American Psychological Association.

Capaldi, E. J. (1966). Partial reinforcement: A hypothesis of sequential effects. *Psychological Review*, *73*, 459–477.

Capaldi, E. J., Miller, D. J., & Alptekin, S. (1989). Multiple-food-unit-incentive effect: Nonconservation of weight of food reward by rats. *Journal of Experimental Psychology: Animal Behavior Processes*, *15*, 75–80.

Carroll, W. R., & Bandura, A. (1987). Translating cognition into action: The role of visual guidance in observational learning. *Journal of Motor Behavior*, *19*, 385–398.

Casey, R., & Rozin, P. (1989). Changing children's food preferences: Parent opinions. *Appetite*, *12*, 171–182.

Catania, A. C. (1975). The myth of self-reinforcement. *Behaviorism*, *3*, 192–199.

Chambers, K. C., Yuan, D., Brownson, E. A., & Wang, Y. (1997). Sexual dimorphisms in conditioned taste aversions: Mechanism and function. In M. E. Bouton & M. S. Fanselow (Eds.), *Learning, motivation, and cognition: The functional behaviorism of Robert C. Bolles*. Washington, DC: American Psychological Association.

Chamorro-Premuzic, T., Swami, V., Terrado, A., & Furnham, A. (2009). The effects of background auditory interference and extraversion on creative and cognitive task performance. *International Journal of Psychological Studies*, *1*, 2–9.

Chappell, J., & Kacelnik, A. (2002). Tool selectivity in a non-mammal, the New Caledonian crow (*Corvus moneduloides*). *Animal Cognition*, *5*, 71–78.

Cherek, D. R. (1982). Schedule-induced cigarette self-administration. *Pharmacology, Biochemistry, and Behavior*, *17*, 523–527.

Chesler, P. (1969). Maternal influence in learning by observation in kittens. *Science*, *166*, 901–903.

Chomsky, N. (1959). Review of B. F. Skinner's *Verbal Behavior*. *Language*, *35*, 26–58.

Chomsky, N. (1988). *Language and problems of knowledge*. Cambridge, MA: MIT Press.

Church, J., & Williams, H. (2001). Another sniffer dog for the clinic? *Lancet*, *358*, 930.

Cialdini, R. B. (1993). *Influence: Science and practice* (3rd ed.). New York, NY: HarperCollins.

Clark, H. B., Rowbury, T., Baer, A. M., & Baer, D. M. (1973). Timeout as a punishing stimulus in continuous and intermittent schedules. *Journal of Applied Behavior Analysis*, *6*, 443–455.

Clark, L. A., Watson, D., & Mineka, S. (1994). Temperament, personality, and the mood and anxiety disorders. *Journal of Abnormal Psychology*, *103*, 103–116.

Clayton, N. S. (2001). Hippocampal growth and maintenance depend on food-caching experience in juvenile mountain chickadees. *Behavioral Neuroscience*, *115*, 614–625.

Colvin, G. (2008). *Talent is overrated: What really separates world-class performers from everybody else*. New York, NY: Penguin.

Conger, R., & Killeen, P. (1974). Use of concurrent operants in small group research. *Pacific Sociological Review*, *17*, 399–416.

Cook, M., & Mineka, S. (1989). Observational conditioning of fear to fear-relevant versus fear-irrelevant stimuli in rhesus monkeys. *Journal of Abnormal Psychology*, *98*, 448–459.

Coombs, D. (Producer). (2013, April 2). *Dr. Watson, I presume* [Radio broadcast]. London, England: BBC Radio 4.

Coon, D. (1998). *Introduction to psychology: Exploration and application* (8th ed.). Pacific Grove, CA: Brooks/Cole.

Coon, D. J. (1994). "Not a creature of reason": The alleged impact of Watsonian behaviorism on advertising in the 1920s. In J. T. Todd & E. K. Morris (Eds.), *Modern perspectives on John B. Watson and classical behaviorism*. Westport, CT: Greenwood Press.

Coren, S. (1994). *The intelligence of dogs: A guide to the thoughts, emotions, and inner lives of our canine companions*. New York, NY: Free Press.

Craig, G. J., Kermis, M. D., & Digdon, N. L. (1998). *Children today* (Canadian ed.). Scarborough, Canada: Prentice-Hall.

Crespi, L. P. (1942). Quantitative variation of incentive and performance in the white rat. *American Journal of Psychology*, *55*, 467–517.

Critchfield, T. S., & Kollins, S. H. (2001). Temporal discounting: Basic research and the analysis of socially important behavior. *Journal of Applied Behavior Analysis*, *34*, 101–122.

Currey, M. (2013). *Daily rituals: How artists work*. New York, NY: Alfred A. Knopf.

Danaher, B. G. (1977). Rapid smoking and self-control in the modification of smoking behavior. *Journal of Consulting and Clinical Psychology*, *45*, 1068–1075.

Darwin, C. R. (1859). *On the origin of species by means of natural selection*. London, England: Murray.

Davey, G. C. L. (1992). Classical conditioning and the acquisition of human fears and phobias: A review and synthesis of the literature. *Advances in Behaviour Research & Therapy*, *14*, 29–66.

Davey, G. C. L., de Jong, P., & Tallis, F. (1993). UCS inflation in the aetiology of a variety of anxiety disorders: Some case histories. *Behaviour Research and Therapy*, *31*, 495–498.

Davis, C., Katzman, D. K., & Kirsh, C. (1999). Compulsive physical activity in adolescents with anorexia nervosa: A psychobehavioral spiral of pathology. *Journal of Nervous and Mental Disease*, *187*, 336–342.

de Waal, F. (2005). *Our inner ape: A leading primatologist explains why we are who we are*. New York, NY: Penguin.

de Waal, F. B. M. (1986). Deception in the natural communication of chimpanzees. In R. Mitchell & N. Thompson (Eds.), *Deception: Perspectives on human and nonhuman deceit*. New York, NY: SUNY Press.

de Waal, F. B. M. (2008). Putting the altruism back into altruism: The evolution of empathy. *Annual Review of Psychology*, *59*, 279–300.

DeAngelis, T. (2010, January). Little Albert regains his identity. *Monitor on Psychology*, *41*(1), 10–11.

Deci, E. L., Koestner, R., & Ryan, R. M. (2001a). Extrinsic rewards and intrinsic motivation: Reconsidered once again. *Review of Educational Research*, *71*, 1–27.

Deci, E. L., Koestner, R., & Ryan, R. M. (2001b). The pervasive negative effects of rewards on intrinsic motivation: Response to Cameron (2001). *Review of Educational Research*, *71*, 43–51.

Deci, E. L., & Ryan, R. M. (1985). *Intrinsic motivation and self-determination in human behavior*. New York, NY: Plenum Press.

Delk, J. L. (1980). High-risk sports as indirect self-destructive behavior. In N. L. Farberow (Ed.), *The many faces of suicide: Indirect self-destructive behavior*. New York, NY: McGraw-Hill.

DeNeys, W. (2006). Developmental trends in decision making: The case of the Monty Hall dilemma. In J. A. Ellsworth (Ed.), *Psychology of decision making in education*. Haupauge, NY: Nova Science Publishers.

Digdon, N., Powell, R. A., & Harris, B. (2014). Little Albert's alleged neurological impairment: Watson, Rayner, and historical revision. *History of Psychology*, *17*, 312–334.

Dingfelder, S. F. (2010, November). A second chance for the Mexican wolf. *Monitor on Psychology*, *41*(10), 20–21.

Dinsmoor, J. A. (1954). Punishment: I. The avoidance hypothesis. *Psychological Review*, *61*, 34–46.

Dollard, J., & Miller, N. E. (1950). *Personality and psychotherapy: An analysis in terms of learning, thinking and culture*. New York, NY: McGraw-Hill.

Domjan, M. (2000). *The essentials of conditioning and learning* (2nd ed.). Belmont, CA: Wadsworth.

Domjan, M. (2015). *The principles of learning and behavior* (7th ed.). Belmont, CA: Wadsworth Cengage Learning.

Dowling, J. E. (1984). Modeling effectiveness as a function of learner-model similarity and the learner's attitude toward women. *Dissertation Abstracts International*, *45* (1-A), 121.

Doyle, T. F., & Samson, H. H. (1988). Adjunctive alcohol drinking in humans. *Physiology and Behavior*, *44*, 775–779.

Drea, C. M., & Carter, A. N. (2009). Cooperative problem solving in a social carnivore. *Animal Behavior*, *78*, 967–977.

Dunlosky, J., Rawson, K. A., Marsh, E. J., Nathan, M. J., & Willingham, D. T. (2013). Improving students' learning with effective learning techniques: Promising directions from cognitive and educational psychology. *Psychological Science*, *14*, 4–58.

Durand, V. M. (1990). *Severe behavior problems: A functional communication training approach*. New York, NY: Guilford.

Dweck, C. S., & Reppucci, N. D. (1973). Learned helplessness and reinforcement responsibility in children. *Journal of Personality & Social Psychology*, *25*, 109–116.

Ehrensaft, M. K., Cohen, P., Brown, J., Smailes, E., Chen, H., & Johnson, J. G. (2003). Intergenerational transmission of partner violence: A 20-year prospective study. *Journal of Consulting and Clinical Psychology*, *71*, 741–753.

Eikelboom, R., & Stewart, J. (1982). Conditioning of drug-induced physiological responses. *Psychological Review*, *89*, 507–528.

Eisenberg, N., McCreath, H., & Ahn, R. (1988). Vicarious emotional responsiveness and prosocial behavior: Their interrelations in young children. *Personality and Social Psychology Bulletin*, *14*, 298–311.

Eisenberger, R. (1992). Learned industriousness. *Psychological Review*, *99*, 248–267.

Eisenberger, R., Carlson, J., Guile, M., & Shapiro, N. (1979). Transfer of effort across behaviors. *Learning and Motivation*, *10*, 178–197.

Eisenberger, R., Masterson, F. A., & McDermitt, M. (1982). Effects of task variety on generalized effort. *Journal of Educational Psychology*, *74*, 499–505.

Eisenstein, E. M., Eisenstein, D., & Smith, J. C. (2001). The evolutionary significance of habituation and sensitization across phylogeny: A behavioral homeostasis model. *Integrative Physiological and Behavioral Science*, *36*, 251–265.

Ellis, N. R. (1962). Amount of reward and operant behavior in mental defectives. *American Journal of Mental Deficiency*, *66*, 595–599.

Epling, W. F., & Pierce, W. D. (1988). Activity-based anorexia: A biobehavioral perspective. *International Journal of Eating Disorders*, 7, 475–485.

Epling, W. F., & Pierce, W. D. (1991). *Solving the anorexia puzzle: A scientific approach*. Toronto, Canada: Hogrefe & Huber.

Epling, W. F., & Pierce, W. D. (1996). An overview of activity anorexia. In W. F. Epling & W. D. Pierce (Eds.), *Activity anorexia: Theory, research, and treatment*. Mahwah, NJ: Erlbaum.

Epstein, R. (1985). Extinction-induced resurgence: Preliminary investigations and possible applications. *Psychological Record*, *35*, 143–153.

Epstein, R. (1997). Skinner as self-manager. *Journal of Applied Behavior Analysis*, *30*, 545–568.

Epstein, R., Lanza, R. P., & Skinner, B. F. (1981). "Self-awareness" in the pigeon. *Science*, *212*, 695–696.

Epstein, S. M. (1967). Toward a unified theory of anxiety. In B. A. Maher (Ed.), *Progress in experimental personality research* (Vol. 4). New York, NY: Academic Press.

Ericsson, K. A. (Ed.). (2009). *Development of professional expertise: Toward measurement of expert performance and design of optimal learning environments*. New York, NY: Cambridge University Press.

Ericsson, K. A., & Charness, N. (1994). Expert performance: Its structure and acquisition. *American Psychologist*, *49*, 725–747.

Ericsson, K. A., Krampe, R. T., & Tesch-Römer, C. (1993). The role of deliberate practice in the acquisition of expert performance. *Psychological Review*, *100*, 363–406.

Eron, L. D., Huesmann, L. R., Lefkowitz, M. M., & Walder, L. O. (1972). Does television violence cause aggression? *American Psychologist*, *27*, 253–263.

Estes, W. K., & Skinner, B. F. (1941). Some quantitative properties of anxiety. *Journal of Experimental Psychology*, *29*, 390–400.

Etscorn, F., & Stephens, R. (1973). Establishment of conditioned taste aversions with a 24-hour CS-US interval. *Physiological Psychology*, *1*, 251–259.

Exton, M. S., von Auer, A. K., Buske-Kirschbaum, A., Stockhorst, U., Gobel, U., & Schedlowski, M. (2000). Pavlovian conditioning of immune function: Animal investigation and the challenge of human application. *Behavioural Brain Research*, *110*, 129–141.

Eysenck, H. J. (1957). *The dynamics of anxiety and hysteria: An experimental application of modern learning theory to psychiatry*. London, England: Routledge & Kegan Paul.

Eysenck, H. J. (1967). *The biological basis of personality*. Springfield, IL: Charles C. Thomas.

Eysenck, H. J. (1968). A theory of the incubation of anxiety/fear response. *Behaviour Research and Therapy*, *6*, 63–65.

Eysenck, H. J. (1976). The learning theory model of neurosis—A new approach. *Behaviour Research and Therapy*, *14*, 251–267.

Falk, J. L. (1961). Production of polydipsia in normal rats by an intermittent food schedule. *Science*, *133*, 195–196.

Falk, J. L. (1971). The nature and determinants of adjunctive behavior. *Physiology and Behavior*, *6*, 577–588.

Falk, J. L. (1977). The origin and functions of adjunctive behavior. *Animal Learning and Behavior*, *5*, 325–335.

Falk, J. L. (1993). Schedule-induced drug self-administration. In F. van Haaren (Ed.), *Methods in behavioral pharmacology*. Amsterdam, Holland: Elsevier.

Falk, J. L. (1994). Schedule-induced behavior occurs in humans: A reply to Overskeid. *Psychological Record*, *44*, 45–62.

Falk, J. L. (1998). Drug abuse as an adjunctive behavior. *Drug and Alcohol Dependence*, *52*, 91–98.

Farroni, T., Johnson, M. H., Brockbank, M., & Simion, F. (2000). Infants' use of gaze direction to cue attention: The importance of perceived motion. *Visual Cognition*, 7, 705–718.

Federal Trade Commission. (2000). *Marketing violent entertainment to children: A review of self-regulation and industry practices in the motion picture, music recording, and electronic game industries*. Washington, DC: Author.

Feigenson, L., & Carey, S. (2003). Tracking individuals via object-files: Evidence from infants' manual search. *Developmental Science*, *6*, 568–584.

Ferster, C. B., & Skinner, B. F. (1957). *Schedules of reinforcement*. New York, NY: Appleton-Century-Crofts.

Finn, J. K., Tregenza, T., & Norman, M. D. (2009). Defensive tool use in a coconut-carrying octopus. *Current Biology*, *19*, R1069–R1070.

Fitch, W. T. (2005). The evolution of language: A comparative review. *Biology and Philosophy*, *20*, 193–230.

Flory, R. K., & Ellis, B. B. (1973). Schedule-induced aggression against a slide-image target. *Bulletin of the Psychonomic Society*, *2*, 287–290.

Foa, E. B., Franklin, M. E., & Kozak, M. J. (1998). Psychosocial treatments for obsessive-compulsive disorder: Literature review. In R. P. Swinson, M. M. Antony, S. Rachman, & M. A. Richter (Eds.), *Obsessive-compulsive disorder: Theory, research, and treatment*. New York, NY: Guilford.

Foa, E. B., Zinbarg, R., & Rothbaum, B. O. (1992). Uncontrollability and unpredictability in post-traumatic stress disorder: An animal model. *Psychological Bulletin*, *112*, 218–238.

Fouts, G. R., & Click, M. (1979). Effects of live and TV models on observational learning in introverted and extroverted children. *Perceptual and Motor Skills*, *48*, 863–867.

Fouts, R. S. (1973). Acquisition and testing of gestural signs in four young chimpanzees. *Science*, *180*, 978–980.

Fox, L. (1962). Effecting the use of efficient study habits. *Journal of Mathematics*, *1*, 75–86.

Fragaszy, D., Izar, P., Visalberghi, E., Ottoni, E. B., & De Oliveira, M. G. (2004). Wild capuchin monkeys (*Cebus libidinosus*) use anvils and stone pounding tools. *American Journal of Primatology*, *64*, 359–366.

Franks, C. M. (1963). Behavior therapy, the principles of conditioning and the treatment of the alcoholic. *Quarterly Journal of Studies on Alcohol*, *24*, 511–529.

Freud, S. (1955). Lines of advance in psychoanalytic therapy. In J. Strachey (Ed. and Trans.), *The standard edition of the complete psychological works of Sigmund Freud* (Vol. 17). London, England: Hogarth Press. (Original work published 1919)

Fridlund, A. J., Beck, H. P., Goldie, W. D., & Irons, G. (2012). Little Albert: A neurologically impaired child. *History of Psychology*, *15*, 302–327.

Furomoto, L. (1971). Extinction in the pigeon after continuous reinforcement: Effects of number of reinforced responses. *Psychological Reports*, *28*, 331–338.

Gailliot, M. T., Baumeister, R. F., DeWall, C. N., Maner, J. K., Plant, E. A., Tice, D. M., & Brewer, L. E. (2007). Self-control relies on glucose as a limited energy source: Willpower is more than a metaphor. *Journal of Personality and Social Psychology*, *92*, 2007.

Galef, B. G., Jr. (1988). Imitation in animals: History, definition and interpretation of data from the psychological laboratory. In T. R. Zentall & B. G. Galef, Jr. (Eds.), *Social learning: Psychological and biological perspectives*. Hillsdale, NJ: Erlbaum.

Gallup, G. G., Jr. (1970). Chimpanzees: Self-recognition. *Science*, *167*, 86–87.

Gandhi, M. K. (1957). *An autobiography: The story of my experiments with truth*. Boston, MA: Beacon Press. (Original work published 1927)

Garcia, J. (1981). Tilting at the paper mills of academe. *American Psychologist*, *36*, 149–158.

Garcia, J., & Koelling, R. A. (1966). Relation of cue to consequence in avoidance learning. *Psychonomic Science*, *4*, 123–124.

Gardner, H. (1993). *Multiple intelligences: The theory in practice*. New York, NY: Basic Books.

Gardner, R. A., & Gardner, B. T. (1969). Teaching sign language to a chimpanzee. *Science*, *165*, 664–672.

Gardner, R. A., & Gardner, B. T. (1975). Evidence for sentence constituents in the early utterances of child and chimpanzee. *Journal of Experimental Psychology: General*, *104*, 244–267.

Gardner, R. A., Gardner, B. T., & Van Cantfort, T. E. (1989). *Teaching sign language to chimpanzees*. New York, NY: State University of New York Press.

Garner, D. M., & Garfinkel, P. E. (1980). Socio-cultural factors in the development of anorexia nervosa. *Psychological Medicine*, *10*, 647–656.

Gay, P. (1988). *Freud: A life for our time*. New York, NY: Norton.

Gist, R., & Devilly, G. J. (2010). Early intervention in the aftermath of trauma. In G. M. Rosen & B. C. Frueh (Eds.), *Clinician's guide to posttraumatic stress disorder*. Hoboken, NJ: Wiley & Sons.

Gleaves, D. H. (1996). The sociocognitive model of dissociative identity disorder: A reexamination of the evidence. *Psychological Bulletin*, *120*, 42–59.

Gold, S. R., Fultz, J., Burke, C. H., & Prisco, A. G. (1992). Vicarious emotional responses of macho college males. *Journal of Interpersonal Violence*, *7*, 165–174.

Gollwitzer, P. M. (1999). Implementation intentions: Strong effects of simple plans. *American Psychologist*, *54*, 493–503.

Gollwitzer, P. M., & Brandstätter, V. (1997). Implementation intentions and effective goal pursuit. *Journal of Personality and Social Psychology*, *73*, 186–199.

Goodall, J. (1990). *Through a window: My thirty years with the chimpanzees of Gombe*. Boston, MA: Houghton Mifflin.

Goodwin, C. J. (2005). *A history of modern psychology* (2nd ed.). Hoboken, NJ: Wiley.

Gottman, J. (1994). *Why marriages succeed or fail: And how you can make yours last*. New York, NY: Simon & Schuster.

Green, L., Fisher, E. B., Perlow, S., & Sherman, L. (1981). Preference reversal and self-control: Choice as a function of reward amount and delay. *Behaviour Analysis Letters*, *1*, 43–51.

Grice, G. R. (1948). The relation of secondary reinforcement to delayed reward in visual discrimination learning. *Journal of Experimental Psychology*, *38*, 1–16.

Griggs, R. A. (2015). Psychology's lost boy: Will the real Little Albert please stand up? *Teaching of Psychology*, *42*, 14–18.

Grosskurth, P. (1991). *The secret ring: Freud's inner circle and the politics of psychoanalysis*. London, England: Jonathan Cape.

Gubernick, D. J., & Alberts, J. R. (1984). A specialization of taste aversion learning during suckling and its weaning-associated transformation. *Developmental Psychobiology*, *17*, 613–628.

Guerra, L. G. G. C., & Silva, M. T. A. (2010). Learning processes and the neural analysis of conditioning. *Psychology & Neuroscience*, *3*, 195–208.

Guevremont, D. C., Osnes, P. G., & Stokes, T. F. (1986). Preparation for effective self-regulation: The development of generalized verbal control. *Journal of Applied Behavior Analysis*, *19*, 99–104.

Guisinger, S. (2003). Adapted to flee famine: Adding an evolutionary perspective on anorexia nervosa. *Psychological Review*, *110*, 745–761.

Gustavson, C. R., Garcia, J., Hankins, W. G., & Rusiniak, K. W. (1974). Coyote predation control by aversive conditioning. *Science*, *184*, 581–583.

Guthrie, E. R. (1952). *The psychology of learning* (Rev. ed.). New York, NY: Harper & Row. (Original work published 1935)

Haggbloom, S. J., Warnick, R., Warnick, J. E., Jones, V. K., Yarbrough, G. L., Russell, T. M., … Monte, E. (2002). The 100 most eminent psychologists of the 20th century. *Review of General Psychology*, *6*, 139–152.

Hagopian, L. P., Fisher, W. W., & Legacy, S. M. (1994). Schedule effects of noncontingent reinforcement on attention-maintained destructive behavior in identical quadruplets. *Journal of Applied Behavior Analysis*, *27*, 317–325.

Hall, G. C. N., Shondrick, D. D., & Hirschman, R. (1993). Conceptually derived treatments for sexual aggressors. *Professional Psychology: Research and Practice*, *24*, 62–69.

Hall, K. R. L., & Schaller, G. B. (1964). Tool-using behavior of the California sea otter. *Journal of Mammology*, *45*, 287–298.

Hanson, H. M. (1959). Effects of discrimination training on stimulus generalization. *Journal of Experimental Psychology*, *58*, 321–334.

Harackiewicz, J. M., Manderlink, G., & Sansone, C. (1984). Rewarding pinball wizardry: Effects of evaluation and cue value on intrinsic interest. *Journal of Personality and Social Psychology*, *47*, 287–300.

Hare, B., Call, J., & Tomasello, M. (2001). Do chimpanzees know what conspecifics know? *Animal Behaviour*, *61*, 139–151.

Hare, B., Melis, A. P., Woods, V., Hastings, S., & Wrangham, R. (2007). Tolerance allows bonobos to outperform chimpanzees on a cooperative task. *Current Biology*, *17*, 619–623.

Harlow, H. F., Harlow, M. K., & Meyer, D. R. (1950). Learning motivated by a manipulative drive. *Journal of Experimental Psychology*, *40*, 228–234.

Harris, B. (1979). Whatever happened to little Albert? *American Psychologist*, *34*, 151–160.

Harris, B. (2011). Letting go of Little Albert: Disciplinary memory, history, and the uses of myth. *Journal of the History of the Behavioral Sciences*, *47*, 1–17.

Haupt, E. J., Van Kirk, M. J., & Terraciano, T. (1975). An inexpensive fading procedure to decrease errors and increase retention of number facts. In E. Ramp & G. Semb (Eds.), *Behavior analysis: Areas of research and application*. Englewood Cliffs, NJ: Prentice-Hall.

Hawkins, R. D., Bailey, C. H., & Kandel, E. R. (2010). The neuronal circuit for simple forms of learning in Aplysia. In G. M. Shepherd & S. Grillner (Eds.), *Handbook of brain microcircuits*. New York, NY: Oxford University Press.

Hayes, K. J., & Hayes, C. (1951). The intellectual development of a home-raised chimpanzee. *Proceedings of the American Philosophical Society*, *95*, 105–109.

Hayes, S. C., Rosenfarb, I., Wulfert, E., Munt, E. D., Korn, Z., & Zettle, R. D. (1985). Self-reinforcement effects: An artifact of social standard setting? *Journal of Applied Behavior Analysis*, *18*, 201–214.

Hayes, S. C., Strosahl, K. D., & Wilson, K. G. (1999). *Acceptance and commitment therapy: An experiential approach to behavior change*. New York, NY: Guilford Press.

Heffernan, T., & Richards, C. S. (1981). Self-control of study behavior: Identification and evaluation of natural methods. *Journal of Counseling Psychology, 28*, 361–364.

Herbranson, W. T., & Schroeder, J. (2010). Are birds smarter than mathematicians? Pigeons (*Columba livia*) perform optimally on a version of the Monty Hall dilemma. *Journal of Comparative Psychology, 124*, 1–13.

Hergenhahn, B. R. (2009). *An introduction to theories of learning* (8th ed.). Englewood Cliffs, NJ: Prentice-Hall.

Herman, L. M., & Forestell, P. H. (1985). Reporting presence or absence of named objects by a language-trained dolphin. *Neuroscience and Biobehavioral Reviews, 9*, 667–681.

Herman, L. M., Kuczaj, S. A., & Holder, M. D. (1993). Responses to anomalous gestural sequences by a language-trained dolphin: Evidence for processing of semantic relations and syntactic information. *Journal of Experimental Psychology: General, 122*, 184 –194.

Herman, L. M., Morrel-Samuels, P., & Pack, A. A. (1990). Bottlenosed dolphin and human recognition of veridical and degraded video displays of an artificial gestural language. *Journal of Experimental Psychology: General, 119*, 215–230.

Herman, L. M., Pack, A. A., & Morrel-Samuels, P. (1993). Representational and conceptual skills of dolphins. In H. L. Roitblat, L. M. Herman, and P. E. Nachtigall (Eds.), *Language and communication: Comparative perspectives*. Hillsdale, NJ: Erlbaum.

Herman, L. M., Richards, D. G., & Wolz, J. P. (1984). Comprehension of sentences by bottlenosed dolphins. *Cognition, 16*, 129–219.

Herrnstein, R. J. (1961). Relative and absolute strength of response as a function of frequency of reinforcement. *Journal of the Experimental Analysis of Behavior, 4*, 267–272.

Herrnstein, R. J. (1966). Superstition: A corollary of the principle of operant conditioning. In W. K. Honig (Ed.), *Operant behavior: Areas of research and application*. New York, NY: Appleton-Century-Crofts.

Herrnstein, R. J. (1969). Method and theory in the study of avoidance. *Psychological Review, 76*, 49–69.

Herrnstein, R. J. (1979). Acquisition, generalization, and reversal of a natural concept. *Journal of Experimental Psychology: Animal Behavior Processes, 5*, 116–129.

Herrnstein, R. J. (1981). Self-control as response strength. In C. M. Bradshaw, E. Szabadi, & C. F. Lowe (Eds.), *Recent developments in the quantification of steady-state operant behavior*. Amsterdam, Holland: Elsevier/North Holland Biomedical Press.

Herrnstein, R. J. (1990). Rational choice theory: Necessary but not sufficient. *American Psychologist, 45*, 356–367.

Herrnstein, R. J. (1997). *The matching law: Papers in psychology and economics*. Cambridge, MA: Harvard University Press.

Herrnstein, R. J., & Heyman, G. M. (1979). Is matching compatible with reinforcement maximization on concurrent variable interval, variable ratio? *Journal of the Experimental Analysis of Behavior, 31*, 209–223.

Herrnstein, R. J., & Hineline, P. N. (1966). Negative reinforcement as shock-frequency reduction. *Journal of the Experimental Analysis of Behavior, 9*, 421–430.

Herrnstein, R. J., & Loveland, D. H. (1975). Maximizing and matching on concurrent ratio schedules. *Journal of the Experimental Analysis of Behavior*, *24*, 107–116.

Heschl, A., & Fuchsbichler, C. (2009). Siamangs (*Hylobates syndactylus*) recognize their mirror image. *International Journal of Comparative Psychology*, *22*, 221–233.

Hicks, J. (1968). Effects of co-observers' sanctions and adult presence on imitative aggression. *Child Development*, *39*, 303–309.

Hinson, R. E., & Poulos, C. X. (1981). Sensitization to the behavioral effects of cocaine: Modification by Pavlovian conditioning. *Pharmacology, Biochemistry, and Behavior*, *15*, 559–562.

Honey, P. L., & Galef, B. G., Jr. (2003). Ethanol consumption by rat dams during gestation, lactation and weaning increases ethanol consumption by their adolescent young. *Developmental Psychobiology*, *42*, 252–260.

Honey, P. L., & Galef, B. G., Jr. (2004). Long lasting effects of rearing by an ethanol-consuming dam on voluntary ethanol consumption by rats. *Appetite*, *43*, 261–268.

Honey, P. L., Varley, K. R., & Galef, B. G., Jr. (2004). Effects of ethanol consumption by adult female rats on subsequent consumption by adolescents. *Appetite*, *42*, 299–306.

Horowitz, A. C. (2003). Do humans ape? Or do apes human? Imitation and intention in humans (*Homo sapiens*) and other animals. *Journal of Comparative Psychology*, *3*, 325–336.

Hothersall, D. (1984). *History of psychology*. New York, NY: Random House.

Houston, A. (1986). The matching law applies to wagtails foraging in the wild. *Journal of the Experimental Analysis of Behavior*, *45*, 15–18.

Howell, A. J., Watson, D. C., Powell, R. A., & Buro, K. (2006). Academic procrastination: The pattern and correlates of behavioural postponement. *Personality and Individual Differences*, *40*, 1519–1530.

Huesmann, L. R. (1986). Psychological processes promoting the relation between exposure to media violence and aggressive behavior by the viewer. *Journal of Social Issues*, *42*, 125–139.

Huesmann, L. R., Moise-Titus, J., Podolski, C.-L., & Eron, L. D. (2003). Longitudinal relations between children's exposure to TV violence and their aggressive and violent behavior in young adulthood: 1977–1992. *Developmental Psychology*, *39*, 201–221.

Hull, C. L. (1932). The goal gradient hypothesis and maze learning. *Psychological Review*, *39*, 25–43.

Hull, C. L. (1934). The rat's speed-of-locomotion gradient in the approach to food. *Journal of Comparative Psychology*, *17*, 393–422.

Hull, C. L. (1943). *Principles of behavior*. New York, NY: Appleton-Century-Crofts.

Hunt, P. S., & Hallmark, R. A. (2001). Increases in ethanol ingestion by young rats following interaction with intoxicated siblings: A review. *Integrative Psychological and Behavioral Science*, *36*, 239–248.

Jacobson, E. (1938). *Progressive relaxation* (2nd ed.). Chicago, IL: University of Chicago Press.

James, W. (1907). The energies of men. *The Philosophical Review*, *16*, 1–20.

James, W. (1983). *The principles of psychology*. Cambridge, MA: Harvard University Press. (Original work published 1890)

Jenkins, H. M., Barrera, F. J., Ireland, C., & Woodside, B. (1978). Signal-centered action patterns of dogs in appetitive classical conditioning. *Learning and Motivation*, *9*, 272–296.

Jenkins, H. M., & Moore, B. R. (1973). The form of the autoshaped response with food or water reinforcers. *Journal of the Experimental Analysis of Behavior*, *20*, 163–181.

Jensen, R. (2006). Behaviorism, latent learning, and cognitive maps: Needed revisions in introductory psychology textbooks. *The Behavior Analyst*, *29*, 187–209.

Job, V., Dweck, C. S., & Walton, G. M. (2010). Ego depletion—Is it all in your head? Implicit theories about willpower affect self-regulation. *Psychological Science*, *21*, 1686–1693.

Job, V., Walton, G. M., Bernecker, K., & Dweck, C. S. (2013). Beliefs about willpower determine the impact of glucose on self-control. *PNAS Proceedings of the National Academy of Sciences of the United States of America*, *110*, 14837–14842.

Job, V., Walton, G. M., Bernecker, K., & Dweck, C. S. (2015). Implicit theories about willpower predict self-regulation and grades in everyday life. *Journal of Personality and Social Psychology*, *108*, 637–647.

Johnson, J. G., Cohen, P., Kasen, S., & Brook, J. S. (2007). Extensive television viewing and the development of attention and learning difficulties during adolescence. *Archives of Pediatric and Adolescent Medicine*, *161*, 480–486.

Jones, B. M. (2011). Applied behaviour analysis is ideal for the development of a land mine detection technology using humans. *The Behavior Analyst*, *34*, 55–73.

Jones, M. C. (1924). The elimination of children's fears. *Journal of Experimental Psychology*, 7, 382–390.

Kaiser, D. H., Sherburne, L. M., & Zentall, T. R. (1997). Directed forgetting in pigeons resulting from reallocation of memory-maintaining processes on forget-cue trials. *Psychonomic Bulletin & Review*, *4*, 559–565.

Kalat, J. W. (1974). Taste salience depends on novelty, not concentration, in taste-aversion learning in the rat. *Journal of Comparative and Physiological Psychology*, *86*, 47–50.

Kamin, L. J. (1969). Predictability, surprise, attention and conditioning. In B. A. Campbell & R. M. Church (Eds.), *Punishment and aversive behavior*. New York, NY: Appleton-Century-Crofts.

Kano, T. (1982). The use of leafy twigs for rain cover by the pygmy chimpanzees of Wamba. *Primate*, *23*, 453–457.

Kantor, T. G., Sunshine, A., Laska, E., Meisner, M., & Hopper, M. (1966). Oral analgesic studies: Penzocine hydrochloride, codeine, aspirin, and placebo and their influence on response to placebo. *Clinical Pharmacology and Therapeutics*, 7, 447–454.

Kaplan, H. I., Sadock, B. J., & Grebb, J. A. (1994). *Kaplan and Sadock's synopsis of psychiatry* (7th ed.). Baltimore, MD: Williams & Wilkins.

Karpicke, J. D., & Blunt, J. R. (2011). Retrieval practice produces more learning than elaborative studying with concept mapping. *Science*, *331*, 772–775.

Katcher, A. H., Solomon, R. L., Turner, L. H., LoLordo, V. M., Overmier, J. B., & Rescorla, R. A. (1969). Heart-rate and blood pressure responses to signaled and unsignaled shocks: Effects of cardiac sympathectomy. *Journal of Comparative and Physiological Psychology*, *68*, 163–174.

Katz, J. L. (1986). Long-distance running, anorexia nervosa, and bulimia: A report of two cases. *Comprehensive Psychiatry*, 27, 74–78.

Katz, J. L. (1996). Clinical observations on the physical activity of anorexia nervosa. In W. F. Epling & W. D. Pierce (Eds.), *Activity anorexia: Theory, research, and treatment*. Mahwah, NJ: Erlbaum.

Kawamura, S. (1963). The process of sub-cultural propagation among Japanese macaques. In C. H. Southwick (Ed.), *Primate social behavior*. New York, NY: Van Nostrand.

Kazdin, A. E. (2011). *Single-case research designs* (2nd ed.). New York, NY: Oxford University Press.

Keesey, R. (1964). Intracranial reward delay and the acquisition rate of a brightness discrimination. *Science*, *143*, 702.

Keith-Lucas, T., & Guttman, N. (1975). Robust single-trial delayed backward conditioning. *Journal of Comparative and Physiological Psychology*, *88*, 468–476.

Kelleher, R. T., & Fry, W. (1962). Stimulus functions in chained fixed-interval schedules. *Journal of the Experimental Analysis of Behavior*, *5*, 167–173.

Kellogg, W. N., & Kellogg, L. A. (1933). *The ape and the child*. New York, NY: McGraw-Hill.

Kimble, G. A. (1961). *Hilgard and Marquis' conditioning and learning* (Rev. ed.). New York, NY: Appleton-Century-Crofts.

Kimble, G. A. (1967). *Foundations of conditioning and learning*. New York, NY: Appleton-Century-Crofts.

King, B. J. (1991). Social information transfer in monkeys, apes, and hominids. *Yearbook of Physical Anthropology*, *34*, 97–115.

Kirsch, L. G., & Becker, J. V. (2006). Sexual offending: Theory of problem, theory of change, and implications for treatment effectiveness. *Aggression and Violent Behavior*, *11*, 208–224.

Kleinke, C. L., Meeker, G. B., & Staneske, R. A. (1986). Preference for opening lines: Comparing ratings by men and women. *Sex Roles*, *15*, 585–600.

Klinger, E. (1975). Consequences of commitment to and disengagement from incentives. *Psychological Review*, *82*, 1–25.

Klinger, E., Barta, S. G., & Kemble, E. D. (1974). Cyclic activity changes during extinction in rats: A potential model for depression. *Animal Learning and Behavior*, *2*, 313–316.

Koehler, O. (1951). The ability of birds to 'count'. *Bulletin of Animal Behaviour*, *9*, 41–45.

Kohlenberg, R. J. (1973). Behavioristic approach to multiple personality: A case study. *Behavior Therapy*, *4*, 137–140.

Kohlenberg, R. J., & Tsai, M. (1991). *Functional analytic psychotherapy: Creating intense and curative therapeutic relationships*. New York, NY: Plenum Press.

Kohler, W. (1939). Simple structural function in the chimpanzee and the chicken. In W. D. Ellis (Ed.), *A course book of gestalt psychology*. New York, NY: Harcourt Brace. (Original work published 1918)

Kohler, W. (1947). *Gestalt psychology: An introduction to new concepts in modern psychology*. New York, NY: Liveright.

Kohler, W. (1959). *The mentality of apes*. New York, NY: Vintage Books.

Kohn, A. (1993). *Punished by rewards*. Boston, MA: Houghton Mifflin.

Kossoff, M. J. (1999, March/April). Gary Player: Swinging hard on life's course. *Psychology Today*, *32*, 58–61, 78, 82.

Koubova, J. (2003). How does calorie restriction work? *Genes & Development*, *17*, 313–321.

Kurzban, R. (2010a). Does the brain consume additional glucose during self-control tasks? *Evolutionary Psychology, 8*, 244–259.

Kurzban, R. (2010b). *Why everyone (else) is a hypocrite: Evolution and the modular mind*. Princeton, NJ: Princeton University Press.

Lakein, A. (1973). *How to get control of your time and your life*. New York, NY: New American Library.

Lang, W. J., Ross, P., & Glover, A. (1967). Conditional responses induced by hypotensive drugs. *European Journal of Pharmacology, 2*, 169–174.

LaRowe, S. D., Patrick, C. J., Curtin, J. J., & Kline, J. P. (2006). Personality correlates of startle habituation. *Biological Psychology, 72*, 257–264.

Lasagna, L., Mosteller, F., von Felsinger, J. M., & Beecher, H. K. (1954). A study of the placebo response. *American Journal of Medicine, 16*, 770–779.

Lefkowitz, M. M., Eron, L. D., Walder, L. O., & Huesmann, L. R. (1977). *Growing up to be violent: A longitudinal study of the development of aggression*. Oxford, MA: Pergamon.

Lepper, M. R., Green, D., & Nisbett, R. E. (1973). Undermining children's intrinsic interest with extrinsic reward: A test of the "overjustification" hypothesis. *Journal of Personality and Social Psychology, 28*, 129–137.

Lerman, D. C., & Iwata, B. A. (1996). Developing a technology for the use of operant extinction in clinical settings: An examination of basic and applied research. *Journal of Applied Behavior Analysis, 29*, 345–382.

Levis, D. J. (1989). The case for a return to a two-factor theory of avoidance: The failure of non-fear interpretations. In S. B. Klein & R. R. Mowrer (Eds.), *Contemporary learning theories: Pavlovian conditioning and the status of learning theory*. Hillsdale, NJ: Erlbaum.

Levis, D. J., & Boyd, T. L. (1979). Symptom maintenance: An infrahuman analysis and extension of the conservation of anxiety principle. *Journal of Abnormal Psychology, 88*, 107–120.

Levitsky, D., & Collier, G. (1968). Schedule-induced wheel running. *Physiology and Behavior, 3*, 571–573.

Lewes, G. H. (1965). *The life of Goethe*. New York, NY: Frederick Ungar.

Lewinsohn, P. M. (1974). A behavioral approach to depression. In R. J. Friedman & M. M. Katz (Eds.), *The psychology of depression: Contemporary theory and research*. New York, NY: Winston/Wiley.

Lewis, K. P., Jaffe, S., & Brannon, E. M. (2005). Analog number representations in mongoose lemurs (*Eulemur mongoz*): Evidence from a search task. *Animal Cognition, 8*, 247–252.

Lichstein, K. L., & Riedel, B. W. (1994). Behavioral assessment and treatment of insomnia: A review with an emphasis on clinical application. *Behavior Therapy, 25*, 659–688.

Lichtenstein, E., & Glasgow, R. E. (1977). Rapid smoking: Side effects and safeguards. *Journal of Consulting and Clinical Psychology, 45*, 815–821.

Lieberman, D. A. (2000). *Learning: Behavior and cognition* (3rd ed.). Belmont, CA: Wadsworth.

Lilienfeld, S. O., Kirsch, I., Sarbin, T. R., Lynn, S. J., Chaves, J. F., Ganaway, G. K., & Powell, R. A. (1999). Dissociative identity disorder and the sociocognitive model: Recalling the lessons of the past. *Psychological Bulletin, 125*, 507–523.

Lindsley, O. R. (1991). Precision teaching's unique legacy from B. F. Skinner. *Journal of Behavioral Education, 1*, 253–266.

Linehan, M. M. (1993). *Cognitive-behavioral treatment of borderline personality disorder*. New York, NY: Guilford.

Linnoila, M., Stapleton, J. M., Lister, R., Guthrie, S., & Eckhardt, M. (1986). Effects of alcohol on accident risk. *Pathologist, 40*, 36–41.

Logue, A. W., Ophir, I., & Strauss, K. E. (1981). The acquisition of taste aversions in humans. *Behaviour Research and Therapy, 19*, 319–333.

Longo, V. D., & Mattson, M. P. (2014). Fasting: Molecular mechanisms and clinical applications. *Cell Metabolism, 19*, 181–192.

Lovaas, O. I. (1987). Behavioral treatment and normal educational and intellectual functioning in young autistic children. *Journal of Consulting and Clinical Psychology, 55*, 3–9.

Lowe, C. F. (1979). Determinants of human operant behavior. In M. D. Zeller & P. Harzem (Eds.), *Reinforcement and the organization of behavior*. New York, NY: Wiley.

Lowe, C. F., Beasty, A., & Bentall, R. P. (1983). The role of verbal behavior in human learning: Infant performance on fixed-interval schedules. *Journal of the Experimental Analysis of Behavior, 39*, 157–164.

Lubow, R. E., & Gewirtz, J. C. (1995). Latent inhibition in humans: Data, theory, and implications for schizophrenia. *Psychological Bulletin, 117*, 87–103.

Luszczynska, A., Sobczyk, A., & Abraham, C. (2007). Planning to lose weight: Randomized controlled trial of an implementation intention prompt to enhance weight reduction among overweight and obese women. *Health Psychology, 26*, 507–512.

Lynch, S. (1998). Intensive behavioural intervention with a 7-year-old girl with autism. *Autism, 2*, 181–197.

MacCorquodale, K. (1970). On Chomsky's review of Skinner's *Verbal Behavior*. *Journal of the Experimental Analysis of Behavior, 13*, 83–99.

MacLean, E. L., Merritt, D. J., & Brannon, E. M. (2008). Social complexity predicts transitive reasoning in prosimian primates. *Animal Behavior, 76*, 479–486.

Maier, S. F., Jackson, R. L., & Tomie, A. (1987). Potentiation, overshadowing, and prior exposure to inescapable shock. *Journal of Experimental Psychology: Animal Behavior Processes, 13*, 260–270.

Maki, W. S., & Hegvik, D. K. (1980). Directed forgetting in pigeons. *Animal Learning and Behavior, 8*, 567–574.

Malone, J. C. (1990). *Theories of learning: A historical approach*. Belmont, CA: Wadsworth.

Malott, R. W. (1989). Achievement of evasive goals: Control by rules describing contingencies that are not direct acting. In S. C. Hayes (Ed.), *Rule-governed behavior: Cognition, contingencies, and instructional control*. New York, NY: Plenum Press.

Malott, R. W., Malott, M. E., & Trojan, E. A. (2000). *Elementary principles of behavior* (4th ed.). Upper Saddle River, NJ: Prentice-Hall.

Malott, R. W., & Suarez, E. A. T. (2004). *Principles of behavior* (5th ed.). Upper Saddle River, NJ: Pearson.

Marks, I. M. (1969). *Fears and phobias*. New York, NY: Academic Press.

Marlatt, G. A., & Gordon, J. R. (Eds.). (1985). *Relapse prevention: Maintenance strategies in addictive behavior change*. New York, NY: Guilford.

Marrazzi, M. A., & Luby, E. D. (1986). An auto-addiction opioid model of chronic anorexia nervosa. *International Journal of Eating Disorders, 5*, 191–208.

Marsh, G., & Johnson, R. (1968). Discrimination reversal following learning without "errors." *Psychonomic Science, 10*, 261–262.

Marten, B., Pearson, M., Kebejian, L., Golden, E., Keselman, A., Bender, M., … & Mattson, M. P. (2007). Sex-dependent metabolic, neuroendocrine, and cognitive responses to dietary energy restriction and excess. *Endocrinology, 148*, 4318–4333.

Martin, G., & Pear, J. (1999). *Behavior modification: What it is and how to do it* (6th ed.). Upper Saddle River, NJ: Prentice-Hall.

Maslow, A. H. (1971). *The farther reaches of human nature*. New York, NY: Viking Press.

Masserman, J. H. (1943). *Behavior and neurosis: An experimental psychoanalytic approach to psycho-biologic principles*. Chicago, IL: University of Chicago Press.

Masters, J. C., Burish, T. G., Hollon, S. D., & Rimm, D. C. (1987). *Behavior therapy: Techniques and empirical findings* (3rd ed.). New York, NY: Harcourt Brace Jovanovich.

Mayou, R. A., & Ehlers, A. (2000). Three-year follow-up of a randomized controlled trial: Psychological debriefing for road accident victims. *British Journal of Psychiatry, 176*, 589–593.

Mazur, J. E. (2002). *Learning and behavior* (5th ed.). Upper Saddle River, NJ: Prentice-Hall.

Mazur, J. E., & Logue, A. W. (1978). Choice in a self-control paradigm: Effects of a fading procedure. *Journal of the Experimental Analysis of Behavior, 30*, 11–17.

McConnell, P. B. (2003). *The other end of the leash*. New York, NY: Ballantine Books.

McCusker, C. G., & Brown, K. (1990). Alcohol-predictive cues enhance tolerance to and precipitate "craving" for alcohol in social drinkers. *Journal of Studies on Alcohol, 51*, 494–499.

McDaniel, M. A., Howard, D. C., & Einstein, G. O. (2009). The read-recite-review study strategy: Effective and portable. *Psychological Science, 20*, 516–522.

McLean, I. G. (Ed.). (2003). *Mine detection dogs: Training, operations and odour detection*. Geneva, Switzerland: Geneva International Centre for Humanitarian Demining.

Melis, A. P., Hare, B., & Tomasello, M. (2006). Engineering cooperation in chimpanzees: Tolerance constraints on cooperation. *Animal Behavior, 72*, 275–286.

Melvin, K. B. (1985). Attack/display as a reinforcer in *Betta splendens*. *Bulletin of the Psychonomic Society, 23*, 350–352.

Mennella, J. A., & Garcia, P. L. (2000). Children's hedonic response to the smell of alcohol: Effects of parental drinking habits. *Alcoholism: Clinical and Experimental Research, 24*, 1167–1171.

Mettke-Hofmann, C., & Greenberg, R. (2005). Behavioral and cognitive adaptations to long-distance migration. In R. Greenberg & P. P. Marra (Eds.), *Birds of two worlds: The ecology and evolution of migration*. Baltimore, MD: Johns Hopkins University Press.

Miller, H. L. (1976). Matching-based hedonic scaling in the pigeon. *Journal of the Experimental Analysis of Behavior, 26*, 335–347.

Miller, N. E. (1960). Learning resistance to pain and fear: Effects of overlearning, exposure, and rewarded exposure in context. *Journal of Experimental Psychology, 60*, 137–145.

Miller, N. E., & Dollard, J. (1941). *Social learning and imitation*. New Haven, CT: Yale University Press.

Miltenberger, R. G. (2012). *Behavior modification: Principles and procedures* (5th ed.). Belmont, CA: Wadsworth Cengage Learning.

Mindell, J. A. (1999). Empirically supported treatments in pediatric psychology: Bedtime refusal and night wakings in young children. *Journal of Pediatric Psychology, 24*, 465–481.

Mineka, S. (1985). Animal models of anxiety-based disorder: Their usefulness and limitations. In A. H. Tuma & J. Maser (Eds.), *Anxiety and the anxiety disorders*. Hillsdale, NJ: Erlbaum.

Mineka, S. (1987). A primate model of phobic fears. In H. Eysenck & I. Martin (Eds.), *Theoretical foundations of behavior therapy*. New York, NY: Plenum Press.

Mineka, S., & Cook, M. (1993). Mechanisms involved in the observational conditioning of fear. *Journal of Experimental Psychology: General, 122*, 23–38.

Mischel, W. (1966). Theory and research on the antecedents of self-imposed delay of reward. In B. A. Maher (Ed.), *Progress in experimental personality research* (Vol. 3). New York, NY: Academic Press.

Mischel, W. (1974). Processes in delay of gratification. In L. Berkowitz (Ed.), *Advances in experimental social psychology* (Vol. 7). New York, NY: Academic Press.

Mischel, W. (2014). *The marshmallow test: Mastering self-control.* New York, NY: Little, Brown, and Company.

Monte, C. F. (1999). *Beneath the mask: An introduction to theories of personality* (6th ed.). New York, NY: Harcourt Brace.

Morgan, C. L. (1900). *Animal behaviour*. London: Arnold.

Morse, A. D., Russell, J. C., Hunt, T. W., Wood, G. O., Epling, W. F., & Pierce, W. D. (1995). Diurnal variation of intensive running in food-deprived rats. *Canadian Journal of Physiology and Pharmacology, 73*, 1519–1523.

Moser, E., & McCulloch, M. (2010). Canine scent detection of human cancers: A review of methods and accuracy. *Journal of Veterinary Behavior, 5*, 145–152.

Mowrer, O. H. (1947). On the dual nature of learning: A reinterpretation of "conditioning" and "problem-solving." *Harvard Educational Review, 17*, 102–150.

Mowrer, O. H. (1960). *Learning theory and behavior*. New York, NY: Wiley.

Mowrer, O. H., & Jones, H. (1945). Habit strength as a result of the pattern of reinforcement. *Journal of Experimental Psychology, 35*, 293–311.

Mulcahy, N. J., & Call, J. (2006). Apes save tools for future use. *Science, 312*, 1038–1040.

Nagel, K., Olguin, K., & Tomasello, M. (1993). Processes of social learning in the tool use of chimpanzees (*Pan troglodytes*) and human children (*Homo sapiens*). *Journal of Comparative Psychology, 107*, 174–186.

Nairne, J. S. (2000). *Psychology: The adaptive mind* (2nd ed.). Pacific Grove, CA: Brooks/Cole.

Newman, A., & Kanfer, F. H. (1976). Delay of gratification in children: The effects of training under fixed, decreasing and increasing delay of reward. *Journal of Experimental Child Psychology, 21*, 12–24.

Newsom, C., Favell, J., & Rincover, A. (1983). The side effects of punishment. In S. Axelrod & J. Apsche (Eds.), *The effects of punishment on human behavior*. New York, NY: Academic Press.

Newton, T. F., Kalechstein, A. D., Tervo, K. E., & Ling, W. (2003). Irritability following abstinence from cocaine predicts euphoric effects of cocaine administration. *Addictive Behaviors, 28*, 817–821.

Nguyen, N. H., Klein, E. D., & Zentall, T. R. (2005). Imitation of a two-action sequence by pigeons. *Psychonomic Bulletin & Review, 12*, 514–518.

Nordin, S., Broman, D. A., Olafsson, J. K., & Wulff, M. (2004). A longitudinal descriptive study of self-reported abnormal smell and taste perception in pregnant women. *Chemical Senses*, *29*, 391–402.

Oaten, M., & Cheng, K. (2006). Improved self-control: The benefits of a regular program of academic study. *Basic and Applied Social Psychology*, *28*, 1–16.

O'Brien, R. M., Figlerski, R. W., Howard, S. R., & Caggiano, J. (1981, August). *The effects of multi-year, guaranteed contracts on the performance of pitchers in major league baseball.* Paper presented at the annual meeting of the American Psychological Association, Los Angeles, CA.

O'Donohue, W., & Ferguson, K. E. (2001). *The psychology of B. F. Skinner*. Thousand Oaks, CA: Sage.

Ono, K. (1987). Superstitious behavior in humans. *Journal of the Experimental Analysis of Behavior*, *47*, 261–271.

Öst, L. (1989). One-session treatment for specific phobias. *Behaviour Research and Therapy*, *27*, 1–7.

Otto the octopus wreaks havoc. (2011, August 10). *The Telegraph*. Retrieved from http://www.telegraph.co.uk/news/newstopics/howaboutthat/3328480/Otto-the-octopus-wrecks-havoc.html

Pack, A. A., & Herman, L. M. (1995). Sensory integration in the bottlenose dolphin: Immediate recognition of complex shapes across the senses of echolocation and vision. *Journal of the Acoustic Society of America*, *98*, 722–733.

Palmer, D. C. (2006). On Chomsky's appraisal of Skinner's *Verbal Behavior*: A half century of misunderstanding. *The Behavior Analyst*, *29*, 253–267.

Patterson, F. G., & Linden, E. (1981). *The education of Koko*. New York, NY: Holt, Rinehart & Winston.

Pavlov, I. P. (1927). *Conditioned reflexes*. (G. V. Anrep, Trans.). London, England: Oxford University Press.

Pavlov, I. P. (1928). *Lectures on conditioned reflexes*. (W. H. Gantt, Trans.). New York, NY: International Publishers.

Pavlov, I. P. (1941). *Conditioned reflexes and psychiatry*. New York, NY: International Publishers.

Pepperberg, I. M. (1992). Proficient performance of a conjunctive, recursive task by an African Grey parrot (*Psittacus erithacus*). *Journal of Comparative Psychology*, *106*, 295–305.

Pepperberg, I. M. (1999). *The Alex studies: Cognitive and communicative abilities of grey parrots*. Cambridge, MA: Harvard University Press.

Pepperberg, I. M. (2007). Grey parrots do not always 'parrot': The roles of imitation and phonological awareness in the creation of new labels from existing vocalizations. *Language Sciences*, *29*, 1–13.

Pepperberg, I. M. (2009). *Alex & me*. New York, NY: Harper Collins.

Pepperberg, I. M., & Sherman, D. (2000). Proposed use of two-part interactive modeling as a means to increase functional skills in children with a variety of disabilities. *Teaching and Learning in Medicine*, *12*, 213–220.

Perin, C. T. (1942). Behavior potentiality as a joint function of the amount of training and the degree of hunger at the time of extinction. *Journal of Experimental Psychology*, *30*, 93–113.

Pfungst, O. (1911). *Clever Hans (The horse of Mr. von Osten): A contribution to experimental animal and human psychology* (Trans. C. L. Rahn). New York, NY: Henry Holt. (Originally published in German, 1907)

Phelps, B. J. (2000). Dissociative identity disorder: The relevance of behavior analysis. *Psychological Record, 50*, 235–249.

Pickens, C. L., Golden, S. A., Adams-Deutch, T., Nair, S. G., & Shaham, Y. (2009). *Biological Psychiatry, 65*, 881–886.

Pierce, W. D., & Epling, W. F. (1995). *Behavior analysis and learning*. Englewood Cliffs, NJ: Prentice-Hall.

Pierce, W. D., & Epling, W. F. (1999). *Behavior analysis and learning* (2nd ed.). Upper Saddle River, NJ: Prentice-Hall.

Pilley, J. W., & Reid, A. K. (2010). Border collie comprehends object names as verbal referents. *Behavioural Processes, 86*, 184–195.

Pinker, S. (1994). *The language instinct: How the mind creates language*. New York, NY: William Morrow.

Plant, E. A., Ericsson, K. A., Hill, L., & Asberg, K. (2005). Why study time does not predict grade point average across college students: Implications of deliberate practice for academic performance. *Contemporary Educational Psychology, 30*, 96–116.

Pliskoff, S. S. (1963). Rate change effects with equal potential reinforcements during the "warning" stimulus. *Journal of the Experimental Analysis of Behavior, 6*, 557–562.

Plotnik, J. M., de Waal, F. B. M., & Reiss, D. (2006). Self-recognition in an Asian elephant. *Proceedings of the National Academy of Sciences, 103*, 17053–17057.

Poling, A., Nickel, M., & Alling, K. (1990). Free birds aren't fat: Weight gain in captured wild pigeons maintained under laboratory conditions. *Journal of the Experimental Analysis of Behavior, 53*, 423–424.

Poling, A., Weetjens, B. J., Cox, C., Beyene, N. W., Durgin, A., & Mahoney, A. (2011). Tuberculosis detection by giant African pouched rats. *The Behavior Analyst, 34*, 47–54.

Poling, A., Weetjens, B. J., Cox, C., Beyene, N. W., & Sully, A. (2010). Using giant African pouched rats (*Cricetomys gambianus*) to detect landmines. *The Psychological Record, 60*, 715–728.

Powell, R. A. (2010). Little Albert still missing. *American Psychologist, 65*, 299–300.

Powell, R. A. (2011). Research notes: Little Albert, lost or found? Further difficulties with the Douglas Merritte hypothesis. *History of Psychology, 14*, 106–107.

Powell, R. A., Digdon, N., Harris, B., & Smithson, C. (2014). Correcting the record on Watson, Rayner, and Little Albert: Albert Barger as "psychology's lost boy." *American Psychologist, 69*, 600–611.

Powell, R. A., & Gee, T. L. (1999). The effects of hypnosis on dissociative identity disorder: A reexamination of the evidence. *Canadian Journal of Psychiatry, 44*, 914–916.

Pravosudov, V. V. (2009). Development of spatial memory and the hippocampus under nutritional stress: Adaptive priorities or developmental constraints in brain development? In R. Dukas & J. M. Ratcliffe (Eds.), *Cognitive Ecology II*. Chicago, IL: University of Chicago Press.

Premack, D. (1965). Reinforcement theory. In D. Levine (Ed.), *Nebraska symposium on motivation* (Vol. 13). Lincoln, NE: University of Nebraska Press.

Premack, D. (1971a). Catching up with common sense or two sides of a generalization: Reinforcement and punishment. In R. Glaser (Ed.), *The nature of reinforcement*. New York, NY: Academic Press.

Premack, D. (1971b). Language in a chimpanzee? *Science, 172*, 808–822.

Premack, D. (1976). *Intelligence in ape and man*. Hillsdale, NJ: Erlbaum.

Premack, D., & Woodruff, G. (1978). Chimpanzee problem-solving: A test for comprehension. *Science, 202*, 532–535.

Prior, H., Schwartz, A., & Güntürkün, O. (2008). Mirror-induced behavior in the magpie (*Pica pica*): Evidence of self-recognition. *Public Library of Science: Biology, 6*, 1642–1650.

Provine, R. R. (1996). Contagious yawning and laughter: Significance for sensory feature detection, motor pattern generation, imitation, and the evolution of social behavior. In C. M. Heyes & B. G. Galef., Jr. (Eds.), *Social learning in animals: The roots of culture*. San Diego, CA: Academic Press.

Pryor, K. (1975). *Lads before the wind: Adventures in porpoise training*. New York, NY: Harper & Row.

Pryor, K. (1999). *Don't shoot the dog: The new art of teaching and training* (Rev. ed.). New York, NY: Bantam Books.

Pychyl, T. A. (2010). *The procrastinator's digest: A concise guide to solving the procrastination puzzle.* Bloomington, IN: Xlibris Corporation.

Rachlin, H. (1974). Self-control. *Behaviorism, 2*, 94–107.

Rachlin, H. (1978). A molar theory of reinforcement schedules. *Journal of the Experimental Analysis of Behavior, 30*, 345–360.

Rachlin, H. (1991). *Introduction to modern behaviorism* (3rd ed.). New York, NY: W. H. Freeman.

Rachlin, H. (2000). *The science of self-control.* Cambridge, MA: Harvard University Press.

Rachlin, H., & Baum, W. M. (1972). Effects of alternative reinforcement: Does the source matter? *Journal of the Experimental Analysis of Behavior, 18*, 231–241.

Rachlin, H., & Green, L. (1972). Commitment, choice and self-control. *Journal of the Experimental Analysis of Behavior, 17*, 15–22.

Rachman, S. (1977). The conditioning theory of fear-acquisition: A critical examination. *Behaviour Research and Therapy, 15*, 375–387.

Rachman, S., & Hodgson, R. J. (1968). Experimentally induced "sexual fetishism": Replication and development. *Psychological Record, 18*, 25–27.

Rachman, S., & Hodgson, R. J. (1980). *Obsessions and compulsions*. Englewood Cliffs, NJ: Prentice-Hall.

Rankin, A. M., & Philip, P. J. (1963). An epidemic of laughing in the Bukoba District of Tanganyika. *Central African Journal of Medicine, 9*, 167–170.

Rathus, S. A., Nevid, J. S., & Fichner-Rathus, L. (2000). *Human sexuality in a world of diversity* (4th ed.). Boston, MA: Allyn & Bacon.

Reed, D. D., Critchfield, T. S., & Martens, B. K. (2006). The generalized matching law in elite sport competition: Football play calling as operant choice. *Journal of Applied Behavior Analysis, 39*, 281–297.

Reese, H. W. (2010). Regarding Little Albert. *American Psychologist, 65*, 300–301.

Reilly, S., & Bornovalova, M. (2005). Conditioned taste aversion and amygdala lesions in the rat: A critical review. *Neuroscience and Biobehavioral Reviews, 29*, 1067–88.

Reiss, D., & Marino, L. (2001). Mirror self-recognition in the bottlenose dolphin: A case of convergent cognition. *Proceedings of the National Academy of Sciences, 98*, 5937–5942.

Remington, B., Roberts, P., & Glautier, S. (1997). The effect of drink familiarity on tolerance. *Addictive Behaviors, 22*, 45–53.

Rendall, D., Owren, M. J., & Ryan, M. J. (2009). What do animal signals mean? *Animal Behavior, 78*, 233–240.

Rescorla, R. A. (1980). Simultaneous and successive associations in sensory preconditioning. *Journal of Experimental Psychology: Animal Behavior Processes, 6,* 207–216.

Rescorla, R. A., & Wagner, A. R. (1972). A theory of Pavlovian conditioning: Variations in the effectiveness of reinforcement and nonreinforcement. In A. H. Black & W. F. Prokasy (Eds.), *Classical conditioning II: Current research and theory*. New York, NY: Appleton-Century-Crofts.

Reynolds, D. K. (1984). *Playing ball on running water*. New York, NY: Quill.

Reynolds, G. S. (1961). Behavioral contrast. *Journal of the Experimental Analysis of Behavior, 4,* 57–71.

Reynolds, G. S. (1975). *A primer of operant conditioning* (2nd ed.). Glenview, IL: Scott, Foresman.

Rickert, V. I., & Johnson, C. M. (1988). Reducing nocturnal awakening and crying episodes in infants and young children: A comparison between scheduled awakenings and systematic ignoring. *Pediatrics, 81,* 203–212.

Riley, A. L., & Clarke, C. M. (1977). Conditioned taste aversions: A bibliography. In L. M. Barker, M. R. Best, & M. Domjan (Eds.), *Learning mechanisms in food selection*. Waco, TX: Baylor University Press.

Riley, A. L., & Wetherington, C. L. (1989). Schedule-induced polydipsia: Is the rat a small furry human? (An analysis of an animal model of human alcoholism). In S. B. Klein & R. R. Mowrer (Eds.), *Contemporary learning theories: Instrumental conditioning theory and the impact of biological constraints on learning*. Hillsdale, NJ: Erlbaum.

Rilling, J. K., Scholz, J., Preuss, T. M., Glasser, M. F., Errangi, B. K., & Behrens, T. E. (2011). Differences between chimpanzees and bonobos in neural systems supporting social cognition. *Social Cognitive and Affective Neuroscience*, 7, 369–379.

Robins, L. N. (1974). A follow-up study of Vietnam veterans' drug use. *Journal of Drug Issues, 4,* 61–63.

Rogers, C. R. (1959). A theory of therapy, personality, and interpersonal relationships, as developed in the client-centered framework. In S. Koch (Ed.), *Psychology: A study of a science* (Vol. 3). New York, NY: McGraw-Hill.

Romanes, G. J. (1884). *Animal intelligence*. New York, NY: Appleton.

Romanes, G. J. (1989). *Mental evolution in man: Origin of human faculty*. London, England: Kegan Paul. (Original work published 1888)

Ross, C. A. (1997). *Dissociative identity disorder: Diagnosis, clinical features, and treatment of multiple personality* (2nd ed.). New York, NY: Wiley.

Ross, C. A., & Norton, G. R. (1989). Effects of hypnosis on the features of multiple personality disorder. *American Journal of Clinical Hypnosis, 32,* 99–106.

Rothschild, J., Hoddy, K. K., Jambazian, P., & Varady, K. A. (2014). Time-restricted feeding and risk of metabolic disease: A review of human and animal studies. *Nutritional Reviews*, 72, 308–318.

Routtenberg, A., & Kuznesof, A. W. (1967). Self-starvation of rats living in activity wheels on a restricted food schedule. *Journal of Comparative and Physiological Psychology, 64,* 414–421.

Rozen, P., Reff, D., Mark, M., & Schull, J. (1984). Conditioned opponent processes in human tolerance to caffeine. *Bulletin of the Psychonomic Society, 22,* 117–120.

Rozin, P., Fischler, C., Imada, S., Sarubin, A., & Wrzesniewski, A. (1999). Attitudes to food and the role of food in life: Comparisons of Flemish Belgium, France, Japan and the United States. *Appetite, 33,* 163–180.

Rumbaugh, D. M. (Ed.). (1977). *Language learning by a chimpanzee: The LANA project.* San Diego, CA: Academic Press.

Russell, J. C., Amy, R. M., Manickavel, V., Dolphin, P. J., Epling, W. F., Pierce, W. D., & Boer, D. P. (1989). Prevention of myocardial disease in JCR:LA-corpulent rats by running. *Journal of Applied Physiology, 66,* 1649–1655.

Russell, M., Dark, K. A., Cummins, R. W., Ellman, G., Callaway, E., & Peeke, H. V. S. (1984). Learned histamine release. *Science, 225,* 733–734.

Russon, A. E., & Galdikas, B. M. F. (1993). Imitation in ex-captive orangutans. *Journal of Comparative Psychology, 107,* 147–161.

Russon, A. E., & Galdikas, B. M. F. (1995). Constraints on great apes' imitation: Model and action selectivity in rehabilitant orangutan (*Pongo pygmaeus*) imitation. *Journal of Comparative Psychology, 109,* 5–17.

Salkovskis, P. M. (1998). Psychological approaches to the understanding of obsessional problems. In R. P. Swinson, M. M. Antony, S. Rachman, & M. A. Richter (Eds.), *Obsessive-compulsive disorder: Theory, research, and treatment.* New York, NY: Guilford.

Sandin, B., & Chorot, P. (2002). Resistance to extinction of conditioned electrodermal responses: A study of the incubation hypothesis. *Psychological Reports, 91,* 37–46.

Sanz, C. M., & Morgan, D. B. (2007). Chimpanzee tool technology in the Goualougo Triangle, Republic of Congo. *Journal of Human Evolution, 52,* 420–433.

Savage-Rumbaugh, E. S. (1993). Language learnability in man, ape and dolphin. In H. L. Roitblat, L. M. Herman, & P. E. Nachtigall (Eds.), *Language and communication: Comparative perspectives.* Hillsdale, NJ: Erlbaum.

Savage-Rumbaugh, E. S., McDonald, K., Sevcik, R. A., Hopkins, W. D., & Rubert, E. (1986). Spontaneous symbol acquisition and communicative use by pygmy chimpanzees *(Pan paniscus). Journal of Comparative Psychology, 115,* 211–235.

Savage-Rumbaugh, E. S., Rumbaugh, D. M., Smith, S. T., & Lawson, J. (1980). Reference: The linguistic essential. *Science, 210,* 922–925.

Savage-Rumbaugh, E. S., Shanker, S. G., & Taylor, T. J. (1998). *Apes, language and the human mind.* New York, NY: Oxford University Press.

Schafe, G. E., & Bernstein, I. L. (1996). Taste aversion learning. In E. D. Capaldi (Ed.), *Why we eat what we eat: The psychology of eating.* Washington, DC: American Psychological Association.

Schlinger, H. D., Derenne, A., & Baron, A. (2008). What 50 years of research tell us about pausing under ratio schedules of reinforcement. *The Behavior Analyst, 31,* 39–60.

Schmidt, R. A., & Bjork, R. A. (1992). New conceptualizations of practice: Common principles in three paradigms suggest new concepts for training. *Psychological Science, 3,* 207–217.

Schmitt, D. R. (2001). Delayed rule following. *The Behavior Analyst, 24,* 181–189.

Schreiber, F. R. (1973). *Sybil.* Chicago, IL: Henry Regnery.

Schusterman, R. J., & Gisiner, R. (1988). Artificial language comprehension in dolphins and sea lions: The essential cognitive skills. *Psychological Record, 38,* 311–348.

Seed, A. M., Clayton, N. S., & Emory, M. J. (2008). Cooperative problem solving in rooks (Corvus frugilegus). *Proceedings of the Royal Society B: Biological Sciences, 275,* 1421–1429.

Seligman, M. E. P. (1971). Phobias and preparedness. *Behavior Therapy, 2,* 307–320.

Seligman, M. E. P. (1975). *Helplessness: On depression, development, and death.* San Francisco, CA: Freeman.

Seligman, M. E. P., & Maier, S. (1967). Failure to escape traumatic shock. *Journal of Experimental Psychology*, *74*, 1–9.

Seligman, M. E. P., Rosellini, R. A., & Kozak, M. J. (1975). Learned helplessness in the rat: Time course, immunization, and reversibility. *Journal of Comparative and Physiological Psychology*, *88*, 542–547.

Seyfarth, R. M., & Cheney, D. L. (1986). Vocal development in vervet monkeys. *Animal Behaviour*, *34*, 1640–1658.

Seyfarth, R. M., Cheney, D. L., & Marler, P. (1980). Monkey responses to three different alarm calls: Evidence for predator classification and semantic communication. *Science*, *210*, 801–803.

Shea, C. H., Wright, D. L., Wulf, G., & Whitacre, C. (2000). Physical and observational practice afford unique learning opportunities. *Journal of Motor Behavior*, *32*, 27–36.

Sheeran, P., & Orbell, S. (1999). Implementation intentions and repeated behaviour: Augmenting the predictive validity of the theory of planned behaviour. *European Journal of Social Psychology*, *29*, 349–369.

Sheeran, P., & Orbell, S. (2000). Using implementation intentions to increase attendance for cervical cancer screening. *Health Psychology*, *19*, 283–289.

Sherry, D. F., & Hoshooley, J. S. (2007). Neurobiology of spatial behavior. In K. A. Otter (Ed.), *The ecology and behavior of chickadees and titmice: An integrated approach*. New York, NY: Oxford University Press.

Sherry, D. F., & Hoshooley, J. S. (2009). The seasonal hippocampus of food-storing birds. *Behavioural Processes*, *80*, 334–338.

Shettleworth, S. J. (2010). *Cognition, evolution and behavior*. New York, NY: Oxford University Press.

Shoda, Y., Mischel, W., & Peake, P. K. (1990). Predicting adolescent cognitive and self-regulatory competencies from preschool delay of gratification: Identifying diagnostic conditions. *Developmental Psychology*, *26*, 978–986.

Shyan, M. R., & Herman, L. M. (1987). Determinants of recognition of gestural signs in an artificial language by Atlantic bottle-nosed dolphins *(Tursiops truncatus)* and humans *(Homo sapiens)*. *Journal of Comparative Psychology*, *101*, 112–125.

Sidman, M. (1960). *Tactics of scientific research: Evaluating experimental data in psychology*. New York, NY: Basic Books.

Siegel, S. (1983). Classical conditioning, drug tolerance, and drug dependence. In R. G. Smart, F. B. Glaser, Y. Israel, H. Kalant, R. E. Popham, & W. Schmidt (Eds.), *Research advances in alcohol and drug problems* (Vol. 7). New York, NY: Plenum Press.

Siegel, S. (1984). Pavlovian conditioning and heroin overdose: Reports by overdose victims. *Bulletin of the Psychonomic Society*, *22*, 428–430.

Siegel, S. (1989). Pharmacological conditioning and drug effects. In A. J. Goudie & M. W. Emmett-Oglesby (Eds.), *Psychoactive drugs: Tolerance and sensitization*. Clifton, NJ: Humana Press.

Siegel, S. (2002). Explanatory mechanisms for placebo effects: Pavlovian conditioning. In H. A. Guess, A. Kleinman, J. W. Kusek, & L. W. Engel (Eds.), *The science of the placebo: Toward an interdisciplinary research agenda*. New York, NY: BMJ Books.

Siegel, S. (2005). Drug tolerance, drug addiction, and drug anticipation. *Current Directions in Psychological Science*, *14*, 296–300.

Siegel, S., Hinson, R. E., Krank, M. D., & McCully, J. (1982). Heroin "overdose" death: The contribution of drug-associated environmental cues. *Science, 216*, 436–437.

Sijbrandij, M., Olff, M., Reitsma, J. B., Carlier, I. V. E., & Gersons, B. P. R. (2006). Emotional or educational debriefing after psychological trauma: Randomised control trial. *British Journal of Psychiatry, 189*, 150–155.

Silvia, P. J. (2007). *How to write a lot: A practical guide to productive academic writing*. Washington, DC: American Psychological Association.

Skinner, B. F. (1938). *The behavior of organisms: An experimental analysis*. Acton, MA: Copley.

Skinner, B. F. (1948a). *Walden II*. New York, NY: Macmillan.

Skinner, B. F. (1948b). "Superstition" in the pigeon. *Journal of Experimental Psychology, 38*, 168–172.

Skinner, B. F. (1950). Are theories of learning necessary? *Psychological Review, 57*, 193–216.

Skinner, B. F. (1953). *Science and human behavior*. New York, NY: Macmillan.

Skinner, B. F. (1956). A case history in scientific method. *American Psychologist, 11*, 221–233.

Skinner, B. F. (1957). *Verbal behavior*. Englewood Cliffs, NJ: Prentice-Hall.

Skinner, B. F. (1967). B. F. Skinner. In E. G. Boring & G. Lindzey (Eds.), *A history of psychology in autobiography* (Vol. 5). New York, NY: Appleton-Century-Crofts.

Skinner, B. F. (1969). *Contingencies of reinforcement: A theoretical analysis*. New York, NY: Appleton-Century-Crofts.

Skinner, B. F. (1971). *Beyond freedom and dignity*. New York, NY: Vintage Books.

Skinner, B. F. (1974). *About behaviorism*. New York, NY: Knopf.

Skinner, B. F. (1983). *A matter of consequences*. New York, NY: Knopf.

Skinner, B. F. (1987). *Upon further reflection*. Englewood Cliffs, NJ: Prentice-Hall.

Skinner, B. F. (1989). *Recent issues in the analysis of behavior*. Columbus, OH: Merrill.

Skinner, B. F., & Vaughan, M. E. (1983). *Enjoy old age: A program of self-management*. New York, NY: Norton.

Skinner-Buzan, D. (2004, March 12). I was not a lab rat. *The Guardian*.

Slater, L. (2004). *Opening Skinner's box: Great psychological experiments of the twentieth century*. New York, NY: Norton.

Smolker, R. A., Richards, A. F., Connor, R. C., Mann, J., & Berggren, P. (1997). Sponge-carrying by Indian Ocean bottlenose dolphins: Possible tool use by a delphinid. *Ethology, 103*, 454–465.

Smoo, A. E., & Resnik, D. B. (2009). *Responsible conduct of research* (2nd ed.). New York, NY: Oxford University Press.

Soares, J. J., & Öhman, A. (1993). Backward masking and skin conductance responses after conditioning to nonfeared but fear-relevant stimuli in fearful subjects. *Psychophysiology, 30*, 460–466.

Sokolowska, M., Siegel, S., & Kim, J. A. (2002). Intraadministration associations: Conditional hyperalgesia elicited by morphine onset. *Journal of Experimental Psychology: Animal Behavior Processes, 28*, 309–320.

Solomon, R. L. (1980). The opponent-process theory of motivation: The costs of pleasure and the benefits of pain. *American Psychologist, 35*, 691–712.

Solomon, R. L., & Corbit, J. D. (1974). The opponent-process theory of motivation: I. Temporal dynamics of affect. *Psychological Review, 81*, 119–145.

Solomon, R. L., Kamin, L. J., & Wynne, L. C. (1953). Traumatic avoidance learning: The outcomes of several extinction procedures with dogs. *Journal of Abnormal and Social Psychology, 48*, 291–302.

Solomon, R. L., & Wynne, L. C. (1953). Traumatic avoidance learning: Acquisition in normal dogs. *Psychological Monographs, 67* (4, Whole No. 354).

Solomon, R. L., & Wynne, L. C. (1954). Traumatic avoidance learning: The principles of anxiety conservation and partial irreversibility. *Psychological Review, 61*, 353–385.

Solvason, H. B., Ghanta, V. K., & Hiramoto, R. N. (1988). Conditioned augmentation of natural killer cell activity: Independence from nociceptive effects and dependence on interferon-beta. *Journal of Immunology, 140*, 661–665.

Spanos, N. P. (1994). Multiple identity enactments and multiple personality disorder: A socio-cognitive perspective. *Psychological Bulletin, 116*, 143–165.

Spanos, N. P. (1996). *Multiple identities & false memories: A sociocognitive perspective.* Washington, DC: American Psychological Association.

Spence, K. W. (1937). The differential response in animals to stimuli varying within a single dimension. *Psychological Review, 44*, 430–444.

Spiegler, M. D., & Guevremont, D. C. (2010). *Contemporary behavior therapy* (5th ed.). Belmont, CA: Wadsworth Cengage Learning.

Staddon, J. E. R. (1977). Schedule-induced behavior. In W. K. Honig & J. E. R. Staddon (Eds.), *Handbook of operant behavior*. Englewood Cliffs, NJ: Prentice-Hall.

Staddon, J. E. R., & Simmelhag, V. L. (1971). The "superstition" experiment: A reexamination of its implications for the principles of adaptive behavior. *Psychological Review, 78*, 3–43.

Stampfl, T. G. (1987). Theoretical implications of the neurotic paradox as a problem in behavior theory: An experimental resolution. *The Behavior Analyst, 10*, 161–173.

Steel, P. (2010). *The procrastination equation: How to stop putting things off and start getting stuff done.* Toronto, Canada: Vintage Canada.

Steketee, G., & Foa, E. B. (1985). Obsessive-compulsive disorder. In D. H. Barlow (Ed.), *Clinical handbook of psychological disorders: A step-by-step treatment manual.* New York, NY: Guilford.

Stevenson-Hinde, J. (1973). Constraints on reinforcement. In R. A. Hinde & J. Stevenson-Hinde (Eds.), *Constraints on learning*. New York, NY: Academic Press.

Stilling, S. T., & Critchfield, T. S. (2010). The matching relation and situation-specific bias modulation in professional football play selection. *Journal of the Experimental Analysis of Behavior, 93*, 435–454.

Streissguth, A. P., Barr, H. M., Bookstein, F. L., Samson, P. D., & Olson, H. C. (1999). The long-term neurocognitive consequences of prenatal alcohol exposure. A 14-year study. *Psychological Science, 10*, 186–190.

Sulzer-Azaroff, B., & Mayer, G. R. (1991). *Behavior analysis for lasting change*. Fort Worth, TX: Holt, Rinehart, & Winston.

Symbaluk, D. G. (1996). The effects of food restriction and training on male athletes. In W. F. Epling & W. D. Pierce (Eds.), *Activity anorexia: Theory, research, and treatment*. Mahwah, NJ: Erlbaum.

Tacitus (Trans. 1956). *Annals of imperial Rome* (M. Grant, Trans.). New York, NY: Penguin.

Task Force on Promotion and Dissemination of Psychological Procedures. (1995). Training in and dissemination of empirically-validated psychological treatments. Report and recommendations. *The Clinical Psychologist*, *48*, 3–24.

Terrace, H. S. (1963a). Discrimination learning with and without "errors." *Journal of the Experimental Analysis of Behavior*, *6*, 1–27.

Terrace, H. S. (1963b). Errorless transfer of a discrimination across two continua. *Journal of the Experimental Analysis of Behavior*, *6*, 223–232.

Terrace, H. S. (1979). *Nim*. New York, NY: Knopf.

Terrace, H. S. (1985). On the nature of animal thinking. *Neuroscience and Biobehavioral Reviews*, *9*, 643–652.

Terrace, H. S., Petitio, L. A., Sanders, R. J., & Bever, T. G. (1979). Can an ape create a sentence? *Science*, *206*, 891–902.

Thigpen, C. H., & Cleckley, H. M. (1957). *The three faces of Eve*. New York, NY: McGraw-Hill.

Thompson, R. F. (1972). Sensory preconditioning. In R. F. Thompson & J. F. Voss (Eds.), *Topics in learning and performance*. New York, NY: Academic Press.

Thompson, T. (1963). Visual reinforcement in Siamese fighting fish. *Science*, *141*, 55–57.

Thorndike, E. L. (1898). Animal intelligence: An experimental study of the associative processes in animals. *Psychological Review Monograph Supplement*, *2*, 1–109.

Thorndike, E. L. (1911/1965). *Animal intelligence*. New York, NY: Hafner.

Thouless, C. R., Fanshawe, J. H., & Bertram, B. C. R. (1989). Egyptian vultures *Neophron percnopterus* and ostrich *Struthio camelus* eggs: The origins of stone-throwing behaviour. *Ibis*, *131*, 9–15.

Thyer, B. A. (1999). Was Carl Jung a behavior analyst? *Journal of Applied Behavior Analysis*, *32*, 533.

Timberlake, W. (1983). Rats' responses to a moving object related to food or water: A behavior systems analysis. *Animal Learning and Behavior*, *11*, 309–320.

Timberlake, W. (1993). Behavior systems and reinforcement: An integrative approach. *Journal of the Experimental Analysis of Behavior*, *60*, 105–128.

Timberlake, W., & Allison, J. (1974). Response deprivation: An empirical approach to instrumental performance. *Psychological Review*, *81*, 146–164.

Timberlake, W., & Grant, D. S. (1975). Autoshaping in rats to the presentation of another rat predicting food. *Science*, *190*, 690–692.

Timberlake, W., & Lucas, G. A. (1989). Behavior systems and learning: From misbehavior to general principles. In S. B. Klein & R. R. Mowrer (Eds.), *Contemporary learning theories: Instrumental conditioning theory and the impact of biological constraints on learning*. Hillsdale, NJ: Erlbaum.

Tinbergen, N. (1951). *The study of instinct*. Oxford: Clarendon Press.

Tinbergen, N. (1963). On aims and methods in ethology. *Zeitschrift für Tierpsychologie*, *20*, 410–433.

Tolin, D. F., & Steketee, G. (2007). General issues in psychological treatment for obsessive-compulsive disorder. In M. M. Antony, C. Purdon, & L. J. Summerfeldt (Eds.), *Psychological treatment of obsessive-compulsive disorder: Fundamentals and beyond*. Washington, DC: American Psychological Association.

Tolman, E. C. (1932). *Purposive behavior in animals and men*. New York, NY: Appleton-Century-Crofts.

Tolman, E. C. (1948). Cognitive maps in rats and men. *Psychological Review*, *55*, 189–208.

Tolman, E. C., & Honzik, C. H. (1930). Degrees of hunger, reward and nonreward, and maze learning in rats. *University of California Publications in Psychology*, *4*, 241–275.

Tomasello, M. (1996). Do apes ape? In B. G. Galef, Jr., & C. M. Heyes (Eds.), *Social learning in animals: The roots of culture*. New York, NY: Academic Press.

Tomie, A. (1996). Self-regulation and animal behavior. *Psychological Inquiry*, 7, 83–85.

Tomie, A., Brooks, W., & Zito, B. (1989). Sign-tracking: The search for reward. In S. B. Klein & R. R. Mowrer (Eds.), *Contemporary learning theories: Pavlovian conditioning and the status of traditional learning theory*. Hillsdale, NJ: Erlbaum.

Tucker, V. A. (2000). The deep fovea, sideways vision and spiral flight paths in raptors. *Journal of Experimental Biology*, *203*, 3745–3754.

Ulrich, R. E., & Azrin, N. A. (1962). Reflexive fighting in response to aversive stimuli. *Journal of the Experimental Analysis of Behavior*, *5*, 511–520.

Valentine, C. W. (1930). The innate bases of fear. *Journal of Genetic Psychology*, *37*, 394–420.

Van der Kolk, B. A. (1989). The compulsion to repeat the trauma: Re-enactment, revictimization, and masochism. *Psychiatric Clinics of North America*, *12*, 389–411.

Van Houten, R. (1983). Punishment from the animal laboratory to the applied setting. In S. Axelrod & J. Apsche (Eds.), *The effects of punishment on human behavior*. New York, NY: Academic Press.

Vargas, J. S. (1990). B. F. Skinner—The last few days. *Journal of Applied Behavior Analysis*, *23*, 409–410.

Verhave, T. (1966). The pigeon as quality control inspector. *American Psychologist*, *21*, 109–115.

Vollmer, T. R., & Bourret, J. (2000). An application of the matching law to evaluate the allocation of two- and three-point shots by college basketball players. *Journal of Applied Behavior Analysis*, *33*, 137–150.

Vos Savant, M. (1990, September 9). Ask Marilyn. *Parade Magazine*, *15*.

Wallace, I., & Pear, J. J. (1977). Self-control techniques of famous novelists. *Journal of Applied Behavior Analysis*, *10*, 515–525.

Wallace, M., & Singer, G. (1976). Schedule induced behavior: A review of its generality, determinants and pharmacological data. *Pharmacology, Biochemistry, and Behavior*, *5*, 483–490.

Waltz, T. J., & Hayes, S. C. (2010). Acceptance and commitment therapy. In N. Kazantzis & M. A. Reinecke (Eds.), *Cognitive and behavioral theories in clinical practice*. New York, NY: Guilford Press.

Wasserman, E. A., & Zentall, T. R. (Eds.). (2006). *Comparative cognition: Experimental explorations of animal intelligence*. New York, NY: Oxford University Press.

Watson, D. L., & Tharp, R. G. (2014). *Self-directed behavior: Self-modification for personal adjustment* (7th ed.). Belmont, CA: Wadsworth Cengage Learning.

Watson, J. B. (1913). Psychology as the behaviorist views it. *Psychological Review*, *20*, 154–177.

Watson, J. B. (1925/1930). *Behaviorism*. New York, NY: Norton. (Original work published 1924)

Watson, J. B., & Rayner, R. (1920). Conditioned emotional reactions. *Journal of Experimental Child Psychology*, *3*, 1–14.

Watson, D. L., & Tharp, R. G. (2014). *Self-directed behavior: Self-modification for personal adjustment*. Belmont, CA: Wadsworth Cengage Learning.

Weindruch, R. (1996, January). Caloric restriction and aging. *Scientific American*, *274*, 46–52.

Weir, A. A. S., Chappell, J., & Kacelnik, A. (2002). Shaping of hooks in New Caledonian crows. *Science*, *297*, 981.

Weiss, H. M., Suckow, K., & Rakestraw, T. L., Jr. (1999). Influence of modeling on self-set goals: Direct and mediated effects. *Human Performance*, *12*, 89–114.

Welker, R. L. (1976). Acquisition of a free-operant-appetitive response in pigeons as a function of prior experience with response-independent food. *Learning and Motivation*, 7, 394–405.

Wells, A., & Papageorgiou, C. (1995). Worry and the incubation of intrusive images following stress. *Behaviour Research and Therapy*, *33*, 579–583.

Wheatley, K. L., Welker, R. L., & Miles, R. C. (1977). Acquisition of barpressing in rats following experience with response-independent food. *Animal Learning and Behavior*, *5*, 236–242.

Wheeler, G. (1996). Exercise, sports, and anorexia. In W. F. Epling & W. D. Pierce (Eds.), *Activity anorexia: Theory, research, and treatment*. Mahwah, NJ: Erlbaum.

Whiten, A. (1998). Imitation of the sequential structure of actions by chimpanzees (*Pan troglodytes*). *Journal of Comparative Psychology*, *112*, 270–281.

Wicks, S. R., & Rankin, C. H. (1997). Effects of tap withdrawal response habituation on other withdrawal behaviors: The localization of habituation in the nematode *Caenorhabditis elegans*. *Behavioral Neuroscience*, *111*, 342–353.

Wilcoxon, H. C., Dragoin, W. B., & Kral, P. A. (1971). Illness-induced aversions in rat and quail: Relative salience of visual and gustatory cues. *Science*, *171*, 826–828.

Williams, B. A. (1981). The following schedule of reinforcement as a fundamental determinant of steady state contrast in multiple schedules. *Journal of the Experimental Analysis of Behavior*, *35*, 293–310.

Williams, B. A. (2010). Perils of evidence-based medicine. *Perspectives on Biology and Medicine*, *53*, 106–120.

Williams, D. R., & Williams, H. (1969). Automaintenance in the pigeon: Sustained pecking despite contingent nonreinforcement. *Journal of the Experimental Analysis of Behavior*, *12*, 511–520.

Williams, H., & Pembroke, A. (1989). Sniffer dogs in the melanoma clinic? *Lancet*, *333*, 734.

Williams, J. L. (1973). *Operant learning: Procedures for changing behavior*. Monterey, CA: Brooks/Cole.

Wilson, C. (1972). *New pathways in psychology: Maslow and the post-Freudian revolution*. New York, NY: Taplinger.

Wilson, E. O. (1984). *Biophilia*. Cambridge, MA: Harvard University Press.

Wilson, G. T. (1997). Behavior therapy at century close. *Behavior Therapy*, *28*, 449–457.

Wilson, J. F., & Cantor, M. B. (1987). An animal model of excessive eating: Schedule-induced hyperphagia in food-satiated rats. *Journal of the Experimental Analysis of Behavior*, *47*, 335–346.

Wolpe, J. (1958). *Psychotherapy by reciprocal inhibition*. Stanford, CA: Stanford University Press.

Wolpe, J. (1995). Reciprocal inhibition: Major agent of behavior change. In W. O'Donohue & L. Krasner (Eds.), *Theories of behavior therapy: Exploring behavior change*. Washington, DC: American Psychological Association.

Woodruff, G., & Premack, D. (1979). Intentional communication in the chimpanzee: Development of deception. *Cognition*, 7, 333–362.

Woods, D. J., & Routtenberg, A. (1971). "Self-starvation" in activity wheels: Developmental and chlorpromazine interactions. *Journal of Comparative and Physiological Psychology*, *76*, 84–93.

Worthington, E. L. (1979). Behavioral self-control and the contract problem. *Teaching of Psychology*, *6*, 91–94.

Yamamoto, S., Yamakoshi, G., Humle, T., & Matsuzawa, T. (2008). Invention and modification of a new tool use behavior: Ant-fishing in trees by a wild chimpanzee (Pan troglodytes verus) at Bossou, Guinea. *American Journal of Primatology*, *70*, 699–702.

Yates, A. (1996). Athletes, eating disorders, and the overtraining syndrome. In W. F. Epling & W. D. Pierce (Eds.), *Activity anorexia: Theory, research, and treatment*. Mahwah, NJ: Erlbaum.

Yin, H., Barnet, R. C., & Miller, R. R. (1994). Spacing and trial distribution effects in Pavlovian conditioning: Contributions of a comparator mechanism. *Journal of Experimental Psychology: Animal Behavior Processes*, *20*, 123–134.

Zeiler, M. D. (1971). Eliminating behavior with reinforcement. *Journal of the Experimental Analysis of Behavior*, *16*, 401–405.

Zelman, D. C., Brandon, T. H., Jorenby, D. E., & Baker, T. B. (1992). Measures of affect and nicotine dependence predict differential response to smoking cessation treatments. *Journal of Consulting and Clinical Psychology*, *60*, 943–952.

Zentall, T. R. (2006). Imitation: Definitions, evidence, and mechanisms. *Animal Cognition*, *9*, 335–353.

Index